THE NATIONAL UNDERWRITER COMPANY

THE TOOLS & TECHNIQUES OF EMPLOYEE BENEFITS AND RETIREMENT PLANNING, 14TH EDITION

Stephan R. Leimberg, John J. McFadden, and C. Frederick Reish

The Tools & Techniques of Employee Benefit and Retirement Planning, 14th Edition, applies the trusted "Tools & Techniques" approach to this complex area, making it easy for you to confidently guide your clients through even the most complex employee benefit and retirement planning processes.

Highlights of the 14th Edition

Now in its 14th edition, the latest release of this very popular resource gets you up-to-date with every single relevant change in these highly regulated areas. But the new *Tools & Techniques of Employee Benefit and Retirement Planning* does more than that. It gives you a vital walkthrough of every issue-providing powerful analysis, techniques, and time-saving tools.

This is the resource that delivers:

- The latest information about qualified and nonqualified deferred compensation planning, including tax, legal, and ERISA requirements.
- An extensive section on health benefits, providing critical information about healthcare reform requirement under the Affordable Care Act (ACA). This includes a detailed timeline of mandates for all sizes of employers.
- A new chapter on ERISA litigation, helping planners and practitioners ensure that their plans are compliant with the latest regulations.
- Increased coverage of the use of life insurance for plan funding techniques.
- Helpful tips about integrating HSAs and FSAs with group health benefits in the post-ACA environment to provide maximum benefits to retain key employees.
- And much more!

Whether you're a newcomer to this area or a seasoned benefits professional, this is the one resource that leads you quickly to the benefits and retirement planning answers you need.

For customer service questions or to place additional orders, please call 1-800-543-0874.

14TH EDITION

The Tools & Techniques of

Employee Benefit and Retirement Planning

LEIMBERG LIBRARY

Stephan R. Leimberg
John J. McFadden
C. Frederick Reish

ISBN 978-1-941627-49-5
Library of Congress Control Number: 2015942388

This publication is designed to provide accurate and authoritative information in regard to the subject matter covered. It is sold with the understanding that the publisher is not engaged in rendering legal, accounting or other professional service. If legal advice or other expert assistance is required, the services of a competent professional person should be sought. – From a Declaration of Principles jointly adapted by a Committee of The American Bar Association and a Committee of Publishers and Associations.

THE NATIONAL UNDERWRITER COMPANY

The National Underwriter Company
4157 Olympic Blvd., Suite 225
Erlanger, KY 41018

Fourteenth Edition

Printed in the United States of America

ABOUT THE NATIONAL UNDERWRITER COMPANY

For over 110 years, The National Underwriter Company has been the first in line with the targeted tax, insurance, and financial planning information you need to make critical business decisions. Boasting nearly a century of expert experience, our reputable Editors are dedicated to putting accurate and relevant information right at your fingertips. With *Tax Facts, Tools & Techniques, National Underwriter Advanced Markets, Field Guide, FC&S®, FC&S Legal* and other resources available in print, eBook, CD, and online, you can be assured that as the industry evolves National Underwriter will be at the forefront with the thorough and easy-to-use resources you rely on for success.

The National Underwriter Company
Update Service Notification

This National Underwriter Company publication is regularly updated to include coverage of developments and changes that affect the content. If you did not purchase this publication directly from The National Underwriter Company and you want to receive these important updates sent on a thirty-day review basis and billed separately, please contact us at (800) 543-0874. Or you can mail your request with your name, company, address, and the title of the book to:

The National Underwriter Company
4157 Olympic Boulevard
Suite 225
Erlanger, KY 41018

If you purchased this publication from The National Underwriter Company directly, you have already been registered for the update service.

National Underwriter Company
Contact Information

To order any National Underwriter Company title, please

- call 1-800-543-0874, 8-6 ET Monday – Thursday and 8 to 5 ET Friday
- online bookstore at www.nationalunderwriter.com, or
- mail to The National Underwriter Company, Orders Department, 4157 Olympic Blvd., Ste. 225, Erlanger, KY 41018

DEDICATION

STEPHAN R. LEIMBERG

To my wife, my best friend, and wisest advisor, Jo-Ann

JOHN J. MCFADDEN

To Rhoda, Susanna, and Diana

ABOUT THE AUTHORS

Stephan R. Leimberg

Stephan R. Leimberg is CEO of LISI, Leimberg Information Services, Inc., at leimbergservices.com, a provider of e-mail/internet news and commentary for professionals on recent cases, rulings, and legislation; CEO of Leimberg and LeClair, Inc., an estate and financial planning software company; and President of Leimberg Associates, Inc., a publishing and software company in Bryn Mawr, Pennsylvania at leimberg.com.

Mr. Leimberg is the author of numerous books on estate, financial, and employee benefit and retirement planning and a nationally known speaker. He is the creator and/or principal author of the entire nine book *Tools & Techniques* series including *The Tools & Techniques of Estate Planning, The Tools & Techniques of Financial Planning, The Tools & Techniques of Employee Benefit and Retirement Planning, The Tools & Techniques of Life Insurance Planning, The Tools & Techniques of Charitable Planning, The Tools & Techniques of Income Tax Planning, The Tools & Techniques of Investment Planning, The Tools & Techniques of Risk Management, and The Tools & Techniques of Practice Management*. Leimberg is co-author, with noted attorney Howard Zaritsky, of *Tax Planning with Life Insurance*, *The Book of Trusts* with attorneys Charles K. Plotnick and Daniel Evans, and *How to Settle an Estate* with Charles K. Plotnick, and *The Buy-Sell Handbook*.

Leimberg is creator or co-creator of many software packages for the financial services professional including *NumberCruncher* (estate planning), *IRS Factors Calculator* (actuarial computations), *Financial Analyzer II, Estate Planning Quickview* (Estate Planning Flow Charts), *Toward a Zero Estate Tax* (PowerPoint Estate Planning Client Seminar), *Gifts That Give, Gifts That Give Back* (Powerpoint Client Charitable Planning Seminar), and Long-Term Care (Powerpoint Client Seminar).

A nationally known speaker, Stephan has addressed the Miami (Heckerling) Estate Planning Institute, the NYU Tax Institute, the Notre Dame Law School and Duke University Law School's Estate Planning Conference, The American Bar Association Planning Techniques for Large Estate and Sophisticated Planning Techniques courses of study, the National Association of Estate Planners and Councils, and the AICPA's National Estate Planning Forum. Leimberg has also spoken to the Federal Bureau of Investigation, and the National Aeronautics and Space Administration.

Leimberg, a 2004 recipient of the National Association of Estate Planners and Councils Distinguished Accredited Estate Planner award, was named 1998 Edward N. Polisher Lecturer of the Dickinson School of Law, and was awarded the Excellence in Writing Award of the American Bar Association's Probate and Property Section. He has been honored as Estate Planner of the Year by the Montgomery County Estate Planning Council and as Distinguished Estate Planner by the Philadelphia Estate Planning Council. He is also recipient of the President's Cup of the Philadelphia Life Underwriters, a three time Boris Todorovitch Lecturer, and the first Ben Feldman Lecturer.

John J. McFadden

John J. McFadden is a tax and pension lawyer and consultant practicing in Philadelphia, PA. His undergraduate degree is from Lehigh University, with a master's degree from the University of Rochester, and a J.D. from Harvard Law School. He has been admitted to the Pennsylvania Bar and the United States Tax Court.

Mr. McFadden is the author of articles in tax and professional journals on such subjects as professional corporations, insured pension plans, retirement plan distributions, and nonqualified deferred compensation. He is the co-author of *Employee Benefits*, 9th Edition, published by Dearborn Financial Publishing, Inc. in 2012.

Mr. McFadden also speaks and consults on tax and compensation planning matters and conducts seminars for financial planners.

C. Frederick Reish

Fred Reish is an ERISA attorney whose practice focuses on fiduciary responsibility, retirement income, and plan operational issues. He has been recognized as one of the "Legends" of the retirement industry by both *PLANADVISER* magazine and *PLANSPONSOR* magazine. Fred is Chair of his firm's Financial Services ERISA Team, which focuses on the services and investments for retirement plans.

Fred has been named "401(k) Industry's Most Influential Person" by *401kWire* and one of RIABiz's "Ten Most Influential Individuals in the 401(k) Industry Affecting RIAs for 2012" He has also received the Commissioner's Award and the District Director's Award by the IRS, the Eidson Founder's Award by the American Society of Professionals & Actuaries (ASPPA), the Institutional Investor and the *PLANSPONSOR* magazine Lifetime Achievement Awards, and the ASPPA/Morningstar 401(k) Leadership Award.

He has written more than 350 articles and four books about retirement plans, including a monthly column on 401(k) issues for *PLANSPONSOR* magazine. Fred co-chaired the IRS Los Angeles Benefits Conference for over ten years, and served as a founding Co-Chair of the NAPA 401(k) Summit.

CONTRIBUTING AUTHORS

Heather B. Abrigo

Heather B. Abrigo is counsel in the Employee Benefits and Executive Compensation Practice Group at Drinker Biddle & Reath, LLP. Heather assists public and private sector plan sponsors, third party administrators and other pension service providers in all aspects of employee benefit, including qualified retirement plan, executive compensation and health and welfare issues. Heather currently serves as vice-chair for ASPPA National Conferences and as a program/steering committee member of the ASPPA Annual Conference and Western Benefits Conference. Heather has written numerous articles and is a frequent speaker on a variety of employee benefits issues.

Robert L. Jensen

Robert L. Jensen is an associate in the Employee Benefits and Executive Compensation Practice Group at Drinker Biddle & Reath, LLP. Rob earned his J.D., *cum laude*, from Seton Hall University School of Law. Rob assists clients regarding a variety of employee benefits and executive compensation matters, including tax-qualified retirement plans, health and welfare benefits, employment, separation, and change in control agreements, non-qualified deferred compensation arrangements, stock options and other equity-based incentive compensation arrangements, as well as employee benefit and executive compensation issues in mergers and acquisitions.

Ryan C. Tzeng

Ryan C. Tzeng is an associate in the Employee Benefits and Executive Compensation Practice Group at Drinker Biddle & Reath, LLP. Ryan earned his J.D. from Loyola Law School and received his B.S. in Managerial Economics from University of California, Davis. Ryan's advises clients in matters involving compliance under 404(c) of ERISA, reporting and disclosure, determination letter applications and voluntary correction program applications, and qualification of state domestic relations orders. Prior to law school, Ryan worked as a third-party administrator and consultant in an employee benefits firm in Northern California.

ABOUT THE PUBLISHER

Kelly B. Maheu, J.D., is Managing Director of the Professional Publishing Division of The National Underwriter Company, a Division of ALM Media, LLC. Kelly has been with The National Underwriter Company since 2006, and served in editorial, content acquisition, and product development roles prior to being named Managing Director.

Prior to joining The National Underwriter Company, Kelly worked in the legal and insurance fields for LexisNexis®, Progressive Insurance, and a Cincinnati insurance defense litigation firm.

Kelly has edited and contributed to numerous books and publications including the *Personal Auto Insurance Policy Coverage Guide, Cyberliability and Insurance, The National Underwriter Sales Essentials Series,* and *The Tools & Techniques of Risk Management for Financial Planners.*

Kelly earned her law degree from The University of Cincinnati College of Law and holds a BA from Miami University, Ohio, with a double major in English/Journalism and Psychology.

ABOUT THE MANAGING EDITOR

Richard H. Cline, J.D., is the Manager, Tax and Insurance Content for the Professional Publishing Division at The National Underwriter Company. He is responsible for both the print and online versions of Tax Facts as well as developing new tax products for our customers.

Richard joined the company in 2013 but has over twenty-five years of tax editing and publishing experience. Prior to joining our team, Richard worked for Lexis-Nexis, CCH, Inc., and PricewaterhouseCoopers.

He has a B.S. degree from Franklin and Marshall College in Lancaster, Pennsylvania, and earned his law degree from Tulane University in New Orleans, Louisiana.

ABOUT THE EDITOR

Jason Gilbert, J.D., M.A., is an assistant editor with the Professional Publishing Division of The National Underwriter Company, a division of ALM Media, LLC. He edits and develops publications related to tax and insurance products, including titles in the *Advisor's Guide* and the *Tools & Techniques* series of investment and planning products. He also develops content for National Underwriter's other financial services publications and online products. He has worked on insurance and tax publications for more than nine years.

Jason has been a practicing attorney for more than a dozen years in the areas of criminal defense, products liability, and regulatory enforcement actions. Prior to joining National Underwriter, his experience in the insurance and tax fields has included work as a Westlaw contributor for Thomson Reuters and a tax advisor and social media contributor for Intuit. He is an honors graduate from Wright State University and holds a J.D. from the University of Cincinnati College of Law as well as a master's degree in Economics from Miami University in Ohio.

EDITORIAL SERVICES

Connie L. Jump, Manager, Editorial Operations

Patti O'Leary, Editorial Assistant

PREFACE

The Tools & Techniques of Employee Benefit and Retirement Planning has become one of the most important and popular resources in the entire Tools & Techniques series. It is intended to serve as an easily accessible, up-to-date guide to creative employee benefit and retirement planning for use by practicing financial planners, insurance agents, accountants, attorneys and other financial services professionals, as well as company managers, human resources departments, and law and graduate school students. The book is designed to meet these professionals' needs for timely, contemporary, and accurate information in this area. Such needs are increasing for two reasons. First, the high direct and indirect expenses involved with recruiting, retaining and ultimately retiring employees mandates a careful search for the combination of benefit and compensation packages that will accomplish an employer's objectives in the most cost effective way. Second, in recent years, there has been a tremendous growth in federal legislation and regulatory activity in the compensation area; this increases the difficulty of designing benefit packages and also the cost (in taxes and potential penalties to employer and employee) of mistakes in benefit and retirement planning.

The Tools & Techniques of Employee Benefit and Retirement Planning covers almost every popular employee benefit arrangement used in business today. Although special consideration is given to employee benefit arrangements as applied to smaller, closely held businesses, most of the benefits described here are used by both small and large companies, and the same tax and other rules apply to both.

As is the case with our companion books, *The Tools & Techniques of Estate Planning*, *The Tools & Techniques of Financial Planning*, *The Tools & Techniques of Income Tax Planning*, *The Tools & Techniques of Investment Planning*, and *The Tools & Techniques of Life Insurance Planning*, in this book each individual tool or technique of benefit or retirement planning is discussed in an easy-to-use format that is aimed at answering the planner's major questions:

- *Brief descriptions* of the benefit planning tool or technique being discussed.
- *Summaries* of the client situations where the particular technique is most often beneficial, including the advantages and disadvantages of each technique.
- *Design features* of the technique and the planning options that are available.
- *Tax implications* describes the federal income, estate and payroll tax implications of the technique to both employer and employee; some state tax aspects are also noted where appropriate.
- *ERISA and other compliance requirements* summarizes the ERISA reporting and disclosure, funding, and other non-tax federal regulatory requirements.
- *Instructions* on how to install the plan provides a summary of the steps that must be taken for an employer to adopt and implement the plan.
- *"Where Can I Find Out More?"* provides a list of references for further study and information.
- *"Frequently Asked Questions"* discusses some specific problems (and their solutions) that are often encountered by planners in connection with the benefit plan.

Where appropriate, some chapters may deviate somewhat from this format in order to provide the best approach to understanding the material.

The authors wish to acknowledge many members of the benefit planning community for their many discussions and critiques over the years have contributed to the perspective taken in this book. In particular, the authors are fortunate to have received substantial technical copy editing assistance from current and previous editors on the staff of The National Underwriter Company and are deeply appreciative of their efforts. We would like to especially thank Joseph C. Faucher, Esq. who contributed a brand new chapter on Fiduciary Litigation. We appreciate Joe's valuable contribution and ability to be flexible in light of the ever evolving changes in the fiduciary arena of employee benefits. We would also like to thank Bruce L. Ashton, Esq. for his assistance with some of the chapters. Lastly, we would like to thank our staff, especially Connie Kang, Rosa Arrendondo, and Santana Mitchell for their organizational skills, patience and assistance in completing this book.

Stephan R. Leimberg
John J. McFadden
C. Frederick Reish
Heather Abrigo
Rob Jensen
Ryan Tzeng

June 2015

CONTENTS

Overview

Compensation-Cash

Compensation-Equity Options

Deferred Compensation-Overview

Deferred Compensation-Rules for Qualified Plans

Deferred Compensation-Defined Contribution Plans

Deferred Compensation-Defined Benefit Plans

Other Employer-Sponsored Deferred Compensation Plans

Health and Disability Plans

Life Insurance Plans

Fringe Benefits

Ethics and Compliance Issues

APPENDICES AND INDEX

For substantive updates to this product please visit: pro.nuco.com/booksupplements

THE PROCESS OF EMPLOYEE BENEFIT PLANNING

CHAPTER 1

INTRODUCTION

The tools and techniques of employee benefit and retirement planning in this book are aimed at helping practitioners with both general and some specific benefit planning issues for employers and their employees. This chapter explains the broad *process* by which the employer's needs are determined and matched-up with the appropriate benefit arrangements.

WHAT BENEFIT PLANS CAN DO

As with any kind of financial planning, every practitioner should know what tools and techniques are at their disposal. In the case of employee benefit plans, two fundamental results may be achieved:

1. *Help employees meet certain financial needs that otherwise cannot be met*. Employee benefits can be used to help employees meet some of their financial needs. For example:

   - Health care costs can be expensive. Health insurance in various forms is a necessity—and the least expensive and simplest form of health insurance or health plan is often a group plan provided by an employer for a group of employees.

   - Retirement saving is difficult for most people: Employer-sponsored plans help promote retirement saving and also provide tax "leverage" for such saving that the employee might not obtain personally.

   - Family protection in the event of an employee's untimely death can be promoted by employer-sponsored plans that are an attractive supplement to private life insurance—and for some employees, are the *only* form of life insurance reasonably available.

2. *Provide unique tax benefits*. Even if an employee is able to meet health care, retirement, and other needs without the employer's help—which is a rare situation—there are dollars-and-cents reasons why an employee benefit plan is the best way to provide for these needs. For example:

   - For qualified retirement plans, employers get an up-front deduction for funding the plan. Employees may not be required to pay taxes on the benefits until they receive them (subject to some exceptions). This tax *deferral* available under an employer plan substantially increases the benefits available at retirement compared with equal amounts of non tax-deferred private savings by the employee.

   - Employer costs for employee health care plans (except for Cadillac Plan as discussed in Chapter 36) are fully deductible *and* the benefits are *completely tax-free* to employees, regardless of amount but again, subject to certain exceptions. Without the employer plan, employees would have to pay for insurance or health care with after-tax dollars, with a tax deduction available only if: (1) the taxpayer itemizes deductions; and (2) the medical expense for the year exceeds the substantial floor for medical expense deductions.

   - Other plans with substantial tax benefits include group-term life insurance plans, dependent care assistance plans, flexible spending accounts, incentive stock options, non-qualified deferred compensation plan, disability plans, and others discussed in this book.

STEPS IN THE PLANNING PROCESS

The process of assisting clients with employee benefit planning can be broken down into six identifiable steps:

1. Meet the client and gather data.
2. Identify the employer's objectives and goals; quantify and prioritize© them.
3. Analyze existing plans to identify weaknesses and needs for design change.
4. Formulate a new overall employee compensation plan and review the advantages but also disadvantages with the client.
5. Communicate the new plan effectively to employer.
6. Develop a program for regular review of the plan's effectiveness legal and compliance.

Step 1: Meet the Client and Gather Data

The planning process begins with fact finding. Only a thorough knowledge of the client's personal and business financial picture can provide the right analysis of benefit plan needs.

Some of the most important information will include:

- An employee census which includes:
    a. a list of all current employees with their ages;
    b. current compensation levels (both anticipated total (Form W-2) income as well as stated salaries);
    c. employment status (full or part-time);
    d. ownership in the business if any; and
    e. dates of employment.
- Data for the current year is mandatory. Similar data for at least five prior years and the employer's projections for the future are extremely useful to the planner.
- Financial information about the employer. Current balance sheets and income statements are mandatory, as well as historical data to give an indication of what level of expenditure the business can sustain for compensation programs.
- Complete information about all existing employee plans—their coverage, funding costs, contract expiration dates, and the like.
- If executive benefit planning for top executives or business owners is a significant consideration—and it usually is—the planner needs information about the executives' individual financial and estate planning situations and needs.

Benefit planners should develop amazing a "fact finder" to record and document the data gathering process.

Planners should remember that formalizing the data gathering process in a fact finder not only provides the information for current planning, but it also documents the *fact* that the planner went through this process of due diligence should any question about the design process ever arise in the future.

Step 2: Identify the Employer's Objectives; Quantify and Prioritize Them

Clients may have conflicting objectives for their benefit plans, unrealistic expectations as to what the plans can accomplish, or an inaccurate idea of the cost of achieving certain objectives. The planner must formulate realistic objectives for the client's compensation planning and must establish an order of priorities. Realistic, achievable goals then become the basis for plan design.

Some benefit plan objectives that clients may formulate include:

- meeting employee needs for health care, lifetime retirement income, and protection against disability and premature death;
- maintaining a program that complements (without duplicating) Social Security and the employee's own efforts in providing for health care, retirement income, and other needs;
- meeting the 4-R needs of the employer: Recruiting, Retaining, Rewarding, and ultimately Retiring employees;
- maintaining a program that matches benefits for nonunion employees with those of comparable union employees;
- providing benefit to those employee benefits of other employers in the industry or in the same geographical area;
- meeting cost targets; providing the most effective benefit package within cost limitations;
- compensating key employees competitively while minimizing costs for non-key employees; and
- maximizing benefits for shareholder or owner-employees

Step 3: Analyze Existing Plans to Identify Weaknesses or Needs for Revision

To what extent do existing plans fail to meet client needs? Here's a checklist:

- Who is covered under the existing plan?
- Who is excluded under the existing plan?
- What benefits are provided?
- What documentation exists? What documentation have employees received—that is, what have they been promised?
- What are the plan's annual costs and in what direction are these costs headed?
- How is the plan funded?
- Who administers the plan—the employer or a third party?
- What are the expiration dates of existing plan contracts and documents?

Step 4: Formulate a New Overall Employee Compensation Plan

A planner does not necessarily have to overhaul an employer's entire compensation package in order to serve the employer well, but it is important that whatever the planner recommends, it should be based on a comprehensive view of the employer's compensation planning needs, and should contribute to the employer's overall goals.

Individual chapters of this book provide detailed information about the advantages and disadvantages of each individual type of benefit plan, with an indication of situations in which that benefit plan will be most useful. But there is no simple formula by which the right mix of benefit plans can be designed to meet an employer's goals. That is an area where the practitioner's diligence, experience and judgment will make a significant difference.

Step 5: Communicate the New Plan Effectively

From the earlier discussion of employer objectives, note that a large part of an employer's goals in instituting employee benefit programs depend on the employees' *subjective reaction* to the plan—how it improves morale, helps recruit and retain employees, complements employee efforts, and the like. Also, from other chapters in this book the planner will note that many types of benefit plans require informed choices by employees in order to be effective.

No matter how well the plan is designed, it will fail to meet those types of goals if it is not communicated effectively and accurately to employees. Thus, effective communication is a great deal more than a soft aspect of plan design; it is just as much a hard, dollars-and-cents matter as drafting documents correctly.

In today's benefit climate, communication with employees is a sophisticated process. First, although employers and planners should try to simplify benefit provisions as much as possible, government regulations and the complexity of the legal environment for benefit plans often make the administration of such plans very complicated. (See Chapter 17 for specific ERISA disclosure requirements.) Second, employees invariably have some degree of skepticism about the value of employer-instituted programs that must be overcome by appropriate types of communication. Finally, the rise of electronic communication among the public in general means that planners can no longer assume that the normal means of communicating information by the employer be adequate. Special efforts must be made.

Employers traditionally have provided a benefits booklet for employees that they can keep for reference concerning benefit plan provisions: Under ERISA, summary plan descriptions are mandatory for many types of plans (see Chapter 17). Employers should not view this as purely a paperwork requirement. On the contrary, a special effort should be made to provide summary plan descriptions that are part of a benefits booklet approach. The booklet should not only meet legal requirements but should also provide information about the employer's benefit plans that is clear and really useful to employees.

Another ERISA requirement is the requirement to provide an individual benefit statement to employees. The statement can be used in a variety of ways including but not limited to a way for the employer to show the employee the full value of the employer's benefit program. Surveys by consulting firms almost invariably show that employees substantially underestimate the value of their benefit plans.

Step 6: Develop a Program for Periodic Review of the Plan's Effectiveness

Benefit plans exist in a dynamic business and government regulatory climate. A business can change drastically in a short time due to new ownership or external or internal business changes. Benefit plans are heavily affected by federal tax laws and Congress—driven by revenue needs—changes the tax laws all too frequently. Thus, no tool or technique of benefit planning is likely to be effective indefinitely without revision.

As part of the planning process, a schedule should be established for reviewing and monitoring plan effectiveness and plan costs. Revision procedures must be developed to assure continuing achievement of the client's objectives.

Finally, as a result of an IRS crackdown on what it considers to be "tax avoidance" transactions, the process of employee benefit planning may also require a review of the rules as stated in IRS Circular 230. If a particular transaction or product structure matches or is "substantially similar to" certain parameters outlined by the IRS, reporting requirements will have to be satisfied by the parties involved; otherwise, stiff penalties will be assessed. For more information, see Chapter 59.

CASH COMPENSATION PLANNING

CHAPTER 2

INTRODUCTION

Although cash compensation—the employee's compensation paid currently (during the year in which it is earned)—is not generally thought of as an employee benefit, it is actually the core of any compensation and benefit package. Any proposed employee benefit has to be compared in effectiveness with equivalent cash compensation. In addition, many employee benefit plans, such as pension and life insurance plans, have benefit or contribution schedules that are based on the employee's cash compensation. Finally, from a tax point of view, cash compensation is not as simple as it might appear. Financial planners must understand the rules to avoid adverse tax results from inappropriate planning.

WHEN IS USE OF SUCH A DEVICE INDICATED?

Opportunities for planning cash compensation primarily arise for employees, including shareholder-employees, of regular or "C" corporations (not "S" corporations). In an unincorporated business or an "S" corporation, all income and losses pass directly through to the owners' tax returns, so there are few compensation planning opportunities.

Advantages

1. Compared with non-cash benefits or deferred payments, cash compensation provides certainty and, therefore, greater security to the employee.

2. Cash compensation tends to set an employee's status in the company and community; the amount of annual salary must be carefully considered for this reason.

3. Cash compensation is an important part of overall financial planning for shareholder-employees of closely held corporations.

4. For employers, cash compensation is preferable to non-cash benefits because it is easier to budget, with no unknown or uncontrollable costs.

5. Cash compensation plans rarely involve design and administrative complexities, including ERISA aspects, which may apply to medical benefits, pensions, and other types of non-cash or deferred compensation.

Disadvantages

1. In general, cash compensation that is paid currently is currently taxable at ordinary income rates.

2. Cash compensation must meet the reasonableness test for deductibility and other tax issues discussed below. In some cases, other forms of compensation can avoid or defer these problems.

TAX IMPLICATIONS

Reasonableness of Compensation

The Internal Revenue Code allows an employer who carries on a trade or business to deduct "a reasonable allowance for salaries or other compensation for personal services actually rendered."[1] This reasonableness test is the main tax issue in determining whether an employer's payments for compensating an employee are deductible. If a company's payment does not meet this reasonableness test, its deduction is disallowed.

In addition to the reasonableness requirement, there is an upper limitation on the amount of compensation paid to certain executives that may be deducted by a publicly held corporation. Generally, no deduction is permitted for compensation in excess of $1,000,000 paid by a publicly held corporation to the company's chief executive officer or any employee who is one of the three highest compensated officers of the company (other than the chief executive officer or chief financial officer).[2] There are, however, exceptions to this rule for compensation payable on a commission basis, and other forms of performance-based compensation.

At a corporate income tax rate of 35 percent, the corporation's deduction saves 35 cents for every deductible dollar. Stated in another manner, the out-of-pocket cost for reasonable (deductible) compensation is 65 cents of each dollar paid, as opposed to one dollar for nondeductible payments. Since state income tax deductibility usually follows the federal rules, the true difference between deductibility and non-deductibility can be even greater.

The IRS does not usually raise the reasonableness issue if salaries are not particularly high. However, as the amount paid and deducted increases, it becomes important for a company to "build a case" that compensation is reasonable. Steps to suggest to a client include:

- Determine compensation levels prior to the beginning of each fiscal year, before salary has been earned, instead of simply determining salaries from year-to-year on a purely discretionary basis. This avoids the impression that the amount of salary is based simply on the amount that shareholder-employees wish to withdraw from the corporation for a given year.

- Written employment contracts should be provided and signed before compensation is earned.

- The company's board of directors should document, in the minutes of directors' meetings, how the amount of salary was determined.

- Court cases and IRS publications mention many factors in determining what constitutes reasonable compensation. These factors, listed below, should be reviewed in documenting the amount of salary and other compensation.

Factors in Determining Reasonable Compensation

Factors mentioned by the courts in "reasonableness of compensation" cases, and by the IRS in its publications, include the following:

- Comparison with compensation paid to executives in comparable positions for comparable employers.

- The employee's qualifications for the position.

- The nature and scope of the employee's duties.

- The size and complexity of the business enterprise.

- Comparison of the compensation paid with the company's gross and net income.

- The company's compensation policy for all employees.

- Economic conditions, including the condition of the industry and the local economy as well as the overall national economy.

- Comparison with dividend distributions to shareholders. Abnormally low dividends can create an inference that a so-called salary payment to a shareholder-employee is really a disguised dividend.

In recent cases, courts have increasingly stressed the "hypothetical independent investor" test. Under this test, the court compares rates of return on investment in the corporation that is under IRS challenge to the rates of return that an independent investor in the same type of business would demand. If the target corporation's rate of investment return is significantly lower, the implication is that corporate profits are being paid out in the form of compensation to employees, which in turn implies that the compensation amounts are unreasonable.

Treatment of Disallowed Compensation

A deduction for compensation that is disallowed because it is unreasonable is treated in various ways depending on the circumstances. IRS regulations state that if a corporation makes excessive payments and such payments are made primarily to shareholders, these payments will be treated as dividends.[3] Dividend treatment is the most typical situation for disallowed compensation. Other types of treatment are possible, depending on the facts. For example, if an employee at some point had transferred property to the corporation, excessive compensation payments could be treated as payments for this property, which would be nondeductible capital expenditures to the corporation.

From the recipient's point of view, in the absence of any other evidence, any excessive payments for salaries or compensation will be taxable as ordinary income to the recipient. In other words, from the employee's point of view, the reasonableness issue may not have much tax effect.

However, if the employee is a shareholder in the corporation, the corporation's tax picture and the possible loss of a compensation deduction at the corporate level can be very important. Note however, that currently, the maximum income tax on certain dividends may be reduced to 15 percent, which may increase compensation planning opportunities for business owners.

Example. Larry Sharp owns 100 percent of Sharp Corporation and is its sole employee. Sharp Corporation earns $400,000 in 2015. If the corporation pays all $400,000 to Larry as deductible compensation, the only tax burden on the $400,000 is the individual income tax that Larry pays. But if the IRS disallows $100,000 of the compensation deduction and treats it as a nondeductible dividend, then Larry now has $300,000 of taxable ordinary income plus $100,000 of dividend income, which will be taxed at 20 percent. The corporation now has $100,000 of additional taxable income. The corporation's tax on this—$22,250—is a direct reduction in Larry's wealth since he is a 100 percent shareholder.

Reimbursement Agreements

Because of the uncertainty of the reasonable compensation issue, companies often enter into reimbursement agreements with employees under which the employee is required to pay back the excessive portion of the compensation to the corporation if the IRS disallows a deduction for compensation. The employee does not generally have to pay income tax on the amount repaid. These agreements can be useful, but they do not necessarily solve the reasonableness problem. In fact, they may be a "red flag" to the IRS examiner. The IRS sometimes asserts that such an agreement is evidence that the corporation intended to pay unreasonable compensation. Therefore, such an agreement can make the compensation even more likely to attract attention during a tax audit and more difficult to defend in litigation.

An agreement to reimburse is rarely in the direct financial interest of the employee, since the employee would usually be better off keeping the money rather than returning it. The employee's tax on any excessive portion is treated as a dividend, so the tax paid from the employee's perspective is the same as if the entire payment was compensation. Reimbursement agreements are primarily used by shareholder-employees where the corporation's tax status is of indirect financial interest to the employee. In those cases, what hurts the corporation hurts the employee as a stockholder.

Timing of Income and Deductions

The tax rules for the timing of a corporation's deduction for compensation are more complicated than one might expect, primarily because the IRS sees potential for abuse in compensation payment situations.

Under the usual tax accounting rules for accrual method taxpayers, an item is deductible for an accounting period if that item has been properly accrued, even if not actually paid. Accrual occurs, for tax purposes, in the taxable year when all events have happened that legally require the corporation to pay the amount—the so-called "all events" test. Usually, the all events test is satisfied as soon as the employee has performed all the services required under the terms of the employment contract. Because of the apparent potential for abuse of compensation arrangements, particularly for closely held businesses, there are specific rules for deducting compensation payments that override the usual accrual rules in some cases. These are summarized below.

If the company uses the cash method of accounting, deductions for compensation cannot be taken before the year in which the compensation is actually paid.

No employer, whether using the cash method or the accrual method, can take a deduction for compensation for services that are not rendered before the end of the taxable year for which the deduction is claimed. Any compensation paid in advance must be deducted pro rata over the period during which services are actually rendered.

Timing of Corporate Deductions for Compensation Payments

The tax rules for timing of deductions distinguish between *current compensation* and *deferred compensation*. If the compensation qualifies as current compensation, then the employer can deduct it in the year in which it is properly accrued to the corporation under the tax accounting accrual rules. If the amount qualifies as deferred compensation, then the employer corporation cannot deduct it until the taxable year of the corporation in which, or with which, ends the taxable year of the employee in which the amount is includable in the employee's income.[4] For example, if an employer sets up a deferred compensation arrangement in 2015 for work performed in 2015 with compensation payable in 2016 and taxable to the employee in 2016, the corporation cannot deduct the compensation amount until 2016.

Whether an amount is considered current or deferred compensation depends on the type of employee:

- For a regular employee—an employee who is not a controlling shareholder or otherwise related to the employer corporation—the IRS takes the position that a plan is deferred compensation if the payment is made more than 2½ months after the end of the taxable year of the corporation.[5] In other words, there is a 2½ month *safe harbor rule*. For example, if a calendar year accrual method corporation declares and accrues a bonus to an employee before the end of 2015, the employer is entitled to a 2015 deduction for the bonus as long as the bonus is paid before March 15, 2016. The employee would include this bonus in income for 2016. However, if the bonus was paid on April 1, 2016—beyond the 2½ month limit—then the employee still includes the amount in income for 2016, but the employer's deduction is delayed until 2016.

- If the employee is related to the corporation (directly or indirectly owns more than 50 percent of the corporation), then the 2½ month safe harbor rule does not apply.[6] Deductions and income are matched in all cases. So, if a calendar year accrual method corporation declares and accrues a bonus to its controlling shareholder before the end of 2015, but pays it on February 1, 2016, the corporation cannot deduct the bonus until 2016.

ALTERNATIVES

1. Taxation can be avoided or deferred by various types of non-cash compensation plans, which are discussed throughout this book. Some examples of plans that defer taxation, usually until cash is actually received by the employee are:

   - nonqualified deferred compensation plans;

   - qualified pension, profit sharing, ESOP, 401(k) and similar plans; and

   - stock option and restricted stock plans.

   Compensation options that are completely tax-free (no taxation, either currently or deferred) include such plans as:

   - health and accident plans (provided that certain nondiscrimination and eligibility requirements are met);

   - disability income plans of certain types;

   - dependent care and educational assistance plans (subject to certain maximum limits on amounts that may be excluded from income by employees);

   - group term life insurance up to $50,000 (unless the plan discriminates in favor of key employees); and

   - the pure death benefit amount from any life insurance plan, even if the premium is currently taxable.

2. Where the employer may lose a deduction for cash compensation due to a reasonableness of compensation problem, part of the compensation might be provided in a form that is both tax-deferred to the employee and deduction-deferred to the employer. This is discussed further under nonqualified deferred compensation plans. The reasonableness of compensation issue does not arise until the year

in which the employer takes the deduction, so deferring the deduction can be helpful.

HOW IS THE PLAN SET UP?

Cash compensation planning is simple and is often not even thought of as a form of employee benefit planning. However, for a complex employment agreement involving cash and other forms of compensation, and in situations where reasonableness of compensation may be an issue, a tax accountant, tax attorney, or financial planner specializing in employee benefits and compensation planning can provide useful guidance.

WHERE CAN I FIND OUT MORE?

1. IRS Publication 334, *Tax Guide for Small Business*, has a simple explanation of the IRS position on the employer's tax treatment of employee pay and benefits. IRS Publication 17, *Your Federal Income Tax*, covers the tax treatment from the employee side. Both these publications are available free from the IRS and are revised annually.

FREQUENTLY ASKED QUESTIONS

Question – If an executive's compensation is based on profits or sales, will it be deemed unreasonable (and therefore nondeductible) if the employer has an unusually good year and the payment is therefore very high?

Answer – The reasonableness of salary is typically tested according to the circumstances existing at the time a profit-oriented compensation agreement is entered into rather than when it is actually paid. Thus, if the percentage or formula itself is not unreasonable at the time the agreement becomes binding on the parties, the actual amount may be deemed reasonable, however high. In addition, the issue of reasonableness can also take into account the element of risk involved to the employee. That is, suppose an employer agrees to pay an employee $100,000, plus 25 percent of profits for the upcoming year. The company has an extremely good year and the employee receives $600,000. While a $600,000 guaranteed salary might be deemed unreasonable, the fact that the executive took some risk in accepting a contingent type of compensation may bring the $600,000 amount within the limits of reasonableness.

Question – What is the significance of cash compensation planning for an employee of an S corporation?

Answer – An S corporation is a corporation that has made an election under federal tax law to be taxed essentially as a partnership. In an S corporation, all corporate income and losses are passed through to stockholders in proportion to their stock ownership. Corporate income is taxable to shareholders whether or not it is actually distributed as dividends. For S corporation shareholder-employees, there is no opportunity to defer taxation of their share of current income, except through a qualified retirement plan (which is discussed in other chapters of this book).

When S corporation shareholders are also employees of the corporation, as is often the case, it is important to distinguish between compensation for services to the shareholder-employees, as opposed to their share of corporate earnings passed through to them from the corporation. This distinction between compensation and dividend income has a significant effect on the various qualified and nonqualified employee benefit plans (discussed later in this book). For example, pension plans and group-term life insurance plans often base their benefits on the employee's compensation income, which does not include any element of income from the corporation that is characterized as a dividend.

CHAPTER ENDNOTES

1. I.R.C. §162(a)(1).
2. I.R.C. §162(m); IRS Notice 2007-49. The limit is $500,000 for certain executives affected by the "troubled assets relief program" (I.R.C. §162(m)(5)), and effective after 2012, a similar rule for certain health insurance executives (I.R.C. §162(m)(6)).
3. Treas. Reg. §1.162-8.
4. I.R.C. §404(a)(5); Reg. §1.404(a)-12(b)(2).
5. Temp. Treas. Reg §1.404(b)-1T, Q 2.
6. I.R.C. §267(a)(2), 267(b)(2).

ANNUAL BONUS PLAN

CHAPTER 3

INTRODUCTION

An annual bonus is an addition to regular salary or compensation that is provided, usually following the end of a calendar or fiscal year, to enable employees to share in a successful year and/or incentivize employees. This chapter discusses the tax and other planning considerations that apply.

WHEN IS USE OF SUCH A DEVICE INDICATED?

1. Annual bonuses are often used in closely held companies to enable shareholder-employees to withdraw the maximum compensation income from the company each year.

2. Annual bonuses are used for managers and executives as an incentive oriented form of compensation, based on the attainment of profit or other performance goals (at the company, business unit, and/or individual level) during the year.

3. Annual bonuses may be used to assist executives in funding cross-purchase buy-sell agreements or in contributing their share of the premium to a split dollar arrangement.

Advantages

1. Bonuses represent an incentive-based form of compensation that is very effective because of the close connection between performance and receipt (i.e., pay-for-performance).

2. A properly designed bonus plan can implement the corporation's strategic objectives.

3. Bonuses allow flexibility in compensation to reflect company performance, both in closely held and larger corporations.

4. Bonus arrangements are flexible and simple to design, within the tax constraints discussed below.

Disadvantages

1. Bonuses generally do not offer an opportunity for the employee to defer taxation of compensation for more than one year (although the requirements of Code section 409A (nonqualified deferred compensation) must be considered when designing an annual bonus plan).

2. Bonuses are limited by the requirement of reasonableness for the deductibility of compensation payments by the employer.

3. Bonuses are taxable to the employee as ordinary income.

TAX IMPLICATIONS

Bonus payments are deductible under the same rules as other forms of cash compensation. These rules are discussed in detail in Chapter 2, but will be covered in summary here as they apply to bonuses.

A bonus, together with other compensation, cannot be deducted unless it constitutes (a) a reasonable allowance for (b) services actually rendered. Factors indicating reasonableness—the first part of the test—are listed in the general discussion in Chapter 2. Also discussed in Chapter 2 is the fact that no deduction is permitted for compensation in excess of $1,000,000 paid to certain top executives of publicly held corporations (unless the compensation is qualified performance-based compensation under Code Section 162(m)), along with certain other limitations.

Bonuses can be very large if they are based on profits or earnings and the company has a very good year. For example, suppose a sales manager receives a $400,000 bonus in addition to his regular $100,000 base salary, under a sales-target bonus formula. Although $500,000 of compensation might, as a general rule, be considered unreasonably high for this type of sales manager, this arrangement might be sustained by the IRS for two reasons:

1. Reasonableness of compensation is often tested in accordance with circumstances existing when the bonus agreement is entered into rather than when the bonus is actually paid.

2. In testing the reasonableness of a bonus, both the IRS and the courts will usually take into account the element of risk involved to the employee. That is, an employee presumably had a choice between a relatively lower amount of guaranteed compensation and a higher amount of contingent compensation. So the two should be deemed equivalent for purposes of testing reasonableness.

Example. A sales manager who receives a $100,000 base salary and a bonus of 10 percent of the gross sales increase in 2015, producing a $400,000 bonus for 2015, probably could not at the beginning of 2015 have negotiated a contract for $500,000 of guaranteed compensation without bonus. The reasonableness of the bonus contract should be based on the reasonableness of the equivalent fixed salary agreement that the sales manager could have negotiated, not on the $500,000 total resulting from taking a chance and then having a good year.

It is important to plan ahead when using bonuses as an employee benefit technique. If reasonableness might become an issue, decide upon a bonus formula well in advance of the time the bonus is paid. (Preferably, in advance of the year in which the bonus will be earned). In other words, a formula for determining a bonus for year-end 2015 should be determined in writing before the beginning of 2015 to help support the reasonableness of the amount.

The timing of income to the employee and deductions to the corporation are governed by the rules discussed in detail in Chapter 2 with regard to cash compensation. Since bonuses are often payable after the end of the year in which they are earned, the "2½ month safe-harbor rule" is important for bonus planning. Under this rule, an accrual method corporation can deduct a compensation payment that is properly accrued before the end of a given year, so long as the payment is made no later than 2½ months after the end of the corporation's taxable year. For instance, for a calendar year accrual method corporation, a bonus earned for services completed in 2015 can be deducted by the corporation for 2015, so long as it is paid on or before March 15, 2016.

Note, however, that the 2½ month rule does not apply to payments to employees who own or control 50 percent or more of the corporation under Code section 267(b). For those employees, the corporation must pay the bonus during its taxable year in order to deduct it during that taxable year.

For regular employees who can make use of the 2½ month safe harbor technique, the ability to move taxable income into the employee's next taxable year is a significant advantage of the bonus form of compensation. For example, a bonus might be earned (and deducted by the corporation) in 2015, paid on March 15, 2016, and the employee could defer the payment of tax to April 15, 2017 (the employee's due date for the 2016 tax return).

The 2½ month rule is also important for the nonqualified deferred compensation rules of Code section 409A. Specifically, if an annual bonus is paid no later than 2½ months following the end of the year in which it is earned, it will not be subject to the complex rules of section 409A.

ALTERNATIVES

1. As with cash compensation in general, as discussed in Chapter 2, taxation can be avoided or deferred by various types of noncash compensation plans that are discussed throughout this book, including qualified pension and profit sharing plans, nonqualified deferred compensation plans, and medical benefit plans.

2. Stock option, incentive stock option (ISO), or restricted stock plans are forms of deferred compensation with many of the same incentive features as a cash bonus plan. These are discussed in later chapters.

HOW ARE THESE PLANS SET UP?

Bonus plans can be informal or even oral. There are no taxes or other legal requirements for a written plan or for filing anything with the government. However, a written plan is often desirable, and in that case employer and employee might want to consult with an attorney experienced in handling employee compensation matters.

FREQUENTLY ASKED QUESTIONS

Question – What are the advantages of a written bonus plan?

Answer – A written agreement has at least two advantages:

First, a written plan, particularly one drafted in advance of the year in which compensation is earned, helps to avoid disallowance of the corporation's deduction on the ground that the amount is unreasonable. Without a written plan, the IRS is likely to claim that a bonus is simply a discretionary payment that is excessive and therefore nondeductible. If this payment is made to a shareholder, the payment may be characterized as a dividend instead of deductible compensation. This means that the corporation will not receive a tax deduction, even though the entire distribution will probably be taxable as dividend income to the shareholder-recipient.

A second reason for a written agreement is that it defines the terms of the bonus and assures the employee of legal grounds to require the corporation to live up to the agreement. The terms of the agreement should be clearly defined for this reason.

Question – If a bonus is based on profits, is there any specific definition of profits that must be used?

Answer – There is no tax or legal reason for any specific definition of profits in a bonus agreement. But it is important to use a clear definition in order to protect against later misunderstandings. Profits can be defined as the amount shown in financial statements, as taxable income for federal income tax purposes, or based upon some other method of defining profits. If the definition relies on company accounting methods or federal tax laws, the agreement should take possible changes in accounting method or the tax laws into account. Paying a bonus may, in itself, affect profits. So, the agreement must specify whether profits are determined before or after bonus payments. For a company with more than one division or subsidiary, an executive may want to tie the bonus to profits in one particular unit rather than the company as a whole.

SEVERANCE PAY PLAN

CHAPTER 4

INTRODUCTION

A severance pay plan is an agreement between employer and employee to make payments after the employee's termination of employment.

Severance pay arrangements are almost completely flexible if characterization as an ERISA pension plan is avoided (see below). If ERISA's pension plan rules do not apply, the plan can cover any group of employees or even a single employee, on any terms and conditions that the employer considers appropriate. For example, provided that ERISA's pension plan rules do not apply to a severance pay arrangement, payments thereunder can be withheld if the employee's service is severed due to misconduct. Severance agreements can be, and often are, negotiated individually with executives.

For a discussion of additional considerations that apply where severance pay is contingent upon a change in corporate ownership, see Chapter 5, Golden Parachute Plan. See also Chapter 55, VEBA Welfare Benefit Trust, for plans that pay severance benefits from pre-funded trust arrangements.

TAX IMPLICATIONS

In general, the tax consequences of a severance pay plan (whether or not it is governed by ERISA, as discussed below) are similar to those of a nonqualified deferred compensation plan. Refer to Chapter 35 for a discussion of further tax considerations.

If the severance payment is characterized as a parachute payment, the employer's deduction may be limited and the employee may be subject to penalty. In general, parachute payments are severance payments that take effect upon changes in business ownership. The parachute rules are discussed in Chapter 5.

Severance payments are deductible by the employer if: (a) the payments are compensation for services previously rendered by the employee, and (b) the payments are reasonable in amount.[1]

Severance payments made pursuant to a written plan or agreement, which is entered into while the employee is still actively at work, should be considered compensation for services in most cases. The promised severance benefits in such a case are considered part of the employer's pay/benefit package, which compensates the employee for services. However, if there is no written plan or agreement in place prior to termination of employment, the IRS could argue that the payment is something other than compensation—such as a gift, a dividend, a buyout payment for the employee's interest in the business, or whatever other characterization might fit the particular facts of the situation. Planners should counsel clients to try to avoid this result by adopting formal severance plans, policies, or agreements.

The reasonableness test which applies to severance pay arrangements is the same test that applies to all forms of compensation payments. (See the discussion in Chapter 2, "Cash Compensation Planning.")

Unfunded Plans

If the severance pay plan is unfunded (i.e., no assets are placed beyond the reach of the employer's creditors), severance payments are taxable to the recipient as compensation income in the year actually or constructively received.[2]

Employers should be aware of the constructive receipt issue concerning severance payments.

Example. Suppose employee Bob Cratchit is terminated on December 24, 2015 and is entitled to an immediate severance benefit of $350 (two weeks' pay). Bob asks his employer to give him a tax break by paying the severance benefit on January 2, 2016, and the employer does so. Technically, Bob has run afoul of the constructive receipt doctrine (see Chapter 33 for discussion); he should report the $350 severance benefit in 2015, because he had an unrestricted right to receive the payments in 2015.

Funded Plans

A severance pay plan is considered to be funded if assets are set aside beyond the reach of the employer's creditors (typically in a trust) solely to pay plan benefits to employees. (The concept of funding is discussed at length in Chapter 35.) Severance pay plans funded through welfare benefit trusts or voluntary employees' beneficiary associations (VEBAs) are of current interest among compensation planners; these are discussed in Chapter 58. If severance pay benefits are funded, the value of the benefit is taxable to the employee in the first year in which he no longer has a substantial risk of forfeiting the benefit. This could result in taxation before the employee has actual or constructive receipt of the benefits. For example, suppose a funded plan provides severance benefits, payable in two equal annual installments, upon the employee's involuntary termination, death, or disability. Unless the plan provides a substantial risk of forfeiture that continues after termination, death, or disability, the full value of the benefits will be taxable in the year in which the employee terminates, dies, or becomes disabled, even if actual payment is spread over two years.

Social Security and Medicare Taxes

The regulations provide guidance on the Social Security tax treatment of nonqualified deferred compensation.[3] According to the regulations, certain welfare benefits are not treated as deferred compensation for FICA purposes. In particular, the IRS believes that severance pay in general is not subject to the special timing rule[4] for nonqualified deferred compensation, which provides that any amount deferred shall be taken into account for FICA purposes, as of the later of: (1) when the services are performed; or (2) when there is no substantial risk of forfeiting the rights to the amount deferred.[5] Thus, severance benefits are generally subject to Social Security and Medicare taxes when received.

ERISA IMPLICATIONS

1. If the severance pay plan requires an ongoing administrative scheme by the employer (i.e., payments are made over a period of time, employer has discretion as to eligibility or level of benefits, etc.), it is likely subject to ERISA. If subject to ERISA, it is either a pension plan or a welfare benefit plan.

2. Labor Department regulations provide that a severance pay plan will not be considered a pension plan, for ERISA purposes, if the following requirements are met:[6]

   - Payments are not contingent, directly or indirectly, upon retirement;
   - The total payments do not exceed twice the employee's annual compensation for the year immediately preceding the termination of employment; and
   - All payments are completed within twenty-four months after termination of employment (or, in the case of a "limited program of terminations," within the later of twenty-four months after termination or twenty-four months after the employee reaches normal retirement age).

   If these conditions are met, the plan will likely be considered a "welfare benefit plan" for ERISA purposes. See Chapter 16 for the reporting requirements applicable to welfare plans.

3. If a severance pay plan does not meet the ERISA pension plan exemption described above, it will be treated essentially as a nonqualified deferred

compensation plan for ERISA purposes. Unfunded plans for a select group of executives may be eligible for the ERISA top hat limited exemption, as discussed in Chapter 33. See also the discussion of this issue in Chapter 55.

4. If the plan covers only a single person and was individually negotiated, some courts have found that ERISA is not applicable because there is no "plan for employees."[7] Therefore, for example, there would be no reporting requirements.

CHAPTER ENDNOTES

1. Treas. Reg. §1.162-7.
2. Treas. Reg. §1.61-2(a).
3. Treas. Reg. §31.3121(v)(2)-1.
4. I.R.C. §3121(v)(2)(A).
5. See Treas. Reg. §31.3121(v)(2)-1(b)(4)(iv).
6. Labor Reg. §2510.3-2(b).
7. See, e.g., *Motel 6, Inc. v. Superior Court*, 195 Cal. App. 3d 1464; 241 Cal. Rptr. 528 (1987). The leading case on this issue is *Fort Halifax Packing Co. v. Coyne*, 48 U.S. 1 (1987).

GOLDEN PARACHUTE ARRANGEMENTS

CHAPTER 5

INTRODUCTION

A golden parachute arrangement is generally a compensation arrangement that provides special or enhanced benefits to executives in the event that their employer undergoes a change ownership or control. Examples of such arrangements include enhanced severance payments if termination occurs in connection with or following a change in control, accelerated vesting of equity incentive awards or nonqualified deferred compensation upon a change in control, retention bonuses paid if executives remain employed through and/or following a change in control, and transaction bonuses.

An executive who accepts employment with a company that is a potential target for acquisition will often insist on a parachute-type compensation arrangement as a matter of self-protection. In addition, employers will sometimes use golden parachute arrangements to incentivize their executives to stick around through the closing of a change in control transaction and for a period of time thereafter. Within limits, such agreements are an acceptable compensation practice.

Compensation arrangements of this type have a potential for abuse: inefficient managers could potentially grant themselves large parachute payments that would act merely as a financial obstacle to acquisition, or would unduly burden successor management. In addition, such arrangements have the effect of helping executives preserve their jobs, encouraging executives to favor a proposed transaction that might not be in the best interests of the shareholders, and/or reducing amounts which might otherwise be paid to the target corporation shareholders. Therefore, Congress added provisions to the Internal Revenue Code that limit corporate deductions for these payments and impose a penalty on the recipient for payments beyond specified limits. These provisions do *not* generally apply, however, to corporations that qualify as S corporations, tax-exempt corporations, certain privately held corporations (see below), partnerships and limited liability companies taxed as partnerships.

Also see Chapter 4 for further considerations in the design of severance pay arrangements.

TAX IMPLICATIONS

Generally, golden parachute arrangements carry the same tax implications as other types of compensation. However, an amount that is characterized as an excess parachute payment is subject to two tax sanctions:

1. no employer deduction is allowed on the excess parachute payment, and

2. the person receiving the payment is subject to a penalty tax equal to 20 percent of the excess parachute payment.[1]

An "excess parachute payment" is defined as the amount of any parachute payment less the portion of the "base amount" that is allocated to the payment. In other words, if a "disqualified individual" (see below) receives potential parachute payments of at least three times his or her base amount (see below), the corporation loses a deduction on the excess amount and the individual is subject to an excise tax on the parachute payments in excess of one times the individual's base amount (the amount in excess of the base amount is the "excess parachute payment"). These calculations are explained in detail below.

Definition of Excess Parachute Payment

In order to be considered an "excess parachute payment," the payment must meet two tests. First, it must be made to a "disqualified individual." A disqualified individual is any employee or independent contractor who (during the twelve-month period prior to the change in control):

1. is an officer;
2. owns more than 1 percent of outstanding shares; or
3. is a highly compensated individual (defined as one of the highest paid 1 percent of company employees, up to 250 employees, making at least $120,000 for 2015[2]).

The second part of the test relates to the nature of the payment itself. To be an excess parachute payment, it must meet the following criteria:[3]

1. the payment is contingent on a change in:
   a. the ownership or effective control of the corporation; or
   b. the ownership of a substantial portion of the assets of the corporation; and
2. the aggregate present value of the payments equals or exceeds three times the individual's base amount (see below).

Also included in the definition of a parachute payment is any payment made under an agreement that violates securities laws.[4]

If an agreement is made within one year of the ownership change, there is a presumption (which is rebuttable) that the payment is contingent on an ownership change.[5] In addition, an event occurring within the period beginning one year before and ending one year after the date of a change in control is presumed to be materially related to (and thus contingent on) the change in control. Pursuant to this rule, payments made upon a termination of employment or service that occurs within the one-year period following a change in control are generally treated as contingent payments.

An excess parachute payment is reduced by any portion of the payment which the taxpayer establishes by clear and convincing evidence is reasonable compensation for personal services actually rendered before the change in control. And any amount that the taxpayer can prove by clear and convincing evidence is reasonable compensation for personal services rendered on or after the change in control will not be treated as an excess parachute payment. Reasonable compensation is determined by reference to either the executive's historic compensation, or amounts paid by the employer or comparable employers to executives performing comparable services.[6]

Disallowance under this provision is coordinated with the Code provision generally disallowing deductions for compensation over $1,000,000; amounts disallowed under one provision are not allowed under the other.[7]

Note that where the payment date of vested compensation is accelerated or the vesting of non-vested compensation is accelerated in connection with a change in control, generally only a portion of the payment is considered a potential parachute payment.

Definition of Base Amount

The "base amount" referenced above refers to the recipient individual's average annualized includable (taxable) compensation for the five taxable years immediately preceding the year in which the change of ownership or control occurs.[8]

Example 1. Roger Flabb, CEO of Wimpp Industries, Inc. has average annualized compensation of $700,000 for the past five years. His severance agreement provides a lump sum severance payment of $2,800,000 in the event he is fired after a corporate takeover. Octopus, Inc. acquires Wimpp in 2015 and Roger is terminated and paid the $2,800,000 in 2015. Of that amount, $700,000 is an excess parachute payment ($2,800,000 – [3 × $700,000]).

Octopus (or whatever corporation pays the amount and is eligible to deduct compensation paid to Roger) is denied a deduction for the $2,100,000 excess parachute payment (the excess of the total $2,800,000 over the $700,000 base amount). The base amount of $700,000 of the severance payment to Roger is deductible by the payor as a compensation payment. Roger must pay income tax on the entire $2,800,000 payment plus a 20 percent penalty tax on the excess parachute payment (20 percent of $2,100,000 or $420,000).

Example 2. Brenda Flabb, Vice President of Wimpp Industries, Inc., earned $100,000 each of the prior five years. She is entitled to two golden parachute payments, one of $200,000 at the time of her termination and a second payment of $400,000 at a future date. Assume that the present value of the second payment is $300,000. Applying the formula above, the portion of the base amount allocated to the first payment would be $40,000 ($200,000/$500,000 × $100,000) and the amount allocated to the second payment would be $60,000 ($300,000/$500,000 × $100,000). Therefore, the amount of the first excess payment is $160,000 ($200,000 – $40,000) and the second excess payment is $340,000 ($400,000 – $60,000).

Exceptions

The parachute rules do not apply to corporations that have no stock that is readily tradable on an established securities market, provided that the payments are approved by a majority of shareholders who, immediately before the change in control, owned more than 75 percent of the voting power of all outstanding stock following disclosure to them of all material facts.[9]

Further, the parachute rules do not apply to payments from qualified retirement plans, simplified employee pension plans and SIMPLE IRAs.[10]

WHERE CAN I FIND OUT MORE?

1. Hevener, Mary B. "Golden Parachutes: Proposed Regulations," *Tax Management Compensation Planning Journal* 17/8, August 4, 1989.

2. Feldman, "A Bird's-Eye View of Golden Parachutes," *Journal of Pension Planning and Compliance*, Spring, 1993.

CHAPTER ENDNOTES

1. I.R.C. §4999.
2. I.R.C. §280G(c).
3. I.R.C. §280G(b)(2).
4. I.R.C. §280G(b)(2)(B).
5. I.R.C. §280G(b)(2)(C).
6. I.R.C. §280G(b)(4); Treas. Reg. §1.280G-1, Q&A 40, 42(a).
7. I.R.C. §162(m)(4)(f). Under I.R.C. §§162(m)(5), 162(m)(6), and 280G(e), these provisions are coordinated with the deduction limitation for executives affected by the "troubled assets relief program" and similar provisions for health insurance executives.
8. I.R.C. §§280G(b)(3)(A), 280G(d)(2). Generally, this means that the amounts that are reported in Form W-2, Box 1 and Form 1099-MISC, Box 7.
9. I.R.C. §§280G(b)(5)(A)(ii), 280G(b)(5)(B); Treas. Reg. §1.280G-1, Q&A 6(a)(2), 7(a).
10. I.R.C. §§280G(b)(5)(A)(i), 280G(b)(6).

STOCK OPTION

CHAPTER 6

INTRODUCTION

A stock option is a formal, written offer that provides employees and other service providers with a right to buy employer stock at a specified price, within specified time limits. Employers often use stock options for compensating executives. Such options are generally for stock of the employer company or a subsidiary.

Options are typically granted to executives as additional compensation at the current market value, with an expectation that the value of the stock will rise, making the option price a bargain beneficial to the individual. Options typically remain outstanding for a period of ten years. If the price of the stock goes down, the individual will not purchase the stock, so he or she does not risk any out-of-pocket loss.

The executive is generally not taxed upon the grant of an option (unless the option has a readily ascertainable fair market value, as described below); taxation is deferred to the time when the option is exercised. Thus, stock options are a form of deferred compensation, with the amount of compensation based upon increases in the value of the company's stock from the date of grant. This equity form of compensation is popular with executives, because it gives them some of the advantages of business ownership.

There are two main types of stock option plans used for compensating executives: (1) incentive stock options (ISO); and (2) nonstatutory stock options. ISOs are a form of stock option plan with special tax benefits; these are discussed in Chapter 7. Nonstatutory stock options will be discussed here.

For an outline of some advanced types of stock option and other plans used for compensating executives, particularly in large corporations, see Appendix C of this book.

WHEN IS USE OF SUCH A DEVICE INDICATED?

1. When an employer is willing to compensate employees with shares of company stock. Many family corporations or other closely held corporations generally do not want to share ownership of the business in this manner. Option plans are most often used by corporations whose ownership is relatively broad, and are common in large corporations whose stock is publicly traded.

2. Where an employer wishes to reward executive performance by providing equity-type compensation—that is, compensation that increases in value as the employer stock increases in value. This has generally been viewed as the perfect incentive for executives, since the executives' interests will be the same as those of shareholders—to increase the value of the corporation. However, recent financial scandals suggest that, at least for CEOs and high executives of large corporations, stock-based compensation may tempt executives to engage in short-term manipulation of the stock price to the detriment of regular shareholders. Executive compensation arrangements should be designed with this caution in mind.

ADVANTAGES

1. Nonstatutory stock option plans can be designed in virtually any manner suitable to an executive or to the employer. There are few tax or other

government regulatory constraints. For example, a stock option plan can be provided for any group of executives, or even a single executive. Benefits can vary from one executive to another without restriction. There are no nondiscrimination coverage or benefit rules.

2. Stock options are a form of compensation with little or no out-of-pocket cost to the company (although stock options generally must be expensed under FASB Accounting Standards Codification Topic 718).

3. Stock options are a form of compensation on which tax to the employee is deferred. As discussed in the Tax Implications section later in this chapter, tax is generally not payable at the time when a stock option is granted to the executive. Taxation to the employee generally occurs when the option is exercised; however, it may be possible to further defer taxation by combining the option with a nonqualified deferred compensation agreement, under which the tax at exercise is further deferred, by restricting or limiting access to the required stock (or stock value) for a period of time or until retirement.[1]

DISADVANTAGES

1. The executive bears the market risk of this kind of compensation. If the market value of stock goes below the option price while the option is outstanding, the employee does not have any actual out-of-pocket loss; however, since the executive will not purchase the stock, there is no additional compensation received. And, after an option is "exercised" (i.e., company stock is purchased by the executive), the executive bears the full market risk of holding company stock.

2. The executive generally must have a source of funds to purchase the stock (and pay taxes due in the year of exercise) in order to benefit from the plan (although some employers will allow for a cashless or "net" exercise).

3. Fluctuation in the market value of the stock may have little or no relation to executive performance. This factor weakens the value of a stock option plan as a performance incentive.

4. The employer's tax deduction is generally delayed until the executive exercises the option and purchases stock. Furthermore, the employer generally gets no further deduction, even if the executive realizes substantial capital gains thereafter. (See "Tax Implications" below for more information).

TAX IMPLICATIONS

1. If an option has no readily ascertainable fair market value (see below) at the time it is "granted" (i.e., transferred to the executive), there is no taxable income to the executive at the date of the grant.[2]

2. The employee has taxable compensation income (ordinary income) in the year when shares are actually purchased under the option. The amount of taxable income to the employee is the "bargain element"—the difference between the fair market value of the shares at the date of purchase and the option price (the amount the executive actually pays for these shares).[3] The employer must withhold and pay federal income tax with respect to this compensation income.

3. The employer does not get a tax deduction at the time an option is granted. The employer receives a tax deduction in the same year in which the employee has taxable income as a result of exercising the option and purchasing shares. The amount of the deduction is the same as the amount of income the employee must include.[4]

Example. Executive Lee was given an option in 2015 to purchase 1,000 shares of Employer Company stock at $100 per share, the market price on the date of grant. The option can be exercised by Lee at any time over the next five years. In 2017, Lee purchases 400 shares for a total of $40,000. If the fair market value of the shares in 2017 is $60,000, Lee has $20,000 of ordinary income in 2017. Employer Company gets a tax deduction of $20,000 in 2017 (assuming that Lee's total compensation meets the reasonableness test), which is the same amount as Lee's compensation income. If Lee re-sells this stock at a gain in a later year, he has capital gain income. Employer Company gets no further tax deduction, even though Lee realizes and reports capital gain income from selling the stock.

---

4. The executive's basis in shares acquired under a stock option plan is equal to the amount paid for the stock, plus the amount of taxable income reported by the executive at the time the option was exercised.[5]

In the example in paragraph (3) above, Lee's basis for the 400 shares purchased in 2017 is $60,000—the $40,000 that Lee paid, plus the $20,000 of ordinary income that he reported in 2017. Therefore, if Lee sells the 400 shares in 2019 for $90,000, he must report $30,000 of capital gain in 2019 (the selling price of $90,000, less his basis of $60,000). Employer Company gets no additional tax deduction in 2019.

5. If the option has a readily ascertainable fair market value at the time of the grant, paragraphs (1) through (4) above do not apply. Instead, it is taxed at the time of the grant, and the employer receives a corresponding tax deduction at that time and the employee has no further taxable compensation income when the option is later exercised.

   An option will be deemed to have a readily ascertainable fair market value if:

   - the option has a value that is determinable as of the time of the grant; and
   - the option can be traded on an established market.[6]

   A non-publicly traded nonstatutory stock option is considered to have a readily ascertainable fair market value on the grant date only if, on that date, it satisfies four conditions:

   a. the option is freely transferable;
   b. the option is exercisable immediately in full;
   c. the option or the stock subject to the option is not subject to any restriction or condition which has a significant effect upon the fair market value of the option; and
   d. the fair market value of the option privilege is readily ascertainable.

FREQUENTLY ASKED QUESTIONS

Question – What is the effect of federal securities laws on stock option plans?

Answer – From the employer viewpoint, it is necessary to determine whether the stock is subject to the registration requirements of federal securities law. Various exemptions from registration may apply to stock provided only to selected executives for compensation purposes, but the existence of such an exemption must be verified. State securities laws may also apply.

Advisors to the executive must determine if any of the resale restrictions of federal securities law apply to the sale of stock acquired under the plan. In addition, the executive may be considered an insider, and subject to the insider trading restrictions upon the resale of stock.

Question – How are stock options treated by the company for accounting purposes?

Answer – Under ASC 718, a company must recognize the cost of options or other share-based award of compensation to an employee at the "grant-date fair value of the award." This cost is recognized over the period during which the employee is required to provide service in exchange for the award of compensation. See Chapter 61, "Accounting for Benefit Plans."

Question – Do the distribution restrictions of Code section 409A, discussed in Chapter 5, apply to a stock option plan?

Answer – Code section 409A and the regulations under that section incorporate a broad definition of deferred compensation that could cover stock options. Unfortunately, applying the 409A distribution restrictions to a stock option plan could destroy the plan's viability, since the option would have to be exercised upon an section 409A permissible payment event (i.e., specified date, separation from service, death, disability, change in control, or unforeseeable emergency).

But the section 409A regulations provide an exception to the application of 409A to options that satisfy certain rules. The most significant rule is that the option price must not be less than the fair market value of the stock at the date of the grant. This rule would penalize discounted options. There may also be other traps in this rule. For example, it may prevent options from being modified in certain respects or extended.

CHAPTER ENDNOTES

1. See Brisendine, "Deferring Tax On Gain From Stock Option Exercises: Does It Work?" *Benefits Law Journal*, Summer 1997. The author's comments in this article are particularly authoritative because he is a former IRS official familiar with IRS positions in this area.
2. I.R.C. §83(e)(3).
3. I.R.C. §83(a).
4. I.R.C. §83(h).
5. Treas. Reg. §§1.61-2(d)(2), 1.83-4(b).
6. Treas. Reg. §1.83-7(b).

INCENTIVE STOCK OPTION (ISO)

CHAPTER 7

INTRODUCTION

An incentive stock option (ISO) plan is a tax-favored plan for compensating executives by granting options to buy company stock. Unlike regular stock options, ISOs generally do not result in taxable income to executives either at the time of the grant or the time of the exercise of the option. If the ISO meets the requirements of Internal Revenue Code section 422, the executive is taxed only when stock purchased under the ISO is sold. (Regular or nonstatutory stock options are discussed in Chapter 6. Also, see Appendix C for a comprehensive outline of stock option and similar plans used for compensating executives, particularly in large corporations.)

WHEN IS USE OF SUCH A DEVICE INDICATED?

ISOs are primarily used by larger corporations to compensate executives. Some closely held corporations grant ISOs that contain put rights (i.e., the right of the employee to sell the acquired stock back to the company at current fair market value), call rights (i.e., the right of the company to purchase the acquired stock from the employee at current fair market value) and/or rights of first refusal (i.e., the company's right to purchase the acquired stock from the employee in the event he or she attempts to sell the stock to a third party).

Advantages

1. Unlike a nonstatutory stock option (see Chapter 6), an ISO is not subject to ordinary income taxes if all of the ISO rules are satisfied.
2. Income from the sale of the stock obtained through exercise of an ISO may be eligible for preferential capital gain treatment.
3. The ISO is a form of compensation with little or no out-of-pocket cost to the company.

Disadvantages

1. The corporation granting an ISO does not ordinarily receive a tax deduction for it at any time.
2. The plan must meet requirements of Code section 422 and related provisions.
3. The exercise price of an ISO must be at least equal to the fair market value of the stock when the option is granted. There is no similar restriction on nonstatutory options, although nonstatutory options must comply with Code section 409A, which means that they generally cannot be granted with an exercise price that is less than the fair market value of the stock on the grant date.
4. As with all stock option plans, the executive gets no benefit unless he is able to come up with enough cash to exercise the option.
5. An executive may incur an alternative minimum tax (AMT) liability when an ISO option is exercised, thus increasing the executive's cash requirements in the year of exercise.

TAX IMPLICATIONS

The executive is not subject to federal income tax on an ISO either at the time the option is granted or at the time he exercises the option (i.e., when he buys the stock). Tax consequences are deferred until the time of disposition of the stock.[1]

Section 422 Rules

In order to obtain this tax treatment for incentive stock options, section 422 prescribes the following rules:

- The terms of the option must not provide that the option will not be treated as an ISO.
- The options must be granted under a written plan specifying the number of shares to be issued through the exercise of ISOs and the class of employees covered under the plan; there are no nondiscrimination rules. The plan can cover key executives only.
- Only the first $100,000 worth of ISO stock granted any one employee—which becomes exercisable for the first time during any one year—is entitled to the favorable ISO treatment. To the extent that the value of the stock exceeds $100,000, this amount is treated as a non-statutory (regular) stock option.
- No option, by its terms, may be exercisable more than ten years from the date of the grant.
- The person receiving the option must be employed by the company granting the option or a related corporation at all times between the grant of the option and three months before the date of exercise (twelve months in the case of permanent and total disability, and no limit in the event of death).
- Stock acquired by an employee under the ISO must be held for at least two years after the grant of the option and one year from the date stock is transferred to the employee. (This requirement is waived upon the employee's death.)
- No additional options may be issued for more than ten years from the date the ISO plan is adopted or approved, whichever occurs first.
- The option must not be transferable (except by will or descent and distribution) and must be exercisable only by the person receiving it.
- Corporate stockholders must approve the ISO plan within twelve months of the time it is adopted by the company's board of directors.
- The exercise price of the option must be at least equal to the fair market value of the stock on the date the option is granted.
- ISOs may not be granted to any employee who owns, directly or indirectly, more than 10 percent of the corporation unless the term of the option is limited to not more than five years and the exercise price is at least 110 percent of the fair market value of the stock on the date of the grant.[2]

Capital Gains

If the executive holds the stock for the periods specified above, (two years after grant and one year after exercise) the gain on any sale is taxed at preferential long-term capital gain rates.

If the stock is sold before the two year/one year holding periods specified above (a disqualifying disposition), the excess of the fair market value of the shares at the time of exercise over the exercise price is treated as compensation income to the executive in the year the stock is sold, depriving the executive of preferential capital gain treatment.[3] In addition, the corporation receives a deduction for the compensation in the event of such a disqualifying disposition.

Example. Executive Flo Through is covered under her company's ISO plan. Under the plan, Flo is granted an option in 2015 to purchase company stock for $100 per share. In January, 2017, Flo exercises this option and purchases 100 shares for a total of $10,000. The fair market value of the 100 shares in January, 2017, is $14,000. In October, 2017, Flo sells the 100 shares for $16,000, resulting in a disqualifying disposition. Flo's taxable gain is $6,000 ($16,000 amount realized less $10,000 cost). Of this amount, $4,000 (fair market value of $14,000 less $10,000 exercise price) is treated as compensation income for the year 2017. The remaining $2,000 is capital gain. The company is allowed a deduction of $4,000 attributable to Flo's exercise of the ISO.

AMT

Although there is no regular income tax to the executive when an ISO is exercised, the alternative minimum tax (AMT) may have an impact. The excess of the stock's fair market value over the option price at the time of exercise is included in the individual's alternative minimum taxable income. (However, if the individual is subject to the alternative minimum tax, his basis in the stock for alternative minimum tax purposes will be increased by the amount included in income.[4])

Employer Deduction

The corporation does not get a tax deduction for granting an ISO. Nor does it get a deduction when an executive exercises an option or sells stock acquired under an ISO plan.[5] However, the corporation *does* get a deduction for the compensation income element that an executive must recognize if stock is sold before the two year/one year holding period, as described in paragraph five above.

WHERE CAN I FIND OUT MORE?

1. *Tax Facts on Investments*, The National Underwriter Co., Cincinnati, OH; revised annually.

CHAPTER ENDNOTES

1. I.R.C. §421(a).
2. I.R.C. §422(b)(6) provides that an incentive stock option can be granted to an individual only if such individual, at the time the option is granted, does not own stock possessing more than 10% of the total combined voting power of all classes of stock of the employer corporation or of its parent or subsidiary corporation.
3. I.R.C. §421(b).
4. I.R.C. §56(b)(3).
5. I.R.C. §§421(a)(2), 421(b).

EMPLOYEE STOCK PURCHASE PLAN (SECTION 423 PLAN)

CHAPTER 8

INTRODUCTION

An employee stock purchase plan (ESPP) under Code section 423 (a qualified ESPP) is a plan for compensating a broad group of employees with purchase rights (i.e., options) to buy stock of the employer company (typically through after-tax payroll deductions) at a discount and without brokerage fees. ESPPs are generally not used for compensating select executives; among other restrictions, ESPP benefits are limited to $25,000 per year and are not available to more than 5 percent owners. See the Stock Option Plan and Incentive Stock Option Plan chapters for the types of option plans used for executive compensation.

The option price in an ESPP is generally 85 percent or more of the market value. The plan generally must cover all full-time employees. The detailed requirements are described further below and are somewhat similar to the requirements of Incentive Stock Options (ISOs) as described in Chapter 7.

The employee is generally not taxed at the grant of a qualified ESPP option or at the time the option is exercised (i.e., the time the stock is purchased by the employee). As long as the appropriate holding period is met, there is no taxation to the employee until the stock is sold. The employee's gain on the sale is taxed as capital gain. Thus, an ESPP is a form of deferred compensation with the amount of compensation based on increases in the value of the company's stock.

WHEN IS USE OF SUCH A DEVICE INDICATED?

1. When an employer is willing to compensate employees with shares of company stock and encourage employee ownership. Many family corporations or other closely held corporations do not want to share ownership of the business in this manner. ESPPs are most often used by corporations whose ownership are relatively broadly held, and are very common in large corporations whose stock is publicly traded.

2. Where an employer wishes to reward executive performance by providing an equity type of compensation—that is, compensation that gives employees an interest in the financial success of the business.

Advantages

1. As a form of equity compensation, it provides an appropriate incentive to employees and aligns them with shareholders.

2. An ESPP is popular with employees as an easy form of savings.

3. An ESPP has little or no out of pocket cost to the company.

4. An ESPP is a form of compensation on which tax to the employee is deferred. Tax is generally not payable until the stock is sold by the employee (see "Tax Implications" section later in this chapter).

Disadvantages

1. The employee bears the market risk of this kind of compensation. After the stock is purchased by the employee, the market price may decline and there

is no compensation to the employee to cover this risk. Studies have shown that employees tend to overrate the value of their company's stock, and are not likely to realize the need to diversify their portfolio.

3. Fluctuation in the market value of the stock is likely to have little or no relation to employee performance where a large group of employees is covered. This factor weakens the value of an ESPP as a performance incentive.

4. As discussed in the Tax Implications section, the employer generally receives no tax deduction under an ESPP.

5. There may be accounting consequences when discounts exceed 5 percent and the plan has a "look-back" provision.

SECTION 423 REQUIREMENTS

Coverage

The plan must cover all employees of the plan sponsor, except that it may exclude:

- employees with less than two years of service,
- employees with customary service of less than twenty hours per week or not more than five months in any calendar year, and
- highly compensated employees (within the definition used for qualified plan purposes under Code section 414(q)).[1]

In addition, no employee who owns more than 5 percent of the company (or a parent or subsidiary) can receive options under an ESPP.[2]

The plan may cover employees of the employer's parent or subsidiary corporation as well as those of the employer.[3]

Benefits and Plan Features

All covered employees must have the same rights and benefits, but the amount of stock purchased can be limited to a uniform percentage of compensation for all employees.[4] The plan can provide for a maximum amount of stock that can be purchased, and in any event no employee can purchase more than $25,000 of stock under an ESPP in any one calendar year.[5] The price for the stock must be not less than the lesser of:

- 85 percent of the fair market value at the time the option for purchase is granted; or
- 85 percent of the fair market value of the stock at the time it is purchased (when the purchase price is determined using the lesser of fair market value at grant and at purchase, the plan contains a "look-back" provision).[6]

A company is not required to offer a 15 percent discount or use a look-back provision.

To participate in an ESPP, employees typically enter into salary reduction agreements to purchase shares during a specified offering period. An offering period may not exceed five years (twenty-seven months if using a look-back provision).

Options under an ESPP are not transferable except by will or the laws of descent and distribution.

TAX IMPLICATIONS

For the Employee

The two main tax benefits for the employee are:

1. The employee has no taxable income at the time the ESPP option is granted.
2. The employee has no taxable income when the ESPP option is exercised (when the employee buys the stock).

In order to receive these two tax benefits, the stock must be held for at least two years after the date the option is granted, and one year after the employee buys the stock. Also, the taxpayer must remain an employee of the company until at least three months before exercising the option.[7] Generally, if the holding period is not met, the result is that the employee will have additional compensation income in the amount of the "bargain" element—the difference between the option price and the fair market value of the stock when the employee purchases it.

If the holding period described above is met, then when the employee sells the stock some of the proceeds will be reported as ordinary compensation income in an amount equal to the lesser of:

- the difference between the option price and the fair market value of the stock at the time the option was granted; or
- the difference between the amount the employee paid for the shares and the fair market value of the shares at the time of the sale.

The rest of the gain on the sale (if any) is capital gain.

Example. Your employer, Y Corporation, granted you an option under its employee stock purchase plan to buy 100 shares of stock of Y Corporation for $20 a share at a time when the stock had a value of $22 a share. Eighteen months later, when the value of the stock was $23 a share, you exercised the option, and 14 months after that you sold your stock for $30 a share. In the year of sale, you must report as wages the difference between the option price ($20) and the value at the time the option was granted ($22). The rest of your gain ($8 per share) is capital gain, figured as follows:

Selling price ($30 × 100 shares)	$ 3,000
Purchase price (option price) ($20 × 100 shares)	– 2,000
Gain	$ 1,000
Amount reported as wages [($22 × 100 shares) – $2,000]	– 200
Amount reported as capital gain	$ 800

For the Employer

The employer receives no tax deduction if the employee meets the holding period described above.[8] However, if the employee must include an amount in income as compensation because the holding period is not met, the employer can deduct this.[9]

REPORTING REQUIREMENTS

An ESPP does not appear to fall within the definition of either a pension or a welfare benefit plan for ERISA purposes.[10] Consequently, there is no reporting requirement (no Form 5500 need be filed) and other ERISA provisions are also inapplicable.

HOW IS THE PLAN SET UP?

The plan must be approved by the stockholders of the granting corporation within twelve months before or after the date the employer adopts the plan.[11] A written plan and notification of employees are desirable steps but not specifically mandated by law.

WHERE CAN I FIND OUT MORE?

IRS Publication 525, Taxable and Nontaxable Income.

CHAPTER ENDNOTES

1. I.R.C. §423(a)(4).
2. I.R.C. §423(b)(3).
3. I.R.C. §423(b)(1).
4. I.R.C. §423(a)(5).
5. I.R.C. §423(a)(8).
6. I.R.C. §423(a)(6).
7. I.R.C. §423(a)(1),(2).
8. I.R.C. §421(a)(2).
9. I.R.C. §421(b).
10. See DOL Reg. §2510.3-1.
11. I.R.C. §423(b)(2).

RESTRICTED STOCK PLAN

CHAPTER 9

INTRODUCTION

A restricted stock plan is an arrangement to compensate executives by giving them shares of stock subject to certain restrictions or limitations. Usually, the stock used in such plans is stock of the employer corporation or its subsidiary.

Company stock is attractive to executives as an element of compensation, because it allows sharing in company growth. To the employer, the use of stock is attractive as a "double incentive" plan for executives, because the terms of the plan can be based on executive performance, and, in addition, increases in the value of the stock may reflect, to some extent, the executive's performance.

Employers often adopt stock plans with restrictions designed to help retain employees or discourage conduct that the employer deems undesirable, such as going to work for a competitor. These restrictions can also serve the employee's interest, by postponing taxation of compensation to the employee.

For an outline of some advanced types of stock and other plans used for compensating executives, particularly in large corporations, see Appendix C.

WHEN IS USE OF SUCH A DEVICE INDICATED?

1. When the employer is willing to create new shareholders of the company. Shareholders of a closely held corporation may not want to share ownership and control of the business outside of the existing group of shareholders.

2. When a corporation wants to provide an executive with an incentive-based form of compensation that aligns the executive's interests with those of the corporation's shareholders. In restricted stock plans, the ultimate amount the executive receives generally depends on the value of the stock. If the plan is well designed, the value of company stock will reflect the executive's performance, at least to some extent.

3. When an employer wants to use a compensation arrangement as a way to attract and retain key employees.

4. When an executive wants an equity-based form of compensation—that is, compensation based on the value of the company's stock. Equity-based compensation allows an executive to share in the upside potential of a company's growth. This type of compensation is particularly useful in the start-up phase of a company, where growth can be very significant.

ADVANTAGES

1. Restricted stock plans can allow deferral of taxation to the employee until the year in which the restricted stock becomes substantially vested. Essentially, this means nonforfeitable, as discussed later in this chapter in the Tax Implications section.

2. A stock plan invests employees with a direct interest in the increase in value of a company's stock. This type of payment, especially when coupled with deferral of taxation, can be much more valuable than straight cash compensation.

3. A restricted stock plan allows an employer to grant an executive an equity interest in the company,

but can call or repurchase it if the executive leaves prematurely or goes to work for a competitor.

4. For non-tax purposes, an executive has all the advantages of stock ownership, such as voting rights, dividends, and appreciation potential, but is not taxed on receipt of the stock to the extent it is not substantially vested.

DISADVANTAGES

1. The employer does not receive a tax deduction for a restricted stock plan until the year in which the property becomes substantially vested and therefore taxable to the executive (unless the executive elects to be taxed earlier under section 83(b), as discussed in the "Tax Implications section).

2. The possibility of a section 83(b) election by the executive means that the employer may not have control of the amount or timing of its tax deduction.

3. S corporations must be certain that the restrictions do not create a second class of stock, which would violate the S corporation one-class-of-stock rule. An S corporation that violates this rule will terminate its S election, thus subjecting all corporate income to taxation at ordinary corporate rates.

   Generally, an S corporation will not be treated as having more than one class of shares so long as all shares confer identical rights to liquidation and distribution proceeds. Thus, guaranteed distributions following a vesting period may violate the rule unless all shares enjoy the same guaranteed distributions. Ordinary contractual arrangements, such as employment agreements, will not be deemed to affect distribution and liquidation proceeds, unless a principal purpose of the arrangement is to circumvent the one-class rule.

4. Issuing new shares of restricted stock dilutes ownership of the corporation. This may be particularly undesirable for closely held corporations. Shareholders of these corporations seldom want to share control or profits, or share company assets upon sale or liquidation of the business.

5. If the change (up or down) in value of the stock is not consistent with the executive's performance, this can be disadvantageous to both employer and executive. If the stock goes up with little or no effort by the executive, other shareholders will be resentful. If the stock drops in value in spite of excellent executive performance, the incentive element of the plan is lost or diminished.

PLAN OBJECTIVES

The types of restrictions used in restricted stock plans can be tailored to meet employer and employee objectives and goals.

Employee Retention

Employers often use stock plans to retain key employees. With this type of objective, for example, stock might be transferred to an employee subject to a restriction that it be forfeited to the company if the employee separates from service prior to a specified period of time (e.g., five years). This simple form of restriction can also be used as a way of keeping retirees tied to the company and providing them with some useful deferral of income. For example, the stock can be transferred to an executive retiree, subject to a provision that the retiree provide consulting services to the employer during a specified time, such as five years. The retiree must, however, be expected to perform substantial services.

Performance

Restricted stock plans can be designed to encourage high performance, by tying vesting to the satisfaction of one or more performance goals. For example, a restricted stock plan might give an executive 1,000 shares of company stock, subject to forfeiture if gross sales in the executive's division do not increase by at least 20 percent within five years. When sales reach the targeted level, the forfeitability restrictions would end. The stock would then belong to the executive without restriction. The advantage of this arrangement over a cash bonus is simply that it increases the security of the benefit to the employee, compared with the employer's mere promise to pay a cash bonus. However, there are some risks, from the employee's point of view, when compared with the stated contingent bonus amount, because the value of the stock could very well go down, even though the employee works effectively and meets or exceeds the designated target sales level.

TAX IMPLICATIONS

Vesting

Under section 83 of the Internal Revenue Code, an employee is not subject to tax on the value of restricted property received as compensation from the employer until the year in which the property becomes substantially vested (unless the employee makes a section 83(b) election to include it in income in the year received, as discussed below).

When an employee has become substantially vested in restricted property, its value is taxed in that year as compensation income.[1] Gain on any subsequent sale of the property is generally taxed as capital gain, as in the case of similar property acquired by any other means.

The definition of substantial vesting in Code section 83 and the regulations thereunder is of great significance in designing restricted stock plans. These plans are obviously much less attractive to employees if they are not carefully designed to provide tax deferral within the rules of section 83.

Example. If an employee receives restricted stock in 2015 that is deemed (for tax purposes) to be substantially vested in 2015, the employee will pay tax in that year (and the corporation will get a corresponding deduction; see below), even if, under state law, the employee does not completely own the stock. In spite of the taxability to the employee, the restrictions on the stock received may still be legally effective under state property law, so that the employee cannot sell the stock in 2015 and realize any cash at that time.

"Substantial Risk of Forfeiture"

Under section 83, property is not considered substantially vested, so long as it is subject to a "substantial risk of forfeiture" and is not transferable by an employee to a third party free of this risk of forfeiture.

The question of whether a substantial risk of forfeiture exists depends on the facts and circumstances in each case. The regulations under section 83 contain various examples and guidelines.

- A substantial risk of forfeiture exists only if the restricted stock is conditioned, directly or indirectly, upon the future performance (or refraining from performance) of substantial services, or upon the occurrence of a condition related to a purpose of the transfer (such as a performance condition) if the possibility of forfeiture is substantial.[2]

- Restricted stock is not subject to a substantial risk of forfeiture if at the time of grant the facts and circumstances demonstrate that the forfeiture condition is unlikely to be enforced. In addition, restricted stock is not subject to a substantial risk of forfeiture to the extent that the employer is required to pay the fair market value of a portion of such restricted stock to the employee upon the return of such property.

- A forfeiture that occurs as a result of a failure to meet certain performance goals, such as a certain level of sales, generally is a substantial risk of forfeiture.[3]

- A requirement that the restricted stock be forfeited if the employee accepts a job with a competitor will not ordinarily be considered a substantial risk of forfeiture unless the particular facts and circumstances demonstrate otherwise. Factors which may be taken into account in determining whether a covenant not to compete constitutes a substantial risk of forfeiture are the age of the employee, the availability of alternative employment opportunities, the likelihood of the employee's obtaining such other employment, the degree of skill possessed by the employee, the employee's health, and the practice (if any) of the employer to enforce such covenants.[4]

Where an employee is an owner or major shareholder of a company, forfeiture provisions may be challenged by the IRS as being insubstantial, because the employee's control or influence over the company can render them relatively ineffective.[5]

As indicated above, property will not be considered subject to a substantial risk of forfeiture if it can be transferred by the employee to another person or entity free of the risk of forfeiture. When employer stock is used in a restricted stock plan, this requirement is usually met by a legend or statement imprinted on share certificates indicating that transfer and ownership of the shares are subject to a restricted property plan. This notifies any prospective buyer or other recipient that the employee is not free to sell, give away, or otherwise transfer the shares without restrictions.

Section 83(b) Election

Under section 83(b), an executive can elect to recognize income as of the date when he receives the restricted property, rather than waiting until it becomes substantially vested. This election must be made within thirty days of receiving the property and must comply with requirements in the IRS regulations.

The amount included in income under section 83(b) election is the excess, if any, of the fair market value of the property at the time of transfer (determined without regard to any restrictions other than "non-lapse" restrictions—see below) over any amount the executive paid for the property.

> *Example.* If the stock is worth $60 per share at the time of receipt and the executive pays nothing for it, under a section 83(b) election, the executive would report ordinary income of $60 per share in the year of receipt.

Why would an executive make a section 83(b) election? Because if a such an election is made, any subsequent appreciation in value of the property is treated as capital gain and taxed at lower capital gain rates. That gain is not subject to tax until the stock is sold. This can be a major consideration in deciding whether to make a section 83(b) election. These elections may also be advantageous in special situations; for example, where the executive wants to maximize taxable income in a particular year in order to offset deductible losses.

When an executive includes an amount in income under a section 83(b) election, the employer gets a tax deduction at that time for the same amount. The employer gets no further tax deduction if the property subsequently increases in value in the hands of the executive, whether or not the executive sells the property. Another disadvantage of the section 83(b) election is that if the stock is forfeited for any reason, no deduction is allowed to the executive for the loss.

The executive making a section 83(b) election is therefore gambling that the stock will increase substantially in value from the date of the election and that the stock will not be forfeited before the executive is able to sell or dispose of it without restriction.

Non-lapse Restrictions

Sometimes the stock received does not have a forfeiture provision as such, but rather has a restriction that reduces the value of the stock to the employee. In that case, the value of the stock is includable in income when received. But the amount includable is less than the full market value.

> *Example.* A plan may provide an employee with a fully vested interest in the stock, but with a provision that the employee cannot resell the stock without first offering it back to the company at a specified price. In that case, because of the "first offer" provision, the value of the stock in the hands of the executive would not be its unfettered market value, but rather a reduced value reflecting the restriction.

A restriction will be taken into account for valuation purposes only if it is a non-lapse restriction—a restriction that, by its terms, will never lapse.[6] The first offer requirement of the type described in the example above would probably qualify as a non-lapse restriction. Whether a restriction constitutes a non-lapse restriction is a facts and circumstances determination. The IRS takes a restrictive view in its regulations and rulings, so non-lapse restrictions are difficult to design.

Employer Deduction

The employer's tax deduction for compensation income to the executive under a restricted stock plan is deferred until the year in which the employee is substantially vested and includes the amount in income. Technically, the employer's tax deduction occurs in the employer's taxable year in which, or with which, the taxable year of the employee in whose income the amount is includable ends.[7] This is the usual rule for the timing of an employer's deduction for deferred compensation payments, as discussed in Chapter 2. As with other types of compensation, the employer is required to withhold and pay tax (although the tax obligations will have to be withheld from other cash compensation or paid by the employee from another source of funds) and meet certain informational requirements.

FREQUENTLY ASKED QUESTIONS

Question – How does a restricted stock plan affect an employer's accounting statements?

Answer – If stock is issued with restrictions based only on continued employment, the excess of the stock's fair market value when issued over the amount paid for it by the executive is a compensation expense for accounting purposes and is charged to earnings on a systematic basis over the related period of employment—the period during which the restrictions are in effect. If restrictions are based on contingent factors such as executive or company performance, the charge to expense can be delayed until the result is known for certain. These rules are set out in the currently effective official accounting statement from the Financial Accounting Standards Board (FASB).[8]

Question – Do federal securities laws apply to restricted stock, and what is their effect?

Answer – Federal securities registration is not generally required if stock is issued without cost, because no "sale" is deemed to occur for securities law purposes. However, the SEC views stock issued to executives as compensation to have been bargained for and thus sold, so the securities laws may apply. Many restricted stock arrangements qualify for one or more of the exemptions from securities registration, typically the "private placement" exemption, whereby registration is not required where securities are issued to a limited number of persons.

Planners must also determine whether executives are restricted under the federal securities laws from re-selling stock acquired under the plan. SEC Rule 144 includes conditions under which such stock can be resold freely. Executives holding stock in a restricted stock plan may also be subject to the anti-fraud provisions of the securities law, such as the insider trading restrictions.

CHAPTER ENDNOTES

1. I.R.C. § 83(a).
2. Treas. Reg. §1.83-3(c).
3. Ibid.
4. Ibid.
5. Treas. Reg. §1.83-3(c)(3).
6. Treas. Reg. §§1.83-5(a), 1.83-3(h).
7. Treas. Reg. §1.83-6(a)(1).
8. ASC Topic 718. See "FASB Proposed Accounting Standards Update: Compensation-Stock Compensation (Topic 718)," (Oct. 23, 2013); available at: www.fasb.org/jsp/FASB/Document_C/DocumentPage?cid=1176163531340&accepted Disclaimer=true.

DESIGNING THE RIGHT RETIREMENT PLAN

CHAPTER 10

INTRODUCTION

This chapter provides an overview of the process of designing a retirement plan for a business client. It is intended to provide a framework for the detailed discussions of *each* type of retirement plan described in the "Retirement Planning" part of this book.

The process of designing the "right" retirement plan for a business can be divided into three broad steps:

Step 1: Gather the relevant facts. The most important factual information is

- an employee census (i.e., a list of all employees with their compensation levels, ages, and years of service for the employer),
- information about existing and past retirement plans, if any, that the employer has maintained, and
- These are essential; but many other details about an employer's business may be important in various cases.

Step 2: Identify employer goals and objectives. In addition to factual information, the planner must develop with the client a list of objectives (broad objectives that can be promoted by a retirement plan, as well as specific goals that will affect plan selection) and their priorities with the employer.

Step 3: Choose plan features that promote the employer objectives. This chapter is a preliminary guide to matching objectives with plan design features. Once the design process has zeroed-in on specific plans or design features, later chapters will provide the necessary details.

ADVANTAGES FOR THE EMPLOYER

The planner must begin with an overall idea of the broad employer objectives that can be promoted by a retirement plan. There are two kinds of employer objectives in this context: (a) broad objectives that favor having some type of retirement plan, such as recruiting the best employees (described below), and (b) narrower goals that will distinguish the benefits of one type of plan from another (explained at "Factors Affecting Plan Selection," later in this chapter).

If it is properly designed and implemented, a retirement plan can promote many employer and employee objectives, the most important of which are listed here. While not every one of these objectives can be met with a single plan—in fact, some are conflicting—it is useful to begin this chapter by noting what pension plans *can* do.

1. *Help Employees with Retirement Saving.* This is the most fundamental reason for retirement plans and it should be treated accordingly. Most employees, even highly compensated employees, find personal savings difficult. It is difficult not merely for psychological reasons, but also because our tax system and economy are oriented toward consumption rather than savings.

   For example, the federal income tax system imposes tax on income from savings (even if it is not used for consumption) with only three major exceptions: (1) deferral of tax on capital gains until realized; (2) exclusion of gain on the sale of a personal residence; and (3) deferral of tax and other benefits for qualified retirement plans and IRAs. In other words, a qualified retirement plan or IRA is one of only three ways our government encourages savings through the tax system, and the benefits of a retirement plan are available only if an employer adopts the plan.

2. *Tax Deferral for Owners and Highly Compensated Employees*. While many employees in all compensation categories can benefit from retirement plans, owners and other key employees typically have more money available for saving, have higher compensation, have longer service with the employer, and often are older than other employees; thus, they can benefit more from retirement plans. When designing a plan for a business owner, a typical objective is to maximize the benefits for the owner (or, in some cases, to minimize the discrimination *against* the highly compensated that is built into some of the qualified plan rules.)

3. *Help Recruit, Reward, Retain, and Retire Employees*. These "four R's" of compensation policy are an important objective in designing retirement plans. The plan can help *recruit* employees by matching or bettering retirement benefit packages offered by competing employers; it can *reward* employees by tying benefits to compensation; it can help *retain* employees by tying maximum retirement benefits to long service; and it can help *retire* employees by allowing them to retire with dignity—without a drastic drop in living standard—when their productivity has begun to decline and the organization needs new members.

4. *Encourage Productivity*. Certain types of plan design can act as employee incentives; this is particularly true of plans whose contributions are profit-based or those providing employee accounts invested in stock of the employer.

5. *Discourage Collective Bargaining*. An attractive retirement plan package—as good as or better than labor union-sponsored plans in the area—can help to keep employees from organizing into a collective bargaining unit. Collective bargaining often poses major business problems for some employers.

QUALIFIED VERSUS NONQUALIFIED RETIREMENT PLANS

All retirement plans involve deferral of part of an employee's compensation for performing services for the employer. Deferred compensation is compensation that is not paid currently—in the year services are performed or shortly thereafter.[1] Retirement plans are either *qualified* or *nonqualified*. Qualified plans receive more favorable tax benefits, but are subject to very stringent government regulation.

The chart in Figure 10.1 summarizes differences between qualified and nonqualified plans.

When Is a Nonqualified Plan Indicated? Chapter 5 discusses in detail when and how nonqualified plans are used. Some highlights:

- nonqualified plans can be designed for key employees without the sometimes prohibitive cost of covering a broader group of employees.
- nonqualified plans can provide benefits to executives beyond the limits allowed in qualified plans.
- nonqualified plans can provide "customized" retirement or savings benefits for selected executives.

TAX ADVANTAGES OF QUALIFIED PLANS

A qualified plan receives tax benefits that are not available for a nonqualified plan. These tax benefits are:

- Amounts paid into the plan—employer contributions and also employee salary reduction contributions—are deductible by the employer (and tax-excludable by the employee) in the year for which they are paid.
- Employees are not taxed in the year that the employer contributes to the plan, even if they are fully vested in their plan benefits at that time.
- The plan itself is a tax-exempt fund. Earnings on plan investments accumulate tax free in the plan and are not taxed currently to the

Figure 10.1

QUALIFIED VERSUS NONQUALIFIED PLANS		
Item	**Qualified Retirement Plan**	**Unfunded Nonqualified Deferred Compensation Plan**
a. Timing of corporation's income tax deduction	Corporation receives a deduction when contributions are made to the plan.	Corporation receives a deduction when benefits are received by employees.
b. Who must be covered by plan	70 percent of nonhighly compensated employees, or alternative test under Code section 410.	Corporation free to discriminate as it sees fit if plan covers only independent contractors or members of management or highly compensated employees.
c. Extent to which benefits may be forfeitable	Must meet ERISA vesting requirements.	The ERISA vesting rules apply only if plan covers rank-and-file employees. If plan covers only independent contractors or a select group of management or highly compensated employees, benefits may be forfeitable in full at all times.
d. Tax treatment of earnings on amount set aside to fund plan	Earning on pre-tax and employer contributions accumulate tax free but will be taxable to employee along with other plan assets when distributed to employee; no income tax deduction for employer.	These earnings will be taxed currently to the employer and will be taxable to the employee when distributed as benefits; however, employer will be entitled to an income tax deduction at that time.
e. Coverage of independent contractors and directors	Only employees are eligible for coverage.	Independent contractors and directors may be covered in the same manner as an employee.

employer or the employee. This significantly increases the effective investment return on plan assets.

- Participants and beneficiaries do not pay taxes until amounts are actually received from the plan, subject to the minimum distribution requirements. Under the minimum distribution rules, payments (and income taxation) can be spread over as many as three life expectances. Also, there are some special benefits for lump-sum distributions. (See Chapter 20.)

- These tax benefits add up to a substantial, quantifiable amount of tax "leverage," as will be shown later in this chapter.

Types of Qualified Plans

Qualified plans are either defined contribution or defined benefit plans. As the names imply, this depends on whether the plan specifies an employer contribution rate on the one hand, or guarantees a specified benefit level on the other. Figure 10.2 shows a brief comparison of defined contribution and defined benefit plans.

Defined Contribution Plans

In a defined contribution plan, the employer establishes and maintains an individual account for each plan participant. When the participant becomes eligible to receive benefit payments—usually at retirement or

Figure 10.2

DEFINED BENEFIT VERSUS DEFINED CONTRIBUTION PLANS		
	Defined Benefit	**Defined Contribution**
Distinguishing characteristic	The amount the participant will receive is specified (A pension is a "definitely determinable benefit")	The amount the employer will contribute is specified
Types of plans	Traditional DB Cash Balance 412(e) (fully insured plan)	401(k) Money purchase plan Stock bonus plan ESOP Traditional profit sharing plan
Advantages	Security to participants Higher deduction for employer Greater value to older employees More likely to provide adequate retirement benefit	Cost control to employer Flexibility to offer more in profitable years Easy to communicate benefits to participants Directed investing offers employees control
Disadvantages	Difficult to explain value of benefit Expensive Not flexible—important that cash flow be stable	Less likely to provide adequate retirement benefit

Source: Presentation titled "Small Business Retirement Planning" by April K. Caudill, J.D., CLU, ChFC, for series of local chapter meetings of the Society of Financial Service Professionals; Copyright 2005, The National Underwriter Company.

termination of employment—the benefit is based on the total amount in the participant's account. The account balance includes employer contributions, employee contributions in some cases, and earnings on the account over all the years of deferral (except for Roth Plans as further described in Chapter 21).

The employer does not guarantee the amount of the benefit a participant will ultimately receive in a defined contribution plan. Instead, the employer must make contributions under a formula specified in the plan. There are two principal types of defined contribution plan formulas:

- *Money purchase pension plan.* Under a money purchase plan, the employer must contribute each year to each participant's account a stated percentage of the participant's compensation. This percentage is usually about 10 percent, although percentages up to twenty five are possible. The money purchase plan is probably the simplest of all types of plans.
- *Profit sharing plan.* A profit sharing plan is a defined contribution plan under which the employer determines the amount of the contribution each year, rather than having a stated contribution obligation. In a profit sharing plan, the employer can decide not to contribute to the plan at all in certain cases. Typically, plan contributions are based on the employer's profits in some manner. If a contribution is made, the total amount must be allocated to each participant's account using a nondiscriminatory formula. Such formulas are usually based on compensation, but service can be taken into account. The allocation formula can also be weighted in favor of plan participants who entered the plan at older ages—using an "age-weighted profit sharing plan" or a "cross-tested (new comparability) plan," as explained later in this chapter.

Profit sharing plans often feature employee contributions, typically with an employer match. For example, the plan could provide that employees may contribute to the plan up to 6 percent of their compensation, with the employer contributing 50 cents for every $1 of employee contribution. This type of plan is referred to as a *thrift* or *savings* plan.

Another variation on the profit-sharing plan design is the *cash or deferred* or *Section 401(k)* plan. Under this type of plan, employees can make tax deferred contributions by electing salary reductions. For 2015, contributions of up to $18,000 annually per employee are permitted. In addition, catch-up contributions of up to $6,000 are permitted for certain employees age fifty or over. Employers often match employee salary reductions in order to encourage employee participation in these plans.

Both of these types of plans are discussed in more detail in separate chapters of this book.

Defined Benefit Plans

Defined benefit plans provide a specific amount of benefit to the employee at normal retirement age. There are many different types of formulas for determining this benefit, as discussed in Chapter 1. These formulas are typically based on the employee's earnings averaged over a number of years of service. The formula also can be based on the employee's service.

These plans are funded actuarially, which means that, for a given benefit level, the annual funding amount is greater for employees who are older at entry into the plan, since the time to fund the benefit is less in the case of an older entrant. This makes defined benefit plans attractive to professionals and closely held business owners; they tend to adopt retirement plans for their businesses when they are relatively older than their regular employees. A large percentage of the total cost for a defined benefit plan in this situation funds these key employees' benefits, as discussed further in Chapter 29.

QUALIFIED PLAN FUNDING VERSUS CASH

The tax advantages of qualified plans mean that an employer's dollar spent on qualified plan benefits is "bigger" than a dollar spent on cash compensation. This is because while the employer gets a current deduction for the cost of the plan, benefits are not taxable to employees until paid. The time value of money "leverages" the value of each employer dollar; the income earned on deferred taxes directly benefits the employee but costs the employer nothing extra.

So why doesn't every employer immediately maximize the qualified plan benefits for every employee, since qualified plan benefits are "cheaper" than cash compensation? The problem is that not every employee *perceives* the same value for qualified plan benefits.

Employees who value retirement benefits most highly include:

- older employees nearing retirement
- long-term employees with substantial vested benefits
- highly compensated employees who can afford to forego substantial cash compensation for retirement benefits
- employees who do not depend on their compensation for basic living expenses—for example, the "supplemental" earner in a two-income family

Employees not in the above four categories may not value and may not want deferred plan benefits—they would rather have immediate cash; in particular:

- younger employees view retirement as a distant prospect and therefore psychologically "discount" the value of retirement benefits
- transitory employees do not expect to stay with an employer long enough to fully vest or accrue substantial benefits
- lower-paid employees cannot afford to forego any substantial amount of cash compensation in return for retirement benefits

In other words, retirement plan design for most employers requires more sophistication than simply "loading up" on benefits. Money spent on plan benefits for employees who do not value these benefits is, in effect, a "pure cost" of the plan. Such costs must not outweigh the value of benefits for those who do want them; otherwise the employer's compensation policy is inefficient and may even be counterproductive.

In designing the plan, a designer must attempt to both (1) maximize the benefits for those who want them and (2) choose a plan design that will be perceived as valuable by the maximum number of employees.

Is a qualified plan cost-effective? For a given client, the threshold question raised by the issues just discussed must be: "Does *any* qualified plan make any sense at all in the client's business?" To illustrate, let's look at what might be viewed as a "worst-case" scenario: the small professional corporation. It is a worst-case situation because the owner or owners are generally much older and higher paid than the rest of the employees; and there is often high turnover among the younger employees. So, the owners want the maximum pension benefits but the rest of the employees probably do not value these benefits much. Thus, the cost of benefits for nonowner employees is about as close to a "pure cost" of providing the owners' benefits as the planner commonly runs into.

> *Example*. Suppose your client, Doctor Leberkrank, age forty-one, and two office employees are the only employees of the doctor's professional corporation. The doctor wants to establish a qualified profit sharing plan that will enable him to contribute the $53,000 annual maximum (as indexed for 2015). A preliminary plan design analysis indicates that in order to do this, a total of $3,000 will have to be contributed annually on behalf of the two office employees, in order to meet the qualified plan nondiscrimination rules. Thus, the doctor's choice is between $53,000 annually of private savings outside the plan or a $56,000 annual contribution to the plan with its accompanying tax deferral benefits.

High required contributions for nonowner employees do not necessarily mean that the plan is not viable. The next step for the planner is then to consider refinements and alternatives:

- Contributions for employees are not really wasted—they're a valuable form of additional compensation for employees. The planner should try to design a plan where these contributions have a maximum perceived value for the employees and, thus, contribute positively to the employer's "4R" (recruiting, retaining, rewarding, and retiring) goals.

- The plan can be redesigned to maximize contributions for the owners and minimize contributions for other employees.

Planning options that can achieve these results are discussed in the next section.

FACTORS AFFECTING PLAN SELECTION

Each type of qualified plan meets some of an employer's planning goals better than the others. Plan design consists of finding the right match between employer's goals and the qualified plan "menu" of choices. The following are some of the most common employer objectives, and the plan design features that are available for customizing the plan to those objectives:

OBJECTIVE: Maximize the Portion of Plan Costs That Benefit Highly Compensated Employees

Many employers, particularly small, closely held companies, view retirement plans as worthwhile only if they provide substantial, tax-sheltered retirement benefits for key employees. The following are the commonly used techniques for doing this:

1. *Defined benefit plans*. Defined benefit plans typically provide the maximum possible proportionate benefits for key employees when key employees, as a group, are older than rank and file employees. This age distribution exists in the majority of small businesses.

   A defined contribution plan allows a contribution of no more than $53,000 (in 2015) annually for an employee—but for a defined benefit plan there is *no* dollar limit on the amount of contributions. Instead, the projected *benefit* (not the contribution) is subject to a limit of the lesser of 100 percent of high three-year average compensation or $210,000 annually (in 2015).[2] Funding the maximum annual benefit for a younger employee generally requires a deductible employer contribution that is less than $53,000 annually, while for an employee who enters the plan at an age greater than approximately 45, the deductible contribution for the maximum benefit is considerably more than $53,000 annually.

   Defined benefit plans can be made even more favorable to key employees by appropriate choices of actuarial assumptions, retirement age and late retirement provisions, form of benefits, and level of Social Security integration. All of these design aspects of defined benefit plans are discussed further in Chapter 29.

2. *Service-based contribution or benefit formulas.* A plan's contribution or benefit formula can be based on an employee's years of service with the employer. This generally benefits the owners and key employees who typically have longer service. Such formulas can be used in defined contribution plans, but are even more effective in defined benefit plans. Defined benefit plans can even provide benefits for *past* service—service prior to establishment of the plan. Of course, the Code's nondiscrimination requirements discussed in Chapter 13 must be satisfied.

3. *Age-weighting and cross-testing.* The age-weighting aspect of a defined benefit plan, which provides favorable funding of benefits for older plan entrants, can also be provided in a defined contribution plan. Where the employer wants to avoid the complexity of the defined benefit approach, age-weighted defined contribution plans should be considered. Figure 10.3 shows a comparison of the various types of plans that allow some degree of age-weighting.

   There are two types of defined contribution plans that tend to favor older employees in this manner: the cross-tested plan, and the fixed formula age-weighted plan. These are described in Chapter 28.

   The cross-tested plan, which is the most commonly used, provides a flat percentage allocation (5 percent of compensation or more) to most rank-and-file employees and the maximum allocation (generally $53,000 (in 2015) under the annual additions limit) for key employees and owners. By projecting contributions to each employee's retirement age and computing the equivalent benefit for this projected accumulation, the benefit structure can generally be shown to be nondiscriminatory under the tax regulations, so long as most of the rank-and-file employees are younger than the highly compensated employees.

   The alternative is to use a fixed age-weighted formula, under which the percentage of compensation contributed for each employee is based actuarially on the employee's age on entering the plan (higher for older employees). This type of plan can be either a profit sharing plan (where employer contributions each year are discretionary) or a pension plan (which requires annual employer contributions). The latter type of fixed-formula age-weighted plan (pension plan) is called a target plan. Target plans are rarely used because of the fixed contribution requirement.

4. *Combinations of defined benefit and defined contribution plans.* Is it possible to contribute the maximum limits for an employee under *both* a defined benefit plan *and* a defined contribution plan? Under ERISA as originally enacted in 1974, the answer was no. However, the "combined plan formula" originally set forth in ERISA and Code section 415(e) was repealed, effective after 1999.[3] It is thus possible to have a defined contribution plan and a defined benefit plan for a participant that provides the maximum benefit under both plans, subject to an overall limitation on employer deductions equal to 25 percent of covered payroll, with certain exceptions.

5. *401(k) plans.* Section 401(k) plans are popular with rank-and-file employees, but designers should not overlook the fact that these plans can be favorable to highly compensated employees as well. The nondiscrimination rules—the ADP and ACP tests[4]—inherently allow a higher rate of contribution for highly compensated employees. However, these rules require maximum participation from nonhighly compensated employees for the highly compensated to fully enjoy the extra contribution levels, so the employer must "sell" the plan to employees in order to maximize the benefits of a 401(k) plan to the owners. In the alternative, a SIMPLE or safe harbor 401(k) plan design could be used (see Chapter 19). These special plan designs allow employers who are willing to meet certain funding and other requirements to *avoid* ADP/ACP testing, as well as to maximize benefits to the highly compensated employees without regard to the participation levels of nonhighly compensated employees.

6. *Social Security integration.* Employers are allowed to "integrate" certain qualified plans with Social

Figure 10.3

AGE WEIGHTED PLANS		
Plan Type	**Characteristics**	**Degree of Age Weighting Permitted**
Traditional defined benefit	• Traditional DB pensions may: • Base benefit on final average pay • Offer early retirement incentives • Require full vesting (3/7 graduated or 5-year cliff)	• Offers highest age weighting ability
Target plan	• Variation on money purchase plan (defined contribution pension); thus subject to minimum funding requirement • Usually weighted for age	• Contributions determined on basis of what is necessary to fund the target benefit
Cash balance plan	• Funded on basis of ultimate benefit, but accounted for like a defined contribution plan	• Some age weighting inherent in plan design but may be required to guarantee accrual rates, interest credits not yet known
Cross tested or new comparability plan	• Usually profit sharing plans • Plan tested on the basis of the benefits it provides • Benefits may be weighted for age or service • Offers age weighting without the costs of DB plan • Exempt from age discrimination requirements	• Ability to compare benefits taking into account assumed rates of growth, allowing smaller contributions for younger employees
Plan designs with NO inherent age weighting	• 401(k) (all types) • Stock bonus plan • ESOP • Traditional profit sharing	• Contributions typically weighted by compensation only • Years of service affect vesting • Some allow permitted disparity (i.e., lower allocations to the extent participant's pay will be replaced with Social Security)

Source: Presentation titled "Small Business Retirement Planning" by April K. Caudill, J.D., CLU, ChFC, for series of local chapter meetings of the Society of Financial Service Professionals; Copyright 2005, The National Underwriter Company. Updated to reflect current information.

Security benefits. The rules for this are very complicated,[5] but in effect they allow a higher rate of qualified plan contributions or benefits for each employee with compensation above a specified level. This reduces employer costs for the qualified plan benefits for lower-paid employees and correspondingly allows greater benefits or contributions for higher-paid employees.

OBJECTIVE: Provide a Savings Medium That Employees Perceive as Valuable

1. *Defined contribution plans*. Every defined contribution plan has an "individual account" for each employee who participates. As a result, the employee knows exactly how much his or her personal benefit is worth from year to year. Defined contribution plans include:

   ESOP/Stock Bonus Plan—Chapter 23

   Money Purchase Pension Plan—Chapter 25

   Profit Sharing Plan—Chapter 22

   Savings Plan—Chapter 24

   Section 401(k) Plan—Chapter 19

   Simplified Employee Pension (SEP)—Chapter 31[6]

   SIMPLE IRA—Chapter 30[7]

   Cross Tested/Age Weighted Plan—Chapter 26

   Tax Deferred Annuity—Chapter 32[8]

   The "savings account" feature of defined contribution plans is often popular with younger employees, who may not expect to stay with the employer until retirement—which in any event seems like a remote contingency to them.

2. *Cash balance plans*. These plans are a type of defined benefit plan that operates very much like a defined contribution plan of the money purchase type. The employer guarantees the principal and interest rate, so the employee assumes no investment risk. However, cash balance plans tend to provide greater benefits to younger employees and those with shorter service, as compared to other defined benefit plans.[9]

3. *Plans with employee participation*. Qualified "savings" plans can allow employees to make after-tax contributions and a Section 401(k) plan[10] permits *before-tax* salary reductions. Such a plan looks to the employee very much like a tax-favored savings account sponsored by the employer.

Figure 10.4 is a chart comparing the advantages and disadvantages of several types of retirement savings alternatives that provide for employee participation. Figure 10.5 shows a comparison and contrast of all the types of plans that involve elective deferrals.

OBJECTIVE: Provide Adequate Replacement Income for Each Employee's Retirement

An employer may wish to adopt a plan that provides an adequate "replacement ratio"—the ratio of postretirement income to that received just before retirement. What is an adequate replacement ratio? Generally speaking, no plan attempts to provide 100 percent of preretirement income, because, apart from the high cost of such a plan (1) an employee's income needs are generally somewhat reduced after retirement and (2) personal savings are deemed to contribute part of the employee's income needs. A higher replacement ratio is necessary for lower-paid employees than for the higher-paid, since fixed costs dominate at lower income levels.

Most early studies indicated that replacement ratios of about 50 to 70 percent were adequate. More recent thinking suggests that higher replacement ratios are desirable. Figure 10.6 gives results of some studies analyzed by the American Society of Pension Professionals & Actuaries (ASPPA). The ASPPA study proposes that the results can be quantified into a formula or "algorithm" under which the pension target for an individual is 85 percent of final pay not exceeding three times the poverty level ($6,810 was the figure used in the ASPPA study), plus 70 percent of any additional final pay. A 2012 study by AON also showed that generally 85 percent should be an adequate replacement ratio for most retirees.

Recent studies have argued that is unrealistic to try to determine a replacement ratio for an entire class of employees. The amount needed to maintain a standard of living in retirement is highly individual, depending on health, longevity, expenditure patterns, and many other factors. One recent study also concludes that the amount needed for retirement is almost always greatly underestimated, and that the actual amount needed is "sobering, if not staggering."[11]

If adequate replacement income is an employer's objective, a defined benefit plan is the best vehicle for the following reasons:

- A defined benefit plan can provide a benefit based on final average compensation, regardless of the employee's years of service

Figure 10.4

ADVANTAGES AND DISADVANTAGES OF ALTERNATIVES WITH EMPLOYEE PARTICIPATION

Savings Alternative	Major Advantages	Major Disadvantages
• After-tax Savings	• No employer action necessary • Complete flexibility for employee	• No tax benefits
• Traditional IRA	• No employer action necessary • Contribution tax-deductible	• Limitation if covered under qualified plan • 10% penalty for withdrawal before age 59½; no loans • $5,500/year maximum (2015) ($6,500 age 50 or older) • Cannot invest in life insurance
• Roth IRA	• No employer action necessary • Withdrawals completely tax-free after waiting period	• Limitation if covered under qualified plan • Waiting period for withdrawals or tax advantages • No tax deductions for contribution • $5,500/year maximum (2015) ($6,500 age 50 or older)
• SIMPLE (Savings Incentive Match Plan for Employees) IRA plan	• Employee can choose amount of saving • Amounts contributed are non-taxable to employee • Tax-free accumulation • Easy for employer to adopt	• Less flexibility for employer than qualified plan • $12,500 limit (2015, indexed) on salary reduction • Relatively complex administration • No forfeitures available for reallocation to long-term employees • No loans permitted • 25% penalty for pre-age 59½ withdrawal during 1st two years of participation; 10% thereafter • Employer must make matching or nonelective contributions • Cannot invest in life insurance
• Thrift (Savings) Plan	• Employee can choose amount of saving • Employer contribution non-taxable to employee • Tax-free accumulation • Employer matching is attractive incentive feature • Liberal loan and withdrawal provisions	• Qualified plan cost and complexity • Employer has fixed, nondiscretionary contribution obligation • Ten percent penalty on pre-age 59½ withdrawal • Must meet Code section 401(m) tests
• Section 401(k) Profit-Sharing Plan	• Employee can choose amount of savings • All or part of contributions can be salary reduction • Amounts contributed are non-taxable to employee • Tax-free accumulation • Hardship withdrawals and loans available	• Qualified plan cost and complexity • $18,000 (2015) annual limit on salary reductions • 401(k) provisions add administrative costs • No forfeitures available for reallocation to long-term employees • In-service withdrawls limited to hardship and loans • Ten percent penalty on pre-age 59½ withdrawal

Figure 10.5

ELECTIVE DEFERRAL PLANS COMPARED

	Traditional 401(k) plan	Safe Harbor 401(k) plan	SIMPLE 401(k) plan	SIMPLE IRA	SAR-SEP (adopted before 1997)
Maximum 2015 salary deferral	$18,000	$18,000	$12,500	$12,500	$18,000
Maximum 2015 catch-up	$6,600	$6,600	$3,000	$3,000	$6,000
Employer limitations	None	None	No more than 100 employees earning greater than $5,000; No other plan covering same employees	No more than 100 employees earning greater than $5,000; No other plan covering same employees	No more than 25 employees
Required contribution	None	Equivalent to 4% match or 3% nonelective, but can satisfy requirements with contributions to other plans	3% match or 2% nonelective; must be made to the SIMPLE 401(k) plan	3% match or 2% nonelective; limited use of 1% match possible for up to 2 years	None
Subject to compensation limit of $265,000 in 2015	Yes	Yes	Yes	No	Yes
Plan loans allowed	Yes	Yes	Yes	No	No
Vesting	Graduated for match amounts (20% after 2 years, 40% after 3, to 100% after 6 years)	100% at all times	100% at all times	100% at all times	100% at all times
Nondiscrimination testing	Yes	No	No	No	Yes
Subject to top heavy rules?	Yes	Generally no (could be if other plans cover same participants)	No	No	Yes

Source: Presentation titled "Small Business Retirement Planning" by April K. Caudill, J.D., CLU, ChFC, for series of local chapter meetings of the Society of Financial Service Professionals; Copyright 2005, The National Underwriter Company. Updated to reflect current information.

Figure 10.6

REPLACEMENT RATIOS					
Preretirement Earnings	**1981 PCPP Study (married couples)**	**Georgia State (1987 study)**	**Georgia State (1991 study)**	**Colin England Study**	**Algorithm**
$ 6,500	86%	—	—	88%	85%
10,000	78%	—	—	85%	85%
15,000	71%	82%	90%	78%	85%
20,000	66%	75%	85%	74%	85%
25,000	—	71%	82%	—	82%
30,000	60%	—	—	68%	80%
40,000	—	68%	77%	—	78%
50,000	50%	66%	73%	73%	76%
60,000	—	66%	71%	—	75%
70,000	—	66%	70%	—	74%
75,000	—	—	—	74%	74%
80,000	—	68%	68%	—	74%
90,000	—	68%	66%	—	73%
100,000	—	—	—	74%	73%

Source: Executive Summary, "National Retirement Income Policy," American Society of Pension Professionals and Actuaries, 1993.

(or a full benefit can be earned after only limited service such as twenty-five years). Defined contribution plans provide benefits that are directly related to service, and a short service employee cannot accumulate a substantial retirement account.

- There is no investment risk taken by the employee in a defined benefit plan—the employer guarantees the benefit (and there is also a limited federal government guarantee of benefits through the Pension Benefit Guaranty Corporation).
- Employer funding of the benefit is mandatory, subject to underfunding penalties, even if the employer's profits drop.
- Maximum life insurance can be provided through a defined benefit plan, providing the fullest protection for beneficiaries even if the employee dies after only a few years of service.

OBJECTIVE: Create an Incentive for Employees to Maximize Performance

1. *Profit sharing plan.* Although a "profit sharing" plan is not technically required to make contributions out of profits, most plans are designed to do so. The profit sharing element provides extra, bonus compensation to participating employees when the business does well, and that acts as an incentive.
2. *ESOP/stock bonus plan.* A plan providing that the employee's account balance is partially or totally invested in stock of the employer has substantial incentive features, paralleling the "equity-based" compensation arrangements often used for executives. The participant's account goes up and down in value with company stock. So, its value depends almost entirely on good performance by the business. If the employee believes that his or her performance has an effect on business results, the plan can be a powerful performance incentive.
3. *Any other defined contribution plan or cash balance plan.* In these plans, employees have an account that begins to grow as soon as they enter the plan. Because of this high visibility, these plans tend to have a better psychological incentive value than defined benefit plans.

OBJECTIVE: Minimize Turnover

1. *Defined benefit plan.* In defined benefit plans, employees are encouraged to stay until retirement because

(1) benefits can be based on years of service; and (2) benefits are generally based on the employee's highest annual compensation. However, defined contribution benefits also continue to grow with each year of service. In many cases, there is no clear type of plan that minimizes turnover, and other features of the compensation and work environment may be dominant.

2. *Graduated vesting*. Plans are often designed with graduated vesting schedules—that is, an employee is not entitled to the full benefit earned until a minimum period of service has passed. Under current law, the longest wait permitted for full vesting in a defined benefit plan is seven years (under the graduated three- to seven-year vesting schedule). The schedule is two to six years for defined contribution plans. Thus, vesting has only a limited effect on employee turnover, and should probably be better viewed as a way for the employer to minimize the cost of covering short-service employees.

OBJECTIVE: Encourage Retirement

Any retirement plan acts to some degree as an incentive to retire, since it makes it possible for the employee to support himself and his dependents after retirement.

However, a defined benefit plan works best to encourage retirement because:

- The plan can be designed to allow full benefits to accrue after a specified period such as twenty-five years, with no further benefits accruing thereafter. Thus, no further benefits can be earned by working for more years thereafter.

- It is relatively easy to design a "subsidized" early retirement benefit in a defined benefit plan by providing a benefit at age sixty-two (or other early retirement age) that is more than the actuarial equivalent of what the retiree would get at age 6sixty-five. This provides an economic incentive to retire early.

- A defined benefit plan makes it relatively easy to design a "window" plan to encourage early retirement. A window plan provides additional retirement benefits, often in the form of deemed additional years of service, that provide additional benefit accruals. These benefits are available to specified employees who retire early during a specified "window" period. Window arrangements are also possible with defined contribution plans, but they generally can take the form only of additional cash bonuses or severance pay. Defined benefit plans are much more flexible in this regard.

OBJECTIVE: Maximize Employer Contribution Flexibility

The most flexible plans from a contribution standpoint are qualified profit sharing plans and SEPs. In these plans, the amount contributed each year can be entirely at the employer's discretion. Contributions can be omitted entirely for a given year without affecting the plan's qualified status. (However, for a profit sharing plan, contributions must be "substantial and recurring" or the IRS may claim that the plan has been terminated.)

Other types of plans are inflexible to one degree or another:

1. Defined benefit plans are subject to the minimum funding requirements of the Internal Revenue Code, and the required annual minimum contribution must be made or the employer is subject to penalty.

   However, it should be noted that the rules for actuarial funding of qualified plans permit some year-to-year variation in the amount that the employer can or must contribute. Thus, in a good year, the employer may contribute the maximum deductible amount, which may tend to reduce the minimum amount that has to be contributed in later years.

2. Defined contribution pension plans (money purchase and target) must have fixed contribution formulas that require a contribution each year based on a percentage of payroll. Failure to make this contribution subjects the employer to minimum funding penalties. The only relief for this is to apply to the IRS for a minimum funding waiver, or to make a timely amendment to the plan to reduce the contribution level.

3. "Matching" plans (e.g., 401(k), savings, and 403(b) plans, as well as SIMPLE IRAs) that

Figure 10.7

RETIREMENT PLANS: MOST TO LEAST FUNDING			
	Most guarantee to employee highest cost	**Moderate guarantees/costs**	**Less guarantee/less cost**
Pensions: Subject to minimum funding standard	Traditional defined benefit plan Section 412(b)(3) plan • Guarantees a definitely determinable benefit at retirement • Often backloaded–more accrual in final years • Offers highest deductible benefit and funding for older employees nearing retirement	Cash balance plan (hybrid defined benefit plan) • Steady accrual throughout working career • Greater portability • More likely than most other plans to provide an adequate (or near adequate) retirement benefit • Level funding	Money purchase pension plan • Defined contribution pension • Required funding, but level amounts • Less necessary since 25% deduction is available with profit sharing plans
Plans with some required funding	Safe Harbor 401(k) plan • Required match or nonelective contribution • Vesting available	SAR-SEPs • Match likely SIMPLE IRA • Required match or nonelective contribution SIMPLE 401(k) plan • Less required match or nonelective contribution • Participation can be limited	SEPs • Flexible funding
Little or no required or promised funding	Traditional 401(k) with small nondiscretionary match • E.g., 2% match • Limited vesting available • Discretionary additional match can be offered • Vesting as to match can be required	Traditional 401(k) with only a discretionary match • Some match probably necessary to pass ADP test • Match can be made in employer stock	Traditional profit sharing plan: • Promises nothing unless employer has a good year • Full vesting can be required 2/6 or 3-year cliff

Source: Presentation titled "Small Business Retirement Planning" by April K. Caudill, J.D., CLU, ChFC, for series of local chapter meetings of the Society of Financial Service Professionals; Copyright 2005, The National Underwriter Company.

require the employer to match employee contributions involve a legally binding commitment by the employer to make the promised matching contributions. Thus, the employer's costs are dependent on employee decisions and out of the employer's control.

Figure 10.7 compares the various types of retirement plans on the basis of funding, from the most secure (such as defined benefit, shown with the darkest shading) to the least (such as profit sharing, shown with the lightest shading).

CHAPTER ENDNOTES

1. For tax purposes, compensation is considered current when it is paid no later than 2½ months after the year in which it is earned. Any compensation paid later than this is considered *deferred*, which means that the employer's tax deduction is deferred also unless the plan is a qualified plan. For a *controlling* employee—one who owns more than 50% of the employer—even the 2½ month rule does not apply (i.e., the compensation must be paid within the year earned for the employer to get a tax deduction for that year).
2. I.R.C. §415(b). Notice 2010-78, 2010-49 IRB 808.
3. I.R.C. §415(e), prior to amendment by SBJPA '99.
4. I.R.C. §401(k)(3).

5. I.R.C. §401(l).
6. A SEP is not technically a qualified defined contribution plan, but from the employee perspective it works the same way.
7. A SIMPLE IRA plan is not technically a qualified defined contribution plan, but from the employee perspective it works the same way. A SIMPLE 401(k) plan, by contrast, is a qualified defined contribution plan.
8. A tax deferred annuity is not technically a qualified defined contribution plan, but from the employee perspective it works the same way.
9. The fact that a cash balance plan is technically a defined benefit plan has no bearing on the planning objectives discussed here.
10. Tax-exempt employers have the option of adopting either a Section 401(k) plan or a Section 403(b) annuity, which provides many of the same advantages. Governmental organizations may not adopt 401(k) plans, but public schools can adopt 403(b) plans.
11. VanDerhei, Employee Benefit Research Institute, "Issue Brief No. 297," September 2006.

PLANNING FOR RETIREMENT NEEDS

CHAPTER 11

INTRODUCTION

Retirement planning is a critical part of the financial services industry. With the baby boomers ranging from middle age to retirement age, the number of individuals with significant savings and retirement planning needs is increasing dramatically. At the same time, the economic and tax complexity of all types of retirement-related financial planning has also increased.

Retirement planning is "interdisciplinary." It combines the skills of the traditional estate planner, the financial planner, and the benefit/compensation planner. The range of issues that must be addressed makes this one of the most challenging of the financial services disciplines.

Retirement planning is also multifaceted because of the broad range of clients that must be served. For example it encompasses advice to clients many years in advance of retirement, as well as to clients at retirement and thereafter. Clients may also range from business owners who are able to use their businesses to help provide retirement benefits, to key executives who can bargain effectively with their employers regarding retirement benefits, to employees who have no significant say in their employee benefit package. All these different types of clients may have needs for retirement planning, as well as sufficient assets to require the services of a planner.

Perhaps no single advisor should attempt to handle all aspects of retirement planning alone. Any person giving advice in these situations should know when it is appropriate to call in an employee benefits expert, a lawyer specializing in estate planning, a knowledgeable portfolio manager, or whatever other specialist is required. However, all financial planners should understand the basics of retirement planning—the broad general approaches, the tools and techniques—and where they fit in.

WHAT ARE THE REQUIREMENTS? Retirement planning is fundamentally composed of three basic steps: (1) assessing the financial needs the client will have at retirement, (2) determining how much of this need will likely be met, based on current assets and income, and (3) establishing a plan for any projected shortfall in cash flow. But before any of these steps can be undertaken, the planner must determine what the client's current assets and income sources are, and evaluate the impact that major financial goals may have on these assets.

CURRENT INCOME SOURCES AND ASSETS

A retirement plan cannot be provided unless the planner has complete and accurate financial information about the client's existing assets and income sources. In fact, "due diligence" in retirement planning *requires* the planner to make every effort to obtain accurate and complete financial information. The planner should be wary of clients who are reluctant to provide such information.

Retirement planning practitioners should develop a "fact finder" for clients that will systematize this process. A sample fact finder, titled Retirement Planning Asset Worksheet (see Figure 11.1) is included at the end of this Chapter. Key Elements of the fact finder are discussed below.

Benefit Plan Information

Retirement planning requires complete information about all employee benefit plans in which the client *and* the client's spouse are currently participating *or have ever participated*. Retirement plans (qualified or nonqualified) and other benefit plans, such as health insurance, life insurance, or even such fringe benefits as membership in company athletic or health clubs after retirement may be significant in the retirement planning process.

In addition to private employer benefit plans, government benefits also should be estimated—Social Security, Medicare, veterans' benefits, and the like.

In order to accurately forecast the level of employee benefits available, the planner needs to see actual benefit plan documents; it is not enough to rely simply on the client's informal impression of what his benefit programs provide. Generally, if a plan provides a Summary Plan Description (SPD), as do most ERISA-affected plans (see Chapter 16), the SPD should be sufficient. For qualified plans, employers are required to provide an individual benefit statement at least once annually. In some cases, the planner might wish to look at the actual underlying plan documents, which the client has the right to request under ERISA. (Companies can charge a reasonable copying fee for providing copies.)

For non-ERISA plans, there often are no formal documentation requirements, so it may be difficult to obtain adequate written information about such benefits. However, most companies provide a "benefits manual" or other literature covering these benefits.

In general, when examining benefit plans, focus on:

- What vested benefits at retirement does the plan now provide—that is, even if the employee terminated employment today?
- What will the plan provide at retirement, if the employee continues working? If the benefits are based on salary, what is a reasonable salary forecast?
- How solid are predictions of future benefits? For example, health benefit plans are currently in constant flux. Can a planner have any confidence that if health benefit plans are even available at retirement fifteen years from now, they will have any resemblance to current benefits? The employer's financial stability also has a bearing on this issue.
- To what extent can the employee control the employee benefits available at retirement? Do employer plans have options available to the employee to change or increase benefits, possibly on a contributory basis? (See the chapters on FSAs (Chapter 38) and Cafeteria Plans (Chapter 40), for example.) Can the employee individually negotiate better or different benefits? At the extreme, an owner or majority shareholder can—and generally should—arrange the company's benefit plans to be consistent with his own individual retirement planning.

Current Asset Information

The planner must have detailed information about the client's current assets and sources of income. Completeness is a must — it is not optional. The fact-finder worksheet at Figure 11.1 includes categories for cash and cash equivalents, investments (detailed by type), and personal assets, including real estate.

Assets must be valued—book value is of little use in developing a financial or retirement plan. Some assets are easy to value; others may be impossible to value with certainty. Asset valuation is discussed in *The Tools and Techniques of Estate Planning*.

Owners of closely held businesses are in a special category. It is difficult to value an interest in a small business, of course. But retirement planning requires more than this. The important factor about a small business interest is not what it is worth now, but what will happen to it in the future—including the extent to which it will continue as a source of income in retirement. In other words, retirement planning for closely held business owners is inextricable from planning for business succession through buy-sell agreements, gifts or sales to successors, or whatever mechanism is set up for continuation of the business or retrieving its value for the owner's benefit.

In obtaining asset information, do not overlook *liability* information. This includes not only traditional debts outstanding, but also legal obligations such as future alimony or child support that involves a recurring obligation, property settlement payments that are outstanding, state or federal tax liabilities outstanding, or fines or judgments not yet fully paid. Many of these are things that clients understandably would rather not think about and they may not be volunteered.

Nonretirement Goals and Objectives

As with estate and financial planning, retirement planning requires the development of a complete profile of the client's financial status, including goals, plans and other anticipated events that may have a significant impact on his retirement assets, such as:

- College or graduate school expenses
- Long-term care for a parent or disabled dependent
- A future windfall, such as an inheritance
- A desire to fund a charitable trust or foundation

These contingencies can be very difficult to value and, unfortunately, they can render a financial or retirement plan nearly worthless if they are ignored. The planner must deal with these issues as well as possible, but must also be willing to "caveat" the ultimate retirement plan—that is, state clearly that the plan does not take into account certain contingencies that potentially exist but are impossible to predict.

HOW IT IS DONE—RETIREMENT NEEDS ANALYSIS

Serious retirement planning must begin well in advance of actual retirement. Although a client far from retirement cannot foresee what his or her life will actually be like after retirement, one way of developing an approximation of retirement needs—at least a good starting point—is to make an estimate of what it costs *now* for a standard of living that the client considers acceptable. By adjusting these amounts for inflation, a reasonable estimate of the total capital needs—the lump sum amount needed at retirement—can be made.

Steps in Calculating Retirement Funding

While detailed planning is appropriate, planners and clients should not expect exactness in all financial planning targets. There are numerous imponderables—future investment return rates, future tax rates, the client's life expectancy, all of which require reasonable assumptions.

There is no perfect method for calculating retirement needs, shortfalls, and savings requirements. It is unlikely that a process requiring twice as much data, or involving twice as many steps, will be twice as accurate. Even if it is conceded that securing more data will result in greater accuracy, this must be balanced against the likelihood that fewer clients will "sit still" for the process. Current savings requirements should be based upon realistic retirement objectives using a process *understood* by the client that produces results *accepted* by the client.

The seven-step planner that follows is adapted from *Field Guide to Financial Planning*, by Donald F. Cady, J.D., LL.M., CLU (National Underwriter, 2013), which includes worksheets and additional information. The seven-step process attempts to achieve both accuracy and usability while striking a balance between detail and simplicity. Income requirements, sources of income, and required savings are all reduced to monthly amounts (most individuals more easily relate to monthly cash flow). Where simplicity produces less than total mathematical accuracy, the process defaults to the more conservative result. Two approaches to determining income requirements are offered, the *replacement ratio method* and the *expense method*.

It is important to remember that these retirement needs calculations are not an end in themselves, but rather a means of moving a client to action, whether that action is allocating more income to savings, becoming more or less aggressive with respect to investment decisions, or planning for a delayed retirement and scaled down lifestyle.

The following steps are designed to determine the required current monthly savings that will meet a future retirement income objective. The tables used for this analysis do not provide for preservation of capital, therefore they contain built-in conservative assumptions. Likewise, in establishing retirement objectives it is usually better to err on the conservative side, by assuming greater longevity, higher income needs, and lower rates of return, than to err on the liberal side. The calculations allow for considering the impact of both inflation and taxes.

Step 1 – Assumptions & Factors to Be Used

In the first step, current age, retirement age, and assumed age of death are used to develop factors for years *to* retirement and years *in* retirement. The selection of an anticipated rate of inflation is critical, because it will determine the inflation factor, a fixed-income factor, and an assets-to-income factor. Assumed rates of return before and after retirement must be chosen to allow for selection of appropriate accumulation factors. For additional information on choosing inflation and rate of return assumptions, see *Tools & Techniques of Investment Planning*.

When estimating income required at retirement one of two approaches can be taken:

a. *Expense method*. This is the "long-form" approach and is probably more accurate than the replacement ratio method (see below). It is best used when a person is close to retirement age. However, there is no guarantee the results will be any more or less accurate than the replacement ratio method, particularly when projecting retirement costs years into the future. An estimate must be made with regard to those expenses that will either increase or decrease in retirement. *Increased expenses* include medical expenses, health care insurance premiums, care of aging parents, and travel and entertainment expenses. *Decreased expenses* might include education costs, life insurance premiums, and clothing.

b. *Replacement ratio method*. This is the "short-form" approach. It is generally considered less accurate but is much easier to use with individuals not yet on the verge of retirement. Generally the target should be a 70 to 90 percent replacement ratio of the client's final average salary.

Step 2 – Inflation Adjusted Income

In this step, income sources are listed (such as Social Security and post-retirement benefits that include an inflation adjustment) whose value today can be estimated and whose future increases are either keyed to or will likely keep up with inflation (both from today to retirement and after retirement). In Step 6, these income sources will be subtracted from income needs that do not have inflation adjustments.

Step 3 – Income from Current Assets

In this step, the value of current assets (and plans) are listed whose value today is either known or can be reasonably estimated, and whose future growth will equal the assumed rate of return before retirement. These include both tax deferred and currently taxed assets.

Step 4 – Income from Future Savings

In contrast to the current assets reflected in Step 3, the assets listed in this step are future amounts intended to be saved on a periodic basis. For example, the current value of a 401(k) plan account might be entered in Step 3, but intended future salary deferral contributions would be entered in Step 4. Note that the seven-step planner assumes the investor's current savings will be continued at the same amount until retirement; however, many investors save more as they approach retirement.

Step 5 – Fixed Income & Amounts Payable at Retirement

In this step, assets or resources are listed that are not expected to be available until retirement but whose value, either income stream or lump sum amount, is known or can be estimated today.

Step 6 – Retirement Cash Flow

This step brings the previous steps together to determine whether there is a retirement income shortfall. First, subtract the inflation-adjusted income (in Step 2) from the income requirement at retirement (in today's dollars). If there is an income requirement, the results are multiplied by an inflation factor in order to determine the income need in retirement age dollars. From this amount subtract the income streams available from current assets (Step 3), future savings (Step 4), and fixed amounts payable at retirement (Step 5). Any other potential sources of income should also be subtracted. The balance equals the retirement income shortfall, if any.

Step 7 – Required Savings

If there is a retirement income shortfall, the additional capital required at retirement to meet this shortfall must be determined, based on annual and monthly savings. Since it may be unrealistic to expect many individuals to commit to a high-level savings program to meet retirement needs many years in the future, this amount should also be redetermined based on an assumption that savings are increased each year (otherwise, savings is assumed to be constant until retirement).

Although necessary for purposes of illustration, it is important to again recognize that rarely, if ever, do investors save at a constant rate over the years, nor do rates of return remain constant. Despite their best intentions, most investors tend to do the bulk of their retirement savings later in life, generally due to rising income and decreasing expenses.

Financial Needs at Retirement

As retirement approaches, the focus will gradually change from accumulation planning toward the need to preserve and make the right decisions about assets the client already has. Decisions that must be addressed at retirement include:

- *Housing*—What should be done with the client's primary residence? What are the client's long range plans for housing? If the client's residence has a considerable market value, it may be tying up a significant portion of his or her net worth. Yet it is important to note that while costs are a critical factor, housing is not entirely a financial decision. The psychological value of circumstances such as outright ownership, low-maintenance housing and geographical location may trump any financial advantages of one form of housing over another.

- *Health care*—What options are available under the client's employee health plans? (See Chapter 36.) What private insurance is necessary to supplement employee benefits and government benefits? What role will Medicare play in the client's plans? How does the Affordable Care Act affect available options? In many cases, the availability of health insurance (or lack thereof) may have a greater effect on the timing of an individual's retirement than the actual retirement income. For an explanation of Medicare and its role in the retirement planning process, see Appendix D.

- *Pensions and Social Security*—Here there are often many possible choices and options; issues include:

    1. How much current income does the client need?

    2. Does the client want to maximize current income or provide for beneficiaries after his (or his and his spouse's) death?

    3. What options are available under the client's benefit plans?

    4. What are the tax consequences of different distribution options—federal income tax, and federal estate and gift taxes, as well as state taxes?

    5. Does the client want to explore possibilities of moving money out of current qualified plans (through a rollover or other option) and investing it in another way—annuities, life insurance, or other investments?

Issues concerning distributions from qualified plans, tax deferred annuities, and IRAs are discussed in Chapter 20 in greater detail. For a discussion of work after retirement and the extent to which it may result in a reduction of Social Security, see Appendix D. Figure 11.2 shows a helpful Retirement Needs Worksheet that can be used in evaluating these issues.

Example. As an illustration of this worksheet, suppose that your client provides information for lines 1 through 9 that indicates he will need $60,000 annually (in current dollars). If the client is ten years from retirement, assuming a 4 percent rate of inflation, this translates to a need for $88,814 (line 14) at retirement ten years from now. Assuming continued 4 percent inflation, a twenty-year payout after retirement, and after-tax investment return of 7 percent, this requires a total capital at retirement (line 21) of $1,374,059.

This worksheet converts everything to a capital equivalent. For example, if the client in the preceding paragraph expects to receive a monthly pension benefit at retirement, it should be converted to its then lump-sum equivalent. If the benefit is worth $300,000, for example, then the client's capital need is reduced to $1,074,059 ($1,374,059 less $300,000).

Capital needs at death. A final aspect of long-range planning that cannot be ignored is preparation for meeting the capital needs the client will have at death. This is a retirement planning issue for two reasons: (1) funding these needs is much more economical when the client begins at a younger age, and (2) in the event of premature death, all the foregoing issues (benefits for a spouse and children, college funding plans, care of a disabled child or spouse, etc.) become a "capital needs at death" issue.

Depending on the type of retirement plan the client participates in, a purchase of life insurance with plan dollars may be an option. If the client is the owner of his or her own business, succession planning is a critical part of retirement planning, since the business may become a source of retirement dollars. For estate planning issues involving retirement assets which may necessitate the purchase of life insurance, see Chapter 18.

Retirement Funding Shortfalls

After the retirement planner has identified the client's current assets and expected future needs, the next critical contribution is the development of a plan for reaching the client's targeted capital needs. All the tools and techniques of financial planning for capital accumulation should be brought to bear on this problem.

Planning requires not only reaching the capital needs targets, but also making sure that the capital is translated appropriately into living expense needs. As noted above, a client's business or personal residence may have a considerable market value on paper, but how will that value contribute to living standards in retirement? Questions like this emphasize the need for planning for liquidity and diversification—here as in all investment planning, but particularly with a focus on retirement needs.

Alternatives for overcoming a retirement funding shortfall may range from a higher savings rate preretirement to a scaled back cost of living either preretirement, postretirement, or both. Some clients may choose to retire later or work part time after retirement. Business owners may choose to adopt a retirement plan that provides a more adequate or more secure retirement benefit.

In attempting to overcome the retirement income gap, some investors may be tempted to make high-risk investments in hopes of gaining higher returns. Another key role of the planner is to steer the investor clear of unnecessary or inappropriate risk. A complete discussion of risk appears in *The Tools & Techniques of Investment Planning*.

Figure 11.1

RETIREMENT PLANNING ASSET WORKSHEET

DATE: ______________________________

Client's Name: ______________________________

Address: ______________________________

Telephone: (home) ____________________(office) ____________________

Business Address: ______________________________

Spouse's Name: ______________________________

Business Address: ____________________ Telephone: ____________________

Figure 11.1 (cont'd)

RETIREMENT PLANNING ASSET WORKSHEET

ASSETS

Valuation as of data prepared unless otherwise indicated.

1. *Cash and cash equivalents*

	Value	Current Return (pretax)
a. checking accounts		
b. saving accounts		
c. money market accounts		
d. life insurance cash values		
Total Cash/Cash Equivalents		

2. *Retirement Plans*
(Do not include defined benefit plans)

	Current balance	Current Return (pretax)
a. IRA		
b. Keogh		
c. Section 401(k)		
d. Section 403(b)		
e. Other defined contribution		
Total Retirement Plans		

Figure 11.1 (cont'd)

3. *Investments*
   (Do not include amounts included in 2 above)

	Fair Market Value	Adjusted Basis	Current Return (pretax)
a. Portfolio Investments			
(1) *money market instruments*			
certificate of deposit	______	______	______
T bills	______	______	______
commercial paper	______	______	______
(2) *fixed-income securities*			
U.S. government	______	______	______
U.S. agencies	______	______	______
municipal bonds	______	______	______
preferred stock	______	______	______
corporate bonds	______	______	______
notes receivable	______	______	______
(3) *common stocks*			
listed	______	______	______
OTC	______	______	______
restricted stock	______	______	______
(4) *other portfolio Investments*			
options	______	______	______
mutual funds	______	______	______
physical assets (collectibles)	______	______	______
b. Passsive Investments			
(1) direct participation investments	______	______	______
(2) real estate (passive)	______	______	______
c. Active Businesses			
(1) value of business owned and operated	______	______	______
(2) real estate (active participation)	______	______	______
Total Investments	______	______	______

Figure 11.1 (cont'd)

4. Personal Assets

	Fair Market Value	Adjusted Basis
a. primary residence	______	______
b. other real estate	______	______
c. household contents	______	______
d. automobiles	______	______
e. other	______	______
Total Personal Assets	______	______

LIABILITIES

1. Short-Term Liabilities
(12 months or less)

	Balance Outstanding	Interest Rate	Monthly Payment	Maturity Date
Consumer credit (credit card & open charge accounts)	______	______	______	______
Personal notes payable	______	______	______	______
Loans from life insurance policies	______	______	______	______
Notes guaranteed	______	______	______	______
Other	______	______	______	______
Total	______	______	______	______

2. Long-Term Liabilities

	Balance Outstanding	Interest Rate	Monthly Payment	Maturity Date
Mortgages on personal residences	______	______	______	______
Loans against investment assets	______	______	______	______
Loans against personal residences	______	______	______	______
Total	______			

Figure 11.1 (cont'd)

3. Other

Deferred taxes	______	______	______	______
Alimony, child support, etc.	______	______	______	______
Judgements, etc.	______	______	______	______
Total	______			

SUMMARY

Assets (fair market value)

Total cash and cash equivalents	______	
Total retirement plans	______	
Total investments	______	
Total personal assets	______	
Total Assets		______

Liabilities (outstanding balances)

Short-term	______	
Long-term	______	
Other	______	
Total Liabilities		______

Figure 11.2

RETIREMENT NEEDS WORKSHEET

Estimated Retirement Living Expenses and Required Capital (in current dollars)

	Per Month × 12 =	Per Year
1. Food		
2. Housing:		
a. Rent/mortgage payment		
b. Insurance (if not included in a.)		
c. Property taxes (if not included in a.)		
d. Utilities		
e. Maintenance (if you own)		
f. Management fee (if a condominium)		
3. Clothing and Personal Care:		
a. Wife		
b. Husband		
c. Dependents		
4. Medical Expenses:		
a. Doctor		
b. Dentist		
c. Medicines		
d. Medical insurance to supplement Medicare		
5. Transportation:		
a. Car payments		
b. Gas		
c. Insurance		
d. License		
e. Car maintenance (tires and repairs)		
f. Other transportation		
6. Recurring Expenses:		
a. Entertainment		
b. Travel		
c. Hobbies		
d. Club fees and dues		
e. Other		
7. Insurance		
8. Gifts and Contributions		
9. Income Taxes (if any)		

Figure 11.2 (cont'd)

	Per Month × 12 =	Per Year
10. Total Annual Expenses (current dollars)	________	$ ________
11. Inflation Rate until Retirement (I)	________	
12. Total Years until Retirement (N)	________	
13. Inflation Adjustment Factor (1 + I)N		× ________
14. Total Annual Expenses (future dollars)		= ________
15. Inflation Rate Postretirement (i)	________	
16. Aftertax Rate of Return (r)	________	
17. Anticipated Duration of Retirement (n)	________	
18. Inflation-Adjusted Discount Factor $a = \frac{1+i}{1+r}$		________
19. Capital Required at Retirement to Fund Retirement Living Expenses: Amt line 14 × $\frac{1-a^n}{1-a}$		$ ________
20. One-Time Expenses		+$ ________
21. Total Capital Need at Retirement		=$ ________

Source: Robert J. Doyle, Jr., *Retirement Planning Handbook*, The American College, Bryn Mawr, PA.

DESIGNING A QUALIFIED RETIREMENT PLAN

CHAPTER 12

INTRODUCTION

This chapter covers the complicated and distinctive steps involved in installing a qualified retirement plan. Each type of qualified plan is covered in more detail in the chapters listed in the table below:

Cash Balance Pension Plan	Chapter 28
Cross-Tested/Age-Weighted Plan	Chapter 26
Defined Benefit Pension Plan	Chapter 27
ESOP/Stock Bonus Plan	Chapter 23
HR 10 (Keogh) Plan	Chapter 29
Money Purchase Pension Plan	Chapter 25
Profit Sharing Plan	Chapter 22
Savings/Match Plan	Chapter 24
Section 401(k) Plan	Chapter 19

This chapter discusses the steps involved in installing or establishing each of these plans. Installing a plan involves various steps, some of which must comply with a fairly strict legal timetable. To help focus this discussion, an installation checklist for a typical qualified plan is set out in Figure 12.1 for reference.

HOW IT IS DONE

Plan Adoption

An employer must adopt a qualified plan during the employer's taxable year in which it is to be effective.[1] (By contrast, simplified employee pension (SEP) can be adopted as late as the tax filing date for the year—see Chapter 31.) The plan sponsor should adopt—and document the adoption of—the plan before the end of the year in which the plan is to become effective. The plan can be made effective to the beginning of the year of adoption. An adoption that is made later and reflected in "backdated" documents is not legally effective for purposes of the tax treatment of a qualified plan.

The reason for this requirement is basically one of tax accounting. An employer cannot obtain a deduction for an expense accrued during a year unless it meets the "all events" test for accrual. That is, all events that make the accrual a legally binding obligation of the employer must have occurred by the end of the tax year. Thus, a qualified plan must have been legally adopted by the end of a particular tax year if the employer wishes to take a tax deduction for contributions to the plan for that year.

A corporation adopts a plan by a formal action of the corporation's board of directors and signing a plan documents and trust agreement, if separate. An unincorporated business should adopt a written resolution in a form similar to a corporate resolution.

If the plan will use a trust for funding, a trust must be established before the end of the year of adoption and must be valid under the law of the state in which it is established. A nominal plan contribution may be required for that purpose. If the plan is to be funded through an insurance contract, the insurer must accept the application for the contract before the end of the year, but the contract need not be formally adopted in final form at that time.

Advance Determination Letter

Because of the complexity of the qualification provisions, and the tax cost of having a plan considered "disqualified" by the IRS, most plan sponsors apply to the IRS for a ruling that the plan provisions meet Code requirements for favorable tax treatment as a qualified plan. This letter is generally referred to as a "determination letter."

Figure 12.1

PLAN INSTALLATION CHECKLIST AND TIMETABLE

ASSUMPTIONS:

1. Employer uses calendar year for tax reporting.
2. Plan is to be effective January 1, 2015.

BEFORE DECEMBER 31, 2014

1. Plan should be drafted in final form and signed by plan sponsor and trustee.
2. Trust agreement must be signed and trust established under state law; or application for group pension contract must be made and accepted by insurance company.
3. Plan must be "communicated to employees." This can be done orally at employee meetings or through a written communication. The summary plan description (SPD) can be used for this purpose simply by distributing it earlier than its regular due date (see below).

BEFORE EMPLOYER'S TAX FILING DATE
(March 15, 2016, with extensions to September 15, 2016 if applied for)

1. Employer must make the 2015 contribution to the plan by this date in order for it to be deductible on the 2015 tax return.

WITHIN 120 DAYS AFTER PLAN IS ADOPTED
(i.e., Board of Directors' resolution)

1. Furnish SPD to participants (see Chapter 16 of this book).

BEFORE FILING APPLICATION FOR DETERMINATION WITH IRS

1. Provide "Notice to Interested Parties" to employees as required by IRS regulations. This is a prescribed formal notice to employees of their rights in connection with the determination letter process. The notice must be provided 10 to 24 days before filing if the notice is mailed, and 7 to 20 days before filing if the notice is posted.

ON OR BEFORE JULY 31, 2014
(and each July 31 thereafter)

1. File Annual Report (Form 5500 series), unless extension is required (see Chapter 13).
2. Application for IRS determination letter should be prepared and filed, if determined necessary (see below)

Technically, a plan does not have to receive a favorable determination letter in order to be qualified. If the plan provisions in letter and in operation meet Code requirements, the plan is qualified and entitled to the appropriate tax benefits. However, without a determination letter, the issue of plan qualification for a given year does not arise until the IRS audits the employer's tax returns for that year. By that time, it is generally too late for the employer to amend the plan to correct any disqualifying provisions. So if the plan has a disqualifying provision or lacks an essential provision, the employer's tax deduction for the year being audited is lost. (In addition, the plan fund will lose its tax-exempt status and employees will become taxable on their vested benefits—a true all-around tax disaster.) A determination letter helps to avoid this problem since auditing agents generally will not raise the issue of plan qualification if the employer has a current determination letter—that is, one that shows the plan complies with current law.

The IRS has adopted submission procedures for plan sponsors to acquire favorable determination letters.[2] These procedures allow plan sponsors to obtain favorable determination letter during the plan's remedial amendment cycle. For new individually designed plans, plan sponsors can file an on-cycle application if their on-cycle submission period ends at least two years after the end of the off-cycle period in which the application is received.

Existing individually designed plans are eligible for a five-year remedial amendment cycle which is generally based on the plan sponsors employer identification number. Volume submitter and prototype plan documents have a six-year remedial amendment cycle.

An additional advantage of the determination letter procedure is that it can extend the time for retroactive amendments. If the determination letter request is filed certain retroactive amendments can be made as long as the determination letter request is still pending.

Determination letter requests are made on IRS Forms 5300 (for custom designed plans) and 5307 (for volume submitter or prototype plans). IRS requirements for documentation of determination letter requests change frequently. Practitioners should consult the annually revised IRS Revenue Procedure on this subject.[3]

The IRS once provided determination letters as a free service, however currently there is a fee schedule. The fee depends on the type of plan and the nature of the advice sought. Form 8717 is filed along with the fee and the form from the appropriate member of the 5300 family. A limited exemption from the fee applies for employers with one hundred or fewer employees, during the first five years of the plan.[4] Also, a limited tax credit for small employers is available (see below) to help defray the costs of implementing a retirement plan.[5]

Voluntary Correction Programs

It is always possible for the IRS to raise the issue that a plan is discriminatory *in operation*—as opposed to merely having discriminatory provisions on paper. A determination letter cannot prevent this. For those plans in which discrimination or other failures have occurred, a combination of voluntary correction programs offers corrective measures ranging from self-correction of insignificant operational errors to correction of document or other errors found during a plan audit. The purpose of these programs, known collectively as the Employee Plans Compliance Resolution System (EPCRS), is to prevent plan disqualification.[6]

VOLUME SUBMITTER AND PROTOTYPE PLANS

Custom design of a qualified plan can be costly because the plan document must be very lengthy to reflect all of the complex requirements of current law. The benefits profession has developed methods to reduce the cost of plan drafting; these are particularly important to smaller employers, since the cost of installation must be spread over relatively few employees.

One of the most common methods of reducing drafting costs is to use a "volume submitter" or "prototype" plan offered by a financial institution as an inducement to use that institution's investment products to fund the plan. Insurance companies, banks, mutual funds, and various service providers frequently offer volume submitter or prototype plans. These plans are standardized plans of various types—e.g., prototype profit sharing or prototype money purchase—that use standardized language approved by the IRS. The plan sponsor has some degree of choice in basic provisions of the plan such as the vesting schedule, the contribution or benefit formula, etc.

A volume submitter plan is distinguished from a prototype in that a volume submitter plan usually refers to a plan under which various employers use a single financial institution for funding, while a prototype plan generally does not commit the plan sponsor to use any particular funding institution or medium.

The use of volume submitter or prototype plans greatly simplifies plan installation in many cases. The fee for adopting a volume submitter or prototype plan is usually much less than the cost of drafting a custom designed plan. The determination letter procedure is also simplified, because the "boilerplate" provisions of the plan have already been approved by the IRS. All the IRS has to do is determine whether the basic vesting schedule, contribution or benefit formula, etc., as applied to the employer in question, is nondiscriminatory.

The cost of drafting a custom designed plan has also been addressed by pension professionals. There are "document preparation services" that will generate documents from their central word processors based on a checklist of plan provisions submitted by the plan installer. Usually, the use of a document preparation service will speed IRS approval of a plan, because the IRS becomes familiar with the standard language used by various document preparers.

TAX CREDIT FOR STARTUP COSTS

Certain small employers are eligible for a business tax credit of up to $500 for startup costs or employee education expenses incurred in connection with the adoption of a retirement plan. The credit is nonrefundable, and may be taken only during the plan's first three years, or for the year preceding the year the plan becomes effective and the first two years of the plan. To be eligible, the employer must have no more than one hundred employees with compensation in excess of $5,000 for the previous year, and the plan must cover at least one non-highly compensated employee. Amounts eligible for the credit include 50 percent of the qualified startup costs paid or incurred during the year. No credit is allowed for the portion of expenses that are used to determine the amount of the credit.[7]

CHAPTER ENDNOTES

1. Treas. Reg. §1.401-1(a)(2). See also *Engineered Timber Sales, Inc. v. Comm'r.*, 74 TC 808 (1980).
2. See Rev. Proc. 2007-44.
3. The 2015 version is Revenue Procedure 2015-6, 2015-1 IRB.
4. P.L. 107-16 (EGTRRA 2001), Sec. 620.
5. See I.R.C. §45E.
6. See Rev. Proc. 2013-12.
7. I.R.C. §45E.

QUALIFIED PLANS: GENERAL RULES FOR QUALIFICATION

CHAPTER 13

INTRODUCTION

The design of qualified pension and profit sharing plans is a complex subject, and the complete details are beyond the scope of this book. However, because of the great importance of these plans in an employer's benefit program and for individual financial and retirement planning, every planner should have a basic understanding of how these plans are structured, what they can do and cannot do, and the rules for "qualifying" these plans.

In order to obtain the tax advantages of qualified plans, complex Internal Revenue Code and regulatory requirements must be met (but special rules apply to church and governmental plans[1]). This chapter will summarize these requirements. The rules have many exceptions and qualifications that will not be covered in detail here.

ELIGIBILITY AND COVERAGE

A qualified plan must cover a broad group of employees, not just key employees/highly compensated employees and business owners. Two types of rules must be satisfied: the "age and service" ("waiting period") requirements, and the "overall coverage" and "participation" requirements.

Minimum waiting period and age requirements are often used in plans to avoid burdening the plan with employees who terminate after short periods of service. However, the plan cannot require more than one year of service for eligibility, and any employee who has attained the age of twenty-one must be allowed to enter the plan upon meeting the plan's waiting period requirement. As an alternative, the plan waiting period can be up to two years if the plan provides immediate 100 percent vesting upon entry. No plan can impose a maximum age for entry. For eligibility purposes, a year of service means a twelve-month period during which the employee has at least 1,000 hours of service.[2]

In addition to the rules restricting age- and service-related eligibility provisions, qualified plan coverage is further regulated through two alternative overall coverage tests. A qualified plan must satisfy one of the two following tests:[3]

1. Ratio percentage test. The plan must cover a percentage of nonhighly compensated employees that is at least 70 percent of the percentage of highly compensated employees covered.

2. Average benefit test. The plan must benefit a nondiscriminatory classification of employees, and the average benefit, as a percentage of compensation, for all nonhighly compensated employees of the employer must be at least 70 percent of that for highly compensated employees (see below).

"Highly compensated" is a concept defined in detail in Code section 414(q) (see below).

In addition, for a *defined benefit* plan to be qualified, it must cover, on each day of the plan year, the lesser of (1) fifty employees of the employer or (2) the greater of (a) 40 percent or more of all employees of the employer, or (b) two employees (or, if there is only one employee, that employee). This test is commonly known as the "50/40 test."[4]

The average benefit test is a two-pronged test—it requires (1) a *nondiscriminatory classification* and (2) the *70 percent average benefit* requirement.[5]

The nondiscriminatory classification test is expanded upon in some detail in the regulations under Section 410(b). First, the regulations provide a "safe harbor" table (Figure 13.1) under which certain plans are deemed to meet the nondiscriminatory classification requirement automatically. The safe harbor test is best explained through an example using the table.

Example. Suppose Average Co. has 700 salaried office employees, including one-hundred highly compensated employees, and 9,300 production employees, of whom 300 are highly compensated. Average Co. would like to maintain a qualified plan just for the office employees. The office plan will not meet the ratio percentage test since its ratio percentage is 25 percent [(600/9,600)/(100/400)]. Does it meet the average benefit test under the regulations? Its nonhighly compensated concentration percentage is 9,600/10,000 or 96 percent. From the table, the "safe harbor" ratio percentage is 23 percent. Since the plan has an actual ratio percentage of 25 percent, it is deemed to meet the nondiscriminatory classification test without actually looking at the classification itself. (Of course, the plan also has to meet the average benefit percentage portion of the average benefit test.)

If a plan's ratio percentage falls between the "safe harbor" and "unsafe harbor" percentages in the table, the IRS will examine the facts and circumstances of the classification to determine whether it is, in fact, discriminatory. If the ratio percentage is *below* the unsafe harbor percentage, the plan is considered automatically discriminatory.[6]

In applying the above coverage tests, certain employees may not be required to be counted, which means that they can effectively be excluded from the plan. One example may include employees included in a collective bargaining unit can be excluded if there was good faith bargaining on retirement benefits.[7]

When the coverage rules are applied, all related employers must be treated as a single employer. Thus, an employer generally cannot break up its business into a number of corporations or other separate units to avoid covering rank-and-file employees. Appendix C discusses these complex rules in further detail.

However, if the employer actually has bona fide "separate lines of business," it is possible to apply the coverage test and the 50/40 test (as necessary) separately to employees in each line of business. This allows plans to be provided only to one line of business, or several different plans tailored to different lines of business.[8]

Highly Compensated—Definition for Employee Benefit Purposes

An employee is a *highly compensated employee* with respect to a plan year if he—

- was a 5 percent owner (as defined for top-heavy purposes) at any time during either the current year or the preceding year; or
- received compensation for the preceding year in excess of $120,000 in 2015, as indexed from the employer, *and* if the employer elects the application of this clause for the preceding year, was in the "top-paid group" for that year.[9]

The "top-paid group" of employees for a year is the group of employees in the top 20 percent, ranked on the basis of compensation paid for the year. For the purpose of determining the top-paid group, the following employees may be excluded: employees with less than six months of service

1. employees who normally work less than 17.5 hours per week;
2. employees who normally work during not more than six months in any year;
3. employees under the age of twenty-one;
4. except as provided by regulations, employees covered by a collective bargaining agreement; and
5. nonresident aliens with no U.S. earned income.

At the employer's election, a shorter period of service, smaller number of hours or months, or lower age than those specified in (1) through (4) may be used.[10]

Former employees are treated as highly compensated employees if (1) they were highly compensated

Figure 13.1

Nonhighly compensated employee concentration percentage	Safe harbor percentage	Unsafe habor percentage	Nonhighly compensated employee concentration percentage	Safe harbor percentage	Unsafe harbor percentage
0-60	50.00	40.00	80	35.00	25.00
61	49.25	39.25	81	34.25	24.25
62	48.50	38.50	82	33.50	23.50
63	47.75	37.75	83	32.75	22.75
64	47.00	37.00	84	32.00	22.00
65	46.25	36.25	85	31.25	21.25
66	45.50	35.50	86	30.50	20.50
67	44.75	34.75	87	29.75	20.00
68	44.00	34.00	88	29.00	20.00
69	43.25	33.25	89	28.25	20.00
70	42.50	32.50	90	27.50	20.00
71	41.75	31.75	91	26.75	20.00
72	41.00	31.00	92	26.00	20.00
73	40.25	30.25	93	25.25	20.00
74	39.50	29.50	94	24.50	20.00
75	38.75	28.75	95	23.75	20.00
76	38.00	28.00	96	23.00	20.00
77	37.25	27.25	97	22.25	20.00
78	36.50	26.50	98	21.50	20.00
79	35.75	25.75	99	20.75	20.00

employees when they separated from service, or (2) they were highly compensated employees at any time after attaining age fifty-five.[11]

The controlled group, common control, affiliated service group, and employee leasing provisions of code section 414 (see Chapter 59) are to be applied before applying the highly compensated employee rules.

NONDISCRIMINATION IN BENEFITS AND CONTRIBUTIONS

Qualified plans must be nondiscriminatory with respect to highly compensated employees either in terms of benefits or in terms of employer contributions to the plan.[12] Some nondiscriminatory formulas will, however, provide a higher benefit for highly compensated employees; for example, contributions or benefits can be based on compensation or years of service.

The application of the nondiscrimination requirements to contributions and benefits are governed by detailed regulations under Code section 401(a)(4). A defined contribution plan will generally be tested under the "contributions" test,[13] although the plan accounts can be converted to benefits and tested under the "benefits" test.[14] However, ESOPs, Section 401(k) plans, and plans with after-tax employee contributions and/or employer matching contributions may not be tested on a benefits basis.[15] Section 401(k) plans and plans with after-tax employee contributions/and or employer matching contributions must continue to meet the special nondiscrimination tests for those plans, as discussed in the chapters referenced.

A defined benefit plan will be nondiscriminatory if it meets a *general* test or a uniformity requirement and one of three "safe harbors."[16] The nondiscrimination rules for defined benefit plans compare the rate at which benefits accrue for highly compensated employees to the rate at which benefits accrue for other employees. The implications of these rules for defined benefit plans are discussed in Chapter 1.

Integration with Social Security

Qualified plan benefit or contribution formulas can be "integrated" with Social Security.[17] In an integrated plan, greater contributions or benefits generally are provided for higher paid employees whose compensation is greater than an amount based on the Social Security taxable wage base. The difference in contributions or benefits permitted under these rules is referred to as "permitted disparity."

Since most employees will receive Social Security benefits when they retire, a calculation of an employee's retirement needs must take these into account. Since Social Security benefits are effectively paid out of employer compensation costs, an employer is permitted by law to take Social Security benefits into account by integrating a qualified plan's benefit formula with Social Security benefits. However, the rules for doing so are quite complex. The details will not be discussed here, but the financial planner should be familiar with the basic integration rules which follow.

Social Security integration benefits employers from a cost point of view since it effectively reduces the cost of the qualified plan. Also, since Social Security provides a higher retirement income, relatively speaking, for lower paid employees, Social Security integration of qualified plans permits such plans to provide relatively greater benefits for highly compensated employees, which is often an employer objective.

Defined Benefit Plans

There are two methods for integrating defined benefit formulas with Social Security: the "excess" method and the "offset" method.

Under the excess method of integration with Social Security, the plan defines a level of compensation called the integration level. The plan then provides a higher rate of benefits for compensation above the integration level. A plan's integration level is an amount of compensation specified under the plan by a dollar amount or formula. Benefits under the plan expressed as a percentage of compensation are lower for compensation below the integration level than they are for compensation above the integration level.[18]

Example. Plan A's integrated formula provides an annual benefit of 30 percent of final average annual compensation plus 25 percent of compensation above the plan's integration level. Labelle, born in 1947, is a participant in plan A. He retires in 2015. Labelle's final average compensation is $70,000. The integration level (rounded covered compensation—see below) is $66,000. Labelle's annual retirement benefit is determined as follows:

- 30 percent of final average compensation of $77,000, or $21,000, plus
- 25 percent of $4,000 ($70,000 – $66,000) or $1000.

The total benefit is $22,000 ($21,000 plus $1,000).

The Code and regulations provide various rules specifying what maximum integration level a plan can use, and how large the percentage spread above and below the integration level can be. As a general rule, a plan's integration level cannot exceed an amount known as *covered compensation*, which is specified by the IRS in a table.

"Covered compensation" is the average of the contribution and benefit base under the Social Security Act for each year during the thirty-five-year period ending with the year in which an employee attains Social Security retirement age.[19] Therefore, the covered compensation amount for each employee depends upon the year in which the employee retires (see Figure 13.2). Under the regulations, a plan may determine an employee's covered compensation by use of a different IRS table that is developed by rounding the actual amounts of covered compensation for different years of birth (see Figure 13.2).[20]

The Code and Treasury regulations also restrict the percentage spread between the benefit as a percentage of compensation above and below the integration level. The "base benefit percentage" is the percentage of compensation that the plan provides for compensation below the integration level, and the "excess benefit percentage" is the percentage of compensation above the integration level.

The excess benefit percentage cannot exceed the base benefit percentage by more than 0.75 percent for any year of service, or participant's years of service up to thirty-five.[21]

Figure 13.2

2015 COVERED COMPENSATION TABLE

Calendar Year of Birth	Calendar Year of Social Security Retirement	2015 Covered Compensation	Calendar Year of Birth	Calendar Year of Social Security Retirement	2015 Covered Compensation
1907	1972	$ 4,488	1945	2011	$ 61,884
1908	1973	4,704	1946	2012	64,560
1909	1974	5,004	1947	2013	67,308
1910	1975	5,316	1948	2014	69,996
1911	1976	5,664	1949	2015	72,636
1912	1977	6,060	1950	2016	75,180
1913	1978	6,480	1951	2017	77,640
1914	1979	7,044	1952	2018	80,004
1915	1980	7,692	1953	2019	82,308
1916	1981	8,460	1954	2020	84,564
1917	1982	9,300	1955	2022	88,884
1918	1983	10,236	1956	2023	90,984
1919	1984	11,232	1957	2024	93,000
1920	1985	12,276	1958	2025	94,920
1921	1986	13,368	1959	2026	96,780
1922	1987	14,520	1960	2027	98,580
1923	1988	15,708	1961	2028	100,320
1924	1989	16,968	1962	2029	101,964
1925	1990	18,312	1963	2030	103,608
1926	1991	19,728	1964	2031	105,204
1927	1992	21,192	1965	2032	106,716
1928	1993	22,716	1966	2033	108,144
1929	1994	24,312	1967	2034	109,464
1930	1995	25,920	1968	2035	110,664
1931	1996	27,576	1969	2036	111,756
1932	1997	29,304	1970	2037	112,716
1933	1998	31,128	1971	2038	113,616
1934	1999	33,060	1972	2039	114,492
1935	2000	35,100	1973	2040	115,308
1936	2001	37,212	1974	2041	116,004
1937	2002	39,444	1975	2042	116,604
1938	2004	43,992	1976	2043	117,072
1939	2005	46,344	1977	2044	117,408
1940	2006	48,816	1978	2045	117,744
1941	2007	51,348	1979	2046	118,080
1942	2008	53,952	1980	2047	118,320
1943	2009	56,628	1981	2048	118,452
1944	2010	59,268	1982 or later	2049 or later	118,500

Figure 13.2 (cont'd.)

2015 ROUNDED COVERED COMPENSATION TABLE	
Calendar Year of Birth	**2015 Covered Compensation Rounded**
1937	$39,000
1938-1939	45,000
1940	48,000
1941	51,000
1942	54,000
1943	57,000
1944	60,000
1945	63,000
1946-1947	66,000
1948	69,000
1949	72,000
1950	75,000
1951-1952	78,000
1953	81,000
1954	84,000
1955-1956	90,000
1957	93,000
1958-1959	96,000
1960-1961	99,000
1962	102,000
1963-1964	105,000
1965-1967	108,000
1968-1969	111,000
1970-1973	114,000
1974-1978	117,000
1979 and later	118,500

Example. If a defined benefit plan provides a benefit of 1% of compensation below the integration level for each year of service, then it can provide not more than 1.75% of compensation above the integration level for each year of service.

Or, for a participant with thirty-five years of service, if the plan provides a benefit of 30% of final average compensation below the integration level, it cannot provide more than 56.25% of compensation above the integration level. (The spread of 26.25% is 0.75% multiplied by thirty-five years of service.)

The difference between the base and excess benefit percentages—the *maximum excess allowance*—can be no greater than the base percentage. Thus if a plan provides 10 percent of final average compensation below the integration level, it can provide no more than 20 percent of compensation above the integration level.[22]

Under the offset method of integration, the plan formula is reduced by a fixed amount or a formula amount that is designed to represent the existence of Social Security benefits.[23] There is no integration level in an offset plan. The Code and regulations provide limits on the extent of an offset for Social Security. In particular, the rules provide that no more than half of the benefit provided under the formula without the offset may be taken away by an offset. For example, if a plan formula provides 50 percent of final average compensation with an offset, even the lowest paid employee must receive at least 25 percent of final average compensation from the plan.

Defined Contribution Plans

Defined contribution plans can be integrated only under the excess method. Generally, if the integration level is equal to the Social Security taxable wage base in effect at the beginning of the plan year ($118,500 for plan years beginning in 2015), the difference in the allocation percentages above and below the integration level can be no more than the lesser of:

1. the percentage contribution below the integration level; or
2. the greater of:
    a. 5.7 percent; or
    b. the old age portion of the Social Security tax rate.[24]

Thus, for a plan year beginning in 2013, if an integrated plan has an integration level of $118,500 and the plan allocates employer contributions plus forfeitures at the rate of 15.7 percent of compensation above the integration level, then it would have to provide at least a 10 percent allocation for compensation below the integration level (making the difference 5.7 percent).

VESTING

Employee contributions and benefits attributable to these contributions must always be 100 percent vested.[25] Benefits attributable to employer contributions to a qualified defined benefit plan must be vested under a specified vesting schedule that is at least as favorable as one of two alternative minimum standards:[26]

1. *Five-year vesting*. A plan's vesting schedule satisfies this minimum requirement if an employee with at least five years of service is 100 percent vested. No vesting at all is required before five years of service. (The rule is three-year cliff vesting for cash balance plans.[27])
2. *Three- to seven-year vesting*. The plan must provide vesting that is at least as fast as the following schedule:

Years of Service	Vested Percentage
3	20
4	40
5	60
6	80
7 or more	100

Employer contributions to a defined contribution plan must vest under a faster vesting schedule that is at least as favorable as one of the following two standards:[28]

1. *Three-year vesting*. A plan's vesting schedule satisfies this minimum requirement if an employee with at least three years of service is 100 percent vested. No vesting at all is required before three years of service.
2. *Two- to six-year vesting*. The plan must provide vesting that is at least as fast as the following schedule:

Years of Service	Vested Percentage
2	20
3	40
4	60
5	80
6 or more	100

This faster vesting schedule is also applicable to top-heavy plans (discussed below).

FUNDING REQUIREMENTS

Employer and employee contributions to a qualified plan must be deposited into an irrevocable trust fund or insurance contract that is for the "exclusive benefit" of plan participants and their beneficiaries.[29] The *minimum funding standard* provides a mathematical calculation of the minimum amount that must be contributed to a qualified pension plan.[30] Pension plans, both defined benefit and defined contribution must meet these annual minimum funding standards or be subject to a penalty. Profit sharing plans are not subject to the minimum funding standards as such, but contributions must be "recurring and substantial" or the IRS can deem the plan to be "wasting" and thus, should be terminated. Substantial and recurring is not clearly defined in the law so that there is always some risk in repeatedly omitting contributions.

The minimum funding standards applicable to defined benefit plans depend on the method by which an annual cost for these plans is determined. The annual cost is based on an *actuarial cost method.*

Actuarial Cost Methods

An actuarial cost method determines the employer's annual cost for a defined benefit plan. Actuaries use a number of different actuarial cost methods, which can be relatively complex mathematically. However, these methods are based on simple principles that should be understood by financial planners even though the computational complexities are left to the actuary. An actuarial cost method develops a series of annual deposits to the plan fund that will grow to the point where as each employee retires the fund is sufficient to fully fund the employee's retirement benefit.

There are two basic ways of spreading these costs over future working careers of employees. Under the *projected benefit* or level funding method, the total cost is divided into equal deposits for each employee's benefit spread over the period remaining until the employee's retirement.

With the *accrued benefit* method the annual deposit is based on the benefit accrued each year. The accrued benefit method produces a generally rising series of deposits for a given employee, because as retirement approaches there is less time to fund each additional piece of accrued benefit. The overall plan cost does not necessarily rise, however, with the accrued benefit method, because employees may enter and leave the plan from time to time.

If a defined benefit plan provides past service benefits, the cost of these can be made part of the annual cost using a projected benefit or accrued benefit method. Alternatively, the past service benefit can be funded separately by developing what is known as an unfunded past service liability or a *supplemental liability.* The supplemental liability is paid off through deposits to the plan fund over a fixed period of years, up to thirty, regardless of actual retirement dates for employees. The use of a supplemental liability can provide additional funding flexibility in many cases.

Projected benefit actuarial cost methods can be either individual or aggregate. With the individual methods, a separate cost is determined for each employee, with the total employer deposit being the sum of all the separate pieces. With the aggregate method, the cost is developed for the employer's payroll as a whole and is expressed as a percentage of payroll.

Because there are so many different approaches in determining the annual cost using an actuarial cost method, there is no one single annual cost applicable to a given defined benefit plan for a given group of employees. Different actuarial methods should be developed giving a variety of annual cost approaches as part of the design stage for a defined benefit plan.

Actuarial Assumptions

Actuarial cost methods depend on making assumptions about various cost factors, since actual results cannot be known in advance. The annual cost developed under an actuarial cost method depends significantly on these assumptions, and there is some flexibility in choosing assumptions. Under the Code, each assumption must be reasonable, within guidelines in the Code and regulations.[31] Actuarial assumptions include:

- investment return on the plan fund
- salary scale—an assumption about increases in future salaries; this is particularly significant if the plan uses a final average type of formula
- mortality—the extent to which some benefit will not be paid because of the death of employees before retirement
- annuity purchase rate—this determines the funds needed at retirement to provide annuities in the amount designated by the plan formula
- the annuity purchase rate, in turn, depends on assumptions about future investment return and post-retirement mortality
- turnover—the extent to which employees will terminate employment before retirement and thereby receive limited or no benefit.

Deduction Limits

Defined Benefit Plans

The deduction limit for a defined benefit plan is based on actuarial considerations and the applicable minimum funding standards under the Code.[32] These rules have been changed, generally providing stricter funding standards for plan years beginning after 2007.[33] Under the current rules the deduction limit is the greater of the minimum funding amount required under Code section 430, or an alternative calculation which includes a "cushion amount."[34] The rules for the "cushion amount" are, in effect, designed to encourage plan sponsors to "overfund" or generously fund the plan. For example, the cushion amount takes into account expected future benefit increases.

Under this rule, the cost of a defined-benefit plan with a group pension contract or trust fund can be relatively flexible for the employer. Between the minimum limit required by the minimum funding standards and the maximum deductible limit, there may be a relatively comfortable range of contributions that can be adjusted according to the employer's specific financial situation.

Defined Contribution Plans

The maximum amount an employer can deduct for contributions to a defined contribution plan depends on the kind of defined contribution plan that is put into place:

1. The deduction limit for profit sharing plans or money purchase pension plans cannot be more than 25 percent of *compensation* paid or accrued during the year to eligible employees participating in the plan.

2. The definition of "compensation" for purposes of the preceding paragraph includes elective deferrals to a qualified plan, 403(b) plan, 457 plan, SEP, SIMPLE, or Section 125 FSA plan.[35] This means that the payroll upon which the 25 percent is based became higher than it was previously, resulting in a higher deduction limit for employer contributions to the plan.

3. For purposes of calculating the total amount that the employer has contributed to a plan, elective deferrals do not have to be counted.[36]

4. The maximum compensation that can be taken into account for each employee in 2015 is $260,000. The following example illustrates the current rules.

Example. ABC Corporation sponsors a 401(k) plan to which ABC's two employees made elective deferrals totaling $10,000 in 2014. ABC's total payroll for the employees covered under the plan totals $100,000. The deduction limit is 25 percent of compensation. Furthermore, the 25 percent limit is based on gross compensation ($100,000), so that ABC's deduction limit is $25,000. Finally, elective deferrals do not count toward the $25,000 limit, so ABC may contribute and deduct as much as $25,000 to its two employees' accounts in addition to the $10,000 of elective deferrals.

Combined Deduction Limit

The current rules expand the deductibility limit for employer contributions to plans that have a combination of defined-benefit and defined-contribution plans. This may provide a way to provide more adequate retirement benefits for employees, and enhance benefits for key employees.

Summarizing these rules:[37]

- In applying the combined limit, contributions to a defined-contribution plan or plans do not count except for amounts greater than 6 percent of aggregate employee compensation. (Note that under older law, elective deferrals also do not count toward the deduction limit).

- Contributions to a single-employer defined benefit plan that is insured by the PBGC do not count toward the combined limit (i.e. the limits for deductions are applied to each plan separately).

- If neither the defined-benefit nor the defined-contribution plan is a multiemployer plan, the limits for deductions are applied to each plan separately).

Most defined-benefit plans are insured by the PBGC, but there are some exceptions, including plans with twenty-five or fewer participants sponsored by a professional service employer, and plans exclusively for "substantial owners."[38]

Example. ABC Company has twenty-two employees, It maintains a profit-sharing plan (no elective deferrals) and a defined-benefit plan, both of which cover all employees and neither of which is a multiemployer plan. For 2015 it contributed the maximum deductible amount to the defined benefit plan and also contributed $200,000 (10 percent of payroll) to the profit-sharing plan. If ABC Company's defined benefit plan is insured by the PBGC, ABC can deduct the full $200,000 it contributed to the profit-sharing plan. If ABC Company's defined benefit plan is not insured by the PBGC, ABC can deduct only $80,000 of the amount contributed to the profit-sharing plan—that is, the amount in excess of 6 percent of compensation ($200,000 – 6% x $2,000,000).

Penalty for Nondeductible Contributions

Generally, there is no advantage in contributing more to a plan than is deductible, because not only is the deduction for the excess unavailable but under Code section 4972, a 10 percent penalty is imposed on the nondeductible portion of the contribution, with some exceptions for combined defined benefit and defined contribution plans. These exceptions are generous and include matching contributions, the first 6 percent of contributions to the defined contribution plan, and certain amounts contributed to a defined benefit plan.

Timing of Contributions

Under the minimum funding rules, contributions will be considered to have been made for a particular tax year if they are made no later than the due date (including extensions) for the employer's tax return.[39] Penalties apply if the minimum funding requirements are not met. Profit sharing plans are not subject to the minimum funding rules.

If a defined benefit plan fails to meet certain funding requirements for a plan year, a quarterly payment requirement must be met in the following plan year. For a calendar year taxpayer, contributions are due April 15, July 15, October 15, and January 15 of the following year; corresponding dates apply to fiscal year taxpayers. A failure to make timely payments subjects the taxpayer to interest on the missed installment.[40]

Each quarterly payment must be 25 percent of the lesser of (a) 90 percent of the annual minimum funding amount or (b) 100 percent of the preceding year's minimum funding amount.[41]

Elective deferral amounts such as salary reductions under 401(k) plans and 403(b) plans cannot be held by employers until the latest contribution date for employer contributions. Such elective deferrals must be deposited no later than the fifteenth day of the month following the payment or payroll withholding of the amounts.[42]

Fiduciary Rules

There are strict limits on the extent to which an employer can exercise control over the plan fund.[43] The plan trustee can be a corporation or an individual, even a company president or shareholder, but plan trustees are subject to stringent federal fiduciary rules requiring them to manage the fund solely in the interest of plan participants and beneficiaries. Loans to employees are permitted within limits (see Chapter 14), but generally the employer is penalized for borrowing from the plan.

LIMITATIONS ON BENEFITS AND CONTRIBUTIONS

To prevent a qualified plan from being used primarily as a tax shelter for highly compensated employees, there is a limitation on plan benefits or employer contributions.

Defined Benefit Limits

Under a defined benefit plan, the highest annual benefit payable under the plan must not exceed the lesser of:

- 100 percent of the participant's compensation averaged over the three years of highest compensation, or
- $210,000 (in 2015, as indexed).[44]

The dollar limit is adjusted in $5,000 increments under a cost-of-living indexing formula.[45]

The dollar limit is also adjusted actuarially for retirement ages earlier than age sixty-two (limit is reduced) or later than age sixty-five (limit is increased).

Defined Contribution Limits

For a defined contribution plan, the "annual additions" (employer contributions, employee salary reductions, employee contributions, and plan forfeitures reallocated from other participants' accounts) to each participant's account is limited. This annual additions limit cannot exceed the lesser of:

- 100 percent of the participant's annual compensation, or
- $53,000[46] (in 2015, as indexed)

The dollar limit is subject to indexing in increments of $1,000.[47]

Compensation Limit

A further limitation on plan benefits or contributions is that only the first $265,000 of each employee's annual compensation (in 2015, as indexed) can be taken into account in the plan's benefit or contribution formula.[48] The $265,000 limit is indexed for inflation in increments of $5,000.[49] Thus, for example, if an employee earns $300,000 annually in 2015, and the employer has a 10 percent money purchase plan, the maximum contribution for that employee would be $26,500 (10 percent of $265,000).

TOP-HEAVY REQUIREMENTS

A *top-heavy* plan is one that provides more than 60 percent of its aggregate accrued benefits or account balances to *key employees*, as defined below.[50] These plans must meet certain additional qualification rules.[51] SIMPLE IRA plans (see Chapter 30), as well as SIMPLE 401(k) plans that allow contributions only under Section 401(k)(11) (see Chapter 19), are exempt from the top-heavy requirements;[52] safe harbor 401(k) plans are generally exempt, subject to limits.[53]

If a plan is top-heavy for a given year, it must provide more rapid vesting than generally required.[54] The plan can either provide 100 percent vesting after three years of service, or six-year graded vesting as follows:

Years of Service	Vested Percentage
2	20
3	40
4	60
5	80
6 or more	100

In addition, a top-heavy plan must provide minimum benefits or contributions for non-key employees.[55]

For defined benefit plans the benefit for each non-key employee during a top-heavy year must be at least 2 percent of compensation multiplied by the employee's years of service, up to 20 percent. The average compensation used for this formula is based on the highest five years of compensation.

For a defined contribution plan, employer contributions during a top-heavy year must be at least 3 percent of compensation.

A *key employee* for purposes of the top-heavy rules is an employee who, at any time during the plan year is:

- an officer of the employer having annual compensation greater than $170,000 (in 2015, as indexed)
- a more-than-5-percent owner of the employer, or
- a more-than-1-percent owner of the employer having annual compensation from the employer of more than $150,000.[56]

For these purposes, no more than fifty employees (or, if lesser, the greater of three or 10 percent of the employees) will be treated as officers.

CHAPTER ENDNOTES

1. Nondiscrimination testing is generally not required by governmental plans. See I.R.C. §§401(a)(5), 401(a)(26), 410(c)(2), 401(k)(3), and 403(b)(12).
2. I.R.C. §410(a).
3. I.R.C. §410(b); Treas. Reg. §1.410(b)-2.
4. I.R.C. §401(a)(26). More lenient rules apply to governmental plans. See Notice 2001-9, 2001-1 CB 375.
5. See Treas. Reg. §1.410(b)-2(b)(3).
6. Treas. Reg. §1.410(b)-4.

7. I.R.C. §410(b)(3).
8. I.R.C. §410(b)(5). The requirement that a separate line of business have at least 50 employees does not apply in determining whether a plan satisfies the 50/40 test on a separate line of business basis. I.R.C. §401(a)(26)(G).
9. I.R.C. §414(q)(1).
10. I.R.C. §414(q)(5).
11. I.R.C. §414(q)(6).
12. I.R.C. §401(a)(4).
13. Treas. Reg. §1.401(a)(4)-2.
14. Treas. Reg. §1.401(a)(4)-8.
15. Treas. Reg. §1.401(a)(4)-2(b)(3).
16. Treas. Reg. §1.401(a)(4)-3.
17. I.R.C. §401(l).
18. I.R.C. §401(l)(3)(A).
19. Treas. Reg. §1.401(l)-1(c)(7).
20. Treas. Reg. §1.401(l)-1(c)(7)(ii)(A). Internal Revenue Bulletin 2014-52, Revenue Ruling 2014-34.
21. I.R.C. §401(l)(4)(A).
22. I.R.C. §401(l)(4)(A).
23. I.R.C. §401(l)(3)(B).
24. I.R.C. §401(l)(2); Treas. Reg. §1.401(l)-2(b)(2). For a required reduction of this percentage for lower integration levels, see Treas. Reg. §1.401(l)-2(d)(4).
25. I.R.C. §411(a)(1).
26. I.R.C. §411(a)(2)(A).
27. I.R.C. §411(a)(13)(B).
28. I.R.C. §411(a)(2)(B).
29. I.R.C. §401(a)(2).
30. I.R.C. §412. For penalties for noncompliance, see I.R.C. §4971.
31. I.R.C. §412(c)(3).
32. See I.R.C. §404.
33. For plan years beginning in 2007 and before, Code section 404(a) provided a limit determined by the largest of three amounts:
    1. The amount necessary to satisfy the minimum funding standard of Code section 412 for the year.
    2. The amount necessary to fund benefits based on past and current service on a level funding basis over the years remaining to retirement for each employee. However, if the remaining unfunded cost of any three individuals is more than 50 percent of the total of the unfunded costs, funding for those three individuals must be distributed over a period of at least five taxable years.
    3. An amount equal to the normal cost of the plan plus, if there is a supplemental liability, an amount necessary to amortize the supplemental liability in equal annual payments over a ten-year period.
34. I.R.C. §404(o).
35. I.R.C. §404(A)(12).
36. See I.R.C. §404(n).
37. See I.R.C. §404(a)(7).
38. ERISA §4021(b).
39. I.R.C. §404(a)(6).
40. I.R.C. §412(m).
41. I.R.C. §412(m)(4).
42. DOL Reg. 2510.3-102(b).
43. ERISA, Part 4 (§401, et seq.). The "prohibited transaction" rules are reiterated in I.R.C. §4975.
44. I.R.C. §415(b).
45. I.R.C. §415(d)(4)(A).
46. I.R.C. §415(c).
47. I.R.C. §415(d)(4)(B).
48. I.R.C. §401(a)(17)(A).
49. I.R.C. §401(a)(17)(B).
50. I.R.C. §416(g)(1)(A).
51. I.R.C. §416(a).
52. I.R.C. §§416(g)(4)(G), 401(k)(11)(D)(ii).
53. I.R.C. §416(g)(4)(H). This rule applies to a plan that consists solely of contributions meeting the requirements of I.R.C. §401(k)(12) and safe harbor matching contributions meeting the requirements of I.R.C. §401(m)(11). Certain variations on the Code's safe harbor plan provisions could trigger the top-heavy rule. See Rev. Rul. 2004-13, 2004-7 IRB 485.
54. I.R.C. §416(b).
55. I.R.C. §416(c).
56. I.R.C. §416(i).

QUALIFIED PLANS: DISTRIBUTIONS AND LOANS

CHAPTER 14

INTRODUCTION

Naturally, when clients have worked hard over the course of many years to save or earn money in a qualified plan; they eventually hope to be able to use that money. There are many circumstances and reasons for wanting to use this money. Some of those circumstances may involve the need to take a loan from the qualified plan. Though the reasons may be diverse and the timing may come at many different ages, there is no questioning the fact that most clients with a qualified plan will want access to the money in that plan someday. Distributions from qualified pension, profit sharing, employer stock plans, and Section 403(b) tax deferred annuity plans are subject to numerous special rules and distinctive federal income tax treatment. Advance consideration of all the potential implications of plan distributions is an important part of overall estate planning.

Given the complex nature of retirement plan distribution rules, this chapter has been organized in sections. Each section will cover a specific area of plan and loan provisions and information. Here is how the chapter is organized,

I. Planning Retirement Distributions
II. Plan Provisions - Required Spousal Benefits
  A. Pre-retirement Survivor Annuity
  B. Qualified Joint and Survivor Annuity
III. Plan Provisions - Other Benefit Options
  A. Defined Benefit Plan Distribution Provisions
  B. Defined Contribution Plan Distribution Provisions
IV. Tax Impact
  A. Nontaxable and Taxable Amounts
  B. Taxation of Annuity Payments
  C. Lump Sum Distributions
  D. Taxation of Death Benefits
  E. Federal Estate Tax
V. Loans
VI. Qualified Domestic Relations Orders (QDROs)
VII. Penalty Taxes
  A. Early Distribution Penalty
  B. Minimum Distribution Requirements and Penalty
VIII. Retirement Plan Rollovers
  A. When Are Rollovers Used?
  B. Tax Treatment of Rollovers
  C. Alternatives to Rollovers

I. PLANNING RETIREMENT DISTRIBUTIONS

As mentioned in the Introduction, distributions from qualified pension, profit sharing, employer stock plans, and Section 403(b) tax deferred annuity plans are subject to numerous special rules and distinctive federal income tax treatment. Advance consideration of all the potential implications of plan distributions is an important part of overall plan design.

Furthermore, in advising clients who are plan participants, a clear understanding of the qualified plan rules is important. A qualified plan or Section 403(b) tax deferred annuity plan can allow employees to accumulate substantial retirement benefits. Even a middle-level employee may have an account balance of hundreds of thousands of dollars available at retirement or termination of employment. Careful planning is important in order to make the right choices of payment options and tax treatment for a plan distribution, to obtain the right result in financial planning for retirement, and also to avoid adverse tax results or even a tax disaster.

The retirement plan distribution rules are astonishingly complicated. They are a maze full of tax traps that have developed in the law over many years, with Congress and the IRS adding new twists and turns almost every year. This chapter is only a basic outline of these rules, but even this basic outline is quite complex.

One way to thread the maze and give some structure to the subject is to look at the issue from the standpoint of advice to a plan participant who is about to retire. What questions need to be asked and what decisions must be made? Typically, the process might proceed by asking and answering these questions—

1. What kinds of distributions does the plan itself allow? The retiree's advisor should review plan documents, particularly the summary plan description (SPD), to determine what options are available. Sections II and III of this chapter discuss these issues.

2. Can and should the distribution be rolled over? (Section VIII explains the issues to be considered.)

3. If periodic payments are chosen, what kind of payment schedule is best?

    - Note the requirement of spousal consent for a payment option that "cuts out" the spouse. (Section II.)

    - Is the payment subject to a 10 percent early distribution penalty? (Section VII.)

    - Are the minimum distribution requirements satisfied? (Section VII.)

    - How will the payments be taxed? (Section IV, A and B.)

4. If a lump sum payment is chosen:

    - Is it eligible for ten-year averaging and if so, is the election beneficial? (Section IV.)

    - How much tax is payable? (Section IV.)

5. What are the potential future estate tax consequences of the form of distribution chosen? (Sections IV E and VII.)

II. PLAN PROVISIONS—REQUIRED SPOUSAL BENEFITS

All pension plans must provide two forms of survivorship benefits for spouses: (1) the "*qualified pre-retirement survivor annuity*" and (2) the "*qualified joint and survivor annuity.*" Stock bonus plans, profit sharing plans, and ESOPs generally need not provide these survivorship benefits for the spouse if the participant's nonforfeitable account balance is payable as a death benefit to that spouse.[1]

Qualified Pre-retirement Survivor Annuity

Once a participant in a plan requiring these spousal benefits is vested, the nonparticipant spouse acquires the right to a pre-retirement survivor annuity, payable to the spouse in the event of the participant's death before retirement. This right is an actual property right created by federal law.

In a defined benefit plan, the survivor annuity payable under this provision of law is the amount that would have been paid under a qualified joint and survivor annuity if the participant had either (1) retired on the day before his or her death (in the case of the participant dying after attaining the earliest retirement age under the plan); or (2) separated from service on the earlier of the actual time of separation or death and survived to the plan's earliest retirement age, then retired with an immediate joint and survivor annuity (in the case of the participant dying before attaining such age).[2] The calculation of joint and survivor annuity amounts is discussed below.

If the plan is a defined contribution plan, the qualified pre-retirement survivor annuity is an annuity for the life of the surviving spouse that is the actuarial equivalent of at least 50 percent of the participant's vested account balance, determined as of the date of death.[3]

The pre-retirement survivor annuity is an automatic benefit. If no other election is made, a pre-retirement survivor annuity is provided. If the plan permits, a participant can elect to receive some other form of retirement survivorship benefit, including no pre-retirement survivorship benefit at all, or survivorship benefits payable to a beneficiary other than the spouse. However, the spouse must understand the rights given up and must consent, in writing, to the participant's choice of another form of benefit.[4]

The right to make an election of a benefit other than the pre-retirement survivor annuity must be communicated to all vested participants who have attained age thirty-two.[5] The participant can elect to receive some benefit other than the pre-retirement survivor annuity at any time after age thirty-five.[6] The participant can also change this election at any time before retirement.

Consideration of "electing out" of the pre-retirement survivorship benefit becomes more important as a participant nears retirement age. Electing out of the pre-retirement survivorship benefit will generally increase the participant's benefit after retirement, unless the plan specifically subsidizes the retirement benefit. Thus, a participant may want to elect out of the benefit to increase the size of the monthly check received during the post-retirement period. Alternatively, the participant may wish to provide a pre-retirement survivorship benefit for a beneficiary other than the surviving spouse.

Such elections must be considered very carefully, particularly by the nonparticipant spouse. Generally a nonparticipant spouse would (and should) not agree to waive this benefit unless the couple's overall retirement planning provides some compensating benefit to the spouse. The existence and amount of any such compensating benefit to the spouse should be documented in connection with the spouse's benefit waiver.

The consent of the nonparticipant spouse to waiver of the pre-retirement survivorship benefit in favor of an optional benefit form selected by the participant must (1) be in writing; (2) acknowledge the effect of the waiver; and (3) be witnessed, either by a plan representative or a notary public.[7] For this reason, full disclosure—in writing—to the nonparticipant spouse must be made, and the spouse should be advised to consult an independent legal (and possibly financial) advisor in connection with the waiver. For large benefits, this advice to the spouse is an extremely important consideration.

Qualified Joint and Survivor Annuity

A qualified joint and survivor annuity is a post-retirement death benefit for the plan participant's spouse. If the plan is subject to these requirements, it must automatically provide, as a retirement benefit, an annuity for the life of the participant with a survivor annuity for the life of the participant's spouse. The survivor annuity must not be between 50 and 100 percent of the annuity payable during the joint lives of the participant and spouse.[8] For example, if $1,000 per month is payable during the joint lives, the annuity to the surviving spouse can be any specified amount from $500 per month to $1,000 per month. The spouse's annuity must be continued even if the spouse remarries.[9]

As with the pre-retirement survivor annuity, a participant may elect to receive another form of benefit if the plan permits. However, as with a qualified pre-retirement survivor annuity, the spouse must consent in writing to the election.[10] An election to waive the joint and survivor form must be made during the ninety-day period ending on the "annuity starting date"—the date on which benefit payments should have begun to the participant, not necessarily the actual date of payment.[11] The waiver can be revoked—that is, the participant can change the election during the ninety-day period. Administrators of affected plans must provide participants with a notice of the election period and an explanation of the consequences of the election within a reasonable period before the annuity starting date.[12]

Since the joint and survivor annuity must be the actuarial equivalent of other forms of benefit, the participant may wish to increase the monthly pension by waiving the joint and survivor annuity and receiving a straight life annuity or some other form of benefit. Just as in the case of the pre-retirement survivorship benefit, discussed above, the nonparticipant spouse's consent to waiver of the joint and survivor annuity in favor of an optional benefit form selected by the participant must (1) be in writing; (2) acknowledge the effect of the waiver; and (3) be witnessed, either by a plan representative or a notary public.[13] It is extremely important that spouses are made aware of what they are giving up if they consent to some other benefit form.

III. PLAN PROVISIONS—OTHER BENEFIT OPTIONS

A qualified plan can offer a wide range of distribution options. Participants benefit from having the widest possible range of options, because this increases their flexibility in personal retirement planning. However, a wide range of options increases administrative costs. Also, the IRS makes it difficult to withdraw a benefit option once it has been established.[14] Consequently, most employers provide only a relatively limited "menu" of benefit forms for participants to choose from.

In addition, a qualified plan generally must provide for "direct rollovers" of certain distributions.[15] Failure to elect a "direct rollover" will subject the distribution to mandatory 20 percent withholding. Plan administrators must provide a written explanation to the distributee of his right to elect a "direct rollover" and the withholding consequences of not making the election.[16] See "Tax Treatment of Rollovers," under Section VIII.

Defined Benefit Plan Distribution Provisions

Defined benefit plans must provide a married participant with a *joint and survivor annuity* as the automatic form of benefit, as described earlier. For an unmarried participant, the plan's automatic form of benefit is usually a *life annuity*—typically monthly payments to the participant for life, with no further payments after the participant's death.

Many plans allow participants to elect to receive some other form of benefit from a list of options in the plan. However, to elect any option that eliminates the benefit for a married participant's spouse, the spouse must consent on a notarized written form to waive the spousal right to the joint and survivor annuity. As discussed earlier, this is not just a legal formality; in consenting to another form of benefit, the spouse gives up important and often sizable property rights in the participant's qualified plan benefit that are guaranteed under federal law.

Typically, plans offer, as an option to the joint or single life annuity, a *period-certain* annuity. A period-certain annuity provides payments for a specified period of time—usually ten to twenty years—even if the participant, or the participant and spouse, both die before the end of that period. Thus, the period-certain annuity makes it certain that periodic (usually monthly) benefits will continue for the participant's heirs even if the participant and spouse die early. Because of this guarantee feature, the annual or monthly payments under a period-certain option are less than they would be under an option where payments end at death (see the typical equivalency table below).

MONTHLY PAYMENTS — VARIOUS ANNUITY FORMS

Assumptions: plan participant aged 65, spouse aged 62, lump sum equivalent at age 65 of $200,000

Form of Annuity	Monthly Benefit
Life	$1,818
Life — 10 years certain	1,710
Life — 20 years certain	1,560
Joint and Survivor — 50%	1,696
Joint and Survivor — 66⅔%	1,626
Joint and Survivor — 100%	1,504

As the above comparison indicates, a period-certain option should be chosen if the participant wants to make sure that his heirs are provided for in case both he and his spouse die shortly after retirement. The reduction in monthly income is relatively small, since it is based on the average life expectancy of all annuitants and assumes that the average annuitant (male or female) lives about twenty years after attaining age sixty-five. Thus, the participant and spouse should consider a period-certain option if they are both in poor health, or if they want to make sure that children (or other heirs) with large financial needs are provided for in the event of their deaths. On the other hand, if the participant wants the largest possible monthly income from the plan, a life annuity should be chosen.

Defined benefit plans may allow a participant to choose a joint annuity with a beneficiary other than a spouse—for example, an annuity for the life of a participant with payments continuing after the parent-participant's death to a son or daughter. Treasury regulations limit the amount of annuity payable to a much younger beneficiary in order to ensure that the participant personally receives (and therefore is taxed on) at least a minimum portion of the total value of the plan benefit and that plan payments are not unduly deferred beyond the participant's death. (See the minimum distribution rules discussed below in Section VII.) Thus, a much younger beneficiary (except for a spouse) generally would not be allowed to receive a 100 percent survivor annuity benefit.

Defined Contribution Plan Distribution Provisions

Defined contribution plans include such plans as profit sharing, 401(k), and money purchase plans. Section 403(b) tax-deferred annuity plans also have distribution provisions similar to defined contribution plans. Some defined contribution plans provide annuity benefits like those in defined benefit plans. In fact, money purchase plans, target benefit plans and Section 403(b) tax deferred annuity plans subject to ERISA must meet the pre-retirement and joint and survivor annuity rules discussed above. Other defined contribution plans do not have to meet these rules if (1) there is no annuity option; and (2) the plan participant's account balance is payable to the participant's spouse in the event of the participant's death.[17] Avoiding the required joint and survivor provisions simplifies plan administration and therefore reduces the plan's cost.

Annuity benefits are computed by converting the participant's account balance in the defined contribution plan into an equivalent annuity. In some plans, the participant can elect to have his account balance used to purchase an annuity from an insurance company. The same considerations in choosing annuity options as have already been discussed would then apply. If the plan offers annuity options, the required joint and survivor provisions apply, as discussed earlier.

Defined contribution plans often provide a lump sum benefit at retirement or termination of employment. Defined contribution plans often also allow the option of taking out non-annuity distributions over the retirement years. That is, the participant simply takes out money as it is needed, subject to the minimum distribution requirements discussed later. Such distribution provisions provide much flexibility in planning.

IV. TAX IMPACT

For many plan participants, retirement income adequacy is more important than minimizing taxes to the last dollar. Nevertheless, taxes on both the federal and state levels must never be ignored, since they reduce the participant's "bottom line": financial security. The greater the tax on the distribution, the less financial security the participant has.

A qualified plan distribution may be subject to federal, state, and local taxes, in whole or in part. This section will focus only on the federal tax treatment. The federal tax treatment is generally the most significant, because federal tax rates are usually higher than state and local rates. Also, many state and local income tax laws provide a full or partial exemption or especially favorable tax treatment for distributions from qualified retirement plans.

Nontaxable and Taxable Amounts

Qualified plans often contain after-tax employee money—that is, contributions that have already been taxed. These amounts can be received by the employee free of federal income taxes, although the order in which they are recovered for tax purposes depends on the kind of distribution.

The first step in determining the tax on any distribution, then, is to determine the participant's cost basis in the plan benefit.

The participant's cost basis can include:[18]

- the total after-tax contributions made by the employee to a contributory plan;
- the total cost of life insurance protection actually reported as taxable income on federal income tax returns by the participant, if the plan distribution is received under the same contract that provides the life insurance protection (If the plan trustee cashes in the life insurance contract before distribution, this cost basis amount is not available. For a person who is now or was self-employed, the cost of life insurance protection is not includable in basis.);[19]
- any employer contributions previously taxed to the employee—for example, where a nonqualified plan later becomes qualified;
- certain employer contributions attributable to foreign services performed before 1963; and
- the amount of any plan loans included in income as a taxable distribution (see V, below).

In-service (Partial) Distributions

If a participant takes out a partial plan distribution before termination of employment (as is provided for in many savings or thrift plans), the distribution is deemed to include both nontaxable and taxable amounts; the nontaxable amount will be in proportion to the ratio of total after-tax contributions (i.e., the employee's cost basis) to the plan account balance (similar to the computation of the annuity exclusion ratio discussed below).[20] Expressed as a formula it looks like this:

$$\text{nontaxable amount} = \text{distribution} \times \frac{\text{Employee's cost basis}}{\text{total account balance}}$$

However, there is a "grandfather" rule for pre-1987 after-tax contributions to the plan. If certain previously existing plans include contributions made before 1987, it is possible to withdraw after-tax money first. That is, if a distribution from the plan is made (at any time, even after 1987) that is *less* than the total amount of pre-1987 after-tax contributions, the entire distribution is received tax free. Once a participant's pre-1987 amount (if any) has been used up, the regular rule applies.[21]

A taxable in-service distribution may also be subject to the early distribution penalty, discussed later. In addition, in-service distributions generally will be subject to mandatory withholding at 20 percent, unless the distribution is transferred to an eligible retirement plan by means of a "direct rollover" (see "Retirement Plan Rollovers," below).[22]

Total Distributions

If the participant begins annuity payments based on the entire account balance, the nontaxable amount will be proportionate to the ratio of total after-tax contributions (i.e., the employee's cost basis) in the plan to the total annuity payments expected to be received (see below). If the participant withdraws his or her entire account balance, the distribution may be eligible for the lump sum distribution treatment discussed below. Total distributions may also be subject to the early distribution penalty, discussed below. In addition, certain distributions may be subject to mandatory withholding at 20 percent, unless such distributions are rolled over by means of a "direct rollover" (see "Retirement Plan Rollovers," below).

Taxation of Annuity Payments

An employee who has no cost basis (described above) for his interest in the plan must include as ordinary income the full amount of each annuity payment (i.e., periodic plan distributions made over more than one taxable year of the employee in a systematic liquidation of the participant's benefit).

If the employee has a cost basis, one of two tables is used to determine the excludable portion of each monthly payment.[23] If the annuity is payable over one life, the table set forth following the paragraph below is used.

Age on annuity starting date	Number of anticipated payments
Not more than 55	360
More than 55-60	310
More than 60-65	260
More than 65-70	210
More than 70	160

Example. Franco retires at age sixty-five with a pension of $2,000 per month payable on a single life basis. His cost basis in the plan is $52,000. From the table, the number of anticipated payments is 260. Franco is deemed to recover $200 ($52,000 divided by 260) of cost basis from each payment. Therefore, of each $2,000 monthly payment, $1,800 is taxable ($2,000 minus $200) and the remaining $200 is recovered tax free. After the entire cost basis is recovered (after Franco receives 260 payments), the entire amount of each subsequent monthly payment is taxable.

If the annuity is payable over two or more lives, the excludable portion of each monthly payment is determined by dividing the employee's investment in the contract by the number of anticipated payments, based on the combined ages of the recipients, as follows:

Combined age of annuitants	Number of payments
Not more than 110	410
More than 110 but not more than 120	360
More than 120 but not more than 130	310
More than 130 but not more than 140	260
More than 140	210

These tables do not apply if the annuitant is age 75 or over, unless there are fewer than five years of guaranteed payments under the annuity.[24] If a lump sum is paid to the taxpayer in connection with the commencement of the annuity payments, it will be taxable as an amount not received as an annuity under Section 72(e), and treated as received before the annuity starting date. Such a taxpayer's investment in the contract will be determined as if the lump sum payment has been received.[25]

After the cost basis is fully recovered, payments received subsequently are taxable in full.[26] If the participant dies before the cost basis is fully recovered, an income tax deduction for the unrecovered basis is allowed on the participant's final income tax return.[27]

If the annuity starting date was before November 19, 1996, different rules were applicable.[28]

Lump Sum Distributions

In some cases, participants may with to take out the entire amount of their retirement benefit from a qualified plan or IRA for retirement purposes. Generally, they will want to roll this distribution over to an IRA or other eligible retirement plan, in order to avoid current taxation on the benefit. There are, however, two special tax benefits for lump sum distributions (from qualified plans only) that are not rolled over and that qualify as "lump-sum distributions" under Code section 402:

- Lump-sum distributions of employer stock from a profit-sharing plan, k stock bonus plan, or ESOP can avoid current taxation of unrealized appreciation; see Chapter 23.
- Certain benefits under prior law are "grandfathered" to individuals who attained age fifty before 1986. Obviously the significance of this tax benefit is rapidly diminishing with the passage of time.

The tax break for lump sum distributions was "ten-year averaging" from 1974 through 1986. For an individual who attained age fifty before January 1, 1986, the ten-year averaging provision is "grandfathered." Such an individual may elect to use ten-year averaging using the 1986 tax rates (taking into account the prior law zero bracket amount).[29]

A further elective grandfather rule imposes a tax rate of 20 percent for the portion of distributions (attributable to pre-1974 accumulations, if any) to participants who attained age fifty before January 1, 1986. Distributees should elect this treatment only if it produces a lower overall tax.

Taxation of Death Benefits

In general, the same income tax treatment applies to death benefits paid to beneficiaries as to lifetime benefits payable to participants. The special lump sum provision can be used by the beneficiary. If the employee had attained age fifty before January 1, 1986, the beneficiary may elect ten-year averaging, even if the participant was not 59½ or older at his or her death.[30] For an annuity distribution, the beneficiary uses the same annuity rules described earlier.

There are also some additional income tax benefits available.

If the death benefit is payable under a life insurance contract held by the qualified plan, the pure insurance amount of the death benefit is excludable from income taxation.[31] The pure insurance amount is the difference between the policy's face amount and its cash value at the date of death.

Example. Ellen Employee, aged sixty-four, dies in 2015 before retirement. Her beneficiary receives a lump sum death benefit of $100,000 from the plan. The $100,000 is the proceeds of a cash value life insurance contract; the contract's cash value at Ellen's death was $60,000. Ellen reported a total of $10,000 of Table 2001 (formerly P.S. 58) insurance costs for this contract on her income tax returns during her lifetime. The taxable amount of the $100,000 distribution to the beneficiary is $100,000 less the following items:

- the pure insurance amount of $40,000 ($100,000 less the cash value of $60,000),
- Ellen's cost basis of $10,000.

The taxable amount of this benefit is therefore $50,000.

Table 2001 rates are generally used in determining the value of life insurance protection after 2000.[32] For prior years, "P.S. 58" rates were used to calculate the value of the protection.[33]

An additional factor in the treatment of death benefits involves rollovers to an IRA; see the discussion later in this chapter.

Federal Estate Tax

The entire value of a qualified plan, IRA, or Roth IRA death benefit is generally subject to inclusion in the decedent's gross estate for federal estate tax purposes, since there is no specific statutory exclusion for these benefits. However, only high-income plan participants (probably less than 1 percent of the population) will actually be subject to estate tax. First, there is a substantial minimum tax credit applicable to the estate tax. This essentially eliminates estate taxes for gross estates of less than $5,430,000 as indexed for 2015. In addition, the unlimited marital deduction for federal estate tax purposes defers federal estate tax on property transferred at death to a spouse in a qualifying manner until the death of the second spouse.[34]

V. LOANS

Because of the 10 percent penalty tax on "early" distributions from qualified plans (see below), a plan provision allowing loans to employees may be attractive. This allows employees access to plan funds without extra tax cost. However, a loan provision increases administrative costs for the plan and may deplete plan funds available for pooled investments.

For participants to borrow from a plan, the plan must specifically permit such loans. Any type of qualified plan (or Section 403(b) tax deferred annuity plan) may permit loans. Loan provisions are most common in defined contribution plans, particularly profit sharing plans. There are considerable administrative difficulties connected with loans from defined benefit plans because of the actuarial approach to plan funding. Loans from IRAs and SEPs are not permitted.

Loans to participants are generally prohibited transactions, subject to penalties unless such loans (1) are exempted from the prohibited transaction rules by an administrative exemption; or (2) meet the requirements set out in Code section 4975(d)(1). The requirements of that section are met if:

(1) loans made by the plan are available to all participants and beneficiaries on a reasonably equivalent basis;

(2) loans are not made available to highly compensated employees in an amount greater than the amounts made available to other employees;

(3) loans are made in accordance with specific provisions regarding such loans set forth in the plan;

(4) the loans bear reasonable rates of interest; and

(5) the loans are adequately secured.[35]

Plan loans may be made from a qualified plan to a sole proprietor, a more-than-10-percent partner in an unincorporated business, and an S corporation employee who is a more-than-5-percent shareholder in the corporation.[36] A loan from a qualified plan (or a Section 403(b) tax deferred annuity) will be treated as a taxable distribution if it does not meet the requirements of Code section 72(p). Section 72(p) provides that aggregate loans from qualified plans to any individual plan participant cannot exceed the *lesser* of:

- $50,000, reduced by the excess of the highest outstanding loan balance during the preceding one-year period over the outstanding balance on the date when the loan is made; or
- one-half the present value of the participant's vested account balance (or accrued benefit, in the case of a defined benefit plan).

A loan of up to $10,000 can be made, even if this is more than one-half of the participant's vested benefit.[37] For example, a participant having a vested account balance of $17,000 could borrow up to $10,000.

Loans must be repayable, by their terms, within five years, except for loans used to acquire a principal residence of the participant.

Interest on a plan loan, in most cases, will be consumer interest, which is generally not deductible by the employee, unless the loan is secured by a home mortgage. Interest deductions are specifically prohibited in two situations: (1) if the loan is to a key employee, as defined in the Code's rules for top-heavy plans (Section 416); or (2) if the loan is secured by a Section 401(k) or Section 403(b) tax deferred annuity plan account based on salary reductions.[38]

VI. QUALIFIED DOMESTIC RELATIONS ORDERS (QDROS)

In general, a qualified plan benefit cannot be assigned or "alienated" by a participant, voluntarily or involuntarily.[39] The idea behind this rule is to protect the participant's retirement fund from attachment by creditors. However, after a series of conflicting state court cases, an exception to this rule was added for the claims of spouses and dependents in domestic relations situations.

This exception permits an assignment of a qualified plan benefit under a *qualified domestic relations order* (QDRO), as defined in Code section 414(p). A QDRO is a decree, order, or property settlement under state law relating to child support, alimony, or marital property rights, which assigns part or all of a participant's plan benefits to a spouse, former spouse, child, or other dependent of the participant. Consequently, a participant's plan benefits are generally part of the negotiable assets in domestic disputes. The Internal Revenue Code does not indicate how such benefits are to be divided; this is a matter of state domestic relations law and the negotiation between the parties. The QDRO provisions of the Code simply provide a means by which state court domestic relations orders can be enforced against plan trustees.

To protect plan administrators and trustees from conflicting claims, a QDRO cannot assign a benefit that the plan does not provide. Also, a QDRO cannot assign a benefit that is already assigned under a previous order.[40]

If, under the plan, a participant has no right to an immediate cash payment from the plan, a QDRO cannot require the trustees to make a cash payment. If an immediate cash settlement is desired, the parties will generally agree to allow the participant to keep the entire plan benefit and pay compensating cash to the nonparticipant spouse. (Such compensating cash payments are not, however, treated as qualified plan distributions to the nonparticipant spouse.) If compensating cash payments are not possible, QDROs have been used to segregate plan assets into a subtrust for the benefit of the spouse making the claim, with cash distributions made at the earliest time that the plan provisions would permit distributions to the participant.

An alternate payee who is the spouse or former spouse of the participant and who receives a distribution by reason of a QDRO may roll over the distribution in the same manner as if he or she were the participant.

VII. PENALTY TAXES

In addition to the complicated regular tax rules, distributions must be planned so that recipients avoid—or at least are not surprised by—tax penalties for withdrawals made too early or too late. These are summarized as follows.

Early Distribution Penalty

This is, in effect, a penalty for making distributions "too soon." Early distributions from qualified plans, Section 403(b) tax deferred annuity plans, IRAs, and SEPs are subject to a penalty of 10 percent of the taxable portion of the distribution.[41] In the case of SIMPLE IRAs, the penalty is increased to 25 percent during the first two years of participation.

The penalty does *not* apply to distributions:

- made on or after attainment of age 59½.
- made to the plan participant's beneficiary or estate on or after the participant's death.
- attributable to the participant's disability.
- that are part of a series of substantially equal periodic payments made at least annually over the life or life expectancy of the participant, or the participant and a designated beneficiary (separation from the employer's service is required, except for IRAs).
- made upon separation from service after attainment of age fifty-five (not applicable to IRAs).
- made to a former spouse, child, or other dependent of the participant under a qualified domestic relations order (not applicable to IRAs).
- to the extent of medical expenses deductible for the year under Code section 213, whether or not actually deducted.
- to pay health insurance costs while unemployed (IRAs only).
- for higher education costs (tuition, fees, books, supplies, and equipment) for the taxpayer, spouse, child, or grandchild (IRAs only).
- to pay acquisition costs of a first home of the participant, spouse, child, grandchild, or ancestor of the participant or spouse, up to a $10,000 lifetime maximum (IRAs only).

"Qualified hurricane distributions" for Hurricanes Katrina, Rita, and Wilma are also exempt from the penalty. The aggregate amount that may be treated as qualified hurricane distributions of an individual (from all eligible retirement plans) is $100,000.[42]

In the case of the periodic payment exception, if the series of payments is changed before the participant reaches age 59½ or, if after age 59½, within five years of the date of the first payment, the tax is generally recaptured. In other words, the penalty that would have been imposed, but for the periodic exception, is imposed, with interest, in the year the change occurs.[43] Detailed guidance on the calculation of such payments and an exception for a "one time election" to lower the payments are set forth in IRS guidance.[44]

Minimum Distribution Requirements and Penalty

Minimum distributions from qualified plans, Section 403(b) tax deferred annuity plans, IRAs, SEPs, SIMPLE IRAs and Section 457 governmental deferred compensation plans must generally begin not later than April 1 of the calendar year following the later of: (1) the calendar year in which the employee attains age 70½; or (2) the year the employee retires.[45] The second (retirement year) alternative is not available for a more-than-5-percent owner of the business sponsoring the qualified plan,[46] or for an IRA owner.

If the annual distribution is less than the minimum amount required, there is a penalty of 50 percent of the amount not distributed that should have been.[47] But a participant can always take out more than the required minimum. The required minimum distribution rules are designed to determine the rate at which income taxes must be paid on the retirement accumulation; the minimum distribution amounts do not have to be spent by the participant, but can be reinvested in a nonqualified investment medium.

Under current regulations,[48] the required minimum distribution each year is generally determined by dividing the account balance (determined as of the last valuation date in the preceding year) by the appropriate number in the lifetime required minimum distribution table set forth in the final regulations (see Figure 14.1).[49]

Figure 14.1

UNIFORM LIFETIME TABLE

Age of Employee	Distribution Period	Age of Employee	Distribution Period	Age of Employee	Distribution Period
70	27.4	86	14.1	101	5.9
71	26.5	87	13.4	102	5.5
72	25.6	88	12.7	103	5.2
73	24.7	89	12.0	104	4.9
74	23.8	90	11.4	105	4.5
75	22.9	91	10.8	106	4.2
76	22.0	92	10.2	107	3.9
77	21.2	93	9.6	108	3.7
78	20.3	94	9.1	109	3.4
79	19.5	95	8.6	110	3.1
80	18.7	96	8.1	111	2.9
81	17.9	97	7.6	112	2.6
82	17.1	98	7.1	113	2.4
83	16.3	99	6.7	114	2.1
84	15.5	100	6.3	115	1.9
85	14.8				

Note that this rule creates a hardship if the value of the account balance declines significantly during the year, since the minimum distribution will be greater fraction of the total than was anticipated. The lifetime minimum distribution factors in Figure 14.1 are generally used regardless of who is named as beneficiary, but note the following:

- A more favorable minimum distribution (lower required annual amount) is available for a participant whose beneficiary is a spouse more than ten years younger than the participant. In this case, a minimum distribution can be determined using the actual joint life expectancy of the participant and the spouse.[50]

- At the participant's death, the minimum distribution to the participant's designated beneficiary is generally based on the beneficiary's remaining life expectancy. Under the current minimum distribution rules, there is likely to be amounts remaining at the owner's death, so the minimum distribution rules for survivors are significant in retirement and estate planning. This is discussed further in Chapter 18 of this book.

- The designated beneficiary for purposes of after-death distributions is determined as of September 30 of the year following the year of the participant's death.

VIII. RETIREMENT PLAN ROLLOVERS

Tax-free "rollovers" of distributions to and from qualified plans, Section 403(b) tax deferred annuity plans, traditional IRAs, SEPs, and eligible Section 457 governmental plans are specifically allowed by the Internal Revenue Code.[51] Thus, rollovers between different types of plans are permitted—for example, from a qualified plan to a Section 403(b) tax deferred annuity. A rollover of a distribution from a SIMPLE IRA during the first two years of participation may be made only to another SIMPLE IRA, except in the case of distributions to which the premature distribution penalty does not apply (see above).[52] The most commonly used form of rollover is a rollover to an IRA from an employer plan at the employee's termination of employment.

If a rollover is made within sixty days of receipt of the distribution and follows statutory rules, the tax on the distribution is deferred; in other words, the receipt is not a taxable event to the participant. However, "eligible rollover distributions" from qualified plans, Section 403(b) tax deferred annuity plans, and eligible Section 457 governmental plans are subject to mandatory withholding at 20 percent, unless the rollover is affected by means of a "direct rollover" (see "Tax Treatment of Rollovers," below.)

When Are Rollovers Used?

1. When a retirement plan participant receives a plan distribution and wants to defer taxes (and avoid any early distribution penalties) on part or all of the distribution.

2. When a qualified retirement plan, Section 403(b) tax deferred annuity plan or eligible Section 457 governmental plan is terminated by the employer, and an individual participant will receive a large termination distribution from the plan, has no current need for the income, and wishes to defer taxes on it.

3. When a participant in a qualified plan, Section 403(b) tax deferred annuity plan, eligible Section 457 governmental plan, or IRA would like to continue to defer taxes on the money in the plan, but wants to change the form of the investment or gain greater control over it.

4. When a spouse receives a death benefit from a plan.

Tax Treatment of Rollovers

1. Any distribution from an "eligible retirement plan"—that is, a qualified plan, Section 403(b) tax deferred annuity plan, eligible Section 457 governmental plan, SEP, or IRA is eligible for rollover, except the following:

    - a required minimum distribution (generally beginning at age 70½),

    - a distribution that is one of a series of substantially equal periodic payments payable (a) for a period of ten years or more, or (b) for the life or life expectancy of the employee or the employee and a designated beneficiary, or

    - a "hardship" distribution.[53]

2. Eligible rollover distributions received from an eligible retirement plan must be either transferred to another eligible retirement plan by means of a "direct rollover," pursuant to the employee's election, or transferred by the participant to the other plan not later than the sixtieth day after the distribution from the plan. A "direct rollover" is defined as an eligible rollover distribution that is paid directly to another eligible retirement plan for the benefit of the distributee. It can be accomplished by any reasonable means of direct payment, including the use of a wire transfer or a check that is negotiable only by the trustee of the new plan or rollover IRA.[54] If the "direct rollover" method is not chosen in the case of a distribution from a qualified plan, Section 403(b) plan, or eligible Section 457 governmental plan, the distribution is subject to mandatory withholding at 20 percent.[55]

   Failure to roll over the distribution within sixty days subjects it to income taxes (although certain employees may be eligible to elect ten-year averaging to cushion the blow, if the distribution qualifies for special averaging). The Secretary of the Treasury has the authority to waive the sixty-day rule where it would be against equity or good conscience to enforce it, including cases of disaster, casualty, or other events beyond the participant's control.[56]

3. Distributions from a rollover IRA are subject to the same rules and limitations as all traditional IRA distributions, discussed in Chapter 20. To summarize, distributions must: (a) begin no later than April 1 of the year after the participant attains age 70½, and (b) be made in minimum amounts, based on a life or joint life payout. Distributions are taxable as ordinary income, without ten-year averaging. Distributions prior to age 59½ are also subject to the 10 percent early withdrawal penalty, subject to the exceptions discussed earlier in this chapter.

4. Loans from a rollover IRA, like loans from any other IRA, are not permitted.

5. If a participant dies before withdrawing all of the rollover IRA account, the death benefit is includable in the deceased participant's estate for federal estate tax purposes. If payable to the participant's surviving spouse in a qualifying manner, the marital deduction will defer estate taxes.

6. If a surviving spouse is the beneficiary of a decedent's IRA or qualified plan, the spouse has unique opportunity to roll over the benefit to the spouse's IRA and, in effect start over as if the benefit were the surviving spouse's own IRA from its inception. Minimum distributions do not need to begin until the spouse's own age 70½, and the spouse can name a new beneficiary for the IRA. This greatly helps with minimum distribution planning because the plan benefit can, in effect be spread over three life expectancies; for example, husband, wife, and child.

7. A nonspouse beneficiary cannot roll a qualified plan benefit over to the nonspouse beneficiary's own IRA at the participant spouse's death. However, the nonspouse beneficiary can roll a qualified plan benefit to an IRA in the name of the decedent. This can help with financial planning, but it does not change the minimum distribution requirements for the decedent's plan benefit.

8. Direct rollovers (conversions) to Roth IRAs are permitted from qualified plans, Section 403(b) tax deferred annuity plans, and eligible Section 457 governmental plans. See Chapter 21 ("Roth IRAs") for more information.

Alternatives to Rollovers

In cases where a rollover IRA is an alternative to leaving the money in the existing qualified plan, it may be better—or no worse—to leave the money in the plan if the participant is satisfied with the qualified plan's investment performance and the payout options available under that plan meet the participant's needs.

Results similar to a rollover IRA can be achieved if the qualified plan distributes an annuity contract to a participant in lieu of a cash distribution. The annuity contract does not have to meet the requirements of an IRA, but the tax implications and distribution restrictions are generally similar.

WHERE CAN I FIND OUT MORE?

1. *Tax Facts on Insurance & Employee Benefits*, National Underwriter Co., Cincinnati, OH; revised annually.

2. IRS Publications 575, *Pension and Annuity Income*, and 590, *Individual Retirement Arrangements*, available from local IRS offices.

CHAPTER ENDNOTES

1. I.R.C. §401(a)(11).
2. I.R.C. §417(c)(1).
3. I.R.C. §417(c)(2).
4. I.R.C. §417(a).
5. I.R.C. §417(a)(3)(B).
6. I.R.C. §417(a)(6)(B).
7. I.R.C. §417(a)(2)(A).
8. I.R.C. §417(b).
9. Treas. Reg. §1.401(a)-11(b)(2). See also Treas. Reg. §1.401(a)-11(g).
10. I.R.C. §417(a)(2).
11. I.R.C. §417(a)(6)(A).
12. I.R.C. §417(a)(3)(A).
13. I.R.C. §417(a)(2)(A).
14. I.R.C. §411(d)(6)(B)(ii); Treas. Reg. §1.411(d)(4), Q&A 1, Q&A 2. This "anti-cutback" rule was eased somewhat for plan years beginning after 2001. I.R.C. §411(d)(6).
15. I.R.C. §401(a)(31).
16. I.R.C. §402(f). The notice must include an explanation of the tax consequences and any restrictions on distributions from the eligible plan receiving the distribution that are different from those applicable to the distributing plan. I.R.C. §402(f)(1)(E).
17. I.R.C. §401(a)(11)(B)(iii).
18. I.R.C. §72(f); Regs. §§1.72-8, 1.72-16(b)(4), 1.402(a)-1(a)(6), 1.403(a)-2; Rev. Rul. 72-149, 1972-1 CB 218.
19. The IRS has stated that it will accept "Table 2001" rates generally for determining the value of life insurance protection after 2001. See Notice 2002-8, 2002-4 IRB 398. For details, see Chapter 17. Table 2001 rates replaced P.S. 58 rates as the proper measure of life insurance protection.
20. I.R.C. §72(e)(8).
21. I.R.C. §72(e)(8)(D).
22. I.R.C. §3405(c)(1).
23. I.R.C. §72(d)(1). This provision is effective for annuity starting dates (i.e., the first date for which an amount is payable) after 1997.
24. I.R.C. §72(d)(1)(E). It would appear that for an annuitant who is 75 or older and whose contract provides for 5 or more years of guaranteed payments, the rules for annuities with a starting date after July 1, 1986 and before November 19, 1996 would be applied.
25. I.R.C. §72(d)(1)(D).
26. I.R.C. §72(b)(2).
27. I.R.C. §72(b)(3).
28. See I.R.C. §§402(a), 72, 403(a); Treas. Reg. §1.72-4(a).
29. Tax Reform Act of 1986, Section 1122(h).
30. Tax Reform Act of 1986, Section 1122(h)(5).
31. Treas. Reg. §1.72-16(c)(4).
32. Notice 2002-8, 2002-4 IRB 398.
33. Rev. Rul. 55-747, 1955-2 CB 228.
34. I.R.C. §§2001(c), 2010(a), 2505(a), 6018(a).
35. I.R.C. §4975(d)(1). Loans from Section 403(b) tax deferred annuity plans are subject to the prohibited transactions rules and penalties if the plan is subject to ERISA. ERISA Sections 408(b), 502(i); Labor Reg. §2550.408b-1.
36. I.R.C. §4975(f)(6)(iii). A similar provision was added to ERISA. For years prior to 2002, such loans were prohibited transactions, subject to penalties. I.R.C. §4975(f)(6), prior to amendment by EGTRRA 2001.
37. I.R.C. §72(p)(2). However, additional security may be required in order to insure that such a loan meets the "adequate security" requirement. See Labor Reg. §2550.408b-1(f)(2).
38. I.R.C. §72(p)(3).
39. I.R.C. §401(a)(13).
40. I.R.C. §414(p)(3).
41. I.R.C. §72(t).
42. I.R.C. §1400Q(a)(1); Notice 2005-92, 2005-51 IRB 1165.
43. I.R.C. §72(t)(4).
44. Rev. Rul. 2002-62, 2002-42 IRB 710, modifying Notice 89-25, 1989-1 CB 662, A-12.
45. A minimum distribution is required for the year in which the participant attains age 70½ or retires, even if the actual distribution is deferred until April 1 of the following year. However, all other minimum distributions must be made during the year to which they apply. So, for example, an individual who attains age 70½ in 2004 and defers the initial minimum distribution to April 1, 2005 must receive two minimum distributions during 2005: the deferred 2004 distribution, and the 2005 distribution.
46. As defined in the top-heavy rules; see I.R.C. §§401(a)(9), 403(b)(10), 408(a)(6), 408(b)(3), and 457(d)(2).
47. I.R.C. §4974.
48. See TD 8987, 67 Fed. Reg. 18988 (4-17-02).
49. See Treas. Reg. §1.401(a)(9)-9, A-2. The rules described here are effective for distributions for calendar years beginning after 2002. Treas. Reg. §1.401(a)(9)-1, A-2. Distributions for 2002 could be made under the 2001 proposed regulations, the 2002 final regulations or earlier 1987 proposed regulations. The 1987 proposed regulations, in effect for years before 2001, were considerably more complicated.
50. See Treas. Reg. §1.401(a)(9)-5, A-4. This joint life expectancy is determined from the Joint and Last Survivor Life Expectancy Table set forth in the final regulations at Treas. Reg. §1.401(a)(9)-9, A-3.
51. I.R.C. §402(c)(8)(B).
52. I.R.C. §408(d)(3)(G).
53. I.R.C. §402(c)(4)(C). Prior to 2002 only hardship distributions from Section 401(k) plans and Section 403(b) plans were prohibited from receiving rollover treatment. EGTRRA 2001 broadened this limitation to include hardship distributions from any eligible retirement plan.
54. Treas. Reg. §1.401(a)(31)-1, A-3.
55. I.R.C. §3405(c)(1).
56. I.R.C. §§402(c)(3), 408(d)(3)(I). Prior to amendments by EGTRRA 2001, there was no legislative basis for waiving the 60-day rule for pre-2002 distributions, even where the delays were the result of erroneous advice or the inaction of third parties.

QUALIFIED PLAN INVESTMENTS

CHAPTER 15

INTRODUCTION

Plan investments are important issues for both employers and employees. In a defined benefit plan, the investment performance significantly affects the amount of the employer's required contributions and therefore its financial results. Good investment performance is also important to plan participants, especially in defined-contribution plans, where plan account balances directly reflect investment results.

This chapter discusses the fiduciary and related rules of ERISA and the Internal Revenue Code, as well as investment strategies and some specific investment issues.

FIDUCIARY REQUIREMENTS OF ERISA AND THE INTERNAL REVENUE CODE

A relationship in which one person holds and administers assets belonging to another is legally described as a "fiduciary" relationship. A funded employee-benefit plan, therefore, involves fiduciary relationships—plan assets are held by a trustee or insurance company, under the direction of the employer, on behalf of plan participants and beneficiaries. The rules governing fiduciary relationships are generally a matter of state law; however, in the case of qualified plans and other employee-benefit plans, federal law (primarily ERISA) has superimposed federal fiduciary requirements that supersede state law, where applicable. While these rules are applicable to most types of employee-benefit plans, they have their greatest impact on qualified pension and profit-sharing plans because the other plans to which they technically apply—welfare-benefit plans—are often insured or unfunded.

The fiduciary rules were generally intended to provide broad protection to employees. Thus, they were not intended to spell out the specific responsibilities of each person involved in designing and maintaining the plan in order to help the employer and trustee. They must be aware of their fiduciary responsibilities to comply with them.

The fiduciary responsibility net is very broad. It includes any person who:

> Exercises any discretionary authority or discretionary control with respect to the management of the plan or exercises any authority or control with respect to the management or disposition of plan assets; renders investment advice for a fee or other compensation, direct or indirect, with respect to any plan asset, or has any authority or responsibility to do so; or has discretionary authority or discretionary responsibility in the administration of the plan.[1]

This definition of fiduciary generally includes the employer, the plan administrator, and the trustee. It also includes a wide variety of other possible targets. However, the government has stated that an attorney, accountant, actuary, or consultant who renders legal, accounting, actuarial, or consulting services to the plan will not be considered a fiduciary solely as a result of performing those services.[2] These rules exclude broker/dealers, banks, and reporting dealers from being treated as fiduciaries simply as a result of receiving and executing buy-sell instructions from the plan. However, if they (or others) make investment recommendations, they may be fiduciaries by virtue of that advice. Furthermore, a person giving investment advice will be considered a fiduciary only with respect to the assets covered by that investment advice.

Every plan must specify a "named fiduciary" in the plan document. The purpose of this requirement is not to limit fiduciary responsibility to named persons; rather it is to provide participants and the government with the ideality of the person(s) ultimately responsible for the plan. Other unnamed fiduciaries can also be included in the legal action, of course.

A fiduciary must:

- discharge its duties to a plan solely in the interest of the participants and beneficiaries;
- act for the exclusive purpose of providing benefits to participants and their beneficiaries and defraying the reasonable expenses of administering the plan;
- act with the care, skill, prudence, and diligence under the prevailing circumstances that a "prudent man" acting in a like capacity and familiar with such matters would use in the conduct of an enterprise of a like character and with like aims;
- diversify the investments of the plan to minimize the risk of large losses, unless under the circumstances it is clearly prudent not to do so; and
- follow the provisions of the documents and instruments governing the plan, unless those provisions are inconsistent with ERISA's provisions.[3]

In interpreting the "prudent man" requirement, labor regulations indicate that the fiduciary, in making an investment, must determine that the particular investment is reasonably designed as part of the plan's portfolio to further the purposes of the plan, and must consider: (1) the composition of the portfolio with regard to diversification; (2) the liquidity and current return of the portfolio relative to the anticipated cash flow requirements of the plan; and (3) the projected return of the portfolio relative to the funding objectives of the plan.[4]

A major exception to the diversification requirement applies to holdings of employer securities and employer real property. An eligible individual account plan (*i.e.*, a profit-sharing, stock-bonus, or employee stock-ownership plan that specifically permits the holding of "employer real property" or "qualifying employer securities") may hold such property in any amount—and may even hold such property as the exclusive assets of the plan.[5]

Fiduciaries can delegate fiduciary responsibilities and, therefore, avoid direct responsibility for performing the duty delegated. For example, the employer can delegate duties relating to the handling and investment of plan assets to a trustee, and the investment management duties can be delegated to an appointed investment manager. The plan must provide a procedure for delegating these duties. However, the delegation of a fiduciary duty does *not* remove all fiduciary responsibility: A fiduciary must prudently select and monitor the appointee (*i.e.*, the service provider) and a fiduciary will be liable (as a "co-fiduciary") for a breach of fiduciary responsibility of any other fiduciary under the following circumstances:

- if the fiduciary participates knowingly in, or knowingly undertakes to conceal, an act or omission of another fiduciary knowing such act or omission is a breach;
- if the fiduciary fails to comply with fiduciary duties in the administration of specific responsibilities that give rise to fiduciary status and, therefore, enables another fiduciary to commit a breach; or
- if the fiduciary has knowledge of a breach by another fiduciary, unless the fiduciary makes reasonable efforts under the circumstances to remedy the breach.[6]

The broad scope of the fiduciary liabilities indicates that, in addition to careful delegation of fiduciary duties to well-chosen trustees and advisors, the employer should consider whether its liability insurance covers any liabilities that might arise out of the fiduciary responsibilities. ERISA specifically prohibits a plan from excusing or exculpating any person from fiduciary liability, but individuals and employers are permitted to have appropriate insurance, and employers can indemnify (*i.e.*, agree to reimburse) plan fiduciaries for losses they might incur as a result of fiduciary duties.

PROHIBITED TRANSACTIONS

In addition to the general fiduciary requirements described above, both the Internal Revenue Code and ERISA include a specific list of "don'ts" for employee-benefit plans, including qualified plans.[7] Under these rules, a "party-in-interest" is forbidden from any of the following, with a number of exceptions described later:

- sale or exchange, or leasing, of any property between the plan and a party in-interest;
- lending of money or other extension of credit between the plan and a party-in-interest;
- furnishing of goods, services, or facilities between the plan and a party-in-interest;
- transfer to, or use by or for the benefit of, a party-in-interest, of any assets of the plan; or
- acquisition, on behalf of the plan, of any employer security or employer real property in excess of the limits described previously in this chapter.

A "party-in-interest" (the Internal Revenue Code uses the term "disqualified person") is defined very broadly, again to bring the largest possible number of persons into the net to provide the maximum protection for plan participants. A party-in-interest includes:

- Any fiduciary, counsel, or employee of the plan.
- A person providing services to the plan.
- An employer, if any of its employees are covered by the plan.
- An employee organization, any of whose members are covered by the plan.
- An owner, direct or indirect, of a 50 percent or more interest in an employer or employee organization described above.
- Various individuals and organizations related to those on the above list, under specific rules given in the Internal Revenue Code and ERISA.[8]

Because of the breadth of the prohibited transaction rules, certain specific exclusions are provided in the law, and the Labor Department is also given the authority to create exceptions to the prohibited transaction rules in certain circumstances.

First, there are the specific statutory exemptions. Loans to participants or beneficiaries are permitted under the rules discussed in Chapter 14. A loan to an ESOP by a party-in-interest is also permitted under certain circumstances to permit the ESOP to function, as described in Chapter 23. Similar provisions permit such a plan to acquire employer securities or real property without violating the prohibited transaction rules. Also, the plan is allowed to pay a reasonable fee for legal, accounting, or other services performed by a party-in-interest. There are provisions permitting various financial services to the plan by a bank or insurance company that is a party-in-interest. Other provisions exempt normal benefit distributions from any possible conflict with the prohibited transaction rules.

In addition to the specific statutory exemptions, the Department of Labor has broad authority to grant an exemption to the prohibited transaction rules for a transaction or a class of transactions after finding that the exemption is administratively feasible, in the interest of the plan and its participants and beneficiaries, and protective of their rights. There are specific administrative procedures for obtaining such exemptions. Pursuant to this authority, the Labor Department has granted, among others, a class exemption permitting the sale of life insurance policies by participants to the plan or by the plan to participants. (See Chapter 18.) Individual exemptions have been granted for a variety of transactions, usually involving a sale to the plan by a party-in-interest of property that represents a particularly favorable investment opportunity for the plan.

Directed Investments. A "defined contribution" (i.e., individual account) plan can have a provision under which a participant can direct that part or all of his account be invested in investment vehicles specified by the participant. If the directed-investment provision of the plan meets requirements in an ERISA regulation, the plan trustees are relieved of fiduciary responsibility for the participant's choice of investments. For administrative convenience, participant investment choices are often limited under the plan to a list of potential investments, usually mutual funds. Under the regulation giving relief to the plan trustees, there must be at least three choices of fund, each of which is diversified.[9]

Penalties. A violation of the prohibited transaction rules can result in a two-step penalty under the Internal Revenue Code, with the initial penalty equal to 15 percent of the amount involved and an additional 100 percent penalty if the transaction is not corrected within a certain time. A violation of the prohibited transaction rules also can result in ERISA penalties equal to 5 percent and can be a breach of fiduciary duty.

Prohibited Transaction Exemption for Investment Advice to Employees. As directed-investment 401(k)-type plans are assuming the major role in employment-based retirement savings it has become increasingly important to provide good investment advice to participants.

The Pension Protection Act of 2006 added an exemption from the prohibited transaction rules for an "eligible investment advice arrangement."[10] The arrangement must be one which either provides for fees that do not vary with the type of investment selected, or which uses a computer model. Additional safeguards also apply.

The new provision should be helpful in providing retirement security for employees. Some commentators, however, have warned of potential abuses that could occur under these arrangements.

UNRELATED BUSINESS INCOME

The trust fund under a qualified plan has a broad exemption from federal income tax similar to that granted to a variety of other institutions and organizations, such as churches, schools, charities, and the like. However, all these tax-exempt organizations are subject to federal income tax on "unrelated business taxable income" (UBTI).[11] Unrelated business taxable income is income of a tax-exempt organization from a trade or business that is not related to the function that is the basis for the tax exemption. For example, if a charitable organization operates a full-time retail store in a shopping center, the store income would be taxable to the charity. However, the charity's tax exemption for its other income probably would not be jeopardized unless the effect of operating the retail store was to shift the focus of the organization totally away from its exempt function.

The basic function of an employee-benefit plan trust is to receive, invest, and distribute plan funds to participants and beneficiaries. Thus, passive investment income of the plan trust is usually not unrelated business income unless the investment is debt-financed, as described in the next paragraph. Problems sometimes arise in distinguishing passive investments from activities that might be considered a trade or business. The law specifically exempts dividends, interest, annuities, and royalties, as well as rents from real property and from personal property leased with real property. However, the wide variety of possible leasing arrangements indicates that each rental arrangement must be looked at on the basis of its own facts and circumstances.

The Internal Revenue Code specifies that income from "debt-financed property" is to be treated by a tax-exempt organization as unrelated business-taxable income.[12] There is, however, an exception for qualified plans holding certain real estate investments that typically are highly leveraged or debt-financed.[13]

INVESTMENT POLICY

Like all investors, a qualified plan investment adviser or asset manager seeks certain objectives, which depend on the interests of plan participants and beneficiaries as well as those of the sponsoring organization. Some specific investment objectives that make up the parts of an overall investment strategy are: appropriate rate of return, safety of principal and adequate liquidity. The pursuit of one of these objectives often will be inconsistent with another; therefore, an overall investment strategy has to strike a balance among them.

Investment Vehicles

The limits set by ERISA allow a qualified plan trustee to invest in a wide range of investment vehicles. Most state laws governing trusts set limits on the types of investments fiduciaries may use in the absence of a specific trust agreement, but allow a trust agreement to expand the permitted category. Qualified plan trust agreements generally are drafted to permit considerable investment flexibility.

The most important investment vehicles, and their relation to the objectives listed above, will be briefly discussed here:

Common Stocks. Historically, common stocks have offered a higher rate of return, with a relatively larger risk (that is, volatility) than other investments, although obviously some stocks are less risky than others. Common stocks can help preserve principal, in that over the long run their value tends to grow at least as fast as inflation. However, this growth is not always experienced in the short term—for example, throughout most of the 1970s, stock values declined in real terms. Common stocks traded on a stock market provide considerable liquidity and a readily determined market value.

Short-Term Debt. Short-term debt instruments are generally considered to be those maturing in less than a year. Some common short-term instruments include certificates of deposit issued by United States or foreign banks, short-term obligations of corporations (e.g., commercial paper), and United States Treasury bills with ninety-day or six-month terms. Such instruments offer significant liquidity, together with a rate of return that is very high, corresponding to current interest rates in periods when these rates are high—but with correspondingly low rates of return when interest rates are low. The risk involved in such instruments depends on the debtor, but can often be low, particularly for government securities.

Long-Term Debt. Intermediate and long-term bonds and other debt instruments have maturity dates extending from several years to as much as fifteen or more years. Corporate bonds are traded on securities exchanges in the same manner as common stocks. The federal government also issues long-term securities. In the long run, long-term securities generally offer higher rates of return than short-term securities, in return for somewhat greater risk. However, United States Treasury securities can provide significant returns with relatively little risk. Long-term instruments are not necessarily illiquid, if they can be sold easily on an exchange.

Real Estate. Real estate investments potentially offer a high rate of return, but as the recent financial debacle made clear, real estate values are volatile, with frequent boom and bust cycles. Qualified plans often invest not only in real estate, but also in mortgages secured by real estate. Even leveraged real estate investments are possible, because of exemptions from the unrelated business income tax (discussed above). However, because the qualified plan is tax exempt, it gets no benefit from the deduction of interest payments, so leveraged investments must be analyzed somewhat differently than for a taxable investor.

Much of the risk typically associated with real estate investments can be reduced by participating in real estate syndications, where the investor owns only a portion of each individual property. Knowledge of the market is essential in real estate investments.

Equipment Leasing. Equipment leasing has been an attractive investment to private investors because of the available tax benefits; these are less important to a tax-exempt organization. However, the rate of return on equipment leasing can be very high and, therefore, such investments may be attractive even without tax benefits. As discussed earlier, it may be necessary to obtain a ruling from the IRS to avoid unrelated business income tax in these situations.

Other Investments. Depending on the economic climate, many types of investments are temporarily attractive—for example, gold, antiques, and other collectibles. Such investments are permitted for certain qualified plans, but not for IRAs or IRA-based plans (see Chapters 20, 21, 30, and 31). Qualified plans can also make use of investment vehicles such as options, commodity futures, puts and calls, and other vehicles typically associated with stock market players. These instruments generally do not play a large part in qualified plan investment strategy, but they may be useful for specific needs.

INVESTMENT STRATEGY

The policy baseline for the investment of qualified plan funds is set by the ERISA rules discussed above—the exclusive-benefit rule, the prudent expert rule, the diversification requirement, liquidity requirements, the plan document itself, and the additional limitations imposed by the prohibited transaction and unrelated business income provisions. Within these constraints, however, a broad range of investment strategies is possible.

ERISA Section 402 requires every qualified plan to adopt a "funding policy and method consistent with the objectives of the plan." In practice, plan administrators usually adopt a very general written statement to meet this statutory requirement, leaving specific investment strategies to the discretion of the employer or the fund manager.

Growth-Oriented Strategies. Trustees governed by fiduciary rules aimed primarily at the preservation of principal generally do not follow aggressive, growth-oriented investment strategies—and pension trustees are no exception. However, qualified plan design offers a number of opportunities for incorporating growth-oriented investment strategies without running into fiduciary problems. Investment in common stocks, for example, is permissible and widespread, as well as investment in various types of pooled equity funds maintained by insurance or investment companies. Defined-contribution plans can use directed investments as discussed above. In directed-investment arrangements plan funds are typically invested in mutual funds or other pooled accounts that offer participants choices of investment strategies—an equity fund, a fixed-income fund, and so on. A defined contribution plan can also be designed to invest primarily in employer securities, which can be viewed as a type of growth-oriented investment strategy.

For defined-benefit plans, there is no provision for participant direction of investments. As a result, the employees, the trustee or an appointed investment manager will need to serve as the fiduciary responsible (and potentially liable) for the investments.

Risk. Most of the ERISA investment rules can be seen as prescriptions for avoiding risk, particularly the risk of large losses (*e.g.*, the requirement for diversification of investments). Within the ERISA limits, however, like any investor, the qualified plan investment manager must balance risk and return.

SOCIAL EFFECTS

Many pension funds are large—not only those funds of large employers but also those held by banks, insurance companies, labor union trustees, and government-employee funds. The issue is sometimes raised whether these organizations should use their clout and target investments, or vote their shares in the companies they hold, in such a way as to serve interests of plan participants and beneficiaries—measures that are above and beyond their narrowly defined interest in achieving maximum investment returns. For example, the issue of excessive compensation for company CEOs (chief executive officers) and top executives is often raised. An example of a more specific set of interests would be the interest of union pension funds in keeping jobs from migrating out of the United States, encouraging union organizing, or requiring companies to provide a safe workplace.

Existing legislation and other law relating to qualified plan investments focuses primarily on fiduciary aspects of the relationship between plan managers and participants; it does not address issues of social policy. That is, it encourages investment managers to invest properly to prevent direct financial losses to participants and beneficiaries, but it does not appear to require them to avoid possible indirect losses resulting from investments that are contrary to participants' and beneficiaries' social and economic interests. The impact of the ERISA fiduciary requirements on this issue is not clear. However, many advisers doubt that a pro-labor or other social-responsibility criterion for investments would be an effective defense for the trustees in the event of consistently low investment returns.

The Department of Labor takes the position that investments must be screened by traditional metrics (for example, potential return and risk), but if that is done and the social aspects do not limit the opportunities then they may be considered.

CHAPTER ENDNOTES

1. ERISA §3(21).
2. DOL Reg. § 2550.408b-2.
3. ERISA §404.
4. DOL Reg. § 2550.404a-1.
5. ERISA §407.
6. ERISA §405.
7. I.R.C. §4975; ERISA §406.
8. I.R.C. §4975; ERISA §406.
9. DOL Reg. § 2550.404c-1.
10. ERISA §408; I.R.C. §4975.
11. I.R.C. §§511, 512, 513, 514.
12. I.R.C. §514.
13. I.R.C. §514(c)(9).

ERISA REPORTING AND DISCLOSURE

CHAPTER 16

INTRODUCTION

The Employee Retirement Income Security Act of 1974—ERISA—is broad legislation that imposes extensive reporting and disclosure requirements on a broad range of employee benefit plans. These provisions require various forms and information to be disclosed to plan participants or filed with the IRS or the Department of Labor.

Under ERISA, employee benefit plans are divided into two types—pension plans and welfare plans. These terms are defined broadly enough that it often makes sense to think of them in terms of their exceptions rather than their definitions. That is, an employee benefit plan should be considered covered by the provisions of ERISA unless there is a specific exemption in ERISA or the regulations interpreting ERISA.

WHICH PLANS ARE EXEMPT FROM ERISA?

The following types of employer plans (both pension and welfare plans) are exempt from most or all ERISA provisions, including the reporting and disclosure requirements:

- plans of state, federal, or local governments or governmental organizations.
- plans of churches, synagogues, or related organizations. (These plans, however, can elect to be covered under ERISA.)
- plans maintained outside the United States for nonresident aliens.
- unfunded excess benefit plans. (These are one type of nonqualified deferred compensation plan, as described in Chapter 33.)
- plans maintained solely to comply with workers' compensation, unemployment compensation, or disability insurance laws.[1]

WHAT IS A "PENSION PLAN" UNDER ERISA?

The term "pension plan" has a much broader meaning under ERISA than under the Internal Revenue Code. ERISA defines an "employee pension benefit plan" and "pension plan" as *any* plan, fund, or program which is established or maintained by an employer or by an employee organization (such as a labor union), or by both, to the extent that by its express terms or as a result of surrounding circumstances the plan, fund, or program (1) provides retirement income to employees, or (2) results in a deferral of income by employees for periods extending to the termination of covered employment or beyond, regardless of the method of calculating the contributions made to the plan, the method of calculating the benefits under the plan, or the method of distributing benefits from the plan.[2]

This definition includes all qualified pension, profit sharing, stock bonus, and similar qualified plans. It also includes some nonqualified deferred compensation plans. (These may, however, be eligible for exemption from ERISA's strict reporting and disclosure requirements—see Chapter 33, at "ERISA Requirements) In general, an ERISA pension plan is any employee benefit plan that involves deferral of an employee's compensation to his or her retirement date or later.

Regulatory Exemptions—Pension Plans

In addition to these exemptions in ERISA itself, Labor Regulations give partial exemption or special treatment for certain pension-like plans.[3] These special regulatory exemptions include the following:

- A *severance pay plan* is not treated as a pension plan if:

  (1) payments do not depend directly or indirectly on the employee's retiring;

  (2) total payments under the plan do not exceed twice the employee's annual compensation during the year immediately preceding the separation from service; and

  (3) all payments to any employee are generally completed within 24 months of separation from service.

  A severance pay plan meeting these criteria need not comply with the reporting and disclosure requirements for pension plans, but must meet the more limited reporting and disclosure requirements for welfare plans discussed below. For example, welfare plans with fewer than 100 participants need not file an annual report (Form 5500 series) if benefits are fully insured or are paid by the employer out of its general assets.

- *Supplemental payment plans* that provide extra benefits to retirees to counteract inflation are exempt from numerous ERISA requirements under Department of Labor regulations.

- *Employer-facilitated IRAs (such as simplified employee pensions (SEPs) and SIMPLE IRAs) and Section 403(b) TDA plans* are, in some cases, either exempt from ERISA's reporting and disclosure requirements or subject to reduced ERISA reporting and disclosure requirements.[4] For details, see the chapters relating to these plans.

Pension Plan Reporting and Disclosure

Pension plans must meet the reporting and disclosure requirements described in the chart at the end of this chapter, with certain exceptions.

Figure 16.1 contains a compliance chart indicating the major reporting and disclosure requirements of ERISA and the timetables for filing or reporting. The latest versions of Forms 5500 and 5500EZ, as well as the related schedules, may be obtained from local IRS offices, or online from the IRS website. Downloaded forms may not be used for filing in some cases.

The following brief explanation of the most important of these reporting and disclosure requirements for pension plans should be helpful in interpreting the significance of these requirements. The major elements of reporting and disclosure are as follows:

1. *The Summary Plan Description (SPD).* The SPD is intended to describe the major provisions of the plan to participants in plain language. An SPD must be furnished automatically to participants within 120 days after the plan is established or 90 days after a new participant enters an existing plan.[5] If plan provisions change, supplements to the SPD must be provided to participants. The contents of the SPD are prescribed by Labor Department regulations, but there is no government form for SPDs. Plans are required to file a copy of their SPD with the Department of Labor (DOL) only if requested to by the DOL.

2. *The Annual Report (Form 5500 series).* This annual financial reporting form must be filed with the IRS each year by the end of the seventh month after the plan year ends.[6] In addition to balance sheets and income statements, an actuary's report (Schedule B, Form 5500) must be included if the plan is a defined benefit plan, and information about any insurance contracts held by the plan must be included on Schedule A, Form 5500.

   The Form 5500 is required to be filed with the Department of Labor. There are many schedules that accompany the Form 5500; however, a plan is required to file only those schedules that apply to its circumstances.

3. *Summary Annual Report.* The summary annual report is a brief summary of financial information from the Annual Report (Form 5500 series) that must be provided to plan participants each year within nine months of the end of the plan year.[7] Labor regulations have essentially reduced this report to a formality. Participants

have a right to see the full Annual Report if they need information about the plan's financial status.

4. *Individual Benefit Statement.*[8] If a participant in a defined benefit plan requests a statement of individual benefits under the plan, the plan administrator must provide it within thirty days. Only one such statement each year needs to be provided.

For defined contribution a plan which allows participants to direct the investments or their account, the plan must provide a benefit statement at least once each calendar quarter. Other defined contribution plans must provide a statement at least once each calendar year, and upon written request by the participant.

Title IV Reporting and Disclosure Requirements

Title IV of ERISA, the plan termination insurance provisions, imposes various reporting and disclosure obligations on certain defined benefit pension plans in an effort to help the Pension Benefit Guaranty Corporation insure and protect pension benefits.

"WELFARE PLANS" UNDER ERISA

A welfare plan (also called a "welfare benefit plan") is defined in Section 3(1) of ERISA as any plan, fund, or program established or maintained by an employer or by an employee organization, or by both, for the purpose of providing for its participants or their beneficiaries, through the purchase of insurance or otherwise, medical, surgical, or hospital care or benefits, or benefits in the event of sickness, accident, disability, death or unemployment, or vacation benefits, apprenticeship or other training programs, or day care centers, scholarship funds, or prepaid legal services. Certain other plans described in federal labor law are also included.

Regulatory Exemptions—Welfare Plans

For welfare plans, Section 2510.3-1 of the Labor regulations provides exemptions and limitations from the applicability of ERISA. The following employment practices and benefits are among those that have been declared by regulation to be exempt from the ERISA reporting and disclosure requirements:

- overtime pay, shift pay, holiday premiums, and similar compensation paid for work done other than under normal circumstances.
- compensation for absence from work due to sickness, vacation, holidays, military duty, jury duty, or sabbatical leave or training programs, if paid out of the general assets of the employer (i.e., not funded in advance).
- recreational or dining facilities or first aid centers on the employer's premises.
- holiday gifts.
- group insurance programs offered to employees by an insurer under which no contribution is made by the employer, participation is voluntary, and the program is not actively sponsored by the employer.
- unfunded tuition reimbursement or scholarship programs (other than Section 127 educational assistance plans—see Chapter 51) that are paid out of the employer's general assets.

Welfare Plan Reporting and Disclosure

All other welfare plans are subject to ERISA reporting and disclosure requirements. However, in general, these are less onerous than those applicable to pension plans.

Small welfare plan exemption. One special rule provides that welfare plans with fewer than one hundred participants need not file an annual report (Form 5500 series) if they are fully insured or are paid out of the general assets of the employer on a pay-as-you-go basis. These plans also do not need to file a Summary Plan Description.[9]

Figure 16.2 sets forth a compliance chart indicating major forms that must be filed with the IRS or Department of Labor or disclosed to participants. Current versions of these forms, as well as the schedules, may be obtained from the local IRS office or online from the IRS website. Downloaded forms may not be used for filing in some cases.

Figure 16.1

MAJOR REPORTING AND DISCLOSURE REQUIREMENTS FOR PENSION PLANS

I. Government Filings

Form	Description	Who Must File	When to File	Where to File
5500	Annual Return/Report of Employee Benefit Plan.	Plan administrator.	On or before last day of seventh month after available — file Form 5558.)	Address indicated in instructions to Form 5500.
5500EZ	Annual Return of One-Participant (Owners and Their Spouses) Plans.	Plan administrator. May be filed for plans that cover only an individual or an individual and spouse who are the owners of a business. May also be filed for partnership plans that cover only partners or partners and their spouses.	Same as Form 5500.	Address indicated in instructions to Form 5500EZ.
Schedule A (Form 5500)	Insurance Information.	Plan administrator, where any plan benefits are provided by an insurance company or similar organization.	Attachment to Form 5500.	Same as Form 5500.
Schedule C (Form 5500)	Service Provider and Trustee Information.	Plan administrator.	Attachment to Form 5500.	Same as Form 5500.
Schedule E (Form 5500)	ESOP Annual Information.	Plan administrator.	Attachment to Form 5500.	Same as Form 5500.
Schedule G (Form 5500)	Financial Schedules.	Plan administrator.	Attachment to Form 5500.	Same as Form 5500.
Schedule MB (Form 5500)	Multi-employer DB Plan and Certain Money Purchase Plan Actuarial Information.	Plan administrator.	Attachment to Form 5500.	Same as Form 5500.
Schedule SB (Form 5500)	Single Employer DB Plan Actuarial Information.	Plan administrator.	Attachment to Form 5500.	Same as Form 5500.
Schedule SSA (Form 5500)	Annual Registration Statement Identifying Separated Participants with Deferred Vested Benefits.	Plan administrator, if plan had participants who separated with deferred vested benefits during the plan year.	Attachment to Form 5500.	Same as Form 5500.

Figure 16.1 (cont'd)

MAJOR REPORTING AND DISCLOSURE REQUIREMENTS FOR PENSION PLANS

I. Government Filings (cont'd)

Form	Description	Who Must File	When to File	Where to File
PBGC Form 1-ES	Estimated Premium Payment (Base premiums for plans with 500 or more participants).	Plan administrator or sponsor of defined benefit plan (with 500 or more participants) subject to PBGC provisions.	Within two months after the end of the prior plan year.	Electronically through www.pbgc.gov.
PBGC Form 1	Annual Premium Payment.	Plan administrator or sponsor of defined benefit plan subject to PBGC provisions.	Varies depending on size of plan.	Electronically through www.pbgc.gov.

II. Disclosure to Pension Plan Participants

Item	Description	Who Must Provide	When Provided
Summary Plan Description	Summary of the provisions of the plan in plain language; includes statement of ERISA rights.	Plan administrator.	New plans: within 120 days after effective date. Updated SPD must be furnished within 210 days of every fifth plan year for plans that have been amended; otherwise SPD must be redistributed every 10 years. New participants: within 90 days after becoming a participant or benefits commence (in the case of beneficiaries).
Summary of Material Modification	Summary of any material modification to the plan and any change in information required to be in summary plan description.	Plan administrator.	Within 210 days after the close of the plan year in which the modification was adopted unless changes or modifications are described in a timely distributed summary plan description.
Summary Annual Report	Summary of annual report Form 5500.	Plan administrator.	Nine months after end of plan year, or within two months after close of extension period for filing plans filing that form.)
Notice of Preretirement Survivor Benefit	Written explanation of preretirement survivor annuity, participant's right to make an election (or revoke election) to waive the annuity, spouse's rights, and effect of election or revocation.	Plan administrator of plan required to provide (see Chapter 6).	Within period beginning on first day of plan year in which participant attains age 32 and ending with close of plan year in which participant attains age 34. Election must be made within the period beginning on the first day of the plan year in which the participant attains age 35 and ending with the participant's death. For individuals who become participants after age 32, plan must provide explanation within three years of first day of plan year they become participants.

Figure 16.1 (cont'd)

MAJOR REPORTING AND DISCLOSURE REQUIREMENTS FOR PENSION PLANS

II. Disclosure to Pension Plan Participants (continued)

Item	Description	Who Must Provide	When Provided
Notice of Joint and Survivor Benefit	Written explanation of joint and survivor annuity, right to make election to waive the annuity, right to revoke waiver, effect of election or revocation, and rights of the spouse.	Plan administrator of plan required to provide (see Chapter 6).	Within reasonable period before annuity starting date. Election must be made no sooner than 90 days before the annuity starting date.
Notice to Terminated Vested Participants	Same information as provided to IRS on Schedule SSA (Form 5500) concerning participant's accrued benefit. Statement must include notice if certain benefits may be forfeited if the participant dies before a particular date.	Plan administrator.	No later than due date for filing Schedule SSA (Form 5500).
Individual Accrued Benefit Statement	Statement of participant's benefit accrued to date based on the latest available data. Statement must include notice of certain benefits may be forfeited if the participant dies before a particular date.	Plan administrator.	Within 30 days of participant's request. Need not be provided more than once in a 12-month period.

Figure 16.2

MAJOR REPORTING AND DISCLOSURE REQUIREMENTS FOR WELFARE PLANS

I. Government Filings

Form	Description	Who Must File	When to File	Where to File
5500	Annual Return/Report of Employee Benefit plan.	Plan administrator.	On or before the last day of the seventh month extension available — file Form 5558.)	Address indicated in instructions to Form 5500.
Schedule A (Form 5500)	Insurance information.	Plan administrator, where any benefits under the plan are provided by insurance company or similar organization.	Attachment to Form 5000.	Same as Form 5500.

II. Disclosure to Welfare Plan Participants and Beneficiaries

Item	Description	Who Must Provide	When Provided
Summary Plan Description	Summary of the provisions of the plan in plain language; includes statement of ERISA rights.	Plan administrator.	New plans: within 120 days after effective date. Updated SPD must be furnished within 210 days of every fifth plan year for plans that have been amended. Otherwise, SPDs must be redistributed every 10 years. New participants: within 90 days after becoming a participant or benefits commence (in the case of beneficiaries).
Summary of Material Modification	Summary of any material modification to the plan and any distributions required to be in summary plan description.	Plan administrator.	Within 210 days after the close of the plan year in which the modification was adopted unless changes or modifications are described in a timely change in information summary plan description.
Summary Annual Report	Summary of annual report Form 5500.	Plan administrator.	Nine months after end of plan year or within two months after close of extension period for filing annual report, if applicable.

CHAPTER ENDNOTES

1. See ERISA §4(b).
2. See ERISA §3(2).
3. Labor Reg. §2510.3-2.
4. See also Labor Regs. §§2520.104-48, 2520.104-49 (SEPs); see also IB 99-1, 64 Fed. Reg. 32999 (6-18-99).
5. ERISA §104(b)(1).
6. ERISA §§103(a)(1)(A) and 104(a)(1); I.R.C. §6058(a).
7. Labor Reg. §2520.104b-10(c).
8. ERISA §105.
9. Labor Reg. §2520.104-20. These plans are relieved of a variety of other reporting and disclosure requirements.
10. This list does not include those notices required as a result of plan design for certain defined contribution plans. (e.g., Qualified Default Investment Alternative Notice, Safe Harbor Notice, Qualified Automatic Contribution Notice, Eligible Automatic Contribution Arrangement).
11. See, Field Assistance Bulletins 2012-02 and 2012-02R for additional information.

ESTATE AND RETIREMENT PLANNING WITH QUALIFIED PLANS AND IRAs

CHAPTER 17

INTRODUCTION

Tax and retirement planners are seeing increasing numbers of a certain type of client who is facing a potential retirement tax disaster. The typical client profile is of an older business owner or executive with a large qualified plan balance (or rollover IRA balance), as well as substantial other assets that will be includable in his or her estate for federal estate tax purposes.

The reason for the potential disaster is the heavy potential tax impact on retirement plan assets. The combination of regular federal (39.6 percent top rate for 2015), state and local (another 10 percent or more in some areas) income taxes; and federal estate taxes (40 percent for 2015) can practically confiscate a qualified plan distribution unless something is done to avoid this result. In a worst-case scenario, the tax rate on $1,000,000 of qualified plan assets included in a decedent's estate could reach a rate of 80 percent.

In addition, planners must make sure that complex technical rules are complied with so that a client's qualified plan assets will actually go where they were intended to go, with the intended tax results. For example, in one private letter ruling, the IRS determined that the marital deduction was not available where a decedent designated a marital trust as an IRA beneficiary, using standard bank forms. The IRS stated that the bank standard forms did not comply with the technical requirements for a marital deduction, and the situation could not be cured by a postmortem amendment of the beneficiary designation.[1]

The courts have generally indicated no inclination to give planners the benefit of the doubt in this complex area. For example, in *Oddi v. Ayco Corp*,[2] a planner erroneously advised taking an immediate taxable distribution from a qualified plan instead of leaving money in and withdrawing (and deferring taxes) over a period of years, and the client was awarded over $400,000 from the planner.

WHEN IS USE OF SUCH A DEVICE INDICATED?

1. When a retiree will have substantial retirement assets at retirement or death.

2. When it is desired to stretch out distributions, so as to defer income taxation.

3. Certain techniques may be useful when there will be a surviving spouse.

Advantages

1. There are various advantages to either a rollover or keeping plan assets where they are (see below).

2. Planning can reduce estate taxes at death.

3. Planning can stretch out distributions, and thus defer income taxation.

Disadvantages

1. There may be various disadvantages to either a rollover or keeping plan assets where they are (see below).

2. Failure to name a beneficiary or to plan can lead to increased taxation.

TAX IMPLICATIONS

1. IRA and qualified plan assets are generally includable in the IRA owner's or plan participant's gross estate for estate tax purposes. A grandfathered exclusion may still be available.

2. A marital deduction is generally available for assets passing to a surviving spouse.

3. Distributions are generally required from IRAs and qualified plans after age 70½ (or retirement, in the case of qualified plans) or death. Distributions are not required from Roth IRAs until after the death of the IRA owner.

4. Distributions are generally fully subject to income tax, except to the extent nondeductible contributions have been made to an IRA or a qualified plan. Qualified distributions from Roth IRAs, including distributions after the death of the IRA owner, are not subject to income tax.

5. When a distribution is included in income, a deduction is available for income tax purposes for estate tax attributable to the IRA or qualified plan being included in the gross estate.

AN ISSUE AT RETIREMENT: ROLLOVER VS. KEEPING IT IN PLAN

For some clients nearing retirement who have large profit sharing accumulations, or otherwise have the option of receiving a lump sum distribution, a preliminary consideration is whether the plan accumulation should be kept in a qualified plan or rolled over to an IRA. There are advantages in each approach. Often a rollover is the appropriate thing to do, but it should not be chosen without considering the options.

Advantages of a Rollover

- If the plan participant is a controlling owner, a rollover may allow him or her to simply terminate the qualified plan, which would then require no further contributions. There is also no further plan administration (filing Form 5500s, etc.) if the plan terminates and all of the assets in the plan have been distributed.

- In an IRA, there may be more investment flexibility in practice since the IRA owner is not dependent on plan trustees and can shop for the best and most flexible IRA arrangement.

- If the plan is subject to the qualified joint and survivor annuity requirement (see below), consent of the participant's spouse is required for the initial rollover, but is not required for subsequent changes in IRA beneficiary designations.

Advantages of Keeping It in a Qualified Plan

- Plan loans may be available, up to the $50,000 maximum limit.

- The plan can invest in life insurance.

- The participant may be able to use ten-year averaging (available only to certain plan participants born before 1936); on a lump sum distribution.

- Qualified plans still have better protection against creditors because of ERISA's anti-alienation rule. The U.S. Supreme Court has clarified the issue of IRA protection in bankruptcy[3] and the application of ERISA protection to qualified plan assets;[4] however, this subject remains complex. Bankruptcy protection remains stronger for qualified plans than for IRAs. The extent to which the ERISA protection applies to business owners is unclear, and is least secure in plans like Keogh plans where the owner is the only plan participant.[5] Note, however, that whatever the status of federal protections, state laws protecting pensions, annuities, insurance, etc., may be available in many states.[6]

- If the plan is a defined benefit plan, PBGC insurance may be applicable within its dollar limits ($60,136 for a sixty-five-year old retiree for plans terminating in 2015). PBGC insurance is not available to a plan "exclusively for substantial owners" or to a plan of a professional service employer that does not at any time have more than twenty-five active participants.[7]

- From the standpoint of the nonparticipant spouse, a qualified plan provides better protection.

Converting to a Roth IRA

A Roth IRA presents unique opportunities for retirement, tax, and estate planning. In many situations, an existing IRA can be rolled over to a Roth IRA. The planner must consider whether this rollover is available to the client and whether it is a good idea.

Some basic aspects of Roth IRAs (see Chapter 21) must be considered:

- There is no limit on the rollover, and it can be a total or partial rollover of an existing IRA.
- The amount rolled over is included in the gross income of the IRA account holder for federal income tax purposes.
- Distributions (principal and interest) from the Roth IRA are received tax free if (1) they are made after a five-year holding period, and (2) they are made after age 59½, death, disability, or for a first-time home purchase.
- No minimum distribution rules apply to the Roth IRA except at death (i.e., at death the beneficiary must take minimum distributions, which are still income tax free, but which lose their Roth IRA character when distributed).

The Economics of the Conversion

A Roth IRA conversion would be a *wash* if (a) taxes had to be paid out of the IRA, (b) only the net amount were going to actually end up in the Roth IRA, and (c) income tax rates were not expected to change, because all factors act equally on the gross IRA amount or the net Roth IRA amount when looking at the net effect of the transaction at any point in the future.

For older clients who will have to start minimum distributions soon, the fact that taxes will have to be paid soon on the traditional IRA minimum distributions makes traditional IRAs less attractive. Since no lifetime minimum distribution requirements apply to Roth IRAs, the distributions and tax on them may be deferred until after death.

If tax dollars can be found from non-IRA sources (without incurring further income taxes) and the full IRA amount can be rolled over to the Roth IRA without pushing up the owner's tax bracket, the Roth conversion is beneficial because the earnings of the Roth IRA are not subject to income tax.

Why Should a Roth IRA Conversion Be Considered (If the Client Is Eligible)?

- The basic economics of the conversion (see above) can be attractive.
- Conversion reduces taxes at death (since income taxes are already paid).
- Conversion provides a source for the unified credit applicable exclusion amount at death. A Roth IRA is better for this purpose than a traditional IRA or qualified plan interest, since a Roth IRA is not an IRD asset (see below).

Negatives of a Roth IRA Conversion

- To get the full benefit from a conversion, the client must come up with non-IRA funds to pay the taxes in the year of conversion.
- The recent increase in the top marginal federal income tax rate makes conversions less advantageous, and the possible effect of more dramatic future tax reform could be adverse. For example, suppose the so-called "flat tax" is enacted, with no taxes on investment earnings? Or income tax is replaced with a consumption tax? Either of these would negate the benefit of conversions to a Roth IRA. Nobody can predict these contingencies.

Nonparticipant Spouse's Rights

The rights of a nonparticipant spouse in qualified plan accumulations is a critical issue. In addition to any rights that exist under state law (these may vary between community property and common law jurisdictions), federal law (under the Retirement Equity Act of 1984, or REA) provides specific rights to the spouse:

1. If the plan is subject to the "qualified joint and survivor annuity" requirement (see Chapter 14), among other requirements, the nonparticipant spouse's consent is required for any change in the beneficiary that reduces the spousal benefit. If the benefit from such a plan

is rolled over to an IRA, spousal consent to the rollover is required. However, after the benefit has been rolled over to an IRA, no further spousal consent is required under federal law for any disposition of the IRA assets.

If there is a rollover, this emphasizes the significance of the initial spousal consent; spouses in this situation should be fully informed of this significance and of their legal rights. It may be advisable for the spouse to have a separate financial or legal advisor in order to prevent later claims that the consent was not an informed one.

2. A stock bonus plan, profit sharing plan, or ESOP does not have to meet the joint and survivor requirement if the participant's nonforfeitable account balance is payable as a death benefit to the spouse.[8] Thus, the spouse must consent to any change in the beneficiary of the death benefit. However, the plan participant can bypass this consent requirement by taking a lump sum distribution (spousal consent is not required at that point) and then disposing of the lump sum in any desired arrangement, also without spousal consent.

   Similarly, amounts in these plans can be rolled over to an IRA without spousal consent (but some plans administratively require spousal consent here, however, to avoid later claims) and the IRA owner is then free to apply IRA assets without spousal consent. Again, particularly where spousal rights are so limited, this situation emphasizes the importance of spouses being informed of their rights and exercising those rights in a prudent manner.

Using a "Frozen" Plan

A frozen plan is one that has been amended to terminate future employer contributions and new plan entrants, but otherwise continues to exist for the benefit of existing participants. For a business-owner retiree, however, using a frozen plan may not be feasible. First, the IRS view is that if the plan continues to exist, the plan sponsor must continue to exist. For many small businesses, the business is likely to end with the retirement of the owner. In addition, Form 5500 must continue to be filed even for a frozen plan, and the plan must be amended to reflect any changes in the law, so administrative costs for a frozen plan can be considerable.

PLANNING RETIREMENT DISTRIBUTIONS

Lump sum or periodic payments. For clients with relatively large account balances, it almost never makes sense to take all the money out and pay taxes on it immediately. For those few who are still eligible for the grandfathered ten-year averaging provision, it would not provide significantly lower tax rates for large distributions. The primary income tax benefit available from qualified plan and IRA accumulations is the potential for long-term tax deferral.

Tax deferral as the basic goal. The current rules for required minimum distributions permit significant long-term tax deferral for qualified accumulations. Attaining maximum tax deferral should be the primary consideration for the planner unless there are compelling nontax reasons for taking distributions faster than required.

The potential for tax deferral can extend over as many as three life expectancies. During the plan participant's lifetime, minimum distributions are calculated over what amounts to a joint and survivor life expectancy (see Chapter 14). If the participant is married and dies before the spouse, the spouse can roll the remaining balance into the spouse's own IRA, and name a younger beneficiary. At the spouse's death, the younger beneficiary can continue payments over the beneficiary's life expectancy.

To understand how to achieve maximum deferral (as well as the alternative results), it's important to understand the minimum distribution rules under Code section 401(a)(9) and, in particular, the final regulations under this section.[9] These are complex and the following is only a summary—often the regulations themselves and IRS rulings must be consulted to resolve questions that arise.

The lifetime minimum distribution requirements were covered in Chapter 14. For complete estate and retirement planning purposes, the rules applicable at the participant's death are also important. The rules for after-death distributions depend on whether the participant dies before or after the required beginning date (RBD) for minimum distributions. As discussed in Chapter 14, the RBD is generally April 1 of the year following the later of (1) the attainment of age 70½ or (2) actual retirement. However, the "actual retirement" option is not available to an owner of more than 5 percent of the business sponsoring the qualified plan, nor to IRAs.

After-death Minimum Distributions

The rules applicable at the participant's death can be summarized as follows:

Beneficiary Is the Participant's Spouse

- *Rollover to IRA.* If the surviving spouse makes a spousal rollover to an IRA, minimum distributions for the surviving spouse's life expectancy do not have to begin until April 1 of the year following the year the *surviving spouse* attains age 70½. The surviving spouse is then subject to the same minimum distribution options as if the surviving spouse were the participant (see Chapter 14). The minimum distribution at that time is based on the Uniform Lifetime Table (see Figure 17.1), Furthermore, the surviving spouse can name a new beneficiary, such as a child.

Example. Christopher dies at age eighty having named his spouse, Patricia, aged seventy-seven, as the beneficiary of his IRA. Patricia rolls the benefit into her own IRA and names their only child, Andy, as beneficiary. During Patricia's lifetime, the same Uniform Lifetime Table (see Figure 17.1) used during Christopher's lifetime is used to calculate the minimum distribution for each year during Patricia's lifetime. For example, in the year following Christopher's death, Patricia's age will be seventy-eight; thus, the distribution period is 20.3 years. After Patricia's death, minimum distributions to Andy are determined based on his single life expectancy (see Figure 17.2), assuming that he is still the beneficiary at that time.

Figure 17.1

UNIFORM LIFETIME TABLE

Age of Employee	Distribution Period	Age of Employee	Distribution Period	Age of Employee	Distribution Period
70	27.4	86	14.1	101	5.9
71	26.5	87	13.4	102	5.5
72	25.6	88	12.7	103	5.2
73	24.7	89	12.0	104	4.9
74	23.8	90	11.4	105	4.5
75	22.9	91	10.8	106	4.2
76	22.0	92	10.2	107	3.9
77	21.2	93	9.6	108	3.7
78	20.3	94	9.1	109	3.4
79	19.5	95	8.6	110	3.1
80	18.7	96	8.1	111	2.9
81	17.9	97	7.6	112	2.6
82	17.1	98	7.1	113	2.4
83	16.3	99	6.7	114	2.1
84	15.5	100	6.3	115	1.9
85	14.8				

- *No rollover*. If the beneficiary is the surviving spouse, but rollover treatment is unavailable or not chosen, distributions must begin by December 31 of the year following the participant's death; but if the deceased participant had not reached age 70½, the distributions can be deferred to December 31 of the year the *deceased participant* would have been 70½.

- Note that, as in the example above, if the surviving spouse survives until the date when the participant was or would have been 70½, minimum distributions are determined over the remaining life expectancy of the surviving spouse. This life expectancy is not a fixed period, but is newly determined (recalculated) each year that the spouse survives, under the table in Figure 17.1. This has the effect of reducing the annual required minimum distribution compared with a fixed life expectancy.

- If the surviving spouse dies before the participant would have been 70½, there is a special rule that treats the spouse as if the spouse were the participant (except that if the spouse has remarried and then dies, the surviving spouse will not be permitted the spousal rollover described above).

Nonspouse Individual Beneficiary

- If the beneficiary is an individual who is not the spouse, minimum distributions must begin as of the end of the year following death, and the amounts are based on the individual beneficiary's life expectancy, determined based on his birthday in the year after the death (using the single life expectancy table; see Figure 17.2). In subsequent years, the applicable distribution period is the life expectancy from the previous year, minus one. In other words, the distribution is made over a fixed period (no recalculation). The same fixed period continues in effect even if the person named as beneficiary at the time of death subsequently dies and leaves the benefit to another heir.

Example. Jack dies at age seventy-six owning an IRA account that is valued at $840,000 as of the end of the year of his death. The sole beneficiary is Sarah his niece, who reaches age fifty-four in the year after Jack's death. The minimum distribution is$27,541, which is calculated by dividing $840,000 by 30.5 (Sarah's single life expectancy). The remaining distribution period is now fixed.

In the next year, the applicable distribution period is 29.5 (30.5 - 1; see Figure 17.2) and so on in future years. In total, distributions can continue for 30.5 years after the death of the participant. This is true even if Sarah dies before the end of the period and leaves the benefit to her heirs.

- If distributions are not begun as of the end of the year following death over the beneficiary's life expectancy, generally the only option is that distributions must be completed by December 31 of the fifth year following the participant's death. Under the five-year rule, there are no minimum distribution requirements for any year other than the fifth year.

No Individual Beneficiary

- *Death before the RBD*. If the participant dies before the RBD, and there is no designated beneficiary as of the end of the year after the employee's death (which would be the case if a nonindividual such as a charity or the estate were named as beneficiary), the entire balance must be distributed by December 31 of the fifth year following the participant's death. Under this option, there are no minimum distribution requirements for any year other than the fifth year.

- *Death on or after the RBD*. If the participant dies on or after the RBD and there is no designated beneficiary as of the end of the year after the employee's death, the distribution period is the participant's life expectancy calculated in the year of death and reduced by one for each subsequent year (again, recalculation is no longer available to determine the required distribution after the participant's death).

Example. Cookie dies at age eighty, having named her estate as the beneficiary of her IRA. Her account balance at the end of the year of her death is $240,000 and her life expectancy is 9.2 (10.2 - 1) in the year following death. The required distribution in the year following death is $26,087 ($240,000/9.2). In each of the

Figure 17.2

SINGLE LIFE TABLE					
Age	Life Expectancy	Age	Life Expectancy	Age	Life Expectancy
0	82.4	38	45.6	75	13.4
1	81.6	39	44.6	76	12.7
2	80.6	40	43.6	77	12.1
3	79.7	41	42.7	78	11.4
4	78.7	42	41.7	79	10.8
5	77.7	43	40.7	80	10.2
6	76.7	44	39.8	81	9.7
7	75.8	45	38.8	82	9.1
8	74.8	46	37.9	83	8.6
9	73.8	47	37.0	84	8.1
10	72.8	48	36.0	85	7.6
11	71.8	49	35.1	86	7.1
12	70.8	50	34.2	87	6.7
13	69.9	51	33.3	88	6.3
14	68.9	52	32.3	89	5.9
15	67.9	53	31.4	90	5.5
16	66.9	54	30.5	91	5.2
17	66.0	55	29.6	92	4.9
18	65.0	56	28.7	93	4.6
19	64.0	57	27.9	94	4.3
20	63.0	58	27.0	95	4.1
21	62.1	59	26.1	96	3.8
22	61.1	60	25.2	97	3.6
23	60.1	61	24.4	98	3.4
24	59.1	62	23.5	99	3.1
25	58.2	63	22.7	100	2.9
26	57.2	64	21.8	101	2.7
27	56.2	65	21.0	102	2.5
28	55.3	66	20.2	103	2.3
29	54.3	67	19.4	104	2.1
30	53.3	68	18.6	105	1.9
31	52.4	69	17.8	106	1.7
32	51.4	70	17.0	107	1.5
33	50.4	71	16.3	108	1.4
34	49.4	72	15.5	109	1.2
35	48.5	73	14.8	110	1.1
36	47.5	74	14.1	111	1.0
37	46.5				

following years, the applicable distribution period is reduced by one, until all amounts are distributed after nine years.

If the participant dies after the required beginning date, in the year of death, the heirs must take the decedent's required distribution (if this distribution was not taken before death) based on the method under which the decedent had been taking distributions. In subsequent years, the required distributions will depend upon who is the chosen beneficiary.

Beneficiary Designation

Under the regulations, the beneficiary for purposes of determining the required distribution is the beneficiary who actually inherits the benefit. Technically, it is the beneficiary determined as of September 30 of the year following death. A "designated beneficiary" must be an individual (that is, not a charity or the participant's estate) if minimum distributions are to be based on the beneficiary's life expectancy. The beneficiary of a trust will not be treated as a designated beneficiary unless the trust satisfies certain requirements (see below).

If there are multiple designated beneficiaries as of September 30 of the year following death (and separate accounts for each participant have not been established), the life expectancy of the oldest beneficiary (with the shortest life expectancy) is used for determining the required distributions. If one of those beneficiaries is a nonindividual, then the participant is deemed to have no designated beneficiary. If there are multiple designated beneficiaries and separate accounts exist, the minimum distributions are calculated separately for each account and taken by each beneficiary over his or her fixed-term life expectancy.

Trust as a Designated Beneficiary

It is often useful in estate planning to designate a trust as beneficiary of an IRA or qualified plan benefit, perhaps to use the optimal marital deduction–unified credit formula approach with respect to the retirement plan assets. If certain requirements of the regulations are met by the trust, a trust beneficiary can qualify as a designated beneficiary, so that the beneficiary's life expectancy can be used to determine the minimum distributions after the participant's death. If the trust has multiple beneficiaries, the age of the oldest beneficiary will be used to determine the minimum distribution.

The regulations set forth the following requirements for a beneficiary of the trust to be treated as designated beneficiary under the minimum distribution rules:

- Beneficiaries of the trust must be identifiable from the trust instrument.
- The trust must be a valid trust under state law, or would be a valid trust except that there is no corpus. The final rules make it clear that the IRS believes that the trust could be a living or testamentary trust.
- The trust must be either be irrevocable, or become irrevocable upon death (i.e., it can be revocable only until the participant's death).
- Certain documentation of the trust provisions (such as a copy of the trust instrument, or a list and description of the beneficiaries) must be provided to the plan administrator.

Under these rules, the usual estate planning trusts (either living or testamentary) that create a marital deduction and unified credit shelter/bypass share at a participant's death can be used as the designated beneficiary of the retirement plan benefits without jeopardizing the use of a beneficiary's life expectancy for the purpose of determining a minimum distribution. However, complex questions remain on this issue.

ESTATE PLANNING FOR QUALIFIED PLAN AND IRA ACCUMULATIONS

Outright gift to spouse. Whenever possible, participants should leave qualified plan or IRA balances to their spouses. This has several advantages:

1. It eliminates federal estate tax at the participant's death through use of the marital deduction.
2. The spouse pays income taxes as distributions are made, thus preserving income tax deferral at least for the spouse's life. If the benefit comes from an IRA, or if the spouse rolls over the benefit into his or her own IRA, the spouse can then choose a beneficiary and extend income tax deferral beyond death and possibly over the lifetime of the beneficiary.[10] However, estate taxes due at the spouse's death may require the estate to dip into retirement plan funds and therefore the amount available for further income tax deferral may be reduced or eliminated.

Leaving as QTIP. An outright transfer of a qualified plan balance to the spouse at the participant's death may be unsuitable for various reasons:

1. the participant desires to provide for ultimate beneficiaries (e.g., children from a prior marriage) that the spouse would not necessarily provide for;
2. the spouse is not considered financially competent; or
3. the spouse is not a U.S. citizen and the marital deduction is not available unless a qualified domestic trust receives the assets.[11]

The use of a QTIP versus an outright gift adds complications. The basic problem is that fund *earnings* cannot accumulate tax-free in a QTIP; QTIP income must be distributed to the spouse.[12] The amount that has to be distributed may be more than is required under the applicable minimum distribution rules. Investment primarily in nonincome producing property to circumvent this rule probably will not work; the trust then might not qualify as a QTIP, and moreover the spouse can force trust property to be made more productive.[13] The IRS has published rules for QTIPs as beneficiaries of qualified plan accumulations;[14] these must be carefully followed or the estate might not qualify for the marital deduction.

SUMMARY

Considerable tax deferral is theoretically possible with qualified plan accumulations. All other things being equal, the goal of the retirement and estate planner in dealing with these accumulations should be to maximize this unique tax benefit by maximizing income tax deferral. As indicated above, deferral can be extended through two deaths by naming the participant's spouse as beneficiary, provided the spouse survives the participant and elects to roll over the amount to his/her own IRA, with a younger child or other heir as beneficiary. This is often referred to as "stretching" the IRA.

However, as an actual blueprint for planning, this has some deficiencies. The desired result—maximum tax deferral—is contingent on (1) the spouse's actually surviving the participant and (2) the possible impact of estate taxes at death; often these cannot be paid without using up the potentially tax-deferrable qualified plan funds.

Possible approaches include:

- Use a pure "game-theory" planning technique; that is, investigate health, genetics, etc., as applied to the participant and spouse, determine probable dates of death and design a distribution plan that minimizes taxes in this "most likely" contingency; or

- Provide a hedge for the plan using life insurance or "pension maximization" as this plan is sometimes described. Use part of the plan balance during the lifetimes of the participant and spouse to purchase life insurance. Second-to-die insurance would be used if both spouses are living and the nonparticipant spouse is the beneficiary; single life insurance on the participant's life would be used otherwise. The insurance generally would be placed in an irrevocable life insurance trust for the benefit of the children or other ultimate beneficiaries. The purpose of this "wealth replacement trust" is to replace the assets lost to federal estate taxation upon the death of the participant or spouse.

WHERE CAN I FIND OUT MORE?

1. *Tax Facts on Insurance & Employee Benefits* (updated annually), The National Underwriter Co. Cincinnati, OH, www.nationalunderwriter.com.

2. Choate, Natalie, *Life and Death Planning for Retirement Benefits* (7th Ed. 2011), available at www.ataxplan.com.

CHAPTER ENDNOTES

1. See Priv. Ltr. Rul. 9220007.
2. 947 F.2d 257 (7th Cir. 1992).
3. See *Rousey v. Jacoway*, 544 U.S. 320 (2005).
4. *Patterson v. Shumate*, 504 U.S. 753 (1992).
5. See, e.g., *Kelly v. Blue Cross*, No. 91-0005L (D.RI 1993), which held that the sole owner of a corporation was not an employee for ERISA purposes, relying on other cases in the First and Sixth Circuits.
6. See *In re Schlein*, 1993 U.S. App. LEXIS 31333 (11th Cir. 1993), holding that ERISA does not preempt state bankruptcy law exemption of pension benefits.
7. ERISA §4021(b).
8. I.R.C. §401(a)(11).
9. Treas. Reg. §§1.401(a)(9)-9; 1.403(b)-3; 1.408-8. These became effective for distributions beginning on or after January 1, 2003. Distributions prior to 2003 were subject to different rules.
10. I.R.C. §408(d). In the case of an IRA, the spouse would treat the IRA as his or her own; in the case of a qualified plan, the spouse would receive a lump sum distribution and roll it over into the spouse's own IRA. I.R.C. §402(c)(9).
11. I.R.C. §2056(d).
12. I.R.C. §2056(b)(7)(B); Rev. Rul. 2000-2, 2000-1 CB 305.
13. Treas. Reg. §20.2056(b)-5(f)(4).
14. See Rev. Rul. 2000-2, 2000 1 CB 305.

Figure 17.3

JOINT AND LAST SURVIVOR TABLE - LIFE EXPECTANCY

Ages	35	36	37	38	39	40	41	42	43	44	45	46	47	48	49	50
35	55.2	54.7	54.3	53.8	53.4	53.0	52.7	52.3	52.0	51.7	51.5	51.2	51.0	50.8	50.6	50.4
36	54.7	54.2	53.7	53.3	52.8	52.4	52.0	51.7	51.3	51.0	50.7	50.5	50.2	50.0	49.8	49.6
37	54.3	53.7	53.2	52.7	52.3	51.8	51.4	51.1	50.7	50.4	50.0	49.8	49.5	49.2	49.0	48.8
38	53.8	53.3	52.7	52.2	51.7	51.3	50.9	50.4	50.1	49.7	49.4	49.1	48.8	48.5	48.2	48.0
39	53.4	52.8	52.3	51.7	51.2	50.8	50.3	49.9	49.5	49.1	48.7	48.4	48.1	47.8	47.5	47.3
40	53.0	52.4	51.8	51.3	50.8	50.2	49.8	49.3	48.9	48.5	48.1	47.7	47.4	47.1	46.8	46.5
41	52.7	52.0	51.4	50.9	50.3	49.8	49.3	48.8	48.3	47.9	47.5	47.1	46.7	46.4	46.1	45.8
42	52.3	51.7	51.1	50.4	49.9	49.3	48.8	48.3	47.8	47.3	46.9	46.5	46.1	45.8	45.4	45.1
43	52.0	51.3	50.7	50.1	49.5	48.9	48.3	47.8	47.3	46.8	46.3	45.9	45.5	45.1	44.8	44.4
44	51.7	51.0	50.4	49.7	49.1	48.5	47.9	47.3	46.8	46.3	45.8	45.4	44.9	44.5	44.2	43.8
45	51.5	50.7	50.0	49.4	48.7	48.1	47.5	46.9	46.3	45.8	45.3	44.8	44.4	44.0	43.6	43.2
46	51.2	50.5	49.8	49.1	48.4	47.7	47.1	46.5	45.9	45.4	44.8	44.3	43.9	43.4	43.0	42.6
47	51.0	50.2	49.5	48.8	48.1	47.4	46.7	46.1	45.5	44.9	44.4	43.9	43.4	42.9	42.4	42.0
48	50.8	50.0	49.2	48.5	47.8	47.1	46.4	45.8	45.1	44.5	44.0	43.4	42.9	42.4	41.9	41.5
49	50.6	49.8	49.0	48.2	47.5	46.8	46.1	45.4	44.8	44.2	43.6	43.0	42.4	41.9	41.4	40.9
50	50.4	49.6	48.8	48.0	47.3	46.5	45.8	45.1	44.4	43.8	43.2	42.6	42.0	41.5	40.9	40.4
51	50.2	49.4	48.6	47.8	47.0	46.3	45.5	44.8	44.1	43.5	42.8	42.2	41.6	41.0	40.5	40.0
52	50.0	49.2	48.4	47.6	46.8	46.0	45.3	44.6	43.8	43.2	42.5	41.8	41.2	40.6	40.1	39.5
53	49.9	49.1	48.2	47.4	46.6	45.8	45.1	44.3	43.6	42.9	42.2	41.5	40.9	40.3	39.7	39.1
54	49.8	48.9	48.1	47.2	46.4	45.6	44.8	44.1	43.3	42.6	41.9	41.2	40.5	39.9	39.3	38.7
55	49.7	48.8	47.9	47.1	46.3	45.5	44.7	43.9	43.1	42.4	41.6	40.9	40.2	39.6	38.9	38.3
56	49.5	48.7	47.8	47.0	46.1	45.3	44.5	43.7	42.9	42.1	41.4	40.7	40.0	39.3	38.6	38.0
57	49.4	48.6	47.7	46.8	46.0	45.1	44.3	43.5	42.7	41.9	41.2	40.4	39.7	39.0	38.3	37.6
58	49.4	48.5	47.6	46.7	45.8	45.0	44.2	43.3	42.5	41.7	40.9	40.2	39.4	38.7	38.0	37.3
59	49.3	48.4	47.5	46.6	45.7	44.9	44.0	43.2	42.4	41.5	40.7	40.0	39.2	38.5	37.8	37.1
60	49.2	48.3	47.4	46.5	45.6	44.7	43.9	43.0	42.2	41.4	40.6	39.8	39.0	38.2	37.5	36.8
61	49.1	48.2	47.3	46.4	45.5	44.6	43.8	42.9	42.1	41.2	40.4	39.6	38.8	38.0	37.3	36.6
62	49.1	48.1	47.2	46.3	45.4	44.5	43.7	42.8	41.9	41.1	40.3	39.4	38.6	37.8	37.1	36.3
63	49.0	48.1	47.2	46.3	45.3	44.5	43.6	42.7	41.8	41.0	40.1	39.3	38.5	37.7	36.9	36.1
64	48.9	48.0	47.1	46.2	45.3	44.4	43.5	42.6	41.7	40.8	40.0	39.2	38.3	37.5	36.7	35.9
65	48.9	48.0	47.0	46.1	45.2	44.3	43.4	42.5	41.6	40.7	39.9	39.0	38.2	37.4	36.6	35.8
66	48.9	47.9	47.0	46.1	45.1	44.2	43.3	42.4	41.5	40.6	39.8	38.9	38.1	37.2	36.4	35.6
67	48.8	47.9	46.9	46.0	45.1	44.2	43.3	42.3	41.4	40.6	39.7	38.8	38.0	37.1	36.3	35.5
68	48.8	47.8	46.9	46.0	45.0	44.1	43.2	42.3	41.4	40.5	39.6	38.7	37.9	37.0	36.2	35.3
69	48.7	47.8	46.9	45.9	45.0	44.1	43.1	42.2	41.3	40.4	39.5	38.6	37.8	36.9	36.0	35.2
70	48.7	47.8	46.8	45.9	44.9	44.0	43.1	42.2	41.3	40.3	39.4	38.6	37.7	36.8	35.9	35.1
71	48.7	47.7	46.8	45.9	44.9	44.0	43.0	42.1	41.2	40.3	39.4	38.5	37.6	36.7	35.9	35.0
72	48.7	47.7	46.8	45.8	44.9	43.9	43.0	42.1	41.1	40.2	39.3	38.4	37.5	36.6	35.8	34.9
73	48.6	47.7	46.7	45.8	44.8	43.9	43.0	42.0	41.1	40.2	39.3	38.4	37.5	36.6	35.7	34.8
74	48.6	47.7	46.7	45.8	44.8	43.9	42.9	42.0	41.1	40.1	39.2	38.3	37.4	36.5	35.6	34.8
75	48.6	47.7	46.7	45.7	44.8	43.8	42.9	42.0	41.0	40.1	39.2	38.3	37.4	36.5	35.6	34.7
76	48.6	47.6	46.7	45.7	44.8	43.8	42.9	41.9	41.0	40.1	39.1	38.2	37.3	36.4	35.5	34.6
77	48.6	47.6	46.7	45.7	44.8	43.8	42.9	41.9	41.0	40.0	39.1	38.2	37.3	36.4	35.5	34.6
78	48.6	47.6	46.6	45.7	44.7	43.8	42.8	41.9	40.9	40.0	39.1	38.2	37.2	36.3	35.4	34.5
79	48.6	47.6	46.6	45.7	44.7	43.8	42.8	41.9	40.9	40.0	39.1	38.1	37.2	36.3	35.4	34.5
80	48.5	47.6	46.6	45.7	44.7	43.7	42.8	41.8	40.9	40.0	39.0	38.1	37.2	36.3	35.4	34.5
81	48.5	47.6	46.6	45.7	44.7	43.7	42.8	41.8	40.9	39.9	39.0	38.1	37.2	36.2	35.3	34.4
82	48.5	47.6	46.6	45.6	44.7	43.7	42.8	41.8	40.9	39.9	39.0	38.1	37.1	36.2	35.3	34.4
83	48.5	47.6	46.6	45.6	44.7	43.7	42.8	41.8	40.9	39.9	39.0	38.0	37.1	36.2	35.3	34.4
84	48.5	47.6	46.6	45.6	44.7	43.7	42.7	41.8	40.8	39.9	39.0	38.0	37.1	36.2	35.3	34.3
85	48.5	47.5	46.6	45.6	44.7	43.7	42.7	41.8	40.8	39.9	38.9	38.0	37.1	36.2	35.2	34.3
86	48.5	47.5	46.6	45.6	44.6	43.7	42.7	41.8	40.8	39.9	38.9	38.0	37.1	36.1	35.2	34.3
87	48.5	47.5	46.6	45.6	44.6	43.7	42.7	41.8	40.8	39.9	38.9	38.0	37.0	36.1	35.2	34.3
88	48.5	47.5	46.6	45.6	44.6	43.7	42.7	41.8	40.8	39.9	38.9	38.0	37.0	36.1	35.2	34.3
89	48.5	47.5	46.6	45.6	44.6	43.7	42.7	41.7	40.8	39.8	38.9	38.0	37.0	36.1	35.2	34.3
90	48.5	47.5	46.6	45.6	44.6	43.7	42.7	41.7	40.8	39.8	38.9	38.0	37.0	36.1	35.2	34.2

Figure 17.3 (cont'd)

JOINT AND LAST SURVIVOR TABLE - LIFE EXPECTANCY

Ages	51	52	53	54	55	56	57	58	59	60	61	62	63	64	65	66
51	39.5	39.0	38.5	38.1	37.7	37.4	37.0	36.7	36.4	36.1	35.8	35.6	35.4	35.2	35.0	34.8
52	39.0	38.5	38.0	37.6	37.2	36.8	36.4	36.0	35.7	35.4	35.1	34.9	34.6	34.4	34.2	34.0
53	38.5	38.0	37.5	37.1	36.6	36.2	35.8	35.4	35.1	34.8	34.5	34.2	33.9	33.7	33.5	33.3
54	38.1	37.6	37.1	36.6	36.1	35.7	35.2	34.8	34.5	34.1	33.8	33.5	33.2	33.0	32.7	32.5
55	37.7	37.2	36.6	36.1	35.6	35.1	34.7	34.3	33.9	33.5	33.2	32.9	32.6	32.3	32.0	31.8
56	37.4	36.8	36.2	35.7	35.1	34.7	34.2	33.7	33.3	32.9	32.6	32.2	31.9	31.6	31.4	31.1
57	37.0	36.4	35.8	35.2	34.7	34.2	33.7	33.2	32.8	32.4	32.0	31.6	31.3	31.0	30.7	30.4
58	36.7	36.0	35.4	34.8	34.3	33.7	33.2	32.8	32.3	31.9	31.4	31.1	30.7	30.4	30.0	29.8
59	36.4	35.7	35.1	34.5	33.9	33.3	32.8	32.3	31.8	31.3	30.9	30.5	30.1	29.8	29.4	29.1
60	36.1	35.4	34.8	34.1	33.5	32.9	32.4	31.9	31.3	30.9	30.4	30.0	29.6	29.2	28.8	28.5
61	35.8	35.1	34.5	33.8	33.2	32.6	32.0	31.4	30.9	30.4	29.9	29.5	29.0	28.6	28.3	27.9
62	35.6	34.9	34.2	33.5	32.9	32.2	31.6	31.1	30.5	30.0	29.5	29.0	28.5	28.1	27.7	27.3
63	35.4	34.6	33.9	33.2	32.6	31.9	31.3	30.7	30.1	29.6	29.0	28.5	28.1	27.6	27.2	26.8
64	35.2	34.4	33.7	33.0	32.3	31.6	31.0	30.4	29.8	29.2	28.6	28.1	27.6	27.1	26.7	26.3
65	35.0	34.2	33.5	32.7	32.0	31.4	30.7	30.0	29.4	28.8	28.3	27.7	27.2	26.7	26.2	25.8
66	34.8	34.0	33.3	32.5	31.8	31.1	30.4	29.8	29.1	28.5	27.9	27.3	26.8	26.3	25.8	25.3
67	34.7	33.9	33.1	32.3	31.6	30.9	30.2	29.5	28.8	28.2	27.6	27.0	26.4	25.9	25.4	24.9
68	34.5	33.7	32.9	32.1	31.4	30.7	29.9	29.2	28.6	27.9	27.3	26.7	26.1	25.5	25.0	24.5
69	34.4	33.6	32.8	32.0	31.2	30.5	29.7	29.0	28.3	27.6	27.0	26.4	25.7	25.2	24.6	24.1
70	34.3	33.4	32.6	31.8	31.1	30.3	29.5	28.8	28.1	27.4	26.7	26.1	25.4	24.8	24.3	23.7
71	34.2	33.3	32.5	31.7	30.9	30.1	29.4	28.6	27.9	27.2	26.5	25.8	25.2	24.5	23.9	23.4
72	34.1	33.2	32.4	31.6	30.8	30.0	29.2	28.4	27.7	27.0	26.3	25.6	24.9	24.3	23.7	23.1
73	34.0	33.1	32.3	31.5	30.6	29.8	29.1	28.3	27.5	26.8	26.1	25.4	24.7	24.0	23.4	22.8
74	33.9	33.0	32.2	31.4	30.5	29.7	28.9	28.1	27.4	26.6	25.9	25.2	24.5	23.8	23.1	22.5
75	33.8	33.0	32.1	31.3	30.4	29.6	28.8	28.0	27.2	26.5	25.7	25.0	24.3	23.6	22.9	22.3
76	33.8	32.9	32.0	31.2	30.3	29.5	28.7	27.9	27.1	26.3	25.6	24.8	24.1	23.4	22.7	22.0
77	33.7	32.8	32.0	31.1	30.3	29.4	28.6	27.8	27.0	26.2	25.4	24.7	23.9	23.2	22.5	21.8
78	33.6	32.8	31.9	31.0	30.2	29.3	28.5	27.7	26.9	26.1	25.3	24.6	23.8	23.1	22.4	21.7
79	33.6	32.7	31.8	31.0	30.1	29.3	28.4	27.6	26.8	26.0	25.2	24.4	23.7	22.9	22.2	21.5
80	33.6	32.7	31.8	30.9	30.1	29.2	28.4	27.5	26.7	25.9	25.1	24.3	23.6	22.8	22.1	21.3
81	33.5	32.6	31.8	30.9	30.0	29.2	28.3	27.5	26.6	25.8	25.0	24.2	23.4	22.7	21.9	21.2
82	33.5	32.6	31.7	30.8	30.0	29.1	28.3	27.4	26.6	25.8	24.9	24.1	23.4	22.6	21.8	21.1
83	33.5	32.6	31.7	30.8	29.9	29.1	28.2	27.4	26.5	25.7	24.9	24.1	23.3	22.5	21.7	21.0
84	33.4	32.5	31.7	30.8	29.9	29.0	28.2	27.3	26.5	25.6	24.8	24.0	23.2	22.4	21.6	20.9
85	33.4	32.5	31.6	30.7	29.9	29.0	28.1	27.3	26.4	25.6	24.8	23.9	23.1	22.3	21.6	20.8
86	33.4	32.5	31.6	30.7	29.8	29.0	28.1	27.2	26.4	25.5	24.7	23.9	23.1	22.3	21.5	20.7
87	33.4	32.5	31.6	30.7	29.8	28.9	28.1	27.2	26.4	25.5	24.7	23.8	23.0	22.2	21.4	20.7
88	33.4	32.5	31.6	30.7	29.8	28.9	28.0	27.2	26.3	25.5	24.6	23.8	23.0	22.2	21.4	20.6
89	33.3	32.4	31.5	30.7	29.8	28.9	28.0	27.2	26.3	25.4	24.6	23.8	22.9	22.1	21.3	20.5
90	33.3	32.4	31.5	30.6	29.8	28.9	28.0	27.1	26.3	25.4	24.6	23.7	22.9	22.1	21.3	20.5

Figure 17.3 (cont'd)

JOINT AND LAST SURVIVOR TABLE - LIFE EXPECTANCY

Ages	67	68	69	70	71	72	73	74	75	76	77	78	79	80	81	82
67	24.4	24.0	23.6	23.2	22.8	22.5	22.2	21.9	21.6	21.4	21.2	21.0	20.8	20.6	20.5	20.4
68	24.0	23.5	23.1	22.7	22.3	22.0	21.6	21.3	21.0	20.8	20.6	20.3	20.1	20.0	19.8	19.7
69	23.6	23.1	22.6	22.2	21.8	21.4	21.1	20.8	20.5	20.2	19.9	19.7	19.5	19.3	19.1	19.0
70	23.2	22.7	22.2	21.8	21.3	20.9	20.6	20.2	19.9	19.6	19.4	19.1	18.9	18.7	18.5	18.3
71	22.8	22.3	21.8	21.3	20.9	20.5	20.1	19.7	19.4	19.1	18.8	18.5	18.3	18.1	17.9	17.7
72	22.5	22.0	21.4	20.9	20.5	20.0	19.6	19.3	18.9	18.6	18.3	18.0	17.7	17.5	17.3	17.1
73	22.2	21.6	21.1	20.6	20.1	19.6	19.2	18.8	18.4	18.1	17.8	17.5	17.2	16.9	16.7	16.5
74	21.9	21.3	20.8	20.2	19.7	19.3	18.8	18.4	18.0	17.6	17.3	17.0	16.7	16.4	16.2	15.9
75	21.6	21.0	20.5	19.9	19.4	18.9	18.4	18.0	17.6	17.2	16.8	16.5	16.2	15.9	15.6	15.4
76	21.4	20.8	20.2	19.6	19.1	18.6	18.1	17.6	17.2	16.8	16.4	16.0	15.7	15.4	15.1	14.9
77	21.2	20.6	19.9	19.4	18.8	18.3	17.8	17.3	16.8	16.4	16.0	15.6	15.3	15.0	14.7	14.4
78	21.0	20.3	19.7	19.1	18.5	18.0	17.5	17.0	16.5	16.0	15.6	15.2	14.9	14.5	14.2	13.9
79	20.8	20.1	19.5	18.9	18.3	17.7	17.2	16.7	16.2	15.7	15.3	14.9	14.5	14.1	13.8	13.5
80	20.6	20.0	19.3	18.7	18.1	17.5	16.9	16.4	15.9	15.4	15.0	14.5	14.1	13.8	13.4	13.1
81	20.5	19.8	19.1	18.5	17.9	17.3	16.7	16.2	15.6	15.1	14.7	14.2	13.8	13.4	13.1	12.7
82	20.4	19.7	19.0	18.3	17.7	17.1	16.5	15.9	15.4	14.9	14.4	13.9	13.5	13.1	12.7	12.4
83	20.2	19.5	18.8	18.2	17.5	16.9	16.3	15.7	15.2	14.7	14.2	13.7	13.2	12.8	12.4	12.1
84	20.1	19.4	18.7	18.0	17.4	16.7	16.1	15.5	15.0	14.4	13.9	13.4	13.0	12.6	12.2	11.8
85	20.1	19.3	18.6	17.9	17.3	16.6	16.0	15.4	14.8	14.3	13.7	13.2	12.8	12.3	11.9	11.5
86	20.0	19.2	18.5	17.8	17.1	16.5	15.8	15.2	14.6	14.1	13.5	13.0	12.5	12.1	11.7	11.3
87	19.9	19.2	18.4	17.7	17.0	16.4	15.7	15.1	14.5	13.9	13.4	12.9	12.4	11.9	11.4	11.0
88	19.8	19.1	18.3	17.6	16.9	16.3	15.6	15.0	14.4	13.8	13.2	12.7	12.2	11.7	11.3	10.8
89	19.8	19.0	18.3	17.6	16.9	16.2	15.5	14.9	14.3	13.7	13.1	12.6	12.0	11.5	11.1	10.6
90	19.7	19.0	18.2	17.5	16.8	16.1	15.4	14.8	14.2	13.6	13.0	12.4	11.9	11.4	10.9	10.5

JOINT AND LAST SURVIVOR TABLE - LIFE EXPECTANCY

Ages	83	84	85	86	87	88	89	90
83	11.7	11.4	11.1	10.9	10.6	10.4	10.2	10.1
84	11.4	11.1	10.8	10.5	10.3	10.1	9.9	9.7
85	11.1	10.8	10.5	10.2	9.9	9.7	9.5	9.3
86	10.9	10.5	10.2	9.9	9.6	9.4	9.2	9.0
87	10.6	10.3	9.9	9.6	9.4	9.1	8.9	8.6
88	10.4	10.1	9.7	9.4	9.1	8.8	8.6	8.3
89	10.2	9.9	9.5	9.2	8.9	8.6	8.3	8.1
90	10.1	9.7	9.3	9.0	8.6	8.3	8.1	7.8

LIFE INSURANCE IN A QUALIFIED PLAN

CHAPTER 18

INTRODUCTION

Life insurance for employees in a qualified plan can often be provided favorably by having the insurance purchased and owned by the plan, using deductible employer contributions to the plan as a source of funds. This chapter deals with the advantages and methods of doing this, as well as the limitations.

WHEN IS USE OF SUCH A DEVICE INDICATED?

1. When employees covered under a qualified plan may have an otherwise unmet life insurance need, either for family protection or estate liquidity.

2. When there are gaps and limitations in other company plans providing death benefits, such as Section 79 group-term life insurance plans, nonqualified deferred compensation plans, and split dollar plans. Planners should consider using life insurance in a qualified plan to fill those gaps or supplement those plans.

3. When a qualified plan for a closely held business or professional corporation is overfunded or close to the full funding limitation for regular trusteed plans, the addition of an incidental life insurance benefit, or a change to fully insured funding, may permit future deductible contributions at a higher rate than before.

4. When life insurance would be attractive to plan participants as an additional option for investing their plan accounts. This technique is most often used in a profit sharing or 401(k) plan, but can be used in other types of defined contribution plans as well.

Advantages

1. The tax treatment of life insurance in a qualified plan, as discussed below, usually provides an overall cost advantage, as compared with individual life policies provided by the employer outside the qualified plan or those personally owned by plan participants.

2. Life insurance provides one of the safest available investments for a qualified plan.

3. The use of appropriate life insurance products for funding a qualified pension plan can help with predictable plan costs for the employer.

4. Life insurance products in a qualified plan can provide employees with retirement benefits guaranteed by an insurance company.

5. The "pure insurance" portion of a qualified plan death benefit (basically, the death proceeds less any policy cash values) is not subject to income tax. This makes it an effective means of transferring wealth.

6. A fully insured plan (one holding only life insurance policies or annuity contracts) is exempt from the minimum funding standard and the actuarial certification requirement of the Internal Revenue Code. This can reduce the administrative cost and complexity of a defined benefit plan. A fully insured plan can also allow a higher initial level of deductible plan contributions than a regular trusteed plan.

Disadvantages

1. Some life insurance policies may provide a rate of return on their cash values which, as compared with alternative plan investments, is relatively low.

2. Policy expenses and commissions on life insurance products may be greater than for comparable investments.

Alternatives

1. Personally owned life insurance.
2. Group-term life insurance. (See Chapter 44.)
3. Life insurance financing in a nonqualified deferred compensation plan.
4. Split dollar life insurance. (See Chapter 45.)

HOW IS IT USED?

Insurance Coverage

Insurance coverage can be provided for all plan participants under a nondiscriminatory formula related to the retirement benefit or plan contribution formula. For example, the amount of insurance for each employee might be specified as one hundred times the expected monthly pension under a defined benefit pension plan. Any insurance-related benefit in the plan must be available on a nondiscriminatory bases.[1]

Insurance coverage can be conditioned on taking a medical exam if this does not result in discrimination in favor of highly compensated employees. For employees who do not "pass" the medical exam, insurance is typically limited to the amount, if any, that can be purchased for them using the amount of premium dollars that would be available if they were insurable.

Turnover costs involved in buying cash value insurance policies can be minimized by having a longer waiting period for insurance than the plan's waiting period for entry (so long as it is not discriminatory). In the interim period, the death benefit for participants not covered by cash value policies can be provided by term insurance. In the past, many plans did not provide insurance for employees who were beyond a specified cutoff age; under current age discrimination law, this probably is disallowed. (See Chapter 62.)

How Much Insurance?—The "Incidental" Test

Life insurance can be used to provide an "incidental" death benefit to participants in a qualified retirement plan, either a defined contribution or defined benefit plan. The IRS considers any nonretirement benefit in a qualified plan to be incidental so long as the cost of that benefit is less than 25 percent of the total cost of the plan. Since this standard by itself is difficult to apply, the IRS has developed two practical tests for life insurance in a qualified plan.[2] If the amount of insurance meets either of the following tests, it is considered incidental:

1. the participant's insured death benefit must be no more than one hundred times the expected monthly benefit; or
2. the aggregate premiums paid (premiums paid over the entire life of the plan) for a participant's insured death benefit are at all times less than the following percentages of the plan cost for that participant:

"ordinary life" insurance	50%
term insurance	25%
universal life	25%

Traditionally, defined contribution plans such as profit sharing plans have used the "percentage limits" in determining how much insurance to provide. Defined benefit plans have typically used the "one hundred times" limit. However, any type of plan can use either limit. It is becoming more common for defined benefit plans to use the percentage limits since the necessary calculations are easily computerized.

Costs for any life insurance held by the plan in excess of a participant's "incidental" benefit limit are not deductible. In addition, if the death benefit exceeds this limit by more than $100,000, it must be disclosed on the tax return as a "listed transaction,"[3] which could result in an IRS inquiry.

LIFE INSURANCE IN DEFINED BENEFIT PLANS

Life insurance is particularly advantageous in defined benefit plans because it *adds to* the limit on deductible contributions. This add-on feature allows greater tax-deferred funding of the plan. That is, a defined benefit plan can be funded to provide the maximum tax-deductible contribution for retirement benefits for each participant. The cost for life insurance can then be added to this amount and deducted.

By comparison, in a defined contribution plan, the costs of the life insurance must be part of the contributions to each participant's account. Using life insurance does not increase the Section 415 annual additions limit for participants' accounts in defined contribution plans. That limit is the lesser of (a) 100 percent of compensation or (b) $53,000 (in 2015, as indexed). This limit applies whether or not life insurance is provided.

Life insurance can be used in defined benefit plans in many ways. Three common approaches will be discussed here: the "combination plan," the "envelope funding" approach, and the fully insured, or "Section 412(e)(3)" plan—formerly Section 412(i).

Combination Plan

In a combination plan, retirement benefits are funded with a combination of whole life policies and assets in a separate trust fund called the "side fund" or "conversion fund." At each participant's retirement, the policies for that participant are cashed in. The participant's retirement benefit is then funded through a combination of the policy cash values and an amount withdrawn from the side fund. (Since whole life policies have a relatively slow cash value buildup, the cash values alone are not usually adequate at age sixty-five to fund the retirement benefit; this is the reason for the side fund.)

This type of funding combines the advantages of an insured death benefit and the investment security of policy cash values, together with an opportunity to invest more aggressively using side fund assets.

Combination plans are very appropriate for funding smaller pension plans—fewer than about twenty-five employees—but can be administratively costly for larger plans due to the number of insurance policies necessary for funding.

The amount of death benefit provided for each employee is usually determined using the 100-to-1 test. The annual cost for the plan each year then consists of the insurance premiums required, plus an amount deposited in the side fund that is determined on an actuarial basis. Actuarial methods and assumptions for the side fund can be varied within reasonable limits, providing some flexibility in funding.

The following example shows how a combination plan works and how it differs from an uninsured plan providing the same retirement benefit:

Example. Dr. X, a sole practitioner physician, adopts a pension plan at age forty-five. His annual compensation is $200,000.

	Insured Plan	Uninsured Plan
Monthly pension at age 65	$ 7,500	$ 7,500
Insured death benefit	750,000	0
Amount required at age 65	900,000	900,000
Less: cash value at age 65	258,750	0
Side fund at 65	641,250	900,000
Level annual deposit at 6% from age 45 to age 65	$16,446	$23,082
Life insurance premium (not considering dividends)	16,343	0
Total annual contribution	32,789	23,082

Note: Future dividends on the life insurance contract can be applied to reduce the annual premium, and typically will reduce it substantially after a number of years.

Envelope Funding

At the opposite pole from the combination plan, where the entire plan is structured around the insurance policies, is the envelope funding approach, where insurance policies are simply considered as plan assets like any other asset. In funding, the actuary determines total annual contributions to the plan to provide both retirement and death benefits provided under the plan. The employer makes the contributions as determined by the actuary. Assets, including insurance policies, are purchased by the plan trustee to fund the costs of both the death benefits and the retirement benefits.

The amount of insured death benefit in this approach is kept within the incidental limits either by providing a death benefit of no more than one hundred times each participant's projected monthly pension, or by keeping the amount of insurance premiums within the appropriate percentage limits (50 percent of aggregate costs for whole life insurance, 25 percent for term insurance, and so on).

The envelope funding approach tends to require lower initial contributions to the plan than a combination plan approach, since the actuary's assumptions are usually less conservative than the assumptions used to determine life insurance premiums. Long-term costs, however, will depend on actual investment results, policy dividends, and benefit and administrative costs of the plan.

Fully Insured Plans

A fully insured pension plan (also known as a Section 412(e)(3) plan, formerly a 412(i) plan[4]) is one that is funded exclusively by life insurance or annuity contracts, and that meets other requirements discussed below. There is no trusteed side fund. Such plans were once common, but the high interest rates of the late 1970s and the bull market of the 1990s lured many pension investors away from traditional insured pension products. Today, however, the advantages of fully insured plans are coming into their own, and life insurance agents and pension sponsors have found these products increasing in popularity. Fully insured plans can offer a solution to the problem of "overfunding" that is still present in some noninsured plans, but even where the overfunding problem is not a factor, the fully insured plan may offer advantages.

A plan is considered fully insured for the plan year if it meets the following requirements:

- the plan is funded exclusively by the purchase of individual insurance contracts. Under the regulations, such contracts can be either individual or group, and can be life insurance or annuity contracts or a combination of both.[5]

- the contracts provide for level annual (or more frequent) premiums extending to retirement age for each individual. However, the employer's cost need not be level, since the regulations permit experience gains and dividends to reduce premiums.[6]

- plan benefits are equal to the contract benefits and are guaranteed by a licensed insurance company. An excessive amount of life insurance may result in the plan failing to satisfy the requirements of Section 412(e)(3).[7]

- premiums have been paid without lapse (or the policy has been reinstated after a lapse).

- no rights under the contracts have been subject to a security interest during the plan year.

- no policy loans are outstanding at any time during the plan year.

Fully insured plans must be nondiscriminatory with respect to rights, benefits and features; thus, for example, the plan may not permit highly compensated employees the right to purchase life insurance contracts from the plan at cash surrender value without providing similar rights to nonhighly compensated employees.[8] The nondiscrimination regulations provide a safe harbor for fully insured plans meeting certain requirements; the benefit formulas of plans satisfying the safe harbor and specified uniformity requirements will be considered to be nondiscriminatory with respect to contributions and benefits.[9]

Other Advantages

Fully insured plans are exempt from the minimum funding requirements. Also, a fully insured plan is eligible for a simplification of the ERISA reporting requirements (Form 5500 series). An insured plan need not file Schedule B, Actuarial Information, with its Form 5500 (or 5500-EZ) and thus does not need a certification by an enrolled actuary.[10] This reduces the cost and complexity of plan administration to some degree.

Finally, a fully insured plan is exempt from the requirement of quarterly pension deposits[11] since that is also tied together with the minimum funding requirements. Fully insured plans are, however, subject to Pension Benefit Guaranty (PBGC) coverage and annual premium requirements.

How Does It Work?

Fully insured funding can be used either with a new plan or an existing plan.[12] The employer can be a corporation or an unincorporated business. Typically, a group type of contract is used, with individual accounts for each participant. All benefits are guaranteed by the insurance company.

The premium is based on the guaranteed interest and annuity rates, which are typically conservative, resulting in larger initial annual deposits than in a typical uninsured plan. (See Figure 18.1.) However, excess earnings beyond the guaranteed level are used to reduce future premiums.

Using excess earnings to reduce future premiums results in a funding pattern that is the opposite of that

Figure 18.1

EFFECT OF INCIDENTAL LIFE INSURANCE BENEFIT ON ANNUAL CONTRIBUTION

Current Age	Age 65 Annual Benefit	Self-Admin. Plan Cost	Split-Fund. Plan Cost	Fully Insured Plan Cost**
35	$91,524	$11,596	$14,705*	$ 26,023
45	91,524	26,716	31,747*	49,168
55	98,064	73,437*	73,437*	134,913

* Full funding limitation.
** Full funding limitation does not apply to fully insured plans.

Source: Lecture by Henry A. Deppe, CLU, inaugurating the Henry Deppe Lecture Series sponsored by The American College.

found in a trusteed (uninsured) plan. In the insured plan, (for a given group of plan participants) the funding level is higher at the beginning of the plan (or the fully insured funding arrangements) and drops as participants move toward retirement. This allows maximization of the overall tax deduction by allowing more of it to be taken earlier. It also often permits deductions for an existing plan that has reached the full funding limitation with uninsured funding. By comparison, a traditional trusteed plan starts with a relatively low level of funding, which increases as each participant nears retirement.

LIFE INSURANCE IN DEFINED CONTRIBUTION PLANS

In defined contribution plans, a part of each participant's account can be used to purchase insurance on the participant's life. The plan can provide:

1. that insurance purchases are voluntary by participants (using a directed account or earmarking provision[13]);
2. that the insurance is provided automatically as a plan benefit; or
3. that insurance is provided at the plan administrator's option (on a nondiscriminatory basis).

The amount of insurance must be kept within the incidental limits already discussed. Usually, defined contribution plans rely on the percentage limits applicable to the type of insurance purchased. For example, if whole life insurance is purchased, aggregate premiums paid from each participant's account must be kept below 50 percent of aggregate contributions to that account. It may be inadvisable to lock the plan into an arrangement requiring premium payments up to the full 50 percent limit. This limits both investment flexibility and employer ability to reduce contributions in lean years. A whole-life premium of about one-third of plan contributions is a conservative guideline.

If a plan has been in existence for a number of years, it may be possible to purchase a considerable amount of insurance in a later year, because the tests are computed in the aggregate.

Example. Suppose a money purchase pension plan has existed for ten years and the employer has contributed $10,000 annually to employee Clyde's account. In the eleventh year, suppose the employer contributes another $10,000 to Clyde's account in the plan. In that eleventh year, an insurance premium amounting to just under $55,000 (50 percent of the $110,000 in aggregate contributions) can be paid out of Clyde's account to purchase whole life insurance.

In some cases, such large purchases of insurance may be justified for planning purposes. The planner must be sure, however, that application of the percentage limits in the future will not prevent the deductible payment of required periodic premiums under the policy.

Profit sharing plans have an additional feature that may allow large insurance purchases. Since profit sharing plans potentially allow in-service cash distributions prior to termination of employment (see Chapter 22), the amount available for an in-service distribution can be used without limit to purchase life insurance. Based on IRS rulings,[14] this means that any employer contribution that has been in the profit sharing plan for at least two years can be used up to 100 percent for insurance purchases of any type as long as the plan specifies that the insurance will be purchased only with such funds.

TRANSACTIONS BETWEEN QUALIFIED PLANS AND PARTICIPANTS

It is often advantageous for the plan to purchase a policy from the insured participant, for example when the participant has become uninsurable. There is a Prohibited Transaction Exemption (PTE)[15] that permits these sales under certain conditions, including a minimum purchase price, and a requirement to offer this opportunity to participants on a nondiscriminatory basis.

It is also often advantageous for a qualified plan to hold life insurance policies for a period of time, paying premiums with plan amounts that have been deducted by the employer, and then rolling out the policy—selling it—to the participant or a related party. However, the requirements of Prohibited Transaction Exemption (PTE) 92-6 must be met.

Under ERISA generally, any purchase of an individual life insurance contract from a qualified plan by a "disqualified person" is a prohibited transaction subject to penalties unless it meets the exemption provided by the Department of Labor in PTE 92-6. Disqualified persons include an owner of 50 percent or more of the business or a member of the family of such an owner.

Many prospective purchasers of an insurance policy from a qualified plan could fall within the definition of a disqualified person. PTE 92-6 exempts sales of life insurance or annuity contracts by an employee benefit plan to a participant or "relative" of the participant. The participant must be the insured under the contract. For purposes of PTE 92-6, a relative is

1. a relative as defined in Section 3(15) of ERISA (spouse, ancestor, lineal descendant, or spouse of a lineal descendent);

2. a member of the family as defined in Code section 4975(e)(6) of the Internal Revenue Code—currently the same list as ERISA Section 3(15); or

3. a sibling of the insured (or a spouse of such sibling), and is the beneficiary under the contract.

If the participant's children are the prospective purchasers of the life insurance contract, they qualify as relatives and should be and generally will be beneficiaries under the contract. Therefore, the exemption of PTE 92-6 would be applicable. The fact that they may only be indirect beneficiaries under an irrevocable life insurance trust, rather than direct beneficiaries, should meet the requirements of PTE 92-6, but there appears to be no authority on this issue.

Other requirements that must be met under PTE 92-6 include:

- The plan, but for the sale, would surrender the contract. (This requirement indicates the need for appropriate language in the plan requiring the plan to surrender the contract upon the death of the insured.)

- If the purchaser is not the insured-participant, the insured-participant must be given an opportunity to purchase the contract first; PTE 92-6 dictates an administrative procedure here that must be followed.

- The purchase price must put the plan in the same cash position as if it had retained the contract, surrendered it, and distributed any vested interest in the plan owed to the participant.

When a life insurance policy is distributed or sold by a qualified plan, it should be valued under the current rules for determining "fair market value."[16]

Valuation Issues

When an insurance policy is transferred to the participant as a plan distribution, like any other distribution of property, its value is taxable as ordinary income. Under Treasury Regulation Section 1.402(a)-1(a)(1)(iii) the amount that has to be included in income by the distributee is the "fair market value" of the property.[17] The Regulation further provides that "policy cash value" and "all other rights under such contract are ... included in determining the fair market value of the contract." If the contract is sold by the plan to a participant or beneficiary in a bargain sale, the excess of the fair market value of the contract over the amount received by the plan is treated as a plan distribution.[18]

As to the actual determination of the fair market value of the contract, the rules were revised in 2005.[19] Under the 2005 guidance, the fair market value of an insurance contract may be determined as the greater of two measures: the "adjusted interpolated terminal reserve (ITR)" or the "adjusted PERC amount." The PERC amount (PERC stands for Premiums, Earnings, and Reasonable Charges) is the aggregate of the premiums paid, plus dividends, plus certain other earnings, minus reasonable charges and distributions. Revenue Procedure 2005-25 discusses these terms in more detail. A parallel rule is provided for variable contracts.

Many techniques such as "pension rescue" and other springing cash value arrangements where cash values rise sharply after the policy is transferred to the plan participant or other person, will not be advantageous under the safe harbor method. For example, in many cases stated cash values were "reduced" by high surrender charges that were not actually charged against the policy, and this practice is not permitted under the safe harbor. As the IRS intends, such arrangements will have to be amended or terminated and future ones will be discouraged.

TAX IMPLICATIONS

For the Participant

The economic value of pure life insurance coverage on a participant's life is taxed annually to the participant at levels specified by the IRS. Generally, the value is taxed at the lower of (a) the IRS "Table 2001" costs (see Figure 18.2) or (b) the life insurance company's actual term rates for standard risks.[20] For years ending before 2002, the "Table P.S. 58" rates issued in earlier guidance by the IRS were used instead of the Table 2001 costs, for purposes of this rule.[21] For periods after 2003, the ability to use an insurer's published rates is much more limited.

Any amount actually contributed to the plan by the participant is subtracted from this amount. (If the participant is an owner-employee in a "Keogh" plan, the taxation is slightly different, as discussed in Chapter 29.)

Example. Participant Lemm, age forty-five, is covered under a defined benefit plan that provides an insured death benefit in addition to retirement benefits. The death benefit is provided under a whole life policy with a face amount of $100,000. At the end of 2014 the policy's cash value is $40,000. The plan is noncontributory (that is, Lemm does not contribute to the plan).

For 2014 Lemm must report an additional $92 of taxable income on his tax returns (sixty times the Table 2001 rate of $1.53 per thousand for a participant age forty-five, to reflect the amount of pure insurance coverage in 2013). The employer is required to report the insurance coverage on Lemm's Form W-2 for the year.

This computation is shown in more detail in the NumberCruncher software illustration in Figure 18.3.

Taxation of Death Benefits

Taxation of an insured death benefit received by a beneficiary can be summarized in the following points:

- The pure insurance element of an insured plan death benefit (the death benefit less any cash value) is income tax free to a participant's beneficiary.[22]

- The total of all Table 2001 (and former P.S. 58) costs paid by the participant can be recovered tax free from the plan death benefit (if it is paid from the same insurance contracts that gave rise to the costs).[23]

- The remainder of the distribution is taxed as a qualified plan distribution.[24] If the decedent participated in the plan before 1987, there may also be some favorable "grandfather" tax provisions for a lump sum distribution that may apply.

Figure 18.2

TABLE 2001 ONE-YEAR TERM PREMIUMS FOR $1,000 OF LIFE INSURANCE PROTECTION					
Attained Age	Premium	Attained Age	Premium	Attained Age	Premium
0	$0.70	34	$0.98	67	$15.20
1	$0.41	35	$0.99	68	$16.92
2	$0.27	36	$1.01	69	$18.70
3	$0.19	37	$1.04	70	$20.62
4	$0.13	38	$1.06	71	$22.72
5	$0.13	39	$1.07	72	$25.07
6	$0.14	40	$1.10	73	$27.57
7	$0.15	41	$1.13	74	$30.18
8	$0.16	42	$1.20	75	$33.05
9	$0.16	43	$1.29	76	$36.33
10	$0.16	44	$1.40	77	$40.17
11	$0.19	45	$1.53	78	$44.33
12	$0.24	46	$1.67	79	$49.23
13	$0.28	47	$1.83	80	$54.56
14	$0.33	48	$1.98	81	$60.51
15	$0.38	49	$2.13	82	$66.74
16	$0.52	50	$2.30	83	$73.07
17	$0.57	51	$2.52	84	$80.35
18	$0.59	52	$2.81	85	$88.76
19	$0.61	53	$3.20	86	$99.16
20	$0.62	54	$3.65	87	$110.40
21	$0.62	55	$4.15	88	$121.85
22	$0.64	56	$4.68	89	$133.40
23	$0.66	57	$5.20	90	$144.30
24	$0.68	58	$5.66	91	$155.80
25	$0.71	59	$6.06	92	$168.75
26	$0.73	60	$6.51	93	$186.44
27	$0.76	61	$7.11	94	$206.70
28	$0.80	62	$7.96	95	$228.35
29	$0.83	63	$9.08	96	$250.01
30	$0.87	64	$10.41	97	$265.09
31	$0.90	65	$11.90	98	$270.11
32	$0.93	66	$13.51	99	$281.05
33	$0.96				

Chapter 20 contains a detailed discussion of the tax treatment and planning options available for an insured death benefit from a qualified plan.

As compared with the tax treatment of life insurance personally owned or provided by the employer outside the plan, there is usually an economic advantage to insurance in the plan, all other things being equal. Insurance outside the plan is paid for entirely with after-tax dollars, so there is no tax deferral. The death benefit of non-plan insurance may be entirely instead of partially tax-free; however, the deferral of tax with plan-provided insurance potentially results in a measurable net tax benefit.

Figure 18.3

TABLE 2001 COMPUTATION*

PART A

INPUT:	Employee's Age	45
INPUT:	Face Amount of Death Benefit	$100,000
INPUT:	Cash Value to Employer	-$40,000
	Net Amount at Risk	$60,000
	Table 2001 Charge	$1.53
	Gross Amount Includible	$92.00
INPUT:	Employee's Contribution	$.00

PART B

INPUT:	Amount of Dividend Paid in Cash to Employee	$.00
INPUT:	Amount of Dividend Used to Reduce Amount of Dividend Premium Contribution	$.00
INPUT:	Amount of Dividend Held at Interest for Employee	$.00
INPUT:	Amount of Dividend – If Cash Value & Death Benefit of Paid Up Additions Are Controlled by Employee	$.00
INPUT:	Amount of Dividend – If Dividends Were Used to Buy One Year Term Insurance for the Employee	$.00
INPUT:	Table 2001 Cost or, If Lower, Published Yearly Renewable Term Cost — If Employer Gets Cash Value of Paid Up Additional Insurance and Employee's Beneficiary Receives Any Balance	$.00
	Reportable Table 2001 Cost	$92.00

Insert company's standard individual 1 year term rates at B1 if lower.

Illustration Courtesy of NumberCruncher Software, Leimberg and LeClair, Inc., P.O. Box 1332, Bryn Mawr, PA 19010.

Qualified plan death benefits are, in general, included in a decedent's estate for federal estate tax purposes.

For the Employer

Employer contributions to the plan, including those used to purchase life insurance, are deductible if the amount of life insurance is within the incidental limits discussed earlier.

FREQUENTLY ASKED QUESTIONS

Question – Can life insurance be used in a Keogh (HR 10) plan?

Answer – A Keogh plan is a qualified plan covering a proprietor or one or more partners of an unincorporated business. Life insurance can be used to provide a death benefit for regular employees covered under the plan, subject to the rules discussed in this chapter. Life insurance can also be provided under the plan for a proprietor or partners. However, slightly less favorable rules apply; these are discussed in detail in Chapter 29.

Question – Can life insurance be used in a Section 403(b) tax deferred annuity plan?

Answer – Life insurance can be provided as an incidental benefit under a tax deferred annuity plan. It is provided on much the same basis as in a qualified profit sharing plan. Covered employees will have Table 2001 (formerly P.S. 58) costs to report as taxable income, as in a regular qualified plan.

Question – Can universal life insurance be used to provide an insured death benefit under a qualified plan?

Answer – Universal life and similar products may be used. However, even though universal life has an investment element like that in a whole life policy, the IRS has taken the view that the "incidental" limits applicable to universal life premiums are the same as those that apply to term insurance. So, if the percentage test is used, aggregate universal life premiums must be less than 25 percent of aggregate plan contributions. This appears to be an overly conservative rule, and may eventually be subject to a court challenge.

Question – How can insurance coverage be continued by a qualified plan after a plan participant has retired or accrued the maximum benefit under the plan?

Answer – If a plan participant's full retirement benefit has accrued, the employer can no longer make deductible contributions to the plan. Several alternatives are available for continuing insurance coverage: (1) the policy can be put on a reduced, paid-up basis; (2) the policy can be sold to the participant for its cash surrender value (possibly financed using a policy loan);[25] (3) the participant can continue to pay premiums (they are nondeductible); or (4) the plan trustee can continue to pay premiums out of fund earnings (Table 2001 (formerly P.S. 58) costs to the participant continue under this alternative).

Question – What types of employers should consider using fully insured plans?

Answer – Fully insured plans might be considered if contributions to an employer's existing, conventionally funded defined benefit plan have been severely reduced by the restrictions on actuarial assumptions or by the full funding limitation. Also, consider fully insured plans for an employer that wants to maximize its initial rate of contribution to a new defined benefit plan, because of particularly good current financial conditions, or because substantial early funding is preferable for any reason, including maximum current tax sheltering.

One caution: if any of the conditions under Section 412(e)(3) that are listed above is not met for a plan year, the plan ceases to be a fully insured plan and must meet the minimum funding requirements for that year. In particular, a failure to make a regular premium payment will terminate fully insured status. Therefore, a fully insured plan is not appropriate for an employer if there is any doubt about its financial ability to make regular premium payments now and in the foreseeable future. A stable business, rather than a boom and bust enterprise, is the best prospect for fully insured funding.

Question – What are the considerations in determining whether fully insured funding is advisable from an economic, investment point of view?

Answer – Employers are likely to wonder if the accelerated tax deduction permitted under fully insured plans is outweighed by an increased overall cost for the plan over the years in which it is in effect. This is not an easy question to answer. In theory, the excess earnings credited to the employer under the contract could provide as good a return on investment as the employer might obtain in a trusteed plan. However, there is no reliable method to predict future earnings, either under the contract or in a trust. Selling a fully insured plan requires "selling the company" so that the employer has confidence that the rate of return will be reasonable. The guarantee features of the contract must be paid for, which implies a lower rate of return in the contract. However, these features are valuable to the employer, since they reduce the downside risk of large losses. Lower administrative costs for fully insured plans must also be factored into the analysis.

Question – Can a participant in a qualified plan have the plan purchase life insurance on the life of another person—a spouse or a business partner, for example?

Answer – Yes; some of the applications of this technique are (1) the purchase of life insurance on a co-shareholder to help fund a buy-sell agreement; or (2) to provide for a beneficiary and avoid estate taxes on the death of the employee-participant.

These "third-party" insurance techniques are primarily used in qualified profit sharing or stock bonus plans because of the need for an "earmarked" or "directed investment" account, as well as rulings prohibiting pension plans from providing third-party insurance.[26] They are discussed further in Chapter 22 and Chapter 23.

A profit sharing plan can also hold "second-to-die" life insurance on the lives of the participant and his or her spouse. This technique is also discussed in the frequently asked questions in Chapter 22.

Question – Can a qualified plan trustee borrow against the cash value of life insurance policies held in the plan?

Answer – Yes, but borrowing by the plan creates "unrelated business taxable income" from any reinvestment of the loan proceeds. For example, if the loan proceeds are reinvested in certificates of deposit, the plan must pay tax on interest income from those certificates.[27]

CHAPTER ENDNOTES

1. Rev. Rul. 2004-21, 2004-10 IRB 544.
2. See e.g., Rev. Rul. 68-453, 1968-2 CB 163; Rev. Rul. 74-307, 1974-2 CB 126.
3. Rev. Rul. 2004-20, 2004-10 IRB 546.
4. Note that the Pension Protection Act of 2006 moved I.R.C. §412(i), unchanged, to Section 412(e)(3) for plan years beginning after 2007.
5. Treas. Reg. §§1.412(i)-1(b), 1.412(i)-1(c).
6. Treas. Reg. §1.412(i)-1(b)(2)(ii).
7. See Rev. Rul. 2004-20, 2004-10 IRB 546. Certain plans holding excessive amounts of life insurance will be classified as "listed transactions."
8. See Rev. Rul. 2004-21, 2004-10 IRB 559.
9. Treas. Reg. §1.401(a)(4)-3(b).
10. Labor Reg. §2520.104-44; Instructions for Schedule B (Form 5500).
11. I.R.C. §412(c)(10).
12. See Rev. Rul. 81-196, 1981-2 CB 107, which allowed an existing split-funded plan to be converted into a fully insured plan. See also Rev. Rul. 94-75, 1994-2 CB 59, imposing certain requirements for uninsured plans that are converted to Section 412(e)(3) plans. The most significant new requirement in this ruling was that the plan must continue to accrue benefits after conversion. Existing plan liabilities must be fully funded in order to make the conversion.
13. ERISA §404(c).
14. See e.g., Rev. Rul. 61-164, 1961-2 CB 99; Rev. Rul. 66-143, 1966-1 CB 79. See also Rev. Rul. 94-76, 1994-2 CB 46 (funds rolled over to profit sharing plan from money purchase plan).
15. PTE 77-7, 42 Fed. Reg. 31575 (June 21, 1977).
16. The original "package" of rulings and regulations was released as IR 2004-21, containing REG-126967-03 (Prop. Treas. Reg. §§1.79-1, 1.83-1, 1-402(a)-1, 69 Fed. Reg. 7384 (February 17, 2004); Rev. Proc. 2004-16, 2004-10 IRB 559; Rev. Rul. 2004-20, 2004-10 IRB 546; and Rev. Rul. 2004-21, 2004-10 IRB 544. The regulations were finalized in 2005.
17. Treas. Reg. §1.402(a)-1(a)(1)(iii).
18. This rule eliminates the implications to the contrary in the old Preamble to PTE 77-8 (the predecessor of PTE 92-6). This change presumably will require a revision of PTE 92-6, which will require joint action by the Department of Labor and the Treasury. One impact of this change is that some of these deemed plan distributions can disqualify the plan, if the pension law or the plan itself does not permit the distribution—for example an in-service distribution from a pension plan is generally impermissible.
19. Rev. Proc. 2005-25, 2005-17 IRB 962, superseding Rev. Proc. 2004-16.
20. Notice 2002-8, 2002-1 CB 398.
21. I.R.C. §72(m)(3); Treas. Reg. §1.72-16(b).
22. Treas. Reg. §1.72-16(c)(4).
23. *Ibid.*; see also Priv. Ltr. Rul. 8539066.
24. I.R.C. §72(m)(3); Treas. Reg. §1.72-16(c).
25. "Springing" cash values—cash values that increase greatly after the policy has been distributed—are subject to IRS scrutiny. Announcement 92-182, Audit Guidelines. Springing cash value contracts were a factor in the development of the valuation guidelines issued with the 2004 package described above.
26. Rev. Rul. 69-523, 1969-2 CB 90.
27. TAM 8445006, citing *Dean v. Simpson*, 35 TC 1038 (1961).

SECTION 401(K) PLAN

CHAPTER 19

INTRODUCTION

A Section 401(k) plan (also known as a "cash or deferred arrangement" or CODA) is a qualified profit sharing or stock bonus plan under which plan participants have an option to put money in the plan or receive the same amount as taxable cash compensation. Contributions are permitted of up to $18,000 annually for years beginning in 2015 plus "catch-up contributions" (see below).[1] Amounts contributed to the plan under these options are not taxable to the participants until withdrawn. Aside from features related to the cash or deferred option, a traditional Section 401(k) plan is much like a regular qualified profit sharing plan described in Chapter 22. SIMPLE 401(k) plans and safe harbor 401(k) plans (see the Frequently Asked Questions at the end of this chapter) vary from the traditional arrangements in that each has a funding requirement; however, such plans are exempt from the special ADP nondiscrimination testing that applies to traditional 401(k) plans.

WHEN IS USE OF SUCH A DEVICE INDICATED?

1. When an employer wants to provide a qualified retirement plan for employees but can afford only minimal extra expense beyond existing salary and benefit costs. Traditional 401(k) plans can be funded entirely from employee salary reductions, except for installation and administration costs. In most plans, however, additional direct employer contributions to the plan will enhance its effectiveness. The plan can be adopted for even a single owner-employee (see the Frequently Asked Questions section at the end of this chapter).

2. When an employer is willing to meet a minimal funding requirement for nonhighly compensated employees and wants to maximize the contributions available to highly compensated employees without annual ADP testing. A SIMPLE 401(k) plan or a safe harbor plan (see the Frequently Asked Questions at the end of this chapter) can offer many of the advantages of a traditional plan, without the nondiscrimination testing.

3. When the employee group has one or more of the following characteristics:

   - Many would like some choice as to the level of savings—that is, a choice between various levels of current cash compensation and tax deferred savings. A younger, more mobile work force often prefers this option.

   - Many employees are relatively young and have substantial time to accumulate retirement savings.

   - Many employees are willing to accept a degree of investment risk in their plan accounts in return for the potential benefits of good investment results.

4. When an employer wants an attractive, "savings-type" supplement to its existing defined benefit or other qualified retirement plan. Such a supplement can make the employer's retirement benefit program attractive to both younger and older employees by providing both security of retirement benefits and the opportunity to increase savings and investment on a tax deferred basis.

5. When the organization is a private taxpaying or tax-exempt organization. Governmental employers may not adopt Section 401(k) plans.

Advantages

1. As with all qualified plans, a Section 401(k) plan provides a tax-deferred retirement savings medium for employees. Employers can also offer a Roth 401(k) feature, which allows after-tax contributions, with tax-free distributions if certain requirements are met (see the Frequently Asked Questions section at the end of this chapter).

2. A Section 401(k) plan allows employees a degree of choice in the amount they wish to save under the plan. The amounts—both as dollar amounts and as percentages of payroll—that can be contributed to 401(k) plans by employees and employers are scheduled for substantial increases (see the Design Features section further in this chapter).

3. The employer's deduction for plan contributions is 25 percent of the total payroll of employees covered under the plan. Furthermore, "total payroll" for purposes of the 25 percent limit includes elective deferral amounts. However, the limit itself does not apply to elective deferral amounts. In other words, an employer may contribute and deduct up to 25 percent in addition to elective deferrals.[2] A higher deduction limit applies to SIMPLE 401(k) plans.

4. Traditional Section 401(k) plans can be funded entirely through salary reductions by employees. As a result, an employer can adopt the plan with no additional cost for employee compensation; the only extra cost is plan installation and administration. The plan may actually result in some savings as a result of lower state or local (but not federal) payroll taxes.

5. In-service withdrawals by employees for certain "hardships" may be permitted; these are not available in qualified pension plans.

Disadvantages

1. As with all defined contribution plans (except target plans), account balances at retirement age may not provide adequate retirement savings for employees who entered the plan at later ages.

2. The annual employee salary reduction under the plan is limited to $18,000 in 2015. (However, employees over age fifty as of the end of the plan year may supplement this amount with "catch-up" contributions of up to $6,000 in 2015, as explained below.) In addition, employers may make matching or nonelective contributions to provide additional tax-deferred savings. For details and scheduled increases of these limits, see "Design Features," below.

3. Because of the "actual deferral percentage" (ADP) nondiscrimination test described below, a Section 401(k) plan can be relatively costly and complex to administer. Safe harbor 401(k) plans and SIMPLE 401(k) plans are not subject to this test; however, both require that certain funding requirements be met. (See the Frequently Asked Questions section at the end of this chapter for the requirements of each of these plans.)

4. Employees bear investment risk under the plan, both before and after retirement. (However, they can also potentially benefit from good investment results.)

DESIGN FEATURES

Salary Reductions

Section 401(k) plans are generally built around salary reduction contributions elected by employees. Automatic enrollment (formerly called "negative election") provisions are also permitted; these are plan provisions whereby the employer contributes a specified portion of each employee's salary to the 401(k) plan unless the employee specifically requests to receive the amount in cash.[3]

Salary reductions must be elected by employees *before* compensation is earned—that is, before they render the services for which compensation is paid. Salary reductions elected after compensation is earned are ineffective as a result of the tax doctrine of "constructive receipt."

The usual practice is to provide plan participants with a salary reduction election form that they must complete before the end of each calendar year. The election specifies how much will be contributed to the plan from each paycheck received for the forthcoming year. Usually the plan will permit the employee to reduce or entirely withdraw the election for pay not yet earned, if circumstances dictate. The plan must restrict each participant's salary reductions to no more than the annual limits set forth in the Code (see below).

The participant is always 100 percent vested in any salary reductions contributed to the plan and any plan earnings on those salary reductions. Even if a participant leaves employment after a short time, his portion of his plan account attributable to salary reductions cannot be forfeited. Usually plan account balances are distributed in a lump sum when a participant terminates employment.

Salary reductions, as well as any other plan contribution which the employee has the option to receive in cash (referred to as "elective deferrals"), are subject to an annual limit. The limit is a "per employee" rather than a "per plan" limit, and one limit applies to both pre-tax elective contributions and Roth contributions. The employee must add together each year all of his or her elective deferrals from:

- Section 401(k) plans;
- salary reduction SEPs (available if established before 1997-see Chapter 31);
- SIMPLE IRAs (see Chapter 30); and
- Section 403(b) tax deferred annuity plans (see Chapter 32).

The total must not exceed the following limits $18,000 for 2015.[4]

In addition to the foregoing salary reductions, employees over fifty (or who will reach age fifty during the plan year) can make "catch-up" contributions. For traditional and safe harbor 401 (k) plans (but not SIMPLE 401(k) plans), the elective deferral limit is increased by $6,000 in 2015.[5]

SIMPLE 401(k) plans are subject to a lower annual elective deferral limit; the limit is $12,500 for 2015.[6] The corresponding fifty-or-over catch-up limit for SIMPLE 401(k) plans is $3,000 for 2015.[7]

Finally, a plan may permit employees to make voluntary contributions to a "deemed IRA" established under the plan. Amounts so contributed reduce the limit for other traditional or Roth IRA contributions. See Chapter 20 for details. Contributions under this provision may also (as with elective deferrals and with other IRA contributions) count toward the nonrefundable "saver's credit" for lower-income taxpayers, explained in the Frequently Asked Questions below.

Employer Contributions

Many Section 401(k) plans provide matching or nonelective employer contributions in order to encourage employee participation and make the plan more valuable to employees. In fact, in the case of safe harbor 401(k) plans and SIMPLE 401(k) plans, the Code requires that the terms of the plan provide for certain matching or nonelective contributions. (See the Frequently Asked Questions section for details.) Section 401(k) plans typically use one or more of the following types of employer contributions:

- *Formula matching contributions.* The employer matches employee salary reductions, either dollar for dollar or under another formula. For example, the plan might provide that the employer contributes an amount equal to 50 percent of the amount the employee elects as a salary reduction. So, if an employee elected a salary reduction of $6,000, the employer would put an additional $3,000 into the employee's plan account.
- *Discretionary matching contributions.* Under this approach, the employer has discretion to make a contribution to the plan each year; the employer contribution is allocated to each participant's plan account in proportion to the amount elected by the participant as a salary reduction during that year. For example, at the end of a year the employer might decide to make a discretionary matching contribution of 40 percent of each participant's salary reduction for the year. Thus, if a participant had salary reductions of $5,000 for that year, the employer would contribute another $2,000 to that participant's account.
- *Pure discretionary or "profit sharing" contributions.* The employer makes a discretionary nonelective contribution to the plan that is allocated simply on the basis of each employee's compensation, without regard to the amount of salary reductions elected by that employee. For example, at the end of a year the employer might decide to contribute another $100,000 to the plan. This contribution would be allocated to plan participants' accounts in the same manner as a discretionary profit sharing contribution, as described in Chapter 22.

- *Formula contributions*. For example, the plan might provide that the employer will contribute 3 percent of compensation to the plan for employees whose annual compensation is less than $50,000. So, for an employee who earned $30,000, the employer would contribute 3 percent, or $900, to that employee's plan account.

Chapter 24, Savings/Match Plan, covers design and advantages of employer matching arrangements as well as the use of certain employee after-tax contributions. Matching contributions may be subject to a test for nondiscrimination under Code Section 401(m). This actual contribution percentage (ACP) test is explained in Chapter 24.

Plan Distributions

Distributions from Section 401(k) plans are subject to the qualified plan distribution rules detailed in Chapter 14. Most plans provide for distributions in a lump sum at termination of employment, which typically are rolled over to IRAs.

Section 401(k) plans can allow participants to make in-service withdrawals (withdrawals before termination of employment); however, there are a variety of restrictions that reduce the availability of such distributions to employees. These restrictions apply whether the plan is a traditional, safe harbor, or SIMPLE 401(k) plan.

First, there is a special rule that Section 401(k) account funds attributable to elective deferrals cannot be distributed prior to occurrence of one of the following:

- retirement
- death
- disability
- severance from employment with the employer
- attainment of age 59½ by the participant
- plan termination (if the employer has no other defined contribution plan other than an ESOP)
- hardship.[8]

"Hardship" is defined more restrictively than many participants may think, as discussed below.

Note also that many pre-retirement distributions will not only be taxable, but will also be subject to the 10 percent early withdrawal penalty tax discussed in Chapter 14. To summarize, a 10 percent penalty tax applies to the taxable amount (amount subject to regular income tax) of any qualified plan distribution; except for distributions:

- after age 59½
- on the employee's death
- upon the employee's disability
- that are part of a series of substantially equal periodic payments following separation from service
- that are paid after separation from service after attaining age fifty-five, or
- that do not exceed the amount of medical expenses deductible as an itemized deduction for the year.[9]

In addition, corrective distributions generally will not trigger the penalty. From this list, it is evident that many "hardship" distributions from a Section 401(k) plan, though permitted by the terms of the plan, will be subject to the 10 percent penalty tax.

Many Section 401(k) plans have provisions for plan loans to participants. A plan loan provision may be extremely valuable to employees because it allows them access to their plan funds without the "hardship" restriction or the 10 percent penalty tax. Plan loans are discussed in detail in Chapter 14.

Hardship Withdrawals

Regulations require that a hardship distribution meet two conditions: (a) the distribution must be necessary in light of immediate and heavy financial needs of the employee, and (b) funds must not be reasonably available from other resources of the employee.

As guidance in interpreting the first requirement, the regulations[10] list the following as meeting the "immediate and heavy" requirement:

- Medical expenses incurred by the participant or the participant's spouse or dependents ("dependent" may include a noncustodial child under certain circumstances, and the medical expense amount is determined without regard to the 7.5 percent floor on itemized deductions).

- Purchase of a principal residence for the participant (mortgage payments do not typically constitute a hardship).
- Payment of tuition, educational fees, and room and board for the next twelve months of post-secondary education for a participant or his spouse, children, or dependents.
- Payments of amounts necessary to prevent the eviction of the participant from his principal residence or from foreclosure on the mortgage.
- Funeral expenses for certain family members.[11]
- Expenses to repair casualty damages to the employee's principal residence.[12]

The second issue—the existence of other resources—is determined on the basis of individual facts and circumstances. To simplify plan administration, there is a "safe harbor" test for this—the requirement will be deemed met if the following circumstances exist:

1. the distribution does not exceed the amount of the immediate and heavy financial need,
2. the employee has obtained all distributions other than hardship distributions and all non-taxable loans available under all plans maintained by the employer, and
3. the plan provides that the employee's elective deferral contributions and nondeductible contributions will be suspended for twelve months after the distribution and that the maximum contribution in the year following the suspension will be reduced by the amount contributed in the prior year.

HOW IT IS DONE

Installation of a Section 401(k) plan follows the qualified plan installation procedures described in Chapter 15.

In addition, elective deferral or salary reduction forms must be completed by plan participants *before* the plan's effective date so that salary reduction elections will be immediately effective. The plan may provide for automatic enrollment, under which a fixed percentage of each employee's salary is contributed unless he elects *not* to participate, so long as each eligible employee is afforded the opportunity to receive the amount as cash or as a contribution.[13]

The success of a traditional Section 401(k) plan in meeting the employer's objectives and passing the ADP test depends on effective communication with employees. Effective employer-employee communication is always important in employee benefit plans, but it is particularly essential for a traditional 401(k) plan because of the active role of employees in the plan.

In those situations where the deferral rates by nonhighly compensated employees severely limit the ability of highly compensated employees to benefit from a traditional 401(k) plan, employers willing to meet certain funding requirements can remove the plan from ADP testing by adopting a safe harbor plan or a SIMPLE 401(k) plan (described below). In both cases, the benefits available to highly compensated employees are unaffected by the participation levels of nonhighly compensated employees.

Investments

Generally, investments traditionally used in qualified profit sharing plans are also used in Section 401(k) plans (see Chapter 15 for details). Employee accounts in the plan fund are usually pooled for investment purposes. Investments tend toward bonds, money market, and liquid, cash-type media. Smaller plans often use a "family" of mutual funds for plan investments. The level of equity investment (common stocks) in Section 401(k) plans is usually lower than in defined benefit plans.

Most plans use a "directed investment" or "earmarking" provision that allows participants some degree of choice in the investment of their plan accounts. Directed investment provisions increase administrative costs of the plan. But they are attractive to employees and, if the directed investment provision meets certain standards set forth in Labor regulations,[14] the employer is relieved of fiduciary responsibility for unsatisfactory results from any investment directed by the participant.

Life insurance is sometimes provided in Section 401(k) plans in much the same way as it is used in a regular profit sharing plan. The use of life insurance in a qualified plan is discussed in Chapter 18.

VARIATIONS OF 401(K) PLANS

In addition to the traditional Section 40(k) plan, there are variations that permit Roth contributions, a SIMPLE set up for small employers, and salary deferral plan that allows a combination of defined benefit and defined contribution plans. Additionally, employers who are worried about nondiscrimination requirements can opt for a "safe harbor" plan which guarantees compliance.

Roth 401(k) Plan

A Roth 401(k) feature is a provision that permits 401(k) plans (as well as 403(b) plans), to offer a "qualified Roth contribution program," which is basically a Roth account for elective deferrals.

Essentially, participants of plans establishing such a program will be able to designate all, or a portion, of their elective deferrals as Roth contributions. The Roth contributions will be included in the participant's gross income in the year made, and then be held in a separate account with separate record keeping. Earnings allocable to the Roth contributions will remain in the separate account.

A "qualified distribution" from a Roth account will not be includable in the participant's gross income, and rollovers will be available only to another Roth account or Roth IRA. The requirements for a "qualified distribution" are nearly identical to those for a Roth IRA (see Chapter 21), except that no exception is permitted for first-time home purchases. In other words, a qualified distribution is any distribution made after the five-year "nonexclusion period" and after the participant has (a) reached age 59½, (b) died or (c) become disabled. (Distributions of excess deferrals are not included in this definition.)

The nonexclusion period is the five-taxable-year period beginning with the earlier of (1) the first year a contribution is made to the Roth account, or (2) if a rollover has been made to the Roth account from another Roth account under another employer plan, the first year a contribution was made to the earlier Roth account.

Aside from being currently included in gross income, amounts designated as Roth contributions under this provision will be treated in all other respects as elective deferrals. They will, together with other elective deferrals, be subject to the otherwise-applicable elective deferral limit (see "Design Features," above); thus, a single total limit will continue to apply to all elective deferrals.[15]

SIMPLE 401(k) Plan

The principal SIMPLE 401(k) plan requirements are:[16]

1. The employer must have one hundred or fewer employees (only employees with at least $5,000 in compensation for the preceding year are counted) on any day in the year.

2. Employees who earned at least $5,000 from the employer in any two preceding years, and are reasonably expected to earn at least $5,000 in the current year, can make salary reduction contributions of up to $12,500 (in 2015, as indexed) annually (the catch-up contribution limit is $3,000 for 2015).

3. The employer is required to make a contribution to the employee's 401(k) account an amount equal to either:

   a. a dollar for dollar matching contribution up to 3 percent of the employee's compensation; or

   b. a nonelective contribution of 2 percent of compensation for all eligible employees earning at least $5,000 (whether or not they elect salary reductions).[17]

4. Employees must be 100 percent vested in all contributions (whether they are salary deferral, matching, or nonelective contributions) at all times.[18] No deferred vesting schedules are available.

5. The limitations on distributions that apply to traditional 401(k) plans apply to SIMPLE 401(k) plans.

A SIMPLE 401(k) plan is deemed to meet the nondiscrimination requirement of Section 401(a)(4) (thus, it is not subject to ADP testing), and it is exempt from the top-heavy rules. However, it is otherwise subject to the reporting, disclosure, fiduciary responsibility, and other requirements for traditional 401(k) plans (e.g., the Section 415 limits, the compensation limit, and the prohibition on state and local governments operating a 401(k) plan).

DB/K Plan

Code Section 414(x) permits a simplified combination defined benefit and 401(k) plan for small employers (between two and five hundred employees). Congress apparently intends this as modest remedy for the decline of defined benefit plans. The two plans would be combined for documentation, administration, and ERISA reporting purposes, but participant's benefits would have to be accounted for separately.

The plans must meet minimum requirements. The defined benefit plan must provide a minimum benefit of final average pay multiplied by the lesser of (1) 1 percent multiplied by years of service or (2) 20 percent. Alternatively, a cash balance formula may be used if it meets minimum pay credit requirements.[19] The defined contribution plan must be a 401(k)-type arrangement with a mandatory employer match of 50 percent, up to 4 percent of compensation. There are also minimum vesting and other requirements. The ADP and 401(m) nondiscrimination tests would be deemed met if the plan complies with 414(x).

These plans may become useful if the administrative burden turns out to be low. In addition, it is possible that they may be attractive to closely held businesses because in some cases they could favor key employees.

Safe Harbor Plan

A safe harbor plan satisfies the ADP test under an alternative safe harbor provided the employer meets a notice requirement and satisfies one of the following contribution requirements:

1. the employer makes a matching contribution of 100 percent of the employee contribution up to 3 percent of compensation, plus 50 percent of deferrals from 3 to 5 percent; or

2. the employer makes a nonelective (nonmatching) contribution for all eligible nonhighly compensated employees equal to at least 3 percent of compensation.[20]

The vesting requirements and withdrawal restrictions that apply to employer contributions in a traditional 401(k) plan are met with respect to all employer contributions (including matching contributions) required under the safe harbor provisions.[21]

The rate of matching contributions for highly compensated employees may not at any time exceed the rate of matching contributions for nonhighly compensated employees.

An alternative matching plan design that produces the same result as the contributions described above may, nevertheless, meet the safe harbor requirements if:[22]

1. the rate of the employer's contribution does not increase as an employee's rate of contribution increases; and

2. the aggregate amount of matching contributions under the alternative formula is at least equal to the aggregate amount of matching contributions that would be made if matching contributions were made on the basis of the percentages described above.

Safe harbor plans are subject to the same elective deferral limits (see "Design Features" above) as traditional 401(k) plans. A safe harbor plan is deemed to meet the nondiscrimination requirement of Section 401(a)(4) (thus, it is not subject to ADP testing), and it is generally exempt from the top-heavy rules.[23] However, it is otherwise subject to the reporting, disclosure, fiduciary responsibility, and other requirements for traditional 401(k) plans (e.g., the Section 415 limits, the compensation limit, and the prohibition on state and local governments operating a 401(k) plan).

TAX IMPLICATIONS

For Employees

Employee elective deferrals (i.e., salary reductions) up to the annual limit ($18,000 in 2015, plus any permitted catch-up contributions) are not subject to income tax to the employee in the year of deferral.[24] However, elective deferrals are subject to Social Security tax (both employer and employee).[25] In other words, even though salary has been deferred for income tax purposes, it is treated as received for Social Security purposes.

Whether the 401(k) plan is a traditional, SIMPLE or safe harbor plan, it is subject to the limits of Code section 415. This means that annual additions to each participant's account are limited to the *lesser of* (a) 100 percent of compensation or (b) $53,000 (in 2015, as indexed).[26] Annual additions include the total of:

- nonelective employer contributions to the participant's account;
- salary reductions or other elective deferrals contributed to the account:
- forfeitures from other participants' accounts; and
- after-tax employee contributions to the account.[27]

Distributions from the plan to employees are subject to income tax when received. Lump sum distributions may be eligible for the special ten-year averaging (for certain employees born before 1936) tax computation available for qualified plans. Not all distributions are eligible for this calculation. Details on the taxation of distributions are discussed in Chapter 14.

Saver's Credit

A limited nonrefundable tax credit, known as the "saver's credit," is available to certain lower income taxpayers who make salary deferrals. Certain lower-income taxpayers may claim a temporary, nonrefundable credit for "qualified retirement savings contributions."[28] "Qualified retirement savings contributions" include elective deferrals to SIMPLE IRAs, as well as other elective deferrals and contributions to Roth or traditional IRAs. (However, the total is reduced by certain distributions received by the taxpayer or his spouse during the prior two taxable years and the current taxable year for which the credit is claimed, including the period up to the due date (plus extensions) for filing the federal income tax return for the current taxable year.) Only the first $2,000 of annual deferrals is eligible for the credit.

The credit is allowed against the sum of the regular tax and the alternative minimum tax (minus certain other credits) and is allowed in addition to any other deduction or exclusion that would otherwise apply. In addition, to be eligible, the taxpayer must be at least eighteen years old by the end of the tax year and must not be claimed as a dependent by someone else or be a full-time student.

The amount of the credit is limited to an "applicable percentage" of IRA contributions and elective deferrals up to $2,000. The "applicable percentages" for 2015 are as follows:

Saver's Credit

Amount of Credit	Joint	Head of Household	Single/ Others
50% of your contribution	AGI not more than $36,500	AGI not more than $27,375	AGI not more than $18,250
20% of your contribution	$36,501 – $39,500	$27,376 – $29,625	$18,251 – $19,750
10% of your contribution	$39,501 – $61,000	$29,626 – $45,750	$19,751 – $30,500
0% of your contribution	more than $61,000	more than $45,750	more than $30,500

For Employers

The sum of all types of employer contributions to a traditional or safe harbor 401(k) plan are deductible by the employer for federal income tax purposes up to a limit of 25 percent of the total payroll of all employees covered under the plan. The employer deduction limit for SIMPLE 401(k) plan contributions is the greater of 25 percent of payroll or the amount of contributions required under the Code for such plans.[29]

Employee elective deferrals (salary reductions) do not have to be counted toward the 25 percent limit for any type of 401(k) plan. In other words, the employer may deduct as much as 25 percent, in addition to the employees' elective deferral amounts.[30]

Example. Anxious Corp. has a traditional 401(k) plan, and its current annual payroll for employees covered under the plan is $400,000. In addition, employee elective deferrals in the current year total $60,000. For the current year, Anxious Corp. can deduct up to a total of $160,000 for the 401(k) plan ([25 percent of $400,000] plus $60,000). Furthermore, the $60,000 of elective deferrals can, but does not have to be, counted as part of this $160,000. (The $60,000 representing elective deferrals is subject to Social Security tax and FUTA—see below).

Elective deferrals are subject to Social Security (FICA) and federal unemployment (FUTA) payroll taxes. Nonelective employer contributions are not. The impact of state payroll taxes depends on the particular state's law. Both elective deferrals and nonelective employer contributions may be exempt from state payroll taxes in some states.

Certain employers adopting a new plan may be eligible for a business tax credit of up to $500 for "qualified startup costs." See Chapter 15 for details.

Nondiscrimination Testing

Elective deferrals in a traditional 401(k) plan must meet a special test for nondiscrimination—the "actual deferral percentage" or ADP test. (No ADP testing is necessary in the case of a SIMPLE 401(k) plan or a safe harbor plan; see the frequently asked questions at the end of this chapter for details.) To meet this requirement, the plan must satisfy, in actual operation, one of two alternative ADP tests as follows:[31]

> *Test 1* – The ADP for eligible highly compensated employees for the plan year is not more than the ADP of all other eligible employees *for the preceding plan year* multiplied by 1.25.
>
> *Test 2* – The ADP for eligible highly compensated employees for the plan year does not exceed the ADP for other eligible employees *for the preceding plan year* by more than 2 percent *and* the ADP for eligible highly compensated employees for the plan year is not more than the ADP of all other eligible employees *for the preceding plan* year multiplied by two.

This ADP testing method is referred to as "prior year testing." As an alternative, the ADP for nonhighly compensated employees for the *current plan year* may be used under either test, but certain restrictions apply to a plan that uses current year testing and later wishes to change to prior year testing. No special restrictions apply to employers wishing to change from prior year testing back to current year testing.[32]

Example. If the ADP for nonhighly compensated employees in 2015 was 3 percent, the ADP for highly compensated employees in 2015 could be as high as 5 percent (3 percent plus 2 percent), using prior year testing. This meets the second test. The plan document must state whether the plan uses current year testing or prior year testing.

"Highly compensated employee" is defined (for this and all qualified plan purposes; see Chapter 13) as an employee who:[33]

- was during the current or preceding plan year, a more than 5 percent owner of the employer, or
- received compensation *for the preceding year* from the employer over $120,000 (in 2015 as indexed) *and* (if the employer elects the use of a "top-paid group" provision) was in the "top-paid group" for the preceding year.

WHERE CAN I FIND OUT MORE?

1. Graduate Course: Qualified Retirement Plans (GS 814), The American College, Bryn Mawr, PA.
2. IRS Publication 560, Retirement Plans for Small Business. This publication is available free from the IRS and is revised annually.
3. *Tax Facts on Insurance & Employee Benefits*, The National Underwriter Company, (updated annually).

FREQUENTLY ASKED QUESTIONS

Question – What kinds of organizations can adopt Section 401(k) plans?

Answer – In general, any private for-profit business can adopt a Section 401(k) plan (whether traditional, SIMPLE, or safe harbor) for its employees; however, the availability of SIMPLE 401(k) plans is limited to employers with 100 or fewer employees.[34] The plan of an unincorporated business can cover partners or a sole proprietor as well as regular employees.

Private (nongovernmental) nonprofit organizations may also adopt 401(k) plans. Certain types of private nonprofits—specifically 501(c)(3) organizations—also have the option of adopting a Section 403(b) tax deferred annuity plan.

Governmental (federal, state, or local) organizations are generally not eligible to maintain a Section 401(k) plan.[35] Both nonprofit and governmental organizations can adopt Section 457 plans (see Chapter 34), which provide some features similar to a Section 401(k) plan.

Question – Can a one-person business (proprietorship or corporation) adopt an individual 401(k) plan for the owner?

Answer – It has always been technically possible for a proprietor or sole shareholder with no employees to adopt a 401(k) plan, but until EGTRRA 2001 changes in the law, there were better alternatives, such as a SEP or SIMPLE IRA.

In 2001, the 401(k) salary reduction limit was increased to its current level, as indexed. In addition, the Section 415 limit (the lesser of 100 percent of compensation or earned income or $53,000 (in 2015)) was also increased. The deduction limit for the business is 25 percent of compensation, but elective deferrals do not count toward the 25 percent limit.

As a result of these changes, a sole owner/plan participant can in 2015 elect a salary reduction of up to $18,000 (plus the fifty-or-over catch-up of $6,000). The company can then contribute an additional amount up to the deductible limit of 25 percent of compensation (but not more than $53,000).

Question – Can a Section 401(k) plan participant make deductible contributions to a traditional IRA as well as salary reductions under a Section 401(k) plan?

Answer – Yes, but only within the reduced deductible IRA limits allowed for active qualified plan participants—see Chapter 20.

Question – How can an employer increase employee participation in its 401(k) plan?

Answer – Employers have an interest in increasing employee participation, both to help meet the ADP tests that permit full deferrals by highly compensated employees, and also to help employees with retirement savings, an area where many employees need a great deal of help, particularly since 401(k) plans are becoming the dominant form of employee pension benefit plan. Some of the tools available to plan designers to increase participation include:

- Matching contributions by employers.
- Safe-harbor or SIMPLE 401(k) plan designs, discussed in the next two questions.
- Employee investment direction provisions. These are popular with employees because they give employees a sense of ownership and control with regard to their accounts. However, studies show that most employees make poor investment choices, so employees need guidance in using investment direction. The new prohibited transaction exemption for investment advice to plan participants (See Chapter 13) may be helpful in making investment direction work for both employer and employee.
- Qualified Automatic Enrollment Arrangement (QACA) (Code Section 410(k)(13). Facilitates automatic enrollment in a 401(k) plan for new employees, subject to a right by the employee to opt out. This provision eliminates many employer concerns by providing that the ADP and 401(m) provisions and the top-heavy provisions are met by a QACA. A QACA must meet specified requirements for automatic deferral, matching or non-elective contributions, vesting, and notice.

Question – Is it better for a 401(k) plan participant to contribute to the 401(k) plan or to use the same amount to pay off a home mortgage?

Answer – With the widespread availability of 401(k) plans, many people must routinely make investment decisions that once only relatively affluent people were faced with. One involves the advisability of paying off existing debt as an alternative to investment. This can be a complex issue. In the case of mortgage interest, if the taxpayer does not itemize deductions, or if the expected return from the 401(k) plan is significantly less than the mortgage interest rate, a mortgage paydown may be better than increasing the 401(k) contribution in some circumstances.[36]

Question – How can an employer provide retirement benefits to replace 401(k) benefits lost by an executive as a result of the $265,000 (in 2015, as indexed) compensation "cap?"

Answer – In applying the ADP test, described under "Tax Implications" above, under Code section 401(a)(17) only the first $265,000 (in 2015) of each participant's salary can be taken into account. This has the effect of imputing a higher ADP percentage for executives than is actually the case. For example, if an executive earns $300,000 and defers $6,000 under the 401(k) plan, although this represents a 2 percent (6,000/300,000) deferral, for ADP purposes in 2015 it would be treated as a 2.26 percent (6,000/265,000) deferral. If this results in excess deferrals under the ADP test, generally the excess deferrals must be returned to highly compensated employees.

Executives in this situation might like a plan under which excess deferrals "pour over" into a nonqualified deferred compensation plan. IRS rulings originally were unfavorable to this approach, on the ground that the election to defer compensation was made too late (i.e., after compensation was earned), but more recent rulings have allowed this approach.[37] Here is an example of how IRS rulings suggest it could be done:

- Executive Nat enters into a salary reduction agreement no later than December 31, 2014 providing for a salary reduction of, say, $20,000 for 2015 to be credited to Nat's account in the Company's nonqualified deferred compensation (NQDC) plan. At this time, Nat also can elect to make an irrevocable "pourover 401(k) election" for 2015 (see below). The company can also agree to provide matching contributions.

- At the end of 2015, and not later than January 31, 2016, the plan administrator performs the ADP test and calculates Nat's elective deferral limit at $8,000.

- Pursuant to the 401(k) plan and the NQDC plan, this $8,000 (more specifically, the lesser of $8,000 or the total 2015 salary reduction, $20,000 in this case) will be paid in cash to Nat not later than March 15, 2016 (and be taxable for 2016) unless Nat has made the pourover 401(k) election for 2015. If Nat has done so, the $8,000 will be contributed directly by the employer to the 401(k) plan. No earnings on amounts held in the NQDC plan will be contributed to the 401(k) plan (relevant only where the "lesser salary reduction" rule applies). [Apparently the principal balance of Nat's account in the NQDC plan will be reduced accordingly, providing for a net 2015 deferral of $8,000 in the 401(k) plan and $12,000 in the NQDC.]

- Any employer matching contributions for Nat required under the 401(k) plan will be taken from employer matching contributions already made under the NQDC plan, and NQDC employer matches will be reduced accordingly.

CHAPTER ENDNOTES

1. I.R.C. §§402(g)(1)(B), 414(v)(2)(B).
2. I.R.C. §§404(a)(3)(A), 404(n). For further explanation of these changes, see Chapter 30, at "Deduction Limits."
3. Rev. Rul. 2000-35, 2000-2 CB 138.
4. I.R.C. §402(g). Note that deferrals from a 457 plan need not be aggregated (see Ch. 34).
5. I.R.C. §414(v)(2)(B)(i). Note that the limit will be lower if the amount of a participant's compensation, (after reduction for other elective deferrals) is less than the catch-up amounts.
6. I.R.C. §§401(k)(11), 408(p)(2)(A)(ii).
7. I.R.C. §414(v)(2)(B)(ii). Note that the limit will be lower if the amount of a participant's compensation, (after reduction for other elective deferrals) is less than the catch-up amounts.
8. I.R.C. §401(k)(2)(B).
9. I.R.C. §72(t).
10. See Treas. Regs. §§1.401(k)-1 through 1.401(k)-4; TD 9169, 69 Fed. Reg. 78144 (December 29, 2004).
11. Funeral or burial expenses must be for the employee's deceased parent, spouse, child or dependents (determined under the definition of dependent in effect before 2005). See Treas. Reg. §1.401(k)-1(d)(3)(iii)(B)(5).
12. The expense must be one that would qualify for the casualty deduction; however, for hardship purposes, the expense is determined without regard to whether the loss exceeds 10 percent of adjusted gross income. See Treas. Reg. §1.401(k)-1(d)(3)(iii)(B)(6).
13. See note 3, above.
14. See DOL Reg. §2550.404c-1.
15. I.R.C. §402A.
16. See I.R.C. §401(k)(11).
17. If this election is made, notice must be provided to employees at least sixty days before the beginning of the plan year. See I.R.C. §401(k)(11)(B)(ii).
18. I.R.C. §401(k)(11)(A)(iii).
19. I.R.C. §414(x)(2)(B)(iii).
20. I.R.C. §§401(k)(12)(B)(i), 401(k)(12)(C).
21. I.R.C. §401(k)(12)(e)(i).
22. I.R.C. §401(k)(12)(B)(iii).
23. I.R.C. §416(g)(3)(H).

24. I.R.C. §402(g).
25. I.R.C. §3121(v)(1).
26. I.R.C. §415(c)(3).
27. I.R.C. §415(c)(2).
28. I.R.C. §25B.
29. I.R.C. §404(a)(3).
30. I.R.C. §404(n).
31. I.R.C. §401(k)(3)(A).
32. I.R.C. §401(k)(3)(A), Notice 98-1, 1998-1 CB 327.
33. I.R.C. §414(q).
34. I.R.C. §§401(k)(11)(D)(i), 408(p)(2)(C)(i). Only employees who earned at least $5,000 of compensation from the employer in the preceding year are counted. In the event that an eligible employer who establishes and maintains a SIMPLE 401(k) plan for one or more years subsequently becomes ineligible (i.e., exceeds the 100-employee limit), it will continue to be treated as eligible for the two years following the last year of eligibility. Special rules apply in the event of a merger or acquisition. See I.R.C. §408(p)(2)(C)(i)(II).
35. I.R.C. §401(k)(4)(B). Certain employers' pre-1987 plans were "grandfathered." See TRA '86, §1116(f)(2)(B); TAMRA '88, §1101(k)(8).
36. See Auster and Sennetti, "Should Participants in a 401(k) Contribute to the Plan or Pay Off Their Mortgages?," *Journal of Pension Planning & Compliance*, Spring 1994, for a discussion of the many factors involved in making this decision.
37. See e.g., Priv. Ltr. Ruls. 199924067, 9807010, 9530038.

TRADITIONAL IRA

CHAPTER 20

INTRODUCTION

A traditional IRA (which stands for either individual retirement account or individual retirement annuity) is a type of retirement savings arrangement under which IRA contributions, up to certain limits, and investment earnings are tax-deferred. That is, interest earned and gains received inside the traditional IRA are free of federal income tax until withdrawn from the IRA.

Traditional IRAs are primarily plans of individual savings, rather than employee benefits. However, their features should be understood. They fit into an employee's plan of retirement savings and, therefore, they influence the form of employer retirement plans to some degree.

Employers can sponsor traditional IRAs for employees, as a limited alternative to an employer-sponsored qualified retirement plan. Employers who have a qualified plan can also sponsor a "deemed IRA" as part of the qualified plan to provide an alternative form of retirement savings for employees. Employer-sponsored IRAs and deemed IRAs are discussed later in this chapter. An arrangement similar to the employer-sponsored IRA which allows greater annual employer contributions is the SEP (simplified employee pension) discussed in Chapter 33. SIMPLE IRA plans involve employee salary reduction contributions and employer matching or nonelective contributions that are contributed to an IRA. SIMPLE plans are discussed in Chapter 30.

See also the chapter on the Roth IRA. The Roth IRA provides benefits comparable to those from a traditional IRA. Detailed comparisons between the two are covered in Chapter 21.

WHEN IS USE OF SUCH A DEVICE INDICATED?

1. When there is a need to shelter current compensation or earned income from taxation.

2. When it is desirable to defer taxes on investment income.

3. When long-term accumulation, especially for retirement purposes, is an important objective.

4. When a supplement or alternative to a qualified pension or profit sharing plan is needed.

Advantages

1. Eligible individuals may contribute up to the maximum annual contribution amount (see below) to a traditional IRA (and up to the maximum annual contribution amount for a spouse if a traditional spousal IRA is available) and possibly deduct this amount from their current taxable income.

2. Investment income earned on the assets held in a traditional IRA is not taxed until it is withdrawn from the account. This deferral applies no matter what the nature of the investment income. It may be in the form of interest, dividends, rents, capital gain, or any other form of income. Such income will generally be taxed only when it is withdrawn from the account and received as ordinary income.

Disadvantages

1. The traditional IRA deduction is limited to the maximum contribution amount each year (and up

to the maximum contribution amount for a spouse if a traditional spousal IRA is available), with phaseout of the deduction if modified adjusted gross income exceeds certain limits and the individual or spouse is an active participant in a tax-favored employer retirement plan, as discussed below.

2. Traditional IRA withdrawals are subject to the 10 percent penalty on early withdrawals applicable to all tax-favored retirement plans.

3. Traditional IRAs cannot be established once an individual reaches age 70½ (except in the case of rollover IRAs) and withdrawals from the account are required by April 1 of the year after the year in which the individual reaches age 70½. For additional information on required distributions, see Chapter 14.

TAX IMPLICATIONS

Contribution Rules

1. There is no required minimum contribution to an IRA. An individual can put aside relatively small amounts each year and still see them grow into a considerable sum for retirement. Also, a contribution does not have to be made every year. It is possible to skip a year or any number of years without jeopardizing the tax-deferred status of the account. However, failure to make contributions reduces the value of the account for tax-shelter purposes and limits the amount of earnings that will build up on a tax-free basis.

2. *Deduction Limits*. The maximum annual deductible IRA contribution for an individual is the lesser of (a) the maximum annual contribution amount or (b) the individual's earned income[1] The maximum annual contribution amount is $5,500 in 2015. For individuals who have attained age fifty before the close of the tax year, an additional catchup contribution amount of $1,000 is available.

3. *Earned Income*. The income must be produced from personal services which would include wages, salaries, professional fees, sales commissions, tips, and bonuses. Unearned income such as dividends, interest, or rent cannot be used in determining the amount of the IRA contribution.

4. *Spousal IRAs*. An additional contribution can be made for a spouse in certain cases. The provision works like this:

Example. If individual Pat's spouse Chris is not working or receives lesser includable compensation for the year than Pat, the couple may contribute up to $5,500 in 2015 to an IRA for Chris, for a total contribution for the couple of up to $11,000. More technically, assuming the "active participant" restrictions below do not apply, the maximum allowable deductible contribution for Chris is the lesser of (1) $5,500 or (2) 100 percent of Chris's includable compensation, plus 100 percent of Pat's includable compensation minus the amount of the deduction taken by Pat for IRA contributions for the year. In order to contribute to a traditional spousal IRA, the couple must file a joint return.[2]

If both spouses have earned income, each can have a traditional IRA. The deduction limit for each spouse with earned income is the maximum annual contribution amount or the 100 percent limit. However, traditional IRA contribution limits are combined with Roth IRAs. The maximum annual contribution amount is reduced for each dollar contributed by the same taxpayer to a Roth IRA.

5. Married couples with two incomes should each establish a separate IRA account. Contributions are based on each separate income and each contribution is a separate tax deduction. This is true even though a couple may live in a community property state.

6. *Active Participant Restrictions*. Income limitations are imposed on the deductibility of traditional IRA contributions for those persons who are "active participants" in an employer retirement plan that is tax-favored—including a qualified retirement plan, simplified employee pension (SEP), Section 403(b) tax deferred annuity plan, or SIMPLE IRA.[3]

A person is an active participant in an employer's retirement plan for a given year if the participant actually receives an employer contribution or accrues a benefit under an employer's defined benefit plan for any part of that year. A person is an active participant in a defined contribution-type plan if any contribution or forfeiture is allocated to his account during the year.

For example, in a qualified profit sharing plan it is possible for an employer to omit making a plan contribution in a given year. For such a year, an employee is generally *not* considered an active plan participant even though covered under the plan, so long as there was no contribution made (or forfeiture allocated) to the employee's account under the plan. But in rare cases (e.g., where an employee is covered by a plan but receives no contribution because the employee worked insufficient hours during the plan year), an employee may be an active participant even if the employee receives no contribution.[4]

Note, however, that an employee is considered an active participant if a contribution is made for the employee by the employer but the employee is not vested in the amount in his account. If the employee stays long enough to become vested, the employee will acquire full rights to that amount, so the employee is considered an active participant for the year in which the contribution was made.

If an otherwise eligible person actively participates in the employer plan, the available traditional IRA deduction is reduced below the maximum annual contribution amount if the AGI of the taxpayer is within the phaseout ranges indicated below, with the deduction eliminated entirely if the AGI is above the upper limit of the phaseout range.

IRA Active Participant AGI phaseout ranges for 2015

Single	Married filing jointly	Married filing separately
$61,000–71,000	$98,000–118,000	$0–10,000

If only one spouse is an active participant, the non-active participant spouse filing a joint return may receive a full IRA deduction if joint income is less than $183,000 (2015). The non-participant spouse may receive a partial deduction if joint income is between $183,000 and $193,000 (2015).

The reduction in the maximum annual contribution amount in the phaseout AGI region is proportional to the amount by which the AGI exceeds the lower limit. For example, suppose that in 2015 a single taxpayer's AGI is $62,000 and he is an active participant under age fifty. The taxpayer is $2,000 into the phaseout region of $10,000, so his annual traditional IRA deduction is reduced by $2,000/$10,000 or 20 percent. This is a reduction of $1,000 (20 percent of $5,000), so the maximum IRA deduction is $4,500 ($5,500 less $1,000).

There is a $200 "floor" under the reduction formula. That is, as long as the taxpayer is below the AGI cutoff level, at least $200 can be contributed and deducted. For example, if the taxpayer in the preceding example had an AGI of $69,900, he could contribute and deduct up to $200.

If neither the individual nor the spouse is an active participant in a qualified retirement plan, simplified employee pension (SEP), Section 403(b) annuity plan, or SIMPLE IRA, they may contribute up to the maximum annual contribution deduction limit, as set out above, and deduct the full amount of the contribution regardless of the level of AGI.

Example 1. Minnie (age thirty-five) and Bill (age forty), a married couple, each earn $75,000 annually. Neither is an active participant in any qualified plan, SEP, Section 403(b) plan, or SIMPLE IRA. For 2015, Minnie and Bill can each contribute and deduct up to $5,500 to their own IRA plan (a total of $11,000 for both).

Example 2. Mabel earns $75,000 annually. Her husband, Alf, has no earned income (although he has investment income over $100,000 annually). Neither spouse is over forty-nine or an active participant in a tax-favored plan. For 2015, Mabel can contribute and deduct up to $5,500 to an IRA for herself and up to $5,500 to an IRA for her spouse (for a total of $11,000) provided they file a joint return.

---

7. *Nondeductible IRAs.* An individual or married couple can also make *nondeductible* traditional IRA contributions, within limits.[5] The limit is the same regardless of income level; it is the *excess of* the maximum annual contribution amount *over* the amount deductible. If the individual or couple makes no deductible contributions, they can therefore contribute up to the maximum annual contribution limit in the case of an individual, and up to an additional maximum annual contribution amount

in accordance with the spousal IRA rules set out above, on a nondeductible basis. Nondeductible contributions will be free of tax when they are distributed, but income earned on such contributions will be taxed. If nondeductible contributions are made to a traditional IRA, amounts withdrawn will be treated as partly tax free and partly taxable. Because nondeductible IRA contributions impose additional accounting problems, and provide generally no better result than simply investing in tax-free or tax-deferred non-IRA investments, most advisers do not recommend them.

For a discussion of nondeductible Roth IRAs, see Chapter 21.

8. *Time Limits*. Eligible persons may establish an IRA account and claim the appropriate tax deduction any time prior to the due date of their tax return, *without* extensions, even if the taxpayer actually receives an extension of the filing date.[6] For most individuals or married couples the contribution cutoff date is April 15th. However, since earnings on an IRA account accumulate tax-free, taxpayers may want to make contributions as early as possible in the tax year. The advantage of making an IRA contribution at the beginning of the year can be seen in the following table which assumes $5,000 annual contributions and a rate of return of five percent.

Years of Growth	Beginning of Year January 1	End of Year December 31	Advantage of Early Contributions
5	$29,010	$ 27,628	$1,381
10	66,034	62,889	3,144
15	113,287	107,893	5,395
20	173,596	165,330	8,266
25	250,567	238,635	11,932
30	348,804	332,194	16,610
35	474,182	451,602	22,580
40	634,199	603,999	30,200
45	838,426	798,501	39,925

The advantage of early contributions continues as the contribution limits increase; of course, the accumulations would be even greater the larger the contributions to the traditional IRA.

9. *Saver's Credit*. Certain lower-income taxpayers may claim a temporary, nonrefundable credit for "qualified retirement savings contributions."[7] "Qualified retirement savings contributions" include elective deferrals to SIMPLE IRAs, as well as other elective deferrals and contributions to Roth or traditional IRAs. (However, the total is reduced by certain distributions received by the taxpayer or his spouse during the prior two taxable years and the current taxable year for which the credit is claimed, including the period up to the due date (plus extensions) for filing the federal income tax return for the current taxable year.) Only the first $2,000 of annual deferrals is eligible for the credit.

The credit is allowed against the sum of the regular tax and the alternative minimum tax (minus certain other credits) and is allowed in addition to any other deduction or exclusion that would otherwise apply. In addition, to be eligible, the taxpayer must be at least eighteen as of the end of the tax year and must not be claimed as a dependent by someone else or be a full-time student.

The amount of the credit is limited to an "applicable percentage" of IRA contributions and elective deferrals up to $2,000 ($4,000 if married jointly). The "applicable percentages" are as follows for 2015:

Amount of Credit	Joint	Head of Household	Single/ Others
50% of first $2,000 deferred	$0 to $36,500	$0 to $27,375	$0 to $18,250
20% of first $2,000 deferred	$36,501 to $39,500	$27,376 to $29,625	$18,251 to $19,750
10% of first $2,000 deferred	$39,501 to $61,000	$29,626 to $45,750	$19,751 to $30,500
0% of your contribution	More than $61,000	More than $45,750	More than $30,500

Example. Joe and Jennifer have an adjusted gross income of $37,000 on a joint return for 2015 and they each contribute $3,000 to a traditional IRA. Neither participates in an employer-provided retirement plan and neither has received any distributions. Not only can Joe and Jennifer each deduct their $3,000 contributions, they each can also claim a tax credit of $400 (20 percent of $2,000) ($800 collectively) on their federal income tax return.

---

10. If more than the maximum allowable amount is contributed in any year, a 6 percent excise tax will be imposed on the excess contribution. However, the 6 percent tax can be avoided by withdrawing the excess contribution and earnings prior to the filing date for the federal income tax return (normally April 15). If the excess contribution plus earnings is not withdrawn by the tax return filing date, the 6 percent excise tax will be imposed in each succeeding year until the excess is eliminated.[8]

Investments

1. IRA contributions are not locked into any one particular investment. First, the IRA participant may select more than one organization that sponsors IRA programs, as long as the total of all investments made each year is within the maximum annual contribution limit. For example, part of the contribution could be placed in a savings account and the remainder in a mutual fund plan. Second, at any time the IRA participant may request an IRA sponsor to transfer IRA assets directly from one sponsoring organization to another; not all IRA sponsors will agree to do this, however. Alternatively, assets may be taken out of an IRA and reinvested with another IRA sponsor within sixty days without any tax consequences. However, the IRA participant is allowed to make this type of transaction from an IRA—a "rollover"—only once every twelve months.[9]

2. IRA funds can be invested in any type of asset, with three specific limitations:

   (a) An IRA cannot be invested in a "collectible" as defined in Code section 408(m). A collectible is any work of art, rug, antique, metal or gem, stamp, coin, alcoholic beverage, or any other item designated as a collectible by the IRS. The IRA can, however, invest in certain state or federally-issued coins.[10]

   (b) IRAs cannot be invested in life insurance contracts.[11]

   (c) Since IRAs cannot make loans to an IRA participant,[12] the participant's note is in effect another type of property the IRA cannot invest in. That is, an IRA owner cannot lend IRA funds to himself or to a related person or business. IRAs can, however, make loans to individuals or companies that are not "disqualified persons" under the prohibited transaction rules,' if the underlying IRA documents permit. For example, Letter Ruling 8723082 states that an IRA owner could make loans from the IRA to an unrelated company that was in the business of owning and managing shopping centers.

Loans

1. An IRA owner cannot borrow from his IRA. Loans from IRAs to the IRA owner or a related party are prohibited transactions subject to penalty.

2. An IRA owner can use the sixty-day IRA rollover provision to, in effect, make a sixty-day interest free loan from an IRA.[13] The owner simply takes the money out, uses it during the sixty-day period, and then deposits it in the same or another IRA on or before the sixtieth day after withdrawal.[14]

Distribution and Rollover Rules

1. An IRA account belongs to the participant and the participant is free to take the money out at any time, in any amount, or leave it in indefinitely. However, the tax penalty provisions described below impose significant penalties that effectively require money to be left in until age 59½ (with some exceptions to the 10 percent early withdrawal penalty) and also require distributions to begin after age 70½ on a joint-life annuity basis or faster.

   If IRA assets are a significant part of the participant's savings, planning for distributions to minimize taxes can be extremely important. The rules (unfortunately very complex) for distributions are discussed in Chapter14.

2. A participant's spouse need not consent to an IRA distribution under federal law. The federal consent requirements enacted under the Retirement Equity Act of 1984 apply to qualified plans but not to IRAs. Spousal consent may be required when a qualified plan distribution is rolled over to an IRA, but distributions thereafter can be made without spousal consent. This underscores the importance of making careful long-range retirement and estate plans for both spouses when a significant qualified plan distribution is rolled over to an IRA. Notwithstanding the absence of federal consent requirements,

however, a spouse's property rights in an IRA account are a matter of state law, and may differ depending on whether the state is a common law or community property jurisdiction.

3. Generally, the entire amount of an IRA distribution including principal and earnings is ordinary income in the year of receipt. However, if nondeductible contributions have been made to the account, they are recovered tax-free. If money is withdrawn periodically in installments or an annuity, only the amount received each year is taxable. If nondeductible contributions have been made, a portion of each payment is received tax-free.

4. The government penalizes certain early withdrawals from IRAs. The early distribution penalty is 10 percent of the taxable amount withdrawn from the IRA.[15] Therefore, IRA contributions should be made from funds that can be left in the account until one of the "non-penalty" events listed below occurs.

   For IRAs, the early distribution penalty (discussed further in Chapter 14) does *not* apply to:

   - distributions made on or after attainment of age 59½,
   - distributions made to the IRA participant's beneficiary or estate on or after the participant's death,
   - distributions attributable to the participant's disability,
   - distributions that are part of a series of substantially equal periodic payments made at least annually over the life or life expectancy of the participant, or the participant and a designated beneficiary,
   - distributions for medical care (in excess of the 10 percent of itemized deduction "floor" for such expenses),
   - distributions to unemployed individuals for health insurance premiums under certain conditions,
   - distributions for higher education costs (tuition, fees, books, supplies and equipment) for the taxpayer, spouse, child, or grandchild, and
   - distributions to pay acquisition costs of a first home for the participant, spouse, child, grandchild, or ancestor of the participant or spouse, up to a $10,000 lifetime maximum.

   The exception for *periodic payments* provides some flexibility and can be very favorable in some cases.

   Example. Suppose Ira Participant decides at age 52 to take some money out of his IRA. Ira can do so without penalty, as long as the amount taken out annually is substantially what the annual payment would be under a life annuity (or joint life annuity) purchased with his IRA account balance. No actual annuity purchase is required.[16] Then, when Ira reaches age 59½, he can withdraw all the rest of the money in his IRA account. Ira doesn't have to continue the annuity payments since he is now relying on a different penalty exception, the exception for payments after age 59½.

   However, if the series of payments is changed before the participant reaches age 59½ or, if after age 59½, within five years of the date of the first payment, the tax that would have been imposed, but for the periodic exception, is imposed with interest in the year the change occurs. In the example above, if Ira Participant had begun receiving payments under the periodic payment exception when he was 57, he would have to continue the annuity payments for at least five years to avoid the penalty.[17]

5. Distributions must begin by April 1 of the year after the year in which age 70½ is reached.[18] The minimum distribution requirements are discussed in Chapter 14.

6. An IRA can be used to receive a "rollover" of certain distributions of benefits from employer-sponsored retirement plans. The distribution must be directly transferred or rolled over to the rollover IRA within sixty days after it is received.[19] IRA rollovers are usually straightforward, but there are some complicated rules in special situations. These are discussed further in Chapter 14.

7. When an IRA owner dies, a somewhat complex pattern of tax rules applies. Planners need to

understand the tax treatment of this common situation in order to prevent unnecessary tax penalties for their clients. These rules are generally designed to prevent IRA distributions from being "stretched out" unduly to increase tax deferral. See Chapter 14 for a detailed discussion.

Employer-Sponsored IRAs

1. *Employer-sponsored IRA*. An employer (or a labor union) can sponsor IRAs for its employees as an alternative to a pension plan. There is no requirement of nondiscrimination in coverage. The IRAs can be made available to any employee or a discriminatory group of employees. Contributions to the IRA can be made either as additional compensation from the employer or as a salary reduction elected by the employee. If the employer contributes extra compensation, it is taxable to the employee, but the employee may be eligible for the IRA deduction. The maximum annual contribution limit for an employer-sponsored IRA is the same as for traditional individual IRAs. Employers may establish payroll deduction IRA plans for employees under Department of Labor guidelines without the arrangement becoming subject to the employee benefit provisions and restrictions of ERISA.[20]

2. *Deemed IRA*. An employer that has a qualified plan, Section 403(b) tax sheltered annuity, or eligible Section 457 governmental plan may allow employees to make voluntary contributions to an account or annuity set up under the plan that meets the rules for traditional IRAs.[21] Such deemed IRAs will not be subject to the Internal Revenue Code rules governing the employer plan but will be subject to the exclusive benefit and fiduciary rules of ERISA (to the extent they apply to the employer plan).

3. *SEP IRA*. An arrangement similar to the employer-sponsored IRA is the simplified employee pension (SEP) discussed in Chapter 31. SEPs allow greater annual employer contributions; however, SEPs require nondiscriminatory coverage of employees.

4. *SIMPLE IRA*. This arrangement involves employee salary reduction contributions and employer matching or nonelective contributions that are contributed to an IRA. See Chapter 30.

WHERE CAN I FIND OUT MORE?

1. Most banks, savings and loans, insurance companies, and brokerage firms actively market IRAs, and can provide brochures describing their IRA plans. These firms will indicate the types of investments available as well as any charges that may be applied to such accounts.

2. IRS Publications 590-A and 590-B, *Individual Retirement Arrangements (IRAs)*.

FREQUENTLY ASKED QUESTIONS

Question – How are IRAs treated for state tax law purposes?

Answer – State tax laws vary, and not every state accords IRAs the same favorable tax treatment as does federal law. Three issues can arise:

1. Is the IRA contribution deductible for state (or local) income tax purposes?

2. Are IRA withdrawals taxable under state income tax law?

3. If an IRA owner takes a deduction for an IRA contribution in State A and then moves to State B, does the owner owe income tax to State A when making an IRA withdrawal? Some states apparently took the position that taxes were due in that situation. However, Title 4 United States Code Section 114, enacted by Congress in 1996, prohibits a state from imposing taxes on certain retirement income (including IRA withdrawals) of individuals who are not residents or legally domiciled in that state.

Question – If a participant's spouse is the beneficiary of the participant's IRA, is the amount eligible for the marital deduction for federal estate tax purposes?

Answer – In general, amounts transferred to a spouse at death are eligible for the marital deduction. There is no problem with this if the spouse receives the IRA directly. However, if a trust for the spouse's benefit receives the IRA assets, the trust must qualify as a qualified terminable interest property (QTIP) trust in order to be eligible for the marital deduction.

In Revenue Ruling 2000-2,[22] the IRS indicated the requirements that must be met for an IRA beneficiary trust to qualify as a QTIP trust. Generally, income must be distributable currently to the spousal beneficiary.

CHAPTER ENDNOTES

1. I.R.C. §§219(a), 219(b).
2. I.R.C. §219(c).
3. I.R.C. §219(g).
4. *Colombell v. Comm'r.*, TC Summ. Op. 2006-184.
5. I.R.C. §408(o).
6. I.R.C. §219(f)(3).
7. I.R.C. §25B.
8. I.R.C. §§4973, 408(d)(4).
9. Prop. Reg. §1.408-4(b).
10. I.R.C. §408(m)(3).
11. I.R.C. §408(a)(3).
12. It is a prohibited transaction under I.R.C. §4975(c)(1)(B).
13. Priv. Ltr. Rul. 9010008.
14. Note, however, that there may be tax consequences with more than one rollover. In *Martin v. Comm'r.*, TC Memo 1992-331, a taxpayer made "rollovers" *from* two separate IRAs within one 12-month period. The Tax Court characterized the second transaction as a distribution taxable under I.R.C. §408(d)(1), noting only that I.R.C. §408(d)(3)(B) states that the rollover exemption can only be used once during any one year period.
15. I.R.C. §72(t).
16. Rules for calculating the annual annuity payment are provided by the IRS in IRS Notice 89-25, 1989-1 CB 662, Question 12. Three methods of calculating payments are listed with approval: (1) use of the minimum distribution rules of Section 401(a)(9); (2) amortizing the account balance over single or joint life expectancies of owner and beneficiary; (3) using an annuity factor using a "reasonable" interest rate and mortality table. See also IRS Publication 590.
17. I.R.C. §72(t)(4).
18. I.R.C. §§408(a)(6), 408(b)(3), 401(a)(9).
19. I.R.C. §408(d)(3)(A)(ii).
20. IB 99-1, 64 Fed. Reg. 32999 (6-18-99).
21. I.R.C. §408(q).
22. 2000-3 IRB 305.

ROTH PLANS

CHAPTER 21

INTRODUCTION

A Roth IRA is a form of IRA under which contributions may be made up to a specified limit (see below) on a nondeductible basis, but withdrawals are tax free within certain limitations. Many provisions relating to Roth IRAs are best understood by comparison with traditional IRAs, so Chapter 20 on traditional IRAs should be reviewed as well.

Roth IRAs, like traditional IRAs, are primarily plans of individual savings. They are an alternative form of a tax-favored individual retirement plan. While they are not employee benefits, their features should be understood by benefit planners since they fit into an employee's plan of retirement savings and therefore they influence the form of employer retirement plans to some degree.

WHEN IS USE OF SUCH A DEVICE INDICATED?

1. Like traditional IRAs, Roth IRAs are indicated when:
   - It is desirable to defer taxes on investment income.
   - Long-term accumulation, especially for retirement purposes, is an important objective.
   - A supplement or alternative to a qualified pension or profit sharing plan is needed.
2. The Roth IRA is indicated as an alternative to a traditional IRA when the particular tax benefits available under the Roth IRA are a better match to the individual's planning needs than the tax benefits from a traditional IRA. (See "Frequently Asked Questions," below.)

Advantages

1. Eligible individuals may contribute up to a specified limit (see below) to an IRA annually.
2. Withdrawals from a Roth IRA after (1) a five-year wait and (2) upon death or disability, for first-time home-buying expenses, or after age 59½ are tax-free in their entirety. That is, the initial investment as well as all investment income, capital gains, or other gains are entirely tax-free at the time of withdrawal.
3. Unlike traditional IRAs, Roth IRA contribution eligibility is not restricted by active participation in an employer's retirement plan.
4. Unlike traditional IRAs, Roth IRA contributions can be made after age 70½.
5. Roth IRAs are not subject to minimum distribution rules until the death of the Roth IRA owner. (For traditional IRAs, minimum distribution rules apply beginning at age 70½. Moreover, minimum distributions from traditional IRAs are generally taxable.)

Disadvantages

1. The Roth IRA contribution is limited each year for each individual, and this limit is reduced for single annual adjusted gross income (AGI) above $116,000 and eliminated entirely for single AGI of $131,000

or more (in 2015). (The corresponding limits in 2015 for joint-return filers are $183,000 and $193,000.)

2. Early Roth IRA withdrawals in excess of contributions are taxed in full and are also subject to a 10 percent penalty on early withdrawals similar to that applicable to traditional IRAs.

TAX IMPLICATIONS

Contribution Rules

1. *Contribution Limits.* The maximum Roth IRA contribution for an individual is the lesser of: (a) the dollar limit ($5,500 in 2015); or (b) 100 percent of the individual's earned income, less contributions to traditional deductible or nondeductible IRAs (not including rollovers to such IRAs).[1] As an example, for 2015, if an individual contributes $3,500 to a traditional deductible IRA, then no more than an additional $2000 can be contributed to a Roth IRA.[2]

   "Earned income" means income from employment or self-employment; investment income cannot be counted. Earned income is computed the same for both traditional and Roth IRAs. For example, taxable alimony payments are included for both types of IRAs.

   For individuals who have attained age fifty before the close of the tax year, an additional $1,000 is allowable.

2. *AGI phaseout.* The contribution limit described in the preceding paragraph is phased out for taxpayers with higher adjusted gross incomes. The phaseout AGI limits in 2015 are:[3]

Unmarried individuals:	$116,000–131,000
Married joint return filers:	$183,000–193,000
Married separate filers:	$0–10,000

   The adjusted gross income used for these limits is "modified" AGI, which excludes taxable income from a conversion of a traditional to a Roth IRA (see below).[4]

   The reduction in the dollar limit in the phaseout AGI region is proportional to the amount by which the AGI exceeds the lower limit. For example, suppose that a single taxpayer's AGI is $119,500. Subtract from that amount $116,000 (single AGI). Divide the result by $15,000 (or $10,000 if filing a joint return, qualifying widow(er), or married filing a separate return and you lived with your spouse at any time during the year). His annual contribution limit is therefore $5,500 less $3,250, or $1,750.

   There is a $200 "floor" under the contribution limit; that is, the taxpayer can always contribute at least $200 until the AGI limit has been completely phased out.

3. *Time Limits.* As with a traditional IRA, eligible persons may establish a Roth IRA account any time prior to the due date of their tax return, without extensions, even if taxpayers actually receive an extension of the filing date.[5] For most individuals or married couples the contribution cutoff date is April 15th. However, since earnings on a Roth IRA account accumulate tax-free, taxpayers may want to make contributions as early as possible in the tax year.

   There is no restriction on contributions to a Roth IRA after the taxpayer reaches age 70½, unlike with a traditional IRA.[6]

4. *Saver's Credit.* Certain lower-income taxpayers may claim a temporary, nonrefundable credit for "qualified retirement savings contributions."[7] "Qualified retirement savings contributions" include contributions to Roth or traditional IRAs, as well as elective deferrals to certain plans. (However, the total is reduced by certain distributions received by the taxpayer or his spouse during the prior two taxable years and the current taxable year for which the credit is claimed, including the period up to the due date (plus extensions) for filing the federal income tax return for the current taxable year.) Only the first $2,000 ($4,000 if married filing jointly) of annual deferrals is eligible for the credit.

   The credit is allowed against the sum of the regular tax and the alternative minimum tax (minus certain other credits) and is allowed in addition to any other deduction or exclusion that would otherwise apply. In addition, to be eligible, the taxpayer must be at least eighteen as of the end of the tax year and must not be claimed as a dependent by someone else or be a full-time student.

   The amount of the credit is limited to an "applicable percentage" of IRA contributions and elective deferrals up to $2,000. The "applicable percentages" for 2015 are as follows:

Amount of Credit	Joint	Head of Household	Single/ Others
50% of first $2,000 deferred	$0 to $36,500	$0 to $27,375	$0 to $18,250
20% of first $2,000 deferred	$36,501 – $39,500	$36,501 – $39,500	$36,501 – $39,500
10% of first $2,000 deferred	$39,501 – $61,000	$29,626 – $45,750	$19,751 – $30,500

5. *Employer-sponsored Roth IRAs.* Employers can sponsor Roth IRAs for employees, as a limited alternative to an employer-sponsored qualified retirement plan. Employers who have a qualified plan can also sponsor a "deemed IRA" as part of the qualified plan to provide an alternative form of retirement savings for employees. See Chapter 20.

6. *Qualified Roth Contribution Programs.* Employers may amend their Section 401(k) or Section 403(b) plan to provide that participants' elective deferrals may be contributed to a "qualified Roth contribution program," which would be a separate account under the Section 401(k) or Section 403(b) plan. Contributions and distributions would be treated generally like Roth IRA amounts.[8]

Distribution Rules

1. Account holders with more than one Roth IRA must treat them as a single account when calculating the tax consequences of distributions from any of them.[9] Distributions from a Roth IRA are tax-free if the distribution meets both of the following requirements:[10]

   (a) The distribution must be made after the five-year period beginning with the first taxable year that the individual made a Roth IRA contribution, and

   (b) The distribution must be

   - made on or after the individual attains age 59½,
   - made to a beneficiary or the individual's estate after the individual's death,
   - attributable to the individual's being disabled ("total and permanent" social security definition of disability), or
   - made for a first-time home purchase.

   The five-year holding period is defined as beginning with the first taxable year for which the account holder has a Roth IRA contribution of any kind. Subsequent rollovers into a Roth IRA will not require the running of a "new" five-year holding period.

   The "first-time homebuyer" exception is somewhat misleadingly titled. It is available for purchasing a principal residence of the individual, spouse, child, grandchild, or ancestor of the individual or spouse. Basically, it can be used at any time if the individual and spouse did not own a principal residence within the preceding two years. The exception can be used more than once. However (and this final rule severely limits the usefulness of this exception), there is a $10,000 lifetime limitation on the use of the first-time homebuyer exception for Roth IRAs.[11]

2. If a Roth IRA distribution is not tax-free under the rules described above, the distribution is subject to federal income tax, except that the total of the original nondeductible contributions are treated as distributed first. Only after all contributions have been distributed will the earnings be deemed to have been withdrawn. In addition, there is a 10 percent penalty imposed on the taxable amount of any distribution, unless the distribution meets one of the exceptions to the 10 percent penalty for early distributions for traditional IRAs (see Chapter 20).[12]

3. There are no minimum distribution requirements at age 70½, as there are for traditional IRAs. The Roth IRA owner can therefore accumulate the fund until death, if this is appropriate.

4. However, at the owner's death, the Roth IRA must be distributed within five years of the owner's death unless the owner has designated a beneficiary. If there is a designated beneficiary, the Roth IRA amount can be distributed over the life or life expectancy of the designated beneficiary as long as distributions begin within one year of the decedent's death.[13] If the beneficiary is the owner's spouse, the surviving spouse can elect to treat the Roth IRA as his or her own. Distributions to beneficiaries after

the owner's death are tax-free to the recipients, but they lose their character as Roth IRAs when distributed; that is, further investment returns on the amounts distributed are currently taxable.

Rollovers

1. A Roth IRA can be rolled over to another Roth IRA tax-free.[14] As with traditional IRA rollovers, the transaction must be completed within sixty days, and only one rollover is permitted within a twelve-month period.

2. A Roth IRA cannot be rolled over to a traditional IRA. A withdrawal can be made from a Roth IRA and contributed to a traditional IRA (deductible or nondeductible) within the annual limit for the year of the contribution. There is also no provision for rolling over a Roth IRA to a qualified plan or tax-deferred annuity (Section 403(b)) plan.

3. A traditional IRA (or any part of a traditional IRA) can be rolled over to a Roth IRA. Distributions from other eligible retirement plans (qualified plans, 403(b) plans, and 457 plans) can also be rolled over to a Roth IRA. A rollover to a Roth IRA is generally referred to as a *conversion* to a Roth IRA.

   The chief disadvantage of conversion is that the entire amount of the traditional IRA that is converted to a Roth IRA is generally taxable to the owner as ordinary income in the year of the conversion. This income is not included in AGI in determining whether the $100,000 limit has been met. Thus conversion accelerates all the taxes on the traditional IRA that could otherwise be deferred within the limits of the minimum distribution rules. To avoid bunching of income into high tax brackets, the conversion can be broken into a series of annual partial conversions.

   See "Frequently Asked Questions," below for criteria for determining whether a Roth IRA conversion is a good idea.

WHERE CAN I FIND OUT MORE?

1. Most banks, savings and loans, insurance companies, and brokerage firms actively market IRAs, and can provide brochures describing their IRA plans. These firms will indicate the type of investments available, as well as any charges that may be applied to such accounts.

2. IRS Publication 590-A and 590-B, *Individual Retirement Arrangements (IRAs)*, covers traditional IRAs and Roth IRAs.

FREQUENTLY ASKED QUESTIONS

Question – If a taxpayer is eligible for the maximum annual contribution to either a traditional or a Roth IRA, which should be chosen?

Answer – The analysis is somewhat complex, but from a strictly accounting viewpoint based on simple assumptions, the Roth IRA tends to provide slightly more money at retirement. However, individual circumstances may dictate otherwise. Figure 21.1 shows a comparison of various features of Roth and traditional IRAs.

The accounting analysis can be found in Auster and Chang, "Roth IRAs or Deductible IRAs: The Contribution and Conversion Decision," *Journal of Pension Planning and Compliance*, Vol. 24, Number 1.

To summarize the difference between the two, first note that if a taxpayer has $4,000 to invest on a before-tax basis, Roth IRAs and traditional IRAs are actuarially equivalent, assuming no change in tax rates.

Example. If a taxpayer invests $4,000 a year in a Roth IRA, this is a net investment of $2,880 (at a 28 percent tax rate). After thirty years at 10 percent, this grows to $473,742, free of taxes. If the taxpayer invests the full $4,000 each year in a traditional IRA, at 10 percent this grows in thirty years to $657,976; after paying 28 percent taxes the net amount is $473,742, the exact same amount as the Roth alternative.

This analysis is incomplete, however, because it fails to recognize that most taxpayers will invest the full $4,000 in the Roth IRA, not $2,880; they will find the tax money somewhere else. Likewise, the analysis thus far does not include contributing the tax savings from the traditional IRA to a side fund.

Example. In the article cited above, a comparison is made between (a) a $4,000 investment in a Roth IRA and (b) a $4,000 investment in a traditional IRA plus the results of investing the

Figure 21.1

COMPARISON OF TRADITIONAL AND ROTH IRA

	TRADITIONAL IRA	ROTH IRA
Contributions must be made out of earned income, not investment income	Yes	Yes
Annual dollar limit	Yes (before-tax). [total for sum of Roth and traditional IRA contributions]	Yes (after-tax). [total for sum of Roth and traditional IRA contributions]
Restrictions based on AGI	No, unless active participant in tax-favored employer plan	Yes, contribution limit phased out between $112,000 and $127,000 (single); $178,000 and $188,000 (joint)
Restrictions on deduction or contribution if active participant in tax-favored employer plan	Yes, deduction limited based on AGI	No
Tax-free buildup during accumulation period	Yes	Yes
Withdrawals tax-free	No	Yes, after waiting period
10% penalty on early withdrawals	Yes	Yes
Required minimum distributions	Yes, beginning at earlier of age 70½ or death	Yes, beginning at death
Can roll over to (another) regular IRA	Yes (once annually)	No
Can roll over to (another) Roth IRA	Yes	Yes
Can roll over to qualified plan, TDA or Section 457 governmental plan	Yes, if plan permits; except nondeductible contributions	No

tax savings from the IRA deduction. For the same investment rates and tax rates, the Roth IRA always produces at least slightly better results. If you add in the fact that traditional IRAs must make minimum distributions beginning at age 70½ and Roth IRAs can be accumulated until death, the Roth IRA looks even better.

If you assume that tax rates increase at retirement, the benefits of Roth IRAs versus traditional IRAs increase further. An assumption that tax rates decrease at retirement improves the traditional IRA performance. Most advisors would hesitate to recommend a course of financial action based on a prediction of income tax rates far in the future (in the last forty years, the maximum federal income tax rate has varied from 28 to 91 percent, with no predictable relation to politics or the economy); so these tax-rate arguments may be academic.

In determining the advantages of a Roth IRA, it's important to take a realistic view of the actual tax burden on distributions from retirement plans. The value of a tax deduction, such as that for a traditional IRA, is determined on the basis of the marginal tax rate in the year the contribution is made to the IRA. However, at retirement, if most of the retiree's income comes from retirement plans, the tax burden is the average rate, which is generally much smaller than the marginal rate.

Question – If I decide to convert my traditional IRA to a Roth IRA, can I move the money back to a traditional IRA within the same year (or before the tax return due date) if that is advantageous (for example if the value of the assets decline, making the tax bite too severe to proceed with the conversion)?

Answer – If the transfer from traditional IRA to Roth IRA was made in a direct trustee-to-trustee transfer, the amount can be "recharacterized" as a traditional IRA under a procedure in the regulations.[15]

Question – Can a Roth IRA invest in stock of the IRA owner's business?

Answer – Yes. However, the IRS is alert to various types of plans which use Roth IRA ownership of company stock as a way to invalidly increase the benefits from the Roth IRA.[16] A plan to invest company stock in an IRA should be examined carefully to make sure that IRS guidelines are considered.

CHAPTER ENDNOTES

1. I.R.C. §§408A(c)(2), 219(b)(5).
2. I.R.C. §408A(c)(2).
3. I.R.C. §408A(c)(3); Treas. Reg. §1.408A-3, Q&A 3.
4. I.R.C. §408A(c)(3)(C)(i); Treas. Reg. §1.408A-3, Q&A 5, Q&A 6.
5. See I.R.C. §219(f)(3). Except for rules added by I.R.C. §408A, Roth IRAs are subject to the same rules as traditional IRAs. I.R.C. §408A(a).
6. I.R.C. §408A(c)(4).
7. I.R.C. §25B.
8. I.R.C. §402A.
9. I.R.C. §408A(d)(4)(A), referencing I.R.C. §408(d)(2).
10. I.R.C. §408A(d)(2).
11. I.R.C. §§408A(d)(5), 72(t)(8).
12. Treas. Reg. §1.408A-6, Q&A 5.
13. I.R.C. §408A(c)(5).
14. I.R.C. §408A(c)(3)(B).
15. Treas. Reg. §1.408A-5.
16. Notice 2004-8, 2004-4 IRB 333.

PROFIT SHARING PLAN

CHAPTER 22

INTRODUCTION

A profit sharing plan is a tax-qualified, defined contribution plan featuring a flexible employer contribution provision. The major characteristics are:

- The employer's contribution to the plan each year can be either a purely discretionary amount (or nothing at all, if the employer wishes) or can be based on some type of formula.
- Each participant has an individual account in the plan. The employer's contribution is allocated to the individual participant accounts on the basis of a formula. The formula may allocate employer contributions in proportion to each employee's compensation for the year, but other types of formulas are permissible so long as it is nondiscriminatory. (*e.g.*, Age-weighted formulas—see Chapter 26.)
- Plan benefits consist of the amount accumulated in each participant's account, which is the total of (a) employer contributions, (b) forfeitures from other employees' accounts, if any (discussed below), and (c) the interest, dividends, capital gains, and other investment return realized over the years on plan assets.

WHEN IS USE OF SUCH A DEVICE INDICATED?

1. When an employer's profits, or financial ability to contribute to the plan, varies from year to year. A profit sharing plan is particularly useful as an alternative to a qualified pension plan where the employer anticipates that there may be years in which no contribution can be made.
2. When the employer wants to adopt a qualified plan with an incentive feature to retain employees.
3. When the employer wants to supplement an existing defined benefit plan. The advantages of a profit sharing plan tend to provide exactly what is missing in a defined benefit plan—and vice versa—so that the two together provide a balanced tax-deferred savings and retirement program.

Advantages

1. Because an employer's financial ability to contribute to a plan may vary from year to year, a profit sharing plan provides flexibility for an employer to increase, decrease or eliminate contributions for a year based on circumstances, such as profitability and cash flow.
2. Contributions can be made even if there are no current or accumulated profits.[1] Even a nonprofit organization can have a qualified profit sharing plan.
3. As with all qualified plans, a profit sharing plan provides a tax-deferred retirement savings medium for employees.
4. The plan is relatively simple and inexpensive to design, administer, and explain to employees.
5. The contributions are tax deductible for the employer and not currently taxed to the participating employees.

Disadvantages

1. Retirement benefits may be inadequate for employees who enter the plan at older ages. This is discussed, with some illustrations, in Chapter 25 relating to money purchase plans. The problem of adequate benefits is even worse in a profit sharing plan than in a money purchase plan because a profit sharing plan does not involve any required minimum annual contribution by the employer. Thus, the ultimate retirement benefits in a profit sharing plan are quite speculative. Some planners argue that a profit sharing plan should be considered primarily as a supplemental form of incentive-based deferred compensation and not as a retirement plan. Note that this disadvantage can be reduced by using an age-weighted formula, as discussed in Chapter 26.

2. Annual additions to a participant's account are limited to the lesser of (a) 100 percent of compensation or (b) $53,000 (in 2015, as indexed). Compensation taken into account for plan purposes is limited to $265,000 (in 2015, as indexed). So for an employee earning $51,000 annually, up to 100 percent of compensation can be contributed to his or her plan account (although contributions are rarely this high), whereas for an employee earning $300,000 annually, a maximum of $53,000 can be contributed—that is, just 17.6 percent of compensation. The relative disadvantage of the allocation to highly compensated employees can be alleviated in part by using an integrated formula (described later in this chapter), or through the use of an age-weighted or cross-tested formula (Chapter 26).

3. Employees bear the investment risk under the plan. While bearing investment risk is a potential disadvantage to employees, from the employer's viewpoint, it is an advantage compared to a defined benefit plan where the employer assumes the investment risk.

4. From the employee's standpoint, profit sharing plans may be disadvantageous because there is no predictable level of employer funding under the plan. However, employees have a right to expect that employer contributions will be "substantial and recurring," as discussed below.

Alternatives

1. Money purchase pension plans are defined contribution plans similar to profit sharing plans except that the employer is *required* to make a contribution to a money purchase plan each year. (See Chapter 25.) Both types of plans allow a contribution (and deduction) of up to 25 percent of each participant's compensation.

2. Cross-tested, age-weighted and target benefit plans are defined contribution alternatives that have some similarities to defined benefit plans. With these plans, the employer contribution percentage can be based on age at plan entry—higher for older entrants. One of these plans may be favorable where the employer wants to provide adequate benefits for older (often key) employees. (See Chapter 26.)

3. Defined benefit plans provide more security of retirement benefits for eligible employees, but are more complex to design and administer and the employer assumes all of the investment risk. (See Chapter 27.)

4. Nonqualified deferred compensation plans can be provided exclusively for selected executives and highly compensated employees. (See Chapter 33.)

5. Individual retirement saving is an alternative or a supplement to an employer plan. But there is little or no tax deduction and tax deferral available except for the limited traditional and Roth IRA provisions (see Chapter 20 and Chapter 21).

See also the discussion in Chapter 10, "Designing the Right Pension Plan."

DESIGN FEATURES

Employer Contribution Arrangements

Employer contributions to a profit sharing plan can be based on either a: (a) discretionary provision; or (b) non-discretionary formula.

Under a *discretionary provision*, the employer can determine each year whether to make a contribution and the amount to be contributed. A contribution can be made to a profit sharing plan even if there are no current or accumulated profits. If the employer desires to make a contribution, any amount up to the maximum deductible limit can be contributed (see discussion of the limit under "Tax Implications" below.

An employer is not required to make a contribution every year under a discretionary provision. However, if too many years go by without contributions, the IRS could determine that the plan has experienced a constructive termination.[2] There is definitive rule for determining whether a discontinuance of contributions has occurred. Rather, the IRS uses a facts and circumstances test based on the following factors: (a) whether there is a reasonable probability that the absence of contributions will continue indefinitely; (b) whether there is an intent to avoid the full vesting requirement; and (c) whether contributions are recurring and substantial.[3] If a constructive termination has occurred, all nonvested amounts in participants' accounts become 100 percent vested.

Under a *non-discretionary formula*, a specified amount or percentage is hardwired into the plan document and such amount must be contributed to the plan annually. For example, a formula might provide that the employer will contribute 10 percent of compensation for all eligible employees. Once a non-discretionary formula has been adopted, the employer is legally obligated to contribute the amount determined under the formula (until such formula is changed by) the employer.

Allocation to Participant Accounts

All profit sharing plans, regardless of how the total amount of employer contributions is determined, must have an allocation formula describing how contributions are divided among the participants' accounts. This allocation formula must not discriminate in favor of highly compensated employees.

Most formulas make allocation to participants on the basis of their compensation as compared with the compensation of all participants.

Example. Participant Fred earns $50,000 this year. Total payroll for all plan participants this year is $500,000. For this year, the employer contributes $100,000 to the plan and the amount allocated to Fred's account is determined as follows:

$$\text{Total employer contribution} \times \frac{\text{Fred's compensation}}{\text{Compensation of all participants}}$$

$$\$100,000 \times \frac{\$50,000}{\$500,000} = \$10,000$$

The allocation to Fred's account equals 1/10 of $100,000, or $10,000.

The plan must define the term "compensation" in a nondiscriminatory way.[4] For example, if compensation is defined to include bonuses and exclude overtime pay, and only highly compensated employees receive bonuses and only lower paid employees receive overtime pay, the formula would likely be discriminatory.

There is a limit on the amount of each employee's compensation that can be taken into account in the allocation formula, as well as for the 25 percent deduction limit discussed below under "Tax Implications." For 2015, the compensation limit is $265,000.[5]

Some profit sharing allocation formulas also take into account the years of service of each employee. Such a formula can satisfy the nondiscrimination requirements by meeting the requirements for one of the safe harbors provided in the regulations or by utilizing cross testing (see Chapter 26).[6]

Alternatively, the allocation formula can be "integrated" with Social Security. An integrated formula defines a level of compensation known as the "integration level." The plan may then provide a higher rate of allocation for compensation above that integration level than the rate for compensation below that integration level. This helps the employer avoid duplicating Social Security benefits that are already provided to the employee, and can reduce the employer's cost for the plan.

Example. For the year 2015, a profit sharing plan has two participants with compensation as shown below. For 2015, the employer contributes $15,000 to the plan. The plan's integration level is $30,000. Under the plan's allocation formula, each participant's account is to receive the maximum permitted percent allocation for compensation above $30,000. (As discussed in the "Frequently Asked Questions," below, integration levels below the taxable wage base—$117,000 in 2015—require a reduction of the 5.7 percent factor. In this case, since the integration level is between 20 percent and 80 percent of the taxable wage base, the factor is 4.3 percent, as shown in column III.) The remaining amount of the employer contribution is allocated in proportion to total compensation. Plan allocations would then be as follows:

Employee	I 2015 Compensation	II Compensation above $30,000	III 4.3% of Excess	IV Allocation of Remainder	V Total Allocation
Al	$100,000	$70,000	$2,800	$10,609	$13,409
Betty	15,000	0	0	1,591	1,591
					$15,000

The amount in column IV is determined as follows: (a) subtract the excess allocations (total of column III) from the $15,000 employer contribution ($15,000 – $2,800 = $12,200); (b) for each participant, this difference ($12,200) is then multiplied by a fraction; the numerator is the participant's total compensation and the denominator is the total payroll of $115,000. This allocation satisfies the permitted disparity regulations. (It should be noted these contribution levels could subject this plan to the top heavy requirements explained in Chapter 13.)

Regulations specify the degree of disparity permitted in a plan—the integration levels and the percentages allowed. Considerations involved in choosing the optimal integration level within the limits of these rules are discussed in the "Frequently Asked Questions," below.

Vesting

Generally, any vesting (nonforfeiture) provision permitted by the Code can be used in a profit sharing plan. Many employers use the graded "two- to six-year" vesting provision. This provides 20 percent vesting after two years of service. Vesting increases by 20 percent for each subsequent year of service and reaches 100 percent after six years of service.[7]

If an employee leaves before becoming fully vested in his or her account balance, the nonvested amount, referred to as "forfeiture," reverts back to the plan. In profit sharing plans, forfeitures are generally used to reduce the amount of employer contributions, pay for plan expenses and if any amounts remain, contributed to remaining participants' accounts as an additional contribution. If forfeitures are allocated to participants' accounts, such amounts must be allocated in a nondiscriminatory manner.[8] This usually requires forfeiture allocation in proportion to participants' compensation rather than in proportion to their existing account balances. In profit sharing plans, the formula for allocating forfeitures is usually the same as the formula for allocating employer contributions to participants' accounts.

Distributions

Benefits from a profit sharing plan are usually payable at termination of employment, at death, at permanent disability or at the plan's stated retirement age. Profit sharing plans usually provide payment in the form of either a lump sum or a series of installment payments. The minimum installment payment must meet the minimum distribution rules discussed in Chapter 14. Some profit sharing plans also offer annuity options with a life contingency, but this is relatively uncommon. (Note, however, that certain plans are subject to the joint and survivor annuity requirements discussed in Chapter 18.)

In addition, profit sharing plans typically allow "in service distributions"—that is, benefits payable before termination of employment. Many plans allow such distributions only in the event of "hardship" as specified in the plan. Typical hardship situations might include medical emergencies, home repair, or educational expenses. Alternatively, many profit sharing plans also allow an in service distribution upon an employee attaining age 59½. However, there is generally a 10 percent early distribution penalty for distributions made to participants before age 59½. This penalty is explained further in Chapter 18.

Because of the 10 percent early distribution penalty, an employer generally elects to have a loan provision in a profit sharing plan. Loan provisions allow participants access to plan funds for emergencies and other financial needs without incurring the tax penalty of an early withdrawal. Plan loans are explained further in Chapter 14.

Investments

Profit sharing plan funds are generally invested: (a) in a pooled account; or (b) by participant directed investment. A pooled account is managed by the employer (through a trustee or insurance company) by a fund manager designated by the employer. Either a trust fund or group or individual insurance contracts can be used. Chapter 18 explains how life insurance can be used in the plan. A plan that allows for participant directed investment, the number of possible investments are generally limited to reduce administrative costs. If the participant-directed account provision meets certain requirements set forth in Department of Labor (DOL) regulations,[9] the plan trustee, plan fiduciary and the employer are generally relieved of any liability for any losses resulting from the investment decisions of a participant. Typically, the plan will offer the participant a choice of mutual fund investments. Under the DOL regulations, at least three diversified choices must be permitted in order for the fiduciaries to be relieved of responsibility for participant investment decisions. However, the employer (or other plan fiduciary) remains legally responsible for prudently selecting and monitoring the investment options.

ERISA Requirements

A profit sharing plan is subject to the ERISA reporting and disclosure rules outlined in Chapter 16.

TAX IMPLICATIONS

For Employers

Employer contributions to the plan are deductible when made, so long as the plan remains "qualified." A plan is qualified if it meets the eligibility, vesting, funding, and other requirements explained in Chapter 16. In addition, the plan must designate that it is a profit sharing plan.[10]

The maximum deductible employer contribution to the plan cannot exceed 25 percent of the payroll of all employees covered under the plan.[11] Any excess over these limits is not only nondeductible, but is also generally subject to a 10 percent penalty.[12] (However, contributions to one or more defined contribution plans that are nondeductible when contributed solely because of the combined plan deduction limit may be subject to an exception from the 10 percent penalty.[13]) Only the first $265,000 (in 2015, as indexed) of each employee's compensation can be taken into account for purposes of this limit.[14]

If an employer maintains a defined benefit plan covering some of the same employees, the total deductible contribution for both plans is limited to 25 percent of compensation of the covered employees (or, if greater, the amount necessary to meet the minimum funding standard for the defined benefit plan, in which case the contribution to the profit sharing plan is not deductible).[15]

Certain employers adopting a plan may be eligible for a business tax credit of up to $500 for "qualified startup costs." See Chapter 27 for details.

For Employees

Assuming the plan remains qualified, taxation for the participating employees is deferred. That is, employer contributions, forfeitures added to a participant's account, and investment earnings on the account are not taxable to a plan participant until withdrawn.[16]

Code section 415 limits annual additions to each participant's account in a defined contribution plan to the *lesser of* (a) 100 percent of the participant's compensation or (b) $53,000 (in 2015, as indexed).[17] In a profit sharing plan, annual additions include:

1. employer contributions;
2. any forfeitures allocated to participants' accounts; and
3. employee contributions, if an employee deferral feature is adopted (e.g., 401(k) feature).[18]

Distributions from a plan must follow the rules for qualified plan distributions. These distribution rules are explained in Chapter 14.

SOCIAL SECURITY INTEGRATION

A "stand alone" profit sharing plan—where the employer has no qualified defined benefit or other plan—is often integrated with Social Security because (1) employer costs are reduced and (2) the employer contribution in an integrated plan is disproportionately allocated to higher paid employees.

If an employer has two or more qualified plans covering even one employee in common, the regulations do not allow both plans to be fully integrated; the degree of integration in one or all plans must be cut back under complex guidelines. Planners generally find that if an employer has both a defined benefit plan and a profit sharing plan covering a common group of employees, it is most favorable to the employer and key employees to maximize the integration in the defined benefit plan and not to integrate the profit sharing plan at all.

The regulations governing permitted disparity (i.e., integration) for defined contribution plans essentially provide as follows:

A defined contribution plan is integrated by providing a higher rate of contributions for compensation *above* a specified earnings level (excess contribution percentage) than for compensation below a specified earnings level (base contribution percentage).[19]

The maximum difference (i.e., the permitted disparity) between the excess contribution percentage and the base contribution percentage depends on the earnings level (integration level) chosen. If the integration level is the taxable wage base (TWB) used for Social Security purposes ($117,000 in 2015), the excess contribution percentage above the integration level cannot exceed the *lesser* of: (a) double the base percentage or (b) the base percentage plus 5.7 percent.[20] For example, if the employer contributes 5 percent for the first $117,000 of compensation, a contribution of up to 10 percent can be made for compensation above that level. If, however, the base contribution percentage is 6 percent of the first $117,000, only an 11.7 percent contribution (not a 12 percent contribution) can be made for compensation above that level.

The regulations do not permit a defined contribution plan to use an integration level greater than the TWB;[21] however, an integration level *below* the TWB can be used. If an integration level below the TWB is chosen, then the permitted disparity is reduced as follows, depending on the amount of the integration level:[22]

- The maximum excess contribution percentage used in a plan where the integration level is 80 percent or more of the TWB ($93,600 to $117,000 in 2015) is the lesser of (a) double the base percentage or (b) the base percentage plus 5.4 percent.

- The maximum excess contribution percentage used in a plan where the integration level is 20 percent or more, but less than 80 percent of the TWB) ($93,600 to $117,000 in 2015) is the lesser of (a) double the base percentage or (b) the base percentage plus 4.3 percent.

Choosing an Integration Level

Most small business owners want to set the integration level at a point that will maximize contributions for owners and key employees. This can be accomplished by carefully looking at the employee census and assessing where a proper cutoff level would be.

Under prior law, the "optimum" integration level for a small business was just above the compensation level of the highest paid nonowner employee. This level gave *only* the owners the benefit of the extra percentage—the permitted disparity—under the integration rules.

Under the current permitted disparity regulations, choosing an optimum integration level is *much more complicated*. Because of the stepwise nature of the reduction in permitted disparity (see above), a reduction in the integration level sometimes increases the owner's benefit from the permitted disparity and in some cases it does not.

In deciding on a reduced integration level, in most cases it will not pay to reduce the integration level if the reduction reduces the owner's benefit level, so certain integration levels are unfavorable.

While in some cases the difference between the optimum integration level and simply using the TWB of $117,000 (in 2015) may be relatively small, can a financial planner afford not to point it out to a client before somebody else does?

PURCHASES OF LIFE INSURANCE

IRS rulings have permitted a participant in a profit sharing account to direct the plan trustee to purchase life insurance on the life of a person in whom he has an insurable interest.[23] Note that the plan must (a) include a "directed investment" (earmarking) provision and (b) permit the purchase of life insurance as directed by the participants. A plan that does not have these two provisions cannot be used for this purpose until it is amended to include the provisions.

The amount of the insurance that can be purchased on the participant's life is governed by the "incidental" limits discussed in Chapter 20. Note that for a profit sharing plan, these rules allow all amounts that have been in the plan for at least two years to be used for insurance. Therefore, profit sharing plans offer an opportunity to provide substantial amounts of insurance using tax-sheltered plan funds.

When an individual and his or her spouse have potentially large estates subject to federal estate tax, the tax becomes payable primarily at the death of the second, not the first, to die. The advantage of a survivorship policy on an individual and spouse is that it provides substantial liquid funds when they are actually needed, and at an annual premium cost substantially lower than that for first-death insurance. If an individual in this situation has a substantial profit sharing account, that account provides a source of funds to pay premiums for this insurance.

As with insurance for the participant alone under a qualified plan, survivorship insurance results in current, annual taxable income to the participant. This income is not measurable under the Table 2001 (formerly P.S. 58) rates, but rather using a lower annual cost reflecting the second-death feature.[24]

If the participant spouse dies first under this arrangement, the policy should be continued outside the plan. The participant (while living) should direct that at his death the policy (which is part of his profit sharing account balance) should be transferred to an irrevocable life insurance trust for the benefit of his family. If the nonparticipant spouse is the first to die, the participant should consider purchasing the policy from the plan, then contributing it to a life insurance trust.

Any purchase of a life insurance contract from the plan by the participant (or other party in interest, such as a relative) will be a "prohibited transaction" subject to penalties unless it meets the requirements set forth by the Department of Labor in Prohibited Transaction Exemption (PTE) 92-6. PTE 92-6 requires the following:

1. the sale must be to a participant, a relative of the participant who is a beneficiary under the contract, an employer, or certain other employee benefit plans;

2. the plan, but for the sale, would surrender the contract;

3. if the purchaser is not the insurance-participant, the insured-participant must be given an opportunity to purchase the contract first; and

4. the purchase price must put the plan in the same cash position as if it had retained the contract, surrendered it, and distributed the participant's vested interest in the plan.

The Department of Labor has clarified and confirmed that the sale of a second-to-die policy covering the participant and his spouse is covered under PTE 92-6.[25] For rules governing the valuation of life insurance policies in this situation, see Chapter 20, Life Insurance in a Qualified Plan, Frequently Asked Questions.

It should be noted that there are no other Treasury or IRS rulings (official or otherwise) which specifically sanction the use of survivorship policies in profit sharing plans.

FREQUENTLY ASKED QUESTIONS

Question – Can a self-employed person adopt a profit sharing plan?

Answer – A self-employed person (sole proprietor or partner in a partnership) can adopt a profit sharing plan covering not only his or her regular employees, if any, but also covering the self-employed person(s). Such a plan is one type of "Keogh" or "HR 10" plan discussed in Chapter 29. Generally the self-employed person is treated the same as regular employees in a profit sharing plan, but there are some special rules that apply.

Question – Can employees make contributions to a profit sharing plan?

Answer – Employees can contribute to the plan on an after-tax basis. For employees to contribute on a pre-tax (salary reduction) basis, the plan must meet the additional requirements of Code section 401(k); these are explained in Chapter 19. Furthermore, if the plan allows employee after-tax contributions, the additional nondiscrimination requirements under Code section 401(m) must be met. These are explained in Chapter 26.

CHAPTER ENDNOTES

1. I.R.C. §401(a)(27)(A).
2. Treas. Reg. §1.401-1(b)(2).
3. Treas. Reg. §1.411(d)-2(d)(1).
4. I.R.C. §414(s). See Treas. Reg. §1.414(s)-1.
5. I.R.C. §401(a)(17).
6. Alternative methods for satisfying nondiscrimination requirements include satisfying a general nondiscrimination test, restructuring or cross-testing (testing defined contribution plans on the basis of benefits). See Treas. Reg. §1.401(a)(4)-2.
7. I.R.C. §411(a)(12).

8. Treas. Reg. §1.401(a)(4)-1(b)(2)(ii).
9. See DOL Reg. §2550.404c-1.
10. I.R.C. §401(a)(27)(B).
11. I.R.C. §404(a)(3).
12. I.R.C. §4972.
13. The exception generally applies to the extent that such contributions do not exceed the greater of (1) 6% of compensation (within the meaning of I.R.C. §404(a) and as adjusted under Section 404(a)(12)) paid or accrued during the taxable year for which the contributions were made, to beneficiaries under the plans; *or* (2) the sum of employer matching contributions plus elective deferrals. See I.R.C. §4972(c)(6)(B).
14. I.R.C. §401(a)(17).
15. I.R.C. §404(a)(7).
16. I.R.C. §402(a).
17. I.R.C. §415(c).
18. I.R.C. §415(c)(2).
19. I.R.C. §401(l)(2). See also Treas. Reg. §§1.401(l)-1, -2, -4.
20. I.R.C. §401(l)(2)(A).
21. I.R.C. §401(l)(5)(A)(ii).
22. Treas. Reg. §1.401(l)-2(d).
23. Priv. Ltr. Ruls. 8445095, 8108110 (co-shareholder).
24. Where the spouse or dependent coverage is available only through the purchase of a rider to the policy on the life of the participant, the cost of the insurance currently includable in the participant's income may not be measured by the actual cost of the rider, but must be measured using the Table 2001 (formerly P.S. 58) rate. See Let. Rul. 9023044.
25. DOL Adv. Op. 98-07A, September 24, 1998.

EMPLOYEE STOCK OWNERSHIP PLANS (ESOPs)

CHAPTER 23

INTRODUCTION

A stock bonus plan is a qualified employer plan—similar to a profit sharing plan—in which participants' accounts are invested in stock of the employer company. An ESOP is a stock bonus plan that the employer can use as a conduit for borrowing money from a bank or other financial institution to purchase employer stock.

Although stock bonus plans and ESOPs are similar in many ways, the following features apply only to an ESOP:[1]

- leveraged loan feature and its prohibited transaction exemption,
- deferral of gain to shareholder who sells stock to the ESOP and buys replacement securities (C corporation only)[2]
- deduction to the company for dividends paid to the ESOP and distributed to participants or used to pay off ESOP loan (C corporation only),
- requirement of funding "primarily" with employer securities, and
- diversification requirement[3]

WHEN IS USE OF SUCH A DEVICE INDICATED?

1. To provide a tax-advantaged means for an employer to offer employees a stake in the company through stock ownership.
2. When estate and financial planning for shareholders would benefit from the additional market for company stock created by a stock bonus plan or ESOP. Moreover, an ESOP not only creates a market but provides the opportunity for estate tax benefits for a sale of stock to the ESOP.
3. To provide employers with the ability to leverage and generate capital for the company through tax-exempt loans.
4. When a company wants to broaden its ownership—for example, to help prevent a hostile takeover of the company.
5. When the business is a corporation. Partnerships do not have stock and thus are ineligible to establish an ESOP or stock bonus plan. S corporations are permitted to establish an ESOP or stock bonus plan; however, they are not eligible for all the tax benefits provided to C corporation ESOPs.[4]

Advantages

1. Employees receive an ownership interest in the employer company, which may provide a performance incentive.
2. A market is created for employer stock of a closely held company, which helps improve liquidity of existing shareholders' assets or estates and helps in business continuity planning.
3. Employees are not taxed until shares are distributed. Furthermore, unrealized appreciation of stock held in the plan might not be taxed to employees at receipt of distributions from the plan. Taxation of the unrealized appreciation can generally be deferred until shares are sold by the employee.

4. The employer receives a deduction either for a cash contribution to the plan or a noncash plan contribution in the form of shares of stock.

5. The overall cost of corporate borrowing can be reduced by using an ESOP.

6. A shareholder can obtain tax benefits by selling stock to the plan.

Disadvantages

1. Since the plan is qualified, all the qualified plan requirements apply—coverage, vesting, funding, reporting and disclosure, and others.

2. Issuing shares of stock to employees "dilutes" (reduces the relative value of) existing shareholders' stock and their control of the company.

3. Company stock may be a very speculative investment. Investment volatility can create employee ill-will either because the plan is not considered very valuable by employees or because employees expect too much from the plan.

DESIGN FEATURES

ESOPs and stock bonus plans are qualified defined contribution plans similar to profit sharing plans. However, participants' accounts are stated in terms of shares of employer stock. Benefits are generally distributable in the form cash rather than employer stock.[5] Dividends on shares can be used to increase participants' accounts or can be paid directly in cash to participants. If dividends are paid directly in cash, the employer gets a tax deduction (see below) and the dividends are currently taxable to the employees.

Employer contributions are either shares of stock, or cash that the plan uses to buy stock.

Plan allocation formulas must not discriminate in favor of highly compensated employees and are typically based on employee compensation. For example, if total payroll of participating employees is $500,000 and the employer contributes stock worth $50,000, an employee earning $10,000 would be allocated $1,000 worth of stock under a compensation-based allocation formula. As with all qualified plans, only the first $265,000 of compensation (in 2015, as indexed) can be used in the plan's allocation formula.[6] The formula for a stock bonus plan can be integrated with Social Security, but this is rarely done. An ESOP formula cannot be integrated.[7]

If shares of the employer company are closely held—that is, not publicly traded on an established securities market—and more than 10 percent of the plan's assets are invested in securities of the employer, then plan participants must be given the right to vote on certain specific corporate issues:

- approval or disapproval of any corporate merger or consolidation, recapitalization, reclassification, liquidation, or dissolution;

- sale of substantially all assets of the trade or business; or

- a similar transaction as prescribed in IRS regulations.[8]

If employer stock is publicly traded, plan participants must be allowed to vote the stock on all issues.[9]

Distributions from stock bonus plans and ESOPs are subject to the same rules applicable to all qualified plans, as described in Chapter 14. For example, distributions prior to age 59½, death, or disability are subject to a 10 percent penalty, with some exceptions. Note, however, that a stock bonus plan or ESOP is generally not required to provide a joint and survivor annuity or other spousal death benefit.[10]

Diversification Provisions

Because of concern about abuses in qualified plans that depend heavily on employer stock, Congress has added a variety of somewhat overlapping provisions requiring investment diversification in various circumstances. These provisions are:

- Code section 401(a)(35) provides diversification rights for participants in any defined contribution plan that holds publicly traded employer securities. The rules apply for all types of plans except for an ESOP (but see below for diversification requirements for certain participants) without employee elective deferrals or matching contributions, and plans with one participant (or one participant and spouse. Under these rules:

- Participants must be allowed to reinvest any part of their elective-deferral or employee-contribution accounts that are invested in employer securities.

- Participants with three years of service must be allowed to reinvest their employer-contribution accounts as well. The plan must provide at least three options for reinvestment. Reinvestments must be permitted at least quarterly. No restrictions can be placed on reinvestments of employer securities that do not apply to other plan assets.

- *Put Options*. Participants can demand that distributions from a stock bonus plan or ESOP be made in the form of employer stock (except in the case of certain S corporation plans). However, if the participant receives stock that is not traded on an established market, the participant has a right to require the employer to repurchase the stock under a fair valuation formula. This requirement is referred to as the "put option."[11]

- To protect employees against unrealistic expectations of stock value, if the stock or securities used in the plan are not traded on an established market, stock valuations used for all plan purposes must be made by an independent appraiser.[12] For more information about the "put option" see the Frequently Asked Questions section at the end of this chapter.

- *Age 55 ESOP Diversification*. Another protective feature is a requirement that participants in ESOPs who have reached age fifty-five and who have at least ten years of participation in the plan be entitled to an annual election to diversify investments in their accounts. For a six-year period after becoming eligible for this election, the participant can elect annually to diversify a total of up to 25 percent of the account balance. In the last year, diversification of 50 percent of the account balance can be elected. (A plan may offer higher percentages of diversification, if desired.) The plan must offer at least three options other than employer stock for diversification.[13]

ESOP Loans

An ESOP is distinguished from a regular stock bonus plan primarily by the "leveraging" feature of an ESOP that enables the employer company to borrow money on a favorable basis.[14] The transaction works like this (see Figure 23.1):

(a) The ESOP trustee borrows money from a lending institution such as a bank (with the loan guaranteed by the employer corporation).

(b) The trustee uses the loan proceeds to purchase stock of the employer from the employer corporation (or from principal shareholders of the corporation).

Figure 23.1

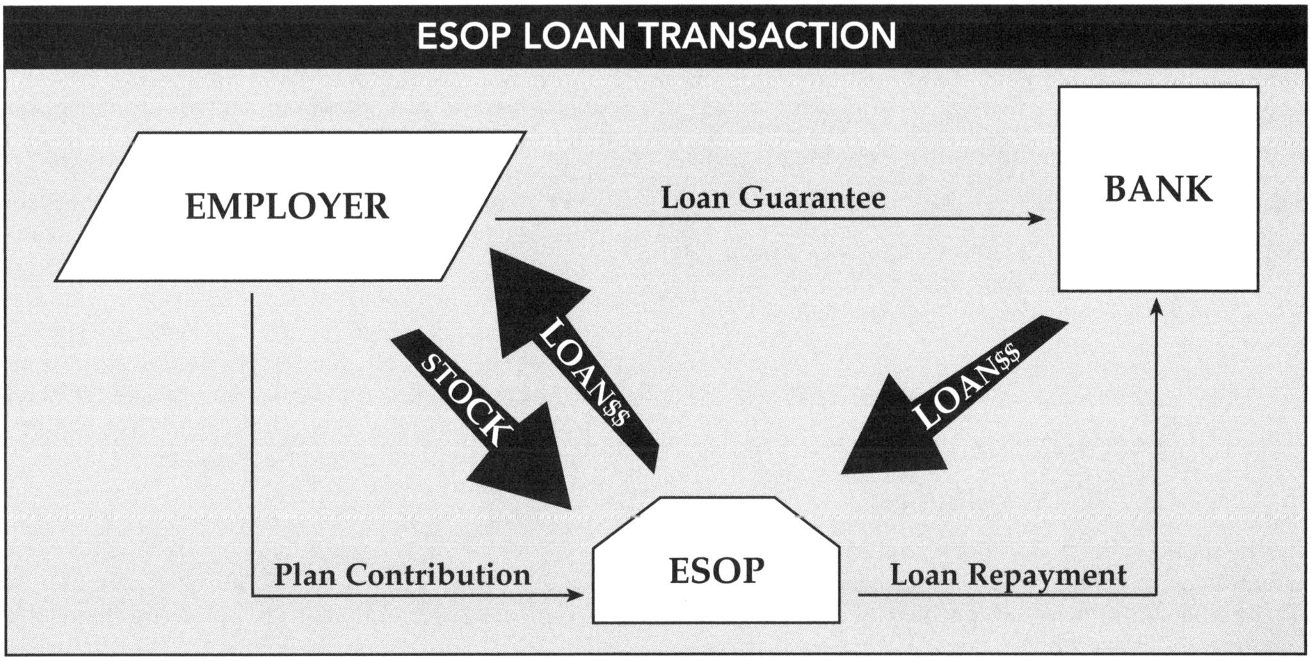

(c) The employer makes tax deductible contributions to the ESOP in amounts sufficient to enable the trustee to pay off the principal and interest of the loan to the bank or other lender.

The net effect of this is that the corporation receives the loan proceeds and repays the loan, both principal and interest, with tax deductible dollars.[15]

ERISA AND OTHER REGULATORY REQUIREMENTS

The plan is subject to the usual ERISA eligibility, vesting, and funding requirements for qualified plans discussed in Chapter 13 and the reporting and disclosure requirements summarized in Chapter 16.

Beyond ERISA requirements, the Internal Revenue Code imposes several other requirements that generally apply to both stock bonus plans and ESOPs, including:

- The Code section 401(a)(35) diversification requirement, except that it does *not* apply to ESOPs with no elective deferrals;
- the "put" option requirement obligating the company to repurchase nonpublicly traded company stock from terminating participants;[16]
- pass-through voting requirements, except that they do not apply to a profit-sharing plan;[17]
- distribution commencement requirements of Code Section 409(o);
- the tax deferral for unrealized appreciation on company stock distributed from the plan in a lump-sum distribution; and
- certain directors and policy-making officers with ESOP or stock bonus accounts may be subject to "insider trading" restrictions under federal securities laws.[18]

TAX IMPLICATIONS

For Employees

The regular annual additions limit for defined contribution plans applies to ESOPs and stock bonus plans. The annual addition to each participant's account cannot exceed the lesser of 100 percent of the participant's compensation or $53,000 (in 2015, as indexed).[19] ESOP plans are subject to the eligibility and vesting rules applicable to all qualified plans (see Chapter 13).

For a C corporation ESOP, deductible employer contributions applied by the plan to the payment of interest on certain loans incurred to acquire employer stock, as well as forfeitures of employer stock acquired with such loans, are excluded from this limit if no more than one-third of the employer contributions applied to the repayment of such loans are allocated to highly compensated employees. This provision is unavailable to S corporation ESOPs.[20]

Taxation to the employee on employer contributions is deferred, as with any qualified plan.[21] An additional tax benefit to employees with a stock bonus plan or ESOP is deferral of tax on unrealized appreciation of stock received in a lump sum distribution.[22]

Example. Suppose an ESOP buys stock for $1,000 and allocates it to participant Farley's account. At retirement twenty years later, the stock is worth $5,000. If Farley receives this stock in a lump sum distribution from the plan, he pays tax only on $1,000. The $4,000 of unrealized appreciation is not taxed until Farley sells the stock. Farley could, however, elect out of this deferred treatment.

For certain employees born before 1936, the taxable amount of any lump sum distribution from a stock bonus plan or ESOP may be eligible for the special ten-year averaging tax treatment for qualified plans.[23]

Shareholders of C corporations that are not publically traded do not have to recognize gain for income tax purposes when they sell shares to an ESOP.[24] To qualify for this treatment, the shareholder must use the proceeds from the sale to purchase "qualified replacement property"—that is, stock or securities of another corporation. The replacement securities take the same basis as the stock sold to the ESOP, and the shareholder does not pay tax until the replacement securities are sold. Many requirements apply; in particular, the ESOP must own at least 30 percent of the employer corporation. Special holding period rules also apply.[25]

For Employers

Employer contributions to the plan are deductible when made, up to an annual limit. The deduction limit for a stock bonus plan or an S corporation ESOP is 25 percent of payroll of employees covered under the plan.[26] For a C corporation ESOP, a higher limit is available—up to 25 percent of covered payroll for amounts used to repay loan principal, with no limit on amounts used to pay interest.[27]

Within certain limitations, a C corporation can deduct dividends paid on stock acquired with an ESOP loan. The dividends must be:

1. paid in cash to plan participants or beneficiaries:
2. paid to the plan and distributed within ninety days to plan participants or beneficiaries;
3. payable as described under (1) or (2) at the election of participants or beneficiaries; or
4. used to make payments on certain loans incurred to acquire employer stock.

Furthermore, the dividends must be nonforfeitable, under the vesting provisions of Code section 411. It is important to note that dividends deducted under these provisions are *not* subject to the special lower tax rates that apply to certain other dividends.[28]

Certain employers adopting a plan may be eligible for a business tax credit of up to $500 for "qualified startup costs." See Chapter 12 for details.

USE IN ESTATE PLANNING

The existence of the ESOP or stock bonus plan as a potential buyer for stock can be very valuable in planning the estate of a shareholder of a closely held business. Such estates are often illiquid because of a lack of a market for the stock, while at the same time the estate may be liable for substantial death taxes because of the inherent value of the stock. The estate planning and related planning opportunities using ESOPs and stock bonus plans for closely held businesses are best illustrated by looking at three typical scenarios: (1) purchase of stock at death; (2) business continuation planning opportunities, (3) in a buy-sell agreement, and (4) simply using the plan as a source of cash.

Purchase of Stock at Death

In most small companies, owners typically expect the company to buy stock from their estate at the shareholder's death. However, for a number of reasons this plan may be difficult to carry out:

- Accumulation of corporate funds can be difficult. Funds to purchase stock must be accumulated by the corporation out of after-tax income, which can be particularly burdensome since corporate tax rates may be higher than individual rates.
- The corporation can purchase life insurance to provide assured funding, but the premiums are not deductible to the corporation, so this is also an accumulation from after-tax income.
- An accumulation of funds at the corporate level may result in exposure to the accumulated earnings tax, particularly if the shareholder is a majority shareholder.
- Receipt by the corporation of otherwise income-tax-free life insurance proceeds may trigger the corporate alternative minimum tax (AMT).
- If insurance is owned by the corporation to fund a buyout, corporate value is increased, which in turn increases the federal estate tax.

Use of an ESOP or stock bonus plan as the purchaser avoids these problems. The corporation gets a deduction for amounts contributed to the plan, and the plan is a tax-exempt entity, so its income is not taxed. Thus, funds accumulate in the plan on a before-tax basis. Also, the plan is not subject to the accumulated earnings tax or the alternative minimum tax. Furthermore, life insurance held in the ESOP will not increase corporate value for purposes of the federal estate tax.

While it may be difficult to accumulate a large amount of cash in the plan, particularly in a short time, the plan can purchase insurance on the shareholder's life as an investment that will provide funds to purchase stock from a shareholder at the shareholder's death.

Should there be a formal plan to carry out this type of stock purchase? Probably not. A shareholder can give the ESOP or stock bonus plan an option to buy his or her shares, but requiring the plan to formally commit to a buyout would probably violate the ERISA fiduciary requirements.

One potentially serious tax problem with this type of plan should be noted—the possibility that the IRS will treat the sale of stock as a dividend paid to the estate by the corporation rather than a sale to the ESOP. Tax-wise, this could greatly increase the cost of the transaction. As a sale, little or no capital gain would be realized by the estate because its basis for the stock would be stepped up to the date of death value. But proceeds from the sale might all be taxable if treated as a dividend, in some cases at low dividend tax rates.

In any event, the IRS is not likely to impose dividend treatment on a sale of stock to an ESOP unless the decedent was a major shareholder. However, the IRS will probably consider all stock held by the decedent and related family members together in determining whether the decedent was a controlling shareholder. In such cases, despite the apparent policy of Congress to encourage stock sales to ESOPs, the IRS may ignore the ESOP and treat the transaction as a dividend paid directly from the corporation to the shareholder, the decedent's estate.

It may be advisable, in doubtful situations, to apply to the IRS for a ruling that the transaction is not a dividend. However, the IRS has announced that it will not issue such a ruling unless the combined beneficial interest of the selling shareholder and all related persons in the stock held in the plan does not exceed 20 percent and certain other representations are made.[29] It may be possible to meet this condition in certain cases by amending the ESOP or stock bonus plan to reduce the stock in the selling stockholder's account below this 20 percent limit.

A final and important incentive for the use of ESOPs in estate planning relates to the tax benefit provided for sales of stock to these plans (see the following section).

Business Continuation

In some circumstances, ESOPs and stock bonus plans can be used to help solve business continuation problems, along with the related estate planning problems.

Example. Suppose Monty Bank owns 100 percent of Knab, Inc., a closely held business with ten employees. Monty's children are not interested in continuing the business.

One way of providing business continuity and a means of selling the stock is to establish an ESOP for Knab, Inc.'s ten regular employees, excluding Monty. This will meet the nondiscrimination requirement for qualified plans, since the plan is permitted to discriminate *against* a highly compensated employee (Monty). Monty sells 49 percent of the shares of Knab, Inc. to the ESOP, using the proceeds of an ESOP loan. Since Monty retains 51 percent, he remains in control of the business.

Knab Inc. is a C corporation that is not publically traded, so Monty recognizes no gain on the sale (see 'Tax Implications" above) but he must reinvest in other securities (generally not a problem) and the replacement securities take the basis of the stock sold to the ESOP. If Monty holds these replacement securities until his death, they receive a stepped-up basis and the gain on the sale to the ESOP will avoid income taxation altogether.

In the years following the sale, shares sold to the ESOP will be allocated to the accounts of the ten employees, with the highest paid employees receiving the most shares. At Monty's death, Monty's heirs will receive his 51 percent share, but they will likely be able to sell these shares to the Knab employees (through the ESOP) at that time since the employees will want to retain control of the business to protect their existing investment in Knab.

Buy-sell Agreements

An ESOP or stock bonus plan can be used to carry out a corporate buy-sell agreement among shareholders. For illustration, take a very simple example with only two major shareholders.

Example. Alf and Ben, each own about half of the corporation's stock, with a relatively small amount held in a stock bonus plan for participants other than Alf and Ben.

The simplest type of arrangement is for the plan trustee to purchase insurance on the lives of Alf and Ben. This insurance is held as key person insurance, since the trust has an insurable interest in the lives of the two business principals. On the death of one shareholder—suppose it is Alf—the trustee collects the insurance proceeds and uses that money to purchase stock from Alf's estate. The stock is reallocated to plan participants. Ben's account will probably receive most of this stock eventually and Ben will retain majority ownership. However, some stock may also be allocated to other participants.

Another arrangement, slightly more formal, makes use of "participant investment direction" or "earmarking," which is permitted under ERISA. With participant investment direction in a qualified plan, a participant is given the right to direct the trustee to invest his or her plan account in specified property. In the example above, Alf would direct the trustee to invest in insurance on Ben's life, and Ben would direct a similar investment in insurance on Alf's life. The insurance proceeds on the death of one owner are therefore used to purchase stock directly for the account of the other owner, with no allocation of stock to other plan participants.

Source of Cash

If the more elaborate plans described above do not apply, a shareholder may be able to establish an ESOP or stock bonus plan simply as a way of turning shares into cash as needed in a lifetime sale.

The issues discussed above, with respect to dividend treatment, apply to a lifetime sale of stock to an ESOP as well. If the shareholder's stock has a low basis—as is often the case in closely held companies—then the capital gain under a "sale" treatment will generate almost as much gain as dividend treatment would. For example, if a shareholder sells stock with a basis of $20,000 to an ESOP for $500,000, the taxable capital gain is $480,000, while dividend treatment could result in taxable dividends of $500,000. Lower tax rates (i.e., 20 percent) generally apply to most long-term capital gains and dividends; however, certain exceptions apply.[30]

HOW TO INSTALL THE PLAN

Plan installation follows the qualified plan installation procedure described in Chapter 13. In addition, if the employer's stock is subject to securities regulation requirements and the employer issues new stock for the plan, a registration statement may have to be filed with federal or state securities regulatory agencies.

FREQUENTLY ASKED QUESTIONS

Question – Does the "put option" impose special obligations on the employer, and if so, how can that obligation be financed?

Answer – The put requirement obliges the employer, not the plan, to repurchase the employee's stock if the employee so demands. An employer must anticipate this need and as part of prudent plan administration insure that liquid funds are available as required. Some methods of financing this requirement are:

- An asset reserve or sinking fund can be maintained by the employer. Such a fund may be unreliable since the employer may be forced to use it in the business during hard times.
- Life insurance can be owned by the employer. Life insurance contracts on plan participants, held by the employer as key-person insurance (owned, paid for, and payable to the employer) can provide funds either in the form of cash values accessible at the employee's retirement, or funds available at the employee's death to reimburse the employer for its outlays.
- Plan assets can be used to repurchase the stock from the employer (if in fact the plan has significant assets other than employer stock).
- Stock can be sold by the employer on the market, if such a market exists.

If the employee group as a whole is relatively old when the plan is adopted, financing the put requirement may be difficult, and consequently the adoption of an employer-stock plan may be imprudent in such a situation. The problem here is somewhat similar to the difficulty in funding an age-weighted or defined-benefit plan for an older group.

Question – Can any type of stock or securities be used in an ESOP?

Answer – Stock used in an ESOP must be either (a) common stock traded regularly on an established market or (b) common stock having a combination of voting power and dividend rights equal to or greater than that of the employer's class of common stock having the greatest voting rights and the class of stock having the greatest dividend rates.[31] If there is only one class of stock, as is often the case with closely held companies, the second test is met.

Question – Can any type of business organization have an ESOP or stock bonus plan?

Answer – Currently, S corporations may adopt ESOPs. However, S corporation ESOPs may be subject to a special penalty if allocations of stock are made to persons owning (or deemed to own) more than 50 percent of the shares in the corporation.[32]

Unincorporated businesses—partnerships or proprietorships—cannot have ESOPs or stock bonus plans because they have no stock.

Finally, a professional corporation may not be able to establish an ESOP or stock bonus plan because state corporate law may require all shareholders of a professional corporation to be licensed professionals.

Question – Can S corporation ownership of employer stock be used as part of a plan to convert nondeductible benefits for corporate shareholders into deductible items?

Answer – Arrangements to do this, which in general are too complex to describe here, are scrutinized closely by the IRS. The Services has adopted a complex regulation package to regulate this type of transaction,[33] and any proposed plan of this type should be adopted only after considering the consequences of this IRS position. Note that somewhat similar planning using Roth IRAs that own corporate stock have also been subject to IRS regulation.[34]

Question – Can a stock bonus plan or ESOP hold life insurance or investments other than employer stock?

Answer – A stock bonus plan is apparently flexible in its investments and can hold the same types and diversity of investments as a regular profit sharing plan.

An ESOP, however, must meet a requirement that it be invested "primarily in employer securities."[35] Neither the IRS nor the Labor Department has issued an official interpretation of this "primarily" requirement, so investments other than employer securities should be very limited. However, some practitioners argue that this requirement means merely more than 50 percent of the assets.

Stock bonus plans and ESOPs can invest in insurance contracts, within the limitations discussed here. However, if the plan participant has the right to name the beneficiary of the death benefit, the amount of insurance is subject to the same "incidental" limitations that apply to qualified profit sharing plans (see Chapter 22).

CHAPTER ENDNOTES

1. See ERISA Sections 407, 408; Code Sections 401(a)(23),(h),(o).
2. I.R.C. §1042.
3. I.R.C. §401(a)(28).
4. See I.R.C. §1361(b)(1)(B). Special rules enacted by EGTRRA 2001 are designed to discourage the use of S corporation ESOPs to primarily benefit a small number of highly compensated employees.
5. Treas. Reg. §§1.401-1(a)(2)(iii); 1.401-1(b)(1)(iii). See also I.R.C. §409(h).
6. I.R.C. §401(a)(17); Notice 2006-98, 2006-46 IRB 906.
7. Treas. Reg. §§1.401(l)-1(a)(4)(ii), 54.4975-11(a)(7)(ii).
8. I.R.C. §§401(a)(22), 409(e)(3).
9. I.R.C. §409(e)(2).
10. I.R.C. §401(a)(11)(c).
11. I.R.C. §§401(a)(23), 409(h).
12. I.R.C. §401(a)(28)(C).
13. I.R.C. §401(a)(28)(B).
14. The prohibited transaction exemption required for ESOP loans is in I.R.C. §§4975(d)(3), 4975(e)(7) and 4975(e)(8).
15. Prior to 1996 legislation, the Code allowed an additional advantage in the form of an exclusion for the lending institution of 50% of the interest income from a loan to an ESOP used to acquire employer securities (provided the ESOP owned more than 50% of the outstanding stock of the employer corporation). This exclusion was repealed, generally effective for loans made after August 20, 1996. I.R.C. §133, prior to repeal by SBJPA '96. However, certain refinancings (of the principal amount immediately before the refinancing) and loans pursuant to a written contract in effect on June 10, 1996 are treated as having been made prior to the effective date of the repeal. SBJPA '96, Section 1602(c).
16. I.R.C. §409(h).
17. I.R.C. §§401(a)(22) and 409(e).
18. See Blair, "Insider Reporting and Short Swing Trading Rules for Qualified Defined Contribution Plans," *Benefits Quarterly*, 1st Quarter 1992.
19. I.R.C. §415(c); Notice 2006-98, 2006-46 IRB 906.
20. I.R.C. §§415(c)(6), 404(a)(9)(B).
21. I.R.C. §§402(a), 403(a).

22. I.R.C. §402(e)(4). If employer securities are distributed in other than a lump sum distribution, the net unrealized appreciation is excludable only to the extent attributable to nondeductible employee contributions. I.R.C. §402(e)(4)(A).
23. I.R.C. §402(d)(4), as in effect prior to repeal after 1999 by SBJPA '96.
24. I.R.C. §1042.
25. I.R.C. §§1042(b)(4), 4978(b)(1).
26. I.R.C. §§404(a)(3), 404(a)(9)(C).
27. I.R.C. §404(a)(9).
28. I.R.C. §§404(k)(2)(A), 404(k)(7); see also I.R.C. §1(h)(11)(B)(ii)(III).
29. See Rev. Proc. 87-22, 1987-1 CB 718.
30. See I.R.C. §1(h)(11).
31. I.R.C. §§4975(e)(8), 409(l).
32. See I.R.C. §§409(p), 4979A. These provisions generally took effect for plan years beginning after 2004, but in the case of ESOPs established after March 14, 2001 and ESOPs holding stock in a corporation that made an S election after March 14, 2001, the rules became effective for plan years ending after March 14, 2001.
33. Treas. Reg. §1.409(p)-1.
34. Notice 2004-8, 2004-4 IRB 333.
35. I.R.C. §4975(e)(7)(A).

SAVINGS/MATCH PLAN

CHAPTER 24

INTRODUCTION

A savings plan (or "thrift plan") is a qualified defined contribution plan that is similar to a profit sharing plan, with features that provide for and encourage after-tax employee contributions to the plan.

A typical savings plan provides for after-tax employee contributions with matching employer contributions. Each employee elects to contribute a certain percentage of his or her compensation, and these employee contributions are matched—either dollar for dollar or under some other formula—by employer contributions to the plan. Employee contributions are not deductible—the employee pays tax on the money before contributing it to the plan.

Although savings plans with only after-tax employee contributions and employer matching contributions were very popular in the past, the after-tax employee contribution approach has more recently been used only as an add-on to a Section 401(k) plan. Some employers adopt a plan that combines all the features of a regular profit sharing plan, a savings plan, and Section 401(k) salary reductions. Some employers may replace the savings plan component with a Roth 401(k) feature, which allows after-tax contributions and tax-free withdrawals after certain requirements are met. See Chapter 19 for details.

"Pure" savings plans, featuring only after-tax employee contributions are rare. However, a savings plan with after-tax employee contributions (often matched by the employer) is sometimes part of a Section 401(k) plan or profit-sharing plan.

WHEN IS USE OF SUCH A DEVICE INDICATED?

1. As an add-on feature to a Section 401(k) plan to allow employees to increase contributions beyond the annual limit on salary reductions under Section 401(k) plans. Unlike Roth 401(k) contributions (see Chapter 19); thrift plan contributions are not subject to the dollar limit on elective deferrals ($18,000 in 2015). However, after-tax contributions are subject to their own complex limitations as discussed under "Tax Implications," below.

2. When the employee group has the following characteristics:

   - Many employees are relatively young and have substantial time to accumulate retirement savings.

   - Many employees are willing to accept a degree of investment risk in their plan accounts in return for the potential benefits of good investment results.

   - There is a wide variation among employees in the need or desire for retirement savings.

3. When the employer wants to supplement the company's defined benefit pension plan with a plan that features individual participant accounts and the opportunity for participants to save on a tax-deferred basis. The use of a combination of plans provides a balanced retirement program.

Advantages

1. As with all qualified plans, a savings plan provides a tax-deferred retirement savings medium for employees. The tax on the employee contributions themselves is not deferred (since they are made on an after-tax basis); however, income taxes on subsequent investment earnings are deferred until distributions are made to employees from the plan.

2. The plan allows employees to control the amount of their savings. Employees have the option of taking all their compensation in cash and not contributing to the plan. (However, if they do so, they generally lose any employer matching contributions under the plan.)

3. Individual participant accounts allow participants to benefit from favorable plan investment results.

Disadvantages

1. The plan cannot be counted on by employees to provide an adequate benefit. First, benefits will not be significant unless employees make substantial contributions to the plan on a regular basis. Furthermore, employees who enter the plan at older ages may not be able to make sufficient contributions to the plan, even if they wish to do so, because of (a) the limits on annual contributions discussed under "Tax Implications," below, and (b) the limited number of years remaining for plan contributions prior to retirement.

2. Employees bear investment risk under the plan. Bearing the investment risk is a potential disadvantage to employees, but from the employer's perspective the shift of risk is a positive feature. Employer costs are lower for a defined contribution plan such as a savings plan, as compared with a defined benefit plan.

3. Since employee accounts and matching amounts must be individually accounted for in the plan, the administrative costs for a savings plan are greater than those for a money purchase or a profit sharing plan without employee contributions.

4. The annual addition to each employee's account in a savings plan is limited to the *lesser of* (a) 100 percent of compensation or (b) $53,000 (in 2015 as indexed).[1] This may limit the relative tax advantage available to highly compensated employees under a savings plan or any other defined contribution plan.

DESIGN FEATURES

Typical savings plans provide after-tax employee contributions with employer matching contributions. Participation in the plan is voluntary; each employee elects to contribute a chosen percentage of compensation up to a maximum percentage specified in the plan. The employee receives no tax deduction for this contribution and the contribution is fully subject to income tax as if it were in the employee's hands.

The employer makes a matching contribution to the savings plan. The employer match can be dollar-for-dollar, or the employer may put in some percentage of the employee contribution. A typical plan might permit an employee to contribute annually any whole percentage of compensation from 1 to 6 percent, with the employer contributing at the rate of half the chosen employee percentage. In this example then, if the employee elected to contribute 4 percent of compensation, the employer would be obligated to contribute an additional 2 percent.

Employer matching contributions are subject to the same vesting requirements as are applied to other defined contribution plans; that is either 100 percent "cliff vesting" after three years, or "graded vesting" starting with 20 percent after two years and increasing by 20 percent each year until 100 percent is reached after six years.[2]

In general, higher paid employees are in a position to contribute considerably more to this type of plan than lower paid employees. To prevent discrimination in savings plans, Section 401(m) imposes tests that effectively limit contributions by highly compensated employees (discussed under "Tax Implications," below). One of the principal administrative burdens in a savings plan is a need to monitor employee contribution levels to be sure the Section 401(m) nondiscrimination tests are met.

Apart from the employee contribution features, savings plans have features similar to profit sharing plans. Emphasis is usually put on the "savings account-like" features of the plan. Usually there are generous provisions for employee withdrawal of funds and for plan loans. Savings plans often feature participant-investment direction or earmarking. Earmarking is usually provided by allowing employees a choice among several specified pooled investment funds (such as mutual funds). However, it is possible, although administratively burdensome, to allow participants to direct virtually any type of investment for their account. If certain Department of Labor regulations are satisfied, the plan trustee and the employer are relieved of fiduciary liability for unsatisfactory investment results from investments chosen by the participant under a participant-directed investment provision.[3] The regulations include the requirement that at least three different diversified investment alternatives be made available to the employee. Life insurance can be used in the plan, as discussed in Chapter 18.

As noted above, many employers adopt a plan that combines all the features of a regular profit sharing plan, a savings plan, and Section 401(k) salary reductions. These combined plans can have one or more of the following features:

- employee after-tax contributions
- employer matching of employee after-tax contributions
- employee (before-tax) salary reductions (Section 401(k) amounts)
- employer matching of Section 401(k) amounts
- employer contributions based on a formula
- discretionary employer contributions
- Roth 401(k) contributions

These are discussed further in Chapter 19.

TAX IMPLICATIONS

For Employers

- Employer contributions to the plan are deductible when made so long as the plan remains "qualified" and separate accounts are maintained for all participants in the plan.[4] A plan is qualified if it meets eligibility, vesting, funding and other requirements discussed in Chapter 13.

- Certain employers adopting a new plan may be eligible for a business tax credit of up to $500 for "qualified startup costs." See Chapter 15 for details.

- The plan is subject to the ERISA reporting and disclosure rules outlined in Chapter 16.

For Employees

- Employee contributions to the plan, whether or not matched, are not tax deductible. (Before-tax employee salary reductions must meet the requirements of Section 401(k) discussed in Chapter 19.)

- Assuming a plan remains qualified, taxation of the employee is deferred with respect to (a) employer contributions to the plan and (b) investment earnings on both employer and employee contributions. These amounts are nontaxable to plan participants until a distribution is made from the plan.[5]

- A plan may permit employees to make voluntary contributions to a "deemed IRA" established under the plan. Amounts so contributed reduce the limit for other traditional or Roth IRA contributions. See Chapter 19 for details.

- Distributions from the plan must follow the rules for qualified plan distributions. Certain premature distributions are subject to penalties. The distribution rules are discussed in Chapter 14.

- Certain employees born before 1936 may be eligible for a ten-year averaging tax calculation on lump-sum distributions. Not all distributions are eligible for this special tax calculation. The rules are discussed in detail in Chapter 14.

Nondiscrimination Testing

In order to be deemed nondiscriminatory (i.e., to prevent the plan from discriminating in favor of highly compensated employees), the plan must meet an *actual contribution percentage* (ACP) test under Code section 401(m). This test is applied to employee contributions, as well as to matching contributions. However, *matching* contributions can meet the ACP test in any of the three ways described below, while employee contributions must be tested under alternative (1) below:

1. The ACP test is satisfied for a plan year if, for highly compensated employees, the average

ratio (expressed as a percentage) of employee contributions (both matched and non-matched) plus employer matching contributions to compensation for the plan year does not exceed the greater of:[6]

a. 125 percent of the contribution percentage (i.e., ratio) for all other eligible employees for the preceding plan year, or

b. the lesser of (a) 200 percent of the contribution percentage for all other eligible employees, or (b) such percentage plus two percentage points for the preceding plan year.

Example. If employee contributions and employer matching contributions for nonhighly compensated employees equaled 6 percent of compensation for the year, those for highly compensated employees could be up to 8 percent (6 percent plus 2 percent) for that year. Under the Code and regulations, the employer may take into account certain 401(k) salary reduction contributions and certain employer plan contributions in meeting this test.[7]

---

2. The ACP test can be satisfied with respect to matching contributions by meeting the requirements for a SIMPLE 401(k) plan (see Chapter 19).

3. A safe harbor plan will satisfy the nondiscrimination test with respect to matching contributions. By design, a safe harbor plan is one that satisfies:

   a. a contribution requirement;

   b. a notice requirement; and

   c. a matching contribution limitation

Under alternative (1), the employer must conduct annual testing to monitor the level of contributions made by nonhighly compensated employees, and then make sure that highly compensated employees do not exceed this level the following year, in order for the plan to remain qualified. Alternatives (2) and (3) are design-based so that annual testing of matching contributions is not necessary, but both include a funding requirement. The safe harbor design generally parallels the requirements for a safe harbor 401(k) plan (described in Chapter 19).

The definition of highly compensated employee for purposes of these tests is the same as that applicable to all benefit plans (and is discussed in detail in Chapter 13).

Safe Harbor Plans

As described above, a safe harbor SIMPLE 401(k) plan must meet three requirements: (1) a contribution requirement; (2) a notice requirement; and (3) a matching contribution limit. These requirements are detailed below.

1. The *contribution requirement* for the safe harbor test states that the employer must make either matching contributions that are:

   a. equal to 100 percent of elective contributions that do not exceed 3 percent of compensation; *plus*

   b. 50 percent of elective contributions that are between 3 and 5 percent of compensation

   Additionally, in no event can the rate for highly compensated employees exceed the rate for nonhighly compensated employees) OR nonelective contributions (on behalf of all employees, equal to at least 3 percent of compensation).

2. Under the *notice requirement*, each employee eligible to participate must, before the plan year begins, be given written notice that:

   a. the plan may be amended during the plan year to provide a nonelective contribution of at least 3 percent; and

   b. if it is, a supplemental notice will be given to eligible employees thirty days prior to the last day of the plan year informing them of the amendment.

   If the plan is amended, the supplemental notice must then be provided to each eligible employee at least thirty days prior to the end of the plan year (i.e., by December 1 for a calendar year).[8]

3. The matching contribution limitation is met if:

   a. no employer match can be made for employee deferrals in excess of 6 percent of compensation;

   b. the rate of match does not increase as the employee deferral rate increases; and

   c. matching contribution rates for highly compensated employees are not greater than those for nonhighly compensated employees.[9]

HOW TO INSTALL A PLAN

Installation of a savings plan follows the qualified plan installation procedures described in Chapter 12.

WHERE CAN I FIND OUT MORE?

Tax Facts on Insurance & Employee Benefits, Cincinnati, OH: The National Underwriter Company (revised annually).

CHAPTER ENDNOTES

1. I.R.C. §415(c).
2. I.R.C. §411(a)(2)(B).
3. DOL Reg. §2550.404c-1.
4. I.R.C. §404(a)(3).
5. I.R.C. §402(a). Recovery of the nontaxable amount differs depending on whether the after-tax contributions were made before 1987 or after 1986. See Chapter 13, "Nontaxable and Taxable Amounts."
6. I.R.C. §401(m)(2).
7. I.R.C. §401(m)(3); Treas. Reg. §1.401(m)-2(a)(5) and (6).
8. Notice 2000-3, 2000-1 CB 413.
9. I.R.C. §§401(m)(11)(a)(i), 401(k)(12)(C).

MONEY PURCHASE PENSION PLAN

CHAPTER 25

INTRODUCTION

A money purchase plan is a qualified employer retirement plan that is, in many ways, the simplest of all qualified plans:

- Each employee has an individual account in the plan. The employer makes annual contributions to each employee's account under a nondiscriminatory contribution formula. Usually, the formula requires a contribution of a specified percentage (up to 25 percent as explained below) of each employee's annual compensation. Annual contributions to the employee's account generally cannot be more than $53,000 (in 2015, as indexed).
- Plan benefits consist of the amount accumulated in each participant's account at retirement or termination of employment. This is the total of employer contributions, interest or other investment return on plan assets, and capital gains realized by the plan on sales of assets in the employee's account.
- The plan may provide that the employee's account balance is payable in one or more forms of annuities equivalent in value to the account balance.

WHEN IS USE OF SUCH A DEVICE INDICATED?

1. When an employer wants to install a qualified retirement plan that is simple to administer and explain to employees.
2. When employees are relatively young and have substantial time to accumulate retirement savings.
3. When employees are willing to accept a degree of investment risk in their plan accounts, in return for the potential benefits of good investment results.
4. When some degree of retirement income security in the plan is desired. (While accounts are not guaranteed unless certain vesting requirements are satisfied, annual employer contributions are required. This provides a degree of retirement security that is intermediate between a defined benefit plan and a profit sharing plan.)
5. When an employer seeks to reward long-term employee relationships.

Advantages

1. As with all qualified plans, a money purchase plan provides a tax-deferred retirement savings medium for employees.
2. The plan is relatively simple and inexpensive to design, administer, and explain to employees.
3. The plan formula can provide a deductible annual employer contribution of up to the lesser of (a) 100 percent of the employee's compensation or (b) $53,000 (in 2015). However, the employer's deduction is limited to 25 percent of covered payroll. Therefore, a money purchase plan typically provides a formula of up to 25 percent of each employee's compensation, with the contribution not exceeding $53,000.[1]
4. Individual participant accounts allow participants to benefit from good investment results in the plan fund.

Disadvantages

1. Retirement benefits may be inadequate for employees who enter the plan at older ages. For example, if an employer contributes 10 percent of compensation annually to each employee's account, the accumulation at age sixty-five for employees with varying entry ages will be as follows, assuming the plan investments earn an average return of 9 percent annually:

Age at plan entry	Annual compensation	Account balance at age 65
25	$35,000	$1,289,022
30	35,000	822,937
40	35,000	323,134
50	35,000	112,012
55	35,000	57,961
60	35,000	22,832

This illustration shows that the "time factor and compound earnings factor" work rapidly to increase account balances. If a closely held corporation that has been in business for many years adopts a money purchase plan, key employees often will be among the older plan entrants. The money purchase plan's failure to provide adequately for such employees, even with their higher compensation levels, can be a serious disadvantage.

However, this is not the whole story—there's another factor in realistic situations that reduces the apparent disparity between long-service and short-service employees. Because salaries increase over time, the long service/short service disparity in the annual pension from a money-purchase plan—as a percentage of final average compensation—is much less than if salaries do not increase. Figure 25.1 shows that, if all salaries increase at 7 percent annually, a fifteen-year employee receives a pension of 19 percent of final average salary while the thirty-five-year employee gets 48 percent of final average salary. This is much less than the disparity resulting

Figure 25.1

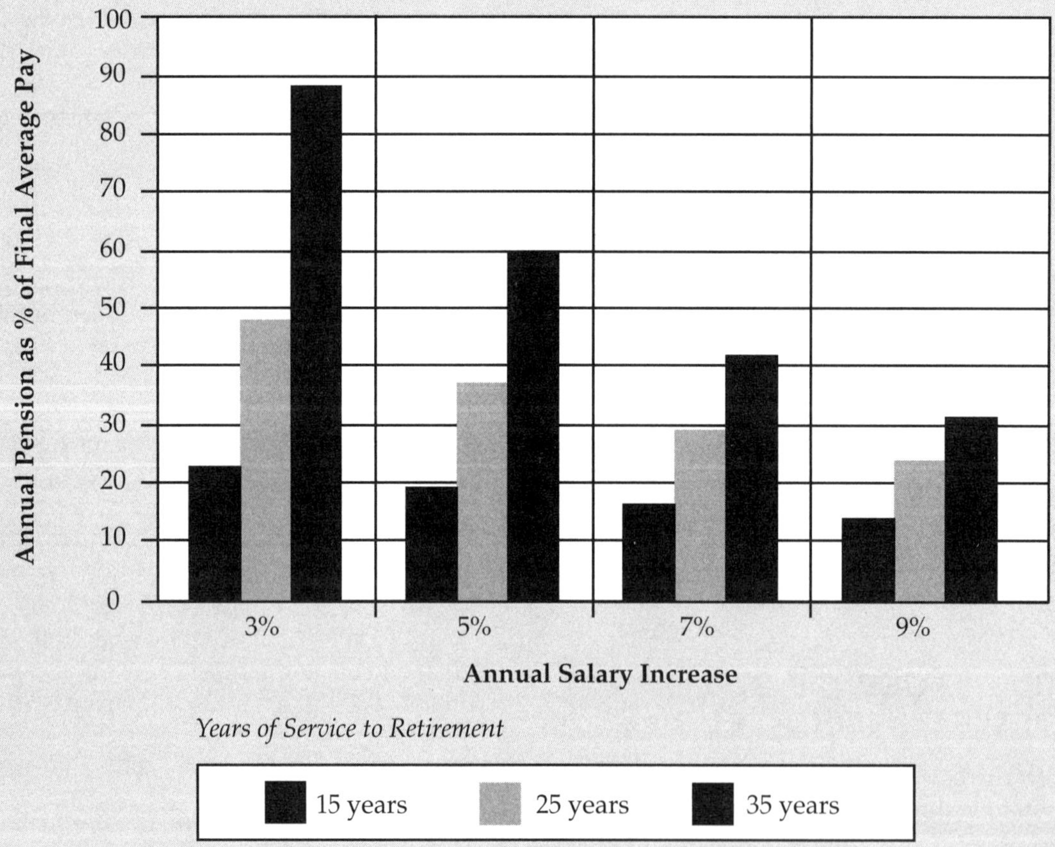

Assumptions: 8% investment return, annual employer contribution of 10% of compensation.

if salaries increase at only 3 percent annually, or do not increase at all. In short, in actual practice a money purchase plan may not be as disadvantageous to shorter service employees as might appear. Note, however, that in recent years salaries of rank-and-file employees have not risen as rapidly with longer service as they did in earlier generations.

2. The annual addition to each employee's account in a money purchase plan is limited to the lesser of (a) $53,000 (in 2015, as indexed), or (b) 100 percent of compensation.[2] This, plus the $265,000 cap on compensation (in 2015, as indexed), limits the relative amount of funding available for highly compensated employees. For example, if an employee earns $300,000 in 2015, no more than $53,000 annually can be contributed for that employee; but that $53,000 is only 20 percent of the $255,000 of the employee's compensation that is allowed to be taken into account, and only 17.6 percent of the actual compensation of $300,000.

3. Employees bear investment risk under the plan. The ultimate amount that can be accumulated under a money purchase plan is very sensitive to investment return, even for an employee who entered the plan at an early age. Figure 25.2 shows this by comparing the ultimate account balance resulting from $1,000 of annual contribution at two different return rates. Also, note that the employee can be significantly disadvantaged if retirement occurs at a time of economic downturn, resulting in an abnormally low retirement fund.

   While bearing investment risk is a potential disadvantage to employees, it does tend to reduce employer costs as compared with a defined benefit plan.

4. The plan is subject to the Internal Revenue Code's minimum funding requirements. Employers are obligated to make the plan contribution each year or be subject to minimum funding penalties. By contrast, under current law, a qualified profit sharing plan (see Chapter 22) permits the same level of deduction to the employer (i.e., 25 percent of payroll) as a money purchase plan, but without the requirement of mandated minimum annual contributions.

Figure 25.2

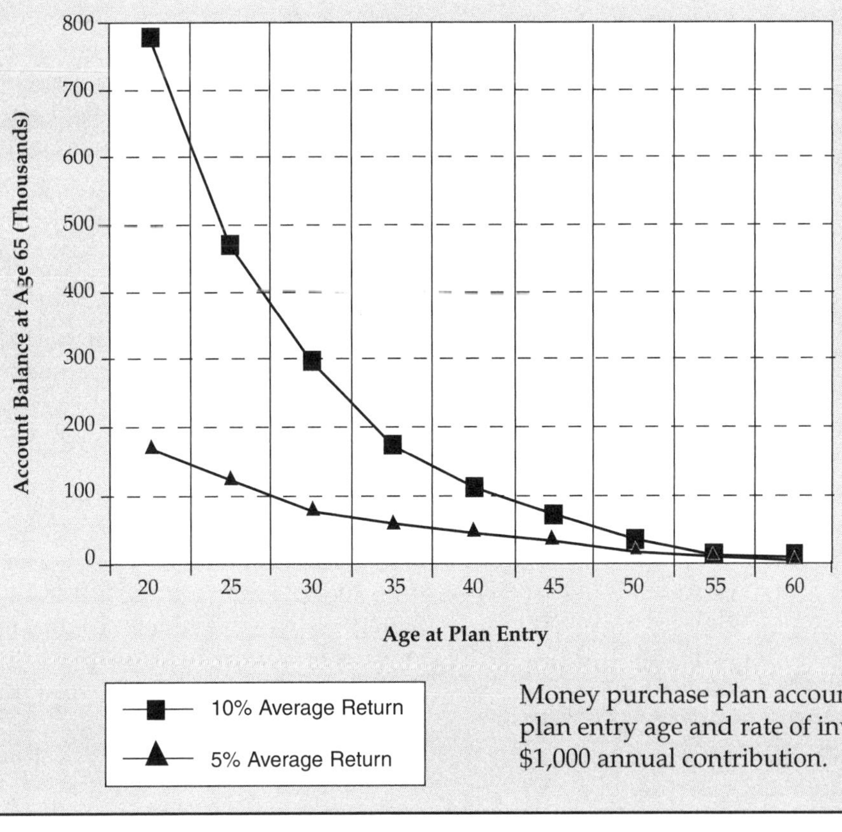

Money purchase plan account balance related to plan entry age and rate of investment return, for $1,000 annual contribution.

DESIGN FEATURES

Most money purchase plans use a benefit formula requiring an employer contribution that is a flat percentage of each employee's compensation. Percentages up to 25 percent may be used - contributions in excess of 25 percent are not tax deductible for the employer. Only the first $265,000 (in 2015, as indexed) of each employee's compensation can be taken into account in the plan formula.[3]

Some money purchase formulas also use a factor related to the employee's service. Service-related factors generally favor owners and key employees. In small, closely held businesses or professional corporations, the use of a service-related factor might result in prohibited discrimination in favor of highly compensated employees. Plan designers generally avoid service-related contribution formulas in these situations.

Nondiscrimination regulations under Code section 401(a)(4) provide safe harbors for money purchase plans with uniform allocation formulas; alternative methods for satisfying nondiscrimination requirements include satisfying a general nondiscrimination test, restructuring, or cross-testing (testing defined contribution plans on the basis of benefits see Chapter 26).[4]

A plan benefit formula can be "integrated" with Social Security (integration is also referred to as "permitted disparity"). This avoids duplicating Social Security benefits already provided to the employee and reduces employer costs for the plan. An integrated formula defines a level of compensation known as the "integration level." The plan then provides a higher rate of employer contributions for compensation above the integration level than the rate for compensation below the integration level.

> *Example*. A money purchase plan specifies an integration level of $20,000 and provides for employer contributions of 14 percent of compensation above the $20,000 integration level and 10 percent below the $20,000 integration level. Employee Art Rambo earns $30,000 this year. The employer contribution to Art's account this year totals $3,400—10 percent of the first $20,000 of Art's compensation plus 14 percent of $10,000 (Art's compensation in excess of the $20,000 integration level).

The Internal Revenue Code and regulations specify the degree of integration permitted in a plan. These rules are discussed further in Chapter 13.

Any of the Code's permitted vesting provisions can be used in a money purchase plan. Since money purchase plans tend to be oriented toward longer service employees, the three-year "cliff vesting" provision (that is, no vesting until three years of service, then 100 percent vesting) is often used.

If an employee leaves before becoming fully vested in his or her account balance, an unvested amount—referred to as a "forfeiture"—is left behind in the plan. Forfeitures can be used to reduce future employer contributions under the plan, to be allocated to remaining participants' account balances as additional contributions or to pay for plan administrative expenses. Adding forfeitures to participants' account balances tends to be favorable to key employees, since they are likely to participate in the plan over a long time period. For this reason, the IRS requires forfeitures to be allocated in a nondiscriminatory manner. This usually requires forfeiture allocation in proportion to participants' compensation, rather than in proportion to their existing account balances.

Benefits in a money purchase plan are usually payable at termination of employment or at the plan's stated normal retirement age. Money purchase plans traditionally provide that the participant's account balance is converted to an equivalent annuity at retirement, based on annuity rates provided in the plan. This is the origin of the term "money purchase." However, it has become more common to provide for a lump sum or installment payment from the plan as an alternative to an annuity. Nevertheless, a money purchase plan, as a condition of qualification, must provide a joint and survivor annuity as the automatic form of benefit even if lump sum or installment payment options are available. The participant, with the consent of the spouse, may elect a different benefit option. This is discussed further in Chapter 14.

"In-service distributions"—that is, benefits payable before termination of employment, are permitted so long as the participant has attained age 59½. Otherwise, distributions of employer contributions or earnings from pension plans are not permitted prior to death, retirement, disability, severance of employment or termination of the plan.[5] However, plan loan provisions are allowable, although relatively uncommon.

Money purchase plan funds may be invested in a pooled account managed (through a trustee or insurance company) by the employer or a fund manager designated by the employer. Either a trust fund or group or individual insurance contracts can be used. Chapter 20 discusses how life insurance can be used in the plan.

TAX IMPLICATIONS

For Employers

- Employer contributions to the plan are deductible when made, so long as the plan remains "qualified."[6] A plan is qualified if it meets eligibility, vesting, funding and other requirements discussed in Chapter 13. In addition, the plan must designate that it is a money purchase pension plan.[7] The deduction is limited to 25 percent of total payroll of the employees covered under the plan.[8]

- The plan is subject to the minimum funding rules of the Code.[9] This requires minimum annual contributions, subject to a penalty imposed on the employer if less than the minimum amount is contributed.[10] For a money purchase plan, the minimum contribution is generally the amount required under the plan's contribution formula. For example, if the plan formula requires a contribution of 20 percent of each participant's compensation, this is generally the amount required to meet the minimum funding rules. Chapter 13 discusses these rules further.

- Certain employers adopting a new plan may be eligible for a business tax credit of up to $500 for "qualified startup costs." See Chapter 15 for details.

- The plan is subject to the ERISA reporting and disclosure rules outlined in Chapter 16.

For Employees

- Assuming the plan remains qualified, taxation of the employee on plan contributions is deferred. Both employer contributions and earnings on plan assets are nontaxable to plan participants until withdrawn.[11]

- Under Code section 415, annual additions to each participant's account are limited to the lesser of (a) 100 percent of the participant's compensation, or (b) $53,000 (in 2015, as indexed).[12] "Annual additions" include employer contributions to the participant's account, forfeitures from other participants' accounts; and employee contributions to the account.[13]

- Distributions from the plan must follow the rules for qualified plan distributions. Certain premature distributions are subject to penalties. The distribution rules are discussed in Chapter 14.

- For certain employees born before 1936, lump sum distributions made after age 59½ may be eligible for a special ten-year averaging tax computation that may reduce tax rates on the benefit. Not all distributions are eligible for these calculations. Chapter 14 covers these rules.

- A plan may permit employees to make voluntary contributions to a "deemed IRA" established under the plan. Amounts so contributed reduce the limit for other traditional or Roth IRA contributions. See Chapters 19 and 20 for details.

ALTERNATIVES

1. Target benefit plans are much like money purchase plans, but the employer contribution percentage can be based on age at plan entry—higher for older entrants. Such a plan may be more favorable where the employer wants to provide adequate benefits for older employees.

2. Profit sharing plans provide more employer flexibility in contributions but less security for participants. The limit on deductible contributions to a profit sharing plan is 25 percent of payroll.

3. Defined benefit plans provide more security of retirement benefits and proportionately greater contributions for older plan entrants, but are much more complex to design and administer.

4. Nonqualified deferred compensation plans can be provided exclusively for selected executives, but the employer's tax deduction is generally deferred until benefit payments are made. This can be as much as twenty or thirty years after the employer's contribution is made.

5. Individual retirement saving is available as an alternative or supplement to an employer plan, but except for certain IRAs, there is no tax deferral.

HOW TO INSTALL A PLAN

Installation of a money purchase plan follows the qualified plan installation procedure described in Chapter 15.

WHERE CAN I FIND OUT MORE?

Graduate Course: Qualified Retirement Plan (GS 814), The American College, Bryn Mawr, PA.

FREQUENTLY ASKED QUESTIONS

Question – Can a self-employed person adopt a money purchase plan?

Answer – A self-employed person can adopt a money purchase plan covering not only his or her regular employees, if any, but also covering the self-employed person(s). Such plans are sometimes referred to as "Keogh" or "HR 10" plans. The self-employed person is treated much the same as the regular employees covered, but there are some special rules and planning considerations that are covered in Chapter 31.

Question – What special issues are involved in money purchase plans covering shareholder-employees in an S corporation?

Answer – S corporations can have money purchase plans that cover shareholder-employees as well as regular employees. However, the plan contribution formula generally cannot provide an employer contribution for all of the shareholder-employee's income from the corporation. The employer contribution formula can be based only on the shareholder's compensation for services rendered to the corporation. Any portion of the shareholder's income that represents dividends must be excluded from the plan formula.

Question – Can an employer fund a money purchase plan using employee salary reductions?

Answer – Salary reductions by employees allowing employee contributions on a before-tax basis are allowed only in

- a profit sharing (Section 401(k) type) plan;
- a salary reduction SEP (simplified employee pension), which had to be adopted before 199 (see Chapter 31);
- a SIMPLE IRA (see Chapter 30); or
- a Section 403(b) tax deferred annuity plan (tax-exempt employers only).

Thus, this kind of funding for a money purchase plan is not available except for a plan "grandfathered" under pre-1974 law.

However, money purchase plans can allow after-tax contributions by employees to increase account balances (permitting greater tax-sheltered investment accumulation) and ultimate retirement benefits. Such after-tax contribution provisions must meet the administratively complex nondiscrimination rules of Code section 401(m). (These are discussed in Chapter 32.) As a result of these rules, after-tax contribution provisions in money purchase plans are uncommon.

CHAPTER ENDNOTES

1. The employer's deduction to a money purchase pension plan cannot exceed the Section 415 annual additions limit for a defined contribution plan. I.R.C. §404(j)(1). For years beginning in 2013, this 415 limit is the lesser of (a) $51,000, or (b) 100% of compensation. I.R.C. §415(c).
2. I.R.C. §415(c).
3. I.R.C. §401(a)(17).
4. See Treas. Reg. §1.401(a)(4)-2.
5. See Rev. Rul. 69-277, 1969-1 CB 116; Rev. Rul. 74-417, 1974-2 CB 131. If money purchase plan assets are "spun-off" to a profit sharing plan, the accounts in the new plan must retain the money purchase restrictions on in-service distributions. However, if the money purchase accounts are "rolled over" to a profit sharing plan (i.e., distributed to participants who then recontribute them to the successor plan), the money purchase plan in-service restrictions no longer apply. Rev. Rul. 94-76, 1994-2 CB 46.
6. I.R.C. §404(a).
7. I.R.C. §401(a)(27)(B).
8. I.R.C. §404(a)(3)(A)(v).
9. I.R.C. §§412(a), 412(h); 430.
10. I.R.C. §4971.
11. I.R.C. §402(a).
12. See I.R.C. §415(c); Notice 2008-102, 2008-45 IRB 1106.
13. I.R.C. §415(c)(2).

CROSS-TESTED/ AGE-WEIGHTED PLAN

CHAPTER 26

INTRODUCTION

An age-weighted contribution allocation formula in a defined contribution plan generally allows higher contribution levels (as a percentage of compensation) for older plan participants. That is, the formula for annual employer contributions or allocations to participant accounts is based not only on the participant's compensation but also on the participant's *age* on entering the plan.

Age-weighting permits account balances of older plan participants to build up in the relatively short time before retirement. In addition, with an age-weighted formula, the employer's plan contributions tend to be weighted toward owners and key employees since in many businesses these employees will be older than rank-and-file employees when the plan is adopted.

The most common type of plan using age-weighting is the *cross-tested plan*, which is often called a *new comparability plan*; other marketing designations are sometimes used. A cross-tested plan does not use a fixed age-weighted formula. Instead, the plan is designed to provide maximized benefits to highly compensated employees, and benefits for other employees are designed to provide the minimum contribution that is required by nondiscrimination regulations under Code section 401(a)(4). A minimum of 5 percent of compensation for the nonhighly compensated employees is generally required, as discussed below.

> *Example.* A plan covering thirteen employees plan might provide for a $53,000 annual contribution for each of the three highly compensated employees, and for the remaining ten employees, the plan would provide a flat percentage of compensation that meets certain tests under the nondiscrimination regulations.

Plans can also be designed using fixed formulas based on each participant's age and compensation. An *age-weighted profit sharing plan* is a profit sharing plan in which the allocation formula contains an actuarial age-weighting factor (i.e., providing a higher allocation for older plan participants). A *target plan* is a pension plan with an age-weighted contribution formula. A target plan, unlike an age-weighted profit sharing plan, requires annual employer contributions to meet the Code's minimum funding standards.

WHEN IS USE OF SUCH A DEVICE INDICATED?

1. When business owners and key employees are generally older than rank-and-file employees and the objective is to provide the maximum contribution for the owners and key employees in a defined contribution plan ($53,000 annually as indexed for 2015), while minimizing costs for covering remaining employees.

2. When the features of a regular defined contribution plan would be attractive to the employer, except that there are older employees whose retirement benefits would be inadequate because of the relatively few years remaining for participation in the plan. The age-weighted formula allows proportionately greater employer contributions for these older employees (greater percentages of their compensation).

3. When the employer is looking for an alternative that provides adequate retirement benefits to older

employees but has the lower cost and simplicity of a defined contribution plan.

4. When an employer wants to terminate an existing defined benefit plan in order to avoid the increasing cost and regulatory burdens associated with these plans. If an age-weighted plan is substituted for the defined benefit plan, in many cases the new plan will provide approximately the same benefits to most employees, and it will be relatively easy to obtain IRS approval for the defined benefit plan termination.

5. When a closely held business or professional corporation has key employees who are approximately age fifty or older and who generally want to contribute less than the annual additions dollar limit of $53,000 (as indexed for 2015). The age-weighted plan is generally the ideal qualified plan to adopt in this situation, because its benefit level is just as high as would be available in a defined benefit plan (given the $53,000 (in 2015) annual restriction), but is much simpler and less expensive to install and administer.

Advantages

1. Retirement benefits can be maximized for employees who enter the plan at older ages. The following comparison of an age-weighted "target plan" (see below) with a money purchase plan illustrates this. The illustration shows how, for a total employer contribution of $12,600 in each case, the annual contribution and retirement benefit vary for three employees, each earning $30,000 annually:

Annual Contribution			Accumulation at 65 (5½% return)	
Employee age at entry	Money Purchase (14%)	Target	Money Purchase	Target
30	$4,200	$1,655	$444,214	$175,000
40	4,200	3,243	226,657	175,000
50	4,200	7,702	99,292	175,000

2. From the viewpoint of a business owner, particularly in a small, closely held business, the feature illustrated in the paragraph above also means that in an age-weighted plan, more of the total employer contributions in the age-weighted plan will likely be allocated to owners and key employees, as compared with a money purchase or other defined contribution plan. This will be the case if the owners and key employees are older than the average of all employees when the plan is adopted.

3. As with all qualified plans, an age-weighted plan provides a tax-deferred retirement savings medium for employees.

4. The age-weighted plan is relatively simple and inexpensive to design, administer, and explain to employees, compared with a defined benefit plan. Plans with fixed age-weighted formulas are more similar in this regard than are cross-tested plans.

5. Individual accounts for participants allow participants to benefit from good investment results in the plan fund.

Disadvantages

1. As with any defined contribution plan, the annual addition to each employee's account is limited to the lesser of (a) 100 percent of compensation, or (b) $53,000 (as indexed for 2015).[1] This limits the relative amount of funding for highly compensated employees. For older employees, a defined benefit plan may allow a much higher level of employer contributions to the plan, as discussed further under "Cross-Tested Plan Design," below.

2. Employees bear investment risk under the plan. While this is a disadvantage to employees, it also tends to reduce employer costs compared to a defined benefit plan. This is because the employer bears the investment risk in a defined benefit plan.

3. A target pension plan is subject to the Code's minimum funding requirements. Employers are obligated to make minimum contributions each year under the plan's contribution formula or be subject to minimum funding penalties. While an age-weighted or cross-tested profit sharing plan is not subject to the minimum funding requirements, contributions must be recurring and substantial as discussed in Chapter 24.

4. If the age-weighted plan is a profit sharing plan, the ultimate benefits to participants are particularly uncertain since the employer is not necessarily committed to any specific funding level and may even omit funding in some years.

5. In the case of a target pension plan or a cross-tested plan, actuarial services may be needed on an annual basis.

CROSS-TESTED PLAN DESIGN

A cross-tested defined contribution plan is designed to meet the nondiscrimination requirements of the regulations under Code Section 401(a)(4) based on the benefits it provides (i.e., it is tested as if it were a defined benefit plan, hence the term "cross testing").

Highly compensated employees are assumed to receive a larger annual allocation, as compared to non-highly compensated employees, up to the maximum amount permitted under the Section 415 annual additions limit (the lesser of $53,000, as indexed for 2013, or 100 percent of compensation). Then, the remaining employees are provided with an allocation that meets the minimum requirements of the cross-testing regulations.

The underlying approach of the cross-testing regulations is to test the plan's benefits available at retirement for nondiscrimination. This is done by projecting the year's contribution for each employee to that employee's retirement age (at an assumed rate of interest) and analyzing the benefit provided by the projected amount, as a percentage of the employee's compensation. If these projected benefits, as a percentage of compensation, do not discriminate in favor of highly compensated employees, then the plan is considered nondiscriminatory.

In order to use cross-testing, the plan must also satisfy a "gateway" requirement, set forth in regulations. Generally, the minimum gateway requirement is satisfied by providing all non-highly compensated employees with contributions equal to no less than one-third of the highest contribution (up to 5 percent of compensation) made to any highly compensated employee[2] Note that this may be higher than the 3-percent-of-compensation minimum required under the top-heavy rules (see Chapter 13).

While the cross-testing rules are complex, a simple example showing their application will illustrate the characteristics and advantages of the cross-tested plan.

Example. Dr. Ace, a solo medical practitioner, has an incorporated medical practice of which he and four others are employees. Dr. Ace is highly compensated and the others are nonhighly compensated within the meaning of the qualified plan rules (see Chapter 13). A cross-tested plan is proposed with the following characteristics:[3]

Participant	Age	Compensation	Plan contribution	% of compensation
Dr. Ace	53	$265,000	$53,000	20
A	55	50,000	2,500	5
B	30	30,000	1,500	5
C	25	30,000	1,500	5
D	25	30,000	1,500	5

The proposed plan provides a contribution of 5 percent of pay to meet the gateway required for the use of cross-testing. The next step is to project the contribution to each participant's age sixty-five, at an assumed rate of 8.5 percent interest (a rate between 7.5 and 8.5 percent must be used;[4] choosing the maximum of 8.5 percent provides the best result for the highly compensated employees).

For Dr. Ace, his $53,000 contribution accumulates to $141,069 at age sixty-five using compound rate of 8.5 percent. The accumulated contribution is then expressed as a life annuity and the annuity as a percentage of compensation is determined.[5] For Dr. Ace, the $141,069 accumulation equates to a $11,395 annuity which is 4.30 percent of his compensation of $265,000.

Participant	Compensation	Plan Contribution	Plan Cont. proj. to Age 65	Projected benefit	Projected Benefit as % of Compensation
Dr. Ace	$265,000	$53,000	$141,069	$11,395	4.30
A	50,000	2,500	5,652	540	1.08
B	30,000	1,500	26,069	2,492	8.31
C	30,000	1,500	39,200	3,746	12.49
D	30,000	1,500	39,200	3,746	12.49

The final step is to test the projected benefit under the coverage tests of Section 410(b). These benefits must satisfy either the ratio percentage test or the average benefit test of that section (see Chapter 13 for a general discussion of Section 410). The ratio percentage test is applied to a hypothetical "plan" consisting of the highly compensated participant (Dr. Ace) and all nonhighly compensated participants whose projected benefits are equal to or greater than those of Dr. Ace. In this case, this consists of Dr. Ace and participants B, C, and D. Under the ratio percentage test, at least 70 percent of the nonhighly compensated employees must be covered. The ratio percentage test is met since the percentage of nonhighly compensated participants who are covered is 75 percent (three out of four), Therefore, this plan meets the requirements of the cross-testing regulations. This test must be done each year.

If there is more than one highly compensated employee in the plan, the test may be more complicated. In that case, the plan must be broken into "rate groups" consisting of each highly compensated participant and all the employees who have projected benefits equal to or greater than the highly compensated participant. The Code section 410 coverage tests are then applied to the rate groups.

Disadvantages of Cross-Tested Plans

Disadvantages of cross-tested plans include:

- Design of the plan is somewhat unstable since hiring of new employees may make the plan suddenly impractical, depending on the age distribution of employees under the new employee census.
- If there are too many rank-and-file employees who are relatively older (ages comparable to that of the highly compensated participants) the cost of the cross-tested plan for the rank and file employees may be higher than that of other alternatives, such as a profit sharing plan integrated with Social Security.
- Similarly, if many highly compensated employees are relatively young, the plan provides fewer advantages as well.
- An analysis of the plan to determine whether it meets the cross-testing requirements must be done at least as often as new employees join the plan, and this can be costly. Software is available, however, for employers to do this "in-house" at relatively low cost.
- Having a plan like this in effect inhibits the hiring of new employees who are relatively old, and this could put the employer in danger of violating age discrimination laws as well as depriving it of the services of valuable and experienced employees with critical skills.

FIXED-FORMULA AGE-WEIGHTED PLANS

Age-Weighted Profit Sharing Plan

An age-weighted profit sharing plan with a fixed age-weighted (actuarial) formula for allocating employer contributions will automatically pass the cross-testing requirements since all participants will (by design) have the same projected benefit as a percentage of compensation. Use of a formula thus reduces the complexity of the plan and the costs of compliance, since periodic cross-testing is not required.

Disadvantages of Fixed-Formula Profit Sharing Plans

Although it is not immediately obvious from the nature of the plan, a fixed-formula plan is more difficult to communicate to employees and more difficult for them to understand than a cross-tested plan. The complicated mechanics of performing cross-testing are not a factor in explaining a cross-tested plan; employees simply understand that their annual allocation is 5 percent of compensation, generally applicable to all but the business owners.

By comparison, a fixed-formula plan has a different percentage of compensation for each age represented in the plan, and employees often have difficulty understanding why this is the case. In the cross-testing example above, if the employee group had a fixed formula plan, the percentage of compensation allocated each year to plan accounts would be much greater for employee A, age fifty-five, than for employees C and D, both age twenty-five. Employees tend to question the fairness of this, particularly younger employees who consider themselves valuable, and who in fact might be making a greater relative contribution to the business than the older employees.

Age-Weighted Pension (Target Benefit) Plan

A pension plan with a fixed age-weighted formula is similar to a profit sharing plan with a fixed formula except that as a pension plan, it is subject to the Code's minimum funding requirements. This means that an annual contribution equal to the amount required under the plan formula *must* be made or penalties are imposed. By comparison, a profit sharing plan is not subject to any annual funding requirement and annual contributions by the employer can be discretionary in amount. Profit sharing contributions can even be omitted in certain years, if permitted by the plan document, as long as they meet the IRS requirement of "substantial and recurring" contributions that applies to all profit sharing plans.

An age-weighted pension plan is generally referred to as a "target" plan since its design (with its requirement of mandatory annual employer funding) implies a funding target at each employee's retirement. However, as a defined contribution plan there is no guarantee of benefits or account balances, and the investment risk remains with the employee as with all defined contribution plans.

The disadvantages of target plans are the employee communication problem described in connection with fixed-formula profit sharing plans, and the inflexibility from the employer's standpoint resulting from the requirement of fixed annual funding.

TAX IMPLICATIONS

For Employers

- Employer contributions to an age-weighted plan are deductible when made, so long as the plan remains "qualified." A plan must meet the eligibility, vesting, funding and other requirements discussed in Chapter 13 to be qualified.

- A target pension plan, but not a profit sharing plan, is subject to the Code's minimum funding rules in code sections 412 and 430. This requires minimum annual contributions, subject to a penalty imposed on the employer if less than the minimum amount is contributed. For a target plan, the minimum funding requirement is generally the amount required under the plan's contribution formula. The minimum funding requirement, therefore, will be satisfied so long as the employer contributes to each participant's account the percentage of compensation required by the plan. Chapter 13 discusses the minimum funding rules further.

- Certain employers adopting a plan may be eligible for a business tax credit of up to $500 for "qualified startup costs." See Chapter 15 for details.

- The plan is subject to the ERISA reporting and disclosure rules outlined in Chapter 16.

For Employees

- Assuming the plan remains qualified, taxation of the employee on plan contributions is deferred. Both employer contributions and earnings on plan assets are nontaxable to plan participants until withdrawn.[6]

- Annual additions to each participant's account are limited to the lesser of (a) 100 percent of the participant's compensation or (b) $53,000 (in 2015, as indexed).[7] "Annual additions" include employer contributions to participants' accounts, forfeitures from other participants' accounts and employee contributions to the account.[8]

- Distributions from the plan must follow the rules for qualified plan distributions. Certain premature distributions are subject to penalties. The distribution rules are discussed in Chapter 14.

- For certain employees born before 1936, lump sum distributions made after age 59½ may be eligible for a special ten-year averaging tax computation. Chapter 14 covers these rules.

- A plan may permit employees to make voluntary contributions to a "deemed IRA" established under the plan. Amounts so contributed reduce the limit for other traditional or Roth IRA contributions. See Chapter 20 for details.

ALTERNATIVES

1. Defined benefit plans provide more benefit security because of the employer and government guarantee of benefit levels. Defined benefit plans also allow greater tax deductible employer contributions for older plan entrants who are highly compensated, because the annual additions limit does not apply. However, defined benefit plans are more complex and costly to design and administer.

2. Money purchase plans offer an alternative similar to target plans, but without the age-related contribution feature.

3. Nonqualified deferred compensation plans can be provided exclusively for selected executives. But with those plans the employer's tax deduction is generally deferred until benefit payments are made. This can be as much as twenty or thirty years after the employer's contribution is made.

4. Individual retirement savings is available as an alternative or supplement to an employer plan, but the amounts that may be subject to deduction or deferral are limited. See Chapters 20 and 21.

HOW TO INSTALL THE PLAN

Installation of an age-weighted plan follows the qualified plan installation procedure described in Chapter 15.

WHERE CAN I FIND OUT MORE?

Graduate Course: Advanced Pension and Retirement Planning I (GS 814), The American College, Bryn Mawr, PA.

FREQUENTLY ASKED QUESTIONS

Question – Can a self-employed person adopt a cross-tested or other age-weighted plan?

Answer – Yes. The plan can cover not only regular employees of the business, but also the self-employed person(s) who own the business—the sole proprietor or partners. Plans covering self-employed persons are known as "Keogh" or "HR 10" plans. These plans are basically the same as regular qualified plans, but some of the special rules that apply are covered in Chapter 29 of this book.

Any contribution or allocation formula applied to self-employed individuals must be based on their "earned income" as contrasted with the "compensation" base for regular employees. The definition of earned income is covered in Chapter 29.

Question – How is an age-weighted formula applied when shareholder-employees of an S corporation are covered?

Answer – For an S corporation, the plan contribution or allocation formula cannot provide an employer contribution for all of the shareholder-employee's income from the corporation. The formula must be based only on the shareholder's compensation for services rendered to the corporation. Any portion of the shareholder's income that represents dividends from the S corporation must be excluded from the plan formula.

CHAPTER ENDNOTES

1. I.R.C. §415(c)(3).
2. Treas. Reg. §1.401(a)(4)-8(b)(1)(iv).
3. This example is based on an example used by Bruce Temkin, MSPA, EA, at an ALI-ABA Course, "Representing the Professional and Closely Held Business," Scottsdale, AZ, Feb. 13-15, 2003.
4. See definition of "standard interest rate," Treas. Reg. §1.401(a)(4)-12.
5. A standard interest rate and mortality table, with no mortality prior to retirement, is used. Treas. Reg. §1.401(a)(4)-8(b)(2)(ii). Standard interest rate and mortality tables are defined in Treas. Reg. §1.401(a)(4)-12. The interest rate is not less than 7.5% and not greater than 8.5%. A list of permissible mortality tables is provided in the regulation.
6. I.R.C. §402(a).
7. I.R.C. §415(c).
8. I.R.C. §415(c)(2).

DEFINED BENEFIT PENSION PLAN

CHAPTER 27

INTRODUCTION

A defined benefit pension plan is a qualified employer pension plan that guarantees a specified benefit level at retirement.

WHEN IS USE OF SUCH A DEVICE INDICATED?

1. When the employer's plan design objective is to provide an adequate level of retirement income to employees regardless of their age at plan entry.

2. When the employer wants to allocate plan costs to the maximum extent to older employees—often key or controlling employees in a closely held business.

3. When an older controlling employee in a small business—for example, a doctor or dentist in a professional corporation—wants to maximize tax-deferred retirement savings.

Advantages

1. As with all qualified plans, employees obtain a tax-deferred retirement savings medium.

2. Retirement benefits at adequate levels can be provided for all employees regardless of age at plan entry.

3. Benefit levels are guaranteed both by the employer and, for some plans (generally larger plans), by the Pension Benefit Guaranty Corporation (PBGC).

4. For an older highly compensated employee, a defined benefit plan generally will allow the maximum amount of tax-deferred retirement saving.

Disadvantages

1. Actuarial and PBGC aspects of defined benefit plans result in higher installation and administration costs than for defined contribution plans.

2. Defined benefit plans are complex to design and difficult to explain to employees.

3. Employees who leave before retirement may receive relatively little benefit from the plan.

4. The employer is subject to a recurring annual funding obligation (that must be paid in quarterly or more frequent installments) regardless of whether, in a given year, it has made a profit or incurred a loss.

5. The employer assumes the risk of bad investment results in the plan fund.

DESIGN FEATURES

Defined benefit plans provide a specified amount of benefit to the plan participant at the plan's specified retirement age—the "normal retirement age."

There are many types of formulas for determining this benefit. The most common formulas can be summarized as the "flat amount," the "flat percentage" and the "unit credit" types. (See Chapter 10 for a discussion of appropriate income replacement percentages in retirement.)

In many plans, these formulas are further modified by "integrating" them with Social Security benefits. Integrating the formula gives the employer some credit for paying the cost of employee Social Security benefits.

It helps to provide a reasonable level of retirement income for all employees by taking Social Security benefits into account. The rules for integrating defined benefit formulas are very complex; they are discussed in more detail in Chapter 13.

Flat Amount Formula

A flat amount formula provides simply a stated dollar amount to each plan participant. For example, the plan might provide a pension of $500 per month for life, beginning at age sixty-five, for each plan participant. Such a plan might require some minimum service to obtain the full amount—perhaps ten or fifteen years of service with the employer—with the benefit scaled back for fewer years of service.

A flat amount formula does not differentiate among employees with different compensation levels, so it would be appropriate only when there is relatively little difference in compensation among the group of employees covered under the plan.

Flat Percentage Formula

Flat percentage formulas are very common; they provide a retirement benefit that is a percentage of the employee's average earnings. For example, the formula might provide a retirement benefit at age sixty-five equal to 50 percent of the employee's average earnings prior to retirement. Under this formula, a participant whose average annual pay was $100,000 prior to retirement would receive an annual pension of $50,000.

Typically a plan will require certain minimum service—such as ten or fifteen years—to obtain the full percentage benefit, with the percentage scaled back for fewer years of service. For example, if the plan provides a benefit of 50 percent of average compensation for an employee who retires with at least ten years of service, it might provide a benefit of only 25 percent of average compensation for an employee who retires at age sixty-five with only five years of service for the employer.

Unit Credit Formula

A unit credit formula is based on the employee's service with the employer.

Example. The formula might provide 1.5 percent of earnings for each of the employee's years of service, with the total percentage applied to the employee's average earnings. Under this formula, a participant with average annual compensation of $100,000 who retired after thirty years of service would receive an annual pension of $45,000 (that is, 1.5 × 30, or 45 percent of $100,000).

There are two methods generally used to compute average earnings for these formulas, the "career-average" and the "final average" methods.

Under the *career average* method, the formula uses earnings averaged over the employee's entire career with the employer. The career-average method takes early and often low-earning years into account, and thus the total benefit may not fully reflect the employee's earning power at retirement.

Under the *final average* method, earnings are averaged over a number of years—usually the three to five years immediately prior to retirement. The final average method usually produces a retirement benefit that is better matched to the employee's income just prior to retirement.

In either a career average or final average formula, only the first $265,000 (in 2015, as indexed) of each employee's compensation is taken into account.[1] In other words, an employee earning $275,000 in 2015 is treated as if compensation were $265,000.

Actuarial Methods

Employers must fund defined benefit plans with periodic deposits determined actuarially to insure that the plan fund will be sufficient to pay the promised benefit as each participant retires. The objective is to accumulate a fund at the employee's retirement age that is sufficient to "buy an annuity" equal to the retirement benefit. (In some plans, annuities are actually purchased at retirement age, but this is not required.)

Example. Suppose the actuary hired by the employer estimates that a pension of $50,000 per year beginning at age sixty-five is equivalent to a lump sum of $475,000 at age sixty-five. In other words, for a given interest rate and other assumptions, the amount of $475,000 deposited at age sixty-five will produce an annuity of $50,000 per year for the life of an individual aged sixty-five. For a participant aged forty-five at plan entry, the employer has twenty years to fund this benefit—that is, to build up a fund totaling $475,000 at age sixty-five.

The actuary will use various methods and assumptions to determine how much must be deposited periodically. As an illustration, a "level annual premium" method (equal annual payment method) with a 6 percent interest assumption would require the employer to deposit $12,180 annually for twenty years in order to build up a fund of $475,000. This shows how investment returns work for the benefit of the employer; the twenty deposits of $12,180 total only $243,600, but at age sixty-five the fund will actually total $475,000 if all annual deposits are made and the fund actually earns a 6 percent investment return annually.

Actuarial methods and assumptions are chosen to provide the desired pattern for spreading the plan's cost over the years it will be in effect. The actuarial method and assumptions often have to be adjusted over the years to make sure that the fund is adequate. It is even possible for a defined benefit plan to become overfunded, in which case employer contributions must be suspended for a period of time.

The actuarial funding approach for defined benefit plans means that, for a given benefit level, the annual funding amount is greater for employees who are older at entry into the plan (see table below), since the time to fund the benefit is less in the case of an older entrant.

AGE/CONTRIBUTION LEVEL FOR DEFINED BENEFIT PLAN

Age at Plan Entry	Annual Benefit at Age 65	Years to fund	Annual Employer Contribution
30	$25,000	35	$1,972
40	25,000	25	4,310
50	25,000	15	10,847

This set of calculations assumes :

- that money deposited before retirement will earn a 7 percent investment return;
- no mortality (i.e., no discount for the possibility that some plan participants may die before retirement); and
- a unisex annuity purchase rate of $1,400 per $10 monthly at age sixty-five (i.e., it will take a deposit of $1,400 at age sixty-five to purchase a lifetime annuity of $10 per month beginning at age sixty-five, for any plan participant, male or female).

This makes defined benefit plans attractive to professionals and closely held business owners; they tend to adopt retirement plans for their businesses when they are relatively older than their regular employees. A large percentage of the total cost for a defined benefit plan in this situation goes to fund these key employees' benefits.

Example. Doctor Retractor, age forty-eight, is a sole practitioner with two office employees, a nurse aged 35 and a receptionist aged twenty-five. The doctor earns $270,000 annually (of which only $265,000 (in 2015) can be taken into account in the plan formula) and the nurse and receptionist earn $30,000 and $20,000 respectively.

The doctor wants to adopt a new qualified plan for his medical practice. Compare the initial cost allocation below for a maximum (i.e., maximum benefit for the doctor) defined benefit plan with that for a maximum defined contribution plan.

The maximum defined contribution plan (for the doctor) provides 20 percent of compensation for each employee. The contribution for the doctor is 20 percent of $265,000 (the compensation limit under Code section 401(a)(17), as indexed for 2015), which equals $53,000, the maximum Section 415 amount for the doctor (in 2015, as indexed).

Assume that the doctor adopts a defined benefit plan that uses the safe harbor for fractional accrual plans (see the Frequently Asked Questions at the end of this chapter). The maximum benefit for the doctor under such a plan is limited because he has only eighteen years remaining until his retirement age of sixty-six (see item three under "Tax Implications" below). Regulations under Section 401(a)(4) require twenty-five years of service for a highly compensated participant to accrue the full benefit. Under the fractional accrual safe harbor, the doctor could accrue

18/25 of the benefit provided to nonhighly compensated participants. Thus, the doctor could receive 18/25, or 72 percent of compensation, provided the nonhighly compensated participants receive a benefit of 100 percent of compensation. The doctor's benefit is 72 percent of his compensation (as limited) of $265,000 (as indexed for 2015), or $190,800.

To back up the employer's funding obligation and safeguard employees, defined benefit plans are insured by the federal Pension Benefit Guaranty Corporation (PBGC) up to specified limits. The employer must pay annual premiums to the PBGC to fund this insurance. Furthermore, the employer is liable for reimbursement to the PBGC for any guaranteed payments the PBGC must make to employees.

"Cash Rich" Plans

Suppose an employer can afford to make substantial contributions to a defined benefit plan. Can a plan be designed with a very low actuarial interest assumptions so that the annual deductible contributions will be maximized?

In designing a plan for a "cash rich" employer an actuary will generally use the lowest reasonable actuarial interest assumption in order to maximize deductible contributions in the early years of the plan, thus maximizing tax deferral. However, Congress and the IRS have restricted the discretion of actuaries to choose relatively low interest assumptions.

The Code requires that all actuarial assumptions be reasonable, including a requirement that in combination, they offer the actuary's best estimate of anticipated experience under the plan.[2] An actuary cannot justify an aggressively low interest rate on the ground that other actuarial assumptions are less aggressive. In years when market rates were higher, the IRS challenged interest rate assumptions lower than 8 percent and retirement ages lower than sixty-five; however, it was repeatedly defeated in the courts and eventually conceded defeat.[3]

A possible alternative for the "cash rich" employer is to use *fully insured* funding for the defined benefit plan. A fully insured plan, also known as a "412(e)(3) plan," is not subject to many of the restrictions on deductible funding and may permit larger plan contributions in the initial years of the plan. Fully insured plans are discussed further in Chapter 18 (Life Insurance in a Qualified Plans).

TAX IMPLICATIONS

1. Employer contributions to the plan are deductible when made.[4]

2. Taxation of the employee on employer contributions is deferred. Contributions and earnings on plan assets are nontaxable to plan participants until withdrawn, assuming the plan remains "qualified."[5] A plan is qualified if it meets the eligibility, vesting, funding and other requirements explained in Chapter 13.

3. Under Code section 415, there is a maximum limit on the projected annual benefit that the plan can provide. For a benefit beginning at age sixty-five, the maximum life annuity or joint and survivor benefit is the lesser of (a) $210,000 (in 2015, as indexed)[6], or (b) 100 percent of the participant's compensation averaged over his three highest-earning consecutive years.

Example. If Foxx retires in 2015 at age sixty-five, and his high three-year average compensation was $60,000, his employer's defined benefit plan cannot provide a life or joint and survivor annuity of more than $60,000 per year. For employee Sharp, who retires in 2015 at age sixty-five with high three-year average compensation of $250,000, the limit is $210,000 annually.

---

4. Distributions from the plan must follow the rules for qualified plan distributions. Certain premature distributions may be subject to penalty taxes. The distribution rules and reporting forms are discussed in Chapter 14.

5. The plan is subject to the "minimum funding" rules of the Code. This requires minimum periodic contributions by the employer, with a penalty if less than the minimum amount is contributed.[7] Chapter 13 explains the minimum funding rules.

6. A defined benefit plan is subject to mandatory insurance coverage by the Pension Benefit Guaranty Corporation (PBGC). The PBGC is a government corporation funded through a mandatory premium

paid by employer-sponsors of covered plans. The premium consists of a flat rate of $57 annually (in 2015) per participant, plus an extra amount calculated on the basis of the plan's unfunded vested benefits, if any.[8] If the employer wants to terminate the plan, the PBGC must be notified in advance and must approve any distribution of plan assets to participants.[9]

7. Certain employers adopting a new plan may be eligible for a business tax credit of up to $500 for "qualified startup costs." See Chapter 15 for details.

8. A plan may permit employees to make voluntary contributions to a "deemed IRA" established under the plan. Amounts so contributed reduce the limit for other traditional or Roth IRA contributions. See Chapter 14 for details.

ERISA REQUIREMENTS

The plan is subject to all the ERISA requirements for qualified plans (participation, funding, vesting, etc.) described in Chapter 12 and the ERISA reporting and disclosure requirements outlined in Chapter 16. The regulations under Code section 401(a)(4) impose rules, with respect to nondiscrimination in benefits, that restrict the design possibilities for defined benefit plans, particularly for business owners who are less than twenty-five years from retirement.

Nondiscrimination Rules

Under the regulations, there is a *general* test for nondiscrimination, with three "safe harbors" available if the plan does not meet the general test.[10]

General test. Although the general test is complex, essentially the effect of it is to require that highly compensated employees covered under the plan not accrue benefits faster than nonhighly compensated employees. For example, suppose a plan is adopted for an employer with two employees: one is aged fifty-five and is highly compensated and the other, nonhighly compensated employee is aged thirty. If the plan provides both participants with a benefit equal to 50 percent of final average compensation, it will not satisfy the general test because the older, highly compensated employee will accrue full benefits in ten years (at age sixty-five) whereas it will take the younger employee thirty-five years to accrue the same benefit.

It should be noted that the general test for nondiscrimination in benefits requires extensive record keeping and actuarial services and, thus, may not be cost effective as compared to the safe harbors, particularly for plans of smaller employers.

Safe Harbors

Three safe harbor exceptions are available for defined benefit plans. Generally, if the benefit formula is uniform and one of the following is satisfied, the plan will be deemed to be nondiscriminatory:

1. *Unit credit plan*: a unit credit plan calculates benefits for each year of service as a percentage of compensation or a fixed dollar amount per year. Generally, the annual accrual rate for any year of service must not be more than 133.3 percent of the accrual rate for any prior year of service.[11]

2. *Fractional accrual plan*: Under this second safe harbor, a plan must satisfy the "fractional accrual" rule as well as certain other requirements. Under the fractional accrual rule, each employee's accrued benefit under the plan as of any plan year before normal retirement age must be determined by multiplying the employee's fractional rule benefit by a fraction: the numerator is the employee's years of service as of the plan year, and the denominator is the employee's projected years of service as of normal retirement age.[12]

Example. If an employee enters the plan at age forty, with twenty-five years to retirement, his benefit after ten years of service cannot be more than 10/25 of the total under the fractional rule.

As the "Doctor Refractor" example earlier in this chapter suggests, the use of this safe harbor limits, but does not eliminate, the favorable aspects of defined benefit plans for older business owners.

3. *Fully insured plan*: The third safe harbor applies to a fully insured insurance contract plan under Code section 412(e)(3) (discussed above) that meets certain benefit accrual requirements.[13]

ALTERNATIVES

1. Money purchase pension plans provide retirement benefits, but without employer guarantees of benefit levels, and with adequate benefits only for younger plan entrants.

2. Target benefit or other age-weighted plans may provide adequate benefits to older entrants, but without an employer guarantee of the benefit level.

3. Cash balance pension plans provide an employer guarantee of principal and investment earnings on the plan fund, but provide adequate benefits only to younger plan entrants.

4. Profit sharing plans, simplified employee pensions (SEPs), stock bonus plans, and ESOPs provide a qualified, tax-deferred retirement savings medium, but the benefit adequacy is tied closely to the financial success of the employer.

5. Section 401(k) plans, savings plans and SIMPLE IRAs provide a qualified, tax-deferred savings medium in which the amount saved is subject to some control by employees themselves.

6. Private retirement saving outside a qualified plan does not provide the same tax benefits as saving within a qualified plan, except in the case of certain IRAs.

See Chapter 10 for a further discussion of planning alternatives.

HOW TO INSTALL A PLAN

Defined benefit plans are installed according to the qualified plan installation procedure outlined in Chapter 15.

WHERE CAN I FIND OUT MORE?

1. Scott, Elaine A., *Simple Defined Benefit Plans: Methods of Actuarial Funding*, Homewood, IL: Dow Jones-Irwin, 1989.

2. Graduate Course: Qualified Retirement Plans (GS 814), The American College, Bryn Mawr, PA.

3. CLU/ChFC/CFP Course: Planning for Retirement Needs (HS 326), The American College, Bryn Mawr, PA.

4. CFP Course: Retirement Planning and Employee Benefits (CFP IV), College for Financial Planning, Denver, CO.

FREQUENTLY ASKED QUESTIONS

Question – At what age is a defined benefit plan more advantageous than a defined contribution plan for tax-deferring the maximum amount of retirement savings?

Answer – Somewhere between age forty and fifty approximately, depending on the actuarial method and assumptions used in the defined benefit plan.

Question – Can an employee be covered under both a defined benefit plan and a defined contribution plan of the same employer?

Answer – Under ERISA, as originally enacted in 1974, there was a required cutback for one or both plans through a complex "combined plan formula," if either plan approached the maximum limits. However, the combined plan formula was repealed, effective after 1999.[14] Consequently, it is possible to have a defined contribution plan and a defined benefit plan for a participant that provide the maximum benefit under both plans. However, this possibility will continue to be limited by Code section 404(a)(7), which imposes a 25 percent of payroll limit (or the required funding for the defined benefit plan, if greater) on total annual employer deductions for the two plans. This limit does not apply if the only contributions under the defined contribution plan are elective deferrals; see Chapter 13.

Question – If the retirement age is less than sixty-five in a defined benefit plan, can the annual funding level be increased because of the shorter time left to fund the benefit?

Answer – Yes. However, the tax benefits of this for highly compensated employees are limited by the fact that the maximum Section 415 limitation on benefits is cut back for retirement earlier than sixty-two.[15] This cutback (to be determined under regulations) limits the deductible annual funding and thus the amount of extra tax deferral available through an accelerated retirement age.

Another factor that has to be taken into account, if acceleration of funding is desired, is that the maximum benefit limit is also cut back proportionately if a participant has participated in the plan for less than 10 years.[16]

Example. Suppose Dr. Drill, a self-employed dentist, aged fifty-seven wants to start a defined benefit plan. If the retirement age is sixty-two in the plan, Dr. Drill will have only eight years of participation at retirement. Assuming that the maximum benefit would be $210,000 (2015 figure) for ten years of participation, the benefit for Dr. Drill will be cut back to 8/10 of that amount, or $168,000 annually.

CHAPTER ENDNOTES

1. I.R.C. §401(a)(17); Notice 2006-98, 2006-48 IRB 906.
2. I.R.C. §412(c)(3). Under pre-1988 law, actuarial assumptions had to be reasonable only in the aggregate.
3. See IR-95-43. For taxpayer victories over the IRS' assault on low interest rate and retirement age assumptions, see *Vinson & Elkins v. Comm'r.*, 93-2 USTC ¶50,632 (5th Cir. 1993); *Rhoades, McKee & Boer v. U.S.*, 93-2 USTC ¶50,425 (W.D.MI 1993); *Wachtell, Lipton, Rosen & Katz v. Comm'r.*, TC Memo 1992-392, aff'd 94-1 USTC ¶50,272 (2d Cir. 1994).
4. I.R.C. §404(a).
5. I.R.C. §§402(a), 403(a).
6. I.R.C. §415(d).
7. I.R.C. §§412, 430.
8. See ERISA §§4006(a)(3)(A)(i) and 4006(a)(3)(E) for an explanation of the calculation of these amounts.
9. ERISA §4041.
10. Treas. Reg. §1.401(a)(4)-3.
11. Treas. Reg. §1.401(a)(4)-3(b)(3).
12. Treas. Reg. §1.401(a)(4)-3(b)(4).
13. Treas. Reg. §1.401(a)(4)-3(b)(5).
14. I.R.C. §415(e).
15. I.R.C. §415(b)(2)(C). The age 62 limited cutback became effective for plan years ending after 2001. For prior years, the cutback applied to retirement ages earlier than 65.
16. I.R.C. §415(b)(5).

CASH BALANCE PENSION PLAN

CHAPTER 28

INTRODUCTION

A cash balance pension plan is a qualified defined benefit plan that provides for annual employer contributions at a specified rate to hypothetical individual accounts that are set up for each plan participant. The employer guarantees not only the contribution level but also a minimum rate of return on each participant's account. A cash balance plan works somewhat like a money purchase pension plan discussed in Chapter 25, but money purchase plans do not involve employer guarantees of the rate of return.

WHEN IS USE OF SUCH A DEVICE INDICATED?

1. When the employees are relatively young and have substantial time to accumulate retirement savings.

2. When employees are concerned with security of retirement income.

3. When the work force is large and the bulk of the employees are middle-income. (Banks and similar financial institutions find this type of plan particularly appealing.)

4. When the employer is able to spread administrative costs over a relatively large group of plan participants.

5. When the employer has an existing defined benefit plan and wishes to convert to a plan that provides a more attractive benefit for younger employees and may lower costs for older employees.

Advantages

1. As with all qualified plans, the cash balance plan provides a tax-deferred savings medium for employees.

2. The employer guarantee removes investment risk from the employee.

3. Plan benefits are guaranteed (within limits) by the federal Pension Benefit Guaranty Corporation (PBGC).

4. The benefits of the plan are easily communicated to and appreciated by employees.

Disadvantages

1. The retirement benefit may be inadequate for older plan entrants—see Figures 28.1 and 28.2.

2. Because of the need for actuarial services, the minimum funding requirements, and the PBGC guarantee, the plan is more complex administratively than qualified defined contribution plans.

3. The shift of investment risk to the employer increases employer costs.

DESIGN FEATURES OF THESE PLANS

A cash balance plan provides a hypothetical individual account for each participant. These hypothetical accounts are credited by the employer at least once a

Figure 28.1

CASH BALANCE PLAN ACCUMULATIONS

Pay credit: 10 percent of compensation
Interest credit: 7 percent annually guaranteed rate

Age at plan entry	Annual compensation	Account balance at age 65
25	$30,000	$640,827
30	30,000	443,739
40	30,000	203,028
50	30,000	80,664
55	30,000	44,349
60	30,000	18,459

Figure 28.2

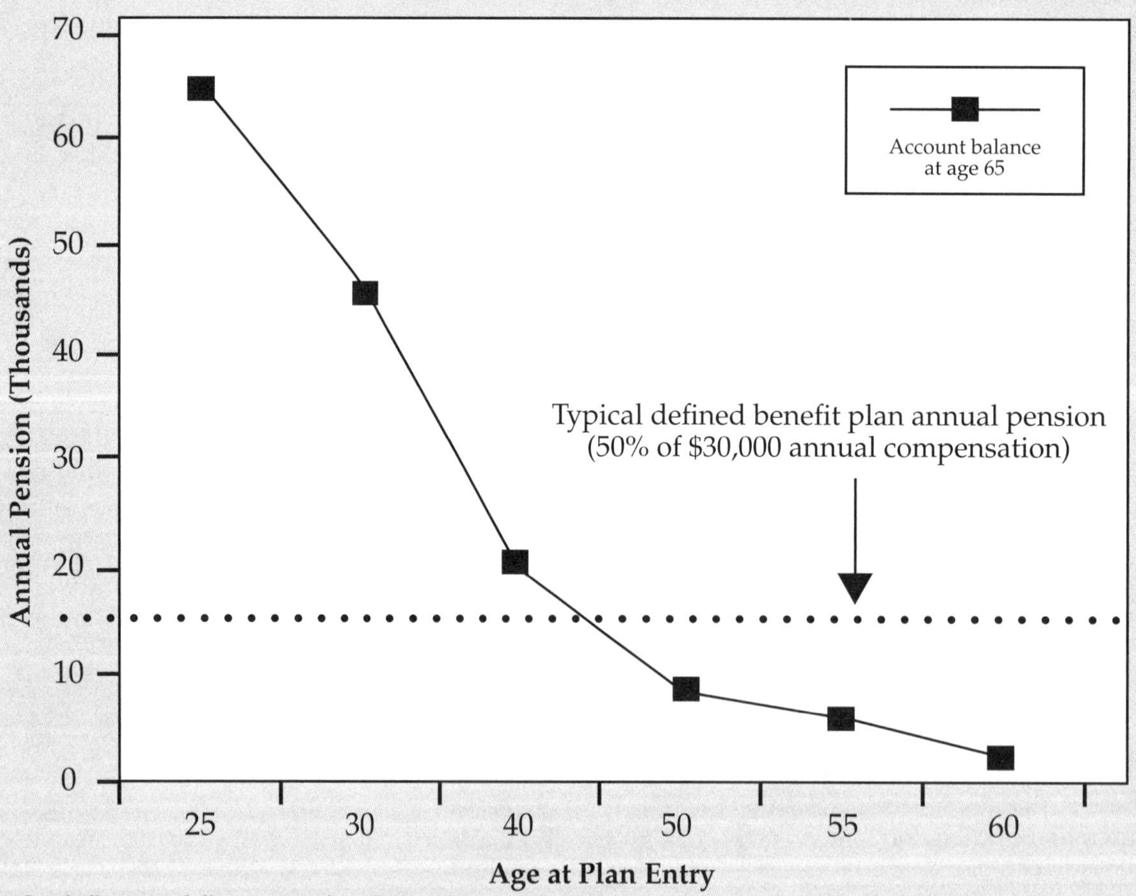

* Graph illustrates dollar amounts from Figure 28.1.

year with two types of credit—the "pay credit" and the "interest credit."

The pay credit uses a formula based on compensation.[1] For example, the plan might require the employer to credit each employee's account annually with a pay credit of 6 percent of compensation. The pay credit formula may also be "integrated" with Social Security. With Social Security integration, compensation below a level specified in the plan—the "integration level"—receives a lesser credit than compensation above the integration level. This reflects the fact that the employer pays Social Security taxes to provide retirement benefits through Social Security. Social Security integration for qualified plans is discussed in Chapter 13 of this book.

The interest credit is an amount of employer-guaranteed investment earnings that is credited annually to each employee's account. The interest credit must follow a formula in the plan and cannot merely be discretionary on the employer's part. For example, the interest credit formula in the plan might provide for each employee's account to be credited annually with a rate of earnings defined as the lesser of (a) the increase in the Consumer Price Index over the preceding year or (b) the one-year rate for U.S. Treasury securities. The plan can allow the employer to credit accounts with actual plan earnings, if these are higher.

In a cash balance plan there are no actual individual accounts, as there are in defined contribution plans. All amounts are pooled in a single fund. Any plan participant has a legal claim on the entire fund to satisfy his or her claim to plan benefits.

The employer's annual cost for the plan is determined on an actuarial basis because of the employer guarantee feature. Investment risk lies with the employer; if actual plan earnings fall below total interest credits for the year, the employer must make up the difference. Employer costs can be controlled primarily by choosing the right kind of formula for the interest credit, one that does not risk uncontrollable and unforeseeable employer obligations. However, the interest credit formula should not be excessively conservative—if actual plan earnings year after year are more than interest credits, plan participants may resent the employer's enrichment and the positive employee relations value of the plan may be lost.

Investment designation by participants (earmarking) is not available in a cash balance plan, because the plan is not technically an individual account plan under ERISA section 404(c). Loans from the plan can be made available, but most employers will not want a loan provision because of the administrative problems resulting from the plan's status as a defined benefit plan without separate participant accounts. Life insurance can be purchased by the plan as an incidental benefit to participants or as a plan investment, under the limitations discussed in Chapter 18.

Modification of Existing Defined Benefit Formula

Some employers that have a traditional defined benefit plan (see Chapter 27) become dissatisfied with the plan because it does not provide an attractive benefit for younger employees, but imposes substantial costs for employees nearing retirement. Termination of the defined benefit plan and substitution of a defined contribution plan would require that most or all existing plan assets would have to be immediately credited to vested participants. However, a less costly alternative might be to revise the existing plan's formula into a cash balance formula.

Generally, the Internal Revenue Code requires that after a conversion of existing defined benefit plan to a cash balance formula, each participant's benefit must be no less than the sum of the actuarial value of the participant's benefit under the old formula at the time of the conversion plus the participant's benefit earned for post-conversion service under the new formula.[2]

If an employer amends a defined benefit plan (or any other plan subject to the minimum funding standards) to adopt a cash balance formula, or makes any other change resulting in a reduction in the rate of future benefit accrual, the plan administrator must provide a prescribed written notice to affected plan participants and beneficiaries. Failure to provide the notice results in a $100 per day penalty.[3] The provision allows for regulations exempting certain plans with fewer than one hundred participants under certain circumstances.

TAX IMPLICATIONS

1. Employer contributions to the plan are deductible when made.[4]

2. Internal Revenue Code section 415(b) limits the benefits provided under the plan to the lesser of $210,000 annually (in 2015, as indexed[5]) or

100 percent of the participant's high three-year average compensation.[6] For a given employee, this is the *defined benefit* plan limit. This limit may be more or less favorable than the defined contribution limit applicable to a comparable money purchase plan.

3. Taxation of the employee on employer contributions is deferred.[7] Both contributions and earnings on plan assets are nontaxable to plan participants until withdrawn, assuming the plan remains "qualified." A plan is qualified if it meets the eligibility, vesting, funding and other requirements explained in Chapter 13.

4. Distributions from the plan must follow the rules for qualified plan distributions. Certain premature distributions are subject to penalties. These distribution rules are discussed in Chapter 13.

5. For certain employees born before 1936, lump sum distributions may be eligible for the special ten-year averaging tax computation available for qualified plans. Not all distributions are eligible; see Chapter 14 for coverage of these rules.

6. The plan is subject to the minimum funding rules of the Internal Revenue Code.[8] This requires minimum contributions, subject to a penalty if less than the minimum amount is contributed in any year. If the plan is not fully funded, the subsequent year's contributions must be made on at least an estimated quarterly basis.[9]

7. Since a cash balance plan is a type of defined benefit plan, it is subject to mandatory insurance coverage by the Pension Benefit Guaranty Corporation (PBGC). The PBGC is a government corporation funded through a mandatory premium paid by employer-sponsors of covered plans. The premium is a flat rate is $35 annually per participant;[10] however, an additional annual premium may be required, depending on the amount of the plan's unfunded vested benefit.[11] If the plan is terminated by the employer, PBGC termination procedures must be followed.

8. Certain employers adopting a plan may be eligible for a business tax credit of up to $500 for "qualified startup costs." See Chapter 15 for details.

9. A plan may permit employees to make voluntary contributions to a "deemed IRA" established under the plan. Amounts so contributed reduce the limit for other traditional or Roth IRA contributions. See Chapter 20 for details.

10. The plan is subject to the additional ERISA reporting and disclosure rules outlined in Chapter 16.

ALTERNATIVES

1. Money purchase pension plans and profit sharing plans build up similar qualified retirement accounts for employees, but without the employer guaranteed minimum investment return. (See the comparison chart in Figure 28.3.)

2. Traditional defined benefit plans provide guaranteed benefits for employees, but are more complex in design and administration. (See the comparison chart in Figure 28.3.)

3. Individual retirement saving is always an alternative or supplement to any qualified plan, but there is no tax deferral except in the case of certain IRAs.

HOW TO INSTALL A CASH BALANCE PLAN

A cash balance plan follows the qualified plan installation procedure discussed in Chapter 15 of this book.

CHAPTER ENDNOTES

1. See also Prop. Treas. Reg. §1.411(b)-2(b)(2)(iii)(D), (E).
2. I.R.C. §411(b)(5)(B) (effective for conversions after June 29, 2005).
3. I.R.C. §4980F.
4. I.R.C. §404(a).
5. Notice 2008-102, 2008-45 IRB 1106.
6. I.R.C. §415(b). This limit is indexed for inflation, in increments of $5,000. I.R.C. §415(d)(4)(A).
7. I.R.C. §402(a).
8. Actuaries differ as to the correct approach in applying the minimum funding rules. For discussion, see Grubbs, "The Cash Balance Plan—A Closer Look," *Journal of Pension Planning and Compliance*, Vol. 15, No. 3 (1989).
9. I.R.C. §412(m).
10. ERISA§4006(a)(3)(A)(i).
11. ERISA §4006(a)(3)(E). This extra premium was formerly "capped" at a maximum of $53 per participant, but after June 30, 1996 there is no cap. URAA '94, Section 774(a).

Figure 28.3

CASH BALANCE VS. CONVENTIONAL PLANS			
	Cash Balance Plan	**Typical Defined Contribution Plan**	**Typical Defined Benefit Plan**
Contribution rate	percentage of salary (with actuarial aspects)	percentage of salary	actuarially determined
Investment risk	employer	employee	employer
Investment earmarking	not available	available	not available
Social Security integration	available	available	available
PBGC cost/coverage	yes	no	yes
401(k) feature	not available	available in profit-sharing plan	not available
Adequate benefit for older entrants	no	no, except for age-weighted plan	yes
Administrative cost	higher	lower (unless 401(k) or earmarking)	higher

HR 10 (KEOGH) PLAN

CHAPTER 29

INTRODUCTION

A Keogh plan, sometimes referred to as an HR 10 plan, is a qualified retirement plan that covers one or more self-employed individuals. A self-employed individual is a sole proprietor or partner who works in his or her unincorporated business. Like all qualified plans, a Keogh plan enables those covered under the plan to accumulate a private retirement fund that will supplement their other pension and Social Security benefits.

A Keogh plan works much like any qualified plan; the details of the various types of qualified plans such as defined benefit or profit sharing plans are discussed in separate chapters of this book. This chapter focuses on the special features of a qualified plan that covers self-employed individuals.

WHEN IS USE OF SUCH A DEVICE INDICATED?

1. When long-term capital accumulation, particularly for retirement purposes, is an important objective of a self-employed business owner.

2. When an owner of an unincorporated business wishes to adopt a plan providing retirement benefits for regular employees as an incentive and employee benefit, as well as retirement savings for the business owner.

3. When a self-employed person has a need to shelter some current earnings from federal income tax.

4. When an employee has self-employment income as well as income from employment, and wishes to invest as much as possible of the self-employment income and defer taxes on it.

Advantages

1. Keogh contributions are deducted from gross income, and tax is deferred until funds are withdrawn from the plan at a later date.

2. Income generated by the investments in a Keogh plan is also tax-deferred until it is withdrawn from the plan. This reinvestment of income and build-up of tax deferred earnings is one of the main features that make Keogh plans attractive.

   For example, the following table shows the results of investing $7,500 annually in a Keogh plan where the rate of return is 8 percent:

Number Of Years	Total Contribution	Tax Deferred Interest	Total Value
5	$ 37,500	$ 10,019	$ 47,519
10	75,000	42,341	117,341
15	112,500	107,432	219,932
20	150,000	220,672	370,672
25	187,500	404,658	592,158

   As can be seen, the tax-deferred earnings portion of the program will eventually exceed the amount of personal annual contributions. This is a strong incentive to start early and continue to make the largest possible contribution to such a plan.

3. Under current law, plan loans to owner-employees are subject to the same rules as are applied to

regular employees (generally up to $50,000 or half the vested benefit).[1]

4. The limits on Keogh plan contributions, as for all qualified plans, are more liberal than those applied to IRAs (individual retirement accounts). IRAs are subject to the following annual contribution limits: $5,500 in 2015 ($11,000 for an individual and spouse). In contrast, the maximum contribution under a defined contribution Keogh plan is $53,000 (in 2015, as indexed). (See the discussion under "Types of Keogh Plans" below regarding how to take advantage of the full $53,000 limit). Thus, a self-employed person may be eligible to contribute more than ten times as much to a Keogh plan as to an IRA. In addition, deductions for IRA contributions may be limited if the individual (or his spouse) is an active participant in a qualified retirement plan (see Chapter 20).

5. From the viewpoint of an employee of an unincorporated business, Keogh plans are advantageous because employees of the business must participate in the plan (within the limits of the coverage requirements for qualified plans described in Chapter 13).

6. Certain employers adopting a plan may be eligible for a business tax credit of up to $500 for "qualified startup costs." See Chapter 15 for details.

Disadvantages

1. Keogh plans involve all the costs and complexity associated with qualified plans. However, for a small plan, particularly one covering only one self-employed individual, it is relatively easy to minimize these factors by using prototype plans offered by insurance companies, mutual funds, banks, and other financial institutions.

2. If a self-employed person has a significant number of employees, the qualified plan coverage requirements, which require nondiscriminatory plan coverage (see Chapter 13), may increase the cost of the plan substantially.

3. As with all qualified plans, there is a 10 percent penalty, in addition to regular federal income tax, for withdrawal of plan funds generally before age 59½, death, or disability (see Chapter 14).

4. Again as with regular qualified plans, benefit payments from the plan generally must begin by April 1 of the later of (a) the year after the plan participant attains age 70½, or (b) the year the participant retires; however, in the case of a more-than-5-percent owner, payments must begin by April 1 of the year after attainment of age 70½, regardless of whether the participant has retired. There is a penalty for noncompliance (see Chapter 14). Thus, Keogh plans, like all qualified plans, cannot be viewed as a means of avoiding income tax, or passing assets to succeeding generations tax free.

5. Life insurance in a qualified plan for a self-employed person, described below, is treated somewhat less favorably than for regular employees.

TYPES OF KEOGH PLANS

In general, any type of qualified plan can be designed to cover self-employed persons. However, the typical Keogh plan covering one self-employed person, and possibly the spouse of the self-employed person, as well as a few employees, is usually designed as a defined contribution plan without a fixed contribution formula (profit sharing type of plan).

Defined Contribution Plans

In a *defined contribution plan*, an annual contribution of any amount up to 25 percent of the total payroll of plan participants is generally deductible.[2] If the plan is the profit-sharing type, plan contributions can even be omitted entirely in a bad year. However, the IRS requires "substantial and recurring" contributions, or the plan may be deemed to have been terminated.[3] This contribution flexibility is very advantageous for a small business, the income of which may fluctuate substantially from year to year.

As with all qualified plans, the compensation base is limited to $265,000 (in 2015, as indexed).[4] This imposes a limit on Keogh profit sharing plans for self-employed persons with earned income of $265,000 or more—an income level that is not unusual for a successful professional. The annual additions limit (see Chapter 13) effectively limits profit sharing plan contributions to $53,000 in 2015.[5]

A partnership or proprietorship may also establish a 401(k) plan, including a solo 401(k) plan (for details, see Chapter 19). Matching contributions made to a 401(k) Keogh plan on behalf of a self-employed person are not treated as elective employer contributions, thus they are not subject to the $18,000 (in 2015) annual limit.[6]

Other Types of Plans

A *money purchase plan* contains a fixed annual contribution formula of up to 25 percent of earned income, for self-employed persons (25 percent of compensation for any regular employees covered under the plan).[7] However, a money purchase plan is subject to the Code's minimum funding requirements (see Chapter 13). These require the employer to make contributions to each employee's and self-employed person's account each year equal to the percentage of compensation stated in the plan. Such contributions are mandatory, regardless of good or bad business results for the year.

A partnership or proprietorship can adopt other types of qualified plans as well. A *defined benefit* plan is attractive to the older self-employed person who is just starting a plan, because the actuarial funding approach allows a greater relative contribution for older plan participants. Often, considerably more can be contributed annually to a defined benefit plan than the $53,000 maximum (in 2015, as indexed) for defined contribution plans.

Partnerships and proprietorships can also adopt cross-tested or other age-weighted plans (see Chapter 26) with self-employed persons as participants. These plans, like defined benefit plans, allow contributions to be weighted (that is, provide contributions equal to a higher percentage of compensation) for older plan entrants, who tend to be the owners of the business.

HOW ARE KEOGHS DIFFERENT FROM OTHER QUALIFIED PLANS?

The unique feature of a Keogh plan, as compared with qualified plans adopted by corporations, is that the Keogh plan covers self-employed individuals, who are not technically considered "employees." This leads to some significant special rules for self-employed individuals covered under the plan.

Earned Income

The most important special rule is the definition of earned income. For a self-employed individual, "earned income" takes the place of "compensation" in applying the qualified plan rules. Earned income is defined as the self-employed individual's net income from the business after all deductions, *including the deduction for Keogh plan contributions*.[8] In addition, the IRS has ruled that the self-employment tax must be computed and a deduction of one-half of the self-employment tax must be taken *before* determining the Keogh deduction.[9]

To resolve the potential complexity of this computation, *IRS Publication 560* specifies the following steps in determining the Keogh deduction:

(1) determine net income from Schedule C income;

(2) subtract one-half of the actual amount of the self-employment tax; and

(3) multiply the result by the "net" contribution rate from the rate table below.

This computation can easily be transferred to a computer worksheet.

Example. Len earns $100,000 of Schedule C income in 2014. His self-employment tax is $14,129.55. (The net income amount of $100,000 is first reduced by 7.65 percent, leaving $92,350 net earnings subject to the self-employment tax. $92,350 x 15.3 (Combined OASDI and HI rate) = $14,129.55.) The deduction for one-half of the self-employment tax then is $7,064.78 (half of $14,129.55).

The Keogh contribution base is thus $100,000 less $7,064.78, or $92,935.23. If the nominal plan contribution rate is 25 percent, the net contribution rate is 20 percent. This rate is applied to the Keogh contribution base and results in a contribution of $18,587.05. (Note that this amount is 25 percent of "earned income," which is equal to $74,348.18 (i.e., the Keogh contribution base of $92,935.23 less the Keogh contribution of $18,587.05).)

The IRS table of "net" contribution rates is as follows:

Self-Employed Person's Rate Table

Column A If the Plan Contribution Rate Is: (shown as a %)	Column B The Self-Employed Person's Rate Is: (shown as a decimal)
1	.009901
2	.019608
3	.029126
4	.038462
5	.047619
6	.056604
7	.065421
8	.074074
9	.082569
10	.090909
11	.099099
12	.107143
13	.115044
14	.122807
15	.130435
16	.137931
17	.145299
18	.152542
19	.159664
20	.166667
21	.173554
22	.180328
23	.186992
24	.193548
25	.200000

Life Insurance

Life insurance can be used as an incidental benefit in a plan covering self-employed individuals, but the tax treatment for the self-employed individuals is different from that applicable to regular employees in a qualified plan.

The entire cost of life insurance for regular employees is deductible as a plan contribution. Employees then pick up the value of the pure life insurance element as extra taxable compensation valued under Table 2001 (formerly the P.S. 58 table).[10] For details, see Chapter 20.

By contrast, for a self-employed individual, the pure life insurance element of an insurance premium is *not* deductible.[11] Only the portion of the premium that exceeds the pure protection value of the insurance is deductible. The pure protection value of the insurance is determined using Table 2001. Since all income and deductions flow automatically to the owners in an unincorporated business, the nondeductible life insurance element in effect becomes additional taxable income to the self-employed individual.

Example. Leo, a self-employed individual, has a Keogh plan providing incidental insurance through a cash value life insurance contract. This year's premium is $3,000, of which $1,200 is for pure life insurance protection and the remainder is used to increase the cash value. Leo can deduct $1,800 of the premium as a plan contribution. The remaining $1,200 is nondeductible. Leo therefore must pay tax on the $1,200 used for pure life insurance protection.

Benefits

Another difference in the treatment of life insurance arises when benefits are paid from the plan. Regular employees have a "cost basis" (a nontaxable recovery element) in a plan equal to any Table 2001 costs they have included in income in the past, so long as the plan distribution is made from the same life insurance contract on which the costs were paid (see Chapter 20). For a self-employed individual, however, Table 2001 costs, while effectively included in income since they were nondeductible, are not includable in cost basis.[12]

TAX AND ERISA IMPLICATIONS

Except for the differences described just above, Keogh plans generally have the same tax and ERISA implications as regular qualified plans. For example, see Chapter 22 for the tax treatment of profit sharing plans.

The annual reporting requirement for qualified plans is simplified for many Keogh plans and other small plans. If a plan covers only the business owner or partners, or the owner or partners and their spouses, the reporting requirement is satisfied by filing Form 5500-EZ.

ALTERNATIVES

1. The disadvantages, if any, of Keogh status of any qualified plan can be eliminated if the business owner incorporates the business and adopts a corporate plan. The owner is then a shareholder

and employee of the corporation. Generally, under current law, it is not advantageous to incorporate a business simply to obtain corporate treatment for qualified plans. Incorporation may result in higher taxes overall and the advantages of corporate plans over Keogh plans are minimal in most cases.

2. A simplified employee pension (SEP) or SIMPLE IRA may be even simpler to adopt than a Keogh plan, particularly if only one self-employed individual is covered. In addition, SEPs can be adopted as late as the individual's tax return filing date, when it is too late to adopt a new Keogh plan. See Chapter 30 for more discussion of SEPs, and Chapter 31 for an explanation of SIMPLE IRAs.

3. Tax deductible IRA contributions may be available if the individual (or his spouse) is not an active participant in a qualified plan. The deduction is subject to cutbacks based on adjusted gross income if the individual (or his spouse) is an active participant in a qualified plan (see Chapter 20). Roth IRAs are also subject to the same limits (see Chapter 21). Because of these limitations, a Keogh plan often permits much greater levels of tax-deferred savings.

HOW TO INSTALL A PLAN

A Keogh plan follows the installation procedure for qualified plans described in Chapter 13. However, in adopting a Keogh plan, it is common to use a "prototype" plan designed by a bank, insurance company, mutual fund, or other financial institution. With a prototype, the sponsoring institution does most of the paperwork involved in installing the plan, at low or nominal cost to the self-employed individual. In return, the self-employed individual must keep most or all of the plan funds invested with that institution.

WHERE CAN I FIND OUT MORE?

1. Banks, insurance companies, and other financial institutions actively market Keogh plans and will usually provide extensive information about their services.

2. IRS Publication 560, *Self-Employed Retirement Plans*, covers Keogh plans in detail. It is revised annually and available free from the IRS.

3. *Tax Facts on Insurance & Employee Benefits*, Cincinnati, OH, The National Underwriter Co. (revised annually).

FREQUENTLY ASKED QUESTIONS

Question – Who can establish a Keogh retirement plan?

Answer – Any sole proprietor or partnership, whether or not the business has employees—for example, doctors, lawyers, accountants, writers, etc. Generally, employees of the business must be included as participants in the plan on the same general basis as the key employees.

Question – Can I collect benefits if I become disabled?

Answer – In the event that any participant in the plan becomes so disabled as to render him or her unable to engage in any substantial gainful activity, all contributed amounts plus earnings may be paid immediately without being subject to a premature distribution penalty.

Question – What happens to my plan if I die?

Answer – In the event that any participant dies, all contributed amounts plus earnings may be immediately paid to the participant's designated beneficiary or estate.

Question – May I set up a Keogh plan in addition to an IRA?

Answer – Yes. If you are eligible to set up a Keogh plan you may also create a traditional or Roth IRA as well. However, because you are an active participant in the Keogh plan, traditional IRA contributions will not be tax deductible if your income is above certain limits (see Chapter 23).

A plan may also permit employees to make voluntary contributions to a "deemed IRA" established under the plan. Amounts so contributed reduce the limit for other traditional or Roth IRA contributions. See Chapter 20 for details.

Question – Can a Keogh plan be established if the self-employed person is covered under a corporate retirement plan of an employer?

Answer – Yes. An individual who works for a regular employer, and is covered under that employer's qualified plan, can establish a separate Keogh plan for an additional business carried on separately as a self-employed individual. For example, an engineering professor at a university may have additional income earned as a consulting engineer for outside clients. A Keogh plan will shelter some of that income from taxation and provide increased retirement savings on a tax-favored basis. The deduction limits for Keogh contributions are not affected unless the individual also controls or owns the regular employer.

For example, suppose an engineer earns $100,000 this year from his university position and is covered under the university's qualified pension plan. The engineer earns an additional $60,000 in consulting fees from outside clients. If he adopts a Keogh money purchase plan for this year, he can contribute and deduct up to 25 percent of *earned income* (see discussion above) to the Keogh plan.

Question – Can a Keogh plan fund be reached by the owner's creditors?

Answer – In general, assets in a qualified plan may have protection under federal law against diversion for any purpose other than providing benefits for the plan participant and his or her beneficiary, including an ERISA prohibition against "assignment or alienation" of benefits.[13] This can protect pension assets from creditors,[14] and even spouses have only the limited rights provided under the qualified domestic relations order (QDRO) provisions (see Chapter 14).

CHAPTER ENDNOTES

1. See I.R.C. §4975(f)(6).
2. I.R.C. §404(a)(3)(A).
3. Treas. Reg. §1.401-1(b)(2).
4. I.R.C. §401(a)(17).
5. I.R.C. §415(c)(1).
6. I.R.C. §402(g)(8).
7. I.R.C. §404(a)(3)(A)(v) was amended by EGTRRA 2001 to clarify that a money purchase plan will be treated in the same manner as a profit sharing plan for purposes of the deduction limit.
8. I.R.C. §401(c)(2).
9. GCM 39807.
10. Notice 2002-8, 2002-1 CB 398.
11. I.R.C. §404(e); Treas. Reg. §1.404(e)-1A(g).
12. Treas. Reg. §1.72-16(b)(4).
13. I.R.C. §401(a)(1), 401(a)(13); ERISA §206(d)(1).
14. The U.S. Supreme Court held that assets in a plan that is qualified under section 401(a) of the Internal Revenue Code and subject to Title I of ERISA (including the anti-alienation requirements of Section 206(d)(1)) are protected in bankruptcy. *Patterson v. Shumate*, 112 S. Ct. 1662 (1992). However, it is important to note that Keogh plans that cover only sole owners or partners (and their spouses) are not considered to cover "employees" within the meaning of Title I of ERISA (see Labor Reg. §2510.3-3) and, thus, are not subject to Title I of ERISA. A line of cases holds that such "plans without employees" are not protected by *Patterson*. See, e.g., *In the Matter of Branch*, 1994 U.S. App. Lexis 2870 (7th Cir. 1994) (unpublished opinion); *In re Hall*, 151 Bankr. 412 (Bankr. W.D. Mich. 1993); *In re Witwer*, 148 Bankr. 930 (Bankr. C.D. Cal. 1992), *aff'd without opinion*, 163 Bankr. 614 (9th Cir. BAP 1994); *In re Lane*, 149 Bankr. 760 (Bankr. E.D.N.Y. 1993).

SIMPLE IRA

CHAPTER 30

INTRODUCTION

A SIMPLE (Savings Incentive Match Plan for Employees) IRA is an employer-sponsored plan under which plan contributions are made to a participating employee's IRA.[1] Tax-deferred contribution levels are significantly higher than the $5,500 (in 2015) limit for traditional and Roth IRAs (see Chapter 20). SIMPLE IRAs feature employee salary reduction contributions (elective deferrals) coupled with employer matching or nonelective contributions.

The term "SIMPLE plan," as used in the Internal Revenue Code refers to a SIMPLE IRA plan. Unlike Section 401(k) plans, SIMPLE IRAs are not required to satisfy the ADP test, but they are subject to additional requirements. See Chapter 19 for details on SIMPLE 401(k) plans.

SIMPLE IRAs are easy to adopt and to administer while providing employees with tax-deferred retirement savings benefits much like those of a qualified plan. However, qualified plans potentially can provide higher contribution levels. An employee's salary reductions under a SIMPLE IRA can be no greater than $12,500 annually (in 2015), plus catch-up amounts of $3,000 (in 2015), if available.[2]

WHEN IS USE OF SUCH A DEVICE INDICATED?

1. When a small employer is looking for an alternative to a qualified profit sharing plan that is easier and less expensive to install and administer. For very small employers, a SIMPLE IRA is one of the simplest types of tax-deferred employee retirement plans available. For larger employers, the cost of installing and administering a regular qualified plan can be spread over enough employees that the advantages of these plans are less significant.

2. When an employer has one hundred or fewer employees and wants an easy-to-administer plan funded through employee salary reductions.

3. Where an individual has a relatively small amount of self-employment income and the SIMPLE IRA contribution limit is higher than that available for any other form of tax-favored plan, such as a Keogh plan or a SEP.

Advantages

1. A SIMPLE IRA can be adopted by completing an IRS form (Forms 5304-SIMPLE or 5305-SIMPLE) rather than by the complex procedure required for qualified plans (described in Chapter 15). However, if the employer adopts a master or prototype qualified plan, the installation costs and complexity may not actually be much greater than that for a SIMPLE IRA, even though the documentation is more voluminous.

2. Assets in a SIMPLE IRA are portable since funding is held entirely in an IRA for each employee and employees are always 100 percent vested in their benefits. Employees own and control their accounts, even after they terminate employment with the original employer.

3. SIMPLE IRA accounts allow participants to benefit from good investment results.

4. A SIMPLE IRA can be funded in part through salary reductions by employees, if the conditions described in "Tax Implications," below, are met.

Disadvantages

1. Employees cannot rely upon a SIMPLE IRA to provide an adequate retirement benefit. First, benefits are not significant unless the employee makes significant regular salary reduction contributions. Such regular contributions are not a requirement of the plan. Furthermore, employees who enter the plan at older ages have only a limited number of years remaining prior to retirement to build up their SIMPLE IRA balances.

2. Annual contributions generally are restricted to lesser amounts than would be available in a qualified plan. SIMPLE IRA salary reduction contributions are limited by a maximum of $12,500 (in 2015). By contrast, traditional 401(k) plans or 403(b) plans have an annual salary reduction maximum of $18,000 (in 2015). The "catch-up" contribution limits are also lower for SIMPLE IRAs ($3,000 in 2015) than for traditional 401(k) plans and 403(b) plans ($6,000 in 2015).

3. Distributions from SIMPLE IRAs are not eligible for the ten-year averaging provisions available for certain qualified plan distributions to employees born before 1936.

4. If an employer adopts a SIMPLE IRA plan, it cannot simultaneously maintain a qualified plan, SEP, 403(a) annuity, 403(b) tax-sheltered annuity, or a governmental plan (other than a Section 457 plan) for that year. However, certain collectively bargained plans will not affect an employer's eligibility to establish a SIMPLE IRA (see the "Tax Implications" section).

5. An employer must make matching contributions equal to 100 percent of an employee's salary reduction up a maximum of 3 percent of compensation or make nonelective contributions equal to 2 percent of compensation.

TAX IMPLICATIONS

For Employers

The employer may deduct contributions (both employee salary reduction amounts and employer matching contributions) to a SIMPLE IRA if certain requirements are met. The principal requirements are:[3]

1. The employer must have one hundred or fewer employees (only employees with at least $5,000 in compensation for the preceding year are counted) on any day in the year.

2. Contributions may be made to an IRA established for each employee.

3. Employees who earned at least $5,000 from the employer in any two preceding years, and are reasonably expected to earn at least $5,000 in the current year, can contribute (through salary reductions) up to $12,500 (as indexed for 2015).

4. Participants who have reached the age of fifty during the plan year may be permitted to make "catch-up" contributions in addition to the limits listed above. The limit for catch-up contributions is $3,000 (as indexed for 2015).

5. The employer is required to make a contribution equal to either:

   a. a dollar for dollar matching contribution up to 3 percent of the employee's compensation (the employer can elect a lower percentage, not less than 1 percent, in no more than two out of the five years ending with the current year);[4] or

   b. a nonelective contribution equal to 2 percent of compensation for all eligible employees earning at least $5,000 (whether or not they elect salary reductions).[5]

Partners and proprietors can be covered under the SIMPLE IRA plan of an unincorporated employer, as well as regular employees. For a person with a limited amount of self-employment income, such as a moonlighting business, the SIMPLE IRA may allow the maximum retirement plan contribution. Alternatives such as Keogh plans and SEPs have various limitations based on percentages of compensation or earned income. The limit for a SIMPLE IRA is not a percentage limit, but a dollar limit of $12,500 (for 2015) on salary reductions, with matching or nonelective contributions required by the employer.[6]

If the employer maintains a SIMPLE IRA, it may not maintain a qualified plan, SEP, 403(a) annuity, 403(b) tax sheltered annuity, or a governmental plan (other than a Section 457 plan) for that year. However, an employer who has only a collectively bargained qualified plan (but not any other qualified plan) may adopt a SIMPLE IRA plan for the non-collectively bargained employees, provided none of the SIMPLE IRA participants are participants in the collectively bargained plan.[7]

Direct employer contributions are not subject to Social Security (FICA) or federal unemployment (FUTA) taxes. However, employee salary reduction contributions are subject to FICA and FUTA.[8] The impact of state payroll taxes depends on the particular state's laws. Both salary reductions and employer contributions may be exempt from state payroll taxes in some states.

Certain employers adopting a new plan may be eligible for a business tax credit of up to $500 for "qualified startup costs." See Chapter 15 for details.

For Employees and Individuals

Each participating employee maintains an IRA for the SIMPLE IRA plan contributions. Employer contributions are made directly to the employee's IRA, as are any employee salary reduction contributions. Employer contributions and employee salary reductions, within the limits discussed above, are not included in the employee's taxable income.[9]

Distributions to employees are generally treated as distributions from a traditional IRA.[10] All the restrictions on traditional IRA distributions apply and the distributions are taxed the same; however, the 10 percent penalty on early distributions is increased to 25 percent during the first two years of participation.[11] Furthermore, while a rollover may be made at any time from one SIMPLE IRA to another SIMPLE IRA, a rollover from a SIMPLE IRA to a traditional IRA during the first two years of participation is permitted only in the case of distributions to which the 25 percent early distribution penalty does not apply.[12] The taxation of traditional IRA distributions is discussed in Chapter 20.

An individual cannot make deductible contributions to his or her own IRA after attaining age 70½. However, employers can make contributions to SIMPLE IRAs (including both matching contributions and salary reductions) for employees who are over age 70½. In fact, the age discrimination law, if applicable, would generally require such contributions to be made.

For purposes of any potential deduction for contributions to a traditional IRA, a SIMPLE IRA participant is treated the same as a participant in a regular qualified plan. That is, if the individual is an "active participant" in the SIMPLE IRA plan, traditional IRA contributions can be made, but the deduction limit of $5,500 (in 2015) is reduced if adjusted gross income (AGI) exceeds certain limits. If the individual is not an active participant in the plan, the full IRA deduction may be available. These rules are discussed in detail in Chapter 20.

An employee covered under a SIMPLE IRA would be considered an active participant in any year in which salary reductions or employer contributions were allocated to his or her account. However, in a year in which no allocation was made to the individual's account, the individual would have any otherwise-available IRA deduction (up to $5,500 in 2015).[13] The higher SIMPLE IRA limit is not available for individual IRA contributions, only for employer contributions or salary reductions under a SIMPLE IRA plan.

Qualified Retirement Savings Tax Credit

Certain lower-income taxpayers may claim a temporary, nonrefundable credit for "qualified retirement savings contributions."[14] "Qualified retirement savings contributions" include elective deferrals to SIMPLE IRAs, as well as other elective deferrals and contributions to Roth or traditional IRAs. (However, the total is reduced by certain distributions received by the taxpayer or his spouse during the prior two taxable years and the current taxable year for which the credit is claimed, including the period up to the due date (plus extensions) for filing the federal income tax return for the current taxable year.) Only the first $2,000 of annual deferrals is eligible for the credit.

The credit is allowed against the sum of the regular tax and the alternative minimum tax (minus certain other credits) and is allowed in addition to any other deduction or exclusion that would otherwise apply. In addition, to be eligible, the taxpayer must be at least eighteen as of the end of the tax year and must not be claimed as a dependent by someone else or be a full-time student.

The amount of the credit is limited to an "applicable percentage" of IRA contributions and elective deferrals up to $2,000 ($4,000 if married filing jointly). The "applicable percentages" are as follows for 2015:

Amount of Credit	Married Filing Jointly	Head of Household	Single/ Others
50% of first $2,000 deferred ($4,000 if married filing jointly)	$0 to $36,500	$0 to $27,375	$0 to $18,250
20% of first $2,000 deferred ($4,000 if married filing jointly)	$36,501 to $39,500	$27,376 to $29,625	$18,251 to $19,750
10% of first $2,000 deferred ($4,000 if married filing jointly)	$39,501 to $61,000	$29,626 to $45,750	$19,751 to $30,500

Example. Max and Erma work for the same employer and together have adjusted gross income of $36,000 on a joint return for 2014. Their employer sponsors a SIMPLE IRA and they each elected to make a salary reduction contribution of $3,000 to the plan. Neither has received any distributions in the current or two preceding taxable years. Max and Erma will be able to exclude their salary reduction contributions as well as each being eligible to claim a credit of $800 jointly ($400 each; 20 percent of $2,000) on their federal income tax return for 2015.

HOW TO INSTALL A PLAN

Installation of a SIMPLE IRA plan can be very easy. The employer completes Form 5304-SIMPLE or Form 5305-SIMPLE. Form 5304-SIMPLE does not provide for a "designated financial institution" for participant investments, while Form 5305-SIMPLE does, which some plan sponsors and participants may find restrictive. Salary reduction elections must be made by employees during a sixty-day period prior to January 1 of the year for which the elections are made. The form does not have to be sent to the IRS or any other government agency.

ERISA REQUIREMENTS

The reporting and disclosure requirements for SIMPLE IRA plans are simplified, particularly if the employer uses Form 5304-SIMPLE or 5305-SIMPLE. The annual report forms (5500 series) are not required for SIMPLE IRA plans.

WHERE CAN I FIND OUT MORE?

IRS Publication 334, *Tax Guide for Small Business*, and Publication 535, *Business Expense Deductions*, available free from the IRS; revised annually.

CHAPTER ENDNOTES

1. The provisions for SIMPLE IRAs are set forth in I.R.C. §408(p). See Chapter 19 and I.R.C. §401(k)(11) for the rules governing SIMPLE 401(k) plans.
2. I.R.C. §408(p)(2)(A)(ii).
3. See I.R.C. §408(p).
4. I.R.C. §408(p)(2)(A)(iii). The compensation limit under I.R.C. §401(a)(17) is not applicable for purposes of the matching contribution; thus, for example, a 3 percent match could reach the maximum limit in 2015 of $12,500 if an employee has compensation of about $416,700 in a year. See also Notice 97-6, 1997-1 CB 353.
5. I.R.C. §408(p)(2)(B). "Compensation" for purposes of the 2 percent nonelective contribution is subject to the limits of I.R.C. §401(a)(17) ($265,000 in 2015). Consequently, the maximum that could be contributed in nonelective contributions for an employee in 2015 would be $5.300 (i.e., 2 percent of $265,000). See I.R.C. §408(p)(2)(B)(ii).
6. SIMPLE IRAs are not subject to the limits of Code section 415, nor to the deduction limits of Code section 404(a); see Chapter 13.
7. I.R.C. §408(p)(2)(D).
8. I.R.C. §§3121(a), 3306(a), 3401(a)(12); Notice 97-6, 1997-1 CB 353.
9. See I.R.C. §§402(k), 402(h)(1), 402(e)(3); Notice 97-6, 1997-1 CB 353.
10. I.R.C. §§402(k), 402(h)(3); General Explanation of Tax Legislation Enacted in the 104th Congress (JCT-12-96), p. 141 (the 1996 Blue Book).
11. I.R.C. §72(t)(6).
12. I.R.C. §408(d)(3)(G). During the two-year period that the 25 percent penalty is imposed, such a transfer would be treated as a distribution from the SIMPLE IRA and a contribution to the regular IRA that does not qualify as a rollover contribution. Notice 97-6, 1997-1 CB 353.
13. Notice 87-16, 1987-1 CB 446, I.
14. I.R.C. §25B.

SIMPLIFIED EMPLOYEE PENSION (SEP)

CHAPTER 31

INTRODUCTION

A simplified employee pension (SEP) is an employer-sponsored plan under which plan contributions are made to the participating employee's IRA. Tax-deferred contribution levels for SEPs are generally significantly higher than the maximum contribution limit for traditional IRAs (see Chapter 20). A SEP provides for employer contributions only, except for existing salary reduction SEPs (SAR-SEPs), which had to be adopted before 1997.

SEPs are easy to adopt and generally simple to administer, while providing employees with the tax-deferred retirement savings benefits of a qualified plan. However, other qualified plans potentially can provide higher contribution levels. Annual SEP contributions are effectively limited to the lesser of 25 percent of compensation or $53,000 (in 2015).[1]

WHEN IS USE OF SUCH A DEVICE INDICATED?

1. When the employer is looking for an alternative to a qualified profit sharing plan that is easier and less expensive to install and administer. For very small employers, a SEP is one of the simplest types of tax-deferred employee retirement plans available. For larger employers (more than about ten employees), the cost of installing and administering a qualified plan can be spread over enough employees that the advantages of a SEP are less significant.

2. When an employer wants to install a tax-deferred plan and it is too late to adopt a qualified plan for the year in question. (Qualified plans must be adopted before the end of the year in which they are to be effective. SEPs can be adopted as late as the tax return filing date for the year in which they are to be effective.)

Advantages

1. A SEP can be adopted by completing IRS Form 5305-SEP rather than by the more complex procedure required for qualified plans (described in Chapter 13). However, if the employer adopts a prototype or volume submitter document for a qualified plan, the installation costs and complexity for such a qualified plan may not be much greater than that for a SEP, even though the documents are much longer.

2. A SEP can be adopted at any time up to the tax return filing date for the year, including extensions. For example, if an incorporated employer uses the calendar year as its fiscal year, the tax return filing date for the 2015 fiscal year is March 15, 2016, with extensions possible to September 15, 2016. Therefore, a SEP could be adopted for 2015 as late as September 14, 2016.

3. SEP assets are portable for employees because the funding vehicle for each employee is an IRA, and employees are always 100 percent vested in their benefits. Employees own and control their SEP-IRAs, even after they terminate employment with the employer sponsor.

4. A SEP provides as much or more flexibility in the amount and timing of contributions as a qualified profit sharing plan. The employer, at its discretion, may elect to make no contributions to the plan in any given year.

5. Individual IRAs allow participants to benefit from good investment; however, participants also assume the risk of bad investment results.

6. A SAR-SEP that was adopted before 1997 can be funded through salary reductions by employees, if the conditions described under "Tax Implications," below, are met.

7. A SEP generally has no annual filing requirements other than the IRS Form 5498, which the financial institution holding the IRAs will generally prepare.

Disadvantages

1. Employees cannot rely solely upon a SEP to provide adequate retirement benefits. First, benefits are not significant unless the employer makes substantial, regular contributions to the SEP, which is not a requirement for a SEP. Second, unless the SEP was adopted prior to 1997 (*i.e.*, a SAR-SEP), no employee salary reduction contributions are not permitted.

2. Annual contributions may be restricted to lesser amounts than would be available in a qualified plan. Although SEPs are subject to the same Code section 415 limit as a defined contribution plan (*i.e.*, the lesser of (a) 100 percent of compensation or (b) $53,000 (in 2015 as indexed), the deduction and exclusion amounts may be lower than they would be for a qualified plan, as explained below.

TAX IMPLICATIONS

For Employers

In a SEP plan, each participating employee maintains a traditional IRA. A SEP may not maintain Roth IRAs.[2] Employer contributions are made directly to the employee's IRA. Employer contributions, within the limits discussed above, are not included in the employee's taxable income.

Partners and proprietors can be covered under the SEP of an unincorporated employer, as well as regular employees. As discussed in Chapter 29 (relating to HR 10 plans), for a partner or proprietor, "earned income" is used in place of compensation in computing SEP contributions.

Note that the above limits are higher than those applicable to SIMPLE IRAs and SIMPLE 401(k) plans (see Chapter 30), so employers with grandfathered salary reduction SEPs may wish to continue them.

If an employer maintains both a SEP and a qualified plan, employer contributions to the SEP reduce the amount that can be deducted for contributions to the qualified plan. Furthermore, if an employer maintains any other qualified retirement plan, it may not use Form 5305-SEP to adopt a SEP.

Certain employers adopting a plan may be eligible for a business tax credit of up to $500 for "qualified startup costs." See Chapter 15 for details.

Employer Contributions

The employer need not contribute any particular amount to a SEP or make any contribution at all. The "recurring and substantial contributions" requirement applicable to qualified profit sharing plans (as discussed in Chapter 22) has no effect on SEPs, so SEP contributions are more flexible than those to a qualified plan. An employer can freely omit any year's contribution to a SEP without any concern about adverse tax consequences.

The employer contribution, if made, must be allocated to plan participants under a written formula that does not discriminate in favor of highly compensated employees. The definition of "highly compensated" is that used for most employee benefit purposes, as discussed in Chapter 13.

SEP formulas must bear a uniform relationship to compensation. That is, the employer contribution provided to each eligible employee must be the same percentage of compensation. However, SEP allocation formulas can be integrated with Social Security under the integration rules applicable to qualified defined contribution plans (discussed in Chapter 13). Also, in the allocation formula, only the first $265,000 (as indexed for 2015) of each employee's compensation can be taken into account.

Direct employer contributions to a SEP are not subject to Social Security (FICA) or federal unemployment (FUTA) taxes. The impact of state payroll taxes depends on the particular state's laws. Both salary reductions and employer contributions may be exempt from state payroll taxes in some states.

An individual cannot make contributions to his or her own traditional IRA after attaining age 70½.

However, employers can make contributions to SEPs for employees who are over age 70½.

Salary Reduction Plans

As noted above, new SEPS were no longer permitted after 1996. Grandfathered SEPs that use salary reductions (SAR-SEPs) are subject to the following rules.

An employer cannot use a salary reduction SEP unless 50 percent or more of the employees eligible to participate elect to make SEP contributions. In addition, rules similar to the "actual deferral percentage" (ADP) test apply to a salary reduction SEP.[3] Under the ADP rules for SAR-SEPs, the deferral percentage for each highly compensated eligible employee who participates must be no more than 1.25 times the ADP of nonhighly compensated eligible employees. For example, if nonhighly compensated employees elect salary reductions averaging 6 percent of compensation, no highly compensated employee can elect more than a 7.5 percent salary reduction.

Salary reductions, but not direct employer contributions, are subject to Social Security (FICA) and federal unemployment (FUTA) taxes.[4] The impact of state payroll taxes depends on the particular state's law. Both salary reductions and employer contributions may be exempt from state payroll taxes in some states.

In addition to the foregoing salary reductions, employees who have reached age fifty during the plan year are generally eligible to make "catch-up" contributions. For salary reduction SEPs, the elective deferral limit is increased by $6,000 (as indexed for 2015) for catch-up contributions.[5]

For Employees and Individuals

For individual IRA purposes, a SEP participant is treated the same as a participant in a regular qualified plan. That is, if the individual is an "active participant" in the plan, individual IRA contributions can be made and deducted, but the deduction is reduced or eliminated if adjusted gross income exceeds certain limits (see Chapter 20 for details). The full IRA deduction may be available to an individual who is not an active participant in a plan.

An employee covered under a SEP or SAR-SEP would be considered an active participant in any year in which salary reductions or employer contributions were allocated to his or her account. However, in a year in which no allocation was made to the individual's account, the individual would have a full individual IRA deduction available (within the limits explained in Chapter 20).[6] The higher SEP limit is not available for individual IRA contributions.

Certain lower-income taxpayers may claim a temporary, nonrefundable credit for "qualified retirement savings contributions."[7] "Qualified retirement savings contributions" include elective deferrals to SIMPLE IRAs, as well as other elective deferrals and contributions to Roth or traditional IRAs. (However, the total is reduced by certain distributions received by the taxpayer or his spouse during the prior two taxable years and the current taxable year for which the credit is claimed, including the period up to the due date (plus extensions) for filing the federal income tax return for the current taxable year.) Only the first $2,000 of annual deferrals is eligible for the credit.

The credit is allowed against the sum of the regular tax and the alternative minimum tax (minus certain other credits) and is allowed in addition to any other deduction or exclusion that would otherwise apply. In addition, to be eligible, the taxpayer must be at least eighteen as of the end of the tax year and must not be claimed as a dependent by someone else or be a full-time student.

Distributions to employees from the plan are treated as distributions from an IRA. All the restrictions on traditional IRA distributions apply and the distributions are taxed in the same manner. The taxation of distributions from traditional IRAs is discussed in Chapter 20.

HOW TO INSTALL A PLAN

Installation of a SEP can be very easy. The employer merely completes Form 5305-SEP. To adopt a SEP, the employer completes the form and signs it prior to the tax filing date for the year in which the SEP is to take effect.[8] The form does not have to be sent to the IRS or any other government agency.

A SEP adopted by filling out Form 5305-SEP is somewhat inflexible since it must follow the provisions set out on the IRS model form. Some of the provisions in this form are more stringent than are actually required by the SEP rules. In particular:

1. The plan set out on Form 5305-SEP is not integrated with Social Security.

2. By its terms, Form 5305-SEP cannot be used if the employer (a) currently maintains a qualified plan, or (b) maintained a qualified defined benefit plan at any time in the past covering one or more of the employees to be covered under the SEP.

If the employer wants to adopt a SEP plan that avoids the limitations of the IRS model form, the plan must be custom designed. Costs for custom designing and installing a SEP are comparable to those for a qualified profit sharing plan.

An employer may deduct contributions to a SEP to the extent such contributions do not exceed 25 percent of the total payroll of all employees covered under the plan.[9] The major SEP coverage requirements are:[10]

- A SEP must cover all employees who are at least twenty-one years of age and who have worked for the employer during three out of the preceding five calendar years. Part-time employment must be considered in determining years of service.
- Employees whose compensation for the calendar year was less than $600 (as indexed for 2015) may be excluded.
- Employees who are covered by a collective bargaining agreement and whose retirement benefits have been the subject of good-faith bargaining may also be excluded.
- Nonresident aliens who received no U.S. source wages, salaries or other personal services compensation from the employer may also be excluded.

ERISA REQUIREMENTS

The reporting and disclosure requirements for SEPs are simplified if the employer uses Form 5305-SEP. The annual report form (5500 series) need not be filed if these forms are used. In other cases, reporting and disclosure requirements are similar to those for a qualified profit sharing plan.

WHERE CAN I FIND OUT MORE?

IRS Publication 334, Tax Guide for Small Business, and Publication 535, Business Expense Deductions, available free from the IRS; revised annually.

CHAPTER ENDNOTES

1. This is the result of the combination of the I.R.C. §415(c) limit (i.e., the lesser of $53,000 (in 2015) or 100 percent of compensation) and the I.R.C. §402(h)(2) exclusion for contributions (which is 25 percent of compensation).
2. I.R.C. §408A(f)(1).
3. I.R.C. §408(k)(6).
4. I.R.C. §§3121(a)(5)(C) and 3306(b)(5)(C).
5. I.R.C. §414(v). Note that the limit will be lower if the amount of a participant's compensation, (after reduction for other elective deferrals) is less than the catch-up amounts.
6. Notice 87-16, 1987-1 CB 446, I.
7. I.R.C. §25B.
8. Prop. Treas. Reg. §1.408-7(b).
9. I.R.C. §404(h)(1)(C).
10. The rules described in this chapter for SEPS are contained in I.R.C. §408(k) unless otherwise indicated in the footnotes. The IRC formerly contained provisions for SEPs funded through salary reductions (SAR-SEPs). No new SAR-SEPs may be adopted after 1996; however, SAR-SEPs existing on December 31, 1996 may continue in effect and add new participants.

TAX DEFERRED ANNUITY

CHAPTER 32

INTRODUCTION

A tax deferred annuity plan (also called a TDA plan or Section 403(b) plan) is a tax deferred employee retirement plan that can be adopted only by certain tax-exempt organizations and certain public school systems.[1] Employees have accounts in a TDA plan to which employers contribute and/or employees contribute through salary reductions.

The benefits of a TDA plan to employees are similar to those of a qualified profit sharing plan, particularly the Section 401(k)-type of plan (see Chapter 19): (1) the TDA contribution is, within limits, not currently taxable to employees; (2) plan account balances accumulate tax-free; and (3) tax on plan contributions and account earnings is deferred until the employee actually withdraws amounts from the plan.

WHEN IS USE OF SUCH A DEVICE INDICATED?

1. When (and only when) the employer organization is eligible under the TDA provisions of the Code. An organization must be one of the following in order to adopt a TDA plan:

    a. A tax-exempt employer described in Code section 501(c)(3). This means that:

        i. The employer must be "organized and operated exclusively for religious, charitable, scientific, testing for public safety, literary, or educational purposes, or to foster national or international amateur sport competition…or for the prevention of cruelty to children or animals."

        ii. The organization must benefit the public, rather than a private shareholder or individual.

        iii. The organization further must refrain from political campaigning or propaganda intended to influence legislation.

    In other words, most familiar non-profit institutions such as churches, hospitals, private schools and colleges, and charitable institutions are eligible to adopt a TDA.

    b. An educational organization with (1) a regular faculty and curriculum and (2) a regularly enrolled student body in attendance that is operated by a state or municipal agency. In other words, most public schools and colleges may adopt a TDA plan. A TDA plan can also be adopted for certain employees outside of the schools who perform services involving the operation or direction of the public school education program.

2. Assuming the employer organization is eligible, the positive indications for a TDA plan are:

    a. When the employer wants to provide a tax deferred retirement plan for employees but can afford only minimal extra expense beyond existing salary and benefit costs. A TDA plan can be funded entirely from employee salary reductions (except for installation and administration costs, which must be paid for by the employer). In most plans, however, some additional employer contribution to the plan can enhance its effectiveness.

b. When the employee group has one or more of the following characteristics:

- Many would like some choice as to the level of savings—that is, a choice between various levels of current cash compensation and tax deferred savings. A younger, more mobile work force often prefers this option.

- Many employees are relatively young and have substantial time to accumulate retirement savings.

- Many employees are willing to accept a degree of investment risk in their plan accounts in return for the potential benefits of good investment results.

c. When an employer wants an attractive, "savings-type" supplement to its existing defined benefit or other qualified plan. Such a supplement can make the employer's retirement benefit program attractive to both younger and older employees by providing security of retirement benefits and the opportunity to increase savings and investment on a tax deferred basis.

Non-governmental, tax-exempt employers are also permitted to offer Section 401(k) plans (see Chapter 19).[2] See the "Frequently Asked Questions," below, for considerations to take into account when choosing between a Section 401(k) plan and a TDA. Also, tax-exempt employers and governmental entities are permitted to maintain SIMPLE IRA plans (see Chapter 30).[3]

Advantages

1. As with qualified plans, a TDA plan provides a tax-deferred retirement savings medium for employees.

2. A salary reduction-type TDA plan allows employees a degree of choice in the amount they wish to save under the plan.

3. TDA plans can be funded entirely through salary reductions by employees. As a result, an employer can adopt the plan with no additional cost for employee compensation; the only extra cost is plan installation and administration. The plan may actually result in some savings as a result of lower state or local (but not federal) payroll taxes.

4. In-service withdrawals by employees are permitted. These are not available in qualified pension plans, although they are available in profit sharing plans.

Disadvantages

1. As with qualified defined contribution plans, account balances at retirement age may not provide adequate retirement savings for employees who enter the plan at later ages.

2. For each employee the annual salary reduction under the plan is subject to the elective deferral limit (see below). However, this amount can be supplemented by employer contributions to provide additional tax deferred savings.

3. Because of the nondiscrimination tests described below, a TDA plan can be relatively costly and complex to administer.

4. Employees bear investment risk under the plan. However, TDA funds are in large part invested in low risk annuity contracts. Only the mutual fund (custodial account—see below) type of TDA investment (and possibly some variable annuity contracts) involves significant investment risk, and employees usually are given a choice of mutual fund investments so they can control the degree of risk.

DESIGN FEATURES

Salary Reductions

Like Section 401(k) plans, TDA plans are generally built around salary reduction contributions elected by employees. A possible alternative is for the employer to provide an annual "bonus" to employees that the employees can either receive in cash or contribute to the plan. "Negative election" provisions are also permitted; these are plan provisions whereby the employer *automatically* contributes a specified portion of each employee's salary to the plan, unless the employee specifically requests to receive the amount in cash. Negative elections have been approved for 401(k) plans as well.[4]

Salary reductions must be elected by employees *before* compensation is earned—that is, before they render the services for which compensation is paid.

Salary reductions elected after compensation is earned are ineffective as a result of the tax doctrine of "constructive receipt."[5]

The usual practice is to provide plan participants with a salary reduction election form that they must complete before the end of each calendar year. The election specifies how much will be contributed to the plan from each paycheck received for the forthcoming year. Usually the plan will permit the employee to reduce or entirely withdraw the election for pay not yet earned, if circumstances dictate. The plan must restrict each participant's salary reductions to no more than the annual limits set forth in the Code (see below). In general, the procedural rules for salary reductions are the same as those for 401(k) plans.[6]

Salary reductions, as well as any other plan contribution that the employee has the option to receive in cash (referred to as "elective deferrals"), are subject to an annual limit. The limit is a "per employee" rather than a "per plan" limit. The employee must add together each year all elective deferrals from:

1. Section 401(k) plans;
2. salary reduction SEPs (available if established before 1997—see Chapter 31);
3. SIMPLE IRAs (see Chapter 30); and
4. Section 403(b) TDA plans.

Note that deferrals from a 457 plan need not be aggregated, creating a "double dip" opportunity; see Chapter 34). The total must not exceed $18,000 (as indexed for 2015).[7]

In addition to the foregoing salary reductions, employees who have reached age fifty during the plan year[8] can make "catch-up" contributions. All participants must have the same right to make this election. Under this catch-up, the elective deferral limit is increased by $6,000 (as indexed for 2015).[9]

The TDA Salary Reduction Catch-Up

TDA plans have an additional catch-up feature that is unique to TDAs. If a covered employee has completed fifteen years of service for the employer, and the employer is (1) an educational organization, (2) a hospital, (3) a home health care agency, (4) a health and welfare service agency, or (5) a church, synagogue or related organization, the elective deferral limit (see above) is increased by an additional sum equal to the least of:

- $3,000;
- $15,000, reduced by the sum of (a) any amounts excluded from gross income for prior taxable years by reason of the catch-up provision, and (b) the aggregate amount of designated Roth contributions for prior taxable years; or
- $5,000 times the employee's years of service with the employer, less all prior salary reductions with that employer.[10]

Notwithstanding these all of these limits, the amount contributed by salary reduction cannot exceed 100 percent of the employee's compensation except that the age-fifty catch-up is not limited by Section 415 limits (see below).[11]

Employer Contributions

Many TDA plans provide for employer contributions, in addition to or instead of salary reduction contributions, in order to encourage employee participation and make the plan more valuable to employees. TDA plans most often use a "formula matching contribution." Under this approach, the employer matches employee salary reductions, either dollar for dollar or under another formula. For example, the plan might provide that the employer contributes an amount equal to 50 percent of the amount the employee elects as a salary reduction. So if an employee elects a salary reduction of $6,000, the employer puts an additional $3,000 into the employee's plan account. Other employer contribution approaches can be used similar to those used in Section 401(k) plans, as discussed in Chapter 19.

The level of employer match can be increased for employees with longer service. However, whenever there are employer contributions, complex nondiscrimination requirements must be met (see below). These impose additional administrative costs for the employer.

Section 415 Limits

A TDA plan is subject to the same limits under Code section 415 as a qualified defined contribution plan.

(See Chapter 13). That is, the annual addition to each participant's account cannot exceed the lesser of (a) 100 percent of compensation or (b) $53,000 (as indexed for 2015). "Annual additions" refers to the total of employer contributions, employee contributions, and forfeitures from other participants' accounts (forfeitures are unlikely in 403(b) plans because of the 100 percent vesting requirement discussed below). The 100 percent limit is applied to the participant's gross compensation, unreduced by any salary reduction contributions to the 403(b) or to a Section 401(k), 457, SIMPLE, or FSA (flexible spending account) plan.

The following are some examples that apply these limits:

Example 1. Employee Bob, age forty-five, earns $80,000 in 2015. He is covered under a TDA plan funded exclusively through employee salary reduction. The maximum amount he may contribute to the TDA plan for 2015 is $18,000.

Example 2. Employee Barb, age thirty-three, earns $90,000 in 2015. She is covered under a TDA plan that provides for salary reductions and employer discretionary contributions. Barb elects a salary reduction of $18,000 for 2015. The employer can contribute up to a total of $35,000 for Barb (a total of $53,000 for 2015).

Example 3. Employee Bill, age forty, earns $10,000 in 2015. His TDA plan provides for salary reductions and discretionary employer contributions. Bill elects a salary reduction of $5,000 for 2015. The employer can contribute up to an additional $5,000, for a total of $10,000 contributed to the plan (100 percent of compensation, unreduced by Bill's salary reduction election). Bill pays taxes currently only on the $5,000 of cash compensation that he receives in 2015.

Nondiscrimination Requirements

Under current regulations,[12] TDA plans (with some exceptions) must satisfy rules similar to the nondiscrimination rules that apply to regular qualified plans, which are discussed in more detail in Chapter 13:

- Rules relating to nondiscrimination in contributions and benefits[13]
- The compensation limit of Section 401(a)(17), which is $265,000 for 2015
- Section 410(b) relating to minimum coverage of nonhighly compensated employees
- Rules aggregating related employers for purposes of testing for nondiscrimination
- "Universal availability" of salary reductions; that is, all employees must be permitted to make elective deferrals (including designation of Roth contributions) if any employee may do so. The employer may require a minimum salary reduction of up to $200 as a condition of participation. Coverage is not required for employees who participate in a Section 401(k) or Section 457 plan, another TDA plan, or certain other employees.[14]

Vesting

The participant is always 100 percent vested in all amounts contributed to the TDA plan by salary reduction and in any plan earnings on those amounts. Even if a participant leaves employment after a short time, his or her plan account attributable to such contributions cannot be forfeited. However, participants need not be immediately vested in employer contributions. Note, though, that plans with employer contributions are generally subject to ERISA and that ERISA imposes minimum vesting standards—that is, 100 percent "cliff" vesting after three years, or graded vesting starting with 20 percent after two years, increasing by 20 percent each year, until 100 percent is reached after six years.[15]

Plan Investments

Generally, all plan funds in TDA plans must be invested in either (1) annuity contracts purchased by the employer from an insurance company, or (2) mutual fund (regulated investment company) shares held in custodial accounts.[16] Many plans provide both types of investments and allow participants full discretion to divide their accounts between the two investment media.

Annuities used in TDA plans can be group or individual contracts, level or flexible premium annuities, or fixed dollar or variable annuities. Face amount certificates providing a fixed maturity value and a schedule of redemptions are also permitted. Annuity contracts can give participants a degree of choice as to investment strategy. For example, the participant can be given a choice of investment mix between equity funds and fixed investment funds.[17]

Plan Distributions

Distributions from TDA plans are subject to the qualified plan distribution rules detailed in Chapter 14. Many plans provide for distributions in a lump sum at termination of employment. However, a plan subject to ERISA must either provide for a qualified joint and survivor annuity as its automatic benefit or provide that if the participant dies, 100 percent of his nonforfeitable benefit will be paid to his surviving spouse unless the spouse is deceased or has consented to another beneficiary.[18]

The current regulations attempt to clarify or interpret overly complex statutory provisions relating to 403(b) plan distributions.[19] There are four categories of 403(b) plan distributions under these rules, as outlined in Figure 32.1.

The definition of hardship in these rules is the same as for 401(k) plans. Note, however, that the maximum amount that can be withdrawn from an elective deferral account for hardship is the principal amount only, not including any earnings on the elective deferral account. (The rules for pre-1989 amounts are more liberal.)

Notwithstanding these rules, distributions may be made to former spouses under the rules for qualified domestic relations orders (QDROs).[21]

All withdrawals are subject to income tax. In addition, many in-service distributions will be subject to the 10 percent early withdrawal penalty tax discussed in Chapter 14, even if the distribution is permitted under the terms of the TDA plan. To summarize, a 10 percent penalty tax applies to the taxable amount (i.e., amount subject to regular income tax) of any qualified plan or TDA distribution, except for distributions:

- on or after age 59½;
- on or after the employee's death;
- attributable to the employee's disability;
- that are part of substantially equal periodic payments (made at least annually) following separation from service and for the life or life expectancy of the employee or the joint lives or joint life expectancies of the employee and his beneficiary;
- that are paid after separation from service after age fifty-five; or
- to the extent that they do not exceed the amount of medical expenses deductible as an itemized deduction for the year.[22]

Many TDA plans have provisions for plan loans to participants. A plan loan provision is extremely

Figure 32.1

403(b) PLAN DISTRIBUTIONS		
Annuity Plan Amounts (Not 403(b)(7) custodial accounts and not amounts attributable to elective deferrals)	**Custodial Account** (403(b)(7) amounts not attributable to elective deferrals)	**Elective Deferral Amounts**
no earlier than the earliest of:	no earlier than the earliest of:	no earlier than the earliest of:
• severance from employment • occurrence of a stated age or stated number of years • disability	• severance from employment • death • disability • attainment of age 59½.	• severance from employment • death • hardship • disability • attainment of age 59½ • plan termination

*Amounts attributable to pre-1989 elective deferrals are subject to different, more complex rules that are beyond the scope of this chapter.[20]

valuable to employees because it allows them access to their plan funds without the 10 percent penalty tax. Plan loans are discussed in detail in Chapter 14.[23]

TAX IMPLICATIONS

1. Employees are not taxed currently on either salary reductions or employer contributions under a TDA plan, so long as these in total do not exceed the limits discussed above.

2. Salary reductions, but not employer contributions, are generally subject to Social Security (FICA) and federal unemployment (FUTA) payroll taxes.[24] The impact of state payroll taxes depends on the particular state's law. Both elective deferrals and employer contributions may be exempt from state payroll taxes in some states.

3. A plan may permit employees to make voluntary contributions to a "deemed IRA" established under the plan. Amounts so contributed reduce the limit for other traditional or Roth IRA contributions. See Chapter 14 for details. Contributions under this provision may also (as with elective deferrals and other IRA contributions) count toward the nonrefundable credit for lower-income taxpayers, explained in the "Frequently Asked Questions," below.

4. Plan participants may exclude from income amounts directly transferred (i.e., from trustee to trustee) from a TDA plan to a governmental defined benefit plan if the transferred funds are used to purchase permissible service credits or to repay contributions or earnings that were previously refunded because of a forfeiture of service credit.[25]

5. Distributions from the plan must follow the rules for qualified plan distributions. Certain premature distributions are subject to penalties. The distribution rules are discussed in Chapter 14.

6. Distributions from the plan to employees are subject to income tax when received. Single sum distributions from TDA plans are not eligible for any special ten-year averaging computations applicable to certain qualified plan distributions.

Credit for Qualified Retirement Savings Contributions

Certain lower-income taxpayers may claim a temporary, nonrefundable credit for qualified retirement savings contributions.[26] Qualified retirement savings contributions include elective deferrals to SIMPLE IRAs, as well as other elective deferrals and contributions to Roth or traditional IRAs. (However, the total is reduced by certain distributions received by the taxpayer or his spouse during the prior two taxable years and the current taxable year for which the credit is claimed, including the period up to the due date (plus extensions) for filing the federal income tax return for the current taxable year.) Only the first $2,000 of annual deferrals is eligible for the credit.

The credit is allowed against the sum of the regular tax and the alternative minimum tax (minus certain other credits) and is allowed in addition to any other deduction or exclusion that would otherwise apply. In addition, to be eligible, the taxpayer must be at least eighteen as of the end of the tax year and must not be claimed as a dependent by someone else or be a full-time student.

The amount of the credit is limited to an "applicable percentage" of IRA contributions and elective deferrals up to $2,000. The "applicable percentages" are as follows for 2015:

Amount of Credit	Joint	Head of Household	Single/ Others
50% of first $2,000 deferred	$0 to $36,500	$0 to $27,375	$0 to $18,250
20% of first $2,000 deferred	$36,501 to $39,500	$27,376 to $29,625	$18,251 to $19,750
10% of first $2,000 deferred	$39,501 to $61,000	$29,626 to $45,750	$19,751 to $30,500
0% of contribution	More than $61,000	More than $45,750	More than $30,500

Example. Joe and Jenny together have adjusted gross income of $38,000 and file a joint return for 2015. Their employer sponsors a TDA plan and they each elected to make a salary reduction contribution of $3,000 to the plan. Neither has received any distributions in the current or two preceding taxable years. Joe and Jenny will be able to exclude their salary reduction contributions as well as each being eligible to claim a joint credit of $800 (20 percent of $2,000—or $400—each) on their federal income tax return for 2015.

ERISA REQUIREMENTS

In general, ERISA applies to a TDA plan to the same extent it applies to a qualified plan. In addition, a plan subject to ERISA must observe its other requirements, including fiduciary requirements and plan requirements protecting spousal benefits. However, TDAs of certain employers may be subject to the ERISA exemption applicable to governmental and church plans. In addition, an ERISA exemption under Labor Department regulations applies to plans that are (1) funded purely through voluntary salary reductions by employees, and (2) not considered "established or maintained by the employer."[27] This exemption permits only minimal employer involvement with the plan.

HOW TO INSTALL A PLAN

Under the regulations, a 403(b) plan must generally have a written defined contribution document including various required provisions described in the regulations.[28] The IRS has developed a prototype plan procedure and other determination letter procedures similar to those applicable to regular qualified plans.[29]

In addition, salary reduction forms must be completed by plan participants before the plan's effective date so that salary reduction elections will be immediately effective.

The success of a TDA plan in meeting the employer's objectives and the nondiscrimination tests depends on effective communication with employees. Effective employer-employee communication is always important in employee benefit plans. But it is particularly essential for a TDA plan because of the active role of employees in the plan.

ROTH 403(B) PLANS

Section 403(b) plans (as well as 401(k) plans) may offer a "qualified Roth contribution program," which is basically a Roth account for elective deferrals. Essentially, participants of plans establishing such a program can designate all, or a portion, or their elective deferrals as Roth contributions. The Roth contributions included in the participant's gross income in the year made, and then held in a separate account with separate record keeping. Earnings allocable to the Roth contributions will remain in the separate account.

A qualified distribution from a Roth account is not includable in the participant's gross income, and rollovers are available only to another Roth account or Roth IRA. The requirements for a "qualified distribution" are nearly identical to those for a Roth IRA (see Chapter 20), except that no exception is permitted for first-time home purchases. In other words, a qualified distribution is any distribution made after the five-year "nonexclusion period" and after the participant has (a) reached age 59½, (b) died, or (c) become disabled. (Distributions of excess deferrals are not included in this definition.)

The nonexclusion period is the five-taxable-year period beginning with the earlier of (1) the first year a contribution is made to the Roth account, or (2) if a rollover has been made to the Roth account from another Roth account under another employer plan, the first year a contribution was made to the earlier Roth account.

Aside from being currently included in gross income, amounts designated as Roth contributions under this provision are treated in all other respects as elective deferrals. They are, together with other elective deferrals, subject to the otherwise applicable elective deferral limit; thus, a single total limit will apply to all elective deferrals.[30]

WHERE CAN I FIND OUT MORE?

Tax Facts on Insurance & Employee Benefits (The National Underwriter Company; published annually).

FREQUENTLY ASKED QUESTIONS

Question – How can a planner determine if an employer organization meets the technical eligibility requirements in the Code?

Answer – Most organizations that are tax-exempt under Section 501(c)(3) have obtained a government ruling letter to that effect. Also, organizations that have been ruled tax-exempt are listed in a government publication available at libraries, and on the IRS web site (http://www.irs.ustreas.gov/bus_info/eo/eosearch.html). Planners should ask the prospective TDA client for a copy of the ruling letter, if any, and keep it in their files. If there is no ruling letter, or if the organization is not a Section 501(c)(3) organization, the planner should at a minimum obtain an attorney's or accountant's written opinion that the organization meets the TDA criteria. In questionable cases, an IRS ruling should be sought.

Question – Can TDA plans cover "independent contractors"—for example, anesthesiologists or radiologists associated with, but not formally employed by, hospitals?

Answer – No. TDA plan participants must be employees of the plan sponsor. The best way for a planner to verify this is to ask the sponsor how these individuals are treated by the sponsor for employment tax purposes—that is, Social Security (FICA) and federal unemployment (FUTA). Employees and independent contractors are treated differently under these taxes (i.e., the employer pays no employment taxes for independent contractors) and the treatment of these individuals in the TDA plan should be consistent.

Question – Can a TDA plan participant make deductible IRA contributions as well as salary reductions under the TDA plan?

Answer – Yes. However, in a year in which an individual makes salary reduction contributions to a TDA plan or the employer contributes to his TDA account, the individual is considered an "active participant" under the IRA rules. IRA contributions are deductible only within the reduced deductible IRA limits allowed for active plan participants (see Chapter 20). There is a phase-out of IRA deductibility based on adjusted gross income. After-tax contributions to a Roth IRA may be made; subject to certain income limitations (see Chapter 20).

Question – Can a TDA participant transfer funds from one annuity contract or mutual fund investment to another without adverse tax effect?

Answer – Yes. The regulations include provisions that allow contract exchanges within the same plan, and plan to plan transfers that are, in general, without adverse consequences to the participant.[31]

There is no income tax or early distribution penalty on a direct transfer. However, some annuity contracts may have a penalty provision for withdrawals that will reduce the net amount available for withdrawal.

Question – Since a 501(c)(3) organization can sponsor both Section 401(k) plans and TDA plans, what are the considerations in choosing between the two?

Answer – Most practitioners believe that TDA plans are generally more favorable in this situation. The advantages of the TDAs include:

- no ADP testing (although employer contributions are subject to Section 401(m) tests);
- no ERISA applicability for salary-reduction-only plans;
- entire plan not disqualified for exceeding salary reduction limit for one employee;[32]
- increased limit on salary reduction contributions for employees who have completed fifteen years of service with certain employers; and
- top-heavy plan rules generally do not apply.
- By contrast, Section 401(k) plans have only a few advantages over TDA plans including:
- a somewhat broader investment flexibility—not limited like TDA plans to annuity contracts and mutual funds; and
- availability of special ten-year averaging for participants born before 1936, a steadily diminishing advantage.

Because of potential complexities in actual situations, however, this choice should always be carefully studied for the individual case at issue.

CHAPTER ENDNOTES

1. Unless other references are provided, the rules in this chapter are found in I.R.C. §403(b).
2. I.R.C. §401(k)(4)(B).
3. I.R.C. §408(p); see also Notice 97-6, 1997-1 CB 353.
4. See I.R.C. §§401(k)(13), 401(m)(12), 414(w). See also Treas. Reg. §1.401(k)-1(a)(3)(ii), 69 Fed. Reg. 78143 (12-29-2004); Rev. Rul.

2000-35, 2000-2 CB 138; General Information Letter to Mark Irwy dated March 17, 2004, at: www.irs.gov/foia/lists/0,id=97728,00.html (in which the IRS stated that there is no special maximum limit on the automatic compensation reduction percentage, and no safe harbor automatic compensation reduction percentage. The compensation percentage reduction for a 403(b) annuity or custodial account is permitted to be any percentage of compensation that would be permitted in the case of an elective contribution or elective deferral made pursuant to an affirmative, explicit election).

5. See Chapter 33, "Nonqualified Deferred Compensation," for discussion.
6. SBJPA '96, Section 1450(a). For the final 401(k) regulations, see 69 Fed. Reg. 78144 (12-29-2004).
7. I.R.C. §402(g).
8. A participant who is projected to attain age 50 before the end of a calendar year is deemed to be age 50 as of January 1 of such year. The necessary rules for coordinating with non-calendar plan years are in final regulations. Treas. Reg. §1.414(v)-1(g)(3).
9. I.R.C. §414(v)(2)(B)(ii).
10. I.R.C. §402(g)(7).
11. I.R.C. §414(v)(3)(a)(1).
12. Treas. Reg. §1.403(b)-5.
13. See I.R.C. §401(a)(4).
14. I.R.C. §403(b)(12)(A)(ii); Treas. Reg. §1.402(b)-5(b).
15. I.R.C. §411(a)(12).
16. Churches and certain related organizations can make TDA plan contributions to retirement income accounts; it seems that such retirement income accounts need not limit their investments to annuities and mutual fund custodial accounts. See I.R.C. §403(b)(9); Conf. Rep. No. 760, 97th Cong., 2nd Sess. 637-638 (TEFRA '82), reprinted in 1982-2 CB 681; Sections 13.3 and 13.3.3 of the final audit guidelines for TDA plans, reprinted in *IRM Handbook 7.7.1, Employee Plans Examination Guidelines Handbook*, Chapter 17 "Section 403(b) Plans," available at: www.irs.ustreas.gov/bus_info/ep/GUIDE.pdf); ERISA §203(a)(2).
17. Under the regulations, effective after 2008, life insurance will *not* meet the definition of an "annuity contract." However, the contract can include "incidental" death benefits, see Chapter 17. See Treas. Reg. §1.403(b)-8(c)(2).
18. ERISA §205.
19. Treas. Reg. §1.403(b)-6.
20. See 1123 (e)(3) of the Tax Reform Act of 1986 and Section 1011A(c)(11) of the Technical and Miscellaneous Revenue Act of 1988.
21. Treas. Reg. §1.403(b)-10(c).
22. I.R.C. §72(t).
23. Note that if the plan is not subject to ERISA (i.e., governmental plans, church plans and certain employee-contribution-only plans—see "ERISA Requirements" in the text), loans are subject to Code section 72(p), but not to ERISA regulations (DOL Reg. §2550.408b-1).
24. I.R.C. §§§3121(a)(5) [FICA] and 3306(b)(5) [FUTA].
25. I.R.C. §403(b)(13).
26. I.R.C. §25B.
27. DOL Reg. §2510.3-2(f).
28. Treas. Reg. §1.403(b)-3(b)(3).
29. Rev. Proc. 2013-22. See also "403(b) Pre-Approved Plan Program - Key Provisions," available from the IRS at: www.irs.gov/Retirement-Plans/403b-Pre-Approved-Plan-Program.
30. I.R.C. §402A.
31. Treas. Reg. §1.403(b)-10(b).
32. I.R.C. §403(b)(1)(E).

NONQUALIFIED DEFERRED COMPENSATION

CHAPTER 33

INTRODUCTION

A nonqualified deferred compensation plan is any employer retirement, savings, or deferred compensation plan for employees that does not meet the tax and labor law (ERISA) requirements applicable to qualified pension and profit sharing plans.

Nonqualified plans are usually used to provide retirement benefits to a select group of executives, or to provide such a select group with supplemental benefits beyond those provided in the employer's qualified retirement plans.

Nonqualified plans do not provide the same type of tax benefit as qualified plans, because, in the nonqualified plan, the employer's income tax deduction generally cannot be taken up front. The employer must wait until the year in which the employee reports income from the deferred compensation plan to take its deduction. However, a nonqualified plan can provide tax deferral for the employee, as well as meet employer and employee compensation and financial planning objectives.

WHEN IS SUCH A DEVICE USED?

1. When an employer wants to provide a deferred compensation benefit to an executive or group of executives, but the cost of a qualified plan would be prohibitive because of the large number of non-executive employees who would have to be covered. A nonqualified plan is ideal for many companies that do not have or cannot afford qualified plans but want to provide key employees with retirement income.

2. When an employer wants to provide additional deferred compensation benefits to an executive who is already receiving the maximum benefits or contributions under the employer's qualified retirement plan.

3. When the business wants to provide certain key employees with tax deferred compensation under terms or conditions different from those applicable to other employees.

4. When an executive or key employee wants to use the employer to, in essence, create a forced, automatic, and relatively painless investment program that uses the employer's tax savings to leverage the future benefits. Since amounts paid by the employer in the future will be tax deductible, the after-tax cost of the deferred compensation will be favorable. For example, if the employer is in a combined federal and state tax bracket of 40 percent, it can pay $50,000 to a retired executive at a net after-tax cost of only $30,000, because its tax deduction saves it $20,000 (40 percent of $50,000).

5. When an employer needs to solve the "four-R" (recruit, retain, reward, or retire) problem. These plans are a fundamental tool in designing executive compensation to meet these issues.

6. When a closely held corporation wants to attract and hold nonshareholder employees. For such employees, an attractive deferred compensation package can be a substitute for the equity-based compensation packages—company stock and stock options—that these employees would expect to receive if they were employed by a publicly held company.

Advantages

1. The design of nonqualified plans is much more flexible than that of qualified plans. A nonqualified plan:

    - allows coverage for a select group of management or highly compensated employees, without any nondiscrimination requirements
    - can provide an unlimited benefit to any one employee (subject to the "reasonable compensation" requirement for deductibility)
    - allows the employer to provide different benefit amounts for different employees, on different terms and conditions

2. A nonqualified plan involves minimal IRS, Department of Labor ("DOL"), and other governmental regulatory requirements, such as reporting and disclosure, fiduciary, and funding requirements.

3. A nonqualified plan can provide deferral of taxes to employees (but the employer's deduction is also deferred). The advantage of deferral is always debated when income tax rates are relatively low and there is some expectation of higher rates in the future. However, if dollars otherwise paid currently in taxes can be put to work over the period of deferral, planners can show advantages in nonqualified plans, even if future tax rates are higher.

4. As has generally been the case historically, the tradeoff in current federal corporate and individual rates for the highest income levels favors deferred compensation, since the marginal individual rate of 39.6 percent is greater than the marginal corporate rate (35 percent).

Example. If an individual pays a $10,000 annual premium for personally owned life insurance, the before-tax cost to that individual is $16,556 ($10,000 multiplied by 1/(1–.396)). If the corporation pays that premium (for example, in a nonqualified deferred compensation plan financed by corporate-owned life insurance) for the same individual, the before-tax cost is $15,385 ($10,000 multiplied by 1/(1 – 0.35)).

While not every situation works out exactly this way, these marginal rates favor corporate financing of deferred compensation, rather than cash bonuses.

Note, however, that the ongoing changes in the tax law can have significant influence on the design of benefit programs of this type and that true long-range stability is not possible in employee compensation planning.

5. A nonqualified plan can be used by an employer as a form of golden handcuffs that help to bind the employee to the company. Since the qualified plan vesting rules do not apply if the plan is properly designed (as discussed below), the plan can provide forfeiture of benefits according to almost any vesting schedule the employer desires and for almost any contingency, such as terminating employment before retirement, misconduct, or going to work for a competitor.

6. Although the plan generally involves only the employer's unsecured promise to pay benefits, some security to the executive can be provided through a rabbi trust (defined below).

7. Assets set aside in some types of informal financing arrangements are available to use for corporate purposes at all times.

Disadvantages

1. The employer's tax deduction is generally not available for the year in which compensation is earned; it must be deferred until the year in which income is taxable to the employee. This can be a substantial period of time—ten, twenty, or even thirty or more years in the future.

2. From the executive's point of view, the principal problem is lack of security as a result of depending only on the employer's unsecured promise to pay. In addition, most of the protections of federal tax and labor law (ERISA) that apply to qualified plans—for example, the vesting, fiduciary, and funding requirements—are not applicable to the typical nonqualified plan.

3. While accounting treatment is not entirely clear (see Appendix F), some disclosure of executive nonqualified plans on financial statements may be required. This would reduce the confidentiality

of the arrangement, which could be considered undesirable by both employer and employee.

4. Not all employers are equally suited to take advantage of nonqualified plans.

    - Because of their pass-through tax structure, S corporations and partnerships cannot take full advantage of nonqualified plans.

    - The employer must be one that is likely to last long enough to make the payments promised under the plan.

    - Special problems exist when tax-exempt or governmental organizations enter into nonqualified plans. See Chapter 34.

OBJECTIVES IN PLAN DESIGN

Through its considerable flexibility, a nonqualified deferred compensation plan can help both the employer and the employee achieve their planning objectives. The plan should be designed to achieve these objectives to the maximum extent possible. Figure 33.1 provides a design worksheet that can be used to illustrate the design process.

Employer Objectives

Employers usually adopt nonqualified deferred compensation plans to provide an incentive to hire key employees, to keep key employees, and to provide performance incentives—in other words, the typical employer compensation policy objectives that apply to other forms of compensation planning.

Plans reflecting employer objectives will typically consider the following types of design:

- Eligibility will be confined to key executives or technical employees that the employer wants to recruit and keep.

- Plan eligibility can be part of a predetermined company policy or the plan can simply be adopted for specific individuals as the need arises.

- Performance incentive features will be included. The features may include benefits or contributions based on salary, increases if specific profits or sales goals are achieved, or benefits related to the value of the employer's stock.

- Termination of employment will typically cause loss or forfeiture of benefits, particularly for terminations followed by undesirable conduct, such as competing with the employer.

- The plan often will not provide immediate vesting of benefits, but vesting will occur over a period of time in order to retain employees.

- It is generally not in the employer's interest to fund the plan in advance or set aside funds for the plan prior to the commencement of benefit payments.

Employee Objectives

An employee's personal financial planning objective is primarily to obtain additional forms of compensation for which income tax is deferred as long as possible, preferably until the money is actually received. Usually it is only highly compensated employees who wish to (or can afford to) defer compensation to a substantial extent, since only they have enough discretionary income to support substantial saving. From the employee's point of view, the tax deferral, and therefore the compounding of dollars that otherwise would be paid currently in taxes, is a major benefit of the plan. In addition, it is possible that plan benefits may be paid when the employee is in a lower marginal tax bracket. (However, due to frequent changes in the tax laws, this factor is difficult to predict.)

An employee who has enough bargaining power to influence the design of a nonqualified deferred compensation plan will favor the following types of provisions:

- Benefit certainty is usually more important than incentive provisions; employees rarely seek contingent features unless the company is definitely growing and the employee wants a benefit based on company growth.

- Employees will want a benefit that is immediately 100 percent vested without forfeiture provisions, for cause or otherwise.

Figure 33.1

NONQUALIFIED DEFERRED COMPENSATION

Design Worksheet

A. EMPLOYER AND EMPLOYEE DATA

Employer ____________________

Employer's address ____________________

____

____________________ Zip __________

Telephone No. (   ) ____________________

Employer I.D. No. ____________________

S corporation election? Yes __________ No __________

Date of S election ____________________

Accounting year ____________________

Company contact (name and title) ____________________

Telephone No. (   ) ____________________

Employee ____________________

Title ____________________

Employee address ____________________

____________________ Zip __________

Telephone No. (   ) ____________________

Social Security No. ____________________

Percent ownership of employer ____________________

Effective date of deferred compensation arrangement ____________________

B. PLAN FORMULA

Formula type (check)

__________ Salary reduction

__________ Salary continuation

__________ Other ____________________

Figure 33.1 (cont'd)

Salary reduction formula (if applicable)

Reduction amount ______________________

Per (month, year, other) ______________________

Date of initial election ______________________

Annual election date thereafter ______________________

Other election date (specify) ______________________

Company contribution, if any ______________________

Conditions on company contribution ______________________

Company guarantee of interest on account balance (check one)

_________ fixed rate of _________ percent

_________ rate based on

______________________ adjusted (how often)__________

Salary continuation formula (if applicable)

Benefits payable at (check)

_________ age 65

_________ other specified age _________

Benefit formula

__________________ percent of compensation monthly

(times years of service)(up to _________ years)

Compensation means

________ Annual compensation over highest _________ years

________ Other (specify) ______________________

____

Offset for other benefits

_________percent of social security benefits actually received

_________percent of qualified retirement plan benefits

Other (describe — e.g., workers compensation, disability)

____

____

Benefit payable at termination of employment prior to retirement

_________ No benefit

_________ Account balance

_________ Vested accrued benefit determined as follows ______________________

____

Figure 33.1 (cont'd)

C. VESTING

Vesting Schedule

__________ Immediate 100 percent vesting

__________ Graduated schedule (specify) ____

____

Forfeiture provisions

__________ None

__________ Forfeiture for ____

____

D. DISABILITY BENEFIT

__________ Disability treated like other termination of employment

or

__________ Special disability provisions

__________ Special benefit computation (specify)____________________________

____

__________ Service continues to accrue for purposes of this plan

Definition of disability ____

____

E. BENEFIT PAYMENT

Options

__________ Lump sum (actuarially equivalent to ____________________________________

__________ Periodic payment options (specify) ______________________________________

____

Optional forms must be elected before ____

____

After benefits commence, payment option (cannot be changed) (can be changed or modified) (annual (other __________) by election prior to ____

After benefits commence, future benefits are forfeited if ________________________________

____

Figure 33.1 (cont'd)

F. DEATH BENEFITS

_________ Benefits forfeited at death

_________ Death benefit payable to named beneficiary or estate if no named beneficiary

_________ Other____

____

Amount of Benefit

_________ Amount that would have been paid to employee at termination of employment

_________ Face amount of insurance contracts (describe contracts)_______________

____

_________ Other ____

____

____

Payment Form

_________ Lump sum only

_________ Beneficiary has same options employee would have had if terminated employment on date of death.

Describe how beneficiary makes elections _________________________

____

_________ Other ____

____

G. FINANCING

_________ Formal funding (specify) _________________________________

____

_________ Informal financing

_________ Insurance contracts (specify) _____________________________

____

_________ Rabbi trust (describe) ___________________________________

____

_________ Third party guarantees, surety bonds, etc.

(describe)____

____

____

_________ No financing arrangement

- Employees like to have funds available for various purposes during employment to the extent possible under the tax law, especially Section 409A (see "Withdrawals During Employment" below).

- Concern for benefit security is significant, and employees will want to explore a rabbi trust.

Types of Benefit and Contribution Formulas

The benefit formula is the basic starting point in designing or explaining a nonqualified deferred compensation plan. Executives covered under the plan want to know first what benefits the plan provides, rather than methods of informally financing those benefits, such as corporate-owned life insurance (COLI) arrangements. Benefit formula design is almost wide open for nonqualified deferred compensation plans; great flexibility is possible and formulas can be designed for the specific needs of specific employees. Some common benefit formula approaches include:

- *Salary Continuation Formula.* Salary continuation generally refers to a type of nonelective nonqualified deferred compensation plan that provides a specified deferred amount payable in the future. A salary continuation plan provides benefits in addition to other benefits provided under other plans and requires no reduction in the covered employee's salary. *For example*: The contract might provide: "At retirement, disability, or death, the XYZ Corporation will pay you or your designated beneficiary $50,000 a year for ten years starting at age sixty-five."

  A salary continuation formula generally uses a defined benefit type of formula to calculate the benefit amount, but the formula is not subject to the limitations applicable to qualified defined benefit plans, such as the limitation on benefits, or the amount of salary used in the formula. A nonqualified salary continuation plan for a selected group of executives with similar formulas for the entire group is sometimes referred to as a SERP (for supplemental executive retirement plan).

- *Salary Reduction Formula.* A salary reduction formula involves an elective deferral of a specified amount of the compensation that the employee would have otherwise received.

  The employer contribution under this type of plan can be in the form of a bonus, without actual reduction of salary. The plan is somewhat similar to a defined contribution type of qualified plan, although the qualified plan restrictions do not apply.

  The amount deferred each year under a salary reduction formula is generally credited to the employee's "account" under the plan. When benefits are due, the amount accumulated in this account determines the amount of payments. Payment is generally in the form of a lump sum, but the account balance can also be paid in an equivalent stream of periodic payments.

  The salary reduction formula generally provides a method by which earnings on the account are credited. These earnings credits can be based upon a specified interest rate, or an external standard, such as Moody's Bond Index, the federal rate or other indexed rate, or the rate of earnings on specified assets.[1]

  In a salary reduction arrangement, the employer has no obligation to actually set assets aside. The participant's account is purely an accounting concept existing only on paper. Thus, when payment becomes due, the employer pays it from its current assets. This points out the fact that all nonqualified deferred compensation plans are essentially based only on the employer's contractual obligation to pay benefits. However, employees may seek some security, as discussed below under "Financing Approaches."

- *Excess benefit plan.* Under ERISA section 4(b)(5), an excess benefit plan that is unfunded is not subject to Title I of ERISA (which contains the reporting and disclosure, participation, vesting, funding, and fiduciary responsibility provisions).[2]

  Excess benefit plans are those designed to provide benefits only for executives whose annual projected qualified plan benefits are limited under the dollar limits of Code section 415 (see Chapter 13). An excess benefit plan makes up the difference between the percentage of pay that top executives are allowed under Section 415 and that which rank and file employees are allowed. In other words, highly compensated employees receive the difference between the amounts payable under their qualified plan and the amount they would have received if there were no benefit limitations under Code section 415.

- *Stock appreciation rights (SARs) and phantom stock formulas.* The benefit formula in the plan can be determined on the basis of the value of a specified number of shares of employer stock, or contributions to a salary-reduction formula can be stated in terms of shares of employer stock rather than cash.

  Generally, no actual shares are set aside, nor are shares of stock necessarily actually distributed. The value of employer stock simply is the measure by which the benefits are valued. Obviously, this type of formula provides a substantial incentive for the executive, and, from the employer viewpoint, matches the size of benefits with company success.

  Phantom stock benefit generally refers to a plan formula based upon an amount of shares of stock, established for an employee when the plan is adopted, with a provision that the employee receives the actual shares or equivalent cash at the date of payment. A SAR formula provides that the employee's future benefits are to be determined by a formula based on the appreciation value of the company's stock over the period between adoption of the plan and the date of payment.

- *Form of Benefits.* Nonqualified deferred compensation plans usually provide payments at retirement in a lump sum or a series of annual payments. Life annuities or joint and survivor annuities for the participant and spouse can also be provided. Since the elaborate restrictions on qualified plan payouts do not apply, considerable design flexibility is available.

Payout Options

Payout options must avoid the triggering of the constructive receipt doctrine—that is, the taxation of benefits before they are actually received by the employee. Constructive receipt problems are discussed further in "Tax Implications," below.

Payout provisions must also comply with the rules of Code section 409A, which penalizes acceleration or delay of the time or schedule of any payment under the plan. The final regulations provide some guidelines:

- The rule is generally not violated if the benefit acceleration doesn't change the timing of income inclusion. For example, the plan could provide a choice between a lump sum and a fully (immediately) taxable annuity contract. The regulations also indicate that a reduction of a vesting requirement (for example from ten years to five years) is permitted, even though this might conceivably provide earlier tax inclusion—for example in a situation where the plan provides for payment on separation from service and the employee quits after seven years of service.[3] Similarly, a Section 457(f) plan (a plan for executives of governmental or nonprofit organizations) may allow a payout to provide for taxes due on a vesting event.[4]

- An accelerated distribution could be permitted if it is not elective and beyond the control of the employee, such as a distribution to comply with a court-ordered divorce settlement or a Federal conflict-of-interest requirement.[5] For example, if federal authorities required a government official to cash out his deferred compensation contract with a company currently doing business with the government rather than allowing it to continue in effect throughout his term of office, creating a scandalous impression of bias and corruption, this would not violate Section 409A(a)(3).

- Payments can be accelerated in order to pay employment taxes (FICA and FUTA) and the income tax withholding resulting from this acceleration.[6] This relief provision is required because in an unfunded plan, FICA and FUTA taxes are payable upon vesting of the amounts involved, while income taxes may not be due until a much later year (the year of receipt or constructive receipt).

- De minimis cashouts of account balances specified under the plan are generally permitted.[7]

The purpose of the non-acceleration rule is to prevent executives from taking money out of a failing corporation when they see financial trouble approaching for the corporation. This is the type of practice involved in the Enron and similar corporate scandals of the last several years, and Congress has decided to try to prevent such practices with Code Section 409A. The rules, however, limit design flexibility in many situations where abusive practices are not likely.

Withdrawals During Employment (Section 409A)

Employees recognize that any kind of deferred compensation plan holds money that they could have received earlier in cash. Thus, certainty of receipt is a very important consideration. Similarly, employees like plan provisions that permit them to make use of the deferred funds when they need them. However, if a deferred compensation plan simply allowed the participant to withdraw from the plan at any time without restriction, the plan would fail to defer income taxes under the doctrine of constructive receipt, as discussed below. Withdrawals must be subject to a restriction or limitation that prevents them from being currently available within the constructive receipt doctrine. Distribution provisions must also comply with the rules of section 409A. Under these rules, plan distributions generally may not be made (without penalty) earlier than one of the following events:

- Separation from service. If the employee is a key employee of a publicly traded company, as defined under the top-heavy rules of Section 416(i), a distribution upon separation from service may not begin until six months after separation.
- Disability. Disability is defined as either the strict Social Security definition of total and permanent disability or disability under an accident and health plan covering employees of the employer, under certain conditions.
- Death of the employee.
- A specified time or fixed schedule.
- A change in ownership or control.
- Occurrence of an unforeseeable emergency. Code section 409A(a)(2)(B)(I) spells out the definition:
  - A severe financial hardship to the participant resulting from an illness or accident of the participant, spouse or dependent
  - Loss of the participant's property due to casualty
  - Other similar extraordinary and unforeseeable circumstances beyond the participant's control
  - The amount can't exceed the amount necessary for the emergency plus taxes on the distribution

The section 409A rules resulted from a view in the Congress and the Treasury Department that prior restrictions on distributions for nonqualified plans were not stringent enough to justify the deferral of taxes on the amounts in question. For example, under prior law, many plans allowed employees to withdraw amounts without restriction except for a "haircut" provision, under which a small penalty (such as 6 percent) was imposed on the amount withdrawn, or the participant was restricted from deferring subsequent compensation for a period such as six months. These haircut provisions will no longer be allowed.

The loss of haircut provisions is arguably the most negative feature of the current law from the employee's standpoint. A haircut provision was an important safeguard: if the employee felt that financial or other conditions within the company might threaten the deferred compensation benefit within the near future, the employee could get his money out under the plan's haircut withdrawal provision. In effect, Congress views the use of this type of safeguard as an abuse, regardless of whether the employee is a high-level executive capable of actually manipulating the situation or just a mid-level executive trying to preserve his retirement funds in a failing or hostile corporate environment.

Termination of Employment

If the plan emphasizes employer objectives, termination provisions will be designed to maximize incentive features and noncompetition and similar provisions. At the extreme, an employer-instituted plan may even provide a complete forfeiture of nonqualified benefits if the employee terminates employment before retirement. Most employer-instituted plans will at least have a vesting schedule under which benefits do not become vested until a specified number of years of service has been attained. Graduated vesting can also be used. As discussed below, if the plan is unfunded, the ERISA vesting provisions generally do not apply and any type of vesting schedule generally can be used.

If an executive's termination of employment results from disability, special benefits may be provided, particularly if the employee has some bargaining power in designing the plan. An employee will generally want benefits paid immediately upon disability. For this purpose, the employee will also want to use a definition of disability that is somewhat less restrictive than the total and permanent disability required for social security disability benefits. A typical disability provision based on employee objectives would provide for disability payments if the employee is no longer able to continue working in his specific profession or executive position. Disability determinations can be shifted to a third party such as an insurer, or a physician chosen by the employer and employee, in order to minimize possible disputes. Note though that if disability is the payment triggering event, the definition of disability must comply with section 409A.

Funded versus Unfunded Plans

In the employee benefit area, the term *funded plan* has a very specialized meaning. In the tax sense, a plan is formally funded if the employer has set aside money or property to pay plan benefits through some means that restricts access to the fund by the employer's creditors—for example, setting assets aside in an irrevocable trust for the exclusive benefit of employees covered under the plan.[8] For ERISA purposes, the Department of Labor (the DOL) has not specifically endorsed this clear-cut definition of funding, but for plans that benefit a select group of management or highly compensated employees, if the plan is unfunded for tax purposes, it probably will be regarded as unfunded for ERISA purposes.[9]

Assets used to informally fund or finance the employer's obligation under a nonqualified plan can be set aside, but if this fund is accessible by the employer's creditors, providing no explicit security to the employee ahead of other employer creditors, the plan is deemed to be unfunded for tax purposes. Such an arrangement is also an unfunded one for ERISA purposes.[10]

Most nonqualified deferred compensation plans are unfunded because of significant tax and ERISA considerations:

- In a funded plan, amounts in the fund are taxable to the employee at the time the employee's rights to the fund become "substantially vested."[11] As discussed in Chapter 9, under the rules of Code section 83, substantial vesting can occur before funds are actually received by the employee.

- Funded plans are generally subject to the ERISA vesting and fiduciary requirements, which create design inflexibility.[12] The vesting rules are the same as these generally applicable to qualified plans.[13]

The vesting and fiduciary rules for funded nonqualified plans are the same as those for qualified plans, as discussed in Chapter 13.[14]

Financing Approaches

Since almost all nonqualified deferred compensation plans are unfunded in the formal sense, employees initiating deferred compensation arrangements are likely to seek ways to increase benefit security. The following approaches are commonly used:

- *Reserve account maintained by employer.* The employer maintains an actual account, invested in securities of various types. There is no trust. Funds are fully accessible to the employer and its creditors. The plan is considered unfunded for tax and ERISA purposes.

- *Employer reserve account with employee investment direction.* With this variation, the employee obtains greater security by having the right to "direct" (select) investments in the account. This right must be limited to a choice of broad types of investment (equity, bonds, family of mutual funds, etc.); the ability to choose specific investments may lead to constructive receipt by the employee.[15] Also, the investment direction by the participant must be advisory only and not binding.[16]

- *Corporate-owned life insurance.* Life insurance policies on the employee's life, owned by and payable to the employer corporation, can provide financing for the employer's obligation under nonqualified deferred compensation plans. With life insurance financing, the plan can provide a substantial death benefit, even in the early years of the plan. This is of significant value to younger employees.

- *Rabbi trust*. A rabbi trust is a trust set up to hold property used for financing a deferred compensation plan, where the funds set aside are subject to the employer's creditors. The IRS has ruled that trusts designed this way do not constitute formal funding in the tax sense. The DOL has a working premise that rabbi trusts meeting with the approval of the IRS will not cause excess benefit plans or top-hat plans to be funded for ERISA purposes.[17] These trusts are referred to as "rabbi trusts" because an early IRS letter ruling involved an arrangement between a rabbi and the employing congregation. The design of rabbi trusts is discussed in the "Frequently Asked Questions," below.

- *Third-party guarantees*. In these arrangements, there is a guarantee from a third party to pay the employee if the employer defaults. The guarantor may be an insurance company or other entity. On occasion, third-party guarantees have received favorable tax treatment.[18] But the law in this area is not entirely clear. Employer involvement raises the possibility that the guarantee will cause the plan to be deemed formally funded for tax purposes.[19] However, it appears that if the employee, independently of the employer, obtains a third-party guarantee, the IRS will not necessarily view the plan as formally funded.[20]

TAX IMPLICATIONS

Constructive Receipt

Under the constructive receipt doctrine,[21] an amount is treated as received for income tax purposes, even if it is not actually received, if it is "credited to the employee's account, set aside, or otherwise made available."

Constructive receipt does not occur if the employee's control over the receipt is subject to a "substantial limitation or restriction." A requirement of a passage of time until money can be received by the employee is usually considered a substantial limitation or restriction.[22] In a typical deferred compensation plan, for example, if the plan provides that an amount is not payable for five years or not payable until the employee terminates employment or retires, it will not be constructively received before that time.

Under the constructive receipt doctrine, the view of the IRS is that an agreement to defer compensation generally must be made before the compensation is earned. In order to defer compensation *after* services have already been performed, the IRS view is that the plan must have a substantial risk of forfeiture of the benefits.[23]

Plan distribution provisions must also be designed to avoid constructive receipt. For example, if the plan provides for distribution in ten equal annual installments, and if the employee can elect, at any time, to accelerate payments, then, under the constructive receipt doctrine, the employee would have to include in income each year the amount that the employee could have elected to receive. As another example, if the plan provides for a payout in ten annual installments with an election at any time to spread payments out further, the constructive receipt doctrine may require taxation under the original ten payment schedule, regardless of any election to further defer payments, unless the plan imposes a substantial risk of forfeiture.[24] A typical forfeiture provision found in nonqualified plan distribution provisions of this type is a requirement that the employee be available for consulting and refrain from competing with the employer. As discussed in Chapter 9, the question of whether this constitutes a substantial risk of forfeiture depends on the specific facts and circumstances of the situation.

Although section 409A generally governs nonqualified deferred compensation, it does not eliminate any other provision of the tax code or common law tax doctrine. Thus, the constructive receipt doctrine continues to apply in addition to section 409A.

Economic Benefit

A compensation arrangement that provides a current economic benefit to an employee can result in current taxation, even though the employee has no current right to receive cash or property. For example, suppose that an employee is covered under a funded nonqualified deferred compensation plan that has an irrevocable trust for the benefit of the employee. Under the economic benefit doctrine, the employee will be taxed as soon as the employee is vested in contributions made to the fund, even though the employee does not, at that time, have a right to withdraw cash.[25] This tax treatment makes funded plans extremely unattractive.

The economic benefit doctrine does not generally affect unfunded plans, and, as discussed earlier, almost all nonqualified deferred compensation plans are unfunded. It is possible that some incidental benefits in the plan could create an economic benefit. This issue has sometimes been raised where the plan includes an insured death benefit. Currently, however, the IRS does not claim that there is an economic benefit resulting from the insured death benefit in a properly designed nonqualified plan.

Although section 409A generally governs nonqualified deferred compensation, it does not eliminate any other provision of the tax code or common law tax doctrine. Thus, the economic benefit doctrine continues to apply in addition to section 409A.

Income Taxation of Benefits and Contributions

Employees must pay ordinary income tax on benefits from unfunded nonqualified deferred compensation plans in the first year in which the benefit is actually or constructively received.

Death benefits from nonqualified plans that are payable to a beneficiary are taxable as income in respect of a decedent to the recipient.

Social Security (FICA) Taxes

Amounts deferred under nonqualified deferred compensation plans are not subject to social security taxes until the year in which the employee no longer has any substantial risk of forfeiting the amount, provided the amounts are reasonably ascertainable.[26] In other words, as soon as the covered executive cannot lose his interest in the plan, he will be subject to social security taxes. Conceivably, this could be earlier than the year of actual receipt.

For example, if the plan provides that benefits are payable at retirement, but the benefits become vested five years after they are earned, then the amounts deferred will enter into the social security tax base five years after they are earned. Note that this is neither the year in which they are earned nor the year they are paid, a circumstance that complicates tax compliance in this situation.

Although part of the social security taxable wage base—the OASDI part—has an annual upper limit ($118,500 for 2015), the Medicare hospital insurance portion is unlimited. The Medicare tax rate is 1.45 percent for the employer and the same rate for the employee. For higher paid executives, the inclusion of deferred compensation in the wage base during a year of active employment will not result in additional OASDI taxes if the executive's current (nondeferred) compensation is more than the OASDI wage base, but additional Medicare taxes will be payable. This factor must be taken into account in designing nonqualified deferred compensation plans.

Federal Estate Tax Treatment

The amount of any death benefit payable to a beneficiary under a nonqualified deferred compensation plan is generally included in the deceased employee's estate for federal estate tax purposes, at its then present value. In other words, the commuted value of payments made to the employee's beneficiary will be included in the employee's gross estate. But such payments will be considered "income in respect of a decedent" (Code section 691 income), and an income tax deduction will be allocated to the recipient of that income for the additional estate tax the inclusion generated. To the extent that payments are made to the employee's spouse in a qualifying manner, the unlimited marital deduction will eliminate any federal estate tax.

A plan can be designed so that the decedent did not have a right to receive the benefit prior to death. A plan designed to provide only death benefits is referred to as a death benefit only (DBO) plan. For employees potentially liable for substantial federal estate taxes, the DBO plan may be an appropriate design. DBO plans are covered in Chapter 47.

Taxation of the Employer

For a nonqualified deferred compensation plan, the employer does not receive a tax deduction until its tax year that includes the year in which the compensation is includable in the employee's taxable income.[27] If the plan is unfunded, the year of inclusion is the year in which the compensation is actually or constructively received. For a formally funded plan, compensation is included in income in the year in which it becomes substantially vested, as discussed earlier.

Payments under a deferred compensation plan, like other forms of compensation, are not deductible unless the amounts meet the reasonableness test discussed in Chapter 2. The same issues can arise with respect to deferred compensation as with regular cash compensation or bonus arrangements.

The reasonableness issue is raised by the IRS in the year in which an employer attempts to take a deduction. For nonqualified deferred compensation, this is generally the year in which the employee includes the amount in income—that is, a year that is later than the year in which the services were rendered. Compensation can be deemed reasonable on the basis of prior service;[28] however, it is possible that a combination of deferred compensation and current compensation received in a given year could raise reasonableness issues, particularly if the deferred amount is very large.

Note that publicly held corporations generally cannot deduct compensation in excess of $1 million per tax year to certain top-level executives (see Chapter 2). Also, businesses that have taken TARP funds may not deduct more than $500,000 paid to certain executives.[29] In addition, covered health insurance providers may not deduct more than $500,000 of compensation paid to applicable individuals.[30]

If assets are set aside in a reserve used to informally finance the employer's obligation under the plan, income on these assets is currently taxable to the employer. Consequently, the use of assets that provide a deferral of taxation can be advantageous. Life insurance policies are often used because their cash value build-up from year to year is not currently taxed. Death proceeds from the policy are also free of tax, except for a possible alternative minimum tax (AMT) liability.

If assets used to finance the plan are held in a rabbi trust, the employer's tax consequences are much the same as if assets were held directly by the employer. For tax purposes, the rabbi trust is a grantor trust. A grantor trust's income, deductions, and tax credits are attributed to the grantor (here, the employer) for tax purposes.

ERISA REQUIREMENTS

Two types of nonqualified deferred compensation plans are eligible for at least partial exemptions from the ERISA requirements. The first exemption is for an unfunded excess benefit plan. This type of nonqualified deferred compensation plan, designed solely to supplement the qualified retirement benefits limited in amount by Code section 415, is not subject to any ERISA requirements.[31] As discussed above, this exemption is rarely available.

The most important ERISA exemption involves a type of plan often referred to as a top-hat plan. Under ERISA, if a nonqualified plan is unfunded and maintained by an employer primarily for the purpose of providing deferred compensation for a "select group of management or highly compensated employees," the plan is exempt from all provisions of ERISA, except for the reporting and disclosure requirements, and ERISA's administrative and enforcement provisions. Top-hat plans can satisfy the reporting and disclosure requirements by providing plan documents, upon request, to the Department of Labor, and by filing a simple, one time statement about the arrangement with the Department of Labor.[32] Figure 33.2 is an example of this simple reporting statement. The reporting statement can also be electronically filed with the DOL.[33]

The term "highly compensated," for this purpose, is not as clearly defined as it is for qualified and other plans (see Chapter 13). The Department of Labor is responsible for interpreting this provision of ERISA and it has not yet issued clear guidelines.[34] However, a plan that covers only a few highly paid executives will probably meet this ERISA exemption.

If a plan does not meet one of these ERISA exemptions, it must generally comply with most of the ERISA provisions applicable to qualified pension plans, including the vesting, fiduciary, minimum funding, and reporting and disclosure provisions.

As a result of these ERISA aspects, almost all nonqualified deferred compensation plans are limited to management or highly compensated employees and are unfunded, even though they may utilize some informal financing methods as discussed earlier.

Finally, the courts have sometimes held that a nonqualified deferred compensation plan was not subject to ERISA because it was not a "plan" within the meaning of ERISA. This ERISA exemption has been generally held to apply to plans covering one or only a few employees, where there was no "ongoing administrative scheme" to maintain the plan.[35] Unless the situation is nearly identical to reported court cases, this exemption is not very practical to rely upon, because it is based on particular facts found by courts in each case, and the result of future court proceedings cannot be easily predicted.

WHERE CAN I FIND OUT MORE?

1. Leimberg et al., *The Tools and Techniques of Estate Planning*, 17th ed., Cincinnati, OH: The National Underwriter Co., 2015.

Figure 33.2

ALTERNATIVE REPORTING AND DISCLOSURE STATEMENT FOR UNFUNDED NONQUALIFIED DEFERRED COMPENSATION PLANS FOR CERTAIN SELECTED EMPLOYEES

To: Top Hat Plan Exemption
Pension and Welfare Benefits Administration
Room N-5644
U.S. Department of Labor
200 Constitution Avenue, N.W.
Washington, D.C. 20210

In compliance with the requirements of the alternative method of reporting and disclosure under Part 1 of Title I of the Employee Retirement Income Security Act of 1974 for unfunded or insured pension plans for a select group of management or highly compensated employees, specified in Department of Labor Regulations, 29 C.F.R. Sec. 2520.104-23, the following information is provided by the undersigned employer.

Name and Address of Employer:____________________________

____

____

Employer Identification Number:____________________________

(Name of employer) maintains a plan (or plans) primarily for the purpose of providing deferred compensation for a select group of management or highly compensated employees.

Number of Plans and Participants in Each Plan:

__________ Plan covering __________ employees (or)

__________ Plans covering __________, __________, and

__________ employees; respectively

Dated ______________________________, 20____

(Name of Employer)

By ____

Plan Administrator

2. Baier, Richard C., Phelan, John, and Richey, Louis R., *The Advisor's Guide to Nonqualified Deferred Compensation*, Cincinnati, OH: The National Underwriter Co., 2014.

FREQUENTLY ASKED QUESTIONS

Question – How is life insurance used to finance an employer's obligation under a nonqualified deferred compensation plan?

Answer – Life insurance can be used in many ways, much like any other asset set aside to finance the plan. Life insurance has several advantages, such as its tax-free build-up of cash values and the availability of substantial death benefits, even in the early years of the plan.

Because of the particular advantages of life insurance, many deferred compensation plans are designed specifically to make use of life insurance financing.

Example. Suppose Crood Petroleum Corporation enters into a deferred compensation agreement with its executive, Frank Furness, under which Frank agrees to defer an anticipated $10,000 annual salary increase in return for the following specified benefits: (1) if Frank dies before retirement, $10,000 a year will be paid to his widow for a period equal to the number of years he was covered under the plan; and (2) if Frank remains employed by Crood until retirement at age sixty-five, he will receive $20,000 per year for ten years, in addition to other company retirement benefits.

Frank's deferred $10,000 per year of compensation would have had an after-tax cost of $6,500 to the corporation if paid currently (assuming a 35 percent marginal corporate tax bracket). The corporation can use this $6,500 instead to finance Frank's benefits by purchasing a life insurance policy on Frank's life. If Frank is age forty-five, about $150,000 of cash value insurance (paid up at sixty-five) can be purchased with this $6,500 annually. The corporation would be both the policyowner and the policy beneficiary and would pay the premiums, which would be nondeductible. (The tax implications of corporate-owned insurance are discussed in detail in Chapter 43.)

If Frank died at age fifty, the corporation would receive approximately $150,000 of tax free policy proceeds (in addition to policy dividends and perhaps interest, but reduced by any corporate AMT liability). It would have paid $32,500 in premiums over the past five years. It is obligated to pay a total of $50,000 ($10,000 a year for five years) to Frank's widow, but since these payments are deductible, their after-tax cost is only $32,500 (65 percent of $50,000). This results in a net gain to the corporation of approximately $85,000 ($150,000 insurance proceeds less $32,500 of premiums and less $32,500 of after-tax cost of benefit payments). (This example does not take into account the time value of money, but to do so does not change the result significantly, since the corporation's loss of the use of five annual premium payments is balanced by being reimbursed in advance for the five years of benefit payments due Frank's widow.)

If Frank had retired before his death, policy cash values and the corporation's current cash flow could be used to finance Frank's annual benefit payments. However, a better solution in most cases is to keep the policy intact and use current corporate cash to make benefit payments. Then, when the employee dies, policy proceeds will reimburse the employer and often add to the company's surplus. This approach is often referred to as "cost recovery" nonqualified deferred compensation.

The employer should purchase enough insurance to offset any corporate AMT liability on the proceeds. Although the AMT should be no more than about 15 percent of policy proceeds, to be on the safe side it is suggested that the employer obtain about 17 or 18 percent more than the amount targeted to meet nonqualified deferred compensation needs.

Question – When should a benefit planner recommend using a rabbi trust?

Answer – Factors indicating that a rabbi trust might be advantageous include (1) a fear that the ownership or management of the business might change before deferred compensation benefits are paid; (2) a situation where new management might be hostile to the key employee in the future and fail to honor its contractual obligation to pay deferred compensation; and (3) situations where litigation to enforce payment of deferred compensation in the future would likely be too costly to be practical.

Question – What costs or risks are involved in the use of a rabbi trust-type of financing arrangement for deferred compensation?

Answer – Costs and risks include: (1) the legal and administrative costs of setting up the rabbi trust agreement in a manner that will meet IRS requirements; (2) the loss of the use of plan assets by the employer corporation (since they must be put in trust for the employee) except in bankruptcy or liquidation; (3) the rate of return on plan assets is limited by trust investments (assets could yield a higher return if invested in the employer's business); and (4) from the employee's standpoint, the employee is not protected against the employer's insolvency.

Question – What provisions should (or should not) be included in a rabbi trust agreement?

Answer – A rabbi trust can be valid without obtaining a specific IRS ruling. However, most clients will either want to obtain a ruling or, at a minimum, will want to use a form of rabbi trust that conforms with IRS' known ruling requirements.

Revenue Procedures 92-64 and 92-65, 1992-2 CB 422 and 428, contain the IRS' ruling position for rabbi trusts. The IRS will generally rule on a nonqualified deferred compensation arrangement using a rabbi trust *only* if the IRS' model rabbi trust (reproduced at the end of this chapter in Exhibit A) is used. If a rabbi trust does not conform with the model, a ruling will be issued only in "rare and unusual circumstances."

The model trust generally conforms with IRS guidelines already well-known from its prior private letter rulings. Optional paragraphs are provided to allow some degree of customization. The model contains some relatively favorable provisions. For example, it allows the use of "springing" irrevocability—that is, a triggering event, like a change of ownership of the employer, can cause the trust to become irrevocable or can obligate the employer to make an irrevocable contribution sufficient to cover its obligations as of the time of the triggering event. Also, the model permits the rabbi trust to own employer stock. However, the model does not contain trigger provisions to allow acceleration of payments if the employer moves toward insolvency; the employee's rights must never be better than those of the employer's general, unsecured creditors. The model rabbi trust also has no provision giving employees investment authority over rabbi trust assets.

While it is somewhat puzzling in light of the IRS' claim that it will not rule on plans using a rabbi trust other than the model trust, Revenue Procedure 92-64 allows the employer to add additional text to the model trust as long as that additional language is not inconsistent with the model language. Typically, this might include provisions required under state law. How much latitude this provides to employers is not clear.

Under IRC Section 409A, some of the more aggressive techniques that have been proposed for financing NQDC plans are penalized. An offshore rabbi trust or similar arrangement (an arrangement where the financing assets are held outside the US) will result in immediate taxation of the deferred compensation to the employee. A rabbi trust or arrangement with a financial trigger—a provision requiring payout if the employer's business drops below certain financial criteria—will similarly be penalized.

Question – Can a corporation provide a nonqualified deferred compensation plan to an executive who is a controlling shareholder (more than 50 percent) in the corporation?

Answer – In principle, a deferred compensation arrangement can be provided for a controlling shareholder under the rules discussed in this chapter. However, the IRS will not issue an advance private letter ruling on the tax effect of such a plan.[36] The IRS will carefully scrutinize such an arrangement because of the controlling shareholder's legal right to require corporate distributions at any time. Here are seven ways to increase the likelihood that the IRS will find that such an arrangement results in deferral of compensation and receives the tax treatment thereof:

(1) Research key cases on point. In particular, see *Casale v. Comm'r., Moline Properties, Inc. v. Comm'r.*, and Revenue Ruling 59-184,[37] which support the proposition that a corporation is a

separate entity from its stockholders as long as the corporation is carrying on a valid business activity and is not a sham. See also *Carnahan v. Comm.*, *Commerce Union Bank v. U.S.*, *First Trust Company of St. Paul v. U.S.*, and Revenue Ruling 77-139,[38] which suggest that mere stock ownership by a plan participant is insufficient to invoke the doctrine of constructive receipt.

(2) Separate the financing of the employer's obligation from the plan itself. For example, if a life insurance policy is to be used, do not match the policy benefit to the promises made. When benefits under the financing vehicle are identical to and directly keyed into the benefits promised under the plan, the IRS will likely deny favorable tax treatment.[39] If the life insurance is maintained by the employer as key employee coverage and is kept totally separate from the agreement, there should be no constructive receipt (or economic benefit) problem.

(3) Include at least one highly compensated person other than a shareholder employee in the plan. The participation of a nonshareholder employee greatly enhances the argument that the plan is for corporate, rather than shareholder, purposes and will be of great help in justifying a corporate income tax deduction when benefits are to be paid.

(4) Create full documentation, in the corporate minutes and in the agreement itself, detailing the advantages to the corporation and the business purpose of the plan. Use wording that indicates that other successful competitive companies are providing similar supplemental compensation in their benefit programs. Incorporate wording from trade journals indicating that this type of plan is often used in the industry as a form of compensation helpful in recruiting, retaining, or retiring employees.

(5) A rabbi trust (discussed above) can be implemented to substantially limit even a controlling shareholder's ability to reach deferred amounts until the occurrence of specific events. The trust should have an independent trustee with the fiduciary responsibility, under state law, to deny access to anyone until the covered person satisfies the plan's triggering criteria (e.g., disability, death, or reaching the specified retirement age). Thus, the rabbi trust negates any "raw power" that a controlling shareholder may have.

(6) Establish an independent compensation review committee with the power to deny benefits to participants who do not meet plan criteria. The committee should actually meet and review the operation of the plan and police its provisions.

(7) Be sure the plan benefits do not fail the "HOG" test[40] by providing overgenerous benefit amounts that would not be provided to nonshareholder employees. Provide that contributions or benefits on behalf of shareholder employees cannot be proportionately greater than those provided to key employees who are not shareholders. In other words, base the plan benefit formula on a reasonable and uniform percentage of salary.

Question – How can an executive determine whether it is better to defer compensation and pay the taxes later or to receive the compensation currently and pay taxes at relatively low income tax rates?

Answer – Because of the uncertainty of future tax rates and investment return, there can never be a certain answer to this question. However, some simple computations can provide a handle on the question. Figure 33.3 shows the break-even point or the number of years of deferral required to make deferral pay, given a higher estimated rate of tax in future years.

As an example of the use of Figure 33.3, suppose an executive is currently in the 28 percent marginal income tax bracket. If the marginal tax rate is assumed to be 40 percent in future years, and investments can earn 9 percent before taxes, then it will take 5.43 years of deferral for deferred compensation to be better than current taxable compensation. Figure 33.3 indicates that deferred compensation is generally still a good idea for a relatively wide range of assumptions and reasonably short periods of deferral.

This computation does not take into account the effect of a corporate tax bracket that is higher than the individual employee's. This situation increases the value of a current tax deduction and accordingly decreases the overall tax value of deferral to the corporation and employee together. Secular trust plans, discussed in the following question, are responsive to this situation.

Figure 33.3

NONQUALIFIED DEFERRED COMPENSATION
(Break Even Point – Years)

Current Tax Rate		28%	28%	28%	28%	28%
Projected Tax Rate		35%	40%	45%	50%	55%
			Years			
Before-tax Return	3%	9.99	15.56	20.42	24.86	29.11
	4%	7.55	11.76	15.43	18.78	21.99
	5%	6.09	9.49	12.44	15.14	17.71
	6%	5.12	7.97	10.44	12.71	14.87
	7%	4.42	6.88	9.02	10.97	12.83
	8%	3.90	6.07	7.95	9.67	11.30
	9%	3.49	5.43	7.12	8.65	10.12
	10%	3.17	4.93	6.45	7.84	9.17
	11%	2.90	4.51	5.91	7.18	8.39
	12%	2.68	4.17	5.46	6.63	7.74
	13%	2.49	3.88	5.07	6.16	7.20

NONQUALIFIED DEFERRED COMPENSATION
(Break Even Point – Years)

Current Tax Rate		33%	33%	33%	33%	33%
Projected Tax Rate		35%	40%	45%	50%	55%
			Years			
Before-tax Return	3%	2.96	9.42	14.96	19.95	24.65
	4%	2.24	7.12	11.31	15.08	18.62
	5%	1.81	5.74	9.12	12.15	15.00
	6%	1.52	4.82	7.65	10.20	12.59
	7%	1.31	4.17	6.61	8.81	10.87
	8%	1.16	3.67	5.83	7.76	9.57
	9%	1.04	3.29	5.22	6.95	8.57
	10%	0.94	2.98	4.73	6.30	7.76
	11%	0.86	2.73	4.33	5.76	7.11
	12%	0.80	2.52	4.00	5.32	6.56
	13%	0.74	2.35	3.72	4.95	6.09

Question – What is a secular trust?

Answer – The secular trust (so named to contrast it with a rabbi trust) is an arrangement that meets two current employee objections to deferred compensation plans: the fear that tax savings will disappear because future tax rates will be very high, and the lack of security to the employee in relying on a formally unfunded plan.

A secular trust is an irrevocable trust for the exclusive benefit of the employee, with funds placed beyond the reach of the employer's creditors. Use of a secular trust is generally thought to result in taxation to the employee in the year in which assets are placed in the trust,[41] with a corresponding deduction to the employer in that year.[42] The amounts already taxed can be distributed tax free to the employee at retirement, even if tax rates have gone up considerably.[43]

Under current tax law where individual rates are higher than corporate rates, the acceleration of the employer's tax deduction does not provide more tax benefit than is lost by the employee in paying tax currently instead of deferring. However, the arrangement provides considerable security of benefits to the employee.

Secular trust designers try to structure secular trusts as grantor trusts, in order to avoid possible double taxation. A grantor trust is generally ignored for tax purposes, with its income and tax reportable directly by the grantor. The IRS has previously ruled favorably on employee-grantor secular trusts, but employers are often more interested in the employer-grantor arrangement, because this allows employers to maintain more control of the trust assets, a major objective in the golden handcuffs type of plan.

Some letter rulings have reached strongly negative results on employer-funded secular trusts.[44] In a complex technical analysis applying Code sections 402(b) and 404(a)(5), the IRS held that an employer-funded secular trust cannot be taxed as an employer-grantor trust. Moreover, the rulings held that employer-funded secular trust earnings can be taxed twice, once to the trust and again to the employees.

At best, these rulings create confusion and uncertainty; a pessimistic view might be that without changes in the Internal Revenue Code, the employer-funded secular trust is not viable for executive compensation planning.

CHAPTER ENDNOTES

1. Amounts representing "interest" credited on unfunded nonqualified deferred compensation cannot be currently deducted as interest under Section 163 by an accrual basis taxpayer. There has been great controversy over the proper timing of an accrual-basis employer's deduction for such amounts, but the current rule seems to be that the deduction must be delayed until such amounts are includable in employee income. *Albertson's, Inc. v. Comm'r.*, 42 F.3d 537 (9th Cir. 1994), *cert. denied*, 516 U.S. 807, 116 S. Ct. 51 (1995), vacating in part 12 F.3d 1529 (9th Cir. 1993), aff'g in part 95 TC 415 (1990) (divided court), en banc rehearing denied, 12 F.3d 1539 (9th Cir. 1994); Notice 94-38, 1994-1 CB 350; Let. Rul. 9201019; TAM 8619006.
2. ERISA §§4(b)(5), 201(7), 301(a)(9), and 4021(b)(8).
3. Treas. Reg. §1.409A-3(j)(1).
4. Treas. Reg. §1.409A-3(j)(4)(iv).
5. Treas. Reg. §1.409A(j)(4)(11) and (iii).
6. Treas. Reg. §1.409A(j)(4)(vi).
7. Treas. Reg. §1.409A(J)(4)(v).
8. While money is not considered "property" subject to the rules of Section 83, a beneficial interest in money transferred or set aside from the claims of the employer's creditors, for example in a trust or escrow account, is Section 83 "property."Treas. Reg. §1.83-3(e).
9. See DOL Regs. §§2520.104-23(a)(1) and 2520.104-23(d)(2); DOL Adv. Ops. 94-31A, 92-13A, 91-16A, 90-14A, 89-22A; see also *Belsky v. First National Life Insurance Co.*, 818 F.2d 661 (8th Cir. 1987) (a plan is unfunded when benefits are paid from the employer's general assets); *Dependahl v. Falstaff Brewing Corp.*, 653 F.2d 1208 (8th Cir. 1981) (a plan is funded when there is property separate from the ordinary assets of the employer to which the employee can look for satisfaction of benefit obligations), aff'g in part 491 F. Supp. 1188 (E.D. Mo. 1980), cert. denied, 454 U.S. 968 (1981) and 454 U.S. 1084 (1981); *Miller v. Heller*, 915 F. Supp. 651 (S.D.N.Y. 1996) (a plan backed by insurance policies is unfunded despite employees' belief that the policies secured their deferred compensation because the language in each agreement clearly defeated their belief); *The Northwestern Mutual Life Ins. Co. v. Resolution Trust Corp.*, 848 F. Supp. 1515 (N.D. Ala. 1994) (insurance policies purchased in conjunction with a deferred compensation plan did not cause the plan to be funded) *Darden v. Nationwide Mutual Insurance Co.*, 717 F. Supp. 388 (E.D.N.C. 1989), aff'd, 922 F.2d 203 (4th Cir.), cert. denied, 502 U.S. 906 (1991) (a pension fund backed by annuities is unfunded when benefits are paid from employer's general assets); *Belka v. Rowe Furniture Corp.*, 571 F. Supp. 1249 (D. Md. 1983) (the distinction between funded and unfunded plans is whether there is property set apart from the employer's general funds for satisfaction of benefit obligations); DOL Adv. Op. 92-01A (refusing to find union arrangement to be an unfunded, dues-financed welfare benefit plan because there was no evidence the benefits were paid out of the union's general assets or that the assets of the arrangement were subject to the union's general creditors).
10. See DOL Adv. Ops. 94-31A, 92-13A, 91-16A, 90-14A, 89-22A.

11. Treas. Reg. §1.83-1(a). If a plan is formally funded through a trust, a special rule may instead tax highly compensated employees each year on their vested accrued benefit in the trust (minus amounts previously taxed). See I.R.C. §402(b)(4).
12. ERISA Sections 201, 401(a).
13. ERISA §203(a)(2).
14. For plan years beginning after December 31, 2001, stricter vesting rules apply to employer matching contributions of employees with at least one hour of service after that effective date. The five-year cliff vesting schedule is reduced to a three-year cliff. Graduated vesting, which previously spanned three-seven years of service is replaced with a two-six year graded vesting schedule (20 percent for each year of service, beginning with the second year, and 100 percent vesting after six years). I.R.C. §411(a).
15. See Rev. Rul. 82-54, 1982-1 CB 11 and rulings cited therein; see also Let. Ruls. 9815039, 9805030.
16. Let. Ruls. 9008043, 8648011; see also Let. Ruls. 9504007, 9332038, 8834015, 8804057, 8607022.
17. E.g., DOL Adv. Op. 92-13A.
18. See *Berry v. U.S.*, 593 F. Supp. 80 (M.D. N.C. 1984) (shareholders of employer corporation guaranteed payment under plan), aff'd per curiam, 760 F.2d 85; *Robinson v. Comm'r.*, 44 TC 20 (1965) (while the issue was not raised by the IRS, payment of deferred prize fight proceeds was guaranteed by corporate fight promoter's parent corporation and one of its major shareholders), acq., 1970-2 CB xxi, 1976-2 CB 2 (correction); Let. Rul. 8906022 (parent guaranteed deferred compensation plan of subsidiary); Let. Rul. 8741078 (same); Let. Rul. 7902082 (shareholders guaranteed payment of corporate termination pay agreement to another shareholder-employee); Let. Rul. 7742098 (same); see also *Childs v. Comm'r.*, 103 TC 634 (1994) (a guarantee does not make a promise secured since the guarantee is itself a mere promise to pay); but see TAM 9336001 (the conclusion that victorious plaintiffs' promise to pay their attorney was funded and secured where they irrevocably ordered defendants' insurers to pay attorney out of plaintiffs' recovery and defendants' insurers paid attorney by buying annuities naming him annuitant was "strengthened" by the fact that a defendant and the defendants' insurers guaranteed to make the annuity payments should the annuity issuer default); compare Let. Rul. 9331006 (protecting benefits by giving employees certificates of participation secured by irrevocable standby letters of credit turned the promise into a secured promise subject to Section 83); Let. Rul. 9443006 (employer's purchase of irrevocable standby letter of credit beyond the reach of its general creditors to back its promise to pay accrued vacation benefits turned promise into a secured promise subject to Section 83).
19. See Let. Rul. 8406012 (current value of protection provided by employer-paid surety bond or other guarantee arrangement constitutes an economic benefit, the cost of which is taxable to the employee); compare Let. Rul. 9241006 (strongly hinting that at least employer-provided surety bonds might secure deferred compensation causing it to be immediately taxable to the extent benefits are substantially vested).
20. See Let. Ruls. 9344038 (employee-purchased indemnification insurance protecting deferred compensation does not accelerate taxation), and 8406012 (employee-purchased surety bond protecting deferred compensation does not accelerate taxation); but compare Let. Rul. 9241006 (suggesting that use of a surety bond to protect deferred compensation could accelerate taxation but not clearly distinguishing between employer-provided and employee-provided bonds).
21. I.R.C. §451.
22. Treas. Reg. §1.451-2(a).
23. Rev. Rul. 60-31, 1960-1 CB 174; Rev. Proc. 71-19, 1971-1 CB 698, as amplified by Rev. Proc. 92-65, 1992-2 CB 428; but see Let. Rul. 9506008 (plan allowing elections to defer bonus payments on or before May 31 of the compensation year with respect to which the deferral will be effective but not imposing forfeiture provisions did not cause constructive receipt).
24. See Rev. Rul. 67-449, 1967-2 CB 173; Rev. Proc. 71-19, 1971-1 CB 698, as amplified by Rev. Proc. 92-65, 1992-2 CB 428; TAM 8632003 (note, though, that the IRS did not analyze whether plan imposed substantial forfeiture provisions); but see *Childs v. Comm'r.*, 103 TC 634 (1994); *Martin v. Comm'r.*, 96 TC 814 (1991); *Veit v. Comm'r.*, 8 TCM 919 (1949).
25. *Sproull v. Comm'r.*, 16 TC 244 (1951), *aff'd per curiam*, 194 F.2d 541 (6th Cir. 1952); Rev. Rul. 72-25, 1972-1 CB 127; Rev. Rul. 68-99, 1968-1 CB 193; Rev. Rul. 60-31, 1960-1 CB 174. A special rule may tax highly compensated employees each year on their vested accrued benefit in the trust (minus amounts previously taxed). See I.R.C. §402(b)(4).
26. I.R.C. §3121(v)(2); Treas. Reg. §31.3121(v)(2)-1. See Notice 94-96, 1994-2 CB 564 for the IRS' enforcement position. Final regulations provide a twist to this special timing rule for certain amounts deferred that are not reasonably ascertainable at the later of (1) the time the services creating the right to the amount deferred are performed; or (2) when there is no substantial risk of forfeiting the right to the amount deferred. See Treas. Reg. §31.3121(v)(2)-1(e)(4)(i).
27. I.R.C. §404(a)(5); Treas. Reg. §1.404(a)-12(b)(1). This rule seems to apply even to amounts credited as "interest" on unfunded deferred compensation by an accrual-basis employer. See footnote 2, above.
28. See, e.g., Acme Construction Co., Inc. v. Comm'r., TC Memo 1995-6; Comtech Systems, Inc. v. Comm'r., TC Memo 1995-4.
29. I.R.C. §162(m).
30. I.R.C. §162(m)(6).
31. ERISA §§4(b)(5) and 4021(b)(8).
32. ERISA §§201(2), 301(a)(3), 401(a)(1), 503, and 4021(b)(6); DOL Regs. §§2520.104-23, 2560.503-1(a), 2560.503-1(b).
33. See www.dol.gov/ebsa/efiletophatplanfilinginstructions.html.
34. The DOL's current position seems to be that the "select group of management or highly compensated employees" is limited to those employees who, by virtue of their position or compensation level, have the ability to affect or substantially influence the design and operation of their deferred compensation plan. E.g., DOL Adv. Op. 92-13A, footnote 1. However, in *Demery v. Extebank Deferred Compensation Plan*, 216 F. 3d 283 (2d Cir. 2000), the Second Circuit held that a plan met the top-hat requirement where it was made available to a group of middle-management employees comprising approximately 15 percent of the company's workforce, and those electing participation amounted to approximately 10 percent of the company's employees.
35. The leading case on this point is *Fort Halifax Packing Co. v. Coyne*, 48 U.S. 1 (Supreme Ct. 1987). However, in *Demery v. Extebank Deferred Compensation Plan*, 216 F. 3d 283 (2d Cir. 2000), the Second Circuit held that a plan met the top-hat requirement where it was made available to a group of middle-management

employees comprising approximately 15 percent of the company's workforce, and those electing participation amounted to approximately 10 percent of the company's employees.

36. This item has been on the IRS' annually revised list of "no ruling" items for many years. See Rev. Proc. 2011-3, 2011-1 IRB 11. Active hostility to controlling shareholder-employee deferred compensation was expressed in a side discussion, or "dictum," in Let. Rul. 8607029, a ruling otherwise favorable to the taxpayer. See also TAM 8828004.

37. *Casale v. Comm'r.*, 247 F.2d 440 (2nd Cir. 1957); *Moline Properties, Inc. v. Comm'r.*, 319 U.S. 436, 63 S. Ct. 1132 (1943); Rev. Rul. 59-184 1959-1 CB 65.

38. *Carnahan v. Comm'r.*, TC Memo 1994-163; *Commerce Union Bank v. U.S.*, 76-2 USTC ¶13,157 (M.D. Tenn. 1976); *First Trust Company of St. Paul v. U.S.*, 321 F. Supp. 1025 (D. Minn. 1970); Rev. Rul. 77-139, 1977-1 CB 278.

39. See *Casale v. Comm'r.*, above, footnote 28; *Goldsmith v. U. S.*, 78-1 USTC ¶9312 (Ct. Cl. Tr. Div. 1978), no appeal (adopted by full court), 586 F.2d 810 (Ct. Cl. 1978). But see Let. Ruls. 8103089 and 7940017.

40. See, e.g., *Willmark Service System, Inc. v. Comm'r.*, TC Memo 1965-294, aff'd, 368 F.2d 359 (2d Cir. 1966).

41. The full picture of the taxation of employees participating in secular trusts is much more complex than this. For the rules applicable to participants in employer-funded secular trusts, see I.R.C. §402(b); Treas. Regs. §§1.402(b)-1(a), 1.402(b)-1(b); Let. Ruls. 9502030, 9417013, 9302017, 9212024, 9212019, 9207010, 9206009. For the rules applicable to employees participating in employee-funded secular trusts, see Let. Ruls. 9450004, 9437011, 9337016, 9328007, 9322011, 9316018, 9316008, 9235044, 9031031, 8843021, 8841023.

42. For more on the employer's deduction in the context of an employer-funded secular trust, see Treas. Reg. §1.404(a)-12(b)(1); Let. Ruls. 9502030, 9417013, 9302017, 9212024, 9212019, 9207010, 9206009. For more on the employer's deduction in the context of an employee-funded secular trust, see Let. Ruls. 9450004, 9437011, 9337016, 9328007, 9322011, 9316018, 9316008, 9235044, 9031031, 8843021, 8841023.

43. The IRS has pointed out that the taxation of distributions from employer-funded secular trusts to highly compensated employees participating in a plan that fails the minimum participation or the minimum coverage tests applicable to qualified plans is unclear. See Let. Ruls. 9502030, 9417013.

44. See Let. Ruls. 9417013, 9302017, 9212024, 9212019, 9207010, 9206009; see also Let. Rul. 9502030.

IRS MODEL RABBI TRUST

TRUST UNDER________PLAN

OPTIONAL

(a) This Agreement made this____day of_____, by and between________(Company) and_________(Trustee);

OPTIONAL

(b) WHEREAS, Company has adopted the nonqualified deferred compensation Plan(s) as listed in Appendix_______.

OPTIONAL

(c) WHEREAS, Company has incurred or expects to incur liability under the terms of such Plan(s) with respect to the individuals participating in such Plan(s);

(d) WHEREAS, Company wishes to establish a trust (hereinafter called "Trust") and to contribute to the Trust assets that shall be held therein, subject to the claims of Company's creditors in the event of Company's Insolvency, as herein defined, until paid to Plan participants and their beneficiaries in such manner and at such times as specified in the Plan(s);

(e) WHEREAS, it is the intention of the parties that this Trust shall constitute an unfunded arrangement and shall not affect the status of the Plan(s) as an unfunded plan maintained for the purpose of providing deferred compensation for a select group of management or highly compensated employees for purposes of Title I of the Employee Retirement Income Security Act of 1974;

(f) WHEREAS, it is the intention of Company to make contributions to the Trust to provide itself with a source of funds to assist it in the meeting of its liabilities under the Plan(s);

NOW, THEREFORE, the parties do hereby establish the Trust and agree that the Trust shall be comprised, held and disposed of as follows:

Section 1. *Establishment Of Trust*

(a) Company hereby deposits with Trustee in trust______[insert amount deposited], which shall become the principal of the Trust to be held, administered and disposed of by Trustee as provided in this Trust Agreement.

ALTERNATIVES—Select one provision.

(b) The Trust hereby established shall be revocable by Company.

(b) The Trust hereby established shall be irrevocable.

(b) The Trust hereby established is revocable by Company; it shall become irrevocable upon a Change of Control, as defined herein.

(b) The Trust shall become irrevocable______[insert number] days following the issuance of a favorable private letter ruling regarding the Trust from the Internal Revenue Service.

(b) The Trust shall become irrevocable upon approval by the Board of Directors.

(c) The Trust is intended to be a grantor trust, of which Company is the grantor, within the meaning of subpart E, part I, subchapter J, chapter 1, subtitle A of the Internal Revenue Code of 1986, as amended, and shall be construed accordingly.

(d) The principal of the Trust, and any earnings thereon shall be held separate and apart from other funds of Company and shall be used exclusively for the uses and purposes of Plan participants and general creditors as herein set forth. Plan participants and their beneficiaries shall have no preferred claim on, or any beneficial ownership interest in, any assets of the Trust. Any rights created under the Plan(s) and this Trust Agreement shall be mere unsecured contractual rights of Plan participants and their beneficiaries against Company. Any assets held by the Trust will be subject to the claims of Company's general creditors under federal and state law in the event Of Insolvency, as defined in Section 3(a) herein.

ALTERNATIVES—Select one or more provisions, as appropriate.

(e) Company, in its sole discretion, may at any time, or from time to time, make additional deposits of cash or other property in trust with Trustee to augment the principal to be held, administered and disposed of by Trustee as provided in this Trust Agreement. Neither Trustee nor any Plan participant or beneficiary shall have any right to compel such additional deposits.

(e) Upon a Change of Control, Company shall, as soon as possible, but in no event longer than____[fill in blank] days following the Change of Control, as defined herein, make an irrevocable contribution to the Trust in an amount that is sufficient to pay each Plan participant or beneficiary the benefits to which Plan participants or their beneficiaries would be entitled pursuant to the terms of the Plan(s) as of the date on which the Change of Control occurred.

(e) Within____[fill in blank] days following the end of the Plan years, ending after the Trust has become irrevocable pursuant to Section l(b) hereof, Company shall be required to irrevocably deposit additional cash or other property to the Trust in an amount sufficient to pay each Plan participant or beneficiary the benefits payable pursuant to the terms of the Plan(s) as of the close of the Plan year(s).

Section 2. *Payments to Plan Participants and Their Beneficiaries.*

(a) Company shall deliver to Trustee a schedule (the "Payment Schedule") that indicates the amounts payable in respect of each Plan participant (and his or her beneficiaries), that provides a formula or other instructions acceptable to Trustee for determining the amounts so payable, the form in which such amount is to be paid (as provided for or available under the Plan(s)), and the time of commencement for payment of such amounts. Except as otherwise provided herein, Trustee shall make payments to the Plan participants and their beneficiaries in accordance with such Payment Schedule. The Trustee shall make provision for the reporting and withholding of any federal, state or local taxes that may be required to be withheld with respect to the payment of benefits pursuant to the terms of the Plan(s) and shall pay amounts withheld to the appropriate taxing authorities or determine that such amounts have been reported, withheld and paid by Company.

(b) The entitlement of a Plan participant or his or her beneficiaries to benefits under the Plan(s) shall be determined by Company or such party as it shall designate under the Plan(s), and any claim for such benefits shall be considered and reviewed under the procedures set out in the Plan(s).

(c) Company may make payment of benefits directly to Plan participants or their beneficiaries as they become due under the terms of the Plan(s). Company shall notify Trustee of its decision to make payment of benefits directly prior to the time amounts are payable to participants or their beneficiaries. In addition, if the principal of the Trust, and any earnings thereon, are not sufficient to make payments of benefits in accordance with the terms of the Plan(s), Company shall make the balance of each such payment as it falls due. Trustee shall notify Company where principal and earnings are not sufficient.

Section 3. *Trustee Responsibility Regarding Payments to Trust Beneficiary When Company Is Insolvent.*

(a) Trustee shall cease payment of benefits to Plan participants and their beneficiaries if the Company is Insolvent. Company shall be considered "Insolvent" for purposes of this Trust Agreement if (i) Company is unable to pay its debts as they become due, or (ii) Company is subject to a pending proceeding as a debtor under the United States Bankruptcy Code.

OPTIONAL

, or (iii) Company is determined to be insolvent by_________[insert names of applicable federal and/or state regulatory agency].

(b) At all times during the continuance of this Trust, as provided in Section l(d) hereof, the principal and income of the Trust shall be subject to claims of general creditors of Company under federal and state law as set forth below.

(1) The Board of Directors and the Chief Executive Officer [or substitute the title of the highest ranking officer of the Company] of Company shall have the duty to inform Trustee in writing of Company's Insolvency. If a person claiming to be a creditor of Company alleges in writing to Trustee that Company has become Insolvent, Trustee shall determine whether Company is Insolvent and, pending such determination, Trustee shall discontinue payment of benefits to Plan participants or their beneficiaries.

(2) Unless Trustee has actual knowledge of Company's Insolvency, or has received notice from Company or a person claiming to be a creditor alleging that Company is Insolvent, Trustee shall have no duty to inquire whether Company is Insolvent. Trustee may in all events rely on such evidence concerning Company's solvency as may be furnished to Trustee and that provides Trustee with a reasonable basis for making a determination concerning Company's solvency.

(3) If at any time Trustee has determined that Company is Insolvent, Trustee shall discontinue payments to Plan participants or their beneficiaries and shall hold the assets of the Trust for the benefit of Company's general creditors. Nothing in this Trust Agreement shall in any way diminish any rights of Plan participants or their beneficiaries to pursue their rights as general creditors of Company with respect to benefits due under the Plan(s) or otherwise.

(4) Trustee shall resume the payment of benefits to Plan participants or their beneficiaries in accordance with Section 2 of this Trust Agreement only after Trustee has determined that Company is not Insolvent (or is no longer Insolvent).

(c) Provided that there are sufficient assets, if Trustee discontinues the payment of benefits from the Trust pursuant to Section 3(b) hereof and subsequently resumes such payments, the first payment following such discontinuance shall include the aggregate amount of all payments due to Plan participants or their beneficiaries under the terms of the Plan(s) for the period of such discontinuance, less the aggregate amount of any payments made to Plan participants or their beneficiaries by Company in lieu of the payments provided for hereunder during any such period of discontinuance.

Section 4. *Payments to Company.*

[The following need not be included if the first alternative under l(b) is selected.]

Except as provided in Section 3 hereof, after the Trust has become irrevocable, Company shall have no right or power to direct Trustee to return to Company or to divert to others any of the Trust assets before all payment of benefits have [*sic*] been made to Plan participants and their beneficiaries pursuant to the terms of the Plan(s).

Section 5. *Investment Authority.*

ALTERNATIVES—[Select one provision, as appropriate.]

(a) In no event may Trustee invest in securities (including stock or rights to acquire stock) or obligations issued by Company, other than a de minimis amount held in common investment vehicles in which Trustee invests. All rights associated with assets of the Trust shall be exercised by Trustee or the person designated by Trustee, and shall in no event be exercisable by or rest with Plan participants.

(a) Trustee may invest in securities (including stock or rights to acquire stock) or obligations issued by Company. All rights associated with assets of the Trust shall be exercised by Trustee or the person designated by Trustee, and shall in no event be exercisable by or rest with Plan participants.

OPTIONAL
,except that voting rights with respect to Trust assets will be exercised by Company.

OPTIONAL
,except that dividend rights with respect to Trust assets will rest with Company.

OPTIONAL
Company shall have the right, at anytime, and from time to time in its sole discretion, to substitute assets of equal fair market value for any asset held by the Trust.

[If the second Alternative 5(a) is selected, the trust must provide either (1) that the trust is revocable under Alternative l(b), or (2) the following provision must by included in the Trust]:

"Company shall have the right at anytime, and from time to time in its sole discretion, to substitute assets of equal fair market value for any asset held by the Trust. This right is exercisable by Company in a nonfiduciary capacity without the approval or consent of any person in a fiduciary capacity."

Section 6. *Disposition of Income.*

ALTERNATIVES—*Select one provision.*

(a) During the term of this Trust, all income received by the Trust, net of expenses and taxes, shall be accumulated and reinvested.

(a) During the term of this Trust, all, or______[insert amount] part of the income received by the Trust, net of expenses and taxes, shall be returned to Company.

Section 7. *Accounting by Trustee.*

OPTIONAL
Trustee shall keep accurate and detailed records of all investments, receipts, disbursements, and all other transactions required to be made, including such specific records as shall be agreed upon in writing between Company and Trustee. Within____[insert number] days following the close of each calendar year and within____[insert number] days after the removal or resignation of Trustee, Trustee shall deliver to Company a written account of its administration of the Trust during such year or during the period from the close of the last preceding year to the date of such removal or resignation, setting forth all investments, receipts, disbursements and other transactions effected by it, including a description of all securities and investments purchased and sold with the cost or net proceeds of such purchases or sales (accrued interest paid or receivable being shown separately), and showing all cash, securities and other property held in the Trust at the end of such year or as of the date of such removal or resignation, as the case may be.

Section 8. *Responsibility of Trustee.*

OPTIONAL
(a) Trustee shall act with the care, skill, prudence and diligence under the circumstances then prevailing that a prudent person acting in like capacity and familiar with such matters would use in the conduct of an enterprise of a like character and with like aims, provided, however, that Trustee shall incur no liability to any person for any action taken pursuant to a direction, request or approval given by Company which is contemplated by, and in conformity with, the terms of the Plan(s) or this Trust and is given in writing by Company. In the event of a dispute between Company and a party, Trustee may apply to a court of competent jurisdiction to resolve the dispute.

OPTIONAL

(b) If Trustee undertakes or defends any litigation arising in connection with this Trust, Company agrees to indemnify Trustee against Trustee's costs, expenses and liabilities (including, without limitation, attorneys' fees and expenses) relating thereto and to be primarily liable for such payments. If Company does not pay such costs, expenses and liabilities in a reasonably timely manner, Trustee may obtain payment from the Trust.

OPTIONAL

(c) Trustee may consult with legal counsel (who may also be counsel for Company generally) with respect to any of its duties or obligations hereunder.

OPTIONAL

(d) Trustee may hire agents, accountants, actuaries, investment advisors, financial consultants or other professionals to assist it in performing any of its duties or obligations hereunder.

(e) Trustee shall have, without exclusion, all powers conferred on Trustees by applicable law, unless expressly provided otherwise herein, provided, however, that if an insurance policy is held as an asset of the Trust, Trustee shall have no power to name a beneficiary of the policy other than the Trust, to assign the policy (as distinct from conversion of the policy to a different form) other than to a successor Trustee, or to loan to any person the proceeds of any borrowing against such policy.

OPTIONAL

(f) However, notwithstanding the provisions of Section 8(e) above, Trustee may loan to Company the proceeds of any borrowing against an insurance policy held as an asset of the Trust.

(g) Notwithstanding any powers granted to Trustee pursuant to this Trust Agreement or to applicable law, Trustee shall not have any power that could give this Trust the objective of carrying on a business and dividing the gains therefrom, within the meaning of section 301.7701-2 of the Procedure and Administrative Regulations promulgated pursuant to the Internal Revenue Code.

Section 9. *Compensation and Expenses of Trustee.*

OPTIONAL

Company shall pay all administrative and Trustee's fees and expenses. If not so paid, the fees and expenses shall be paid from the Trust.

Section 10. *Resignation and Removal of Trustee.*

(a) Trustee may resign at any time by written notice to Company, which shall be effective____[insert number] days after receipt of such notice unless Company and Trustee agree otherwise.

OPTIONAL

(b) Trustee may be removed by Company on____[insert number] days notice or upon shorter notice accepted by Trustee.

OPTIONAL

(c) Upon a Change of Control, as defined herein, Trustee may not be removed by Company for____[insert number] year(s).

OPTIONAL

(d) If Trustee resigns within____[insert number] year(s) after a Change of Control, as defined herein, Company shall apply to a court of competent jurisdiction for the appointment of a successor Trustee or for instructions.

OPTIONAL

(e) If Trustee resigns or is removed within____[insert number] year(s) or a Change of Control, as defined herein, Trustee shall select a successor Trustee in accordance with the provisions of Section 11(b) hereof prior to the effective date of Trustee's resignation or removal.

(f) Upon resignation or removal of Trustee and appointment of a successor Trustee, all assets shall subsequently be transferred to the successor Trustee. The transfer shall be completed within____[insert number] days after receipt of notice of resignation, removal or transfer, unless Company extends the time limit.

(g) If Trustee resigns or is removed, a successor shall be appointed, in accordance with Section 11 hereof, by the effective date of resignation or removal under paragraph(s) (a) [or (b)] of this section. If no such appointment has been made, Trustee may apply to a court of competent jurisdiction for appointment of a successor or for instructions. All expenses of Trustee in connection with the proceeding shall be allowed as administrative expenses of the Trust.

Section 11. *Appointment of Successor.*

OPTIONAL

(a) If Trustee resigns or is removed in accordance with Section 10(a) [or (b)] hereof, Company may appoint any third party, such as a bank trust department or other party that may be granted corporate trustee powers under state law, as a successor to replace Trustee upon resignation or removal. The appointment shall be effective when accepted in writing by the new Trustee, who shall have all of the rights and powers of the former Trustee, including ownership rights in the Trust assets. The former Trustee shall execute any instrument necessary or reasonably requested by Company or the successor Trustee to evidence the transfer.

OPTIONAL

(b) If Trustee resigns or is removed pursuant to the provisions of Section 10(e) hereof and selects a successor Trustee, Trustee may appoint any third party such as a bank trust department or other party that may be granted corporate trustee powers under state law. The appointment of a successor Trustee shall be effective when accepted in writing by the new Trustee. The new Trustee shall have all the rights and powers of the former Trustee, including ownership rights in Trust assets. The former Trustee shall execute any instrument necessary or reasonably requested by the successor Trustee to evidence the transfer.

OPTIONAL

(c) The successor Trustee need not examine the records and acts of any prior Trustee and may retain or dispose of existing Trust assets, subject to Sections 7 and 8 hereof. The successor Trustee shall not be responsible for and Company shall indemnify and defend the successor Trustee from any claim or liability resulting from any action or inaction of any prior Trustee or from any other past event, or any condition existing at the time it becomes successor Trustee.

Section 12. *Amendment or Termination.*

(a) This Trust Agreement may be amended by a written instrument executed by Trustee and Company. [Unless the first alternative under 1(b) is selected, the following sentence must be included.] Notwithstanding the foregoing, no such amendment shall conflict with the terms of the Plan(s) or shall make the Trust revocable after it has become irrevocable in accordance with Section 1(b) hereof.

(b) The Trust shall not terminate until the date on which Plan participants and their beneficiaries are no longer entitled to benefits pursuant to the terms of the Plan(s) [unless the second alternative under 1(b) is selected, the following must be included:], "unless sooner revoked in accordance with Section 1(b) hereof." [*Sic*] Upon termination of the Trust any assets remaining in the Trust shall be returned to Company.

OPTIONAL

(c) Upon written approval of participants or beneficiaries entitled to payment of benefits pursuant to the terms of the Plan(s), Company may terminate this Trust prior to the time all benefit payments under the Plan(s) have been made. All assets in the Trust at termination shall be returned to Company.

OPTIONAL

(d) Section(s)________[insert number(s)] of this Trust Agreement may not be amended by Company for_____[insert number] year(s) following a Change of Control, as defined herein.

Section 13. *Miscellaneous.*

(a) Any provision of this Trust Agreement prohibited by law shall be ineffective to the extent of any such prohibition, without invalidating the remaining provisions hereof.

(b) Benefits payable to Plan participants and their beneficiaries under this Trust Agreement may not be anticipated, assigned (either at law or in equity), alienated, pledged, encumbered or subjected to attachment, garnishment, levy, execution or other legal or equitable process.

(c) This Trust Agreement shall be governed by and construed in accordance with the laws of__________.

OPTIONAL

(d) For purposes of this Trust, Change of Control shall mean: [insert objective definition such as: "the purchase or other acquisition by any person, entity or group of persons, within the meaning of section 13(d) or 14(d) of the Securities Exchange Act of 1934 ("Act"), or any comparable successor provisions, of beneficial ownership within the meaning of Rule 13d-3 promulgated under the Act) of 30 percent or more of either the outstanding shares of common stock or the combined voting power of Company's then outstanding voting securities entitled to vote generally, or the approval by the stockholders of Company of a reorganization, merger, or consolidation, in each case, with respect to which persons who were stockholders of Company immediately prior to such reorganization, merger or consolidation do not, immediately thereafter, own more than 50 percent of the combined voting power entitled to vote generally in the election of directors of the reorganized, merged or consolidated Company's then outstanding securities, or a liquidation or dissolution of Company or of the sale of all or substantially all of Company's assets"].

Section 14. *Effective Date.*

The effective date of this Trust Agreement shall be________, 20[___].

SECTION 457 PLAN

CHAPTER 34

INTRODUCTION

Code section 457 provides rules governing all nonqualified deferred compensation plans of governmental units, governmental agencies, and also non-church controlled tax-exempt organizations. A plan designed to comply with these rules is referred to as a Section 457 plan.

WHEN IS USE OF SUCH A DEVICE INDICATED?

Any nonqualified deferred compensation plan adopted by an employer that is an affected organization generally must comply with the rules discussed here.

DESIGN FEATURES

What Employers Are Covered by Section 457?

Section 457 applies to nonqualified deferred compensation plans of:

1. A state, a political subdivision of a state (such as a city, township, etc.), and any agency or instrumentality of a state or political subdivision of a state (for example, a school district or a sewage authority); and

2. Any organization exempt from federal income tax, except for a church or synagogue or an organization controlled by a church or synagogue.[1]

Limit on Amount Deferred

Under Section 457, plans that include limits on the amounts deferred are subject to favorable tax treatment; these are generally referred to as *eligible* Section 457 plans. Plans providing greater deferral, generally designed for executives, are referred to as *ineligible plans*; these are discussed in the Frequently Asked Questions section of this chapter.

Basic Limit

For an eligible plan, the amount deferred annually by the participant cannot exceed the lesser of (1) 100 percent of the participant's compensation or (2) an applicable dollar amount, which is $18,000 as indexed for 2015.[2]

In determining these limits, all Section 457 plans in which an individual participates must be aggregated.

Example. Sam, age forty-five, works for two governmental employers, Municipal Salt Works and also Municipal School District, earning a $30,000 salary from each. Both employers maintain a Section 457 plan. Sam participates in both plans, but for 2015 Sam's total contribution to both plans is limited to $18,000. This amount can be allocated between the plans in any manner consistent with the plans' provisions.

But Section 457 salary reduction contributions do not reduce contributions to another type of salary reduction plan such as a Section 403(b) or Section 401(k) plan. This presents an opportunity for a "double dip."

Example. Municipal School District maintains both a 457 plan and a 403(b) plan. Max, age forty, works for Municipal School District and earns $40,000. For 2015, Max can contribute

> $18,000 to the School District's 457 plan and also contribute $18,000 to the School District's 403(b) plan, for a total salary reduction contribution of $36,000.[3]

The 100 percent of compensation limit applies to gross compensation before salary reductions. For example, Max in the example in the preceding paragraph is considered to have $40,000 of compensation for purposes of the 100 percent limit (not $40,000 less salary reductions). Obviously, this rule increases the available salary reduction contribution considerably in certain situations like this one.[4]

Fifty-or-over Catch-up Contributions

All participants in a plan of a governmental employer (but not a private tax-exempt organization) who are aged fifty or over are eligible for additional salary reduction contributions of $6,000 (in 2015).[5]

Notwithstanding this amount the fifty-or-over catch-up can't exceed the excess of the participant's compensation over all regular elective deferrals. However, the Section 415 limitation (annual additions to participant's accounts can't exceed the lesser of $53,000 (2015) or 100 percent of compensation) does not limit the use of the fifty-or-over catch-up.

> *Example 1.* If a participant over age fifty in 2015 has compensation of $18,500 and has regular salary reductions of $18,000, the catch-up for 2015 cannot exceed $500.

> *Example 2.* A participant over age fifty in 2015 with annual compensation of $100,000 has regular annual additions of $53,000 to various defined contribution plans of the employer. The participant is nevertheless eligible for the full $6,000 catch-up (2015) in addition.

Old three-year catch-up provision for 457 plan participants. To complicate matters a bit further, there is an "old" three-year catch-up provision for 457 plans that still applies, as discussed below. The fifty-or-over catch-up provision is not available for a participant who is eligible for a higher catch-up under this old three-year provision.[6] The three-year catch-up provision applies during the participant's last three years prior to the plan's normal retirement age.[7] During those last three years, the limit on deferrals is increased to the lesser of:

1. twice the amount of the regularly applicable dollar limit; or

2. the sum of:

    a. the otherwise applicable limit for the year; plus

    b. the amount by which the applicable limit in preceding years exceeded the participant's actual deferral for those years.[8]

The old three-year catch-up rule applies to all eligible 457 plans, not just eligible 457 governmental plans. Under the *old* three-year catch-up rule, during the last three years prior to the plan's normal retirement age, an eligible participant in an eligible 457 governmental plan may defer the greater of

1. the regular applicable dollar amount plus the catch-up amount permitted under Code section 414(v) (which are not subject to any otherwise-applicable limitation of Code section 457(b)(2)); or

2. the amount permitted under the "new" three-year catch-up provisions of section 457(b)(3).[9]

Timing of Salary Reduction Elections

Employee elections to defer compensation monthly under Section 457 must generally be made under an agreement entered into before the beginning of the month.[10]

Distribution Requirements

Plan distributions cannot be made before:[11]

1. The calendar year in which the participant attains age 70½;

2. Severance from employment;[12] or

3. An "unforeseeable emergency," as defined in regulations. The definition of unforeseeable emergency is discussed in the Frequently Asked Questions.

A participant can elect to receive an involuntary cashout up to $5,000 from his account under a tax-exempt nongovernmental organization's plan, if no amount has been deferred by the participant for two years, and there has been no prior distribution. A cashout distribution in excess of $1,000 (and, by definition, less than or equal to $5,000) must be automatically transferred to an individual retirement plan (e.g., IRA) unless the participant affirmatively elects to have the distribution transferred to another eligible retirement plan or to take the distribution in cash.[13] The Department of Labor has issued final safe harbor regulations governing involuntary automatic rollovers.[14]

A participant may make a one-time election, after amounts are available and before commencement of distributions, to defer commencement of distributions.[15]

Minimum distributions must be made under the rules of Section 401(a)(9),[16] which apply to qualified plans as well; the minimum distribution rules are discussed in Chapter 14.

The qualified plan rules of Section 414(p) regarding Qualified Domestic Relations Orders (QDROs) apply to Section 457 plans.[17]

Coverage and Eligibility

There are no specific coverage requirements for Section 457 plans. For a governmental organization, the plan can be offered to all employees, or to any group of employees, even to a single employee.

However, most private non-governmental tax-exempt organizations are subject to ERISA. Therefore, the ERISA eligibility rules may apply to the Section 457 plan of the tax-exempt organization. The eligibility requirements would be the same as those applicable to a nonqualified deferred compensation plan for a taxable employer, as discussed in Chapter 33. Such plans can avoid the ERISA rules if they are structured to take advantage of specific ERISA exemptions, such as the exemption for unfunded plans covering only a select group of management or highly compensated employees—the "top-hat" group.[18]

Funding

Nongovernmental tax-exempt organizations. A Section 457 plan for such organizations may not be funded. However, "financing" the plan with insurance or annuity contracts is allowed and is almost always appropriate. The employer can, and in most cases should, finance its obligations under the plan by setting aside assets in advance of the time when payments will be made. Life insurance or annuity contracts are often used for this purpose.

If the employer purchases life insurance contracts to finance the plan, there is no current life insurance cost to employees, as long as the employer retains all incidents of ownership in the policies, is the sole beneficiary under the policies, and is under no obligation to transfer the policies or pass through the proceeds of the policies. This favorable result applies even if the contracts are purchased at the option of participants.[19] However, as with all deferred compensation plans, benefits to participants and their beneficiaries, including death benefits, are not excludable as life insurance proceeds, even if life insurance is used to finance the plan.[20]

For the plan of a tax-exempt organization that is subject to ERISA, the no-funding requirement of Section 457 may conflict directly with certain ERISA requirements, such as the funding and exclusive purpose requirements; this issue has not yet been resolved.[21] One way to eliminate the conflict is to limit participation in the plan to a select group of management or highly compensated employees—the "top-hat" group.

Governmental organizations. Governmental plans *must* be funded—that is, they must hold plan assets in trusts or custodial accounts.[22] If such plans hold life insurance contracts for participants, by analogy with the rules for qualified plans, employees should pay income tax on the value of current life insurance protection,[23] and the death proceeds from the life insurance contracts should be free of income tax to their beneficiaries. (See Chapter 18). However, as of this writing, neither the IRS nor Congress has clarified this issue.

TAX IMPLICATIONS

1. Since the employer sponsoring a Section 457 plan does not pay federal income taxes, deductibility is not an issue.

2. Certain lower-income taxpayers may claim a temporary, nonrefundable credit for qualified retirement savings contributions.[21] Qualified retirement savings contributions include elective deferrals to SIMPLE IRAs, as well as other elective deferrals and contributions to Roth or traditional IRAs. (However, the total is reduced by certain

distributions received by the taxpayer or his spouse during the prior two taxable years and the current taxable year for which the credit is claimed, including the period up to the due date (plus extensions) for filing the federal income tax return for the current taxable year.) Only the first $2,000 of annual deferrals is eligible for the credit.

The credit is allowed against the sum of the regular tax and the alternative minimum tax (minus certain other credits) and is allowed in addition to any other deduction or exclusion that would otherwise apply. In addition, to be eligible, the taxpayer must be at least eighteen as of the end of the tax year and must not be claimed as a dependent by someone else or be a full-time student.

The amount of the credit is limited to an "applicable percentage" of IRA contributions and elective deferrals up to $2,000. The "applicable percentages" are as follows for 2015:

Amount of Credit	Joint	Head of Household	Single/ Others
50% of first $2,000 deferred	$0 to $36,500	$0 to $27,375	$0 to $18,250
20% of first $2,000 deferred	$36,501 to $39,500	$27,376 to $29,625	$18,251 to $19,750
10% of first $2,000 deferred	$39,501 to $61,000	$29,626 to $45,750	$19,751 to $30,500
0% of contribution	More than $61,000	More than $45,750	More than $30,500

Example: Max and Erma together have adjusted gross income of $38,000 for 2015. Their government employers sponsor an eligible Section 457 governmental plan and they each elected to make a salary reduction contribution of $3,000 to the plan. Neither has received any distributions in the current or two preceding taxable years. Max and Erma will be able to exclude their salary reduction contributions as well as each being eligible to claim a joint credit of $800 (20 percent of $2,000—or $400—each) on their federal income tax return ($800 if married filing jointly) for 2015.

---

3. A plan may permit employees to make voluntary contributions to a deemed IRA established under the plan. Amounts so contributed reduce the limit for other traditional or Roth IRA contributions. See Chapter 22. Contributions under this provision may also (as with elective deferrals and other IRA contributions) count toward the nonrefundable credit for lower-income taxpayers, explained in the Frequently Asked Questions below.

4. Employees (or their beneficiaries) include Section 457 *governmental* plan distributions in income when they are paid. Employees (or their beneficiaries) include Section 457 non-governmental, tax-exempt plan distribution in income when they are actually paid or otherwise made available.[25] Even if life insurance financing is used, benefits are taxable; see the Frequently Asked Questions.

   However, if a nonqualified deferred compensation plan of a governmental or tax-exempt employer does not comply with Section 457, compensation deferred is included in the employee's income in the first taxable year in which there is no substantial risk of forfeiture of the rights to the compensation. Any distributions from an ineligible plan are treated in the same manner as annuity distributions under Section 72.[26] The implications of this are discussed in the Frequently Asked Questions section of this chapter.

5. Section 457 plan distributions are not eligible for the grandfathered lump sum ten-year averaging treatment available for qualified plans.[27]

6. Plan participants may exclude from income amounts directly transferred (i.e., from trustee to trustee) from a Section 457 plan to a governmental defined benefit plan and used to purchase permissive service credits. Likewise, a participant may use such directly transferred amounts to repay contributions or earnings that were previously refunded because of a forfeiture of service credit, under either the transferee plan or another Section 457 plan maintained by a governmental employer in the same state.[28]

7. Participants in an eligible Section 457 plan of a governmental employer may rollover distributions to an IRA or other eligible plan, under the same rules that apply to rollovers from qualified plans—see Chapter 14.[29] The direct rollover (direct trustee-to-trustee) provisions applicable to qualified plans also apply to governmental Section 457 plans.[30] In addition, participants in any eligible plan (including those of tax-exempt nongovernmental organizations) can roll over

a Section 457 plan distribution to another Section 457 plan without incurring income tax on the amount rolled over.[31]

ERISA REQUIREMENTS

Governmental employers and church-related organizations are not subject to ERISA. However, tax-exempt private employers will encounter the ERISA compliance problems discussed above.

ALTERNATIVES

Tax-exempt employers can adopt qualified pension and profit sharing plans for employees. In addition, certain tax-exempt organizations can adopt Section 403(b) plans that provide as good or better benefits for employees than a Section 457 plan (see Chapter 32, Tax Deferred Annuity).

Tax-exempt organizations (but not governmental entities) can adopt 401(k) plans (see Chapter 19).[32] Also, tax-exempt employers and governmental entities are permitted to maintain SIMPLE IRA plans,[33] and tax-exempt organizations (but not governmental entities) are permitted to maintain SIMPLE 401(k) plans.[34] (See Chapter 30, Simple IRAs).

Governmental employers can also adopt governmental pension plans similar to qualified private plans. However, since the Section 403(b) type of plan is not available to governmental employers (except state and local governments with respect to employees performing services for public schools), such employers are more likely to use Section 457 plans to supplement a pension plan (see Chapter 32, Tax Deferred Annuity).

The design of nonqualified deferred compensation plans for top management employees of governmental and tax-exempt employers is discussed in the Frequently Asked Questions section.

HOW TO INSTALL A PLAN

A written plan containing the provisions described above should be adopted. Also, forms must be furnished to employees to carry out any salary reduction elections. For tax-exempt private employers subject to ERISA, the same ERISA requirements applicable to nonqualified deferred compensation will apply. These are discussed in Chapter 33.

WHERE CAN I FIND OUT MORE?

1. *Tax Facts on Insurance & Employee Benefits*, Cincinnati, OH: The National Underwriter Co. (revised annually).

2. O'Meara and Anderson, "Section 457 Plans," *Journal of Pension Planning and Compliance*, 1992.

FREQUENTLY ASKED QUESTIONS

Question – How can a governmental or tax-exempt employer provide a substantial deferred compensation benefit for an executive or key employee for whom the annual dollar limit would be inadequate?

Answer – The following statutory provisions would allow deferred compensation beyond the annual dollar limit, and planners should investigate these where executive compensation plans are desired.

Grandfathered plans. Grandfather provisions applicable to Section 457 may preserve some existing deferred compensation plans. These grandfather provisions apply to nonelective and elective plans. In the case of *governmental employers*, Section 457 does not apply to nonelective deferred compensation that was deferred before July 14, 1988, or to amounts deferred on or after that date under a written agreement in effect on July 14, 1988 that provided for deferral of a fixed amount or under a fixed formula. For nonelective plans of *nongovernmental tax-exempt employers*, the effective date is apparently January 1, 1988.[35]

Nonemployee plans. Nonelective deferred compensation plans for nonemployees—for example, doctors working for hospitals as independent contractors—are not subject to Section 457. However, for this exception to apply, all such nonemployees (other than those who have not satisfied any applicable initial service requirement) must be treated the same under the plan, with no individual variations.[36]

"Ineligible" or Forfeitable plans. The most general provision that allows escape from the annual dollar limit is Section 457(f). Under this section, if an employee defers more than the annual dollar limit, the deferred amount is not necessarily taxed immediately; it is taxed in the first taxable year in which there is *no substantial risk of forfeiture*. Thus, if a deferred compensation plan has forfeiture provisions, amounts greater than the annual dollar limit can be deferred until the year in which the forfeiture provision lapses.

An extension of the forfeiture provision agreed to before it expires may be acceptable to extend deferral of taxation.[37] However, the IRS probably would not accept a plan with a "rolling" forfeiture—that is, a provision designed for regular annual extensions.

Example. An employer subject to Section 457 might provide supplemental deferred compensation to selected executives, in amounts greater than the annual dollar limit, with a provision that the amount deferred would not be payable unless the executive served a full term under a multi-year contract. Taxation on the amount deferred would not occur until the year in which each executive served the full term and the deferred amounts became nonforfeitable.

The IRS has approved forfeitable deferred compensation plans of this type for employers subject to Section 457,[38] and this should be considered an appropriate technique of executive compensation for governmental and nonprofit employers.

A major problem in designing such plans is to develop forfeiture provisions that are substantial enough to defer taxes (see Chapter 35), but are nevertheless acceptable to the executive. Another major design problem occurs at retirement. In general, it is very difficult to design a bona fide, substantial forfeiture provision that extends past the executive's retirement. Consequently, Section 457(f) amounts generally are taxable in full no later than the year of the executive's retirement. If deferral past retirement is essential, other techniques, such as equity-type split dollar plans, might be investigated.

Note also that Section 457(f) plans are subject to the restrictions of Code Section 409A distribution and other rules (see Chapter 33).

Severance pay plans. A bona fide severance pay arrangement is not subject to the Section 457 limits.[39] See Chapter 4.

Question – What constitutes an unforeseeable emergency that would permit distributions from a Section 457 plan?

Answer – The current regulations under Section 457 define unforeseeable emergency as severe financial hardship to the participant resulting from a sudden and unexpected illness or accident of the participant or a dependent, a loss of property due to casualty, or other similar extraordinary and unforeseeable circumstances arising as a result of events beyond the control of the participant.[40]

The regulations specifically mention that the purchase of a residence or college education of children is not considered an unforeseeable emergency. Any amount distributed from the plan as the result of an emergency cannot exceed the amount reasonably needed to satisfy the emergency.

CHAPTER ENDNOTES

1. I.R.C. §§457(e)(1), 457(e)(13).
2. I.R.C. §457(e)(15).
3. I.R.C. §402(g)(3)(D). See PLR 2009-34012 (20 April 2009).
4. I.R.C. §457(e)(5).
5. I.R.C. §414(v)(2)(B)(i).
6. I.R.C. §414(v)(6)(C).
7. I.R.C. §457(b)(3).
8. I.R.C. §457(b)(3).
9. I.R.C. §457(e)(18).
10. I.R.C. §457(b)(4); Treas. Reg. §1.457-2(g).
11. I.R.C. §§457(b)(5), 457(d)(1).
12. After December 31, 2001, distributions may be made upon "severance from employment," rather than upon "separation from service." I.R.C. §457(d)(1)(A)(ii), as amended by EGTRRA 2001 §646. Under prior law, a Section 457 plan (like a 401(k) plan) could not make amounts available before the earliest of: (1) the calendar year in which the participant attains age 70½; (2) the date when the participant separates from service; or (3) the date when the participant is faced with "an unforeseeable emergency." The "same desk rule" (which is also applicable to 401(k) plans) provides that an employee is not considered to have separated from service when he continues on the same job for a different employer as a result of a liquidation, merger, consolidation, or similar event involving his former employer. A severance from employment occurs when a participant ceases to be employed by the employer sponsoring the plan. An employee may experience a severance of employment without experiencing a separation from service.

13. I.R.C. §401(a)(31)(B).
14. EGTRRA 2001 §657(d); 29 CFR Part 2550, RIN 1210-AA92, 69 Fed. Reg. 58018 (September 28, 2004).
15. I.R.C. §457(e)(9).
16. I.R.C. §§457(b)(5), 457(d)(1)(B), 457(d)(2). For distributions prior to 2002, Section 457 plans are also subject to special distribution rules under I.R.C. §457(d)(2), prior to amendment by EGTRRA 2001.
17. The qualified plan rules regarding QDROs under Section 414(p) apply to Section 457 plans for years beginning after December 31, 2001, so that a Section 457 plan will not violate the restrictions on distributions under Section 457(d) by making a QDRO distribution. I.R.C. §414(p). Under prior law, such distributions were not permitted.
18. See DOL News Release 86-527, [September 1985 – December 1987 transfer binder] Pens. Plan. Guide (CCH) ¶23,720C.
19. Priv. Ltr. Rul. 9008043.
20. See Treas. Reg. §1.457-1(c).
21. The IRS has recognized this "catch 22"–that a plan subject to Title I of ERISA will not be able to satisfy the Code's requirement that the plan be unfunded. See Notice 87-13, 1987-1 CB 432, at 444, Q&A-25; Priv. Ltr. Rul. 8950056. Section 457 plans for nongovernmental tax-exempt organizations are generally subject to Title I of ERISA unless they are structured to take advantage of specific exemptions from ERISA coverage. DOL News Release 86-527, [September 1985 – December 1987 transfer binder] Pens. Plan. Guide (CCH) ¶23,720C. The most significant exemptions are for (1) top-hat plans (i.e., unfunded plans maintained primarily for the purpose of providing deferred compensation for a select group of management or highly compensated employees); and for (2) unfunded excess benefit plans (i.e., unfunded plans maintained solely for the purpose of providing benefits for certain employees in excess of the limitations imposed by Code section 415). See ERISA Sections 3(36), 4(b)(5), 201(2), 301(a)(3), 401(a)(1), 503. Unless a Section 457 plan for a nongovernmental tax-exempt organization is structured to take advantage of an ERISA exemption, it will be subject to ERISA and will probably be unable to satisfy the Code's requirement that the plan be unfunded.
22. I.R.C. §457(g).
23. For taxable years ending after December 31, 2001, the Internal Revenue Service has stated that it will no longer treat or accept the P.S. 58 rates as a proper measure of current life insurance protection for federal tax purposes. Instead, taxpayers may use Table 2001 (see Chapter 18) to determine the value of current life insurance protection on a single life provided under a qualified retirement plan.
24. I.R.C. §25B.
25. I.R.C. §457(a). For distributions made before 2002, a participant or beneficiary in any eligible Section 457 plan must include deferred compensation (and income thereon) in gross income for the tax year in which it is paid or otherwise made available. I.R.C. §457(a), prior to amendment by EGTRRA 2001.
26. I.R.C. §457(f).
27. I.R.C. §402(e)(4)(D)(i).
28. This rule is effective for transfers made after December 31, 2001. I.R.C. §457(e)(17).
29. I.R.C. §457(e)(16).
30. I.R.C. §457(d)(1)(C).
31. I.R.C. §457(e)(10).
32. I.R.C. §401(k)(4)(B).
33. I.R.C. §408(p); see also Notice 98-4, 1998-2 IRB 25.
34. I.R.C. §401(k)(4)(B); I.R.C. §408(p).
35. Section 1107 of the Tax Reform Act of 1986 extended Section 457 to apply to nongovernmental tax-exempt organizations effective after 1986, but in Section 1107(c)(3)(B), a grandfather provision exempted nonelective plans that were in writing on August 16, 1986, so long as they remain unmodified. Section 6064(d)(3) of the Technical and Miscellaneous Revenue Act of 1988 extended the grandfather provision to plans of governmental organizations, with an effective date of July 14, 1988. Letter Ruling 9629022 appears to indicate that the IRS's position is that the grandfathering date is January 1, 1988 for nonelective plans of nongovernmental tax-exempt organizations. See also Notice 88-8, indicating that the IRS would not enforce Section 457 for nonelective deferred compensation plans for taxable years of employees beginning before January 1, 1988. Since the Letter Ruling applies only to the taxpayer on whose behalf the ruling was issued and because it addressed only *nonelective* plans, a cautious practitioner must remain mindful of the August 16, 1986 date for elective plans of nongovernmental, tax-exempt clients.
36. I.R.C. §457(e)(12).
37. Compare Priv. Ltr. Rul. 9431021 (postponing vesting date of restricted stock would not trigger taxation of stock as long as future services required of employee were and would continue to be substantial). This ruling has generated some controversy. See, e.g., the comments of Thomas A. Brisendine, Branch 2 Chief of the Office of Associate Counsel, Employee Benefits/Exempt Organizations in 22 Pens. & Ben. Rep. (BNA) 1099-1100 (1995).
38. See, e.g., Priv. Ltr. Ruls. 9429007, 9008059, 8831022. Letter Ruling 9008059 involved a nonprofit (Section 501(c)) employer that had *two* Section 457 plans, both maintained only for a select group of management and highly compensated employees (the top hat group). Plan One provided benefits within the $7,500 limits (and had graduated vesting) while Plan Two provided supplemental additional benefits that were forfeited if employment was terminated prior to normal retirement age for reasons other than death or disability.
39. I.R.C. §457(e)(11).
40. Treas. Reg. §1.457-6.

DESIGNING THE RIGHT HEALTH BENEFIT PLAN

CHAPTER 35

INTRODUCTION

Health care plans are among the most popular and important employee benefits and are expected to remain so, particularly in view of the aging of the population. However, the design of these plans is in a state of great change. Employers are faced with problems associated with both the rising costs of medical procedures and an aging work force. In addition, employers must deal with new requirements under the Patient Protection and Affordable Care Act and other related new legislation (all of which will be referred to here as the Affordable Care Act for simplicity). The Affordable Care Act mandates sweeping changes in the health insurance area, including employer health care plans for employees. These new rules are phased in over the period from 2011 to 2018. The article at the end of this chapter briefly explains the rules for employers, and there is a chart showing the timing of the phase-in of these rules.

The purpose of this chapter is to provide a broad outline for the design of an appropriate health care plan, based on the planning tools discussed in detail in later chapters.

WHAT HEALTH BENEFITS DO EMPLOYEES WANT?

The first step in adopting a new benefit design or changing an existing design is to make a preliminary determination of the types of health benefits that will be most valued by employees. In smaller firms, this can often be done by personal interviews and management's personal knowledge of the company's employees. Larger firms often use questionnaires designed by benefit consultants.

The make-up of the employee group may provide some typical responses. For example, a younger work force will typically want to maximize benefits for childbirth and pediatric care, while an older work force will want adequate coverage for major medical expenses. However, employers should not simply accept generalizations, but should make an effort to determine what employees actually want.

Where there is a wide variety in the health care needs perceived by the employees, designers should consider making use of the tools that allow employees to choose the benefits provided by the employer's dollars. Some of these tools are discussed in detail in other chapters in this book:

- Flexible Spending Accounts—Chapter 38
- Health Savings Accounts—Chapter 39
- Cafeteria Plans—Chapter 40

PLAN DESIGN FEATURES

In designing a health insurance plan to provide appropriate benefits, three aspects are vitally important:

1. Efficient delivery of the benefits.
2. Meeting the employer's cost constraints.
3. Positive employee perception of the plan.

Employers should consider plans designed along the lines of traditional health insurance, as discussed in Chapter 36, as well as alternatives, such as Health Maintenance Organizations, which are also addressed in Chapter 36. But modern benefit design requires consideration of a much broader range of options.

For many years, health care costs increased faster than the rate of inflation. Although the rate of increase has slowed somewhat recently, it is expected that this trend will continue. While employees expect health care coverage as a standard employee benefit, they are naturally resistant to accepting less cash compensation in return for health benefits. Thus, employers are coming under increasing cost pressures in this area. Employee resistance may be diminished by education in health care economics and tax policy. This is illustrated by the success of premium conversion plans (discussed in Chapter 40).

Traditional health insurance plans (discussed in Chapter 36) are *postpaid* plans—that is, plans that reimburse (or pay directly) *after* the employee has independently chosen a physician or other provider and undergone the medical or other procedure. Although there are methods for designing cost controls into such plans, with traditional health insurance the fundamental "levers" of cost control are outside the employer's control.

In the past decade, the concept of managed health care has become an accepted and familiar option in the design of health care plans. Managed health care is a broad concept, aimed at getting the basic cost management into the hands of employers—the people who pay for the product. Managed health care includes the use of prepaid health care plans, such as HMOs (discussed in Chapter 36). However, the concept is a broader one that can use a variety of delivery methods for health care services.

In designing health care plans, employers and benefit specialists must consider managed health care concepts. There is no one type of plan that can be described as a managed health care plan. Managed health care is a set of tools and techniques that can be used to design a health care plan to meet employer—and also employee—needs and cost requirements. This procedure also must now consider the requirements of the Affordable Care Act that will become applicable over the next several years.

Tools and Techniques for Managed Health Care

Designers of modern health care plans for employers should consider one or more of the following recognized health care management tools and techniques:

1. *Prospective pricing*. A prospective price for health care services is one that is negotiated by the employer (or by a provider or consultant on behalf of the employer) *before* the year in which the health services will be provided to covered employees.

   An HMO is an example of this type of pricing. However, prospective pricing can be used in other types of health care arrangements, such as a Preferred Provider Organization (PPO). A PPO is a group of providers with whom an employer negotiates per-unit charges for various types of health services. Employees covered under the employer's health plan are channeled or steered toward these providers, usually by providing a lower employee share of the cost if the employee uses the PPO members.

   Why would a health care provider be willing to agree to prospective pricing? Apart from cost pressures that are causing consumers to increasingly demand such arrangements, there is a potential benefit to the doctor, hospital, medical group, or other provider in prospective pricing. While prospective pricing requires the health care provider to assume the risk of cost overruns, the provider also gets the benefit of cost savings not anticipated. And since prospective pricing creates incentives to keep costs down, it can contribute to reducing or slowing health care cost inflation in the long run.

2. *Negotiated discounts*. As either a supplement or an alternative to prospective pricing, employers can negotiate to obtain health services at discounted prices. For example, a hospital might agree to charge the covered employees 75 percent of the hospital's usual and customary rate for hospitalization. However, if the hospital raises its usual and customary rates over the period of the agreement, the amount charged under the plan also goes up, with the discount in effect, so costs are not absolutely controlled.

3. *Channeling*. In order to maximize the benefit of negotiated and prepaid rates, employees must be encouraged, as much as possible, to utilize providers who operate under these rate agreements. HMOs and PPOs are examples of health care delivery systems that involve channeling. Channeling can also be provided in plan design by providing more favorable cost sharing for utilization of the preferred providers.

4. *Bundling of services*. If a health plan agrees to a per-diem room and board rate with a hospital and the hospital becomes dissatisfied with its revenues during the term of the agreement, there is an incentive for the hospital to try to make up its losses on room charges by increasing pharmacy, laboratory, and other ancillary charges. *Bundling* is a concept designed to avoid this type of "end run" around a pricing agreement. The price negotiated with a provider for a given type of services is arranged to cover the broadest possible range of services connected with a hospital stay or other covered medical event. For example, the agreement would provide a specified price for all hospital charges for a patient whose gall bladder is removed.

5. *Capitation payment*. Under traditional contracts, health care providers have a built-in incentive to maximize utilization, since they get paid only when a procedure is actually done. One cost-saving answer is a *capitation* payment—a flat monthly or periodic fee to the provider per plan participant, regardless of the number of procedures the provider actually performs. This helps remove the financial incentive to order tests and procedures that are of relatively little benefit to the patient. Moreover, a simple capitation payment agreement can eliminate the need for complicated fee negotiations in many situations.

6. *Peer review*. Peer review is a concept under which a decision to perform medical or surgical procedures on a patient is reviewed by professional colleagues of the physician or provider who first sees the patient. Peer review is built into group practice systems, such as HMOs and clinics. Its importance in health benefit plan design lies in the recognition that a large number of medical and surgical procedures currently being performed are unnecessary—unnecessary, that is, in the view of the medical profession itself. Peer review helps to avoid unnecessary procedures, and thus plays an important role in controlling costs.

7. *Utilization review*. Utilization review is similar to peer review, but is more specifically targeted. An example of utilization review is a requirement in an employer's health benefit plan that covered employees must obtain a second surgeon's opinion in order to be covered for (or to receive full coverage for) specified surgical procedures. These specified procedures are typically those most likely to be recommended unnecessarily.

8. *Quality review*. The quality review concept attempts to insure that health services provided to employees meet minimum quality levels and, thus, do not simply lead to further medical costs. With quality review, the employer's health plan provides full coverage only for facilities that meet minimum requirements, professional groups with minimum credentials, or procedures that follow established medical norms.

9. *Cost sharing*. Cost sharing by requiring deductibles and copayment is a familiar method of holding down an employer's health insurance costs. Currently, good plan design involves creative use of these devices to actually *encourage* employees to use alternative, lower cost methods of providing equivalent health care. For example, the plan should provide an equal or higher employer share for outpatient services than for equivalent inpatient hospital services, so that the plan does not discourage utilization of less costly outpatient alternatives.

10. *Lifestyle management*. The employer should develop programs that encourage employees to stay healthy—an obvious way to reduce health care costs. Exercise programs, weight-loss, and no-smoking programs, in addition to many others, can be considered.

Defined Contribution Health Plans

An emerging trend in health care plans is the defined contribution health plan. The term defined contribution is used to describe various health plan models. What they all have in common, however, is that they shift the payment and selection functions from employers to employees. Most of these defined contribution models could be provided within the existing employer-provided health insurance system, through the use of cafeteria plans or otherwise. But they could also be structured to allow employees to purchase health insurance directly from carriers, and some have suggested that they may even result in new forms of risk pooling for health care services. Employers are attracted to defined contribution health plan models because they are perceived as permitting employers to avoid future legislation, regulations, and litigation, that is expected to result from the public's growing disenchantment with managed care, and thus enable the employer to control health care cost increases. These models also dovetail nicely with the trend of giving workers more control over their benefits, as illustrated by the growth in 401(k) plans.

The Health Savings Account (HSA) is a fairly recent development by which the government encourages the use of the defined contribution approach to health plans. With an HSA, the employee is covered under a high deductible health insurance contract and the employee makes contributions (or the employer makes contributions on behalf of the employee) to an IRA-like account that is used to pay for medical expenses. HSAs are discussed further in Chapter 39, which includes a chart comparing HSAs with other alternative methods of providing health insurance.

Health Benefits for Executives

Does the employer want to provide health benefits for selected executives over and above benefits provided for employees in general? Congress's first attempt to impose such rules, Code section 89, proved unworkable and was repealed. Currently, PPACA requires insured group plans to meet nondiscrimination requirements that formerly applied only to uninsured arrangements, with an exception for certain existing ("grandfathered") plans. The options for executive health plans are discussed in Chapter 37.

SMALL BUSINESS HEALTH PLAN TAX CREDIT

An eligible small business can receive a tax credit for part of the cost of health care for its employees.[1] Form 8941 is filed to claim the credit.

Eligibility

- The plan must pay a uniform percentage of at least 50 percent of the cost of health care coverage for covered workers.

- The employer must have fewer than twenty-five full-time workers or equivalent (e.g., fifty half-time workers). Owners or family members are not counted for this purpose.

- The average wage for employees must be less than $50,000; owners and family members' compensation is generally not included for this purpose.[2]

Amount of Credit

- The credit is an amount up to 35 percent (25 percent for tax-exempt employers) of the cost of health care for employees. This rate increases to 50 percent (35 percent for tax-exempts) in 2014 and thereafter.

- The maximum credit applies to firms with fewer than ten workers and phases out as the number of workers increases, up to twenty-five workers.

- The credit phases out for average wages between $25,000 and $50,000.

PLAN DESIGN AND MAINTENANCE

Designing and maintaining a health benefit plan has the following components:

- Plan design
- Communication with employees
- Financing the plan
- Claims administration
- Claims payment
- Periodic plan review and updating
- Compliance with federal and state regulatory requirements

There are many ways to split responsibilities for these various plan components. A very large corporation may perform all of these responsibilities itself, while at the other extreme, a small employer might delegate all of them to a traditional health insurer.

Increasingly, however, specialized organizations have become available to carry out specific responsibilities in the most cost-effective manner. For example, there are many independent firms that contract to do claims administration for employers or insurers. Similarly, plan design is often done by specialized benefit consulting firms that do not take on any of the other responsibilities, although often they recommend organizations for this purpose.

For the employer, finding the right people and organizations for these responsibilities can be as important to the cost-effective delivery and positive perception of benefits as plan design itself.

AFFORDABLE CARE ACT

The following is a brief summary of the significant parts of the Affordable Care Act and related legislation that may affect employers who have or are considering adoption of a health benefit plan for their employees. In general, Act provisions that primarily affect insurance companies or individuals are not covered here. Figure 35.1 outlines the timeline of implementations of various parts of the ACA, the most important of which are discussed in detail below. A complete discussion of all these extensive changes is beyond the scope of this book.

Definitions

Note some definitions that are applicable to items in the timetable:

Grandfathered Plan - A plan with at least one participant enrolled on March 23, 2010. The plan can admit new entrants without losing grandfather status. Regulations indicate how much other change can be made to the plan without losing grandfather status. Starred (*) requirements in Figure 35.1 below do not apply to grandfathered plans.

Essential Benefits - Ambulatory patient services; emergency care services; hospitalization; maternity and newborn care; mental health and substance abuse disorder services; prescription drugs; rehabilitative and habilitative services & devices; laboratory services; preventive and wellness services and chronic disease management; pediatric services, including oral and vision care.

Employer Mandate - Applies to employers with an average of fifty or more full-time employees (defined as employees who average thirty or more hours weekly). There is no actual mandate, but rather a penalty that is imposed on any covered employer who (a) does not offer minimum essential benefits or offers such coverage only on an unaffordable basis or (b) has at least one full-time employee who qualifies for federal premium assistance for coverage through an exchange.

Individual Mandate - Every individual must obtain minimum essential health insurance coverage. An individual's existing employer-sponsored or individual plans may qualify for this requirement. If not, the individual must obtain coverage; federal premium subsidies are available based on income. States may establish exchanges under which individuals or small employers may purchase insurance at group rates. If a state does not establish an exchange individuals and small employers may purchase from a federal exchange for that state. The exchanges may be made available to both small and large employers in 2017 and thereafter.

Individual Mandate

Beginning in 2014, individuals are required to obtain minimum essential health coverage for themselves and their dependents or pay a monthly penalty tax for each month without coverage. The monthly penalty tax is one-twelfth of the greater of the dollar penalty or gross income penalty amounts. The dollar penalty is an amount per individual of:

- $95 for 2014 (capped at $285 per family)
- $325 for 2015 (capped at $975 per family)
- $695 for 2016 (capped at $2085 per family)

These dollar penalties will be indexed for inflation starting in 2017.

The gross income penalty is a percentage of household income in excess of a specified filing threshold of:

- 1 percent for 2014
- 2 percent for 2015
- 2.5 percent for 2016 and later

In no event will the maximum penalty amount exceed the national average premium for bronze-level exchange plans for families of the same size.

Figure 35.1

AFFORDABLE CARE ACT IMPLEMENTATION

Provisions Already Implemented			
Effective in 2011 and earlier	*Effective in 2012*	*Effective in 2013*	*Effective in 2014*
• For essential benefits, a plan may place no annual limits that are less than $750,000 for 2011, $1.25 million for 2012; and $2 million for 2013, with some exceptions • No lifetime limits on essential benefits • No recission of benefits except for fraud or misrepresentation • No preexisting condition exclusions for participants under age 19 • Coverage must extend to adult children up to age 26 • HSA, HRA, or FSA cannot reimburse for over-the-counter drugs • Plan must allow choice of pediatrician, gynecologist, and obstetrician without referral* • Emergency services must be covered without preauthorization and must be treated as in-network* • Internal appeal and external review provisions required* • Must cover immunization and preventive care without cost-sharing*	• Prescribed summary of coverage and benefits must be provided • Reporting requirements to Dept. of Health and Human Services (HHS) go into effect* • Group health plans must provide recommended preventive health services without cost sharing and must adjust the services covered in accordance with changes to recommended preventive services guidelines*	• Health FSAs limited to $2,500 annually (see Chapter 38) • Medicare Part D subsidy repealed • For employers issuing at least 250 W-2s, W-2s for tax years 2012 and beyond must show employer and employee payments for certain health care items[3]	• Individual mandate applicable • State and federal exchanges open for individuals and small employers • No annual limits on essential benefits • Out of pocket expenses limited to $6,350 per individual and $12,770 per family except for "separately administered" benefits • No preexisting condition exclusions for any participant • Waiting period for group coverage limited to ninety days • No discrimination based on health status* • No discrimination on health care providers acting within the scope of their license* • Coverage for clinical trials mandated*
New Provisions			
Effective in 2015	*Effective in 2016*	*Effective in 2017*	*Effective in 2018*
• Employer mandate applies to employers with 100 or more employees • Out-of-pocket expenses limits are $6,600 for self only coverage and $13,200 for other than self-only coverage* • HDHP limits are $6,450 for individuals and $12,900 for families • IRS Form 6055 reporting minimum essential coverage provided in 2015 (due 1/31/2016) • No discrimination in favor of highly compensated employees*†	• Employer mandate applies to employers with 50 to 99 employees who meet certain conditions, though employer contributions may be based on 2014 levels	• Employer mandate standardized for all employers with 50 or more employees • Large employers may purchase coverage from the exchanges	• 40% "Cadillac Tax" on high-cost plans—a 40% excise tax on plan costs that exceed $10,200 annually for self-only coverage, or $27,500 for family coverage. These amounts are indexed for inflation.

*: Provision does not apply to grandfathered plans.
†: The health plan nondiscrimination rules are dependent on IRS adoption of regulations, which has not occurred at the time of print.

Minimum essential coverage includes Medicare, Medicaid, CHIP, TRICARE, individual insurance, grandfathered plans, and eligible employer-sponsored plans. Workers compensation and limited-scope dental or vision benefits are not considered minimum essential health coverage.

Individuals can demonstrate that they have complied with the individual mandate by filing Form 6055 outlining the coverage provided by their employers starting in 2015.

Employer Mandate

Starting in 2015 Employers with one hundred or more full-time equivalent (FTE) employees will be required to offer their full-time employees (FTEs) minimum essential health coverage or pay a fine of up to $2,000 per year for each FTE in excess of thirty FTEs if any employee receives a premium tax credit on a state health insurance exchange.

If an employer provides minimum essential health coverage to its FTEs, but fails to pay at least 60 percent of its actuarial value or the coverage is considered unaffordable (costs more than 9.5 percent of household income), then the employer must pay a penalty of up to $3,000 per year for each FTE who receives the premium credit on an exchange, but not more than would be owed for the $2,000 per year penalty. An FTE is defined as an employee who is employed for thirty or more hours per week, calculated on a forty-hour work week. This provision also applies to grandfathered plans.[4]

If employer has on average one hundred or more Full-Time (including full-time equivalents) Employees and fails to offer coverage to a full-time employee for any day of a calendar month, that employee is treated as not having been offered coverage during the entire month.[5]

Employers with Fiscal Year Health Plans

The employer mandate retains it's effective of January 1, 2015. However, employers with non-calendar (fiscal) year plans can be subject to the mandate based on the start of their 2015 plan year rather than on January 1, 2015, and other transition relief where certain conditions are met, as follows:

1. *Pre-2015 Fiscal Year Plan Eligibility Transition Relief*. Pre-2015 eligibility transition relief applies to employees, whenever hired, who are:

   a. eligible for coverage on the first day of the 2015 plan year under the eligibility terms of the plan as of February 9, 2014 (whether or not they elected coverage); and

   b. offered affordable coverage that provides minimum value effective no later than the first day of the 2015 plan year.

   Where these two conditions are satisfied, the employer will not be subject to a potential employer shared responsibility payment until the first day of the 2015 plan year. This relief applies only to employees to whom coverage was previously offered by the employer. Thus, penalties may still be imposed for the months in 2015 that are part of the plan year commencing in 2014 for employees to whom coverage was not previously offered.

2. *Significant Percentage Fiscal Year Plan Transition Relief (all employees)*. No employer mandate penalty applies for any month before the first day of the plan year beginning in 2015 for employees who are offered affordable coverage that provides minimum value by the first day of the 2015 plan year if as of any date in the twelve months ending on February 9, 2014, an employer:

   a. covers at least one-quarter of its employees (full-time and part-time) under its non-calendar year plan; or

   b. offered coverage under the plan to one-third or more of its employees during the open enrollment period that ended most recently before February 9, 2014.

   To qualify for this relief, the employee must not have been eligible for coverage as of February 9, 2014 under any group health plan maintained by his or her employer that has a calendar year plan year.

   Unlike the pre-2015 eligibility transition relief discussed above, an employer that qualifies for this relief and who offers affordable, minimum value coverage commencing with the 2015 plan year has no Code section 4980H exposure for periods before the 2015 plan year. Relief under this and the next transition rule applies for the period before the first day of the first non-calendar year plan year beginning in 2015 but only for employers that maintained non-calendar year plans as of December 27, 2012, and only if the plan year was not modified after December 27, 2012, to begin at a later calendar date.

70 Percent Offer in 2015

For 2015 (and for any calendar months during a non-calendar year plan year beginning in 2015 that fall in 2016), the 95 percent offer of coverage threshold is lowered to 70 percent. Thus, in 2015, an employer will be in compliance if employer offers coverage to at least 70 percent of full-time employees and dependents in 2015 (unless the employer qualifies for the 2015 dependent coverage transition relief, discussed below), although an employer will owe penalty if at least one of the full-time employees receives a premium tax credit for coverage in the public marketplace, which may occur because the employer did not offer coverage to that employee or because the coverage the employer offered was either unaffordable or did not provide minimum value.

Dependent Coverage

In order to avoid exposure for the employer mandate penalty, an employer must offer coverage not only to full-time employees but also their dependents (but not spouses). The final regulations provide transition relief to plan years that begin in 2015 if the employer takes steps during the 2015 plan year toward satisfying this requirement in 2016. The transition relief applies to employers for the 2015 plan year for plans under which:

- dependent coverage is not offered;
- dependent coverage that does not constitute minimum essential coverage is offered; or
- dependent coverage is offered for some, but not all, dependents.

This relief is not available, however, if the employer had offered dependent coverage during either the plan year that begins in 2013 or the 2014 plan year and subsequently eliminated that offer of coverage.

Small Employers

Employers with between fifty and ninety-nine FTEs have a one-year delay in the employer mandate, until January 1, 2016 (and for non-calendar-year plans, any calendar months during the plan year beginning in 2015 that fall in 2016) if:

1. the employer certifies it did not lay off employees during the period beginning on February 9, 2014 and ending on Dec. 31, 2014 to fall below the one-hundred-employee threshold and that employer did not reduce any coverage it was already offering; and

2. during the period beginning on February 9, 2014 and ending on Dec. 31, 2014, employer does not eliminate or materially reduce the health coverage, if any, offered as of February 9, 2014. An employer will not be treated as eliminating or materially reducing health coverage if, for each employee who is eligible for coverage on February 9, 2014:

    a. the employer offers to make a contribution toward the cost of employee-only coverage that is either:

        i. at least 95 percent of the dollar amount of the contribution the employer was making toward the coverage in effect as of February 9, 2014; or

        ii. at least the same percentage of the cost of coverage that the employer offered to contribute toward coverage in effect as of February 9, 2014;

    b. benefits offered as of February 9, 2014 at the employee-only coverage level does not change, or, if it does, the coverage after the change provides minimum value; and

    c. eligibility under the employer's group health plans is not amended to narrow or reduce the class or classes of employees (or the employees' dependents) to whom coverage under those plans was offered as of February 9, 2014.

Note that small employers that qualify under the above requirements must still report coverage provided to employees for 2015.

Reporting Requirements

All employers providing minimum essential coverage must file information with the IRS and plan participants.[6] (Effective for calendar years beginning on and after Jan. 1, 2015, after one-year delay.)

Large employers and employers with at least fifty full-time equivalent employees must submit annual health insurance coverage returns to the FTEs and the IRS. The returns must certify whether the employer offers healthcare insurance to its employees and, if so, describe the details regarding plan participation, applicable waiting periods, coverage availability, the lowest cost premium option under the plan in each enrollment category, and other information.[7]

Out-of-pocket Expense Limits

Healthcare reform's requirement that health insurance individual and small group plans cap how much consumers must pay out-of-pocket each year for medical care will take effect as scheduled in 2014 for some and 2015 for others.

For 2014 and thereafter, the health reform law requires that private insurance plans offered in the individual and small group markets[8] limit how much in cost-sharing charges — deductibles, copayments, and coinsurance — that people enrolled in a plan must pay each year for covered benefits provided by the plan's network of health care providers. The requirement does not apply to "grandfathered" plans or to self-insured employer plans, large group employer plans, or large group market insurers.[9]

In 2015, the maximum out-of-pocket limit will be $6,600 for an individual and $13,200 for a family (the same as for HSA compatible high deductible plans).[10] The deductible cannot exceed $2,000 for a plan covering a single individual or $4,000 for any other plan.[11]

The agencies interpret the annual deductible limit as applying only to employers and insurers in the individual and small group markets for non-grandfathered plans.[12] In the case of a plan using a network of providers, cost sharing paid by, or on behalf of, an individual for benefits provided outside of such network does not count toward the annual limitation on cost sharing or the annual limitation on deductibles.[13]

However, employer plans that have "separately administered" benefits, such as a primary package of health benefits and a different insurer or administrator for other benefits, such as prescription drugs, need not comply until 2015.[14] Employer plans with separately administered benefits that qualify for the delay must apply some out-of-pocket limits. These plans must ensure that their primary package of health benefits has an out-of-pocket limit of no more than $6,600 for individuals and $13,200 for families. A separately administered benefit, such as prescription drugs, that already has an existing limit on out-of-pocket costs must also comply with the limits of $6,600 for individuals and $13,200 for families in 2015.[15]

"Cadillac" Tax

Beginning in 2018, a 40 percent nondeductible excise tax is imposed on "coverage providers" that provide high-cost health care coverage to the employer's employees. Coverage providers include:

- the health insurer for fully insured plans
- the employer with respect to self-insured plans, HSA or Archer MSA contributions; and
- in all other cases, the "person that administers the plan."

The tax applies to "applicable employer-sponsored coverage," which is coverage under a group health plan:

1. that is made available to an employee by an employer; and
2. that either:
   a. is actually excludable from gross income under Code section 106, or
   b. would be excludable if it were employer-provided coverage within the meaning of Code section 106[16]

The excise tax is imposed on the "excess benefit" provided to the employees. There is no exception to the tax for grandfathered plans.

"Excess benefit" is determined by comparing the cost of the actual coverage provided (calculated using rules similar to those for determining COBRA premiums) that exceeds annual limits. For 2018, the annual limit for employee-only coverage is $10,200 per year (as adjusted by a "health cost adjustment percentage" or

HCAP) and $27,500 per year (as adjusted by the HCAP) for coverage other than employee-only.

The HCAP takes into account year-to-year increases in the cost of health care coverage, including increases attributable to age and gender differences.

WHERE CAN I FIND OUT MORE?

1. *2015 Healthcare Reform Facts*, National Underwriter, updated annually.
2. IRS, "Questions and Answers on Employer Shared Responsibility Provisions Under the Affordable Care Act"[17]

CHAPTER ENDNOTES

1. I.R.C. §45R.
2. I.R.C. §45R(e)(1).
3. I.R.C. §6051(a).
4. I.R.C. §4980H.
5. For January 2015, if an employer offers coverage to a full-time employee no later than the first day of the first payroll period that begins in January 2015, the employee will be treated as having been offered coverage for January 2015.
6. PPACA §1502; I.R.C. 6055.
7. PPACA §§1311(e)(3), 10104; PHSA §2715A; I.R.C. §5056.
8. A group health plan shall ensure that any annual cost sharing imposed under the plan does not exceed the limitations provided for under paragraphs (1) and (2) of section PPACA §1302(c).
9. "Standards Related to Essential Health Benefits, Actuarial Value, and Accreditation," 45 CFR Parts 147, 155, and 156, 78 Fed. Reg. 12834, 12837 (Feb. 25, 2013); Department of Labor, "FAQs About the Affordable Care Act Implementation Part XII," Q/A-1 available at: www.dol.gov/ebsa/faqs/faq-aca12.html.
10. PPACA §1302(c)(1)(A); I.R.C. §223(c)(2)(A)(ii).
11. PPACA §1302(c)(2)(A).
12. HHS Reg. §156.130(b); "Standards Related to Essential Health Benefits, Actuarial Value, and Accreditation," 45 CFR Parts 147, 155, and 156, 78 Fed. Reg. 12834, 12837 (Feb. 25, 2013).
13. HHS Reg. §156.130(c).
14. Department of Labor, "FAQs About the Affordable Care Act Implementation Part XII," Q/A-2, available at: www.dol.gov/ebsa/faqs/faq-aca12.html.
15. Id.
16. I.R.C. §4980I(d)(1)(A).
17. Available at: www.irs.gov/Affordable-Care-Act/Employers/Questions-and-Answers-on-Employer-Shared-Responsibility-Provisions-Under-the-Affordable-Care-Act.

GROUP HEALTH PLANS

CHAPTER 36

INTRODUCTION

Health insurance is the most common employee benefit. About 99 percent of large employers (those with over 200 employees) provide health insurance for employees, and about 59 percent of smaller employers,[1] Health insurance is widespread as an employee benefit not only because it meets a critical employee need, but also because it receives almost unique tax benefits. If the plan meets the rules discussed below, the entire cost is deductible to employers, but nothing is includable in employees' taxable income as a result of plan coverage or payment of plan benefits. Thus, health insurance is a completely tax-free form of employee compensation.

There are two main types of health insurance plans:

- prepaid plans, in which health care providers are paid in advance of providing services; and

- postpaid plans, which pay health care providers for services rendered, or reimburse employees for payments to providers.

The principal form of prepaid plans is the Health Maintenance Organization, or HMO. This chapter will focus primarily on postpaid plans, which are the traditional form of health insurance. See also Chapter 39, which discusses Health Savings Accounts (HSAs), a growing portion of the health insurance business.

Employer health insurance plans are significantly affected by the Affordable Care Act (PPACA), which President Obama signed into law, includes changes in various federal statutes including ERISA, the Internal Revenue Code, and others. The provisions of this law are phased in over several years through 2018. A chart summarizing the complete act and its effective dates is included in Chapter 35, "Designing the Right Health Care Plan."

Beginning in 2015, employers with an average of fifty or more full-time employees (thirty or more hours weekly) during the preceding calendar year will be subject to a penalty if they:

1. do not offer "minimum essential coverage" as defined by the Act to substantially all full-time employees or offers such coverage and it is unaffordable or does not provide minimum value; and

2. have at least one full-time employee who qualifies for federal premium assistance for coverage purchased through an exchange (described below).

There is a "grandfather" provision under which less stringent requirements (see Chapter 35) apply to a plan in existence on March 23, 2010. The plan can admit new entrants without losing grandfather status. Regulations indicate what changes can be made to the plan without losing grandfather status.

The central feature of the Affordable Care Act (PPACA) is the "individual mandate." Under this requirement, every individual must obtain minimum essential health insurance coverage. An individual's existing employer-sponsored or individual plans may qualify for this requirement. If not, the individual must obtain coverage; federal premium subsidies are available based on income.

States must establish "exchanges" under which individuals or small employers may purchase insurance at group rates. The exchanges may be made available to both small and large employers in 2017 and thereafter.

A complete discussion of the Affordable Care Act is beyond the scope of this book. A good reference is Alson Martin's, *Healthcare Reform Facts*, Cincinnati, OH, National Underwriter Company (updated annually).

PLAN DESIGN FEATURES

Health insurance plans provided by employers are usually complicated and may even be customized to some degree, particularly for larger employers. However, three fundamental types of plan design are usually identified: (1) the basic plan; (2) the major medical plan; and (3) the comprehensive plan.

Basic Plan

A basic plan primarily provides health care services that are connected with hospitalization. The types of benefits provided in a basic plan are:

1. *Inpatient hospital charges*, such as room and board, nursing care, supplies, and other hospital expenses.

2. *In-hospital visits by physicians.* Home or office visits are not covered in a basic plan.

3. *Surgical fees*, including surgeons' fees as well as anesthesiologists' and other surgical assistants' fees. These plans often cover fees for surgical procedures performed in a doctor's office or at an outpatient facility—not just those performed on patients admitted to a hospital.

Major Medical Plan

A major medical plan covers medical services excluded from basic plans. For this reason, it is sometimes referred to as a "supplemental major medical plan." Although the objective of the plan is to fill gaps in basic coverage, few plans cover all medical expenses. Routine doctors' office visits are usually excluded. Also, most plans do not cover dental, vision, and hearing care, although employers often provide these through separate plans.

Comprehensive Plan

The comprehensive type of plan combines the coverage of basic and major medical plans in a single plan. This is currently the dominant type of plan. Many employers have replaced basic and major medical plans with comprehensive plans.

ACA Essential Benefits

The new health care law includes a definition of "essential benefits" that will have an effect on plan design. Specifically, insured health plans in the individual and small group markets must include an "essential health benefits package" and employer-sponsored self-insured health plans, insured large group health plans, and grandfathered health plans are prohibited from imposing annual and lifetime dollar limits on any essential health benefits they offer. Essential benefits include:

- ambulatory patient services
- emergency services
- hospitalization
- maternity and newborn care
- mental health and substance abuse disorder services
- prescription drugs
- rehabilitative and habilitative services and devices
- laboratory services
- preventive and wellness services and chronic disease management
- pediatric services, including oral and vision care.[2]

These will be further defined by regulation.

BENEFIT STRUCTURE

Many health plans do not pay the full cost of covered benefits. Major medical and comprehensive plans in particular, but also some basic plans, use deductibles and coinsurance to reduce plan costs by requiring employees to share benefit costs.

Deductibles

A deductible is an amount of initial expense specified in the plan that is paid by the employee toward covered benefits. For example, if the plan has a $200 deductible, the participant pays the first $200 of covered expenses, and the plan covers the rest, up to a specified limit. Deductibles are usually computed annually.

> *Example.* If the deductible is $500 and a covered individual incurs $400 of doctors' bills covered under the plan between January and November, the plan does not pay anything. However, if the same individual incurs an additional covered medical expense of $200 in December, the $500 deductible will have been satisfied and the plan will pay the $100 in excess of the deductible.

Some plans have carryover provisions to avoid an unfair impact of the deductible. For instance, with a three-month carryover provision, medical bills incurred during the last three months of the year can be used toward the next year's deductible. Thus, if an individual has a serious illness in December and incurs a $1,000 medical expense, subsequent bills in January and thereafter will not be subject to another deductible.

Most deductibles are *all-causes* deductibles—that is, the deductible is cumulative over the year or other period, even though the medical bills may reflect many different illnesses or medical conditions. However, some plans have *per-cause* deductibles. Under a per-cause deductible, the deductible amount must be satisfied for each separate illness or other medical condition.

Most employee plans use a *per-family* deductible as well as individual deductibles to minimize the payment burden for families. For example, the plan may have a $200 per individual deductible, but also a provision under which the plan pays for all covered expenses in full when total expenses for all family members exceed $500.

Coinsurance

Under a coinsurance provision, the plan participant is responsible for a specified percentage, usually 20 percent, of covered expenses. For example, if a plan has a $100 deductible, and a participant incurs expenses of $1,100 during the year, the plan pays $800 of these and the participant pays the rest (the $100 deductible plus 20 percent of the remaining $1,000 of expenses).

The participant's 20 percent share can become burdensome quickly in the event of a major illness, so good plan design requires an upper dollar limit on the participant's share. The participant's costs are usually limited to several thousand dollars on an annual basis (called an out-of-pocket maximum).

Maximum Coverage Limits

Traditionally, many benefit plans had upper lifetime limits on the amount that the plan would pay for any one individual's medical expenses. However, under the ACA a group health plan or health insurance coverage may not have a lifetime or annual limit on essential benefits.

Finally, in designing cost-sharing provisions in health plans for future years, employers will have to consider the employer-mandate provisions that take effect in 2015. (See Figure 35.1 in Chapter 35 for a timeline of the implementation of the major ACA initiatives.) Broadly speaking, these impose penalties on plans that do not provide minimum essential coverage, or that are unaffordable to employees (generally, cost more than 9.56 percent of household income) or provide less than 60 percent of the total cost of benefits for any full-time employee.[3]

PLAN FUNDING

Employers fund postpaid-type health plans in one or a combination of three ways:

(1) commercial insurance company contracts;

(2) Blue Cross/Blue Shield contracts; and

(3) "self-funding" or self-insurance.

Commercial Insurers

A health insurance contract from a commercial insurance company usually provides reimbursement to employees for their expenses for covered medical procedures. Some insurers may pay health care providers directly, however. Reimbursement is usually limited to the "usual, customary, and reasonable" (UCR) charges for a given procedure in the employee's geographical area. Thus, an employee may not receive full reimbursement for a medical claim if the insurer's claims department considers the amount charged to be greater than the UCR amount.

Premiums for commercial health insurance contracts reflect six elements:

1. expected benefit payments;
2. administrative expenses;
3. commissions;
4. state premium taxes;
5. risk charges; and
6. return on the insurer's capital allocated to the contract (profit).

For groups of fifty employees or more, premiums are usually "experience-rated." That is, the insurer keeps separate records for the employer group and adjusts charges to reflect above- or below-average benefit utilization by the group itself.

Blue Cross/Blue Shield

Blue Cross and Blue Shield plans were originally designed by organizations of hospitals and physicians in order to facilitate the payment of hospital and doctor bills. Blue Cross and Blue Shield plans generally provide direct payment in full to "participating" hospitals and doctors for medical benefits provided to covered employees. A participating hospital or doctor is one that agrees to pre-established rates and billing schedules with Blue Cross or Blue Shield. If an employee is admitted to a hospital or uses a doctor that is not participating, the Blue Cross or Blue Shield plan pays or reimburses on a UCR basis.

Blue Cross and Blue Shield plans can be obtained by individuals as well as by employers. A basic principle of the "Blues" is to offer coverage to any individual who requests it and to provide terminating employees under an employer plan with the ability to convert to an individual product.

Blue Cross (for hospital bills) and Blue Shield (for doctors' bills) are nonprofit organizations operating within a given geographical area. However, they must meet standards prescribed by their national associations. Federal tax law provides that these organizations are taxed on a basis similar to insurance companies.

Self-Funding

With self-funding (self-insurance), the employer pays claims and other costs directly, either on a pay-as-you-go basis (that is, the employer pays claims out of current operating revenues as they are incurred by covered employees), or out of a reserve fund accumulated in advance. (However, as indicated below, the employer can accelerate its tax deductions for health and accident plans only to a limited extent, even if a fund is accumulated in advance.)

Self-funding can be combined with an insurance contract which provides "administrative services only" (an ASO contract). Also, the employer can obtain a "stop-loss" insurance contract, under which plan claims above a stated level are assumed by the insurer. This protects the employer against large unanticipated losses.

A self-funded plan should not be confused with a Health Reimbursement Arrangement (HRA). An HRA is a plan designed to supplement existing insured health plans and to provide special tax benefits. These plans are discussed in Chapter 37.

Health Maintenance Organization (HMO)

A Health Maintenance Organization, (HMO), is an organization of physicians or other health care providers that provides a broad and nearly complete range of health care services on a prepaid basis. An HMO is an alternative to traditional health insurance. Generally, the provisions of the Affordable Care Act apply to an employer plan that uses an HMO on the same basis as other types of health insurance.

As an alternative to traditional health insurance, HMOs are attractive to younger employees and employees with many dependents, because the HMO typically covers all medical expenses without significant deductibles or co-pay provisions. Where such employees are predominant in an employer's work force, the employer may get the most perceived value for its benefit dollar by offering an HMO, or choice of HMOs, as its health benefit plan.

The tax treatment of payments to HMOs and benefits received is the same as that for health insurance. Eligibility and coverage requirements, including the COBRA provisions, are also the same as for health insurance.

HMO Advantages

1. HMOs typically cover more health care services than traditional health insurance, with fewer deductibles and lower co-payments.

2. HMOs are said to emphasize preventive medicine, and thus control overall costs better than plans which pay only when employees are hospitalized or sick.

HMO Disadvantages

1. An HMO subscriber generally must receive care from a doctor or other service provider who is part of the HMO. Except for certain emergencies, the HMO will not pay for services of non-HMO providers.

2. The cost advantage, if any, of HMOs may be due to the fact that they enroll younger and healthier participants than traditional health insurance plans, which emphasize coverage for major medical procedures. In time, therefore, it is argued that the cost advantage of HMOs will diminish.

HMO Benefit Structure

Conventional health insurance reimburses employees for expenses or pays providers for health care as required by covered employees. By contrast, an HMO either employs the providers or contracts directly with providers (see the discussion below on types of HMOs). The providers agree to provide medical services to HMO subscribers when required, in return for an annual payment determined *in advance*. Each subscriber to the HMO (or employer who sponsors the plan) pays a fee based on the HMO's projected annual cost.

As a result of this arrangement, the HMO assumes the risk that services required will cost more than the annual payment. In other words, the HMO has an incentive to hold down the costs of health care to subscribers. In theory, these reduced costs will be passed along in the form of reduced costs to the HMO subscribers or to employers who pay for the plan.

HMO subscribers generally must use physicians and other health care providers who are part of the HMO contractual arrangement. Exceptions are usually allowed for emergency services out of the HMO's geographic area, and for medical specialties not available within the HMO, if referred by the primary HMO physician. In return for this reduction in freedom of choice, HMO plans provide for almost all health care services, including routine physician visits. Usually there are no deductibles. There may be a small co-payment fee for some services. For example, subscribers may be required to pay $10 for each visit to a doctor's office and $5 for each prescription.

Types of HMOs

HMOs are organized in one of three ways:

1. The *staff model* HMO is an HMO organization that directly employs doctors and other health care providers who provide the HMO's services to subscribers.

2. The *group practice* or medical group model involves contracts between the HMO and a medical group or groups that provide services to subscribers. The individual doctors and other providers are not directly employed by the HMO as an entity.

   Both staff model and group practice HMOs are sometimes referred to as *closed panel* plans, because subscribers must use doctors and other providers who are employed by the HMO or under contract to the HMO.

3. The *individual practice association* or IPA plan, under which the HMO is an association of individual doctors or medical groups that practice in their own offices. Most see non-HMO as well as HMO patients. These plans are often referred to as *open panel* plans, since HMO subscribers can choose any doctor who is part of the IPA. In some areas, many doctors participate in these plans, giving HMO subscribers a wide range of choice.

The structure of an HMO is relevant to an employer's benefit planning in that different types of HMOs may have varying attractiveness to employees. Many employees may be reluctant to give up their own doctors in order to sign up with an unfamiliar closed-panel type of HMO. On the other hand, the choice of doctors in a large IPA plan may be appealing. The IPA may even include some employees' own doctors already. So, an HMO affiliation may effectively change nothing from some employees' viewpoints except to drastically lower the cost of their doctor bills.

The appeal of HMOs in a given geographical area depends in large part on the local medical community's support of the HMO concept. If local doctors and hospitals, particularly the most prestigious ones, are in favor of HMOs, then many local health care providers will join HMOs. HMO subscribers will then have almost the same amount of choice as they would in a conventional insured plan.

ELIGIBILITY AND COVERAGE

Employer health insurance plans generally cover all employees. Employees are usually covered immediately upon being hired, or after a brief waiting period for coverage, which may not exceed ninety days under the ACA. Some employers maintain separate plans for collective bargaining unit employees or other identifiable groups.

Internal Revenue Code Eligibility and Coverage Requirements

The tax law provides certain requirements for employer group health plan coverage, subject to a penalty for noncompliance. Broadly, the requirements are:

1. Exclusion of participants for preexisting conditions is prohibited.[4]

2. Participants may not be excluded (or required to pay an extra premium) on the basis of:

    a. health status;

    b. medical condition (physical or mental);

    c. claims experience;

    d. receipt of health care;

    e. medical history;

    f. genetic information;

    g. evidence of insurability; or

    h. disability.[5]

3. The plan may not restrict benefits for any hospital length of stay in connection with childbirth for the mother or newborn child to less than forty-eight hours (ninety-six hours for caesarean births).[6]

4. Limits on benefits for mental illness must be no more restrictive than those for medical or surgical benefits.[7]

5. A health benefit plan may not discriminate with respect to premiums or benefits on the basis of an individual's genetic characteristics.[8]

6. The plan must offer coverage to adult children up to age twenty-six.[9]

7. An insurer in the individual and small group markets must cover essential benefits (as described above).[10]

Check the Affordable Care Act timetable in Figure 35.1 for some additional provisions similar to those listed above. Some provisions do not apply to governmental plans, or to plans that have fewer than two participants who are current employees. Other complex exclusions also apply.[11]

For noncompliance with these provisions, the penalty is generally $100 per day for each individual, up to a total of the lesser of:

- 10 percent of the employer's payments under group health plans in the previous year; or

- $500,000.[12]

This is the same penalty amount that applies to COBRA violations (see below).

COBRA Continuation of Coverage

An employer's adoption of any kind of health plan for employees results in an additional due to certain provisions in the Consolidated Omnibus Budget Reconciliation Act of 1985 (COBRA), under which the employer is subject to penalties unless the plan makes available continuation of health plan benefits for certain employees and their dependents after termination of employment and certain other qualifying events.[13]

There is an exemption for small employers—the COBRA continuation provisions apply for a given year only if the employer had twenty or more employees on a typical business day in the preceding year. Final regulations provide that an employer is considered to have employed fewer than twenty employees during a calendar year if it had fewer than twenty employees on at least 50 percent of its typical business days during that year.[14] Only common law employees are taken into account for purposes of the small-employer exception. Self-employed individuals, independent contractors, and directors are not counted.[15]

In the case of a multiemployer plan, a small-employer plan is a group health plan under which each of the employers contributing to the plan for a calendar year normally employed fewer than twenty employees during the preceding calendar year.[16] Government and church plans are also exempt.

Health plan coverage must be continued for eighteen months after termination of employment or reduction in hours of employment, other than for gross misconduct.[17] In general, the employer must provide the option to continue dependent coverage for thirty-six months after the following qualifying events which result in a loss of coverage:

- death of the employee;
- divorce or legal separation of the covered employee;
- the employee's entitlement to Medicare benefits; and
- a child ceasing to be a dependent for plan purposes.

If following a loss of coverage due to termination of employment or reduction in hours a qualified beneficiary is determined to have been disabled during the first sixty days of COBRA coverage, coverage must be continued for twenty-nine months (or when disability ends, if earlier).

If an employee is on leave under the Family and Medical Leave Act of 1993 (FMLA) and does not return to work, the COBRA qualifying event generally is deemed to take place on the last day of the FMLA leave.[18]

Continuation coverage can be terminated before the thirty-six, twenty-nine, or eighteen-month period if:

- the employer terminates its health plan for all employees;
- the qualified beneficiary becomes entitled to benefits under Medicare after electing COBRA coverage;
- a qualified beneficiary ceases to be disabled before the end of the extended twenty-nine-month coverage period;
- the beneficiary fails to pay his or her share of the premium; or
- the beneficiary becomes covered under any other plan providing medical care. However, if the new plan excludes a pre-existing condition, the employee must be allowed to continue coverage for the full COBRA period.

The employer can require the former employee or beneficiary to pay part of the cost of continuation coverage. However, this former employee or beneficiary's share cannot be more than 102 percent of the cost to the plan of coverage for similarly situated beneficiaries with respect to whom a qualifying event has not occurred. This is true whether the cost is paid by the employer or employee. The premium for an employee disabled at the time of his termination or reduction in hours may be as much as 150 percent of the plan cost after the eighteenth month of continuation coverage.

The penalty for noncompliance with these requirements is, generally, a tax of $100 a day during the period that any failure with respect to a qualified beneficiary continues.

Employees and beneficiaries must be notified of their right to continuing coverage when they become covered under the plan and when a qualifying event occurs. A model notification form from the Department of Labor is reproduced in Figure 36.1. Similar information must be provided in the plan's Summary Plan Description (SPD).

The COBRA continuation requirements apply to any kind of group health care coverage, including HMOs and self-funded or noninsured plans. However, the covered employee has the right only to continue the kind of coverage that existed during employment. For example, the employer must offer continuing HMO coverage to an employee covered under an HMO, but the employer need not offer alternative health insurance, although the employer can do so if it wishes. Note, however, that an employee on COBRA continuation coverage must be given the same right to switch coverage during an "open enrollment" period that is available to an active employee.

Figure 36.1

FINANCING OF RETIREE MEDICAL BENEFITS

	Advantages	Disadvantages
Pay-As-You-Go	• low initial cash flow • simplicity • no nondiscrimination requirements	• FASB standards require liability • increasing cash flow requirements • burdens future management/ shareholders
Earmarked Corporate Assets	• demonstrates responsible financial management • money managers can manage portfolio like pension fund • no nondiscrimination requirements	• no tax deduction until benefits are paid • investment income taxable • rate of return could be inadequate
Corporate-Owned Life Insurance	• offset to balance sheet liability • tax-free investment accumulation • policy loan interest deductible (up to $50,000 loan on each key person) • death benefits tax-free • potentially high rate of return • no nondiscrimination requirements	• high initial cash requirements • no tax deduction until benefits are paid
Increased Pension Benefits	• no FASB balance sheet liability except for increased pension • tax-free accumulation • deductibility of contributions	• nondiscrimination requirements • benefits taxable to employees • Sec. 415 limits for higher paid
Incidental Qualified Plan Benefit (401(h))	• deductibility of contributions • tax-free accumulation	• nondiscrimination requirements • contributions cannot exceed 25% of pension plan contributions • reduces maximum pension • tax deductions do not reflect future medical cost inflation
VEBA	• deductibility of contributions	• tax deductions do not reflect future medical cost inflation under Sections 419, 419A • nondiscrimination requirements • earnings in excess of current claims subject to UBIT (Un-related Business Income Tax)

COBRA's continuing coverage requirement does not contain a preemption of state law in states that require more generous continuing coverage in certain situations. Therefore, planners must continue to be aware of state continuation requirements applicable to their clients.

Continuing Health Coverage for Retirees

Some employers want to continue company-paid health benefits for retirees, either for all employees or for a selected group. Rising costs as well as new developments in the tax and accounting treatment of such plans have required many of these plans to be redesigned.

The key issue is the method of funding or financing the plan. There is no one best way to design these plans, so the planner must weigh the advantages and disadvantages of each approach and fit it with the employer's unique situation. Currently, the alternatives are:

1. *Pay-as-you-go*. With this alternative, there is no advance funding or financing; health insurance premiums are simply paid each year after the covered employee retires. This alternative is simple and offers the lowest initial cost. There are no nondiscrimination requirements at this point if the plan is insured,[19] so the plan can be offered only to selected executives. However, costs of such plans can rise unpredictably and burden future cash flow of the company. Under FAS 106 (see Chapter 61) a current accrual must nonetheless be made, so current earnings are reduced. Also, the employer's tax deduction for the payment is deferred to the year in which the premiums are actually paid.

2. *Earmarked corporate assets*. Under this approach, the plan is essentially a pay-as-you-go arrangement, but to provide a better indication of responsible financial management the corporation sets aside specified assets to offset the additional liability that the FASB rules would impose.

3. *Corporate-owned life insurance*. This is again a variation on the pay-as-you-go approach, but with a dedicated corporate asset reserve in the form of corporate-owned life insurance. The insurance is maintained on the life of each covered employee, with the corporation as owner and beneficiary. The tax-free cash buildup of the policy is used to pay the after-tax cost of health insurance premiums for retired employees. When the insured employee dies, the tax-free death benefit allows the company to recover part or all of its costs for the plan.

4. *Increase pension benefits*. Under this alternative, there is no formal health insurance continuation plan for retirees (except for the required COBRA coverage), but pension benefits are increased to provide employees with additional money to pay insurance premiums. This alternative allows a current deduction to the employer for the extra costs and tax-free accumulation of investment returns, but the pension nondiscrimination rules require that the increased benefits be provided to all employees covered under the pension plan. Also, the employee must pay taxes on the increased pension benefit, so the potentially tax-free nature of the health insurance benefit is lost. Also, there is no certainty or even reasonable expectation that the increased benefits will, in fact, cover health insurance costs incurred many years after retirement.

5. *Incidental benefit in qualified plan*. Under this approach, continued health insurance coverage is provided as an incidental benefit under a qualified pension or profit sharing plan. The health insurance coverage is funded as part of the plan cost. Under Code Section 401(h), the fund for health insurance must be kept in a separate account for each participant. Neither health insurance costs nor benefit payments are taxable income to the employee,[20] which means that the 401(h) alternative has the same tax benefit as direct health insurance coverage. Incidental benefits in a qualified plan are limited to 25 percent of the aggregate contributions to the plan after establishment of the 401(h) account,[21] and many actuaries consider this limit inadequate for funding the full potential liability.

6. *Key employees*. Coverage of key employees in a Section 401(h) arrangement adds some extra complexities that have led some planners to recommend against covering key employees in 401(h)-type plans. First, there must be

separate, individual 401(h) accounts for each key employee.[22] The total amount allocated to a key employee for pension plus incidental medical or other benefits is subject to the $53,000 (as indexed for 2015) annual additions dollar limitation under Code Section 415, which may limit the ability to prefund medical benefits for key employees in some cases.[23] The definition of "key employee" in these rules is that used for purposes of the top-heavy rules, Code Section 416(i). (See Chapter 13.)

7. *VEBA or other trust fund*. Here assets are set aside to meet the future insurance liability in a separate trust fund. A VEBA is a tax-exempt arrangement that can be used for this purpose. (VEBAs are discussed in detail in Chapter 55.) The approach is similar to using a Section 401(h) account, but the limits on contributions are not subject to the 25 percent incidental benefit rule, but rather to the rules for prefunded welfare benefits under Sections 419 and 419A. Although a VEBA is generally tax exempt, the rules for "unrelated business taxable income" as applied to a VEBA in this situation would generally tax most of the VEBA's income.[24] VEBAs must meet nondiscrimination rules[25] similar to those for qualified plans, so the benefits cannot be provided just to a selected group of executives.

The chart in Figure 36.1 summarizes the advantages and disadvantages of these approaches to preretirement financing of retiree medical benefits.

TAX IMPLICATIONS

1. The employer may deduct the cost of health insurance premiums in an insured plan or benefits paid in an self-insured plan as a general business expense. Plan administrative expenses are also deductible.

2. Deductions for prefunding medical benefits (that is, setting funds aside and deducting amounts for medical benefits to be paid in future years) are limited under rules set out in Code sections 419 and 419A. Generally, for a given year an employer can deduct expenditures for medical benefits up to a limit equal to the total of (a) the direct costs of the plan for the year—claims paid plus administrative costs, plus (b) contributions to an asset account up to 35 percent of the preceding year's direct costs.

3. The employee does not have taxable income (a) when the employer pays insurance premiums, (b) when benefits are paid, or (c) when the plan reimburses the employee for covered expenses (unless the employee is considered highly compensated and the plan is a discriminatory noninsured medical expense reimbursement plan).[26]

4. The employee is eligible for an itemized medical expense deduction under Code section 213 for

   a. any portion of health insurance premiums paid by the employee;

   b. unreimbursed out-of-pocket costs resulting from deductibles or coinsurance; and

   c. any other medical expenses eligible for a Section 213 deduction.

   The Section 213 deduction is available only if the taxpayer itemizes deductions on the tax return. The deduction is limited to the amount by which the total of all eligible medical expenses exceeds 10 percent of the taxpayer's adjusted gross income (7.5 percent for taxpayers sixty-five or older).

ERISA AND OTHER REQUIREMENTS

An employer's health and accident plan is a "welfare benefit plan" subject to the ERISA requirements discussed in Chapter 16.[27]

WHERE CAN I FIND OUT MORE?

1. Beam, Burton T., Jr. and John J. McFadden, *Employee Benefits*, 9th ed. Chicago, IL: Dearborn Financial Publishing, Inc., 2012.

2. *Tax Facts on Insurance & Employee Benefits*, Cincinnati, OH: *The National Underwriter Co.*, (revised annually).

3. Cady, Donald F., *Field Guide to Estate Planning, Business Planning, & Employee Benefits*, Cincinnati, OH: *The National Underwriter Co.*, (revised annually).

FREQUENTLY ASKED QUESTIONS

Question – Can employee premiums for a group health plan be paid on a pre-tax basis under a cafeteria plan?

Answer – Yes. Cafeteria plans are discussed further in Chapter 40.

Question – Can a self-employed person (sole proprietor or partner in an unincorporated business) or S corporation shareholder-employee be covered under his business's health insurance plan and obtain any tax advantage?

Answer – A self-employed person or S corporation shareholder-employee can be covered under a business's health insurance plan. This may provide a more economical means of obtaining health benefits than individual insurance, because of the group underwriting of an insured employer plan.

The cost of health insurance for a self-employed individual or a more than 2 percent shareholder-employee in an S corporation would ordinarily not be a deductible expense to the business because the self-employed individual is not considered an employee (and a more than 2 percent S corporation shareholder-employee is treated as a partner for fringe benefit purposes). However, a special provision, Code section 162(l), permits a special deduction in order to equalize the treatment of incorporated and unincorporated businesses in this regard. Under section 162(l), a self-employed individual is entitled to a business expense deduction equal to the amount paid for health insurance. The deduction cannot exceed the self-employed individual's earned income for the year from the trade or business with respect to which the plan is established. The deduction cannot be used to reduce self-employment income subject to self-employment tax. Rules are provided to prevent duplication of deductions for other medical insurance covering the taxpayer or itemized medical expense deductions.

Question – Can an employer use the excess assets in an "overfunded" pension plan to fund retiree medical benefits?

Answer – An employer with an overfunded pension plan can amend the plan to add postretirement health insurance as an additional incidental benefit. The amount allocated to all incidental benefits cannot exceed 25 percent of the aggregate plan contributions after establishment of the 401(h) account.[28] If a plan is at the full funding limit, it is not allowed to make any further actual contributions for pension purposes, so (since 25 percent of zero is zero) no additional deductible contributions for medical benefits can be made.

Code section 420 allows an employer to make a transfer of excess pension assets to a Section 401(h) account without the employer having to pay either regular income tax or the pension reversion excise tax on the amount transferred. This provision, however, includes complex restrictions and regulatory requirements. Also, transferred assets may not be used for postretirement health benefits for key employees as defined in Code section 416(i).

It also appears unfeasible to withdraw excess funding from a qualified plan and transfer it to a VEBA to fund retiree benefits. The IRS apparently views this withdrawal as a pension reversion to the employer, which is fully income taxable to the employer and is also subject to the 20 percent pension reversion penalty tax under Code section 4980.

Question – How is health plan coverage for retirees reflected by the employer for accounting purposes?

Answer – The accounting profession's Financial Accounting Standards Board (FASB) has adopted a standard for accounting treatment of postretirement benefits other than pensions (FAS 106). This standard requires employers to reflect the promise of future benefits on an accrual basis—that is, as benefits are earned, rather than when they are ultimately paid out. Accounting requirements for benefit plans are discussed further in Appendix F.

Question – May an employer drop retiree health insurance coverage after an employee has retired?

Answer – This is a complex issue involving both federal law (ERISA) and the interpretation of the retiree's employment contract, which often results in litigation.

As a practical matter, the best way for an employer to maintain flexibility is to have a clear "reservation of rights" clause in its collective bargaining agreements, its plan documents, and other

Figure 36.2

Model COBRA Continuation Coverage Election Notice
(For use by single-employer group health plans)

IMPORTANT INFORMATION: COBRA Continuation Coverage and other Health Coverage Alternatives

[*Enter date of notice*]

Dear: [*Identify the qualified beneficiary(ies), by name or status*]

This notice has important information about your right to continue your health care coverage in the [*enter name of group health plan*] (the Plan), as well as other health coverage options that may be available to you, including coverage through the Health Insurance Marketplace at www.HealthCare.gov or call 1-800-318-2596. **You may be able to get coverage through the Health Insurance Marketplace that costs less than COBRA continuation coverage.** Please read the information in this notice very carefully before you make your decision. If you choose to elect COBRA continuation coverage, you should use the election form provided later in this notice.

Why am I getting this notice?

You're getting this notice because your coverage under the Plan will end on [*enter date*] due to [*check appropriate box*]:

- ☐ End of employment
- ☐ Death of employee
- ☐ Entitlement to Medicare
- ☐ Reduction in hours of employment
- ☐ Divorce or legal separation
- ☐ Loss of dependent child status

Federal law requires that most group health plans (including this Plan) give employees and their families the opportunity to continue their health care coverage through COBRA continuation coverage when there's a "qualifying event" that would result in a loss of coverage under an employer's plan.

What's COBRA continuation coverage?

COBRA continuation coverage is the same coverage that the Plan gives to other participants or beneficiaries who aren't getting continuation coverage. Each "qualified beneficiary" (described below) who elects COBRA continuation coverage will have the same rights under the Plan as other participants or beneficiaries covered under the Plan.

Who are the qualified beneficiaries?

Each person ("qualified beneficiary") in the category(ies) checked below can elect COBRA continuation coverage:

- ☐ Employee or former employee
- ☐ Spouse or former spouse
- ☐ Dependent child(ren) covered under the Plan on the day before the event that caused the loss of coverage
- ☐ Child who is losing coverage under the Plan because he or she is no longer a dependent under the Plan

Figure 36.2 (cont'd)

Are there other coverage options besides COBRA Continuation Coverage?

Yes. Instead of enrolling in COBRA continuation coverage, there may be other more affordable coverage options for you and your family through the Health Insurance Marketplace, Medicaid, or other group health plan coverage options (such as a spouse's plan) through what is called a "special enrollment period." Some of these options may cost less than COBRA continuation coverage.

You should compare your other coverage options with COBRA continuation coverage and choose the coverage that is best for you. For example, if you move to other coverage you may pay more out of pocket than you would under COBRA because the new coverage may impose a new deductible.

When you lose job-based health coverage, it's important that you choose carefully between COBRA continuation coverage and other coverage options, because once you've made your choice, it can be difficult or impossible to switch to another coverage option.

If I elect COBRA continuation coverage, when will my coverage begin and how long will the coverage last?

If elected, COBRA continuation coverage will begin on [*enter date*] and can last until [*enter date*].
[*Add, if appropriate*: You may elect any of the following options for COBRA continuation coverage: [*list available coverage options*].
Continuation coverage may end before the date noted above in certain circumstances, like failure to pay premiums, fraud, or the individual becomes covered under another group health plan.

Can I extend the length of COBRA continuation coverage?

If you elect continuation coverage, you may be able to extend the length of continuation coverage if a qualified beneficiary is disabled, or if a second qualifying event occurs. You must notify [*enter name of party responsible for COBRA administration*] of a disability or a second qualifying event within a certain time period to extend the period of continuation coverage. If you don't provide notice of a disability or second qualifying event within the required time period, it will affect your right to extend the period of continuation coverage.

For more information about extending the length of COBRA continuation coverage visit http://www.dol.gov/ebsa/publications/cobraemployee.html.

How much does COBRA continuation coverage cost?

COBRA continuation coverage will cost: [*enter amount each qualified beneficiary will be required to pay for each option per month of coverage and any other permitted coverage periods.*]

Other coverage options may cost less. If you choose to elect continuation coverage, you don't have to send any payment with the Election Form. Additional information about payment will be provided to you after the election form is received by the Plan. Important information about paying your premium can be found at the end of this notice.

You may be able to get coverage through the Health Insurance Marketplace that costs less than COBRA continuation coverage. You can learn more about the Marketplace below.

What is the Health Insurance Marketplace?

The Marketplace offers "one-stop shopping" to find and compare private health insurance options. In the Marketplace, you could be eligible for a new kind of tax credit that lowers your monthly premiums and

Figure 36.2 (cont'd)

cost-sharing reductions (amounts that lower your out-of-pocket costs for deductibles, coinsurance, and copayments) right away, and you can see what your premium, deductibles, and out-of-pocket costs will be before you make a decision to enroll. Through the Marketplace you'll also learn if you qualify for free or low-cost coverage from **Medicaid** or the **Children's Health Insurance Program (CHIP)**. You can access the Marketplace for your state at www.HealthCare.gov.

Coverage through the Health Insurance Marketplace may cost less than COBRA continuation coverage. Being offered COBRA continuation coverage won't limit your eligibility for coverage or for a tax credit through the Marketplace.

When can I enroll in Marketplace coverage?

You always have 60 days from the time you lose your job-based coverage to enroll in the Marketplace. That is because losing your job-based health coverage is a "special enrollment" event. **After 60 days your special enrollment period will end and you may not be able to enroll, so you should take action right away.** In addition, during what is called an "open enrollment" period, anyone can enroll in Marketplace coverage.

To find out more about enrolling in the Marketplace, such as when the next open enrollment period will be and what you need to know about qualifying events and special enrollment periods, visit **www.HealthCare.gov**.

If I sign up for COBRA continuation coverage, can I switch to coverage in the Marketplace? What about if I choose Marketplace coverage and want to switch back to COBRA continuation coverage?

If you sign up for COBRA continuation coverage, you can switch to a Marketplace plan during a Marketplace open enrollment period. You can also end your COBRA continuation coverage early and switch to a Marketplace plan if you have another qualifying event such as marriage or birth of a child through something called a "special enrollment period." But be careful though – if you terminate your COBRA continuation coverage early without another qualifying event, you'll have to wait to enroll in Marketplace coverage until the next open enrollment period, and could end up without any health coverage in the interim.

Once you've exhausted your COBRA continuation coverage and the coverage expires, you'll be eligible to enroll in Marketplace coverage through a special enrollment period, even if Marketplace open enrollment has ended.

If you sign up for Marketplace coverage instead of COBRA continuation coverage, you cannot switch to COBRA continuation coverage under any circumstances.

Can I enroll in another group health plan?

You may be eligible to enroll in coverage under another group health plan (like a spouse's plan), if you request enrollment within 30 days of the loss of coverage.

If you or your dependent chooses to elect COBRA continuation coverage instead of enrolling in another group health plan for which you're eligible, you'll have another opportunity to enroll in the other group health plan within 30 days of losing your COBRA continuation coverage.

Figure 36.2 (cont'd)

What factors should I consider when choosing coverage options?

When considering your options for health coverage, you may want to think about:

- Premiums: Your previous plan can charge up to 102 percent of total plan premiums for COBRA coverage. Other options, like coverage on a spouse's plan or through the Marketplace, may be less expensive.
- Provider Networks: If you're currently getting care or treatment for a condition, a change in your health coverage may affect your access to a particular health care provider. You may want to check to see if your current health care providers participate in a network as you consider options for health coverage.
- Drug Formularies: If you're currently taking medication, a change in your health coverage may affect your costs for medication – and in some cases, your medication may not be covered by another plan. You may want to check to see if your current medications are listed in drug formularies for other health coverage.
- Severance payments: If you lost your job and got a severance package from your former employer, your former employer may have offered to pay some or all of your COBRA payments for a period of time. In this scenario, you may want to contact the Department of Labor at 1-866-444-3272 to discuss your options.
- Service Areas: Some plans limit their benefits to specific service or coverage areas – so if you move to another area of the country, you may not be able to use your benefits. You may want to see if your plan has a service or coverage area, or other similar limitations.
- Other Cost-Sharing: In addition to premiums or contributions for health coverage, you probably pay copayments, deductibles, coinsurance, or other amounts as you use your benefits. You may want to check to see what the cost-sharing requirements are for other health coverage options. For example, one option may have much lower monthly premiums, but a much higher deductible and higher copayments.

For more information

This notice doesn't fully describe continuation coverage or other rights under the Plan. More information about continuation coverage and your rights under the Plan is available in your summary plan description or from the Plan Administrator.

If you have questions about the information in this notice, your rights to coverage, or if you want a copy of your summary plan description, contact [*enter name of party responsible for COBRA administration for the Plan, with telephone number and address*].

For more information about your rights under the Employee Retirement Income Security Act (ERISA), including COBRA, the Patient Protection and Affordable Care Act, and other laws affecting group health plans, visit the U.S. Department of Labor's Employee Benefits Security Administration (EBSA) website at **www.dol.gov/ebsa** or call their toll-free number at 1-866-444-3272. For more information about health insurance options available through the Health Insurance Marketplace, and to locate an assistant in your area who you can talk to about the different options, visit **www.HealthCare.gov**.

Keep Your Plan Informed of Address Changes

To protect your and your family's rights, keep the Plan Administrator informed of any changes in your address and the addresses of family members. You should also keep a copy of any notices you send to the Plan Administrator.

Figure 36.2 (cont'd)

COBRA Continuation Coverage Election Form

Instructions: To elect COBRA continuation coverage, complete this Election Form and return it to us. Under federal law, you have 60 days after the date of this notice to decide whether you want to elect COBRA continuation coverage under the Plan.

Send completed Election Form to: [*Enter Name and Address*]

This Election Form must be completed and returned by mail [*or describe other means of submission and due date*]. If mailed, it must be post-marked no later than [*enter date*].

If you don't submit a completed Election Form by the due date shown above, you'll lose your right to elect COBRA continuation coverage. If you reject COBRA continuation coverage before the due date, you may change your mind as long as you submit a completed Election Form before the due date. However, if you change your mind after first rejecting COBRA continuation coverage, your COBRA continuation coverage will begin on the date you submit the completed Election Form.

Read the important information about your rights included in the pages after the Election Form.

I (We) elect COBRA continuation coverage in the [*enter name of plan*] (the Plan) listed below:

Name　　Date of Birth Relationship to Employee　　SSN (or other identifier)

a. ____

[*Add if appropriate*: Coverage option elected: ____________________]

b. ____

[*Add if appropriate*: Coverage option elected: ____________________]

c. ____

[*Add if appropriate*: Coverage option elected: ____________________]

______________________　　______________________

Signature　　Date

______________________　　______________________

Print Name　　Relationship to individual(s) listed above

____

____

______________________　　______________________

Print Address　　Telephone number

Figure 36.2 (cont'd)

Important Information About Payment

First payment for continuation coverage

You must make your first payment for continuation coverage no later than 45 days after the date of your election (this is the date the Election Notice is postmarked). If you don't make your first payment in full no later than 45 days after the date of your election, you'll lose all continuation coverage rights under the Plan. You're responsible for making sure that the amount of your first payment is correct. You may contact [*enter appropriate contact information, e.g., the Plan Administrator or other party responsible for COBRA administration under the Plan*] to confirm the correct amount of your first payment.

Periodic payments for continuation coverage

After you make your first payment for continuation coverage, you'll have to make periodic payments for each coverage period that follows. The amount due for each coverage period for each qualified beneficiary is shown in this notice. The periodic payments can be made on a monthly basis. Under the Plan, each of these periodic payments for continuation coverage is due [*enter due day for each monthly payment*] for that coverage period. [*If Plan offers other payment schedules, enter with appropriate dates*: You may instead make payments for continuation coverage for the following coverage periods, due on the following dates:]. If you make a periodic payment on or before the first day of the coverage period to which it applies, your coverage under the Plan will continue for that coverage period without any break. The Plan [*select one*: will *or* will not] send periodic notices of payments due for these coverage periods.

Grace periods for periodic payments

Although periodic payments are due on the dates shown above, you'll be given a grace period of 30 days after the first day of the coverage period [*or enter longer period permitted by Plan*] to make each periodic payment. You'll get continuation coverage for each coverage period as long as payment for that coverage period is made before the end of the grace period. [*If Plan suspends coverage during grace period for nonpayment, enter and modify as necessary*: If you pay a periodic payment later than the first day of the coverage period to which it applies, but before the end of the grace period for the coverage period, your coverage will be suspended as of the first day of the coverage period and then retroactively reinstated (going back to the first day of the coverage period) when the periodic payment is received. This means that any claim you submit for benefits while your coverage is suspended may be denied and may have to be resubmitted once your coverage is reinstated.]

If you don't make a periodic payment before the end of the grace period for that coverage period, you'll lose all rights to continuation coverage under the Plan.

Your first payment and all periodic payments for continuation coverage should be sent to:

[*enter appropriate payment address*]

employment agreements, as well as its ERISA-required Summary Plan Descriptions (SPDs). This clause should clearly state that the employer reserves the right to change or withdraw the benefit at any time, both before and after the retirement of any covered employee. The procedure by which this change would be made should be specified and the company should strictly follow this procedure.[29] Although this may not prevent lawsuits by aggrieved employees, it will put the employer in the best possible position if these benefits must be revoked at some time in the future.

CHAPTER ENDNOTES

1. Employee Health Benefits 2007 Annual Survey-Report, Kaiser Family Foundation et al. Health coverage by small employers declined from 68 percent in 2000, but coverage by large employers held steady at 99 percent. The percentage of uninsured individuals was 16.7 percent in the United States as a whole in 2009, varying by state from 4.4 percent in Massachusetts to 26.1 percent in Texas.
2. PPACA §1302(b).
3. I.R.C. §4980H.
4. I.R.C. §9815, incorporating provisions of Public Health Service Act §2704 and other sections of PHSA.
5. I.R.C. §9802. This existing provision (also PHSA §2705) is broadened effective 2014 under PPACA—see note 5, above.
6. I.R.C. §9811.
7. I.R.C. §9812. Effective 2010, this provision is expanded to include substance abuse treatment and other provisions (under the Mental Health Parity and Addiction Equity Act of 2008).
8. I.R.C. §9802(b)(3).
9. PHSA §2714; see note 5 above.
10. PHSA §2707.
11. I.R.C. §9831.
12. I.R.C. §4980D.
13. I.R.C. §4980B.
14. Treas. Reg. §54.4980B-2, A-5.
15. Treas. Reg. §54.4980B-2, A-5.
16. Treas. Reg. §54.4980B-2, A-5.
17. The definition of "gross misconduct" is not provided under COBRA, but has been developed through case law, often based on state law definitions.
18. Notice 94-103, 1994-2 CB 569.
19. I.R.C. §105(h).
20. Treas. Reg. §1.72-15(h). See Priv. Ltr. Rul. 8747069.
21. I.R.C. §401(h), last paragraph.
22. I.R.C. §§401(h)(6), 415(l); Treas. Reg. §1.401-14(c)(2).
23. I.R.C. §§415(l)(1), 415(c)(1)(B), 415(c)(2).
24. IRC Sections 512(a)(3)(E)(iii), 419A(c)(2).
25. I.R.C. §505.
26. I.R.C. §§105, 106.
27. Treas. Reg. §2510.3-1.
28. I.R.C. §401(h), last paragraph; Treas. Reg. §1.401-14(c)(1)(i).
29. *Curtis-Wright Corporation v. Schoonejongen*, 514 U.S. 73 (1995).

ALTERNATIVES TO GROUP HEALTH PLANS

CHAPTER 37

INTRODUCTION

Under a Health Reimbursement Arrangement (HRA), an employer reimburses covered employees for specified medical (health and accident) expenses. These reimbursements come directly from corporate funds rather than from a third party insurer. An HRA is used:

1. as a substitute for health insurance (although as a result of the Affordable Care Act, stand-alone HRAs generally are not a viable option);

2. as a supplement to provide payments for medical expenses not covered under the company's health insurance plan (such as dental expenses); or

3. to pay for medical expenses in excess of the limits in the company's health insurance plan.

The tax objective of the plan is to provide tax-free benefits to the covered employees and obtain a corresponding employer tax deduction for the benefits paid. HRAs are employer-funded accounts. Employees are not permitted to contribute their own funds.

HRAs were often used in the past to provide extra benefits for selected groups of executives. However, current tax law denies tax benefits to highly compensated employees if a self-insured plan does not meet the nondiscrimination tests of Code section 105(h), as described below.

HRAs are generally subject to the requirements of the Affordable Care Act. See the discussion and timetable for these provisions in Chapter 35.

WHEN IS USE OF SUCH A DEVICE INDICATED?

1. In combination with a high deductible health plan.

2. Where an employer would like to provide employees with medical benefits beyond those provided by the basic medical coverage already in force.

PLAN DESIGN FEATURES

Basically, an HRA is simple. The company adopts a plan by corporate resolution specifying:

- the group of employees covered;

- the types of medical expenses that will be reimbursed; and

- any limits or conditions on payment by the company.

When an employee incurs medical expenses subject to reimbursement, the employee submits a claim to the employer. The employer then reimburses the employee, provided that the claim is covered under the plan.

The plan's objective is to provide tax-free benefits to employees. Benefits will be tax free if: (1) they qualify as medical expenses under the Code; and (2) (for a highly compensated employee) the plan is nondiscriminatory under Code section 105(h), as discussed below under the Tax Implications.

A broad range of expenses can qualify as medical expenses under an HRA. This is one of the advantages of these plans—the plan can cover expenses often not available under health insurance plans. For example, an HRA can cover full dental expenses including orthodontia, and even items such as swimming pools prescribed by a physician for treatment of a condition such as arthritis.

Any expense that could be deducted by an individual as an itemized medical expense under Code section 213 is eligible for tax free reimbursement under an HRA. See Figure 37.1 for a partial list of items that have been approved for deduction under Section 213, and, thus, are eligible for tax free reimbursement under an HRA. Note that section 213 has some specific exclusions; in particular, cosmetic surgery. Also, there are no tax benefits for nonprescription (over-the-counter) drugs except for insulin.[1]

TAX IMPLICATIONS

1. The employer may deduct 100 percent of the cost of benefits paid to employees under the plan. Plan administrative expenses are also fully deductible.[2]

2. Deductions for prefunding medical benefits (that is, setting funds aside and deducting amounts for medical benefits to be paid in future years) are limited under rules set out in Code sections 419 and 419A. Generally, for a given year, an employer can deduct expenditures for medical benefits up to a limit equal to the total of (a) the direct costs of the plan for the year—claims paid plus administrative costs, plus (b) contributions to an asset account up to 35 percent of the preceding year's direct costs.

3. The employee does not have taxable income when benefits are paid. Benefits are tax-free when medical expenses are paid directly to doctors or hospitals, or when the plan reimburses the employee for covered expenses.[3] Highly compensated employees may have to pay taxes on the reimbursements to the extent that the plan is discriminatory under the Section 105(h) rules described below. See the Frequently Asked Questions for further discussion.

4. The employee is eligible for an itemized medical expense deduction under Code section 213 for any medical expenses not covered by the HRA or other employer health insurance plan. The Section 213 deduction is available only if the taxpayer itemizes deductions on the tax return. The deduction is limited to the amount by which the total of all eligible medical expenses exceeds 10 percent of the taxpayer's adjusted gross income (7.5 percent for taxpayers sixty-five or older).

Nondiscrimination Rules

Health reimbursement arrangements that are funded on a "pay as you go" basis are generally considered self-insured for tax purposes, and therefore are governed by nondiscrimination rules found in Code section 105(h). Failure to comply with these rules means that plan benefits will be taxable to highly compensated employees. Section 105(h) defines a highly compensated individual as one who is:

1. one of the five highest paid officers;

2. a shareholder who owns more than 10 percent of the company's stock; or

3. is among the highest paid 25 percent of all employees.

Non-highly compensated employees receive benefits tax-free even in a discriminatory plan. The nondiscrimination rules require the plan to pass both a *benefits test* and a *coverage test*.

The *benefits test* for an HRA is simple: all benefits provided for highly compensated individuals under the plan must be provided for all plan participants.

The coverage test is slightly more complex. Under this test the plan must:

- benefit 70 percent or more of all employees;

- benefit 80 percent or more of all employees who are eligible to participate in the plan if at least 70 percent of all employees are eligible to participate; or

- benefit a classification of employees, established by the employer, that does not discriminate in favor of highly compensated individuals.

Certain categories of employees can be excluded from these tests:

- employees who have not completed three years of service;

Figure 37.1

DEDUCTIBLE MEDICAL EXPENSES*

- **Professional Services of**
  - Christian Science Practitioner
  - Oculist
  - Unlicensed practitioner if the type and quality of his services are not illegal
- **Equipment and Supplies**
  - Abdominal supports
  - Air conditioner where necessary for relief from an allergy or for relieving difficulty in breathing
  - Arches
  - Autoette (auto device for handicapped person), but not if used to travel to job or business
  - Back supports
  - Contact lenses
  - Cost of installing stair-seat elevator for person with heart condition
  - Elastic hosiery
  - Eyeglasses
  - Fluoridation unit in home
- **Medical Treatments**
  - Acupuncture
  - Diatheray
  - Healing services
  - Hydrotherapy (water treatments)
- **Medicines**
  - Drugs
  - Patient medicines
- **Miscellaneous**
  - Birth control pills or other birth control
  - Braille books —excess cost of braille books over cost of regular editions
  - Clarinet lessons advised by dentist for treatment of tooth defects
  - Convalescent home — for medical treatment only
  - Face lifting operation, even if not recommended by doctor
  - Fees paid to health institute where the exercises, rubdowns, etc., taken there are prescribed by a physician as treatments necessary to alleviate a physical or mental defect or illness
  - Hair transplant operation
- **Miscellaneous (cont'd)**
  - Practical or other non-professional nurse for medical services only; not for care of a healthy person or a small child who is not ill
  - Costs for medical care of elderly person, unable to get about, or person subject to spells
  - Hearing aid
  - Heating devices
  - Invalid chair
  - Orthopedic shoes
  - Reclining chair if prescribed by doctor
  - Repair of special telephone equipment for the deaf
  - Sacroiliac belt
  - Special mattress and plywood bed boards for relief of arthritis of spine
  - Truss
  - Wig advised by doctor as essential to mental health of person who lost all hair from disease
  - Navajo healing ceremonies ("sings")
  - Sterilization
  - Vasectomy
  - Whirlpool baths
  - Vitamins, tonics, etc., prescribed by doctor — but not if taken as food supplement or to preserve your general health
  - Kidney donor's or possible kidney donor's expenses
  - Legal fees for guardianship of mentally ill spouse where commitment was necessary for medical treatment
  - Nurse's board and wages, including social security taxes you pay on wages
  - Remedial reading for child suffering from dyslexia
  - Sanitarium and similar institutions
  - "Seeing-eye" dog and its maintenance
  - Special school costs for physically and mentally handicapped children
  - Wages of guide for a blind person
  - Telephone-teletype costs and television adapter for closed caption service for deaf person

* A partial list of items which the IRS or the courts have held to constitute deductible medical expenses.

Figure 37.1 (cont'd)

NONDEDUCTIBLE MEDICAL EXPENSES*

- Antiseptic diaper service
- Athletic club expenses to keep physically fit
- Babysitting fees to enable you to make doctor's visits
- Boarding school fees paid for healthy child while parent is recuperating from illness. It makes no difference that this was done on a doctor's advice
- Bottled water bought to avoid drinking fluoridated city water
- Cost of divorce recommended by psychiatrist
- Cost of hotel room suggested for sex therapy
- Cost of trips for a "change of environment" to boost morale of ailing person. That doctor prescribed the trip is immaterial
- Dance lessons advised by doctors as physical and mental therapy or for the alleviation of varicose veins or arthritis; however, the cost of a clarinet and lessons for the instrument were allowed as deduction when advised as therapy for a tooth defect
- Deductions from your wages for a sickness insurance under state law
- Domestic help — even if recommended by doctor because of spouse's illness. But part of cost attributed to any nursing duties performed by the domestic is deductible
- Funeral, cremation or burial, cemetery plot, monument, mausoleum
- Health programs offered by resort hotels, health clubs and gyms
- Illegal operation and drugs
- Marriage counseling fees
- Maternity clothes
- Premiums, in connection with life insurance policies, paid for disability, double indemnity or for waiver of premium in event of total and permanent disability or policies providing for reimbursement of loss of earnings or a guarantee of a specific amount in the event of hospitalization
- Scientology fees
- Special food or beverage substitutes — but excess cost of chemically uncontaminated foods over what would have ordinarily been spent on normal food was deductible for allergy patients
- Toothpaste
- Transportation costs of a disabled person to and from work
- Traveling costs to look for a new place to live on doctor's advice
- Travel costs to favorable climate when you can live there permanently
- Tuition and travel expenses to send a problem child to a particular school for a beneficial change in environment
- Veterinary fees for pet; pet is not a dependent
- Weight reduction or stop smoking programs undertaken for general health, not for specific ailments
- Your divorced spouse's medical bills. You may be able to deduct them as alimony

* A list of some expenses which have been held *not* deductible.

- employees who have not attained age twenty-five;
- part-time or seasonal employees;
- employees in a collective bargaining unit if there has been good faith bargaining on the health plan issue; and
- nonresident alien employees who received no U.S. income.

Internal Revenue Code Eligibility and Coverage Requirements

The tax code provides certain requirements for group health plan coverage subject to a penalty for noncompliance. "Group health plan" is broadly defined and apparently includes HRAs.[4] Broadly, the requirements are:

1. Participants may not be excluded (or required to pay an extra premium) on the basis of:

   a. health status;

b. medical condition, whether physical or mental;

c. claims experience;

d. receipt of health care;

e. medical history;

f. genetic information;

g. evidence of insurability; or

h. disability.[5]

2. The plan may not restrict benefits for any hospital length of stay in connection with childbirth for the mother or newborn child to less than forty-eight hours (ninety-six hours for Caesarean births).[6]

3. Limits on benefits for mental illness must be no more restrictive than those for medical or surgical benefits.[7]

These provisions do not apply to governmental plans or to plans that have fewer than two participants who are current employees. Other complex exclusions also apply.[8]

The penalty for noncompliance with these provisions is generally $100 per day for each individual up to a total of the lesser of: (1) 10 percent of the employer's payments under group health plans in the previous year; or (2) $500,000.[9] This is the same penalty amount that applies to COBRA violations.

COBRA Continuation of Coverage

An employer's adoption of any kind of health plan for employees results in an additional due to certain provisions in the Consolidated Omnibus Budget Reconciliation Act of 1985 (COBRA), under which the employer is subject to penalties unless the plan makes available continuation of health plan benefits for certain employees and their dependents after termination of employment and certain other qualifying events.[10]

There is an exemption for small employers—the COBRA continuation provisions apply for a given year only if the employer had twenty or more employees on a typical business day in the preceding year. Final regulations provide that an employer is considered to have employed fewer than twenty employees during a calendar year if it had fewer than twenty employees on at least 50 percent of its typical business days during that year.[11]

Only common law employees are taken into account for purposes of the small-employer exception. Self-employed individuals, independent contractors, and directors are not counted.[12] In the case of a multiemployer plan, a small-employer plan is a group health plan under which each of the employers contributing to the plan for a calendar year normally employed fewer than twenty employees during the preceding calendar year.[13] Government and church plans are also exempt.

Health plan coverage must be continued for eighteen months after termination of employment or reduction in hours of employment, other than for gross misconduct.[14] In general, the employer must provide the option to continue dependent coverage for thirty-six months after the following qualifying events which result in a loss of coverage:

- death of the employee;
- divorce or legal separation of the covered employee;
- the employee's entitlement to Medicare benefits; and
- a child ceasing to be a dependent for plan purposes.

If following a loss of coverage due to termination of employment or reduction in hours a qualified beneficiary is determined to have been disabled during the first sixty days of COBRA coverage, coverage must be continued for twenty-nine months (or when disability ends, if earlier).

If an employee is on leave under the Family and Medical Leave Act of 1993 (FMLA) and does not return to work, the COBRA qualifying event generally is deemed to take place on the last day of the FMLA leave.[15]

Continuation coverage can be terminated before the applicable period if:

- the employer terminates its health plan for all employees;
- the qualified beneficiary becomes entitled to benefits under Medicare after electing COBRA coverage;

- a qualified beneficiary ceases to be disabled before the end of the extended twenty-nine-month coverage period;
- the beneficiary fails to pay his or her share of the premium; or
- the beneficiary becomes covered under any other plan providing medical care. However, if the new plan excludes a pre-existing condition, the employee must be allowed to continue coverage for the full COBRA period.

The employer can require the former employee or beneficiary to pay part of the cost of continuation coverage. However, this former employee or beneficiary's share cannot be more than 102 percent of the cost to the plan of coverage for similarly situated beneficiaries with respect to whom a qualifying event has not occurred. This is true whether the cost is paid by the employer or employee. The premium for an employee disabled at the time of his termination or reduction in hours may be as much as 150 percent of the plan cost after the eighteenth month of continuation coverage.[16]

The penalty for noncompliance with these requirements is, generally, a tax of $100 per day during the period that any failure with respect to a qualified beneficiary continues.

The COBRA continuation requirements are discussed further in Chapter 36.

ERISA AND OTHER REQUIREMENTS

An employer's HRA is a welfare benefit plan subject to the ERISA requirements discussed in Chapter 16. For Form 5500 filing purposes, stop loss insurance is not a plan asset that must be reported on Schedule A, Form 5500.[17]

AFFORDABLE CARE ACT IMPLICATIONS

As a group health plan, an HRA is generally subject to the Affordable Care Act (ACA). Among other things, the Affordable Care Act contains certain market reforms, including a prohibition on annual benefit limits.

By definition, an HRA imposes an annual benefit limit and thus raises the issue of whether an HRA can be offered under the Affordable Care Act. (The annual benefit limit reform does not apply to a plan that covers fewer than two current employees. This also means that an employer could maintain a retiree-only HRA without violating the market reform requirements, since it would not cover any current employees.)

Assuming the employer's health plan does cover its current workforce, it could provide an HRA if this feature is "integrated" with a group health plan because, viewed together, there would be no annual limit. In other words, the group health plan generally would not be permitted to impose an annual limit. Even though one element of the health plan, the HRA, itself has a limit, this does not cause the plan to violate the requirement. (Note, however, that the HRA may not be integrated with individual insurance.)

"Integration" (i.e., combining an HRA with general group health plan coverage) requires that covered employees have other non-HRA group health plan benefits. This can be done either through the plan of the employer that maintains the HRA or the plan maintained by the employer of the employee's spouse. The employee must also be given the opportunity to opt out and waive HRA coverage annually.

WHERE CAN I FIND OUT MORE?

1. Beam, Burton T., Jr. and John J. McFadden, *Employee Benefits*, 9th ed. Chicago, IL: Dearborn Financial Publishing, Inc., 2012.

2. *Tax Facts on Insurance & Employee Benefits*, Cincinnati, OH: The National Underwriter Co. (Revised annually).

3. Leimberg, Stephan R., et al., *The Tools & Techniques of Estate Planning*, 17th ed. Cincinnati, OH: The National Underwriter Co., 2015.

4. Cady, Donald F., *Field Guide to Estate Planning, Business Planning, & Employee Benefits*, Cincinnati, OH: The National Underwriter Co. (Revised annually).

FREQUENTLY ASKED QUESTIONS

Question – Is there ever any advantage in designing an HRA that discriminates by covering only specific executives?

Answer – The consequence of not meeting the nondiscrimination requirements is only that:

1. part or all of plan reimbursements (the excess reimbursements, as computed under the complex Section 105(h) rules) are taxable to highly compensated employees;

2. taxable excess reimbursements must be reported by the employer on the employee's Form W-2.

The employer does not lose any part of its deduction for a discriminatory plan.

The excess reimbursement in a discriminatory plan is either:

1. if the plan provides a benefit to a highly compensated employee but not to other participants, the excess reimbursement is the amount of such benefit that is reimbursed; or

2. if the benefit is provided to both non-highly and highly compensated employees but on a discriminatory basis, the excess reimbursement is the amount reimbursed to the highly compensated participant, multiplied by the total amount reimbursed to all highly compensated participants for the year, over the total amount reimbursed to all employees for the year.[18]

Example: Suppose that a plan provides eligibility for medical reimbursement immediately upon hire to Hal Gall, a highly compensated executive, but under the plan all other employees must be employed for four years before they are covered. In 2015, Hal is reimbursed $6,000 for hospital and surgical expenses for his knee surgery. In 2015, amounts reimbursed under the plan to all highly compensated participants totaled $30,000 out of a total of $90,000 of reimbursements. Hal's excess reimbursement for 2015 is

$$\$6{,}000 \times \frac{\$30{,}000}{\$90{,}000} = \$2{,}000$$

Thus, for 2015, Hal must report $2,000 of the $6,000 reimbursement as additional taxable income. The remaining $4,000 of the reimbursement is tax free.

If there is a case where these consequences are not objectionable, a discriminatory plan may be useful. The consequences of a discriminatory plan can be alleviated by paying bonuses to highly compensated employees—taxable to employees and deductible to the employer—to cover the amount of tax generated by "excess reimbursements" taxed to the employee. Such a plan may still provide some tax advantage, if the employer's outlay exceeds the employee's tax cost. And the cost may be substantially less than providing the benefit on a nondiscriminatory basis.

Question – Can a partnership provide HRA benefits to a partner on a favorable tax basis?

Answer – In a Technical Advice Memorandum (TAM), the IRS took a very unfavorable position with respect to HRAs for the self-employed. Based on a technical reading of the various relevant Code provisions, the IRS asserted that the HRA did not constitute "insurance," and therefore implied that the benefit *payments* were taxable income.[19] Under this view, a partner receiving reimbursement for a serious medical condition might have hundreds of thousands of dollars of additional taxable income in a year which the partner spent mostly in the hospital or otherwise out of service.

Question – May a participant in an HRA roll over unused amounts from an HRA to a Health Savings Account (HSA)?

Answer – Not currently. For tax years beginning before 2012, an HRA could permit a plan participant, one time per arrangement, to make a *qualified HSA distribution*.[20] A qualified HSA distribution was an employer-to-trustee transfer from an HRA to an HSA. The rollover could not exceed the lesser of the balance in the HRA on September 21, 2006, or the date of distribution. A qualified HSA distribution was be treated as a rollover contribution to the HSA and did not count toward the annual HSA contribution limit. (See Chapter 39 for more information.)

CHAPTER ENDNOTES

1. I.R.C. §106(f).
2. Treas. Reg. §1.162-10(a).
3. I.R.C. §105(b).

4. I.R.C. §§9832(a), 5000(b)(1).
5. I.R.C. §9802.
6. I.R.C. §9811.
7. I.R.C. §9812.
8. I.R.C. §9831.
9. I.R.C. §4980D.
10. I.R.C. §4980B.
11. Treas. Reg. §54.4980B-2, A-5.
12. Treas. Reg. §54.4980B-2, A-5.
13. Treas. Reg. §54.4980B-2, A-5.
14. The definition of "gross misconduct" is not provided under COBRA, but has been developed through case law, often based on state law definitions.
15. Notice 94-103, 1994-2 CB 569.
16. For workers involuntarily terminated between September 1, 2008 and December 31, 2009, the American Recovery and Reinvestment Act of 2009 provides a subsidy of 65% of the COBRA premium for a period of nine months. The employer or health insurance provider provides full coverage for an employee payment of 35% of the premium, and the employer or provider is entitled to a government subsidy payment for the rest. This benefit is phased out for higher incomes beginning at $125,000 single/$250,000 joint returns. ARRA 2009 Section 3001 et seq.
17. DOL Adv. Op. 92-02A.
18. I.R.C. §105(h)(7).
19. TAM 9320004.
20. I.R.C. §106(e).

FLEXIBLE SPENDING ACCOUNT

CHAPTER 38

INTRODUCTION

A flexible spending account, or FSA, is a type of benefit offered under a cafeteria plan—a plan under which employees can choose between cash and specified benefits—that is funded through salary reductions elected by employees each year. The two most common types of benefits offered through an FSA under a cafeteria plan are medical reimbursement (commonly referred to as a health FSA) and dependent care assistance (adoption assistance may also be offered, but it is not a common FSA benefit).

Health FSAs are significantly affected by recent healthcare legislation discussed here as the Affordable Care Act. This legislation included changes in various federal statutes including ERISA, the Internal Revenue Code, and others. The provisions of this law are phased in over several years through 2018.

WHEN IS USE OF SUCH A DEVICE INDICATED?

1. When an employer wants to expand employee benefit choices without significant extra out-of-pocket costs (or possibly realize some actual dollar savings). Some situations where benefit choices are desirable:

   - Where the employer's medical plans have large deductibles or coinsurance (co-pay) provisions

   - Where there is a need for benefits that are difficult to provide on a group basis, such as dependent care.

2. Where the costs of an employee benefit plan, such as health insurance, have increased and the employer must impose additional employee cost sharing in the form of deductibles or coinsurance, the health FSA approach minimizes employee outlay since the FSA converts after-tax employee expenditures to before-tax expenditures.

3. The FSA provides a tax benefit for employees (tax exclusion for medical reimbursement and dependent care assistance benefits) that is not available through any other plan.

4. Because of administrative costs, FSAs are usually only practical for medium and large businesses. Most FSAs involve employers with twenty-five or more employees, but the plan can be considered for as few as ten employees. Also, see the discussion relating to simple cafeteria plans in Chapter 40.

Advantages

1. Since it is a type of benefit offered under a cafeteria plan, the FSA provides employees with a choice as to whether to receive compensation in cash or benefits, and what form the benefits will take (i.e., medical reimbursement or dependent care assistance).

2. The FSA is funded through employee salary reductions, which means that no extra outlay by the employer is required, except for administrative costs.

3. The FSA may result in a reduction in some employment taxes paid by the employer, since taxable payroll is reduced.

4. Salary reductions elected by employees to fund FSA benefits under a cafeteria plan are not subject

to federal income, FICA, and most state and local income taxes.

Disadvantages

1. An FSA must meet all of the complex nondiscrimination requirements for cafeteria plans (see Chapter 40). Monitoring compliance with these rules raises administrative costs. Also, particularly in some closely held corporations, there could be a loss of tax benefits to highly compensated employees if the nondiscrimination rules are not met.

2. FSAs require employees to evaluate their personal and family health and dependent care expenses and file a timely election form every year. They must estimate—at the end of each year—the amount that will be required for covered expenses in the following year. This is sometimes both confusing and difficult, and some employees may not fully utilize the plan because of the perceived complexity or paperwork involved. Others may not want to risk the forfeiture required of any funds left in the account at the end of the year (see Step 6 in "How It is Done," below).

3. FSAs involve a certain level of administrative costs.

4. IRS proposed regulations require an employer to be "at risk" regarding the total annual amount an employee elects to allocate to his or her health FSA (see further discussion in Frequently Asked Questions).

5. Once made, FSA benefit elections are generally fixed for the entire plan year, unless a qualifying life event occurs.

6. FSA benefits cannot be provided to self-employed persons, including partners and sole proprietors.

HOW IT IS DONE

Suppose an FSA plan is to be effective January 1, 2015. The essential step before this date is to obtain effective employee salary reduction elections. Thus, the plan must be designed, communicated to employees, and the salary reduction forms must be designed and furnished to employees before January 1, 2014. (See enrollment form in Figure 38.1 at the end of this chapter.)

Formal plan documents for the FSA must be drafted and adopted by the employer. (All are incorporated under a cafeteria plan.) To be effective January 1, 2015, a corporation would have to formally adopt these documents, with a written resolution of the board of directors, before the end of the corporation's taxable year in which the effective date—January 1, 2015—falls. For example, a calendar-year corporation would have to formally adopt these plans no later than December 31, 2015. The steps required to enact a plan are explained in detail below.

Step 1: The employer decides what benefits are to be provided in the FSA (medical reimbursement and/or dependent care assistance) and adopts a written cafeteria plan to provide these benefits, if not already in place. For example, the employer might decide that the FSA will allow employee salary reductions to be applied to:

a. medical expenses, such as deductibles and co-pays, not covered under the health insurance plan (but note that health FSA deferrals are subject to an annual limit of $2,550 per employee, subject to cost of living adjustments)

b. expenses of dependent care

Step 2: The employer advises employees to review their benefit needs toward the end of each year and estimate their next year's expenses for items covered in the plan.

Step 3: Before the end of the calendar year, employees file with the employer a written election to reduce salary by the amount they choose (the amount they estimate that they will spend on covered benefits) and allocate it among the benefits in the plan. Figure 38.1, at the end of this chapter, illustrates a sample enrollment form. The chosen salary reduction goes into a "benefit account." The benefit account is a book account—it is not actually funded by the employer in most cases.

Step 4: Each employee keeps a record of expenses in each benefit category and makes a claim on the plan for reimbursement. Claims can be made on a quarterly or other basis for administrative convenience. Figure 38.2, at the end of this chapter, is an example of a sample claim form. Administration of these plans has become highly sophisticated, and some employers and benefit administrators manage claims by distributing specialized debit cards to employees that can be used only for FSA-reimbursable purchases.

Step 5: Employer reimbursements to employees under the plan are free of income tax.

Step 6: At the end of the year, if anything is left in the employee's benefit account, it is forfeited (although most plans provide for a run-out period, typically three months, following the end of the plan year in which to submit claims for expenses incurred during the plan year). It cannot be carried over to the next year.

But the plan can include a "grace period" provision under which expenses up to 2½ months after the end of the year can be covered under the preceding year's FSA account. This requires careful planning by the employee. In addition, in lieu of a grace period, a health FSA may allow for unused balances of up to $500 from a plan year to be carried over to a subsequent plan year.

Example. Suppose employee Patella earns $40,000 per year and is covered under an FSA having the features noted in this discussion. On December 31, 2014, having reviewed his probable benefit needs for 2015, he files an FSA election with his employer to reduce his 2015 salary by $2,000. The $2,000 will go into his FSA benefit book account, and he elects to allocate it as follows:

- $1,500 for medical expenses covered under the health FSA (Patella anticipates orthodontic expenses during 2015 for his daughter, Rubella)
- $500 for expenses under the dependent care plan (Patella plans to send his daughter, age eleven, to summer day camp costing about $500)

If Patella's expenses run as expected, the FSA will have turned $2,000 of nondeductible after-tax expenditures into before-tax payments, saving Patella the federal income, FICA and state and local income tax on $2,000, and saving the employer the employment taxes on $2,000 of compensation paid.

If Patella's covered expenses are higher, he will simply lose the tax benefits that would have been available if he had made a larger salary reduction election.

But if Patella's expenses are less than predicted, he will actually forfeit the amount remaining in his FSA benefit account at the end of the year except to the extent of any grace period or carryover provision in the plan. The amount forfeited may be used to pay reasonable administration expenses, reduce required salary reductions, or provide cash refunds.

DESIGN FEATURES

An FSA is a benefit under a cafeteria plan under Code section 125, and it must meet all the complex rules prohibiting discrimination in favor of highly compensated employees and prohibiting a concentration of benefits among the key employees. These rules are discussed in detail in Chapter 40.

In general, these rules will be satisfied if all employees are allowed to participate and if benefits, as a percentage of compensation, are approximately equal for all employees. If the employer wants more selective coverage and benefits, compliance with the nondiscrimination rules must be carefully analyzed.

The cost of noncompliance with the rules is not disqualification of the plan as a whole. Rather, the tax benefits for highly compensated employees only are lost.

On the practical side, the critical design feature is *adequate employee communication*, so that employees use the plan, and the employer's efforts in instituting the plan pay off in employee appreciation.

Benefits

Employers can include the following types of benefits in an FSA arrangement:

- Medical reimbursement, including anything not covered in the health insurance plan—dental care, eyeglasses, hearing aids, etc.

The potentially wide range of this option is discussed further in Chapter 42 of this book. Note that payments for drugs are included only if the drugs are prescription drugs, or insulin. In other words, over-the-counter drugs are not included unless they are prescribed by a doctor.

- Dependent Care Reimbursement (see Chapter 50).
- Adoption assistance, though this is uncommon.

TAX IMPLICATIONS

For Employees

Employee salary reductions applied to FSA benefits are not subject to income tax, though highly compensated employees may be taxed on these benefits if the plan is discriminatory. Further, key employees may lose the tax benefits of an FSA if their benefits, as a percentage of compensation, are too large (see Chapter 40).

Salary reductions, to be effective for tax purposes, must be made before the compensation is earned. IRS regulations require FSA elections to be made annually before the beginning of the calendar year for which the salary reduction is to be effective.

For Employers

The employer may deduct the amounts it pays to reimburse employees for covered expenditures. Also, the employer's payroll subject to payroll taxes is reduced by the amount of any employee salary reductions under an FSA. Payroll taxes include:

- FICA (Social Security);
- FUTA (federal unemployment tax);
- state unemployment taxes; and
- workers' compensation.

State laws relating to unemployment taxes and workers' compensation may vary and should be checked.

ERISA, COBRA, AND HIPAA REQUIREMENTS

Health FSAs are subject to ERISA (unless maintained by a government entity or a church plan). Although exempt from any requirement of advance funding and follow the rules applicable to welfare benefit plans under ERISA (see Chapter 16), health FSAs must comply with ERISA's written plan, summary plan description, and formal claims procedure requirements.

Health FSAs must also comply with COBRA and HIPAA (unless an exception applies).

Dependent care assistance programs are not subject to ERISA, COBRA or HIPAA.

WHERE CAN I FIND OUT MORE?

1. IRS Publication 969, Health Savings Accounts and Other Tax-Favored Health Plans.
2. Beam, Burton T., Jr. and John J. McFadden, *Employee Benefits*, 9th ed. Chicago, IL: Dearborn Financial Publishing, Inc., 2010.

FREQUENTLY ASKED QUESTIONS

Question – Is an employee locked-in for a full year to his or her FSA salary reduction amount and benefit allocation, or can it be changed during the year?

Answer – Changes are not generally allowed unless there are major life events that affect benefit needs. The regulations list marriage, divorce, death of a spouse or child, birth of a child or addition of a dependent, and loss of a spouse's job as some of the permitted qualifying events.

Question – Since FSA salary reductions eliminate Social Security taxes on the salary reduction, are Social Security benefits also affected?

Answer – If an FSA salary reduction reduces an employee's wages below the taxable wage base for the year ($118,500 for 2015), then Social Security benefit credit for that year will also be reduced. This probably will not reduce an employee's ultimate Social Security retirement benefit by very much, but it may deter FSA participation by lower-paid employees. It is advisable for employers to investigate exactly how much effect this will have and communicate it to employees to allay any unreasonable fears they may have. Also, for a relatively low cost, employers can provide an insurance or annuity benefit or qualified plan supplement to compensate employees for this loss.

Question – Are FSA salary reductions recognized for state or local income tax purposes?

Answer – If state or local income taxes are based on federal taxable income—as most are—then salary reductions are generally effective for state tax purposes. But state and local laws vary.

Question – Is there a dollar limit on annual salary reductions in an FSA plan?

Answer – The separate employee benefit plans that are part of an FSA program may have their own dollar limits. For example, there is a $5,000 annual limit for dependent care plans (see Chapter 53). Also, employers often limit salary reductions to a relatively small amount in order to meet the nondiscrimination rules of IRC Section 125. If the plan permits large salary reductions, highly compensated employees are likely to use the plan disproportionately. Regulations require the plan to specify a maximum dollar limit or a maximum percentage of compensation.[1] In addition, the employer may wish to limit the amount at risk. See discussion below.

There is a limit of $2,550, as indexed in subsequent years, applicable to an employee's contributions to a health FSA.

Question – If an employee uses up his or her benefit account allocated to one form of benefit, can amounts allocated to another form of benefit be reallocated?

Answer – The IRS takes the position that there can be no such "crossover" of benefit allocations between medical FSAs and dependent care FSAs during the year. This emphasizes the importance (and difficulty) of careful employee planning in making the annual salary reduction election and allocation of the benefit account.

Question – What are the implications of the IRS position that an employer must be "at risk" with respect to health benefits in an FSA?

Answer – Proposed regulations[2] state that the health FSA will not be tax-free if the plan eliminates all "risk of loss" to an employer. In effect, this forces the employer to be a health insurer with respect to the health care reimbursement aspect of the FSA. In other words, the full amount of a participant's health care reimbursement for the entire year must be available at all times.

Example. Suppose a law firm's FSA plan covers employee Ben DeLaws. Ben elects in December 2014 to reduce his 2015 salary by $100 per month (a total of $1,200 for 2015) and use the salary reduction amount for health benefits under the FSA plan. In February, 2015, Ben's daughter incurs orthodontia expenses of $1,000 which are covered under the plan. Can the plan reimburse Ben in March 2015 only the $200 that he has contributed so far, and reimburse the remaining $800 as Ben makes further salary reduction FSA contributions over the rest of 2015? The IRS says no; Ben is entitled to reimbursement of the entire $1,000 (at the subsequent claims period under the plan). If Ben quits his job and goes to work for another firm in June, 2015, he will never have contributed enough to the FSA to cover this reimbursement and his prior employer will have to cover the difference. This is what the IRS means by "risk of loss."

In light of this IRS position, it appears advisable for employers to recognize the rights of employees to receive full current reimbursement of health FSA claims even before their health FSA accounts have accumulated enough to pay the claim.

CHAPTER ENDNOTES

1. For further discussion, see Baxendale and Coppage, "Choosing Between the Child Care Credit and Flexible Accounts," *Taxation for Accountants*, May, 1993.
2. See IRS Notice 2012-40.

Figure 38.1

(Name of Employer)
FLEXIBLE SPENDING ACCOUNT (FSA)
ENROLLMENT — 2013

Each employee must complete this form before December 31, 2012 and return it to the employer.

Name: ______________________________ Social Security No. _______________

( ) NO, I do not wish to enroll in the FSA for 2013. I understand that I cannot enroll at any other time during the 2013 Plan Year.

( ) YES, I elect to enroll in the FSA, effective January 1, 2013, and authorize the employer to reduce my pay by the following amount(s):

*an allocation for anticipated health expenses .... $__________
*an allocation for dependent care expenses (not to exceed $5,000) .... $__________

Total (Not to exceed $[0,000]) .... $__________

I understand that the salary reduction I have elected for health expenses are recorded separately from the salary reduction for dependent care costs. If there is money recorded in one account at the end of the year, it is not transferable to meet expenses in the other category.

I understand that I cannot suspend, increase or decrease my salary reductions during the 2013 Plan Year unless I experience a major "life event" as described in federal regulations.

I understand that any money remaining in my Flexible Spending Account at the end of the 2013 Plan Year will be forfeited by me.

I have received a written explanation of the Flexible Spending Account. I understand that the employer cannot be responsible for any tax liabilities which may subsequently occur as a result of my FSA participation.

______________________________ ______________

Your signature *Date*

Figure 38.2

(Name of Employer)
FLEXIBLE SPENDING ACCOUNT (FSA)
EMPLOYEE REIMBURSEMENT REQUEST

INSTRUCTIONS:
When to file a reimbursement request form:

This form is to be filed every time you request reimbursement under the FSA for *eligible health expenses* or for *dependent care expenses*. Please submit your original bills or cancelled checks with this form. Legible photocopies are acceptable.

HEALTH EXPENSES
I authorize reimbursement of the health expenses indicated below through my FSA. I certify that, to the best of my knowledge, the expenses I am submitting would qualify as tax deductible medical expenses. I further certify that these expenses are not reimbursable under any other plan, including a plan of another employer that covers me, my spouse or another member of my family.

(1)	(2)	(3)	(4)
DESCRIPTION OF ELIGIBLE EXPENSES	DATE INCURRED	TOTAL AMOUNT OF BILL	AMOUNT PAID BY ANY OTHER PLAN

(5)	(6)
FSA Col. (3) - Col. (4)	EXPENSES FOR: NAME (If dependent, relationship and date of birth)

Figure 38.2 (cont'd)

DEPENDENT CARE EXPENSES

I authorize reimbursement of the expenses indicated below through my FSA. I certify that, to the best of my knowledge, the expenses I am submitting meet the requirements of employment-related dependent care expenses. If married, I further certify that these expenses, together with any other dependent day care expenses already reimbursed through FSA, do not exceed the lesser of my earned income or the earned income of my spouse. I also certify that my spouse was employed on the date these expenses were incurred.

(1)	(2)	(3)	(4)
Name of Individual or Organization Providing Dependent Care Service	Provider Social Security or I.D. Number	Date Incurred	Total Amount of Bill

(5)	(6)
FSA CLAIM	EXPENSES FOR CARE OF: (Name, relationship, age)

Employee Name: ____________________ Social Security No. ____________

______________________________ ______________

Employee Signature Date

Plan Administrator ____________________ Date ____________

HEALTH SAVINGS ACCOUNT (SECTION 223 PLAN)

CHAPTER 39

INTRODUCTION

A Health Savings Account (HSA) is a plan that provides tax benefits to qualified individuals covered by a high deductible health plan (HDHP) for amounts accumulated to pay health care expenditures. An HSA can be provided for employees by an employer or can be set up by individuals or organizations.

The major features are:

- annual individual or employer contributions up to $3,350 for an individual or $6,650 for a family (for 2015) to an IRA-like plan (deductible or excludible from income tax) that pays qualified medical expenses; combined with;

- a "high-deductible" health plan with at least a $1,300 individual deductible or $2,600 family deductible and a maximum limit of $6,450 or $12,900 (for 2015) on annual out-of-pocket expenses; and

- the ability to accumulate savings because amounts not used for medical expenses can continue to grow tax-free.

WHEN IS USE OF SUCH A DEVICE INDICATED?

HSAs may provide employers a way to save on health insurance costs or offer an exit strategy for high cost plans.

HSAs also have potential value for self-employed individuals and their families as an alternative to conventional individual health insurance plans for those not covered under employer plans.

Advantages

1. HSAs offer tax-saving opportunities to individuals who are eligible for them or can arrange eligibility by having a high-deductible plan. If an individual is eligible for an HSA and has enough discretionary income to make contributions, it appears that there is little reason not to set up the HSA and make contributions.

2. Employee contributions to an HSA can be made on a pre-tax basis through a cafeteria plan. Employer contributions are not included in employees' income and are not subject to income or FICA tax withholding.

3. Unused funds in HSA accounts are not forfeited at year-end as with FSA-type cafeteria arrangements. Excess funds simply grow tax-free inside the HSA.

4. There is no actual requirement that HSA account balances be used to pay a participant's medical expenses. The amount that can be accumulated is considerable: an annual contribution of $5,000 will grow to more than $400,000 after thirty years at 6 percent.

5. The 10 percent penalty for early distributions has fewer exceptions than that for IRAs, so the HSA fund is not quite as flexible as an IRA. However, a participant in an employer's qualified plan can contribute to an HSA (but not an IRA) regardless of income.

6. Proponents of HSAs have stated that if people use what they see as their own money for health care expenditures, they will shop wisely and the free market will optimize health care costs. Pessimists predict instead that without first-dollar insurance

coverage, people will put off going to the doctor until their condition requires really costly medical intervention.

Disadvantages

1. HSAs are not appropriate as a technique for providing benefit plans tailored to selected executives. (See Frequently Asked Questions.) HSAs also do not seem likely to substantially extend health insurance coverage to people who are currently uncovered.

2. Although employers have an opportunity to save money on health insurance by adopting high deductible plans along with HSAs, the downside is that lower-income employees are likely to see this change as a drastic cut in benefits. They may not feel they have enough discretionary income to make adequate contributions to the HSA (almost $500 monthly for a family). However, as the costs of regular employer-sponsored continue to rise the HSA amount is becoming comparable to the amount employees may be expected to pay under an employer's regular plan.

3. Taxpayers in lower brackets get less tax benefit from the tax deduction/exclusion structure of the HSA provisions; in fact the benefit may be zero for the very lowest-paid who pay no income taxes. Also, the potential "doughnut-hole" in coverage (discussed in the Frequently Asked Questions) will have its primary impact on families who use up most of their HSA accounts each year. Thus, the amount of health costs that must be funded by the general public may increase as these employees utilize emergency rooms and other publicly subsidized facilities.

4. Some health-insurance economists argue that if an employer offers an HSA/high-deductible plan as an alternative to regular health insurance, there will be adverse selection, since younger, healthier, and higher-income employees will choose the HSA, resulting in higher premiums for the regular insurance covering the older and sicker members of the group and possibly the eventual disappearance of such coverage.

ELIGIBILITY

The basic requirement for eligibility is that an individual must be covered under a high-deductible health plan.[1] There is no restriction to small businesses, and in fact, HSAs do not have to be linked to a business at all, and can be adopted by any individual who qualifies.

A high deductible health plan[2] is a plan that has:

- an annual deductible of at least $1,300 for an individual or $2,600 for a family (2015 figures); and

- an annual out of pocket limit (deductibles, co-payments, etc., not including premiums) not exceeding $6,450 for an individual or $12,900 for a family (2015 figures).

A high deductible health plan can be insured or—for an employer—self-insured.[3]

The individual covered under a high deductible plan is not eligible if he is also covered under a non-high deductible plan. For example, an individual is not eligible for HSA coverage if his spouse has a non-high deductible plan that covers him or if he or his spouse participates in a health FSA.

The individual can be eligible for an HSA even though covered by certain types of permitted insurance that don't have high deductibles; these include coverage for accidents, disability, dental care, vision care, long-term care, workers' compensation, hospitalization insurance paying a certain sum per day of hospitalization, and insurance for a specified disease or illness.[4]

Also, a plan including low deductible or first-dollar coverage for preventive care can qualify as a high-deductible plan.[5] Certain network plans are eligible as high deductible plans even though out-of-pocket limits for out-of-network coverage are higher than the $6,450/$12,900 limits.[6]

If an individual is covered under a separate prescription drug program with a lower deductible, the individual is apparently ineligible since the drug plan is a non-high-deductible plan.[7]

An individual entitled to Medicare is not eligible for an HSA. Thus, HSA contributions will generally cease after attaining age sixty-five.[8]

An individual who may be claimed as a dependent on another person's tax return is not eligible for an HSA.[9]

An HSA plan may be adopted by an employer for employees, or an individual may adopt it on his own.

If an employer adopts an HSA for employees, there does not seem to be any requirement for coverage of any minimum percentage of employees or prohibition against a plan that covers only highly compensated employees. However, there is a comparability requirement for employer contributions, discussed below.

Nondiscrimination Rules

In assessing whether there is an executive benefit loophole in the HSA provisions, beginning in 2011 all employer health benefit plans are subject to the nondiscrimination rule of Code section 105(h), except for grandfathered plans. The penalty for noncompliance is significant, as discussed in Chapter 35. Accordingly, the possibilities of using HSAs to provide executive-only plans are very limited for the future.

If an employer does make contributions to HSAs on behalf of its employees, it must make comparable contributions to the HSAs for all comparable participating employees for each coverage period during the calendar year. Comparable contributions are defined as contributions that are either (1) the same amount or (2) the same percentage of the annual deductible limit under the high deductible health plan.[10]

Comparable participating employees are all employees who (1) in the same category of employee and (2) have the same category of coverage. Category of employee refers to full-time employees, part-time employees, and former employers. (But highly compensated employees are not treated as comparable participating employees to non-highly compensated employees.)

Category of coverage refers to self-only and family-type coverages. Family coverage may be subcategorized as:

1. self plus one;
2. self plus two; and
3. self plus three or more.

Subcategories of family coverage may be tested separately, but under no circumstances may an employer contribute less to a category of family coverage with more covered persons.[11]

Employer contributions made to HSAs through a cafeteria plan under Code section 125, including matching contributions, are not subject to the comparability rules, but are subject to the section 125 nondiscrimination rules (see Chapter 40).[12]

CONTRIBUTIONS

The maximum contribution to an HSA is a monthly limit. For coverage during the full year 2015, the monthly limits add up to $3,350 annually for an individual and $6,650 for a family.[13]

The contribution limit is a per-individual (or family) limit, and all HSAs covering the individual are aggregated for this purpose.

There is a catch-up addition of $1,000 per tax year for individuals age fifty-five or older.[14]

For example, if a spouse participates in an individual's plan, the basic limit is equal to the family limit, and each spouse age fifty-five or over is eligible for a separate catch-up ($8,650 for 2015 for two spouses over fifty-five).

No contributions (regular or catch-up) can be made after the individual reaches age sixty-five and becomes entitled to Medicare. Excess contributions are treated similarly to excess IRA contributions.

Contributions may be made:

(1) directly by an individual;

(2) through salary reductions under an employer cafeteria (Section 125) plan; or

(3) directly by employers.[15]

FUNDING

HSA plans must be funded.[16] Funds are held with a qualified trustee or custodian, similar to IRAs. The establishment of the fund requires no IRS permission or involvement of an employer. Contributions must be in cash. The HSA fund is not subject to income tax. The fund may not be invested in life insurance contracts,[17] and is otherwise subject to the same investment restrictions as an IRA.

The trustee or custodian of an HSA is not required to provide the high-deductible health insurance, but it is expected that marketers will sell the two products (insurance and investment account) in tandem to make the package more attractive.

Assets in an HSA can accumulate without limit. If they are not used each year for qualified medical expenses, they are not forfeited. Neither do unused amounts reduce the participant's contribution limit in the future. Whatever amount remains in the HSA account when the participant reaches age sixty-five is treated much like an IRA accumulation thereafter, except that it can be used tax-free to pay medical expenses in the future (see "Tax Implications").

A covered individual can withdraw funds from his HSA at any time, but there may be a penalty if amounts withdrawn are not used for qualified medical expenses (see Tax Implications).

PLAN BENEFITS

Participants in HSAs can use the funds in their plans to pay for qualified medical expenses for themselves, their spouses, and dependents. Distributions from the plan for this purpose are not taxable to the participants. Qualified medical expense means any expense eligible for an itemized medical expense deduction under Code Section 213(d).[18] This is a very broad category of expenses including some items that are almost never covered under health insurance, such as special schools for children with psychological conditions or heated swimming pools for arthritics. Cosmetic surgery, however, is not included. Also, beginning in 2011, non-prescription drugs are not included.[19] Finally, no more can be paid from the plan than the amount in the participant's account.

HSA plan funds cannot be used to pay the employee's share of health insurance premiums (co-pays). However, HSA distributions can be used to pay for:

1. qualified long-term care insurance;
2. COBRA continuation payments;
3. health care while receiving unemployment compensation; or
4. Medicare Part A or B; and
5. certain other payments including employer-sponsored retiree health insurance premiums.[20]

Individuals (not plan trustees or employers) are responsible for proving that amounts are paid for qualified medical expenses. While there is no standardized ay of reporting these expenditures right now, the IRS is likely to provide a form for this purpose in the future.

The "Doughnut Hole"

An HSA plan together with its companion high-deductible insurance plan may have a "doughnut hole" in its coverage because of the gap between the maximum contribution level and the maximum out-of-pocket limit. For example, if a family high-deductible insurance plan limits out-of-pocket expenses to the maximum of $12,900, and the family contribution for the year is $6,650 (2015 figures), there is a potential gap of $6,250 of uninsured expenses with no coverage from the HSA fund (assuming no carryovers from prior years in the HSA fund) that must be paid out-of-pocket with no tax benefit except presumably the possibility of an itemized medical-expense deduction under Code section 213. Plans should be designed with this problem in mind.

Another similar issue arises when an individual incurs medical expenses that are below the deductible but exceed the amount in the individual's HSA account. For example, this might happen in the early part of the year where the individual has been making monthly deposits for family coverage and the total in the HSA account is $800. If this individual incurs a $1400 medical expense, the $600 must be paid out of pocket. And of course since the expense is below the deductible, there is no insurance coverage. These examples illustrate the point that there is no insurance as such in an HSA plan for expenses below the high deductible threshold.

TAX IMPLICATIONS

Contributions

Contributions made by an individual are deductible above-the-line (that is, regardless of whether the individual itemizes deductions).[21] An individual cannot double-dip by taking an itemized medical expense deduction for contributions or reimbursed expenses.

Contributions by the employer either directly or under a Section 125 cafeteria plan are deductible by the employer, not taxable to the employee, and not subject to FICA and FUTA taxes (Social Security and federal unemployment).[22]

Contributions from Partnerships and S Corporations

Generally, the partnership can treat these amounts as partnership distributions or guaranteed payments.

If they are partnership distributions, they are not deductible to the partnership and do not affect the distributive shares of the partners. (That is, they don't change the amount of partnership income taxed to any partner). If they are treated as guaranteed payments, they are deductible to the partnership. These guaranteed payments are taxable to the partner who receives them, and are not excluded from income as part of a Section 106 accident or health plan. They are also included in the partner's net earnings from self-employment for self-employment tax purposes.

S corporation payments to the HSA of a more than 2 percent shareholder follow the pattern of partnership guaranteed payments. They are includible in income of the shareholder, with no exclusion under Code section 106. The shareholder is subject to FICA (regular Social Security tax) instead of the self-employment tax. However, FICA exceptions for sickness or accident payments may be available.[23]

Distributions

An individual can make contributions to an HSA for a family member who is eligible—for example, a son or daughter who needs some financial support. The eligible son or daughter in this case would take the deduction for the HSA contribution. However, as noted above, an individual who may be claimed as a dependent on another person's tax return is not eligible for an HSA.

Distributions from an HSA are tax-free to the extent used to pay for qualified medical expenses, even if the medical expenses are paid at a time when the individual is not eligible for HSA coverage, for example after an individual has enrolled in Medicare.[24]

Distributions other than for qualified medical expenses are taxable and subject to a 20 percent penalty. However, the 20 percent penalty does not apply if the distribution is made after the account beneficiary's death, disability, or attainment of age sixty-five.[25]

ERISA IMPLICATIONS

An HSA provided by an employer is considered an employee welfare benefit plan that is subject to the ERISA requirements discussed in Chapter 16. If an individual adopts an HSA plan without employer involvement, ERISA does not apply.

IRA ROLLOVERS

A taxpayer may, once in his lifetime, transfer money from an IRA to an HSA (called a *qualified HSA funding distribution*).[26] Because the transfer counts toward the taxpayer's annual HSA contribution limit, it is not truly a rollover in the usual sense of the word.

The qualified HSA funding distribution must be a trustee-to-trustee transfer from an IRA to an HSA in an amount that does not exceed the annual HSA contribution limitation for the taxpayer. If the taxpayer fails at any time during the following tax year to be an eligible individual, he must include in his gross income the total amount of all qualified HSA funding distributions and pay a 10 percent penalty tax.

ALTERNATIVES

Since HSAs add to—rather than replace—other arrangements (even existing Archer MSAs are grandfathered rather than terminated), we're left with an alphabet soup of possible health plans for employees, in addition to all the variations on conventional health insurance.

Chapter 35 discusses the broad range of alternatives. The following chart describes some of the differences between HSAs and various other alternative employee-plan arrangements besides conventional health insurance. HRAs are discussed in detail in Chapter 37, and FSAs in Chapter 38.

FREQUENTLY ASKED QUESTIONS

Question – What is the difference between HSAs and Archer Medical Savings Accounts?

Answer – In 1996 Congress enacted a pilot program for a new approach to providing tax benefits for health care expenses called the Medical Savings Account (MSA). This was also called an Archer MSA after one of the sponsors. It was limited to small businesses (fifty or fewer employers) and the program was to be closed once 750,000 taxpayers were covered.[27]

The results of this program were inconclusive and coverage never reached the 750,000 limit. The Congressional sponsors were committed to the

Figure 39.1

TYPE OF PLAN	HSA	ARCHER MSA	HRA (Health Reimbursement Arrangement)	FSA (Flexible Spending Arrangement)
High-deductible insurance required?	Yes	Yes	No	No
Contribution limit?	\$3,250/\$6,650 family for (2015)	65%–75% of plan deductible	None	\$2,550 subject to cost of living increases
Can it be used to pay health insurance premiums?	No	No	Generally, no	No
Individual contributions allowed?	Yes	Yes, if no employer contributions for the year	No	No
Individual salary-reduction contributions?	Yes	Yes	No	Yes
Employer contributions?	Yes	Yes	Yes	Yes
Benefits taxable?	No, if used for qualified medical expenses	No, if used for qualified medical expenses	No, to extent benefits are nondiscriminatory	No, if used for qualified medical expenses
Unused accounts forfeited annually?	No	No	Employers may permit carryover	Yes (grace period and limited carry-over may apply)
Funded plan required (trustee or custodian)?	Yes	Yes	No	No
Antidiscrimination rule?	Yes—Sec. 105(h) plus "Comparability" rule	Yes—Sec. 105(h) plus "Comparability" rule	Yes—Sec. 105(h)	Yes—Sec. 125 plus Sec. 125 Cafeteria Plan rules

concept and as part of the Medicare Prescription Drug Act of 2003, the idea behind Archer MSAs was expanded and made permanent in the form of the Health Savings Account or HSA. No new Archer MSAs may be adopted.

Like HSAs, Archer MSAs are similar to employer-sponsored IRAs providing medical expense benefits. The employer's role is primarily to provide payroll deductions or direct contributions (subject to nondiscrimination requirements) and also possibly to provide a "high-deductible" health insurance plan.

In order to participate in an MSA, the employee must be covered under a high deductible health insurance plan. The deductible range (for 2015) for individual coverage is \$2,200 to \$3,300, with an out-of pocket limitation of \$4,450. For family coverage these numbers are \$4,450, \$6,650, and \$8,150 respectively.

An MSA works like an IRA devoted to paying the employee's unreimbursed medical expenses and those of his spouse and dependents. Contributions by the employee are deductible from the employee's income for tax purposes and contributions by the employer to the MSA are not includible in the employee's income. Unlike an IRA, however, distributions from the MSA, when used to cover medical expenses that would be eligible for the Code section 213 itemized medical expense deduction, are not taxable to the employee. Distributions from an MSA used for other purposes are subject to income tax, plus an additional penalty tax of 20 percent unless the distribution is made after age sixty-five or upon death or disability.

Generally, the effect of an MSA is similar to that of a Flexible Spending Account (FSA) devoted to medical expenses, except that there is no risk of loss provision in an MSA. MSA balances that are unused at the end of the year can be carried over and used for medical expenses in subsequent years.

Contributions to an MSA are subject to an annual limitation (an aggregate of monthly limitations) which is a percentage of the deductible of the required high deductible health plan. For an individual, it is 65 percent of that deductible and 75 percent for family coverage.

If an employer contributes to an MSA, there is a comparability rule designed to prevent discrimination in favor of highly compensated employees.

Question – May a taxpayer roll over unused balances from Health Reimbursement Arrangements (HRAs) or health Flexible Spending Accounts (health FSAs)?

Answer – There is no current provision for such rollovers. Through 2011, a participant in an HRA or a health FSA was able, one time per arrangement, to make a qualified HSA distribution.[28] A qualified HSA distribution was a true rollover contribution to the HSA and did not count toward the annual HSA contribution limit.

CHAPTER ENDNOTES

1. I.R.C. §223(c)(1).
2. I.R.C. §223(c)(2).
3. Notice 2004-2, 2004-2 IRB, Q-7, indicates that a self-insured medical reimbursement plan sponsored by an employer can qualify as a high-deductible health plan.
4. I.R.C. §223(c)(3).
5. I.R.C. §223(c)(2)(C).
6. Notice 2004-2, Q-4.
7. Rev. Rul. 2004-38, 2004-15 IRB 717; Rev. Proc. 2004-22, 2004-15 IRB 727.
8. I.R.C. §223(b)(7). Technically, the deduction limit is reduced to zero beginning with the first month of Medicare enrollment.
9. I.R.C. §223(b)(6).
10. I.R.C. §§4980E, 4980G; Treas. Reg. §54.4980G-4, A-1.
11. Treas. Reg. §§54.4980G-3, A-5; 54.4980G-4, A-1.
12. Notice 2004-50, 2004-33 IRB 196, A-47.
13. I.R.C. §223(b).
14. I.R.C. §223(b)(3).
15. I.R.C. §106(d).
16. I.R.C. §223(d).
17. I.R.C. §223(d)(1)(C).
18. I.R.C. §223(d)(2)(A).
19. I.R.C. §220(d)(2)(A).
20. I.R.C. §§223(d)(2)(B), (C).
21. I.R.C. §62(a)(19).
22. Notice 2004-2, 2004-2 IRB 269.
23. Notice 2005-8, 2005-4 IRB 368.
24. I.R.C. §223(f).
25. I.R.C. §223(f)(4).
26. I.R.C. §§408(d)(9), 223(b)(4)(C).
27. Archer Medical Savings Accounts are governed generally by I.R.C. §§220 and 4980E.
28. I.R.C. §§106(e), 223(c)(1)(B)(iii).

CAFETERIA PLAN

CHAPTER 40

INTRODUCTION

A cafeteria plan is one under which employees may, within limits, pay for certain qualified benefits on a pre-tax basis. In other words, employees make a choice between taxable cash and non-taxable benefits. Small employers (One hundred or fewer employees) can adopt a simple cafeteria plan with rules that are simpler than those for regular plans.

Certain benefits offered under cafeteria plans are significantly affected by recent healthcare legislation discussed here as the Affordable Care Act. This legislation included changes in various federal statutes including ERISA, the Internal Revenue Code, and others. The provisions of this law are phased in over several years through 2018. A chart summarizing the Affordable Care Act and its effective dates is included in Chapter 35.

WHEN IS USE OF SUCH A DEVICE INDICATED?

1. When employers want to allow their employees to pay for their benefits (e.g., medical, dental, vision, flexible spending account, etc.) on a pre-tax basis in order to reduce tax liability.

2. To help attract and retain employees.

ADVANTAGES

1. Cafeteria plans help give employees an appreciation of the cost of their benefit package.

2. Salary reduction contributions to a cafeteria plan to pay for qualified benefits are not subject to federal income tax, FICA tax, and most state and local income taxes.

3. Employers do not pay FICA and FUTA tax on salary reduction contributions to a cafeteria plan.

4. Offset premium increases through tax savings.

DISADVANTAGES

1. Cafeteria plans can be somewhat complex and expensive for the employer to set-up and administer, especially if flexible spending account (FSA) plans are involved. Costs involved with establishing and administering a cafeteria plan include drafting a plan document, drafting, distributing and collecting benefit elections forms (or setting up an online benefit election process), and performing required nondiscrimination testing.

2. Complex tax requirements apply to the plan under section 125 of the Internal Revenue Code; these are simplified under a section 125(j) simple cafeteria plan for eligible small employers.

3. Once made, elections under a cafeteria plan generally cannot be changed during the plan year, unless certain qualified life events or special enrollment opportunities occur.

4. Salary reduction contributions to cafeteria plans could lower compensation amounts for purposes of benefits under other employee benefit plans (e.g., 401(k)).

HOW IT IS DONE

1. All employees are offered the following elective benefits:

   - medical insurance for employee and dependents;

- dental insurance for employee and dependents;
- vision insurance for employee and dependents; and
- supplemental group term life insurance on the life of the employee.

2. Each employee may elect to receive cash (i.e., his or her salary) or purchase one or more of the above qualified benefits on a pre-tax basis.

Example. John Lee, an employee, makes an irrevocable election during open enrollment for the 2015 plan year to purchase medical and dental insurance for himself and his spouse for that plan year. The total premium cost to John for such benefits is $500 per month. During the 2015 plan year, John's salary is reduced by $500 per month, for a total of $6,000 for the year. John and his spouse are covered by the elected medical and dental insurance. Assuming that John's federal tax rate is 25 percent and the FICA tax rate is 7.65 percent, John would save $1,959 in taxes for the 2015 plan year by paying for his benefits on a pre-tax basis under his employer's cafeteria plan.

TAX IMPLICATIONS

1. A cafeteria plan must comply with the provisions of Code section 125. This code section provides an exception from the "constructive receipt" doctrine for cafeteria plans. Under that doctrine, an employee is taxed on money or property that he has a free election to receive, even if he chooses not to receive it. So, if the terms of section 125 are not met in a cafeteria plan, an employee is taxed on the value of any taxable benefits available from the plan, even if the participant chooses nontaxable benefits, such as medical insurance.

2. Under section 125 and its regulations, only certain benefits—qualified benefits—can be made available in a cafeteria plan.[1] Qualifying benefits include cash and most tax-free benefits provided under the Code (e.g., medical, dental and vision benefits, supplemental group term life insurance on the life of the employee, health and dependent care flexible spending accounts, and health savings accounts), *except*:

   - Archer Medical Savings Account contributions under section 106(b)—however, Health Savings Account contributions under section 106(d) are permitted;
   - scholarships and fellowships under Code section 117;
   - educational assistance provided under a plan governed by Code section 127;
   - employee discounts (for example, those for department store employees), no-additional-cost services (for example, standby airline travel for airline employees), and other fringe benefits provided under Code section 132;[2]
   - retirement benefits, such as qualified or nonqualified deferred compensation—however, a 401(k) arrangement can be included;[3] and
   - long-term care insurance.[4]

3. There are nondiscrimination requirements for cafeteria plans:

   Participation. The plan must be made available to a group of employees in a manner that does not discriminate in favor of highly compensated individuals.[5] A highly compensated individual, for this purpose, is one who is an officer, a shareholder owning more than 5 percent of the employer, a highly compensated employee, or the spouse or dependent of any of these.[6] The following safe-harbor eligibility provision is permitted: the plan will not be considered discriminatory if it benefits a group of employees under a classification that does not discriminate in favor of highly compensated individuals *and* it covers all employees with three years of service beginning no later than the first day of the plan year after the three years' service is attained.[7]

   Benefits. The plan must not discriminate in favor of highly compensated participants as to contributions and benefits.[8] Also, qualified benefits provided to key employees (officers with annual compensation in excess of a specified dollar limit ($170,000 for 2015), more-than-5-percent owners, and more-than-1-percent owners with compensation over $150,000) under the plan must not exceed, in value, 25 percent of the aggregate value of plan benefits provided to all employees.[9]

If these nondiscrimination tests are not met by the plan, the result is that the pre-tax salary reduction contributions used to pay for qualified benefits become taxable to highly compensated employees or key employees—but not to regular employees.

In addition, any type of benefit offered under the plan must meet its own nondiscrimination tests—for example, any group term life insurance offered under the plan would also have to meet the nondiscrimination requirements of Code section 79. These requirements are discussed in the chapters of this book covering these plans.

In many cases, it is not difficult to meet the nondiscrimination tests. In other cases, the result of not meeting the tests—some taxation to highly compensated employees only—may not be objectionable in view of the overall advantages of the plan.

SIMPLE CAFETERIA PLAN

An eligible small employer may adopt a simple cafeteria plan under the provisions of Code section 125(j). The advantage of a simple plan is that it provides a safe harbor (automatic compliance if the 125(j) provisions are met) for the nondiscrimination requirements described above for regular cafeteria plans, as well as any separate nondiscrimination requirements that apply to group term life insurance, self-insured medical expense reimbursements, and dependent care assistance plans offered under the simple cafeteria plan.[10]

An eligible small employer is one with an average of one-hundred or fewer employees on business days during either of the two preceding years. Once the plan is established, the employer can continue it until its employment level reaches 200 employees.[11]

The rules for simple cafeteria plans include simplified minimum participation and contribution requirements that do not discriminate in favor of key employees or highly compensated employees, as these terms are defined for qualified plan purposes (see Chapter 12).[12]

ALTERNATIVES

The FSA, or flexible spending account, is a qualified benefit offered under a cafeteria plan funded through salary reductions. It is not an alternative, but a special type of cafeteria plan benefit that should be thoroughly investigated whenever cafeteria benefits are considered—see Chapter 38. FSA-type arrangements can make use of the "simple cafeteria plan" rules discussed above.

HOW ARE THESE PLANS SET UP?

1. First, the employer must decide on a plan design. This involves a survey of employee needs and employer costs, and a business decision as to the best alternative.

2. A written plan must be drafted and adopted by the employer. IRS or other governmental approval of the plan is not necessary.

3. Employee election (choice of benefit) forms must be designed and distributed to employees. Generally, employees must make benefit choices in advance of the year in which the benefits are earned.[13] For example, for benefits to be earned and used in 2015, employees must complete and file their election forms with the employer before the end of 2014 (although there are certain exceptions for employees who are hired or become eligible during the year).

4. Communication with employees is the most important element in the success of a cafeteria plan; these plans are often complicated.

WHERE CAN I FIND OUT MORE?

1. Beam, Burton T., Jr. and John J. McFadden, *Employee Benefits*, 9th ed. Chicago, IL: Dearborn Financial Publishing, Inc., 2010.

CHAPTER ENDNOTES

1. I.R.C. §125(d)(1)(B).
2. I.R.C. §125(f).
3. I.R.C. §125(d)(2).

4. I.R.C. §125(f).
5. I.R.C. §125(b)(1)(A).
6. I.R.C. §125(e).
7. I.R.C. §125(g)(3).
8. I.R.C. §125(b)(1)(B).
9. I.R.C. §125(b)(2).
10. I.R.C. §125(j)(6).
11. I.R.C. §125(j)(5).
12. I.R.C. §(j)(3),(4).
13. Prop. Treas. Reg. §1.125-1, Q&A 15.

SICK PAY (SHORT-TERM DISABILITY)

CHAPTER 41

INTRODUCTION

A sick pay or short-term disability plan is a plan that continues employees' salary or wages for a limited time during periods of illness or other disability. Generally, sick pay or short-term disability payments do not extend beyond about six months. Programs covering disabilities lasting longer than six months are generally considered long-term disability programs, and are discussed in Chapter 42.

WHEN IS USE OF SUCH A DEVICE INDICATED?

Almost all employers have a broad based program providing some sick pay for short absences from work. This is a high visibility benefit that employees count on and appreciate.

An employer may want to provide special favorable short-term disability programs for selected executives. Under current law, such plans can be provided on a discriminatory basis. That is, the employer can choose: (1) who will be covered; (2) the level of benefits, which can vary from employee to employee; and (3) the terms and conditions of coverage.

DESIGN FEATURES

Most employers divide short-term coverage into two types of plans: (1) sick pay; and (2) short-term disability plans. Although there is some overlap in these concepts, *sick pay* generally refers to uninsured continuation of salary or wages (usually 100 percent replacement) for a short period of time beginning on the first day of illness or disability. A *short-term disability plan* is one that goes into effect when the employee's sick pay benefits run out and extends until the six month limit has been reached, when the employer's long-term disability plan (if any) and Social Security disability go into effect. Short-term plans, as defined this way, can be and often are insured.

Sick Pay

Sick pay benefits are usually provided for a broad group of employees. However, an employer can have a plan for selected executives, only, or a plan with more favorable benefits for executives.

Usually, only full-time employees are covered under sick pay plans. The employer can define the term full-time for this purpose in any reasonable manner; the 1,000-hour year of service definition applicable to qualified plans does not apply.

The duration of sick pay benefits is often tied to the length of an employee's service. For example, there may be no benefits until an employee has completed three months of service, then the plan will provide full benefits. Or, duration of benefits can be graded, based on service. For example, employees may be entitled to twenty days of sick pay annually after ten years of service, with the number of days of sick pay reduced for shorter service. One danger in providing increasingly generous sick pay as a "benefit" is that employees may come to believe that they are expected to take advantage of such sick days and abuse the benefit.

Some sick pay plans allow carryover of unused benefits. For example, if an employee is entitled to ten days of sick pay in 2015 and uses only five of them, then the plan could allow the employee to carry over these five days to 2016, thus having fifteen days of sick pay available in 2016. Plans allowing carryovers usually provide some maximum limit on the sick pay available for any one year. Usually, no more than six months of sick pay can be accumulated.

If long periods of sick pay are allowed, benefits are often reduced below 100 percent of salary after a specified period of time (such as thirty days). This reduces employer costs and helps to phase in the long-term benefits available, which usually do not provide 100 percent salary replacement.

Preventing sick pay abuse is a major management problem in many organizations. Some employers require a physician's certificate to obtain sick pay, particularly if the employee's absence is longer than one week. In some organizations, management simply accepts the idea that employees will take whatever sick days are available and limits them accordingly or simply designates a number of days as paid leave whether or not those days are specified for illness. Generally speaking, absenteeism is a symptom of management problems that cannot be solved simply by the design of employee benefit programs.

Short-Term Disability Plans

A short-term disability plan fills the gap between sick pay and the employer's long-term disability plan, if any. These plans are often insured, particularly for smaller employers, since the employer's liability to continue a disabled employee's salary for six months or so can be a considerable burden.

The design of short-term plans, particularly if they are insured, is similar to the long-term plans discussed in Chapter 42. However, there are some significant differences:

- Short-term plans often have broader coverage than long-term plans. An employer's long-term plan may be limited to selected executives.
- Short-term plans often require less service for coverage. Long-term plans may be reserved for career employees, such as those with five or more years of service.
- The definition of disability is typically more generous (i.e., easier to meet) in a short-term plan than in a long-term plan. Usually the "regular occupation" definition is used. That is, disability in a short-term plan is typically defined as the total and continuous inability of the employee to perform any and every duty of his or her regular occupation.

Coverage exclusions in insured short-term plans are similar to those in long-term plans, as discussed in Chapter 42. As with long-term plans, the Civil Rights Act of 1964 prohibits exclusion of pregnancy-related disabilities if the employer has fifteen or more employees. (State civil rights laws may apply even to smaller employers.)

TAX IMPLICATIONS

For Employers

The employer can deduct payments made directly to employees under a sick pay or short-term disability plan, as compensation to employees. The employer can also deduct premium payments made under an insured plan. Like all compensation deductions, these payments are subject to the reasonableness requirement described in Chapter 2.

Disability insurance premiums paid by the employer under the plan are not considered wages subject to employment taxes (FICA—Social Security; FUTA—federal unemployment).[1] Generally, disability insurance premiums are not subject to state employment taxes either, but individual state laws should be consulted.

For Employees

In some insured plans, employees pay part of the cost of the plan, usually through payroll deductions. These payments are not tax deductible by the employee.

Employer payments of premiums under an insured disability plan do not result in taxable income to the employee.[2]

Benefit payments under an employer-paid plan are fully taxable to the employee as received (subject to the credit described below) if the plan was fully paid for by the employer. If the employer paid only part of the cost, then only a corresponding part of the benefit is taxable, again subject to the credit. For example, if the employer paid 75 percent of the disability insurance premiums and the employee paid the remaining

25 percent, only 75 percent of the disability benefit received by the employee would be taxable.[3]

IRS regulations specify the time over which the employer and employee percentages are to be measured for this purpose. For group disability insurance, generally, payments over the three year period prior to the disability are taken into account in determining the percentages paid by employer and employee.[4]

Disability benefits are subject to federal income tax withholding if paid directly by the employer. If paid by a third party, such as an insurance company, withholding is required only if the employee requests it.[5]

Disability benefits attributable to employer contributions are subject to Social Security taxes for a limited period at the beginning of a disability. Thereafter, they are not considered wages subject to Social Security tax.[6]

Disability Credit

If an employee receiving benefits meets the total and permanent disability definition, a limited tax credit reduces the tax impact of disability payments for lower-income recipients.[7] Because of this definition, the credit has little or no impact on most employees receiving sick pay or short-term benefits, but it may come into effect for more serious or long-term conditions.

Total and permanent disability (the Social Security definition) means a condition under which the individual "is unable to engage in any substantial gainful activity by reason of any medically determinable physical or mental impairment which can be expected to result in death or which has lasted or can be expected to last for a continuous period of not less than twelve months."[8] This is the strictest disability definition that is commonly used for any purpose.

Generally, the disability credit is calculated by taking the maximum amount subject to the credit (see below) and subtracting one-half of the amount by which the taxpayer's adjusted gross income exceeds the AGI limits (see below). The credit is equal to 15 percent of this amount. IRS Publication 524 describes the credit in detail. The table below shows the maximum amounts eligible for the credit, the limitations to Adjusted Gross Income (AGI), and the maximum credit that may be obtained.

MAXIMUM AMOUNT SUBJECT TO CREDIT	
Single Person	$5,000
Joint Return (where one spouse is a qualified individual)	$5,000
Joint Return (where both spouses are qualified individuals)	$7,500
Married Filing Separately	$3,750
ADJUSTED GROSS INCOME LIMITS	
Single Person	$17,500
Married Filing Jointly	$20,000
Married Filing Separately	$12,5000
MAXIMUM CREDIT	
Single Person	$750
Joint Return (where one spouse is a qualified individual)	$750
Joint Return (where both spouses are qualified individuals)	$1,125
Married Filing Separately	$562.50

For individuals who have not attained age sixty-five during the year, the maximum amount subject to the Section 22 credit is limited to taxable disability income received, if that is less than the amount shown in the table above. For individuals age sixty-five and older, the Section 22 credit is a credit for the elderly (rather than a disability credit), the individual need not be disabled, and the maximum amount subject to the credit is not limited to taxable disability income received.

This tax credit is even further reduced by 15 percent of any tax-free income received by the employee from a pension, annuity, or disability benefit, including Social Security. Since most disability plans are integrated with Social Security benefits, this further reduction makes the credit even less valuable.

In view of all the reductions applicable to this credit, and the extremely low AGI limits on full availability, the credit is a minor factor in the design of disability benefits, and plays practically no part in designing benefits for executives.

ERISA REQUIREMENTS

A sick pay or short-term disability income plan is considered a welfare benefit plan under ERISA (see Chapter 16), unless it is considered a "payroll practice" (i.e., payment of an employee's normal compensation, out of the employer's general assets, on account of periods of time during which the employee is physically or mentally unable to perform his or her duties, or is otherwise absent for medical reasons).[9] Unless a payroll practice, such plans require:

1. a written summary plan description;

2. the naming of a plan administrator; and

3. a formal written claims procedure by which employees can make benefit claims and appeal denials.

The plan is not subject to the eligibility, vesting, or funding requirements of ERISA. The plan administrator must provide plan participants with a Summary Plan Description (SPD).

WHERE CAN I FIND OUT MORE?

1. Beam, Burton T., Jr. and John J. McFadden, *Employee Benefits*, 9th ed. Chicago, IL: Dearborn Financial Publishing, Inc., 2012.

2. *Tax Facts on Insurance & Employee Benefits*. Cincinnati, OH: The National Underwriter Co. Revised annually.

CHAPTER ENDNOTES

1. I.R.C. §§3121(a)(2), 3306(b)(2).
2. I.R.C. §106(a).
3. I.R.C. §§104(a)(3), 105(a); Treas. Reg. §1.105-1(d).
4. Treas. Reg. §§1.105-1(d), 1.105-1(e).
5. I.R.C. §3402(o).
6. I.R.C. §3121(a)(4).
7. I.R.C. §22.
8. I.R.C. §22(e)(3).
9. DOL Reg. §2510.3-1(b)(2).

LONG-TERM DISABILITY AND LONG-TERM CARE INSURANCE

CHAPTER 42

INTRODUCTION

Long-term disability insurance is an employer-sponsored program to provide disability income to employees who are disabled (unable to work) beyond a period specified in the plan, usually six months. Such plans are designed to supplement the Social Security disability coverage available to almost all employees. Disability income under an employer plan usually continues for the duration of the disability, or until death. The plan is usually funded through an insurance contract, particularly for smaller employers.

A long-term care plan is an employer-provided benefit similar to health insurance. Benefits generally cover nursing home or home health expenses for chronically ill beneficiaries; these are items not traditionally included in a health care plan. Tax benefits are similar to those for employer-provided health insurance—premium costs are deductible to the employer, and premiums and benefits are nontaxable to the employee or beneficiary within certain limits.

LONG-TERM DISABILITY INSURANCE

When is the Use of Such a Device Indicated?

1. When employees have a need for income to provide for themselves and their families in the event of long-term disability.

   Unfortunately, disability is a common event. It is more likely that an employee will become disabled before age sixty-five than that he or she will die before sixty-five. Social Security disability benefits are available only for severe disabilities, and Social Security benefit levels are not adequate for highly paid employees to maintain their standard of living. Disability income plans are very common as employee benefits because of the great perceived need for them. They would be even more common, or more generous, if it were not for their high cost to employers. The question employers face is not so much whether there is a need for these programs, but rather how they can be financed.

2. When an employer wants to provide a special benefit for executives, if the company has no regular long-term disability program for all employees, or if the regular program provides limited benefits. Under current law, employers can provide disability plans on a discriminatory basis—that is, special plans can be provided for selected executives only. The employer is free to choose (1) who will be covered; (2) the amounts of coverage provided (amounts can vary from employee to employee); and (3) the terms and conditions of coverage.

Eligibility

Since long-term disability plans provided by employers are not subject to nondiscrimination rules (unless provided through a cafeteria plan—See Chapter 40 for the cafeteria plan nondiscrimination rules), the employer has great flexibility in deciding who is covered under the plan. Many plans cover only full-time salaried employees, or only a select group of executive employees. This reduces plan costs, not only because fewer employees are covered, but also because experience in many firms indicates that disability claims are more frequent among non-salaried employees. Some plans simply use the approach of covering only employees above a specified salary level. Exclusions like these in an employer plan are not necessarily grossly inequitable to lower paid employees, because Social Security disability benefit levels—income replacement ratios—are relatively satisfactory for lower paid employees.

Most long-term disability plans require a waiting period of three months to a year before an eligible employee becomes covered.

Definition of Disability

The plan's definition of disability is very important in establishing its cost to the employer. The definition can be strict or liberal, or somewhere in between. Three common definitions will illustrate the range of options:

- The *Social Security* (or "total and permanent") definition of disability is defined as a condition under which the individual "is unable to engage in any substantial gainful activity by reason of any medically determinable physical or mental impairment which can be expected to result in death or which has lasted or can be expected to last for a continuous period of not less than twelve months." This is the strictest (i.e., least favorable to the employee) definition that is commonly used.

- The *qualified for* definition of disability is defined as the total and continuous inability of the employee to engage in any and every gainful occupation for which he or she is qualified or shall reasonably become qualified by reason of training, education, or experience. This definition is more liberal than the Social Security definition since it does not require the disabled employee to be incapable of any gainful employment, only employment for which the employee is qualified. This definition, or some variation of it, is commonly used in employer long-term disability plans.

- The *regular occupation* (or *own occupation*) definition of disability is defined as the total and continuous inability of the employee to perform any and every duty of his or her regular occupation. Although this definition is often used in short-term disability plans (see Chapter 41), it is generally too liberal for an employer's long-term plan. However, if the plan is designed purely as an extra benefit for a selected group of executives, a liberal definition might be used. Most individual disability policies also use a liberal definition, since individuals, for themselves, tend to define disability in terms of inability to do their current job.

As these definitions indicate, most long-term disability plans require total disability in order to receive benefits. However, some plans provide payments for partial disabilities, particularly if the partial disability is preceded by a total disability. This may encourage rehabilitation and return to gainful employment, which is desirable for both employer and employee.

Disability plans usually contain specific exclusions under which benefits will not be paid even if the definition of disability is otherwise met. Common exclusions are (1) disabilities during periods when the employee is not under a physician's care; (2) disabilities caused by an intentionally self-inflicted injury; and (3) disabilities beginning before the employee became eligible for plan coverage.

Benefit Formulas

Long-term plans generally do not provide 100 percent of pre-disability income. The principal reason for this, from the employer's viewpoint, is to avoid disincentives to return to work. Insurers generally do not underwrite plans providing too high a replacement ratio. Disability income amounts of 50 to 70 percent of pre-disability income are typical.

Benefits are usually integrated with disability benefits from other plans. For example, a plan's benefit formula might provide that the disability benefit from the employer is 70 percent of the employee's pre-disability compensation, less disability benefits from specified other sources. This provides the employee with the desired 70 percent disability income level, but the employer only pays whatever additional amount is required after other sources are taken into account. Typical sources of disability benefits, other than the disability plan itself, include:

- Social Security
- workers' compensation
- retirement plans (qualified and nonqualified)
- other insurance
- earnings from other employment

Integration with other plans can use either a full (dollar-for-dollar) offset of the disability benefit by the other income sources, or an integration formula of some kind can be used, under which benefits from the employer plan are reduced by something less than a dollar-for-each-dollar of other disability benefits. There are no federal tax law restrictions on integration similar to those applicable to qualified retirement plans. This means that the employer is free to design any kind of integration formula that meets its cost limits and other objectives for the plan.

Tax Implications

1. Employer contributions to disability income plans, either insurance premium payments or direct benefit payments under an uninsured plan, are deductible as employee compensation. Like all compensation deductions, they are subject to the reasonableness requirement described in Chapter 2.

2. In some plans, employees pay part of the cost of the plan, usually through payroll deductions. These payments are not deductible by the employee.

3. Employer payments of premiums under an insured disability plan do not result in taxable income to the employee.[1]

4. Benefit payments under an employer plan are fully taxable to the employee (subject to the credit described below) if the plan was fully paid for by the employer. If the employer paid part of the cost, only a corresponding part of the benefit is taxable, again subject to the credit. For example, if the employer paid 75 percent of the disability insurance premiums and the employee paid the remaining 25 percent, only 75 percent of the disability benefit received by the employee is taxable.[2]

   IRS regulations specify the time over which the employer and employee percentages are to be measured for this purpose. For group disability insurance, generally, payments over the three-year period prior to the disability are taken into account in determining the percentages paid by employer and employee.[3]

5. *Disability credit*. If an employee receiving benefits meets the total and permanent disability definition, a limited tax credit (known as a "Section 22 credit') reduces the tax impact of disability payments for lower-income recipients.[4] Because of this definition, the credit has little or no impact on most employees receiving sick pay or short-term benefits, but it may come into effect for more serious or long term conditions.

   Total and permanent disability (the Social Security definition) means a condition under which the individual "is unable to engage in any substantial gainful activity by reason of any medically determinable physical or mental impairment which can be expected to result in death or which has lasted or can be expected to last for a continuous period of not less than twelve months."[5] This is the strictest disability definition that is commonly used for any purpose.

   Generally, the disability credit is calculated by taking the maximum amount subject to the credit and subtracting one-half of the amount by which the taxpayer's Adjusted Gross Income (AGI) exceeds the AGI limits. The credit is equal to 15 percent of this amount.[6] The maximum amounts eligible for the credit, the limitations to AGI, and the maximum credit that may be obtained are shown below:

MAXIMUM AMOUNT SUBJECT TO CREDIT	
Single Person	$5,000
Joint Return (where one spouse is a qualified individual)	$5,000
Joint Return (where both spouses are qualified individuals)	$7,500
Married Filing Separately	$3,750

ADJUSTED GROSS INCOME LIMITS	
Single Person	$17,500
Married Filing Jointly	$20,000
Married Filing Separately	$12,500

MAXIMUM CREDIT	
Single Person	$750
Joint Return (where one spouse is a qualified individual)	$750
Joint Return (where both spouses are qualified individuals)	$1,125
Married Filing Separately	$562.50

   For individuals who have not attained age sixty-five during the year, the maximum amount subject to the Section 22 credit is limited to taxable disability income received, if that is less than the amount shown in the table above.

This tax credit is even further reduced by 15 percent of any tax-free income received by the employee from a pension, annuity, or disability benefit, including Social Security. Since most disability plans are integrated with Social Security benefits, this further reduction makes the credit even less valuable.

In view of all the reductions applicable to this credit, and the extremely low AGI limits on full availability, the credit has become a minor factor in the design of disability benefits.

6. Disability insurance premiums paid by the employer under the plan are not considered wages subject to employment taxes (FICA—Social Security; FUTA—federal unemployment).[7] Generally, disability insurance premiums are not subject to state employment taxes either, but individual state laws should be consulted.

7. Disability benefits are subject to federal income tax withholding if paid directly by the employer. If paid by a third party, such as an insurance company, withholding is required only if the employee requests it.[8]

8. Disability benefits attributable to employer contributions are subject to Social Security taxes for a limited period (six months generally) at the beginning of a disability. Thereafter, they are not considered wages subject to Social Security tax.[9]

ERISA Requirements

A long-term disability insurance plan is considered a welfare benefit plan under ERISA (see Chapter 16). Such plans require a written Summary Plan Description (SPD), the naming of a plan administrator, and a formal written claims procedure by which employees can make benefit claims and appeal denials. The plan is not subject to the eligibility, vesting, or funding requirements of ERISA. The plan administrator must provide plan participants with a summary plan description.

LONG-TERM CARE PLANS

When Is the Use of Such a Device Indicated?

The use of long-term care pans as an employee benefits is rare, but there are certain circumstances in which employers may wish to consider it:

1. When an employer wishes to provide an additional tax-favored benefit to employees that might be too expensive for the employees to consider without the employer's involvement.

2. When the employee group is relatively old (the aging baby boomer group), conscious of the significant need for help with potential long-term care expenses, and appreciative of employer assistance in providing this.

Plan Design

Tax benefits for long-term care are relatively new. It is still not entirely clear what form the majority of employer plans will ultimately take, or whether these plans will be widely accepted. However, certain aspects of these plans can be noted:

- Long-term care insurance is expensive and most employer-sponsored plans probably will require substantial payments by employees; many might require employees to pay the full cost. This limits potential tax benefits because, unlike the employer's tax deduction for premium payments that is generally allowable in full, the employee's tax deductions are limited by the floor for medical expense deductions (see subsequent discussion).

- The employee's share of premiums, if any, cannot be paid from a cafeteria or flexible spending account type of plan.[10] This eliminates one of the most potentially promising methods of covering employee payments under such plans.

- Long-term care, in general, is underwritten similarly to health insurance both as an employee benefit and for purposes of individual policies. Because of limitations on the ability of employers to provide this benefit on a cost-effective basis, individual policies may become more common than employer plans.

- For purposes of the tax benefits under these plans, the definition of long-term care insurance is strictly limited (see subsequent discussion) and plans generally will tend to be tailored to comply with this definition in order to receive tax benefits.

- The COBRA continuation coverage requirements (described in Chapter 36) do not apply to long-term care plans.[11] Further, certain provisions relating to preexisting conditions and other portability issues do not apply to long-term care plans if the plan is offered separately.[12]

- Subject to the portability requirements and general civil rights and similar nondiscrimination requirements applicable to all types of employee compensation, an employer can make a long-term care plan available to any employee or any group of employees.

- The plan apparently can cover spouses and dependents on the same basis as a health insurance plan.

Tax Implications

If a plan meets the Code's definition of a qualified long-term care insurance contract[13] it is treated for tax purposes the same as an accident and health insurance contract. A qualified long-term care insurance contract is any insurance contract if:

a. the only insurance protection provided under the contract is coverage of qualified long-term care services;

b. the contract does not pay or reimburse expenses that are reimbursable under Medicare;

c. the contract is guaranteed renewable;

d. the contract has no cash surrender value or other monetary value;

e. refunds of premiums are used to reduce future premiums or increase future benefits; and

f. certain consumer protection requirements are met.

Qualified long-term care services means specified services provided to a chronically ill individual as defined in Code section 7702B. For purposes of determining how much of the benefit payments may be excluded from income there is a per diem limitation that is indexed for inflation ($330 per day in 2015).

Treatment as a qualified long-term care insurance contract carries with it the same tax treatment as an accident and health contract. In the case of an employer plan:

- the employer's premium payments are tax-deductible under Code Section 162(a);

- the employer's payment of the premium does not result in taxable income to the covered employee;[14] and

- benefits under the plan are not taxable to the employee or beneficiary subject to certain limitations.[15]

Medical Expenses Deduction

If the employee pays part or all of the cost of the plan, premiums that do not exceed certain dollar limits are treated as medical expenses available for an itemized deduction under Code section 213 for medical expenses subject to the floor of 10 percent of adjusted gross income (7.5 percent for those over age sixty-five). In 2015, the dollar limits are:

Age attained before close of tax year:	Limitation on premiums
40 or less	$ 380
41 through 50	710
51 through 60	1,430
61 through 70	3,800
Over 70	4,750

Similarly, unreimbursed expenses for qualified long-term care services for the taxpayer or his spouse or dependents are eligible for the section 213 itemized deduction, again subject to the 10 percent floor.

A self-employed person may deduct 100 percent of premiums for a qualified long-term care insurance contract. However, the deductible premiums are first limited to those eligible for the section 213 itemized deduction described previously.[16]

Erisa Requirements

An employer's long-term care plan is a welfare benefit plan subject to the ERISA requirements discussed in Chapter 16.

WHERE CAN I FIND OUT MORE?

1. Beam, Burton T., Jr. and John J. McFadden, *Employee Benefits*, 9th ed. Chicago, IL: Dearborn Financial Publishing, Inc., 2012.

2. *Tax Facts on Insurance & Employee Benefits*, Cincinnati, OH: The National Underwriter Co. Revised annually.

3. Sadler, Jeff, *How to Sell Disability Income Insurance*, Cincinnati, OH: The National Underwriter Co., 2005.

4. Forman, Stephen D. and Sadler, Jeff, *The Advisor's Guide to Long-Term Care*, 2nd edition, Cincinnati, OH: The National Underwriter Co., 2014.

FREQUENTLY ASKED QUESTIONS

Question – What are the alternatives to the classic employer-paid long-term disability plan?

Answer – When an employer considers providing a disability income to an executive or group of executives, the advantages and disadvantages of an employer-paid plan versus individual disability insurance must be weighed.

The employer plan results in no current taxable income to the employee, and thus provides deferral of taxes. Disability benefits are, however, fully taxable, except for a credit which benefits only low-income employees. This raises some planning issues. The amount of disability benefit for a particular employee may be, and in fact usually is, much more than what the employer paid for it. Thus, the total tax bill to the employee is usually larger if the employee does in fact become disabled. Also, if tax rates increase, each dollar of taxable disability income may be subject to more tax in the future than the value of a dollar's worth of current tax exclusion (ignoring the time value of money).

These factors may make individual disability income policies, or a group policy paid for totally by the employee, more attractive to some executives than an employer-paid long-term disability plan. An employee-paid policy results in no current tax deduction, but benefits are free of tax. The cost of the policy to the executive can be minimized or eliminated if the employer pays additional compensation or an annual bonus in the amount of the employee's cost for the coverage, plus the income tax on the bonus itself—a so-called "double bonus" plan.

Question – Is there any type of disability plan that provides *both* employer payment of deductible premiums and non-taxation of benefits to the employee?

Answer – Under Code section 105(c), disability benefits are tax-free if the amount of benefit is:

1. based on permanent loss of use of a member or function of the body; and

2. is computed by reference to the nature of the injury and not to the period the employee is absent from work.

This Code provision is intended primarily to cover plans such as Accidental Death and Dismemberment (AD&D) plans that pay a lump sum for loss of a leg, eye, etc. However, some planners have made use of this exclusion as a substitute for traditional disability insurance. This is done by designing a plan that pays a stated amount for a heart attack, for arthritis, or for other specified conditions, with benefits based on a schedule in the plan and not specifically on the employee's compensation. These benefits can be paid by the employer directly, or in some cases can be paid out of a qualified pension or profit sharing plan.

Another approach—one with less validity—that is sometimes used in order to get the best of both worlds is to design a plan under which the decision as to whether the employer or the employee pays premiums is postponed to the last possible time each year. This permits an employee to opt for employee payment if he or she becomes disabled during the year. However, if all the facts about such a plan were known to the IRS, it would probably be viewed as a sham—that is, treated as an employer-paid plan if an employee becomes disabled.

However, the following plan design would probably pass muster for tax purposes: the plan provides for the employee to choose (in advance) cost-sharing of premiums each year from zero to 100%. Just before the beginning of each year the employee would choose whatever share was appropriate under the circumstances. If the employee was in poor health, he could choose 100% employee-paid coverage for the following year, so that benefits under the plan, if he becomes disabled during that year, would be tax-free. Since there is no certainty that the employee will actually become disabled, the employee's election is subject to a real economic risk and should be valid for tax purposes.[17]

CHAPTER ENDNOTES

1. I.R.C. §106(a).
2. I.R.C. §§104(a)(3), 105(a); Treas. Reg. §1.105-1(d).
3. Treas. Reg. §§1.105-1(d)-(e).
4. I.R.C. §22.
5. I.R.C. §22(e)(3).
6. IRS Publication 524 describes the credit in detail.
7. I.R.C. §§3121(a)(2), 3306(b)(2).
8. I.R.C. §3402(o).
9. I.R.C. §3121(a)(4).
10. I.R.C. §125(f).
11. I.R.C. §4980B(g)(2) provides that the health care continuation rules (COBRA) do not apply to coverage under a "...plan substantially all of the coverage under which is for qualified long-term care services...." There is no such specific exclusion under Code section 4980D relating to preexisting conditions and other portability requirements.
12. I.R.C. §§9831, 9832(c).
13. I.R.C. §7702B(b).
14. I.R.C. §106(a).
15. I.R.C. §105. See also I.R.C. §7702B(d).
16. I.R.C. §162(l).
17. See Priv. Ltr. Rul. 200312001, Nov. 13, 2002.

DESIGNING THE RIGHT LIFE INSURANCE PLAN

CHAPTER 43

INTRODUCTION

This chapter summarizes the steps in designing a life insurance plan for executives that will meet identified employer and employee objectives. The design of plans for selected executives, rather than broad groups of employees, is stressed here. For the broad employee group, insurance planning generally emphasizes the group term plans discussed in Chapter 44.

STEPS IN DESIGNING A LIFE INSURANCE PLAN

Step 1: Identify Insurance and Capital Accumulation Needs

Do executives have specific identifiable needs for death benefits or capital accumulation programs that can be financed with life insurance? The business's dollars for executive benefits should be focused toward actual and perceived needs.

Insurance and capital accumulation needs are widespread; the two most common situations involve:

- the need for family protection for the younger executive to cover family support needs in the event of premature death; and
- the need for accumulation of liquid funds in the executive's estate to cover taxes and expenses, or to carry out the transfer of a closely held business interest.

Step 2: Analyze Existing Plans

The employer's existing plans must be analyzed to determine whether and to what extent these plans meet the needs identified. To the extent possible, it is also advisable to take the executive's personally owned insurance into consideration.

Employer plans that can provide death benefits or capital accumulation include:

- Group term life insurance.
- Pension, profit sharing and other qualified plans. These plans almost always provide some form of death benefit, even if there is no specific life insurance benefit in the plan. Benefits from these plans are discussed in Chapter 12. Specific life insurance benefits from qualified plans are discussed generally in Chapter 18.
- Nonqualified deferred compensation plans. What benefits are provided if the employee dies before or after retirement? How is the plan financed? Are specific assets set aside to meet the employer's obligation?
- Other insurance plans of the employer such as split dollar, death benefit only, or other similar arrangements.

Step 3: Identify Objectives

What are the employee and the employer intending to accomplish with the plan? How are the objectives prioritized? Some common objectives in designing life insurance plans include:

- provide life insurance protection at the lowest possible cost;
- provide the maximum feasible death benefits;

- design a plan with the lowest tax cost (or the maximum tax leverage);
- maximize the employee's federal estate tax marital deduction;
- enhance cost effectiveness of the plan by giving the employer (or in some cases the employee) control of policy cash values; and
- address portability (or nonportability). The executive generally wants maximum portability, while the employer might want to use the plan as a way of tying a key person to the company—the "golden handcuffs" concept.

Step 4: Design the Plan

When needs and objectives have been analyzed, the planner can then match these needs and objectives with the right type of plan(s). Other chapters in this book cover the major tools of life insurance planning in detail:

- Bonus or Section 162 life insurance—Chapter 3
- Split dollar life insurance—Chapter 45
- Insurance financing of nonqualified deferred compensation plans—Chapter 33
- Death benefit only plans—Chapter 47
- Life insurance in qualified plans—Chapter 18

Figure 43.1 compares some major characteristics of these different types of plans.

Figure 43.1

MAJOR CHARACTERISTICS OF LIFE INSURANCE PLANS

	Split Dollar	Bonus Insurance	Insurance in Qualified Plan	Insurance Financing of Nonqualified Deferred Compensation Plan	DBO
Tax deduction for employer outlay	None	Yes (deductible compensation)	Yes (within "incidental" limits)	Deduction deferred to year paid*	Deduction deferred to year paid**
Current taxable income to employee	Term cost** less employee contribution	Bonus amount fully taxable	Term cost** less employee contribution	None	None
Recovery of employer outlay	Yes	No	No	No	No
Amount of death benefit for employee	Amount at risk (standard plan)	Full death proceeds	Full death proceeds	Full death proceeds "leveraged" by employer's tax deduction	Full death proceeds "leveraged" by employer's tax deduction
Income taxation of death benefit to employee's beneficiary	Generally tax-free	Tax-free	Amount at risk is tax-free	Fully taxable as received	Fully taxable as received
Federal estate tax treatment	Includible to extent of incidents of ownership	Includible to extent of incidents of ownership	Includible to extent of incidents of ownership	Value of deferred comp. benefits included	Excluded (noncontrol employee)

* Note, however, that the deduction is based, not on what the employer paid into the plan, but on the much larger amount the employer pays out.

** Table 2001 rates (P.S. 58 rates may be used for certain split dollar arrangements entered into before January 28, 2002) or one-year term cost if lower. Vested cash values in a split dollar plan may also be currently income taxable; see Chapter 45.

GROUP TERM LIFE INSURANCE

CHAPTER 44

INTRODUCTION

A group-term life insurance plan provides insurance for a group of employees—typically ten or more employees—under a group insurance contract held by the employer. If the plan qualifies under Code section 79, the cost of the first $50,000 of insurance is tax-free to employees.

Group term life insurance plans are generally fairly easy to administer and rely heavily on group insurance contracts provided by the insurer. In addition to group insurance contracts, it is also advisable to adopt a written plan meeting the Section 79 requirements listed below. Employers should also monitor the implementation of the plans to make sure the plan is complaint with the nondiscrimination requirements discussed below.

WHEN IS USE OF SUCH A DEVICE INDICATED?

Because virtually all employees have at least some basic need for life insurance, and as there are few other ways to obtain tax-free life insurance, most employers would find it difficult to find reasons not to provide a group term plan, at least at levels up to the $50,000 tax-free limit. Employees also usually have the expectation – if they are working for a larger employer – that this benefit will be made available to them.

At levels above $50,000, group term plans may be a cost effective way to provide a life insurance benefit, both for employer and employee. However, group term coverage may have costs and other disadvantages for coverage of amounts over $50,000; these disadvantages have led planners to investigate the "carve-out" concept discussed below.

Alternatives

1. Life insurance in a qualified plan. (See Chapter 18.)
2. Split dollar life insurance. (See Chapter 45.)
3. Death benefit only (employer death benefit). (See Chapter 47.)
4. Personally owned insurance.

SECTION 79 REQUIREMENTS

The regulations for Code section 79 require group-term insurance to have the following characteristics in order to obtain the $50,000 exclusion:[1]

1. It must provide a *general death benefit*. Accident and health insurance, including double indemnity riders, and travel accident insurance are not considered part of the Section 79 plan. Also, life insurance as an incidental benefit in a qualified pension or profit sharing plan is not considered part of the Section 79 plan.

2. It must be provided to a *group of employees* as compensation for services. The group can be all employees or a group defined in terms of employment-related factors—union membership, duties performed, etc.—or a group restricted solely on the basis of age or marital status. (Nondiscriminatory coverage requirements also apply, as discussed below.) The plan cannot cover company shareholders who are not employees, or a group consisting only of shareholder-employees.

3. The insurance policy must be *carried directly or indirectly by the employer*. This requirement is met if the employer pays any part of the cost of the plan.

4. Insurance amounts for employees must be determined under a *formula that precludes individual selection*. The formula must be based on factors such as age, years of service, compensation, or position in the company.

The plan can, however, provide a given level of coverage to persons in a position defined such that only a few (but at least more than one) highly compensated employees are in that category. (However, note the nondiscrimination rules discussed above.)

Nondiscrimination Requirements

Code section 79 prescribes rules to prevent discrimination in favor of key employees ("key employee" is defined under the top-heavy rules of Code section 416(i)). The nondiscrimination requirements do not apply to plans of churches, synagogues, or certain related organizations.

If these rules are not met, key employees lose the tax exclusion for the first $50,000 of coverage. Because coverage above $50,000 is included in taxable income, key employees must include the cost of the entire amount of coverage at the greater of Table I rates (see Figure 44.1) or the actual cost.

Coverage Rules

The plan must:

- benefit at least 70 percent of all employees;
- benefit a group of which at least 85 percent are not key employees;
- benefit a nondiscriminatory classification of employees, as determined by the IRS; or
- in a cafeteria (Section 125) plan, meet the Code section 125 nondiscrimination rules (see Chapter 40).[2]

Benefit Rules

1. Benefits must not discriminate in favor of key employees.

2. All benefits available to key employees must be available to other plan participants.[3]

3. Life insurance coverage equal to the same percentage of compensation for all participants will not violate the benefit nondiscrimination rule. There is no dollar limit on the amount of compensation that can be taken into account for this purpose.[4]

Who Can Be Excluded

In applying the percentage tests, the following may be excluded:

- employees who have not completed three years of service;
- part-time or seasonal employees; and
- employees not included in the plan who are part of a collective bargaining unit that has engaged in good faith bargaining on the issue of death benefits.

Do all employees of the company have to receive life coverage equal to the same percentage of compensation? Not necessarily. The company can set up two or more plans, having different benefit formulas, as long as each plan meets the coverage rules.

Example. Employer has 600 employees; 500 are nonunion hourly employees and 100 are salaried; of the 100 salaried, 10 are key employees. Plan 1 provides group insurance equal to 1x compensation for all hourly employees. Plan 2 provides group insurance equal to 2x compensation for all salaried employees. Both plans meet the coverage requirements (Plan 1: 100% of participants are not key employees; Plan 2: 90% of participants are not key employees; both percentages are greater than 85%.)

Group Life Insurance Carve-Out for Executives

An executive covered under a company's group term life insurance plan (Section 79 plan) may be able to obtain a better benefit if the executive is taken out of the group plan and given a separate individual policy provided by the employer. A group of selected executives can be similarly treated. Removing these executives does not affect the qualified status of the group term plan for the remaining employees.[5]

Advantages of Carve-Out Coverage over Group Term

1. Executives can be provided with more insurance than would be available under a group-term plan. A group term plan requires the same multiple of salary for all employees while the carve-out plan formula can be selective and discriminatory.

2. The plan can provide cash growth, which is a portable benefit for the executive. In a group term plan, coverage after retirement can be provided only by an expensive policy conversion or by purchasing new individual coverage.

3. Cost to the employer can be favorable.

4. Carving out the discriminatory benefits in a group-term plan can save an otherwise discriminatory plan.

How to Structure the Carve-Out Coverage

All of the methods used to finance executive life insurance are generally available for carved-out benefits; that is:

- bonus or Section 162 plans
- split dollar plans
- death benefit only plans

For a comparison of carve-out with regular group-term coverage, see Figure 44.1.

The IRS has taken a position that could create problems with the carve-out concept. In a Technical Advice Memorandum (TAM), the IRS concluded that the insurance for the carved-out group in question was itself a group term plan subject to Section 79 rather than a split dollar plan as the designers intended.[6] The IRS concluded that the carve-out split dollar plan had all four of the characteristics of Section 79 group-term insurance described under "Requirements of Section 79 Regulations," above. Accordingly, it was governed by Section 79 and taxation to employees was based on Table I (see Figure 44.1) rather than the Table 2001[7] or equivalent applicable to split dollar plans (see Chapter 45).

It would appear that in order for carve-out programs to work as intended, the carve-out coverage will need to be actively designed to avoid Section 79 status. If the carve-out coverage involves a split dollar plan, it may be possible to avoid Section 79 status if the plan provides more than a pure insurance benefit—that is, if the split dollar plan is an equity-type plan as described in Chapter 45. However, the full implications of the current IRS position on carve-outs as described in the TAM are not completely clear.

Small Groups

Under the Section 79 regulations,[8] group insurance for fewer than ten employees qualifies for the tax exclusion under Section 79 if:

- it is provided for all full-time employees, and
- the amount of protection is computed either as a uniform percentage of compensation, or on the basis of coverage brackets established by the insurer under which no bracket exceeds 2½ times the next lower bracket and the lowest bracket is at least 10% of the highest bracket.

For example, a plan dividing employees into four classes with insurance amounts according to the following brackets would meet the test in the regulations:

Class A:	$ 10,000
Class B:	25,000
Class C:	50,000
Class D:	100,000

Eligibility and amount of coverage may be based on evidence of insurability but this must be determined solely on the basis of a medical questionnaire completed by the employee and not by requiring a physical examination.

Meeting the under-ten employee regulations described in this answer is no guarantee that the plan will also be deemed nondiscriminatory. An under-ten employee plan must also meet the Section 79 nondiscrimination requirements.

Figure 44.1

GROUP TERM VS. CARVE-OUT		
	Group term	**Carve-out**
Income tax to employee	1. First $50,000 is income tax free. 2. Coverage over $50,000 is taxed at Table I rates (cannot use insurer's lower term rate).	1. All coverage is taxable (except for DBO arrangement). 2. Generally, coverage is taxed at lower of P.S. 58 (Table 2001 after 2001) rates or insurer's term rate.
Premium deductibility to corporation	Fully deductible	Varies; bonus-type plan is fully deductible, nondeductible if corporation is beneficiary.
Cost to corporation	Rises if group ages; experience-rated (rises if group mortality or incidence of policy conversion at 65 increases).	Most plans involve level-premium insurance contracts with guaranteed premium.
Nondiscrimination coverage requirements	Section 79 coverage requirements apply; if not met, key employees lose the $50,000 exemption.	None
Benefit nondiscrimination requirements	Section 79 requirements apply; generally benefits must be uniform percentage of compensation for all participants.	None; coverage can vary from executive to executive.
Underwriting	Group, with guaranteed issue	Generally individual
Treatment at retirement	Coverage usually terminates or is reduced sharply because of increasing employer cost; also, higher Table I rates past age 64 increase cost to employee.	Can be continued beyond retirement with no increased employer cost; employee cost is Table 2001 or lower term cost.
Use of cash value or permanent insurance	May result in unfavorable taxation to covered employee.	Enhances planning flexibility

ERISA REQUIREMENTS

A group term plan is a welfare benefit plan subject to the ERISA requirements discussed in Chapter 16. ERISA requires that the plan must be established and maintained in writing, plan documents must provide for one or more named fiduciaries. The named fiduciaries, who administer the plan, and the plan document must provide a procedure for amending the plan and specify the basis on which payments are to be made to and from the plan. Additionally, the plan must provide a claims review procedure. The plan must also meet the Code section 79 requirements described above.

TAX IMPLICATIONS

1. The cost of the first $50,000 of group term insurance provided for each employee is tax-free to the employee. Key employees may lose this benefit

if the plan does not meet the Section 79 nondiscrimination rules discussed above. The cost of any discriminatory coverage (including any coverage over $50,000) is included in the key employee's income at the greater of the Table I rates or the actual cost.[9]

2. For the cost of nondiscriminatory coverage above $50,000, the amount taxable to the employee is determined on a monthly basis.[10] The amount of coverage in excess of $50,000 is multiplied by the Table I rates.[11] The annual taxable amount is the sum of the monthly amounts, less any premiums paid by the employee.

TABLE I: RATES FOR GROUP TERM INSURANCE

5-year age bracket	Cost per $1,000 of insurance for One-month period[12]
Under 25	$ .05
25 to 29	.06
30 to 34	.08
35 to 39	.09
40 to 44	.10
45 to 49	.15
50 to 54	.23
55 to 59	.43
60 to 64	.66
65 to 69	1.27
70 and above	2.06

NOTE: Age of the employee is attained age on the last day of the employee's taxable year (generally December 31).

Example. Suppose a thirty-two-year-old employee was covered under a group term plan providing insurance of $100,000 for all twelve months of the year, and the employee paid $30 for this coverage for the year. The amount of coverage in excess of the $50,000 tax-free level is $50,000 ($100,000 – $50,000). Using Table I, 50 times $0.08 equals $4.00 of monthly cost, which multiplied by twelve months equals $48. The employee paid $30, and the difference of $18, is taxable income for the year.

---

3. The death benefit from the insurance is tax-free to the beneficiary, just as if the insurance was personally owned.

4. Premiums paid by the employer for group term life insurance of employees are deductible business expenses.

5. The employer must pay employment taxes on the extra compensation that each employee includes in income as a result of plan coverage with insurance amounts over $50,000 or any coverage or benefits included by reason of the nondiscrimination rules.[13] Employment taxes include FICA (Social Security) and FUTA (federal unemployment tax). State unemployment and workers' compensation taxes may apply in some states—state laws vary and should be checked in each case.

6. Proceeds of group term life insurance are includable in the insured's estate if they are payable to, or for, the benefit of the insured's estate; or if at death the insured holds any incident of ownership regardless of who is named as beneficiary.[14] The proceeds may be removed from an employee's estate if certain requirements are met.[15]

USING POLICIES WITH PERMANENT BENEFITS

Under certain conditions a group policy can provide a permanent benefit. A policy is considered to provide a permanent benefit if it provides an economic value extending beyond one policy year. For example, a policy with a cash surrender value would be considered to provide a permanent benefit.

A policy with a permanent benefit may be treated as part of a group term plan if:

- the amount of death benefit considered part of the group term plan is specified in writing; and

- the group term portion of the death benefit each year complies with a formula in the regulations.

If permanent insurance is used in a group term plan, the cost of the permanent benefit, less any amount contributed by the employee towards that permanent benefit, is included in the employee's taxable income for the year. The regulations contain a formula for computing the annual cost of permanent benefits.[16]

Group Universal Life Insurance Programs

Group Universal Life Insurance Programs (GULPs) are universal life insurance arrangements for a group of employees. These programs provide covered employees with the advantages of universal life coverage (variation in the timing and amount of premiums, and cash values with attractive rates of investment return) as well as the advantages of group underwriting (convenience for employees, reduced costs, and coverage without evidence of insurability, within limits).

Group universal life contracts can be used as part of a plan of group term insurance meeting the requirements of Section 79 and the regulations. However, application of this Code section to a GULP plan does not produce a good tax result due to the rules for taxing "permanent" insurance benefits contained in Section 79. Thus, most GULP plans are designed specifically to *avoid* the application of Section 79. This can be done by using an employee-pay-all arrangement and structuring coverage through a third party (such as a trustee) so that the policy is not deemed to be "carried directly or indirectly by the employer" as required under Section 79. Planning requires close adherence to technical requirements and must be done with the advice of an expert.[17]

It is possible to provide Section 79 group term insurance up to the tax-free level, and also provide the GULP benefit as a (non-Section 79) supplement to the Section 79 plan, if adequate coverage for group underwriting can be obtained.

WHERE CAN I FIND OUT MORE?

1. *Tax Facts on Insurance & Employee Benefits*, Cincinnati, OH: The National Underwriter Co. (revised annually).

2. Cady, Donald F., *Field Guide to Estate Planning, Business Planning, & Employee Benefits*, Cincinnati, OH: The National Underwriter Co. (revised annually).

FREQUENTLY ASKED QUESTIONS

Question – Can group term insurance be provided for self-employed persons or S corporation shareholders?

Answer – The exclusion from taxable income of the cost of the first $50,000 of group term insurance under Code Section 79 is not available to self-employed persons—partners or proprietors—or to shareholders of S corporations who own more than 2 percent of the corporation. (These more-than-2-percent shareholders are treated as partners for employee benefit purposes.)

However, self-employed persons and more-than-2-percent shareholders of S corporations can be included in the insured group for purposes of determining group coverage and premiums. The full cost of such insurance is taxable to the individual covered. (See Appendix B.)

Question – Should dependent coverage be included in a group term plan?

Answer – A small amount of dependent coverage in a group term plan is treated favorably for tax purposes. Dependent coverage is regarded as a de minimis fringe that is not included in income (see Chapter 51) if the face amount of employer-provided group term life insurance payable on the death of a spouse or dependent of an employee does not exceed $2,000.[18] Additional dependent coverage can be provided by the employee on an after-tax basis, without affecting the nontaxability of the employer-paid $2,000 of insurance.

CHAPTER ENDNOTES

1. Treas. Reg. §1.79-1.
2. I.R.C. §79(d)(3).
3. I.R.C. §79(d)(2).
4. I.R.C. §79(d)(5). Prior to its repeal by P. L. 101-140, Section 89 included a $200,000 limit on the amount of compensation that could be taken into account. P. L. 101-140 also includes a provision that even if Section 79 coverage is provided through a Section 501(c)(9) VEBA (see Chapter 55), the limit applicable to VEBAs in general under Code Section 505(b)(7) does not apply in determining whether the requirements of Section 79 are met. P. L. 101-140, Section 204(c).
5. In Letter Ruling 9701027, the IRS found that a plan could permit employees with coverage in excess of $50,000 to reduce the amount of their coverage without violating the "individual selection" rule of Section 79.
6. TAM 200002047. TAMs are applicable only to a specific taxpayer, but as indications of IRS positions they command considerable deference in planning.
7. Formerly the P.S. 58 table.
8. Treas. Reg. §1.79-1(c).

9. I.R.C. §79(d)(1).
10. Treas. Reg. §1.79-3.
11. Treas. Reg. §1.79-3(d)(2).
12. Treas. Reg. §§1.79-3(d)(2), 1.79-3(e).
13. I.R.C. §3121(a)(2)(C); See Notice 88-82, 1988-2 CB 398 for current FICA reporting rules.
14. I.R.C. §2042.
15. See Rev. Rul. 72-307, 1972-1 CB 307 which modified Rev. Rul. 69-54, 1969-1 CB 221. See also *Estate of Max J. Gorby v. Comm'r.*, 53 TC 80, acq. 1970-1 CB xvi; *Landorf v. U.S.*, 408 F.2nd 461 (1969).
16. Treas. Reg. §§1.79-1(b), 1.79-1(d).
17. TAM 200502040 illustrates how the IRS makes this complex analysis.
18. Notice 89-110, 1989-2 CB 447.

SPLIT DOLLAR LIFE INSURANCE

CHAPTER 45

INTRODUCTION

Split dollar life insurance is an arrangement, typically between an employer and an employee, in which there is a sharing of the costs and benefits of the life insurance policy. (Split dollar plans can also be adopted for purposes other than providing an employee benefit—for example, between a parent corporation and a subsidiary, or between a parent and a child or in-law.) Usually split dollar plans involve a splitting of premiums, death benefits, and/or cash values, but they may also involve the splitting of dividends or ownership.

Under the classic approach, the employer corporation pays that part of the annual premium that equals the current year's increase in the cash surrender value of the policy. The employee pays the balance, if any, of the premium. In the long run this provides a low outlay protection incentive for selected employees to stay with the employer. If the insured employee dies, the corporation recovers its outlay (an amount equal to the cumulative cash value) and the balance of the policy proceeds is paid to the beneficiary chosen by the employee.

Split dollar plans can be used for various purposes between parties who don't have an employer-employee relationship (for example, for intra-family gift or estate planning). However, this chapter will focus entirely on the use of split dollar for employee compensation purposes.

WHEN IS USE OF SUCH A DEVICE INDICATED?

1. When an employer wishes to provide an executive with a life insurance benefit at low cost and low outlay to the executive. Split dollar plans are best suited for executives in their thirties, forties, and early fifties because the plan requires a reasonable duration in order to build up adequate policy cash values and the cost to the executive[1] can be excessive at later ages.

2. When a pre-retirement death benefit for an employee is a major objective, split dollar can be used as an alternative to an insurance-financed nonqualified deferred compensation plan.

3. When an employer is seeking a totally selective executive fringe benefit. An employer can reward or provide incentives for employees on a pick and choose basis. Neither the coverage, amounts, nor the terms of the split dollar arrangement need to meet nondiscrimination rules that add cost and complexity to many other benefit plans.

4. When an employer wants to make it easier for shareholder-employees to finance a buy out of stock under a cross purchase buy-sell agreement or make it possible for non-stockholding employees to effect a one-way stock purchase at an existing shareholder's death. This helps establish a market for what otherwise might be unmarketable stock while providing an incentive for bright, creative, productive employees to remain with the company and increase profits.

Advantages

1. A split dollar plan allows an executive to receive a benefit of current value (namely, life insurance coverage) using employer funds, with minimal tax cost to the executive.

2. In most types of split dollar plans, the employer's outlay is at all times fully secured. At the employee's death or termination of employment, the employer is reimbursed from policy proceeds for its premium outlay. The net cost to the employer for the plan is merely the loss of the net after-tax income the funds could have earned while the plan was in effect. If a split dollar plan is treated as a loan, the employer may recognize taxable income as part of the transaction.

3. Many types of split dollar designs are possible so the plan can be customized to meet employer and employee objectives and premium paying abilities.

Disadvantages

1. The employer receives no tax deduction for its share of premium payments under the split dollar plan.

2. The employee must pay income taxes each year on the current cost of life insurance protection under the plan (less any premiums paid by the employee). This cost may be determined by using either, one-year term insurance rates published by the insurance company, or Table 2001 rates, as discussed in the Design Features section of this chapter.

3. The plan must remain in effect for a reasonably long time (ten to twenty years) in order for policy cash values to rise to a level sufficient to maximize plan benefits.

4. The plan must generally be terminated at approximately age sixty-five, because the employee's tax cost for the plan rises sharply at later ages.

5. Plans that provide for an employee share in the policy's cash value (i.e., equity-type split dollar plans) were attractive in the past because they provide a savings or investment benefit for the employee, but under current regulations the tax treatment of these plans is unfavorable.

DESIGN FEATURES

In a split dollar arrangement between employer and employee, at least three aspects of the policy can be subject to different types of split: (1) the premium cost, (2) the cash value, and (3) the policy ownership. Following is a brief discussion of these variations, their advantages and disadvantages, and when they are used.

Premium Cost Split

There are four major categories of premium split: (1) the classic (or standard) split; (2) the level premium plan; (3) an employer-pay-all plan; and (4) an offset plan.

Classic Split

The classic or *standard* split dollar plan under which the employer pays a portion of the premiums equal to the increase in cash surrender value of the policy for the year, or the net premium due, if lower. (See Figure 45.1.) The employee pays the remainder of the premium.

Advantages of this approach are that the employer's risk is minimized (because the cash value is enough to fully reimburse its outlay even if the plan is terminated in the early years) and the plan is (arguably) simple to design and explain.

The principal disadvantages are that the employee's outlay is very high in the initial years of the plan, when cash values increase slowly, and the tax benefits available are not maximized under this option, as discussed in Tax Implications, below.

Level Premium Plan

The *level premium* plan, under which the employee's premium share is leveled over an initial period of years, such as five or ten. This alleviates the large initial premium share required of the employee under the standard arrangement. If the plan stays in existence long enough the employee and employer ultimately pay nearly the same total amount as under the standard arrangement.

The disadvantage of the level premium plan is that if the plan is terminated in the early years, the policy cash value is not sufficient to fully reimburse the employer for its total premium outlay. This possibility should be considered in drafting the split dollar agreement.

Employer-pay-all Plan

The *employer pay all* arrangement, with the employer paying the entire premium and the employee paying nothing. This arrangement is used when the employee's funds to pay for the plan are severely limited. The employee's cost in this arrangement is limited to the Table 2001 cost of pure insurance coverage that must

Figure 45.1

"STANDARD" PLAN

WHOLE LIFE
FACE AMOUNT: $100,000
DIVIDENDS APPLIED TO BUY ONE-YEAR TERM INSURANCE, REMAINDER TO REDUCE PREMIUM
MALE AGE: 40
FIRST-YEAR PREMIUM = $2,298.00

		Premium Split		Payment on Death	
Year	Guar. Cash Value	Paid by Employer	Paid by Employee	To Employer	To Employee's Beneficiary
1	0	0	2,298	0	100,000
2	1,700	1,700	598	1,700	98,300
3	3,600	1,900	219	3,600	100,000
4	5,500	1,900	189	5,500	100,000
5	7,500	2,000	60	7,500	100,000
6	9,500	2,000	32	9,500	100,000
7	11,500	2,000	0	11,500	100,000
8	13,600	1,974	0	13,474	100,126
9	15,700	1,948	0	15,421	100,279
10	17,800	1,926	0	17,347	100,453
Total		17,347	3,396		
Average		1,735	340		
11	20,000	1,905	0	19,252	100,748
12	22,200	1,888	0	21,141	101,059
13	24,400	1,864	0	23,004	101,396
14	26,700	1,869	0	24,874	101,826
15	29,000	1,866	0	26,740	102,260
Total		26,740	3,396		
Average		1,783	226		
16	31,300	1,870	0	28,609	102,691
17	33,700	1,879	0	30,488	103,212
18	36,000	1,895	0	32,383	103,617
19	38,400	1,926	0	34,309	104,091
20	40,900	1,969	0	36,278	104,622
Total		36,278	3,396		
Average		1,814	170		

be reported by the employee as taxable income. If the split dollar plan is treated as a loan, the reportable income by the employee is measured by Code section 7872 (see "Tax Implications" below).

As with the level premium plan, if the plan is terminated early, the policy cash value will not fully reimburse the employer outlay; again, the agreement between the employer and employee should address this problem.

Offset Plan

The *offset* plan, under which the employee pays an amount equal to the Table 2001 cost, if applicable, for the coverage (or if less, the net premium due) each year. The employer pays the balance of the premium. The purpose of this arrangement is to zero out the employee's income tax cost for the plan, as discussed below.

As a further refinement, the employer can reduce the employee's out-of-pocket cost for this arrangement by paying a tax deductible bonus to the employee equal to the employee's payment under the split dollar plan. The employer might want to go a step further and pay an additional amount equal to the tax on the first bonus as a double bonus.

The offset arrangement is an advantageous one that is commonly used. However, as with most variations on the standard plan, the employer remains exposed to some risk if the plan is terminated early, because the cash value will be less than the employer's outlay in some cases. The split dollar agreement should deal with this issue.

Cash Value and Death Proceeds Split

The purpose of the split of cash value or death proceeds is to reimburse the employer, in whole or in part, for its share of the premium outlay, in the event of the employee's death or termination of the plan.

At the employee's death, any policy proceeds not used to reimburse the employer go to the employee's designated beneficiary. This provides a significant death benefit in the early years of the plan, one of the principal objectives of a split dollar plan.

Most plans are designed to provide cash value growth sufficient to reimburse the employer after a number of years. The excess cash value can also benefit the employee, by allowing the plan to provide an attractive investment element (in a sense, a deferred compensation or pension element) in addition to the death benefit. Some plans are designed primarily to maximize this element.

The following are commonly used cash value/death proceeds split arrangements:

1. the employer's share is the *greater* of:
    a. the aggregate premiums it has paid; or
    b. the policy's cash value;
2. the employer can recover only up to the amount of its aggregate premiums paid; or
3. the employer is entitled to the entire cash value.

If a plan terminates early—usually when the employee terminates employment before the plan has matured—the cash value of the policy may not be sufficient to fully reimburse the employer for the aggregate premium payments it has made. The plan can provide that the employee is personally responsible to reimburse the employer in that event. As a practical matter, however, it may be difficult to enforce such a requirement, particularly if the amount is insufficient to justify the costs of a lawsuit. (A practical suggestion is to make sure that the company's severance pay arrangement, if any, allows recovery of any such amount out of severance pay otherwise due.)

Policy Ownership

There are two methods of arranging policy ownership under a split dollar plan: the endorsement method and the collateral assignment method. These two types have several variations based on the details of the plans. The general information for each method, though, remains similar.

Endorsement Method

Under the endorsement method, the employer owns the policy and is primarily responsible to the insurance company for paying the entire premium. The beneficiary designation provides for the employer to receive a portion of the death benefit equal to its premium outlay (or some alternative share), with the remainder of the death proceeds going to the employee's designated beneficiary. An endorsement to the policy is filed with the insurance company under which payment to the employee's beneficiary cannot be changed without consent of the employee (or, in some cases, a designated third person where the employee wishes to avoid incidents of ownership for estate tax purposes).

Advantages of the endorsement method are:

- greater control by the employer over the policy;
- simpler installation and administration; the only documentation required (except for possible ERISA requirements described below) is the policy and endorsement;
- avoidance of any formal arrangement that might be deemed to constitute a "loan" under current regulations, general tax principles, or for purposes of state laws prohibiting corporate loans to officers and directors; and
- if the company owns an existing key employee policy on the employee, it can be used directly in the split dollar plan without change of ownership. (Using an existing policy may be important if the employee has developed health problems since the policy was issued.)

Similar to the collateral assignment method, discussed next, endorsement split dollar can be either contributory or non-contributory with respect to the insured's portion of the premium payments.

A variant of the endorsement method is called reverse-split dollar. This variant involves the roles of the parties to the arrangement being reversed. If the parties are the employee and employer (typically the case), then the employee would own the policy and endorse a portion of the death benefit to the employer. The viability of reverse split dollar has been severely compromised by Notice 2002-592.[2]

Collateral Assignment Method

Under the collateral assignment method, one party (either the employee or employer) pays a portion of the premium and as a result of receives a collateral interest in the policy cash value and death benefit (Collateral Assignee). The other party is the owner of the policy (Policy Owner) and is entitled to receive any cash value and death benefit not collaterally assigned to the Collateral Assignee.

There are two variations of the collateral assignment method, (1) non-contributory, and (2) contributory. In non-contributory, the collateral assignee pays the entire premium.

In contributory, the policy owner (often the employer) pays a portion of the premium. The employer then makes interest-free loans of the amount of the premium the employer has agreed to pay under the split dollar plan (these may or may not be treated as loans for income tax purposes). To secure these loans, the policy is assigned as collateral to the employer. At the employee's death, the employer recovers its aggregate premium payments from the policy proceeds, as collateral assignee. The remainder of the policy proceeds are paid to the employee's designated beneficiary. If the plan terminates before the employee's death, the employer has the right to be reimbursed out of policy cash values; the employee continues as the owner of the policy.

Some advantages of the collateral assignment method include:

- it arguably gives more protection to the employee and the employee's beneficiary; and
- it is easier to implement using existing insurance policies owned by the employee.

There are two types of collateral assignment split dollar arrangements – equity split-dollar and non-equity split-dollar. These two types are discussed in more detail in our companion book, *The Tools & Techniques of Life Insurance Planning*.

TAX IMPLICATIONS

Split dollar arrangements entered into before September 18, 2003 were taxed under the "economic benefit theory." (The "Frequently Asked Questions" section below outlines the transition rules that remain in effect for plans that were issued before this date.) Under the economic benefit theory, the amount of economic benefit received by an employee each year was determined using the IRS table that values the pure insurance coverage for the employee.[3] The taxation of equity-type plans[4] and policy rollouts when the arrangement terminated were then unclear.

Under the current Treasury regulations, there are two mutually exclusive regimes for taxing split dollar arrangements:[5] (1) the economic benefit regime; and (2) the loan regime.

1. *Economic benefit regime.* The economic benefit regime applies to (1) endorsement-type plans, and (2) collateral assignment plans that are not equity-type plans.[6] Under the economic benefit regime, the pure death benefit amount applicable to the employee is valued each year under Table 2001 and this amount, less any amount contributed by the employee to the plan, is taxed to the employee. The employee is also taxed on the amount of equity in the policy's cash value, if any, that the employee gains access to during the taxable year.

2. *Loan regime.* The loan regime, in effect, applies mainly to collateral assignment equity-type plans (technically, it is the default treatment for arrangements that don't qualify for economic benefit treatment). Under the loan regime, the premium amounts provided by the employer that benefit the employee are treated as loans to the employee from the employer. If the arrangement carries no stated interest rate, the loan is considered a "demand loan" that is taxed under the rules of Code Section 7872 (see Chapter 53).[7]

Rollout Rules

The Treasury regulations specifically provide that when a contract is transferred to the employee (typically when the split dollar plans is terminated or when the employee terminates employment), the employee has income equal to the fair market value of the policy, less the sum of (1) any amount paid by the employee to the employer for the policy, plus (2) the amount the employee took into income as an economic benefit for equity buildup or for current life insurance protection.[8] Amounts contributed by the employee for insurance protection (Table 2001 amounts) are not included in the employee's basis.[9] Taxation under this rule occurs in the year determined under Section 83—that is, the year in which the contract is no longer subject to a risk of forfeiture.

Death Benefits

Death benefits from a split dollar plan—both the employer's share and the employee's beneficiary's share—are generally income tax free.[10]

The tax-free nature of the death proceeds is lost if the policy has been transferred for value in certain situations. The transfer for value trap should be carefully avoided in designing split dollar plans.[11]

The following transfers of insurance policies are exempt from the transfer for value rules—in other words, they will not cause the loss of the death proceeds' tax-free nature:

(a) a transfer of the policy to the insured;

(b) a transfer to a partner of the insured or to a partnership of which the insured is a partner;

(c) a transfer to a corporation of which the insured is a shareholder or officer; or

(d) a transfer in which the transferee's basis is determined in whole or in part by reference to the transferor's basis (i.e., a substituted or carryover basis).

Some precautions for avoiding potential transfer for value situations in split dollar plans are as follows:

- Do not initiate the plan by transferring an existing corporate-owned key employee policy to a third-party beneficiary.
- Do not start the plan by transferring an employee-owned policy to the corporation unless the employee is a shareholder or officer.
- At termination of the plan, do not transfer the corporation's interest in the policy to a third party beneficiary; although there are some arrangements where this presents no problem, it is better to make such a transfer to the insured.

If the employee had no incidents of ownership in the policy, the death benefit is not includable in the employee's estate for federal estate tax purposes unless the policy proceeds are payable to the employee's estate.[12] If an employee is potentially faced with a federal estate tax liability, all incidents of ownership in the policy should therefore be assigned irrevocably to a third party, a beneficiary or a trust. Proceeds generally should be payable to a named personal beneficiary and not to the employee's estate.

If the employee is a controlling shareholder (more than 50 percent) in the employer corporation, the *corporation's* incidents of ownership in the policy will be attributed to the majority shareholder. The current IRS position is that even if the corporation has only the right to make policy loans against its share of the cash value, this is an incident of ownership that will be attributed to the controlling shareholder and cause estate tax inclusion of the policy death proceeds.[13]

For a majority shareholder, the only way to avoid estate tax inclusion is for not only the employee but also the employer to get rid of the incidents of ownership. The corporation can avoid such incidents by retaining no rights of ownership in the policy, including any policy contract provisions or riders relating to the split dollar agreement. One procedure for accomplishing this is for the employee's personal beneficiary to be the original purchaser of the policy, and the beneficiary to enter into the split dollar agreement with the corporation on a collateral assignment basis.

Gift Taxes

There may be federal gift tax consequences if a person other than the employee owns the insurance policy used in a split dollar plan. The transfer of the policy from the employee to another party is a gift subject to tax. In addition, there is a continuing annual gift if the employee pays the premiums. There is also a continuing annual gift by the employee if the *employer* pays premiums, because this employer payment represents compensation earned by the employee that is indirectly transferred to the policyowner.[14] Such potentially taxable gifts may avoid taxation if they qualify for the annual gift tax exclusion ($14,000, as indexed for 2015). Gifts made directly to beneficiaries generally qualify, while gifts to insurance trusts may be considered "future interests" that do not qualify for the gift tax exclusion.

ERISA REQUIREMENTS

A split dollar plan is considered an employee welfare benefit plan and is subject to the ERISA rules applicable to such plans, as discussed in Chapter 16.

A welfare plan can escape the ERISA reporting and disclosure requirements, including the Form 5500 filing and the summary plan description (SPD) requirement, if it is an insured plan maintained for a select group of management or highly compensated employees.[15] Most split dollar plans qualify for this exception. If the plan covers more than a select group, it must provide SPDs to participants. If the plan covers fewer than one hundred participants, the SPD need not be filed with the DOL.[16]

ERISA further requires a written document, a "named fiduciary," and a formal claims procedure for split dollar plans.[17]

USE IN PARTNERSHIPS AND S CORPORATIONS

Generally, split dollar does not work as a way of using corporate dollars for owners of S corporations or unincorporated entities. with an S corporation split dollar plan on several shareholder-employees, the effect is to reallocate the cost of the plan toward the majority shareholder. Most majority shareholders will not be interested in such an arrangement. The results are generally the same for partners and proprietors.

Example. Suppose an S corporation earns $50,000 after paying a $100,000 salary to its sole shareholder-employee Lionel. The corporation proposes to pay $10,000 of this as premiums for a split dollar insurance program for Lionel. Lionel's taxable income *with* the split dollar plan: $150,000 (plus possible Table 2001 costs, although it is not clear that double taxation is required). *Without* the split dollar plan, Lionel's taxable income is also $150,000. At best, the split dollar plan risks taxation on the premium plus the Table 2001 costs, and using the corporation in this manner provides no advantage over holding the insurance personally.

Split dollar can sometimes work in unincorporated businesses. First, it does work for key (non-shareholder) employees of an S corporation or unincorporated business, because they are not subject to the income pass-through that applies to owners.

Split dollar may also work for owners where an S corporation's taxable income is reduced to zero through carryovers, depreciation, etc. Then the use of corporate funds for split dollar insurance for a shareholder-employee does not affect taxable income.

Another possible use for split dollar for a shareholder of an S corporation applies where saving gift taxes, not income taxes, is the object. For example, suppose an S corporation shareholder-employee wants to set up an irrevocable insurance trust for his children. He will make gifts to the trust to pay premiums, which puts the entire premium into his gift tax base and to the extent the annual exclusion is exceeded, this will reduce his lifetime exclusion or result in gift taxes. If, however, the plan is set up as a split dollar arrangement between the trust and the S corporation, the shareholder-employee's annual gift will be equal only to his Table 2001 or one-year term premium costs. This will be below the annual exclusion ceiling for considerable amounts of insurance for many years in some cases.

WHERE CAN I FIND OUT MORE?

1. *Tax Facts on Insurance & Employee Benefits*, Cincinnati, OH: *The National Underwriter Co.* (revised annually).

2. Cady, Donald F., *Field Guide to Estate, Employee, & Business Planning*, Cincinnati, OH: *The National Underwriter Co.* (revised annually).

3. Leimberg, Stephan R., Doyle, Robert J. Jr., and Buck, Keith A. *The Tools & Techniques of Life Insurance Planning*, 6th edition, Cincinnati, OH: The National Underwriter Co., 2015. Chapter 41 deals specifically with split dollar plans.

FREQUENTLY ASKED QUESTIONS

Question – What is the impact of a split dollar plan on corporate earnings for accounting purposes?

Answer – Many corporate managers, particularly in publicly held corporations, are concerned that adoption of various executive compensation plans may cause a charge to corporate earnings for financial reporting purposes. The tendency in the accounting profession is toward requiring charges to earnings for most types of executive compensation, and the Financial Accounting Standards Board (FASB) is currently considering accounting rules in this area.

Under the rules currently in effect, however, there would not be a charge to earnings under a "standard" split dollar plan such as that in Figure 45.1, because the corporation controls the cash value of the policy and the premium outlay is always balanced by a cash value increase owned by the corporation.

Question – What are the transition rules currently in effect for split dollar plans entered into before September 18, 2003?

Answer – The transitional rules (from Notice 2002-8) are as follows:[18]

- Arrangements entered into before September 18, 2003, will have no current tax on the equity buildup. This provision removes a threat that was implicit in earlier IRS pronouncements.

- Arrangements entered into before September 18, 2003, will not be treated as terminated with a rollout and transfer of property subject to Section 83 as long as life insurance protection continues to be treated as an economic benefit to the employee.

- For arrangements entered into before September 18, 2003, the parties will have the option of treating premium payments as loans under any reasonable effort to comply with Section 7872.

- Notice 2002-8 retained Table 2001, which replaced the P.S. 58 table for valuing economic benefit. No such table was included in the regulations, but it is believed that Table 2001 will be replaced at some time in the future. Notice 2002-8 contains other rules regarding which term rates to use.

- Arrangements entered into before January 28, 2002, can continue to use the P.S. 58 rates if those rates are stated in the split dollar plan. Since the Table 2001 rates are lower than the P.S. 58 rates, this is useful only for limited purposes.

- Arrangements entered into before the effective date of future guidance (i.e., before September 18, 2003) can use Table 2001.

- Arrangements entered into before September 18, 2003, can use an insurer's lower term premium rate in lieu of P.S. 58 or Table 2001 rates. However, after December 31, 2003, the published insurer rates may not be used "(i) unless the insurer generally makes the availability of such rates known to persons who apply for term insurance coverage from the insurer, and (ii) the insurer regularly sells term insurance at such rates to individuals who apply for term insurance coverage through the insurer's normal distribution channels."

CHAPTER ENDNOTES

1. As determined by Table 2001, formerly P.S. 58.
2. In Notice 2002-59, the IRS stated that one party cannot use inappropriately high current term insurance rates, prepayment of premiums, or other techniques to confer policy benefits other than current life insurance protection on another party.
3. Rev. Rul. 64-328, 1964-2 CB 11.
4. In the equity split dollar arrangement, the employer's interest in the policy value was limited at all times to the aggregate premiums it had paid. Thus, after the policy cash value reached the level of the aggregate employer premium payments, the employee began receiving a gradually increasing interest in the investment build-up in the policy. The ability to receive an increasing interest in the cash value made this plan what is referred to as an "equity split dollar" plan.
5. "Split-dollar arrangement" is defined broadly, Treas. Reg. §1.61-22(b).
6. Treas. Reg. §§1.61-22(b)(3), 1.61-22(c), and 1.61-22(d)(2).
7. Treas. Reg. §1.7872-15.
8. Treas. Reg. §1.61-22(g)(1).
9. Treas. Reg. §1.61-22(f)(2).
10. I.R.C. §101(a)(1).
11. I.R.C. §101(a)(2).
12. I.R.C. §2042.
13. Rev. Rul. 82-145, 1982-2 CB 213.
14. Rev. Rul. 78-420, 1978-2 CB 67.
15. Labor Reg. §2520.104-24.
16. Labor Reg. §2520.104-20.
17. ERISA §402(a).
18. 2002-1 CB 398.

KEY EMPLOYEE LIFE INSURANCE

CHAPTER 46

INTRODUCTION

Key employee life insurance, sometimes included within the broader description of corporate-owned life insurance or COLI, is insurance on a key employee's life owned by the employer, with the death benefit payable to the employer. Technically, key employee insurance is designed to compensate the employer for the loss of a key employee and is not an employee benefit for the key employee. However, in closely held corporations, key employee insurance can be used to indirectly benefit shareholder-employees by providing a source of liquid assets in the corporation. Key employee policies make assets available from policy cash values during the employee's lifetime and from the policy proceeds on the death of the employee. These assets can be used to finance the employer's obligation under one or more employee benefit plans.

WHEN IS USE OF SUCH A DEVICE INDICATED?

1. When a corporation will incur an obligation to pay a specified beneficiary or class of beneficiaries at an employee's death under a Death Benefit Only (DBO) plan (see Chapter 47).

2. When an employer has a nonqualified deferred compensation arrangement with one or more key executives or other employees and needs a way to finance its obligation upon the death of the employee. For example, such a plan might provide a benefit of $50,000 a year for ten years if the employee lives to retirement or $50,000 a year for ten years to a designated beneficiary if the employee dies either before or after retirement (see Chapter 33).

3. When a closely held corporation anticipates a need for liquid assets upon the death of a key employee to stabilize the corporation financially and enable it to continue contributing to employee benefit plans for surviving employees.

4. When a shareholder-employee expects the corporation to buy stock from his or her estate as part of an estate plan and the corporation needs additional liquid assets to carry out such a purchase.

TAX IMPLICATIONS

For Employees

There is no income tax to a key employee or the key employee's estate when the corporation owns the policy, pays the premiums, and receives death proceeds from key employee life insurance.

Corporate-owned key employee life insurance may have some effect on the federal estate tax payable by the deceased key employee's estate. The value of corporate stock held by a decedent at death is included in the decedent's gross estate for federal estate tax purposes. If the corporation held life insurance on the decedent's life, the insurance proceeds increase the value of the corporation and, therefore, can be included in the value of the stock held by the decedent.

The general rule for key employee life insurance, where the corporation is the beneficiary, is that the insurance proceeds are taken into account in valuing the decedent's stock, but not necessarily included in the decedent's estate dollar for dollar.[1] However, in many situations the IRS attempts to increase the value of the stock as much as possible where the corporation held key employee life insurance.

If the insured key employee was a majority shareholder (more than 50 percent), the tax law provides that policy proceeds, to the extent payable to or for the benefit of a party other than the corporation or its creditors, will be taxed in the insured key employee's estate as life insurance.[2] For this reason, policy proceeds of corporate-owned life insurance should generally be payable only to the corporation or its creditors.

For Employers

Corporate-paid premiums on life insurance on the life of a key employee, where the corporation is the owner and beneficiary of the life insurance contract, are not deductible for federal income tax purposes.[3]

The death proceeds of key employee life insurance are tax-free when paid to the corporation, except for the potential application of the Alternative Minimum Tax (AMT) discussed below.[4]

If the corporation has accumulated earnings of more than $250,000 ($150,000 for certain service corporations) then the further accumulation of income to pay life insurance premiums for key employee insurance potentially exposes the corporation to the accumulated earnings tax. There are, however, many exceptions to the application of this tax. The purchase of life insurance to cover the potential loss of a bona fide key employee should not result in a significant risk of accumulated earnings tax exposure in most cases.

AMT

Key employee life insurance involves some potential corporate exposure to the corporate Alternative Minimum Tax (AMT). The purpose of the AMT is to require corporations to pay a minimum level of income tax on actual economic income, even if taxable income has been reduced by significant amounts of tax-exempt or tax-preferred income. The AMT is a tax computed on a base of reported income plus certain tax preferences. Generally, a corporation must pay the larger of its regular tax or the AMT.[5] Certain small corporations are exempt from AMT (generally, average gross receipts of $7,500,000 or less).[6]

The AMT is imposed on a base of Adjusted Minimum Taxable Income (AMTI). The AMTI includes regular income plus tax preferences. In addition, there is included in the AMTI an amount equal to 75 percent of the excess of corporate adjusted current earnings over the AMTI (computed without regard to the adjustment for current earnings), with various adjustments.[7]

Adjusted current earnings includes amounts that are income for accounting purposes and treated as "earnings and profits" but are not included in taxable income.[8] IRS regulations indicate that both death proceeds (in excess of the taxpayer's basis) and the annual increases in cash value are part of adjusted current earnings.[9]

The corporate AMT is equal to 20 percent of AMTI reduced by a $40,000 exemption which is phased out at the rate of 25 percent of AMTI exceeding $150,000. In other words, the exemption disappears for AMTI that is equal to or greater than $310,000 ($310,000 exceeds $150,000 by $160,000 and 25 percent of $160,000 is $40,000).

A simple example will illustrate the impact of AMT on corporate-owned life insurance:

Example. Professional Services, Inc. (PSI) has regular taxable income of $200,000. Also, PSI receives $300,000 of net death proceeds from corporate-owned term life insurance. PSI's regular income tax on $200,000 is $61,250. The AMT is computed as follows:

Taxable income		$200,000
AMTI without adjustment for current earnings		200,000
Current earnings	$500,000	
Less AMTI w/o adjustment	– 200,000	
	$300,000	
75% of 300,000		$225,000
AMTI		425,000
Exemption amount		0
AMTI less exemption		425,000
AMT (20% of AMTI less exemption)		85,000
Less regular tax		– 61,250
Additional tax		$ 23,750

This example shows an additional tax of $23,750, which is 7.9 percent of the insurance proceeds of $300,000. In general, the maximum tax that can be imposed on death proceeds is 20 percent of 75 percent of the death proceeds, or 15 percent.

Although the AMT is unfavorable to corporate-owned life insurance, its maximum impact is not extreme. Furthermore, the best way to avoid the impact of the AMT is to purchase additional life insurance, to insure that the corporation receives the full amount expected, after AMT.

ALTERNATIVES

Personally owned insurance can provide estate liquidity and funds to meet the needs of beneficiaries. Corporate funds can be used indirectly by paying extra compensation to the employee as discussed in Chapter 3. This extra compensation is deductible so long as it meets the reasonableness test discussed in Chapter 2. In a situation where the corporation's marginal income tax bracket is higher than the employee's, personally owned insurance may provide a better tax result.

WHERE CAN I FIND OUT MORE?

1. *The Tools and Techniques of Estate Planning*, 17th ed. Cincinnati, OH: The National Underwriter Co., 2015.

2. *The Tools and Techniques of Life Insurance Planning*, 6th ed., Cincinnati, OH, The National Underwriter Co., 2015.

3. CLU/ChFC Course: Planning for Business Owners and Professionals (HS 331), The American College, Bryn Mawr, PA.

4. Graduate Courses: Advanced Estate Planning (GS 815 and 816), The American College, Bryn Mawr, PA.

CHAPTER ENDNOTES

1. Treas. Reg. §20.2031-2(f).
2. Treas. Reg. §20.2042-1(c)(6).
3. I.R.C. §264(a)(1).
4. I.R.C. §101(a)(1).
5. I.R.C. §§55 and 56.
6. I.R.C. §55(e).
7. I.R.C. §56(g).
8. I.R.C. §312.
9. Treas. Reg. §1.56(g)-1(c)(5).

DEATH BENEFIT ONLY (DBO) PLAN

CHAPTER 47

INTRODUCTION

A Death Benefit Only plan (DBO) sometimes referred to as an employer-paid death benefit or a survivor's income benefit plan is a plan by which an employer defers employee compensation and pays it to the employee's designated beneficiary at the employee's death. No benefit is payable in any form to the employee during his or her lifetime.

WHEN IS USE OF SUCH A DEVICE INDICATED?

1. The DBO plan is most valuable in the case of a highly compensated employee who: (1) expects to have a large estate; and (2) faces significant federal estate tax liability because the estate will be payable to a nonspouse beneficiary (i.e., will not be able to fully use the estate tax marital deduction). If the covered employee owns 50 percent or less of the corporation's stock and the plan is properly designed, the benefit from a DBO plan is not subject to federal estate tax.

2. The plan can be used for selected employees as a supplement to qualified retirement plan benefits. Under current law, maximum qualified plan benefits to highly compensated employees may be significantly limited. A DBO plan can provide extra benefits not affected by such limitations.

3. The plan can be used to replace a split dollar plan (see Chapter 48) where the cost to the employee of the current insurance protection is increasing rapidly because of age—usually after age sixty.

4. A DBO plan can be used for deferring compensation of younger employees with families and a need for insurance. The DBO plan can be converted to full nonqualified deferred compensation with lifetime benefits when the employee's value to the employer has increased to the point where this is indicated.

Advantages

1. If the covered employee is not a controlling (more than 50 percent) shareholder, properly designed DBO benefits can be kept out of the deceased employee's estate for federal estate tax purposes.

2. The plan's death benefit provides valuable estate liquidity and a source of immediate and continuing cash to the beneficiary upon the employee's death.

3. The benefit is not taxable to the employee during lifetime.

4. The plan can be financed by the employer through the purchase of life insurance, which provides funds to pay the death benefit and avoids current tax on investment returns under the policy. (Some alternative minimum tax—AMT—on the death proceeds may be payable at the corporate level.)

Disadvantages

1. The entire benefit is income taxable to the beneficiary—as ordinary income. This applies even if the benefit is financed using life insurance.

2. Keeping the death benefit out of the gross estate requires very careful plan design and avoidance of

technical tax traps, thus limiting flexibility in plan design.

3. The employer-corporation's tax deduction for the plan is deferred until the benefit is paid and the beneficiary includes the payments received in income. The employer must wait to take the deduction, even if it sets funds aside in advance (such as through the purchase of a life insurance contract).

Alternatives

There are several alternatives that may allow an employer to achieve many of the same benefits as a DBO plan:

1. Group-term life insurance.

2. Life insurance in a qualified plan.

3. Split dollar life insurance.

4. Individually owned life insurance (perhaps paid for through additional bonus compensation from the employer).

DESIGN FEATURES

The plan's benefit formula can take many forms:

1. The simplest formula is a fixed dollar amount—for example, $50,000 for each employee covered under the plan, or $10,000 per year for five years.

2. Benefits can be based on average compensation over a period of years—for example, the death benefit might be equal to a year's salary averaged over the five years prior to death.

3. Benefits are often related loosely to the death benefit under an insurance policy on the employee's life that is owned and purchased by the employer, in order to finance the plan. For example, suppose the employer and employee agree that the employee's salary will be reduced by $100 per month, or agree to extra employer payments of $100 per month, that will be used toward the premiums on an insurance policy. If the $1,200 per year will buy approximately a $50,000 life insurance policy for that employee, given his age and health, then the death benefit under the plan will be $50,000. Note, however, that most planners recommend against tying the benefit directly, dollar-for-dollar, to a life insurance policy. The plan should be designed to avoid any inference that it is simply the purchase of life insurance for the employee.[1]

HOW TO INSTALL A PLAN

Except for a voluntary plan (see Frequently Asked Questions), there should always be a written plan adopted in advance of the time that payments are to be made under the plan. The plan document can be simple, but it should specify

1. the amount of the benefit;

2. what employee or group of employees is entitled to it; and

3. that the benefit is intended as compensation for services to be rendered by the employee.

Nothing has to be filed with the government, except for the possible ERISA requirements listed earlier.

Financing the Plan

Many plans are informally funded—a better term to use is financed—through the corporation's setting aside an asset or combination of assets that is designed to grow to the point where benefit payments can be made from it. The amount, however, must be available to corporate creditors. The IRS does not consider this type of arrangement to be a fund for tax purposes, and the Department of Labor (which administers ERISA) probably will not consider this type of arrangement to be a fund for ERISA purposes.[2]

One of the most common types of investment for this type of fund is life insurance, since the insurance guarantees that adequate amounts will be available, even if the employee dies at a relatively young age.

Example. Suppose the plan provides a $100,000 death benefit to a key executive. The employer corporation expects to be in a 34 percent tax bracket when the benefit is paid. The corporation purchases a $66,000 policy on the employee's life. The corporation is owner and beneficiary of the policy and pays the premiums. The corporation's premium payments are nondeductible. If the employee dies, the corporation pays out $100,000 to the beneficiary and it deducts $100,000 as compensation, which saves $34,000 in taxes. The $66,000 in death proceeds from the policy is tax-free to the corporation, assuming no AMT tax. These proceeds reimburse the corporation for its out-of-pocket cost.

If the benefit is to be paid to the beneficiary over a period of years, rather than in a lump sum, the amount of life insurance needed by the corporation is further reduced. This is because investment earnings received by the corporation on the policy death proceeds are available to help fund the benefit payments.

TAX IMPLICATIONS

Benefits paid to the employee's beneficiary are taxable in full to the beneficiary as ordinary income.[3] The tax implications for the employee's estate and the employer are discussed below.

For the Employee's Estate

The death benefit from the plan will not be included in the deceased employee's estate so long as:

- the plan does not provide any benefits payable during the employee's lifetime; and

- the employee does not have the right to change the beneficiary, once the plan is established.[4]

In determining whether the plan pays lifetime benefits, the IRS will look beyond the DBO plan itself. Another plan that provides benefits during lifetime can be taken into account for this purpose, even if the employee never actually lives to collect those benefits.[5] Thus, a DBO plan will not be excluded from an employee's estate, if the employer also maintains a nonqualified deferred compensation plan providing lifetime benefits. The two plans will be linked together for this purpose and the estate tax exclusion will be lost. However, a *qualified* pension or profit sharing plan is not taken into account for this purpose, so those plans can be provided in addition to DBOs.[6] After several court cases on the issue,[7] the IRS also now agrees that an employer's long-term disability benefit plan will not taint a DBO, unless the disability plan requires that the employee be "retired on disability" to receive benefits.[8]

For the Employer

The benefit payments are deductible to the corporation when paid, so long as they constitute reasonable compensation for the services of the deceased employee in prior years. See Chapter 2 of this book for a detailed discussion of the "reasonableness" test. The reasonableness issue is most likely to be raised by the IRS if the decedent was a majority or controlling stockholder, particularly if the beneficiary is also a stockholder.

The IRS may also question whether the death benefit payment was for services actually rendered by the employee, as required for deductibility under Code section 162. This issue is most likely to be raised where: (1) the deceased employee was a majority shareholder; or (2) where there was no written agreement to pay the benefit prior to the employee's death.

If the corporation's deduction is disallowed for this reason, the amount could be treated as a nondeductible dividend, or, in unusual cases, as a gift by the corporation, with deductibility limited to $25 under Code section 274(b).

ERISA REQUIREMENTS

Whether a DBO plan is a pension plan or a welfare benefit plan for ERISA purposes is not clear.[9] These plans, if provided to a select group of management or highly compensated employees, should not come within the funding requirements of ERISA. However, if they are formally funded, many ERISA requirements apply. This is discussed in detail in Chapter 33, Nonqualified Deferred Compensation. Therefore, formal funding (where the employee has rights to the fund ahead of corporate creditors) is undesirable.

In either case, if the plan is unfunded and limited to a select group of management or highly compensated employees the "top hat" group it should be exempt from most of the provisions of ERISA.[10]

If such a DBO plan is considered a pension plan, it should be exempt from ERISA's participation, vesting, funding, and fiduciary responsibility requirements; the plan will be subject to ERISA's reporting and disclosure requirements and ERISA's administrative and enforcement provisions, but such a plan should be able to satisfy the reporting and disclosure requirements through a streamlined procedure including a simple notice to the Department of Labor (see Chapter 33, Nonqualified Deferred Compensation, for details and a sample notification form).[11]

If such a DBO plan is considered a welfare benefit plan, it will be (like all welfare benefit plans) exempt from ERISA's participation, vesting, and funding requirements, and it will be relieved of ERISA's reporting and disclosure requirements, except for the requirement that it submit plan documents to the Secretary of Labor upon request; the plan would appear to be subject to at least some of ERISA's fiduciary responsibility requirements and to ERISA's administrative and enforcement provisions.[12]

If the plan covers a broader group of employees, the full scope of ERISA's requirements—including vesting, funding, and reporting and disclosure requirements—may apply.[13] The vesting and funding requirements are discussed in Chapter 13 of this book and the reporting and disclosure requirements are summarized in Chapter 16.

WHERE CAN I FIND OUT MORE?

1. *The Tools and Techniques of Estate Planning*, 17th ed. Cincinnati, OH, The National Underwriter Co., 2015.

2. *The Tools and Techniques of Life Insurance Planning*, 6th ed. Cincinnati, OH, The National Underwriter Co., 2015.

FREQUENTLY ASKED QUESTIONS

Question – What mistakes in plan design or other circumstances would cause an employer death benefit to be included in the employee's estate?

Answer – The promise of the employer to pay a death benefit to a specified beneficiary, in return for the employee's promise to continue working for the employer, is considered a transfer by the employee of a property right.[14] If the agreement gives the employee the right to change the beneficiary, that retention of the power to designate who will enjoy the "transfer" has been held by the IRS to cause estate tax inclusion.[15]

If the beneficiary's right to receive the death benefit is conditioned on surviving the employee, and the employee retained a right to direct the disposition of the property (for example, where the death benefit is payable to the employee's spouse, but if the spouse does not survive the employee, the death benefit is payable to the employee's estate), that reversionary interest may cause inclusion.[16]

If the beneficiary is a revocable trust established by the employee, the right to alter, amend, or revoke the transfer by changing the terms of the trust would cause inclusion.[17]

Another problem relates to an employee who is also a controlling (more than 50 percent shareholder). The IRS argues that such an individual, by virtue of his or her voting control, has the right to alter, amend, revoke, or terminate the agreement. Therefore, the benefit should be includable in the estate of such an individual.[18]

If the employee already has postretirement benefits, such as a nonqualified deferred compensation agreement that pays a retirement benefit, the IRS could claim that the preretirement death benefit plan and the postretirement deferred compensation plan should be considered as a single plan. This would cause the present value of the death benefit to be treated, for estate tax purposes, as if it were a joint and survivor annuity; the present value of the death benefit would be includable in the deceased employee's estate.[19]

If the death benefit is payable to a trust over which the employee had a general power of appointment, the IRS might argue that the employee had a power of appointment over the death proceeds, which would result in inclusion for estate tax purposes.[20]

If the death benefit is funded with life insurance on the employee's life and the employee owned the policy or had veto rights over any change in the beneficiary, the IRS would probably attempt to include the policy proceeds because of the employee's incidents of ownership.[21]

Question – What is the advantage of a voluntary DBO plan?

Answer – A voluntary DBO is a payment not made under a contract or plan, but rather at the employer's discretion, after the employee's death. Such a payment probably will not be included in the employee's estate, because neither the employee nor the beneficiary possessed any right to compel the employer to pay the benefit and, therefore, there was no transfer to the employee.[22] However, if the employee owned more than 50 percent of the company's stock, the IRS is likely to argue for inclusion, for the reasons discussed above, even in this type of plan.

Even though there is no formal contract in this type of plan, it may be satisfactory, since the employee can reasonably expect the benefit to be paid in many cases. However, in other situations, this expectation may not be enough. The benefit will then provide the employee no peace of mind or financial security, and a written plan should be adopted.

CHAPTER ENDNOTES

1. See *Dependahl v. Falstaff Brewing Corp.*, 491 F. Supp. 1188 (E.D. Mo. 1980), *aff'd in part*, 653 F.2d 1208 (8th Cir. 1981), *cert. denied*, 454 U.S. 968 (1981) and 454 U.S. 1084 (1981); Department of Labor (DOL) Advisory Opinion 81-11A, regarding conditions under which life insurance is not considered a "plan asset"; see also *Belsky v. First National Life Insurance Co.*, 818 F.2d 661 (8th Cir. 1987); *Miller v. Heller*, 915 F. Supp. 651 (S.D.N.Y. 1996); *The Northwestern Mutual Life Ins. Co. v. Resolution Trust Corp.*, 848 F. Supp. 1515 (N.D. Ala. 1994); *Darden v. Nationwide Mutual Ins. Co.*, 717 F. Supp. 388 (E.D.N.C. 1989), *aff'd*, 922 F.2d 203 (4th Cir.), *cert. denied*, 502 U.S. 906 (1991), *Belka v. Rowe Furniture Corp.*, 571 F. Supp. 1249 (D. Md. 1983); DOL Advisory Opinions 94-31A, 92-22A, 92-02A.
2. See Chapter 35, Nonqualified Deferred Compensation, at "Funded versus Unfunded Plans," and the authorities cited in that discussion; see also Labor Reg. §2520.104-24; DOL Advisory Opinions 93-14A, 92-24A, 92-22A, 92-02A, 81-11A.
3. If the decedent died on or before August 20, 1996, up to $5,000 can be excluded as an employee death benefit under Code Section 101(b) if the employee did not have vested rights to the benefit immediately before death. This employee death benefit exclusion has been repealed for decedents dying after August 20, 1996. SBJPA '96, Section 1402.
4. See the frequently asked question above relating to "mistakes in plan design."
5. Treas. Reg. §20.2039-1(b).
6. *Est. of Fusz v. Comm'r.*, 46 TC 214 (1966), acq. 1967-2 CB 2; Rev. Rul. 76-380, 1976-2 CB 270.
7. *Est. of Wm. V. Schelberg v. Comm'r.*, 79-2 USTC ¶13,321 (2d Cir. 1979), *rev'g*, 70 TC 690 (1978); *Est. of Glen J. Van Wye v. U.S.*, 82-2 USTC ¶13,485 (6th Cir. 1982).
8. The IRS has announced that it will follow the *Schelberg* decision in all circuits. See *Looney v. U.S.*, Docket No. 83-8709 (11th Cir., motion filed 1-26-84).
9. The definitions of "pension plan" and "welfare benefit plan" for ERISA purposes are sufficiently vague that a DBO plan could arguably be characterized as either (or perhaps both). See ERISA Sections 3(1), 3(2)(A); Labor Reg. §2510.3-1; see also *Dependahl*, above.
10. See ERISA Sections 201(1), 201(2), 301(a)(1), 301(a)(3), 401(a), 401(a)(1), 503, 4021(a), 4021(b)(6); Labor Regs. §§2520.104-23, 2520.104-24, 2560.503-1(a), 2560.503-1(b). If a DBO plan is considered *both* a pension plan and a welfare benefit plan, it might not be able to take advantage of the exemptions from ERISA's participation, vesting, funding, and fiduciary responsibility requirements available to an unfunded plan maintained primarily for the purpose of providing deferred compensation to the top hat group. The argument would be that because such a plan's benefits are equally pension and welfare benefits, such a plan does not *primarily* provide deferred compensation. See ERISA Sections 201(2), 301(a)(3), 401(a)(1). Under a similar argument, such a hybrid plan might also be ineligible for the streamlined reporting and disclosure procedure available to an unfunded pension plan *primarily* providing deferred compensation to the top hat group. See Labor Reg. §2520.104-23. The merit of such arguments is unclear, and they are subject to counter-arguments. For example, a potential response might point out that the top hat exemptions are not written in terms of a plan that is *primarily a pension plan*; they are written in terms of a *plan primarily providing deferred compensation*, and welfare benefits can be considered deferred compensation just as readily as can pension benefits—for they are a form of future compensation for current services. Thus, the response might conclude, a plan that is equally a pension plan and a welfare benefit plan could still provide deferred compensation primarily (or even solely!). The merits of this argument, too, are unclear.
11. ERISA Sections 201(2), 301(a)(3), 401(a)(1), 503; Labor Regs. §§2520.104-23, 2560.503-1(a), 2560.503-1(b). The streamlined procedure for satisfying the reporting and disclosure requirements is also available to pension plans providing benefits to the top hat group (1) exclusively through employer-paid insurance contracts or policies, or (2) through employer-paid insurance contracts or policies and from the employer's general assets. Labor Reg. §2520.104-23.
12. ERISA Sections 201(1), 301(a)(1); Labor Reg. §2520.104-24; See ERISA Sections 401(a), 503; Labor Reg. §2560.503-1(a). The almost complete exemption from the reporting and disclosure requirements also extends to welfare plans providing benefits to the top hat group (1) exclusively through employer-paid insurance contracts or policies, or (2) through employer-paid insurance contracts or policies and from the employer's general assets. Labor Reg. §2520.104-24. A creative argument might (1) point out that the exemptions from ERISA's participation, vesting, funding, and fiduciary responsibility requirements for an unfunded plan maintained primarily for the purpose of providing deferred compensation to the top hat group are written in terms of a *plan* rather than in terms of a *pension plan*, (2) claim that a DBO plan's promised death benefits are nothing but deferred compensation—that is, future compensation for current services—and (3) conclude that regardless of whether a

DBO plan is characterized as a pension plan or a welfare benefit plan it should still be able to take advantage of the exemptions from ERISA's participation, vesting, funding, and fiduciary obligations for an unfunded *plan* maintained primarily for the purpose of providing *deferred compensation* to the top hat group. The merits of this argument are not clear.

13. Welfare benefit plans are not subject to ERISA's Title I participation, vesting, and funding requirements, nor to ERISA's Title IV plan termination insurance provisions. See ERISA Sections 201(1), 301(a)(1), 4021(a)(1).
14. See, e.g., *Est. of Fried v. Comm'r.*, 445 F.2d 979 (2d Cir. 1971); *Est. of Bernard L. Porter v. Comm'r.*, 442 F.2d 915 (1st Cir. 1971).
15. I.R.C. §2036; Rev. Rul. 76-304, 1976-2 CB 269.
16. I.R.C. §2037; *Est. of Fried v. Comm'r.*, 54 TC 805 (1970), *aff'd*, 445 F.2d 979 (2nd Cir. 1971), *cert. denied*, 404 U.S. 1016 (1972); Rev. Rul. 78-15, 1978-1 CB 289.
17. I.R.C. §2038.
18. *Est. of Levin v. Comm'r.*, 90 TC 723 (1988). The IRS' position in this case was a reversal of an earlier private ruling, TAM 8701003.
19. I.R.C. §2039; *Est. of Fusz v. Comm'r.*, 46 TC 214 (1966).
20. I.R.C. §2041.
21. I.R.C. §2042.
22. *Edith L. Courtney v. U.S.*, 84-2 USTC ¶13580 (N.D. Ohio 1984).

DESIGNING THE RIGHT PACKAGE OF FRINGE BENEFITS

CHAPTER 48

INTRODUCTION

Fringe benefits are noncash compensation benefits to employees. Most miscellaneous fringe benefits not discussed in other chapters of this book are governed by Code section 132, which determines whether the benefits are taxable to employees. The IRS publishes a "Taxable Fringe Benefits Guide" that contains much useful information in this regard.[1] This chapter covers:

- employee discounts;
- no-additional-cost services;
- company cafeterias and meal plans;
- qualified transportation;
- qualified retirement planning services;
- gyms and athletic facilities;
- "working condition fringes"; and
- "de minimis fringes"

EMPLOYEE DISCOUNTS

Employers in the retailing business often provide employees with discounts on merchandise sold in the employer's stores. For example, a department store may provide a 10 percent discount on clothing purchased by employees.

Advantages

Discounts on merchandise are almost as valuable as cash to employees, but are very inexpensive for the employer because the employer can still make a profit on the items sold (or at least recover its cost) but does not have to bear the full cost of marketing and selling the items to the public.

In the retail fashion industry, discounts serve the retailer's interest in promoting its products by allowing sales employees to wear the retailer's fashion items (which they otherwise could not afford) on the job.

Tax Implications

Employee discounts are not includable in the employee's taxable income if the following conditions are met:

1. For a highly compensated employee (see definition below), the discount is excludable from income only if the discount is available on substantially the same terms to each member of a classification of employees and does not discriminate in favor of highly compensated employees. For example, if a department store provided discounts only to its executives, most of whom fell under the highly compensated definition, the discounts would be taxable income, but only to those executives who were highly compensated.

2. The discount does not exceed the employer's gross profit percentage on the item. Gross profit percentage is the percentage of the ordinary retail price equal to:

$$\frac{\text{sales price less cost for all such items}^{2}}{\text{sales price for all such items}}$$

3. The items discounted must be property offered for sale to customers in the ordinary course of the line of business of the employer in which

the employee is working.[3] However, real estate or investments are not available for employee discount programs, even if the employer is in the business of selling real estate or investment products.

4. Employee discounts can be offered not only to active employees but also to:

   a. retired and disabled employees;

   b. surviving spouses of employees; or

   c. spouses or dependent children of employees.

5. Dependent child includes either an actual dependent for tax purposes, or a child under age twenty-five both of whose parents are deceased.[4]

NO-ADDITIONAL-COST SERVICES

Service businesses can provide discounted services to employees at low cost, but with considerable perceived value to the employees. Probably the best-known example of this type of fringe benefit is the free or discounted standby air travel available to some airline employees.

Advantages

Free or discounted services to employees may be almost as valuable to them as cash, but they can be provided at almost no marginal cost to the employer if they primarily involve excess capacity that provides no revenue to the employer.

Tax Implications

Services provided free or discounted to employees are not includable in the employee's taxable income if the following conditions are met:

1. For a highly compensated employee (see definition below), the value of the services used is excludable from income only if the services are available on substantially the same terms to each member of a classification of employees that does not discriminate in favor of highly compensated employees. For example, if an airline provided free standby air travel only to its executives, most of whom fell under the highly compensated definition, the value of any trips taken by highly compensated employees would be taxable income to them. Trips taken by nonhighly compensated employees would not be taxable.

2. Either of the following two conditions must be satisfied:

   a. The employer must incur no substantial cost (including foregone revenues) in providing such service to the employee (determined without regard to any amount paid by the employee). For example, providing hotel employees free hotel accommodations on a standby basis—that is, where the rooms are not otherwise booked—would meet this condition, because there would be no foregone revenue, and no substantial additional cost to the employer. However, providing free hotel room reservations, thus "bumping" paying customers, would not meet this condition.[5]

   b. Alternatively, if services are discounted to employees, the discount cannot be more than 20 percent of the price at which the services are offered by the employer to regular customers.[6]

3. The services must be those offered for sale to customers in the ordinary course of the line of business of the employer in which the employee is working.[7] For example, if a corporation operates both a hotel and an airline, employees of the hotel business can be provided with free standby hotel rooms in the employer's hotel, but not standby air transportation.

Unrelated employers in the same line of business—for example, two unrelated airlines—can enter into reciprocal written agreements under which employees of both can obtain nontaxable services from either one of the employers.[8]

No-additional-cost services can be offered not only to active employees but also to (1) retired and disabled employees, (2) surviving spouses of employees, or (3) spouses or dependent children of employees. Dependent child includes either an actual dependent for tax purposes or a child under age twenty-five both of whose parents are deceased.[9] In addition, for air travel, parents of employees can be included in the plan.[10]

COMPANY CAFETERIAS AND MEAL PLANS

Employers often provide cafeterias or dining rooms for employees for various business reasons: (1) time is saved by having employees eat on the premises rather than travel to outside restaurants; (2) nearby restaurants may be too expensive for many employees; (3) the work environment is enhanced by providing company dining facilities; and (4) employees may even talk business at lunch and trade ideas or make business decisions.

Employers can almost always deduct the cost of these facilities as business expenses. The significant tax question is: are the meals taxable to employees? The rules are surprisingly complicated.

There are two types of cafeteria/dining room/meal plans provided by an employer for employees that do not result in extra taxable income to employees: (1) a Section 119 "on-premises" plan, and (2) a Section 132(e)(2) "on or near" plan.[11]

Any *other* meals or meal plans, other than these two types, that are furnished to employees working at their regular workplace will constitute taxable income to the employee to the extent of the fair market value of the meal. However, meals and lodging furnished to employees who are working away from home are not taxable to the employees.[12]

Section 119 On-premises Plan

If an employer furnishes meals for employees, or their spouses or dependents, the value of the meals is excluded from the employee's income if:

- the meals are for the "convenience of the employer"; and
- the meals are furnished on the business premises of the employer.[13]

The issue of whether the plan serves the convenience of the employer is a factual one, with guidelines set out in the regulations under Code section 119.

If more than half of the employees are provided with meals that meet the above tests, all meals provided to employees on business premises are excluded from income.[14]

There is no requirement that the meals must be furnished for all employees or a broad or nondiscriminatory classification of employees.

The tax treatment of the plan is the same whether or not employees must pay for the meals, in full or in part. The amount the employee pays for individual meals is not tax-deductible by the employee. However, if the plan is structured so that the employee is *required* to pay a fixed periodic charge for the plan (not on a per-meal basis), then the fixed periodic charge is excluded from the employee's income for tax purposes.[15]

Section 132(e) On-or-near Plan

If an employer operates an eating facility for employees, the value of meals is not taxable to employees if the following conditions are met:[16]

- the eating facility is located on or near the business premises of the employer;
- revenue derived from the facility normally equals or exceeds the direct operating costs of the facility. The direct operating costs are the costs of food and beverages and labor performed directly at the eating facility.[17]
- if the employee is highly compensated (see definition below) the meal is taxable unless access to the eating facility is available on substantially the same terms to each member of a group of employees that is defined in a nondiscriminatory way.

In other words, an executives only dining room (including even a separate, posh dining room next to the employee mess[18]) can result in taxation of the meal's value to the executive, unless the plan meets the requirements of a code section 119 on-premises plan.[19]

QUALIFIED TRANSPORTATION

A qualified transportation fringe is a plan that provides one or more of the following benefits for employees:[20]

- transportation in a commuter highway vehicle;
- a transit pass for use on a transit system (public or private); or
- qualified parking.

Advantages

1. The value of these benefits can be considerable in some cases. They are provided tax-free to employees while the cost is fully deductible to employers.

2. Qualified transportation fringes, unlike other fringe benefits, can be provided to employees on a cash-option (salary reduction) basis.[21] For example, the employer can offer a group of employees the choice of receiving a monthly transit pass worth $50 or $50 more in cash that month. Those who choose the transit pass do not pay federal income taxes on its value; only those who choose the cash option must pay taxes on the $50 monthly benefit.

   By contrast, if an employer offered another fringe benefit on this basis, all employees would be taxable on the value of the benefit, whether they took cash or not.

   Example. If a department store offered employees a choice between $50 worth of monthly discounts on store merchandise or $50 monthly in cash, all employees covered by the plan would have $50 of taxable monthly income, whether or not they chose the cash option. Fringe benefits other than qualified transportation fringes must be offered as an employer-paid extra only, not under a cash option, or they lose their tax-free nature.

   ---

3. There are no nondiscrimination requirements for qualified transportation fringes. For example, parking can be provided tax-free (up to the monthly limit described below) even if it is available only to selected executives. Planners of executive compensation programs, particularly for executives working in downtown office buildings, should make note of the compensation opportunity potentially available here.

Available Benefits

Commuter highway vehicle. This benefit is available for transportation in vans seating at least six passengers and running on commuting trips when it is at least half-full. (This half-full provision is evidently designed to exclude chauffeured executive limos, etc.) The van can be operated by the employer or a contractor hired by the employer.[22] Tax-free benefits are limited to an aggregate per-employee monthly limit of $130 (in 2015) worth of transportation in commuter highway vehicles and transit passes.[23]

Qualified bicycle commuting. Employers can reimburse up to $20 per month (2015 figure) tax-free for bicycle expenses to an employee who uses a bicycle to commute to work.[24] This amount may not be claimed in any month in which the employee is eligible for the parking or transit pass exclusions.

Transit pass. A transit pass applies to mass transit as normally understood, as well as costs for a van operated as a business by a third party (not the employer or a contractor hired by the employer) and having at least a six-passenger capacity.[25] As indicated, a $130 (in 2015) monthly aggregate limit applies for transit passes together with commuter highway vehicle benefits.

Parking. Although many employees probably do not think of parking as an employee benefit, particularly if they work in suburban locations, the value of parking to employees can be considerable.

Under the tax law, parking provided to employees is excludable from their taxable income up to $175 per month (as adjusted for inflation, $250 in 2015).[26] To qualify, the employer must provide the parking arrangement on or near the employer's place of business or near a location from which the employee can board some type of commuter vehicle.[27]

Although it is relatively easy to determine the value of a parking space in a commercial lot or garage, valuing spaces at suburban office or plant facilities may be a problem. The IRS has simplified this somewhat by taking the position that the value of the parking is zero if nobody but an employee would pay to park in the lot or garage.[28]

QUALIFIED RETIREMENT PLANNING SERVICES

An employee and spouse may exclude from their income the value of certain retirement planning services provided by the employer maintaining their qualified retirement plan.[29] The exclusion will not be available to highly compensated employees, unless the services are also available, on substantially the same basis, to all employees that would normally be provided education and information regarding the employer's qualified plan.[30]

The services that may be excluded are not limited to information regarding the employer's qualified retirement plan. Thus, the services may include general advice regarding the employee's and the spouse's overall plan for retirement of which the employer's qualified plan is only a part.[31] Services such as tax preparation, and accounting, legal, or brokerage services are excluded, without regard to whether they relate to retirement planning.

GYMS AND ATHLETIC FACILITIES

An athletic facility available to employees is tax-free to them if:

1. it is located on the premises of the employer (but this can be somewhere other than the employer's *business* premises and can be either owned or leased);[32]

2. it is operated by the employer; and

3. substantially all of the facility's use is by employees, their spouses, and their dependent children.[33]

There are no nondiscrimination requirements for this provision. That is, an athletic facility that is provided only for selected executives is tax-free to the executives if it meets the three requirements listed above.[34]

WORKING CONDITION FRINGES

Code section 132 contains a general provision that if an employer provides property or services to an employee, the value of these is not taxable to the employee if, had the employee paid for them himself, that payment would be allowable as an employee business expense deduction.[35] Such employer-provided property or services are referred to as "working condition fringes."

For example, if an employee is driven to an away-from home work location in the company limousine, the value of that transportation is not taxable to the employee. This is because if the employee himself paid for travelling to a work location away from home, such costs would be deductible to him.

In the case of company cars and car expense reimbursement plans, the IRS has woven a vast web of regulation out of this seemingly simple provision, as discussed in Chapter 49.

DE MINIMIS FRINGE

A final general rule in the fringe benefit area is a provision of Code section 132 that property or services provided to the employee are not taxable to him if their value is so small as to make accounting for them "unreasonable or administratively impractical."[36] Such benefits are referred to as de minimis fringes after the legal term *de minimis* which means among the small things (that can be ignored).

Unfortunately, employers and employees still have to worry whether the IRS will agree that a small thing is small enough to be ignored. While the IRS is apparently not yet concerned about used pencils that employees take home from the office, there are many doubtful areas. Some current guidelines from the IRS regulations appear in Figure 48.1.[37]

DEFINITION OF HIGHLY COMPENSATED

For purposes of the fringe benefit rules that include nondiscrimination provisions, the definition of highly compensated employee is the same one used for qualified pension and profit sharing plans.[38]

In summary, a highly compensated employee is any employee who, during the year or the preceding year:

1. was at any time an owner of *more* than 5 percent of the business; or

2. received compensation from the employer in excess of $80,000 (as indexed, $120,000 for 2015).[39]

CHAPTER ENDNOTES

1. Internal Revenue Service, January 2011. See also IRS Publication 15-B, Employers Tax Guide to Fringe Benefits.
2. I.R.C. §132(c)(2)(A). Regulations provide details for calculating this percentage.
3. I.R.C. §132(c)(4).
4. I.R.C. §132(h).
5. I.R.C. §132(b).
6. I.R.C. §132(c)(1)(B).

7. I.R.C. §132(b)(1). For airlines, certain affiliated airlines are deemed to be in the same line of business. I.R.C. §132(j)(5).
8. I.R.C. §132(i).
9. I.R.C. §132(h).
10. I.R.C. §132(h)(3).
11. The two Code sections dealing with meals for employees, 119 and 132, were enacted at different times and are not coordinated. The only provision dealing with the overlap is Section 132(l), and it is not explicit and subject to differing interpretations. The interpretation adopted in this chapter is that meals are tax-free to employees if they meet *either* of these two Code provisions. For a discussion of the relationship of these provisions, see "Unraveling Recent Tax Law Changes for Free Meals to Employees at On-Premises Facilities," *Weekly Alert*, RIA, August 13, 1998.
12. See IRS Publication 463.
13. I.R.C. §119(a).
14. I.R.C. §119(b)(4).
15. I.R.C. §119(b)(3).
16. I.R.C. §132(e)(2).
17. Treas. Reg. §1.132-7(b).
18. Treas. Reg. §1.132-7(a)(1)(ii).
19. See note 11 as to whether Code sections 119 and 132 are alternatives. A discriminatory executives-only dining facility could meet the requirements of Section 119, but it should be noted that the "convenience of the employer" test in the latter section must then be met; it has no counterpart in Section 132. "Convenience of the employer" appears to be a tough test to meet. See TAM 9143003.
20. I.R.C. §132(f)(1).
21. I.R.C. §132(f)(4).
22. I.R.C. §§132(f)(5)(B), 132(f)(5)(D).
23. I.R.C. §132(f)(2)(A).
24. I.R.C. §132(f)(1)(D).
25. I.R.C. §132 (f)(5)(A).
26. I.R.C. §132(f)(2)(B), 132(f)(6).
27. I.R.C. §132(f)(5)(C).
28. Notice 94-3, 1994-1 CB 327, Q-10.
29. I.R.C. §132(a)(7).
30. I.R.C. §132(m)(2).
31. I.R.C. §132(m)(1).
32. Treas. Reg. §1.132-1(e)(2).
33. I.R.C. §132(j)(4).
34. Treas. Reg. §1.132-1(e)(5).
35. I.R.C. §132(d). The two-percent floor on itemized deductions is not considered. Treas. Reg. §1.132-5(a)(1)(vi).
36. I.R.C. §132(e).
37. Treas. Reg. §1.132-6.
38. I.R.C. §414(q).
39. Notice 2010-78, 2010-49 IRB 808.

Figure 48.1

NOT TAXABLE	
Occasional money for meals or local transportation, not provided on a regular or routine basis	Occasional cocktail parties, group meals, picnics
Taxi fare for commute outside of normal work hours to or from unsafe area (employee must include only first $1.50 per trip in income but highly compensated must include full fare)	Traditional noncash birthday or holiday gifts with a "low" fair market value
Occasional typing of personal letters by company secretary	Occasional theater or sports tickets
Occasional personal use of copying machine (machine must be used 85% for business)	Coffee, doughnuts, or soft drinks
	Local telephone calls
	Flowers, gifts for illness, reward, family crisis
TAXABLE	
Season theater or sports tickets	Group-term life insurance on spouse or child
Commuting use of company car more than one day per month	Use of company apartment, lodge, etc. for weekend
Membership in private club	

COMPANY CAR OR REIMBURSEMENT PLAN

CHAPTER 49

INTRODUCTION

A car is often an essential business tool for an employee or someone who is self-employed. Employers often provide cars or reimburse expenses for business use of personally owned vehicles. Company cars or car expense reimbursement plans are not employee benefits as such, since their purpose is not actually to compensate the employee. However, an employer's policy regarding business use of cars is often viewed as part of the employer's fringe benefit package.

There are three possible types of arrangements between an employer and employee regarding business use of cars:

(1) *Company car*. The business can provide the car directly to the employee.

(2) *Reimbursement plan*. The business can reimburse the employee for costs incurred in using the employee's car for business.

(3) *No plan*. The employee or self-employed person can assume the costs of business use of the car and deduct them on his or her tax return. (The employee's salary or other compensation implicitly will reflect the fact that the employee assumes this burden.)

For an employee, the first scenario—the company car—generally provides the best tax result, since it can allow all business related car expenses to be excluded from taxable income in all cases. A reimbursement approach, or the unreimbursed use of the employee's car (scenarios two or three) may not allow full deductions since the employee must deduct car expenses as a miscellaneous expense. These are subject to a 2 percent of adjusted gross income floor, as discussed later in this chapter under the heading Reporting.

For a self-employed person, all business related car expenses are deductible without a 2 percent floor.

The tax rules for car expense deductions are inordinately complicated, apparently because Congress and the IRS believe that taxpayers often abuse these provisions. This chapter will summarize the rules for handling deductions and reimbursements for car use.

COMPANY CARS

Because of the administrative complexity of company car plans, company cars are provided primarily where employees use them substantially for business or commuting. They are also provided as a fringe benefit for selected executives in high tax brackets.

Advantages

1. The company car approach can maximize tax benefits for the employee by avoiding the 2 percent of adjusted gross income floor for miscellaneous itemized deductions.

2. Companies can maintain maximum control over the cars employees use in business (type of car, maintenance, etc.)

Disadvantages

1. Companies must bear the capital investment costs of car ownership. With the termination of the

investment credit and less favorable depreciation rules, such an investment has fewer tax benefits than in past years.

2. Companies must bear substantial administrative costs. In particular, if the car is used for personal purposes to a significant extent, the company must bear the burden of determining the value of personal use if the employee is to avoid the 2 percent floor limitation on miscellaneous itemized deductions (see the rules discussed below).

Tax Treatment of Employer

In a company car plan, the employer is the owner of the car and is entitled to deductions for depreciation, as well as for any other expenses it actually pays.

Employer Reporting

The employer must report the value of car availability to affected employees. There are basically three options for reporting:

1. The employer can report the entire value of car availability on the employee's W-2 and the employee can claim a deduction for business use. In this case, the employee is subject to the 2 percent floor requirement for miscellaneous itemized deductions;

2. The employer can determine the amount of personal or commuting use and report that only; or

3. If the plan meets the requirements for a written plan (discussed later in Employee Recordkeeping), the employer can report only commuting use for which the employer has not been reimbursed by the employee.

The employer must withhold Social Security (FICA) and FUTA on the amount reported, but the employer can elect not to withhold federal income tax on this amount.[1] If so, the employee may have to increase withholding or estimated tax payments to avoid an underpayment penalty.

The employer can elect a special accounting rule under which fringe benefits, such as company cars, provided during the last two months of a calendar year can be treated as provided during the following calendar year.[2] If the employer elects this treatment, the employee must follow it also.

Valuation of Car Availability

The taxable value of a car to an employee is the amount an unrelated third party would charge for its use in an arms-length transaction.[3] A comparable lease value can be used.

Alternatively, the employer can elect one of three special valuation rules; if the employer does so, the employee must use either the same rule that the employer elected or the general arms-length rule.[4] The three special rules are:

- A lease value from the IRS' Annual Lease Value Table.[5]

- A mileage rate of 57.5 cents per mile (in 2015) for all business use.[6] To use the mileage rate the car must be: (1) used more than 50 percent in business; (2) used each weekday in an employer sponsored commuting pool; or (3) driven at least 10,000 miles during the year and used primarily by employees. Also, the standard mileage rate cannot be used to value the use of any luxury car subject to the depreciation limitations of Code Section 280F.[7]

- A commuting valuation rule of \$1.50 per one-way commute or \$3.00 per round trip. To use this rule, the employer must have (and enforce) a written policy that the employee must commute in the vehicle and cannot use the vehicle for other than minimal personal use. This election is unavailable to control employees (directors and certain officers and owners—discussed later).[8]

Tax Treatment of Employee

To the extent used for business, providing a car to an employee is a working condition fringe under Code section 132 and, thus, its value is not included in income. (See Chapter 48.) If the car is used for commuting or for personal purposes, the amount included in the employee's income for the year is:

$$\frac{\text{personal/commuting miles}}{\text{total miles}} \times \text{value of car availability}$$

See the Frequently Asked Questions section at the end of this chapter for a definition of commuting.

The employee is entitled to a business deduction for any expenses the employee actually pays for business use of the automobile (such as gasoline, etc.). The employee is also entitled to a deduction to the extent of business use if the employer chooses to report 100 percent of the car's availability value on the employee's W-2. (In that case, the employee's deduction on Form 2106, line 27 is the business use percentage of the total amount reported on the W-2.)

However, if the employee claims a deduction in either situation, it must be reported on Schedule A as a miscellaneous deduction and is therefore subject to the 2 percent of adjusted gross income limitation for such deductions. In other words, the most advantageous company car plan will be one which minimizes or eliminates the need for the employee to claim any business expense deductions.

Employee Recordkeeping

If the car is used partly for business and partly for personal use, the employee must keep records substantiating the business use. These are necessary either to allow the employer to determine the amount of business use, or to allow the employee to claim a business deduction if the employer reports 100 percent of the car's value on the employee's W-2 (see above).

However, if the car is used only for business and commuting, with minimal personal use, the employee does not have to keep records if:

1. the company has a written policy statement (meeting requirements set out in IRS Regulations) of no personal use except for commuting;
2. the employee is not a control employee (director, officer earning $50,000 or more, employee earning $100,000 or more, or 1 percent or more owner);
3. the employer reports the commuting value on the employee's W-2 to the extent the commuting value is not reimbursed to the employer; and
4. the employee is required, for bona fide noncompensatory business reasons, to travel to or from work in the vehicle.[9]

REIMBURSEMENT PLANS AND "NO PLANS"

The IRS recognizes three types of reimbursement plans:

1. An *accountable plan* is one that requires the employee (a) to adequately account to the employer for expenses and (b) return any excess reimbursement to the employer.
2. A *nonaccountable plan* is one that *either* (a) does not require the employee to adequately account to the employer, or (b) allows the employee to keep excess reimbursements.
3. *No plan*—that is, the employer does not reimburse directly at all, and the employee is responsible for paying expenses and is entitled to any deduction for them. However, the employer can indirectly reimburse the employee in this situation by increasing salary or paying a bonus.

The IRS table shown in Figure 49.1 summarizes the employer and employee reporting treatment under these three situations. The IRS table shown in Figure 49.2 summarizes when local transportation expenses are deductible.[10]

REPORTING

Employer W-2 reporting requirements have been discussed above.

For an *employee* claiming a car expense deduction, Form 2106 must be filed. A simplified Form 2106-EZ may be used in certain situations using the standard mileage rate. The deductible amount determined on Form 2106 is entered on the employee's Schedule A, Form 1040, as a miscellaneous deduction. Miscellaneous deductions, in total, are allowable only to the extent that they exceed 2 percent of the employee's adjusted gross income.

A *self-employed person* does not file Form 2106. Instead, car expenses are computed and entered as a deduction on Schedule C, "Income From Business or Profession." There is no 2 percent of adjusted gross income limitation on Schedule C deductions.

WHERE CAN I FIND OUT MORE?

The rules in this area are extremely complex. A summary of these rules is found in IRS Publication 463, *Travel, Entertainment, Gift, and Car Expenses*, and IRS Publication 535, *Business Expenses*. IRS regulations under Code sections 61, 132, and 274 also deal with car expenses.

Figure 49.1

REPORTING TRAVEL, ENTERTAINMENT, GIFT AND CAR EXPENSES AND REIMBURSEMENTS

Type of Reimbursement (or Other Expense Allowance) Arrangement	Employer Reports on Form W-2	Employee Reports on Form 2106[1]
Accountable Plan		
Actual expense reimbursement Adequate accounting made and excess returned	No amount.	No amount.
Actual expense reimbursement Adequate accounting and return of excess both required but excess not returned	Excess reported as wages in Box 1.	No amount.
Per diem or mileage allowance up to federal rate Adequate accounting made and excess returned	No amount.	All expenses and reimbursements *only* if excess expenses are claimed. Otherwise form is not filed.
Per diem or mileage allowance up to the federal rate Adequate accounting and return of excess both required but excess not returned	Excess reported as wages in Box 1. Amount up to the federal rate is reported only in Box 12—it is not reported in Box 1.	No amount.
Per diem or mileage allowance exceeds the federal rate Adequate accounting up to the federal rate only and excess not returned	Excess reported as wages in Box 1. Amount up to the federal rate is reported only in Box 12—it is not reported in Box 1.	All expenses (and reimbursements reported on Form W-2, box 12) *only* if expenses in excess of the federal rate are claimed. Otherwise, form is not filed.
Nonaccountable Plan		
Either adequate accounting or return of excess, or both, not required by plan	Entire amount is reported as wages in Box 1.	All expenses.
No Reimbursement Plan	Entire amount is reported wages in Box 1.	All expenses.

[1] You may be able to use Form 2106-EZ. See *Completing Forms 2106 and 2106-EZ* in Chapter 6 of IRS Pub. 463.

Figure 49.2

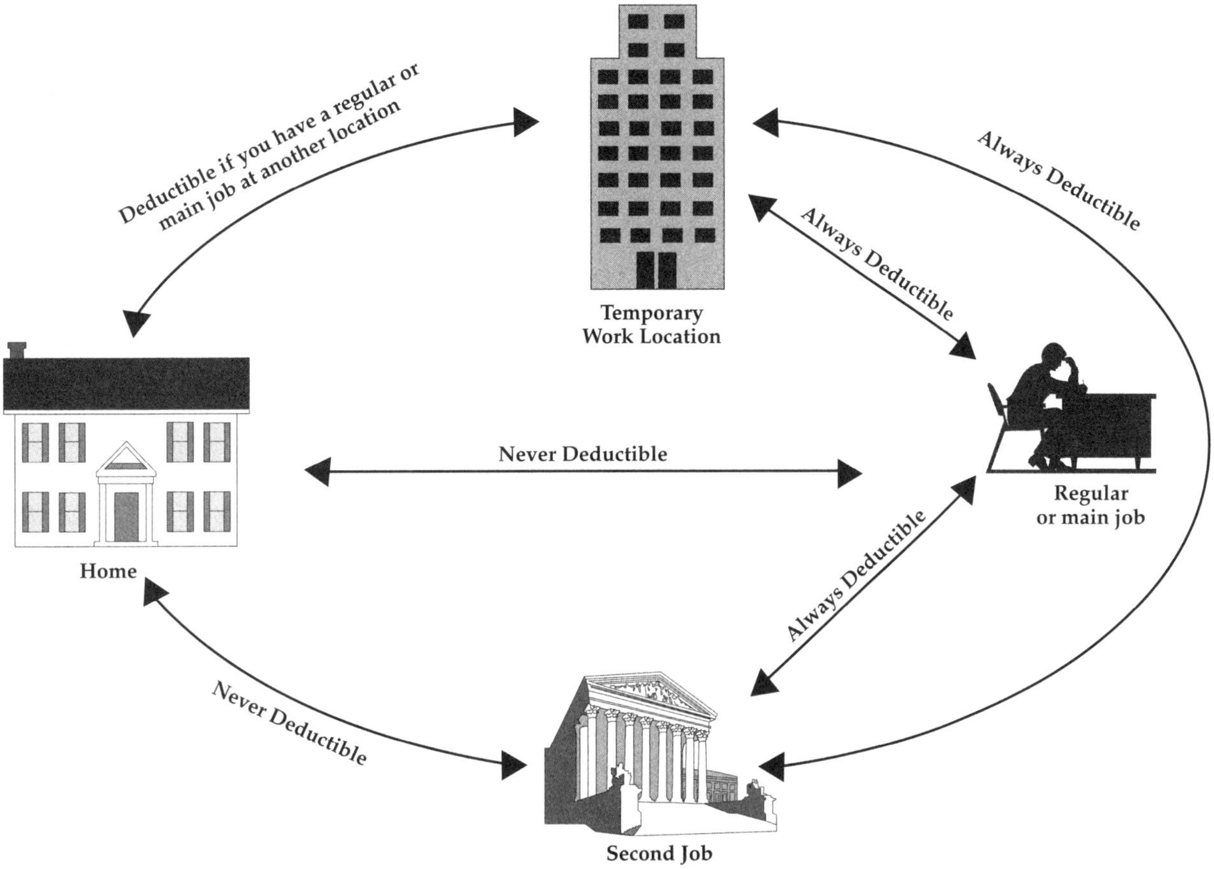

Home: The place where you reside. Transportation expenses between your home and your main or regular place of work are personal commuting expenses.

Regular or main job: Your principal place of business. If you have more than one job, you must determine which one is your regular or main job. Consider the time you spend at each, the activity you have at each, and the income you earn at each.

Temporary work location: A place where your work assignment is irregular or short-term, generally a matter of days or weeks. Unless you have a regular place of business, you can only deduct your transportation expenses to a temporary location *outside* your metropolitan area.

Second job: If you regularly work at two or more places in one day, whether or not for the same employer, you can deduct your transportation expenses of getting from one workplace to another. You cannot deduct your transportation costs between your home and a second job on a day off from your main job.

FREQUENTLY ASKED QUESTIONS

Question – Is interest on a car loan deductible as a business expense?

Answer – Interest on a car loan is not deductible by most taxpayers. However, if the taxpayer is self-employed, the interest is deductible as a Schedule C deduction, to the extent of business use of the car.

Question – What types of getting to work trips are business expenses as opposed to commuting?

Answer – The IRS has persistently attempted to crack down on alleged abuses in this area. Some current IRS positions:

- Using a car telephone for business calls, carrying tools or instruments, or having advertising signs on your car will not cause a commute to be considered a business trip.

- If you work at two different workplaces, the cost of getting from one place to the other is deductible as a business expense. The cost of traveling between an office at home and other work locations is a deductible business expense *if* the home office is the principal place of business. But a commute to and from home to a part-time job is not a deductible expense. See the IRS chart in Figure 49.2.

- You can deduct the round-trip cost of travel from your home to a temporary work assignment (i.e., where work is initially expected to last for a year or less and actually does last for a year or less) if the temporary work is located outside the metropolitan area where you live.[11]

Question – How does the car expense deduction differ if the car is used 50 percent or less (as opposed to more than 50 percent) for business purposes?

Answer – The amount of the deduction allowed for depreciation is computed in a different, less favorable way if the car is used 50 percent or less for business.

If the car is used 50 percent or less for business, the taxpayer must compute depreciation on a straight-line basis over a five-year period. Neither accelerated depreciation nor the Section 179 election to expense[12] can be used.

Question – When can the standard mileage rate be used to compute car business expenses?

Answer – Generally, whenever a taxpayer wants to deduct car business expenses, there is a choice between determining the actual expenses and using the simpler standard mileage rate. The mileage rate for 2015 is 57.5 cents per mile for all business use.[13]

In order to use the standard mileage rate the taxpayer must choose the standard mileage rate method for the first year in which the car was placed in service in business. If actual expenses (using certain accelerated depreciation) are used in the first year, the mileage rate cannot be used in later years. But if the mileage rate is used in the first year the taxpayer can change to actual expenses in later years.

CHAPTER ENDNOTES

1. I.R.C. §§3121(a)(20), 3402(s).
2. Ann. 85-113, 1985-31 IRB 31; see Treas. Reg. §1.61-21(c)(7).
3. Treas. Reg. §1.61-21(b)(4).
4. Treas. Reg. §1.61-21(b)(4).
5. Treas. Reg. §1.61-21(d)(2).
6. Rev. Proc. 2010-51, 2010-51 IRB 1; IR 2010-119, 12/3/2010.
7. Treas. Reg. §1.61-21(e)(1)(iii).
8. Treas. Reg. §1.61-21(f).
9. Treas. Regs. §§1.61-21(f), 1.132-5(f), 1.274-6T(a)(3), 1.274-6T(d).
10. These tables are found in IRS Pub. 463, *Travel, Entertainment, Gift, and Car Expenses*, revised annually.
11. Rev. Rul. 99-7, 1 CB 361.
12. Treas. Reg. §1.179-1(d).
13. IR 2010-19, 12/3/2010.

DEPENDENT CARE ASSISTANCE PLAN

CHAPTER 50

INTRODUCTION

A dependent care assistance plan reimburses employees for daycare and other dependent care expenses or provides an actual daycare center or similar arrangement. If the program is properly structured, the daycare expenses are deductible to the employer under Code section 162 and non-taxable to the employee under Code section 129. (See Frequently Asked Questions.) The dependent care plan can be funded using employee salary reductions under a Flexible Spending Account (FSA) described in Chapter 38.

WHEN IS USE OF SUCH A DEVICE INDICATED?

1. When an employer wants to attract and keep employees by offering non-taxable ways to pay for the expenses of caring for small children or other dependents during working hours.

2. To provide an attractive tax benefit to all employees who have dependent care expenses.

Advantages

1. The plan can be helpful in recruiting and keeping relatively low-paid employees who have dependent care needs.

2. The employer gets more benefit for each dollar spent on this form of compensation as opposed to cash compensation because benefits paid under a properly structured dependent care assistance program are tax-free to the employees.

3. The plan can be funded partially or entirely through FSA salary reductions.

Disadvantages

1. A fully subsidized daycare or other dependent care program can be expensive while a partially subsidized program may not be helpful in attracting and keeping employees.

2. A substantial daycare program may be seen by nonparticipating employees as discriminatory in favor of participating employees.

Alternatives

One alternative to dependent care assistance programs is the informal coverage of these expenses for selected employees through extra compensation or bonuses. However, this extra compensation is fully taxable to the employee.

DESIGN FEATURES

1. Dependent care can be provided in kind.[1] For example, the employer can provide a daycare and after school center for employees' children right on the business premises or contract with a nearby center to provide daycare.

2. Alternatively, the benefit can be provided through full or partial reimbursement of qualifying employee expenses for dependent care. This is the approach usually taken when the plan is funded

through employee salary reductions as part of an FSA plan.

3. A dependent care assistance plan must be in writing.[2]

TAX IMPLICATIONS

The costs of the plan are deductible to the employer as employee compensation.

If the plan meets the requirements of Code section 129, the benefits are non-taxable to participating employees. The amount of benefits excluded annually by the employee—the value of the services provided directly plus any employer reimbursements of expenses paid by the employee—cannot be more than the employee's earned income or, if the employee is married, the lesser of the employee's or spouse's earned income. Furthermore, the total amount excluded by the employee is limited to $5,000 annually, or $2,500 if the employee is married and files a separate return.[3]

In order to claim the exclusion for dependent care assistance benefits under Section 129 the taxpayer must report the correct name, address and taxpayer identification number of the care provider on his tax return.[4]

Permissible Benefits

Dependent care assistance eligible under Section 129 can be provided only to: (a) a child under age thirteen for whom the employee-taxpayer is entitled to take a dependency deduction on the income tax return; or (b) a taxpayer's dependent or spouse who is physically or mentally unable to care for himself *and* who has the same principal place of abode as the taxpayer for more than one-half of the taxable year.[5]

Qualifying expenses must be for care alone, not for education above the kindergarten level. The following are items that qualify as care:[6]

- preschool and nursery school expenses (full tuition and fees for these programs);
- before-and-after-school programs for children under age thirteen;
- summer camp for children under age thirteen (however, expenses for overnight summer camp do not qualify);
- cost of a housekeeper/sitter for children or other dependents cared for at home.

However, payments to a child under age nineteen or to a child that the employee is entitled to a personal exemption for do not qualify.

Effect on the Dependent Care Tax Credit

Current law prohibits "double dipping" by taxpayers who pay child care expenses qualifying for the child care credit and who participate in a company sponsored dependent care assistance program.[7]

An employee's tax benefit from the child care credit is reduced to the extent he or she uses a company plan to cover expenses. Specifically, the maximum amount of qualifying expenses ($3,000 for one child; $6,000 for two or more children) a taxpayer may use for the child care credit is reduced dollar-for-dollar by amounts paid through a company plan. For example, if a company plan reimburses an employee with two children $4,000 for child care expenses in 2015, only $2,000 ($6,000 – $4,000) of additional child care expenses paid by the employee will qualify for the child care credit.

As a result, all employees who have child care expenses exceeding $6,000 and who may participate in a company sponsored dependent care assistance program must choose between the company plan and the child care credit.

The choice depends on the employee's tax rate and whether or not amounts that would otherwise be allocated to child care under the company plan can be allocated to other benefits. For example, if the company dependent care assistance plan is part of a cafeteria plan or FSA salary-reduction plan where the employees can choose to allocate the amount that would otherwise go to child care expenses to fund other benefits such as medical expenses, health insurance premiums, or life insurance, the employees will generally be better off if they elect benefits other than child care reimbursements from their company plan. In this way they still get the full benefit of the company plan and may take the child care credit for the child care expenses they pay with after-tax dollars separately from the plan.

However, if the company plan does not allow the employees to use the amount that would otherwise go to child care expenses to fund other benefits, or for those employees who cannot fully use the other benefits that may be elected, the choice between the company plan and the child care credit depends on their tax rate (taxable income), filing status, and Adjusted Gross Income (AGI).

The child care credit is equal to 35 percent of qualified expenses for persons with an AGI of $15,000 or less. The credit is reduced by one percentage point for each $2,000 of AGI above $15,000 with a floor of 20 percent for persons with AGI over $43,000.[8] Therefore, for each dollar of qualifying child care expenses the tax savings range from 35 cents to 20 cents for AGIs ranging from $15,000 to $43,000 and above.

In contrast, if child care expenses are reimbursed through a company salary-reduction plan, the tax savings will depend on the person's tax rate, which depends on taxable income and filing status. Employees whose taxable income falls in the 15 percent tax bracket will save only 15 cents on each qualifying dollar of child care expenses reimbursed through a company plan. Consequently, they should clearly opt out of the company plan and use the child care credit because they will save between 5 and 20 cents more on the dollar. However, if taxable income falls in a tax bracket above 25 percent, the employees will save at least 25 cents on each qualifying dollar of child care expenses reimbursed through the company plan. For these levels of taxable income the tax savings with the company plan will always equal or exceed the tax savings from the child care credit.

NONDISCRIMINATION TESTING

Section 129(d) imposes a variety of nondiscrimination rules. Contributions or benefits must not discriminate in favor of highly compensated employees, as defined in Code section 414(q) (see Chapter 16). The plan must cover a group that the IRS finds nondiscriminatory.

Nondiscrimination testing may exclude:

1. employees with less than one year of service;
2. employees who are less than twenty-one years old; and
3. employees in a collective bargaining unit if there has been good faith bargaining on dependent care.

Benefits for all employees who own more than 5 percent of the employer—and their spouses and dependents—cannot be more than 25 percent of the total benefits each year.

The average benefits provided to employees who are not highly compensated must be at least 55 percent of the average benefits provided to highly compensated employees. In applying this benefit test the employer can elect to exclude employees earning less than $25,000 (or a lower specified amount) if the plan is funded through salary reductions.

Failure to meet these rules makes plan benefits taxable, but only to highly compensated participants.[9]

ERISA AND OTHER REQUIREMENTS

The plan is considered a welfare benefit plan for ERISA purposes. This requires a written plan document, a Summary Plan Description (SPD) explaining the plan that is provided to employees, a designated plan administrator, and a formal claims procedure. (Chapter 16 details these requirements more fully.)

Further, Section 129 requires that the employer provide each employee with an annual statement of the expenses incurred in providing the prior year's benefits by January 31 of each year.[10]

HOW TO INSTALL A PLAN

ERISA and the Internal Revenue Code require a written plan and an SPD but no governmental approval. Some employers may want to obtain an IRS ruling stating that the plan complies with Section 129 if there are plan features, such as liberal benefits or limited employee eligibility, that raise compliance questions.

WHERE CAN I FIND OUT MORE?

1. IRS Publication 503, *Child and Dependent Care Expenses* (annual IRS publication available at: www.irs.gov).
2. IRS Publication 334, *Tax Guide for Small Business* (annual IRS publication available at: www.irs.gov).
3. Beam, Burton T., Jr. and John J. McFadden, *Employee Benefits*, 9th ed. Chicago IL: Dearborn Financial Publishing, Inc., 2012.

FREQUENTLY ASKED QUESTIONS

Question – Can an unincorporated business have a dependent care plan covering partners or proprietors as well as regular employees?

Answer – Yes. Section 129 allows self-employed individuals—partners or proprietors—to be treated as employees under the plan.[11] As with regular employees, dependent care benefits are excluded from the income of partners or proprietors who are covered by the plan.

Question – What is the tax credit for employer-provided child care facilities?

Answer – Employers that provide child care for their employees may be able to claim a tax credit for the expenses associated with the expenses of providing the child care. The amount of the credit is 25 percent of certain child care expenditures and 10 percent of certain child care resource and referral expenditures. This credit may not exceed $150,000 for any tax year.[12]

There are recapture rules if the qualified child care facility ceases operation within ten years of starting up or if there is a change in ownership in the child care facility. (However, special rules may apply if the purchaser agrees to assume the recapture liability.) If a taxpayer uses this credit with respect to property, the basis of the property is reduced by the amount of the credit. Also, no other deductions or credits may be taken for payments that result in this tax credit.

CHAPTER ENDNOTES

1. I.R.C. §§129(a)(1), 129(e)(8).
2. I.R.C. §129(d)(1).
3. I.R.C. §§129(a)(2), 129(b)(1).
4. I.R.C. §129(e)(9).
5. I.R.C. §§21(b), 129(e)(1).
6. I.R.C. §§21(b)(1), 21(B)(2), 129(c), 129(e)(1); Treas. Reg. §1.21-1(d)(5).
7. I.R.C. §21(c).
8. I.R.C. §21(a)(2).
9. I.R.C. §129(d)(1).
10. I.R.C. §129(d)(7).
11. I.R.C. §§129(e)(3), 129(e)(4).
12. I.R.C. §45F.

EDUCATIONAL ASSISTANCE PLAN

CHAPTER 51

INTRODUCTION

An employer's educational assistance plan pays or reimburses employees for expenses incurred in educational programs aimed at improving job skills. Some broader plans provide assistance for education even if not job-related, or for education for children or dependents of employees.

Section 127 of the Code allows an employer to provide a broader range of educational reimbursements to *employees* (but not dependents or others) on a tax-free basis. Such amounts are excludable from the employee's gross income.[1]

Advantages

1. Employers benefit from improvement in employee skills through education that the employee might not be able to afford otherwise.

2. Properly structured job-related educational benefits are not taxable income to employees.

Disadvantages

1. A program that is too broad may simply train an employee for a job with another employer.

2. Educational benefits beyond certain limits are taxable as compensation to the employee.

PLAN DESIGN

A broad range of educational benefits can be included in a Section 127 plan, including primary, secondary, undergraduate, and graduate programs as well as most other legitimate education programs. A Section 127 plan must be in writing. However, it need not be funded in advance and does not have to be approved in advance by the IRS. Eligible employees must be notified of the program.

Under the plan, an employer can make payments up to a maximum of $5,250 annually for tuition, fees, books, supplies, and equipment for educational programs for an employee. Payments under the plan are deductible by the employer and excludable from the employee's gross income. The employer may pay these expenses directly, provide the education directly, or reimburse employees for expenditures they make.

Courses taken by employees and covered under the plan need not be job-related. However, course benefits may not involve sports, games, or hobbies unless they relate to the employer's business or is required as part of a degree program.

Section 127 provides no tax benefits for tools or supplies retained by the employee after completion of the course or for meals, lodging, or transportation. A plan may provide benefits to former employees, including retired, disabled, or laid-off employees.[2]

TAX IMPLICATIONS

For Employees

There are several tax benefit provisions available to individuals incurring educational expenses, reimbursed or otherwise:

- An itemized deduction can be claimed for these amounts as employee business expenses. This deduction is available only if the employee itemizes deductions, and is subject to the 2-percent-of-adjusted-gross-income floor on total miscellaneous deductions under Code section 67.

- The taxpayer may be eligible for the American Opportunity Tax Credit (AOTC) and Lifetime Learning tax credits. These are described in detail in IRS Publication 970.

An individual can deduct job-related educational expenses—including not only tuition but incidental expenses such as transportation, books, and supplies, if the education:

- maintains or improves a skill required in the individual's employment; or

- is expressly required by the individual's employer as a condition of keeping the individual's job.

Job-related educational expenses are not deductible as a trade or business expense under Code section 162 if they do not meet these requirements. The IRS specifies that the costs for two types of education are not deductible: (1) education required to meet the minimum qualification requirements for an individual's present employment; and (2) education that qualifies the individual for a new trade or business.[3]

Example 1. Suppose an individual who has not completed a law degree begins working with a law firm on the understanding that the degree will be completed. Expenses for completing the law degree are nondeductible because they are incurred simply to meet the minimum qualification requirements of the individual's current job.

Example 2. For a tax accountant in an accounting firm, law school expenses could be deductible if the accountant can prove to the IRS that the education will maintain or improve the accountant's skills as a tax expert.

Example 3. For an English teacher, expenses for law school probably would not be deductible since they would not maintain or improve skills in the teacher's existing job and would be seen as training to qualify in a new trade or business.

Expenses for travel to the facility where the coursework is being offered are not deductible as job-related educational expenses.[4]

For Employers

Employer reimbursements to employees for job-related educational expenses are deductible by the employer as compensation.[5]

To the extent that the employer's deduction for reimbursements is matched by a corresponding deduction at the employee level, the educational assistance plan provides the employee with a form of tax-free income.[6]

Usually an employer's educational assistance plans are designed to reimburse only the deductible job-related expenses, both to provide the tax benefit and because the deductible job-related expenses will be the ones that the employer will be most interested in subsidizing. For example, it does not make sense for an employer to pay for education that qualifies an employee for a career with a different company.

Employer reimbursements of employee expenses for educating their children or other dependents are taxable income to the employee and deductible as compensation by the employer. For a highly compensated employee, such payments may create a question as to whether the overall compensation meets the reasonableness of compensation test for deductibility. This test is discussed in Chapter 2.

ERISA AND OTHER REQUIREMENTS

An employer's educational assistance plan may be considered a welfare benefit plan for ERISA purposes, which means that the plan should be in writing, with a written claims procedure, and a Summary Plan Description (SPD) must be furnished to employees. If the plan is funded (most plans are not) additional requirements may apply. The ERISA rules are summarized in Chapter 16.

A Section 127 plan must not discriminate in coverage in favor of highly compensated employees. In addition, there is a nondiscrimination rule for benefits: not more than 5 percent of the total amount paid or incurred annually by the employer for educational assistance under the plan may be provided for employees who are shareholders or owners of at least 5 percent of the business.

There should be a written plan, especially if the plan covers more than a few employees, but the document can be a simple one. An SPD should be drafted and distributed to meet ERISA requirements. No government approval is required, nor is it usually recommended. A request for an IRS ruling can be made if there are any tax questions.

WHERE CAN I FIND OUT MORE?

1. IRS Publications 17, *Your Federal Income Tax*, and 970, *Tax Benefits for Education*, cover the deduction for educational expenses. They are revised annually and available from the IRS online.

2. Beam, Burton T., Jr. and John J. McFadden, *Employee Benefits*, 9th ed. Chicago, IL: Dearborn Financial Publishing, Inc., 2012.

FREQUENTLY ASKED QUESTIONS

Question – What is an educational benefit trust and how is it used?

Answer – An educational benefit trust is an arrangement under which an employer creates a trust fund to pay educational expenses for dependents of employees covered under the plan. Typically, this is used as an executive benefit, but it can also be provided to a larger group of employees or all employees.

Under current tax law, there is little, if any, tax advantage to this type of plan. The employer can deduct amounts paid into the trust fund for plan purposes. However, under Code section 419, the deduction is limited to the amount of benefits provided during the year. In other words, the employer cannot accelerate deductions by setting up the trust fund rather than paying benefits directly.

To the employee, benefits are taxable when they are paid to dependents for educational expenses. The amount paid to an employee's dependent is considered additional compensation income to the employee.

CHAPTER ENDNOTES

1. I.R.C. §127(a).
2. Rev. Rul. 96-41, 1996-2 CB 8.
3. Treas. Reg. §1.162-5.
4. I.R.C. §274(m)(2); but see Treas. Reg. §1.162-5(e).
5. Treas. Reg. §1.162-10.
6. Reimbursements are considered a "working condition fringe" under I.R.C. §132(d). Reimbursements can discriminate in favor of highly compensated employees. A written plan is not required.

LEGAL SERVICES PLAN

CHAPTER 52

INTRODUCTION

A legal services plan (sometimes referred to as a prepaid legal services plan) is an employer-funded plan that makes legal services available to employees when needed. The expenses of the plan are deductible to the employer. Benefits are generally taxable as compensation to the employees.

WHEN IS USE OF SUCH A DEVICE INDICATED?

In theory, any group of employees can benefit from the advantages of these plans. However, in practice they are used primarily by larger employers for employees in collective bargaining units. Such plans are usually funded through multiemployer trusteeships sponsored by labor unions. Group insurance for funding these plans is also available but is not yet widely used.

Advantages

1. Many employees, particularly middle and lower income employees, are not well-served by the traditional fee-for-service system of delivering legal services and, as a result, often do without a lawyer when they really need one. For example, many middle income people do not have adequate legal advice in tax and domestic matters. A legal services plan provides these services without additional employee expenditure.

2. Legal expenses, such as the cost of a criminal trial, can be the kind of catastrophic expense that is best provided through an insurance-type or group benefit program such as a legal services plan.

Disadvantages

1. Because most employees rarely need a lawyer, or rarely perceive the need for one, a legal services plan may not be fully appreciated by employees compared with other forms of employee compensation.

2. Funding and administering a legal services plan is difficult in light of the limited availability of group legal insurance or multiemployer arrangements.

3. Some employers fear that a legal services plan will make it more likely that employees will sue the employer in the event of a dispute. However, legal services for actions by employees against the employer can be (and usually are) excluded from the plan.

4. Either employer expenditures for the plan or the value of legal services provided will be taxable income to covered employees.

DESIGN FEATURES

1. Generally, any group of employees can be covered.

2. Benefits are usually provided on either a *scheduled* or a *comprehensive* basis.

   With a *scheduled* plan only those benefits listed in the plan are provided. Most plans provide at least the following benefits:

   - legal consultations and advice on any matter;

   - preparation of wills, deeds, powers of attorney, and other routine legal documents;

- personal bankruptcy;
- adoption proceedings;
- defense of civil and criminal matters;
- juvenile proceedings; and
- divorce, separation, child custody, and other domestic matters.

A plan that provides *comprehensive* benefits pays for all legal services, with specified exclusions. The most common exclusions include:

- audits by the IRS;
- actions against the employer, the plan, or a labor union sponsoring the plan;
- contingent fee cases or class action suits; and
- actions arising out of the employee's separate business transactions.

3. Some plans provide benefits on an indemnity basis, that is, by reimbursing the employee for covered expenditures. In that case, benefits are usually limited to a flat amount for a given legal service or a maximum hourly rate. There may also be a maximum annual benefit such as $1,000.

Prepayment-type plans are more common than indemnity plans. In a prepayment plan there is no direct expenditure by employees. In a *closed-panel* prepayment plan, the most common type, employees must obtain covered services from specified groups of lawyers who are either employed by or under contract with the plan (similar to an HMO—see Chapter 35).

In an *open-panel* prepayment plan employees can choose their own lawyer or choose a lawyer from an approved list. The lawyer must agree in advance to a fee schedule set by the legal services plan. A plan can combine both the closed panel and open panel approaches, allowing occasional use of top legal specialists for serious matters, while routine matters are handled by the closed panel.

TAX IMPLICATIONS

1. Costs of a legal services plan are deductible to the employer,[1] with certain limitations:

   a. as with all deductions for employee compensation, the overall compensation of each employee must meet the "reasonableness" test discussed in Chapter 2;

   b. if the plan is funded in advance, the amount of deductible advance funding is limited to approximately the benefits provided during the taxable year plus administrative expenses.[2]

2. Employees are taxed as follows:[3]

   a. If the plan is prefunded by the employer—for example, if the employer pays a group legal insurance premium to an insurance company—the employee is taxed on his or her share of the premium at the time the employer pays it, *if* the employee is fully vested in the benefit (legally entitled at that time to receive benefits under the plan). The benefits should then be received tax-free.

   b. If the employer pays for benefits out of current revenues as employees receive benefits, the employee is taxed on the value of benefits as they are received.

WHERE CAN I FIND OUT MORE?

Beam, Burton T., Jr. and John J. McFadden, *Employee Benefits*, 9th ed. Chicago IL: Dearborn Financial Publishing, Inc., 2012.

CHAPTER ENDNOTES

1. I.R.C. §162(a)(1).
2. See generally I.R.C. §419.
3. The rules discussed here are the general rules for inclusion under Code sections 61 and 83. There is no longer a specific Code provision providing a tax benefit for certain legal services; Code Section 120 expired for taxable years beginning after June 30, 1992.

LOANS TO EXECUTIVES

CHAPTER 53

INTRODUCTION

Many employers make loans available to executives, usually restricted to loans for specified purposes. Typically such loans are interest-free or made at a favorable interest rate. Also, under Treasury regulations, certain split dollar plans may be treated as loans (see Chapter 45).

WHEN IS USE OF SUCH A DEVICE INDICATED?

Employers rarely act as an unrestricted bank for executives. However, loan programs can be extremely attractive as a compensation supplement to help executives meet cash needs in special situations. Loans are typically offered for the following:

- Mortgage or bridge loans to help in the purchase of a home, where the employee is moving from one of the employer's business locations to another.
- College or private school tuition for members of the executive's family.
- Purchase of stock of the employer through a company stock purchase plan or otherwise.
- Meeting extraordinary medical needs, tax bills, or other personal or family emergencies such as divorce settlement costs.
- Purchase of life insurance.
- Purchase of a car, vacation home, or other expensive item.

Advantages

1. Although the tax rules discussed in the Tax Implications section provide no tax advantage to executive loans, such loans still provide a valuable benefit by (a) making cash available where regular bank loans might be difficult to obtain and (b) providing loans at a favorable rate of interest.

2. Certain types of loans are generally exempt from the complex tax rules for below-market loans:

   a. mortgage and bridge loans made in connection with an employment-connected relocation;

   b. de minimis loans aggregating less than $10,000 (see "Tax Implications," below); and

   c. low interest loans without significant tax effect on the lender or borrower.

3. The cost of a loan program to the employer is only the administrative cost (plus the loss of interest on the loan, if any) compared to what the employer could have obtained by another type of investment or investment in the business itself.

4. There are no nondiscrimination rules for executive loan programs. Loans can be provided to selected groups of executives or even a single executive. The terms, amounts, and conditions of executive loans can be varied from one executive to another as the employer wishes.

Disadvantages

1. The tax rules for below-market loans are complicated and confusing, which increases the

administrative cost of the loan program for both employer and employee.

2. The tax treatment of term loans (as opposed to demand loans) is unfavorable—the employee must include a substantial portion of the loan in income immediately in some cases.

3. The employer must bear the cost of administering the loan (for example, determining whether the loan should be granted, monitoring the payback, and advising the executive as to the tax consequences), and also must bear the risk of default (either losing the money altogether or the costs of foreclosure on a house or other asset used as collateral).

TAX IMPLICATIONS

Tax Rules for Loans

The following tax rules apply if a loan is

1. below-market[1] loan;
2. compensation-related;[2] and
3. a demand loan—a loan payable in full at any time upon demand of the lender. A demand loan also includes any loan:
   a. where the interest arrangements are conditioned on the future services of the employee; and
   b. of which the interest benefits are not transferable by the employee.[3]

Most executive loan programs involve loans that meet these definitions. Term loans—those payable at a specified time in the future—are discussed in the Frequently Asked Questions at the end of this chapter.

For federal income tax purposes, interest on a loan meeting conditions (a), (b), and (c) is treated as three transactions combined—the actual transaction plus two deemed transactions:

1. Interest *actually* paid by the executive borrower is taxable income to the company (lender) and that interest payment may be deductible by the borrower, subject to the usual limitations on interest deductions. For example, if the loan qualifies as a home mortgage loan, the interest is fully deductible, but if it is a personal loan not secured by a home mortgage, it is generally nondeductible.

2. The employer is treated as if it paid additional compensation to the employee in the amount of the difference between the actual rate of interest and the Applicable Federal Rate.[4] This additional compensation income is deductible by the employer (within the usual reasonable compensation limits) and is taxable to the executive.

   The Applicable Federal Rate (AFR) is published monthly by the IRS as a Revenue Ruling (which appears monthly in the Internal Revenue Bulletin). For demand loans, the AFR is the short-term semiannual rate. For a term loan, the AFR is the short-term, mid-term, or long-term rate in effect as of the day the loan was made, also compounded semiannually. Each of these figures can be found in Table 1 of each month's Revenue Ruling establishing the AFR. If the loan is of a fixed principal amount that remains outstanding for the entire calendar year, the blended annual rate (published in July of each year) is the AFR.[5]

3. The executive is treated as if he paid the amount in (2), above, to the employer. This amount is additional taxable income to the employer. The amount is deductible by the executive borrower, again under the usual limitations on interest deductibility.

Example. Executive Flint borrows $100,000 from her employer. Assume that interest at the applicable federal rate for Year 1 would be $6,000, but actual interest under the loan agreement is only $2,000. This loan results in additional taxable compensation income to Flint for year 1 of $4,000 ($6,000 less $2,000). If interest is deductible (for example, if the loan qualifies as a home mortgage loan), Flint can deduct $6,000 (the actual $2,000 paid plus the deemed $4,000) as an interest payment. Flint's employer can deduct $4,000 as compensation paid to Flint for year 1, regardless of whether Flint can deduct any of the interest.

Are these loans advantageous to the employee in light of these rules? Yes, because with a low interest loan it still costs the employee less to borrow money even if it results in additional taxable income.

Example. Suppose that in the previous example executive Flint had not been able to deduct any interest on the loan. Then, in this worst-case scenario, Flint would have had additional taxable income of $4,000; at a marginal rate of 30 percent, this would result in an additional tax of $1,200. The total cost of borrowing for year 1, therefore, would be the actual interest paid ($2,000) plus the additional tax ($1,200), or a total of $3,200. By comparison, a loan at the applicable federal rate (which presumably is close to the actual market rate) would have cost Flint $6,000 in year 1.

Exceptions to the Loan Rules

1. *Mortgage and bridge loans.* The rules described above do not apply to certain mortgage and bridge loans used to help an employee purchase a house in connection with the employee's transfer to a new principal place of work. In other words, such loans are treated for tax purposes by the employer and employee just as they are actually negotiated, without any deemed transactions.

   The following requirements must be met in order to qualify for the mortgage loan exception:[6]

   a. the loan is compensation-related and is a demand or a term loan, as defined earlier;

   b. the new principal residence is acquired in connection with the transfer of the employee to a new principal place of work (which meets the distance and time requirements for a moving expense deduction under Code section 217—see Chapter 54);

   c. the executive certifies to the employer that he or she reasonably expects to be entitled to and will itemize deductions while the loan is outstanding;

   d. under the loan agreement, loan proceeds may be used only to buy the executive's new principal residence; and

   e. the loan is secured by a mortgage on the new principal residence of the employee.

   A bridge loan must satisfy the requirements above, as well as the following additional requirements:[7]

   a. the loan must be payable in full in fifteen days after the old principal residence is sold;

   b. the aggregate principal of all bridge loans must not exceed the employer's reasonable estimate of the equity of the executive and his spouse in the old residence; and

   c. the old residence must not be converted to business or investment use.

2. *De minimis loans.* The below-market rules do not apply to a compensation-related loan for any day on which aggregate loans outstanding between the company and the executive do not exceed $10,000, provided that tax avoidance is not one of the principal purposes of the interest arrangements.[8] A husband and wife are treated as one borrower for this purpose.[9]

3. *No tax effect.* A loan is exempt from the below-market rules if the taxpayer can show that the interest arrangements will have no significant effect on any federal tax liability of the lender or borrower.[10] In making this determination the IRS will consider

   a. whether items of income and deduction generated by the loan offset each other;

   b. the amount of such items;

   c. the cost to the taxpayer of complying with the below-market loan rules; and

   d. any non-tax reasons for structuring the transaction as a below-market loan.[11]

ERISA AND OTHER REGULATORY IMPLICATIONS

An executive loan program does not appear to fall within the definition of either a welfare benefit plan or a pension plan for ERISA purposes. Therefore, ERISA requirements should not apply and a Form 5500 need not be filed.

Federal Truth in Lending requirements may conceivably apply.[12] Employers should investigate the Truth in Lending requirements if they extend more than twenty-five loans (or more than five loans secured by dwellings) in a calendar year. The Truth in Lending requirements primarily involve additional paperwork, but failure to meet them could result in penalties.

As part of the wave of corporate governance regulation arising out of the Enron collapse and similar events in 2001 and 2002, Congress enacted the Sarbanes-Oxley Act, which contains a range of corporate accountability provisions. Included in the Act is a provision that prohibits any publicly traded corporation from making a personal loan to any director or executive officer. The law does not apply to loans to employees who are not directors or officers, nor does it apply to loans of corporations that are not publicly traded.

ALTERNATIVES

Because of the administrative cost and complexity of loan programs, employers may wish to investigate alternatives that would provide substantially the same benefits to executives. These could include:

- loans by the employer at full market rates, but "bonus" the interest cost to the executive as additional compensation.
- guarantees by the employer of regular bank loans taken out by executives. This works best where the bank is one with which the employer has an established business relationship.

FREQUENTLY ASKED QUESTIONS

Question – How is a term loan to an executive treated for tax purposes?

Answer – A term loan is defined in the below-market loan rules as any loan that is not a demand loan.[13] Generally, a term loan is one with a fixed payment date such as five years—that is, a loan that does not by its terms have to be paid back until a specified date in the future.

A term loan is deemed to be below-market if the amount loaned is more than the present value of all payments due under the loan.[14] The present value is determined with a discount rate based on the Applicable Federal Rate (AFR).

If a below-market compensation-related loan is made, the executive (borrower) is treated as if he immediately received an amount equal to the excess of (a) the amount of the loan, over (b) the present value of all payments required to be made under the loan.[15]

Example. Suppose employer Rocks, Inc. lends executive Rubble $40,000, interest-free, payable in five years. Assume that based on the AFR for the first year of the loan, the present value of the loan is $22,000. Rubble is treated as having received additional compensation income of $18,000 ($40,000 less $22,000) in the first year of the loan. Rocks, Inc. can deduct this $18,000 as additional compensation paid (subject to the reasonable compensation rules). Over the five-year period of the loan, Rubble is also treated as paying interest to Rocks, Inc. at the applicable federal rate on the deemed "unpaid amount" of $22,000, and Rocks, Inc. must include this interest in income.

The $10,000 de minimis rule for term loans is similar to the one for demand loans; however, once a term loan has exceeded $10,000, it continues to be subject to the below-market loan rules, even if the balance later falls below $10,000.[16]

CHAPTER ENDNOTES

1. I.R.C. §7872(e)(1) defines below-market loans; a demand loan is a below-market loan if interest is payable on it at a rate less than the "applicable federal rate" in effect for the loan period.
2. I.R.C. §7872(c)(1)(B) provides that a below-market loan is compensation-related if it is directly or indirectly between (1) an employer and an employee, or (2) an independent contractor and the person for whom the independent contractor provides services.
3. I.R.C. §7872(f)(5). The IRS is given authority to issue regulations treating any loan with an indefinite maturity as a demand loan.
4. The actual calculation is complicated; the rules are given in detail in the proposed treasury regulations under Code Section 7872.
5. Rev. Rul. 86-17, 1986-1 CB 377.
6. Temp. Treas. Reg. §1.7872-5T(c)(1)(i).
7. Temp. Treas. Reg. §1.7872-5T(c)(1)(ii).
8. I.R.C. §7872(c)(3).
9. I.R.C. §7872(f)(7).

10. Temp. Treas. Reg. §1.7872-5T(b)(14).
11. Temp. Treas. Reg. §1.7872-5T(c)(3).
12. See Title I of the Consumer Protection Act, as amended, 15 U.S.C. 1601 *et seq*.
13. I.R.C. §7872(f)(6).
14. I.R.C. §7872(e)(1)(B).
15. I.R.C. §7872(b)(1).
16. I.R.C. §7872(f)(10).

MOVING EXPENSE REIMBURSEMENT

CHAPTER 54

INTRODUCTION

Many companies reimburse employees' moving expenses connected with changes in job location. While the reimbursements are taxable income to the employee, the moving expenses may be deductible from the employee's gross income. Moving expense reimbursement, therefore, not only helps employees bear a major expense but can be a form of tax-free compensation for employees.

WHEN IS USE OF SUCH A DEVICE INDICATED?

Because of the major benefits of a moving expense reimbursement to employees, employers should consider it whenever it is consistent with their recruitment and staffing needs.

Advantages

1. A company may have to recruit executives and employees from a wide geographical area; reimbursing moving expenses can help induce a prospective employee to change jobs.

2. Larger companies with more than one geographical location can encourage mobility of their employees among company locations by adopting a moving expense reimbursement policy.

3. A moving expense reimbursement can be a tax-free form of compensation for employees.

4. Employers have complete flexibility in designing moving reimbursement plans. Reimbursement can be offered only to selected employees or even a single employee. Amounts and terms of reimbursement can be varied from employee to employee, and reimbursement can be offered as needs arise without having to adopt a formal plan in advance.

Disadvantages

1. The *distance* test (see Tax Implications) requires an employee's new main job location to be at least fifty miles farther from the employee's former home than the old main job location was in order to deduct moving expenses.

2. An employee may not deduct expenses for house hunting or expenses for selling, buying, or leasing a residence.

TAX IMPLICATIONS

For Employers

1. Moving expense reimbursements to employees or to third parties (moving companies, etc.) on behalf of employees are deductible by the employer as compensation expenses if, together with all other forms of compensation, the amount is reasonable (the reasonable compensation test).

2. Reimbursement amounts must be reported as compensation on the employee's Form W-2 for the year. The employer does not have to withhold taxes if it reasonably believes that the employee will be entitled to an offsetting deduction; however, withholding is required on nondeductible moving expense reimbursements.[1]

3. There are no coverage or nondiscrimination rules that limit employer and employee deductions for moving expenses to nondiscriminatory plans. Reimbursement can be provided for whatever employee the employer chooses, and in whatever amounts the employer considers appropriate.

For Employees

Employees can deduct moving expenses as an above-the-line deduction (subtracted from gross income), if certain requirements are met.[2] The deduction is subject to a variety of typically complex rules and limitations:

1. the *distance* test;
2. the *time* test; and
3. limitations on the *types of expenses* that are deductible.

There are no dollar limits on otherwise deductible expenses.

Distance test. A move meets the distance test if the new main job location is at least fifty miles farther from the employee's former home than the old main job location was. For example, if the employee's old job location was ten miles from his home, the distance test is satisfied if the new job location is at least fifty miles from the old home. Distances are measured by the shortest of the more commonly traveled routes.[3]

Time test. To deduct moving expenses, the employee must work full time for at least thirty-nine weeks during the first twelve months after arriving at the new job location. The regulations contain numerous complex exceptions to and variations on this rule.[4]

Types of expenses deductible. Deductible moving expenses include only the reasonable costs of the following:[5]

(a) packing, crating, and moving household goods and personal effects (personal effects include a car and household pets; moving expenses include the costs of connecting and disconnecting utilities);

(b) storage and insurance within any consecutive thirty-day period after moving out of the former home and before delivery to the new home;

(c) traveling to the new home—a $0.23 per mile allowance for 2015 can be used for travel in the employee's own car.[6] The cost of meals is *not* deductible as a moving expense.

Nondeductible expenses. The following expenses are *not* deductible as moving expenses:[7]

- home improvements to help sell the old home;
- loss on sale of the old home;
- mortgage penalties;
- forfeiture of club dues or entry fees;
- any part of the purchase price of the new home;
- real estate taxes;
- car registration or driver's license fees;
- reinstalling carpets or draperies;
- storage charges other than as described earlier; and
- expenses for house hunting and expenses for selling, buying, or leasing a residence.

Reporting by Employee. An employee claiming a moving expense deduction, whether or not the employer provided any reimbursement, must file Form 3903; copies of this form can be obtained from the IRS website at www.irs.gov.

ERISA AND OTHER IMPLICATIONS

A moving expense reimbursement plan does not appear to fall within the definition of either a pension or welfare benefit plan for ERISA purposes.[8] Consequently, there is no reporting requirement (so no Form 5500 needs to be filed), nor do any other ERISA provisions apply.

WHERE CAN I FIND OUT MORE?

IRS Publication 521, *Moving Expenses*, at: www.irs.gov.

FREQUENTLY ASKED QUESTIONS

Question – Suppose you change jobs to a more distant location and try commuting from your old home for several years, then decide it is too difficult and move closer to the new job. Are moving expenses deductible then?

Answer – The IRS position is that moving expenses are not closely related to work at the new job location (and therefore not deductible) unless they are incurred within one year from the date the employee first reported to work at the new job. However, the expenses can be deducted if the employee can show that circumstances did not permit a move within one year, such as the need for children to complete high school in the old location. The IRS probably would not view the circumstances in the question as justifying a moving expense deduction.[9]

Question – If an employer wants to protect an employee against obtaining an inadequate price on the forced sale of a residence when moving, what is the best way to do it?

Answer – If the employer simply reimburses the employee for any reduction in house/sale proceeds, the reimbursement is taxable income to the employee, and it is not offset by any moving expense or other tax deduction. (Capital losses on the sale of a personal residence by an individual are nondeductible.[10])

It is better from a tax standpoint for the employer to actually buy the house from the employee. Any capital gain (up to $250,000 per taxpayer, if certain requirements are met) that the employee realizes on the sale will generally be excludable under Code section 121. The sale price should be the fair market value as determined by an independent real estate appraiser. Although this price may legitimately be higher than a "forced sale" price, it should not exceed the fair market value, as any excess over fair market value could be deemed to be additional compensation income to the employee.

CHAPTER ENDNOTES

1. I.R.C. §3401(a)(15).
2. I.R.C. §62(a)(15).
3. I.R.C. §217(c). However, if the *new* home is farther from the new job location than the old home was, the moving expenses are not deductible on the ground that the move is not related to starting work. Treas. Reg. §1.217-2(a)(3). For example, suppose the old home was 5 miles from the old job. You change job locations to a location 55 miles from the old home. You then move to a new home 60 miles from the new job. The distance test is met because the new job location is at least 50 miles farther from your old home, but moving expenses are not deductible because the move actually produces a longer commute than if you had stayed put. However, you can deduct the moving expenses if you can show that the 60-mile commute takes less time and money than the 55-mile commute from your old home, or if you are required as a condition of employment to live in the new home.
4. I.R.C. §217(c)(2); see also Treas. Reg. §1.217-2(c)(4).
5. The list given here is a summary of the rules in I.R.C. §217(b), Treas. Reg. §1.217-2(b), and IRS Publication 521.
6. IRS Publication 521.
7. Treas. Reg. §1.217-2(b)(3); see also IRS Publication 521.
8. See DOL Reg. §2510.3-1.
9. See Treas. Reg. §1.217-2(a)(3), Ex. (2).
10. Treas. Reg. §1.165-9(a). If a corporation purchases the house from an employee and later sells it at a loss, the loss is treated by the corporation as a capital loss. *Azar Nut Co. v. Comm'r.*, 931 F.2d 314 (5th Cir. 1991).

VEBA WELFARE BENEFIT TRUST

CHAPTER 55

INTRODUCTION

A Voluntary Employees Beneficiary Association (VEBA) is not a benefit plan as such—it is a type of fund into which employers make deposits that will be used to provide specified employee benefits in the future. For example, an employer can contribute funds on a regular basis to a VEBA that provides covered employees with a death benefit payable to their named beneficiary.

A VEBA can be either a trust or a corporation, but is generally a trust. It is set up by an employer unilaterally or through collective bargaining to hold funds used to pay benefits under specific employee benefit plans.[1] Income of the VEBA is exempt from regular income tax if the VEBA meets the requirements of section 501(c)(9) of the Internal Revenue Code.

WHEN IS USE OF SUCH A DEVICE INDICATED?

1. When an employer wants to provide benefit security for all covered employees by placing funding amounts in trust, for the exclusive benefit of employees and beyond the reach of corporate creditors.

2. When an employer wants to accelerate deductibility of employee benefit costs by prefunding those costs. Accelerated deductions are available only in limited situations, if at all (see Employer's Deduction in Tax Implications).

Advantages

1. Benefit security for individual employees is enhanced by using a VEBA, since there is an irrevocable trust for the exclusive benefit of employees and protection against reversion of funds to the employer.

Disadvantages

1. Installing and administering a VEBA can be relatively complex and costly. Smaller employers will find these plans feasible only if they use a vendor of packaged plans provided to groups of employers.

2. Use of a multiple-employer plan, which is often the only practical way to utilize a VEBA, means that the employer loses some degree of control over the plan's design, investments and even to some extent, the tax consequences of the plan.

3. A reversion of assets to the employer is effectively prohibited[2] (in contrast to qualified pension and profit-sharing plans, where reversions are allowed subject to a penalty). This means that the plan must be carefully designed to avoid overfunding and potential losses of funding intended for owner-employees.

VEBA DESIGN ISSUES

Who Must Be Covered?

1. A plan funded through a VEBA must generally cover more than one employee.[3]

2. Coverage generally must be broad. It is possible to design VEBA-funded plans that do not cover all employees, but excluding employees brings the planner into a fearsome thicket of overlapping,

complex, and unclear rules designed to prevent discrimination. In summary, these are as follows:

- Provisions in the section 501(c)(9) regulations that result in a loss of the VEBA's tax exemption if violated.[4]

- A separate code section providing specific nondiscrimination rules for VEBA-funded plans.[5] Full regulations under this section have not yet been issued by the IRS.

- Nondiscrimination provisions in the Code applicable to each separate benefit plan included in the VEBA plans. For example, a group term life insurance plan funded through a VEBA must meet the provisions of Code section 79.[6]

In many cases these rules require such broad coverage that relatively few employees can be excluded from VEBA plans. Because the savings to be gained through excluding employees often do not outweigh the tax risks and expense of compliance with these rules, many VEBA plans simply cover all employees.

3. The direct result of failing to meet the nondiscrimination rules is loss of tax exemption of the VEBA, which may not be a severe sanction if the VEBA has relatively little taxable income (by having invested in life insurance or tax-free bonds, for example). However, plans that are funded through the VEBA may have their own coverage requirements with various consequences for failure to have broad enough coverage.

4. Under the VEBA rules, generally, a plan providing a disproportionate share of benefits to owner-employees will not be tax exempt.[7]

What Kinds of Benefits Can Be Provided?

The VEBA regulations list the following as permitted VEBA benefits:[8]

- life insurance before and after retirement;

- other survivor benefits;

- sick and accident benefits; and

- other benefits, including vacation and recreation benefits, severance benefits paid through a severance pay plan (discussed below), unemployment and job training benefits, and disaster benefits.

The following are among items specifically *prohibited* as VEBA benefits: savings, retirement, or deferred compensation plans; coverage of expenses, such as commuting expenses, accident or homeowners' insurance covering damage to property, and other items unrelated to maintenance of the employee's earning power.[9]

Any plan funded through a VEBA, in addition to being subject to whatever nondiscrimination rules apply to that type of plan (for example, the section 79 rules for group term life insurance, etc.), is also subject to the VEBA benefit nondiscrimination rules of Code section 505. In particular, section 505(b)(7) limits compensation used in the plan's benefit formula to $265,000 annually (as indexed for 2015). This is the same compensation limit that applies to qualified plans under Code section 410(a)(17). For example, if a plan provided a death benefit of double the employee's compensation for all employees, the death benefit for an employee earning $500,000 would be limited to $530,000 (in 2015) rather than $1,000,000.

TAX IMPLICATIONS

Taxation of Employees

Premium payments or other funding deposits to the fund by the employer are generally not taxable to employees; that is, they are treated the same as if there was no VEBA and the employer maintained the plan without a VEBA.

Benefits payable to employees or beneficiaries are, in general, subject to the same income tax treatment as if they were paid directly by the employer.

Life Insurance. If the VEBA includes a life insurance (death benefit) plan, the value of life insurance protection is taxable (measured either by the Table 2001 rates or some other measure, as applicable; see Chapter 18). If the plan qualifies as a group term plan under the rules of section 79, the cost of the first $50,000 of protection is tax-free to the employees and additional insurance coverage is taxed under the Table 2001 rates.

Life insurance proceeds paid directly by a commercial insurer to a beneficiary on group term policies held by a VEBA are income tax free to beneficiaries.[10] It is unclear whether proceeds paid under a whole life policy are entirely income tax free, or are taxed similarly to life insurance proceeds received under a qualified plan (see Chapter 18).

For federal estate tax purposes, life insurance held by a VEBA can be kept out of the participant's estate by avoiding incidents of ownership, just as with personally owned insurance. If an irrevocable beneficiary designation is made at least three years before death, the policy proceeds will not be includible in the estate.

Taxation of the VEBA

Income of a VEBA is exempt from regular income tax if all the requirements of Code sections 501(c)(9) and 505 are met, as discussed above.

An organization will not be treated as a tax-exempt VEBA unless it notifies the IRS.[11] This is generally accomplished by filing within fifteen months from the end of the month in which the VEBA was organized an application for recognition of exempt status (Form 1023).[12]

Generally, VEBA income set aside (to provide for appropriate benefits and reasonable costs of administering those benefits) in excess of the Section 419A account limits (calculated without reference to any reserve for postretirement medical benefits) is subject to taxation as Unrelated Business Taxable Income (UBTI) under Code sections 511 and 512. (Any VEBA income derived from an unrelated trade or business regularly carried on by the VEBA is also subject to such taxation.)

These rules relating to UBTI are applicable even if the VEBA is part of a ten-or-more-employer plan under Section 419A(f)(6).[13] Since maximum tax deduction benefits derive from funding 419A(f)(6) plans far in excess of the Section 419A limits (discussed in the Frequently Asked Questions), to some extent this UBTI exposure nullifies the advantage of the tax-exempt status of the VEBA for purposes of funding a 419A(f)(6) plan. Funding with life insurance or tax-free investment vehicles can eliminate or minimize UBTI exposure.

Employer's Deduction

In general, an employer can deduct actuarially reasonable contributions to a VEBA that are designated to fund the benefits provided through the VEBA. Deductions are generally subject to the same limits as if the benefit were provided directly; these are found in Code Sections 419 and 419A. These sections provide that deductions are generally limited to the current annual cost of benefits, with a small reserve provision for benefits or claims incurred but not paid.

If cash value life insurance contracts are used to fund VEBA or welfare benefit trust benefits, it probably will not be possible for the employer to deduct the entire premium for the contract in the year paid. The IRS has severely disapproved of this tax-leveraging practice in numerous notices and rulings, denying deductibility and in some cases imposing other sanctions.[14]

ERISA AND OTHER REQUIREMENTS

ERISA treatment of benefits funded through a VEBA is the same as the treatment of any individual benefit plan funded by any other means. The use of a VEBA does not create or remove any reporting and disclosure, fiduciary, or other requirement otherwise applicable to the benefit plan.

A VEBA is subject to the filing requirement discussed in the Taxation of the VEBA section.

WHERE CAN I FIND OUT MORE?

1. Amoroso, "Computing Deduction Limits for Contributions to Welfare Benefit Plans," *Journal of Taxation*, September 1992.

2. Stiefel and Roth, "VEBAs Revisited as Funding Mechanisms—After DEFRA," *Benefits Law Journal*, Winter 1989/1990.

3. Weiss, "The Multiple Employer Welfare Benefit Trust," *Journal of the American Society of CLU & ChFC*, March 1990.

FREQUENTLY ASKED QUESTIONS

Question – Can an employer recover excess assets in a VEBA when it terminates after paying out all benefits due to participants?

Answer – No, the VEBA regulations effectively provide that when a VEBA is terminated, all excess assets must be paid out to covered employees.[15] Also, under

Code section 4976, there is generally a 100 percent penalty tax imposed when a portion of a welfare benefit fund reverts to an employer. What this means in practice is that an employer must avoid overfunding a plan funded through a VEBA.

Question – How are VEBA assets allocated when a plan terminates?

Answer – As indicated in the preceding question, plan assets cannot revert back to the employer. A VEBA must include a nondiscriminatory formula under which excess assets are allocated to plan participants.[16] For example, assets could be allocated under a formula as follows:

$$\text{Participant's share} = \frac{\text{Participant's compensation during period of participation}}{\text{Total compensation of all participants for all plan years}} \times \text{Excess Plan Assets}$$

Since this formula would tend to increase the share of long-term key employees, consideration should be given to restricting the number of years of participation used in the numerator to five years, for example.

Question – Can plan participants borrow from a VEBA?

Answer – Loans from VEBAs are not permitted except in times of distress, which appears to be strictly interpreted by the IRS.[17]

CHAPTER ENDNOTES

1. See Treas. Regs. §§1.501(c)(9)-2(a)(1), 1.501(c)(9)-2(c)(1), 1.501(c)(9)-3.
2. Generally, an organization will not be a tax-exempt VEBA if the written instrument creating the organization provides for the distribution of its assets upon dissolution to the contributing employers or if state law (in the state in which the organization was created) provides for such distribution. Treas. Reg. §1.501(c)(9)-4(d). Additionally, Code Section 4976 generally imposes a 100% penalty tax when a portion of a welfare benefit fund reverts to an employer.
3. Relevant parts of the Code's definition of a welfare benefit fund are written in the plural: a welfare benefit fund is, in part, a fund providing welfare benefits to "employees or their beneficiaries." Language describing VEBAs in a similarly plural fashion has been held to require that a VEBA provide benefits to more than one employee. I.R.C. §419(e)(1)(b). See also Rev. Rul. 85-199, 1985-2 CB 163.
4. See Treas. Regs. §§1.501(c)(9)-2(a)(2), 1.501(c)(9)-4(b).
5. I.R.C. §505(b).
6. See I.R.C. §505(b)(3).
7. Treas. Regs. §§1.501(c)(9)-2,(a)(2), 1.501(c)(9)-4(b). See also GCMs 39818 (1990), 39801 (1989).
8. Treas. Reg. §1.501(c)(9)-3.
9. Treas. Reg. §1.501(c)(9)-3(f).
10. See, e.g., Priv. Ltr. Ruls. 8534048, 8352022, 8035066, and 8025100.
11. I.R.C. §505(c).
12. Temp. Treas. Reg. §1,505(c)-1T, Q&A-3, Q&A-4, Q&A-5, and Q&A-6.
13. I.R.C. §512(a)(3)(E)(i); Temp. Treas. Reg. §1.512(a)-5T, Q&A-3.
14. These include Treas. Reg. §1.419A(f)(6)-1; (relating to 10-or-more employer plans), Notice 2003-24, 2003-1 CB 853 (purported collectively bargained plans); Rev. Rul. 2007-65, 2007-45 IRB 949; Notice 2007-83, 2007-45 IRB 960; and Notice 2007-84, 2007-45 IRB 963 (relating to single employer plans). The Tax Court as affirmed by the Second Circuit has agreed with this IRS view, M. Curcio, CA-2, 2012-2 USTC para 50,512.
15. See Treas. Reg. §1.501(c)(9)-4(d).
16. Ibid.
17. Treas. Reg. §1.501(c)(9)-3(f). This regulation provides that permissible VEBA benefits do not include "the provision of loans to members except in times of distress (as permitted by section 1.501(c)(9)-3(e))." That regulation provides examples of acceptable VEBA benefits, but only explicitly mentions loans once: stating that VEBAs may provide "temporary living expense loans ... at times of disaster (such as fire or flood) ...." Treas. Reg. §1.501(c)(9)-3(e). On a different but related issue, an IRS General Counsel's Memorandum has suggested that a loan from a VEBA to the employer might jeopardize the VEBA's tax-exempt status. GCM 39884 (1992).

KNOWING THE RULES: GOVERNMENT REGULATIONS AND HOW TO FIND THEM

CHAPTER 56

An employer can pay its top executives as much as it wants to; the federal government does not regulate this except for a very general reasonableness limit on the amount of salary payments that can be deducted and a maximum cap of $1,000,000 on deductible compensation for certain executives. By contrast, federal tax law specifically limits the maximum pension benefit that an employer can provide to an employee.

There are innumerable other detailed federal laws and regulations effective in the employee benefits area; just to pick another one at random, the government specifies, to the day, when an employer must allow an employee to begin participating in the employer's pension plan.

Why does the federal government micromanage an employer's benefit programs? What is the impact of this extensive regulation on the employee benefit planner, and how can the planner keep up with the rules? That's the subject of this chapter.

WHY THE RULES EXIST

Maintaining income of individuals when they cannot support themselves has been a major governmental concern. Governments are not always happy at being handed this responsibility but usually end up with it if it is not picked up somewhere else in society. So, governments have always tried to encourage private organizations to act in this area. This is one reason why charitable institutions are exempt from tax.

When the American economy started to become mainly industrial around the beginning of the 20th century, the need for retirement plans increased because the industrial economy tended to break up the traditional supportive, extended farm family, and industry provided less work for the aged than farming. The government became involved in retirement plans in a twofold way.

First, in the 1920s the federal government began encouraging private, employer-sponsored retirement plans by providing two kinds of tax benefits: (1) pension funds were made tax exempt;[1] and (2) employer contributions to plan funds were made currently deductible even though benefits were not paid until later years.[2] The second big federal initiative in the retirement plan area was, of course, the adoption of the Social Security system in the 1930s at a time when private pension plans were in great decline.

Since the 1940s, private pension plans have revived to an enormous degree; assets in these plans now amount to more than five *trillion* dollars—a pot of money constituting as much as 10 percent of the nation's *total capital*.

However, something else has grown as fast as or even faster than the dollars in pension funds: the words, paragraphs, pages, and volumes of federal statutes, court cases, rulings, and regulations based on the simple, original 1920s tax benefit arrangements for private pension plans. How does the government justify the sometimes almost unbelievable complexity of this regulatory scheme? Three reasons are generally given; two are respectable, while the third is questionable:

- The government loses substantial revenue by providing tax benefits for retirement and other benefit plans. So, it has to make sure that benefits go where they are most needed so that the tax "expenditure" is cost effective.

- Private saving for retirement should be encouraged so that individuals do not become dependent on the government; but such saving should not fail to help those who really need the retirement benefit. There have to be rules so that plans do not simply benefit highly compensated employees who have other sources of retirement income.

- The government can gain a lot of tax revenue—without the political pain of "raising taxes"—by fine-tuning the employee benefit law to reduce tax benefits for certain plan participants. Historically, the most notorious example of this was the "reforms" of the 1982 tax law (the Tax Equity and Fiscal Responsibility Act of 1982) that virtually undid the tax reductions that had just been passed the year before (the Economic Recovery Tax Act of 1981). Year after year, fine-tuning adds page after page to federal laws and regulations. Last year's fine-tuning scheme is seldom repealed; it is merely added to or amended.

What's the significance of all this history and government policy to the benefit planner? Just two points have to be made:

- Understanding the rules is a lot easier if you know where they come from. For example, can you adopt a plan provision that gives extra benefits to one or more employees who are not highly compensated? You can search the federal law until doomsday and you will not find the answer to this in so many words. But if you understand what the law is trying to do, you will understand immediately that this kind of provision usually will not violate the law.

- If you know what kinds of concerns motivate our Congress, you can give your clients useful advice about potential future changes in the law. While nobody can predict tax law changes in detail, it is pretty safe to say, for example, that prohibiting discrimination in favor of highly compensated employees will continue to be an important policy consideration.

THE RULES

Planners need to understand where the employee benefit plan rules are and how to find them. They also must understand the significance of the rules; for example, some rules are binding on everybody, while certain other authorities are merely sources of information about the government's position on a certain issue in case the issue should get into court.

Government regulation is expressed through the following, in order of importance: (1) the statutory law; (2) the law as expressed in court cases; (3) regulations of government agencies; (4) rulings and other information issued by government agencies.

Statutory Law

The law as expressed by statutes passed by the U.S. Congress is the highest level of authority and is the basis of all regulation; the court cases, rulings, and regulations are simply interpretations of the statute. If the statute was detailed enough to cover every possible case, there theoretically would not be any need for anything else. But despite the best efforts of Congressional drafting staffs, the statutes cannot cover every situation.

Benefit planners should become as familiar as possible with the statutory law since it is the basis for all other rules, regulations, and court cases. One of the main causes for confusion among non-experts is a lack of understanding of the relative status of sources of information. That is, while a rule found in the Internal Revenue Code is controlling, a statement in an IRS ruling or instructions to IRS forms may be merely a matter of interpretation that is relatively easy to "plan around."

In the benefits area, the sources of statutory law are:

- *Internal Revenue Code (the Code).* The tax laws governing the deductibility and taxation of pension and employee benefit programs are controlling. These are found primarily in Code sections 401-424, with important provisions also in Sections 72, 83, and other sections.

- *Employee Retirement Income Security Act of 1974 (ERISA), as amended, and other labor law provisions.* Labor law provisions such as ERISA govern the non-tax aspects of federal regulation. These involve plan participation requirements, notice to participants, reporting to the federal government, and a variety of rules designed to safeguard any funds that are set aside to pay benefits in the future. There is some overlap between ERISA and the Code in the areas of plan participation, vesting, prohibited transactions, and others.

- *Pension Benefit Guaranty Corporation (PBGC).* The PBGC is a government corporation set up under ERISA in 1974 to provide termination insurance for participants in qualified defined benefit plans up to certain limits. In carrying out this responsibility, the PBGC regulates plan terminations and imposes certain reporting requirements on covered plans that are in financial difficulty or in a state of contraction.

- *Securities laws.* The federal securities laws are designed to protect investors. Benefit plans may involve an element of investing the employee's money. While qualified plans are generally exempt from the full impact of the securities laws, if the plan holds employer stock, a federal registration statement may be required and certain securities regulations may apply.

- *Civil Rights laws.* Benefit plans are part of an employer's compensation policies, and these plans are therefore subject to the Civil Rights Act of 1964, prohibiting employment discrimination on the basis of race, religion, sex, or national origin.

- *Age Discrimination.* The Age Discrimination in Employment Act of 1967, as amended, has specific provisions aimed at benefit plans.

- *Disabled Employees.* The Americans with Disabilities Act of 1990 generally prohibits an employer from discriminating against a person on the basis of the person's disability in the areas of employment, public services and transportation, public accommodations and telecommunication services.

- *State legislation.* ERISA contains a broad preemption provision under which the provisions of ERISA supersede any state laws relating to employee benefit plans. If ERISA does not deal with a particular issue, however, there may be room for state legislation. For example, there is considerable state legislation and regulation governing the types of group-term life insurance contracts that can be offered as part of an employer plan. There are also certain areas where states continue to assert authority even though ERISA also has an impact—for example, in the area of creditors' rights to pension fund assets.

Court Cases

The courts enter this picture primarily when a specific taxpayer decides to appeal a tax assessment made by the IRS. The courts do not act on their own to resolve tax or other legal issues. Consequently, the law as expressed in court cases is a crazy-quilt affair that offers some answers but often raises more questions than it answers. However, after statutes, court cases are the most authoritative source of law. Courts can and do overturn regulations and rulings of the IRS and other regulatory agencies.

A taxpayer wishing to contest a tax assessment has three choices: (1) the Federal District Court in the taxpayer's district; (2) the United States Tax Court; or (3) the United States Court of Federal Claims.[3] Tax law can be found in the decisions of any of these three courts.

All three courts are equally authoritative. Most tax cases, however, are decided by the U.S. Tax Court, because it offers a powerful advantage: the taxpayer can bring the case before the Tax Court without paying the disputed tax. The other courts require payment of the tax, followed by a suit for refund.

Decisions of the Federal District Court and the United States Tax Court are appealed to the Federal Circuit Court of Appeals for the applicable federal judicial circuit—the United States is divided into eleven of these circuits. Decisions of the United States Court of Federal Claims are appealed to the Court of Appeals for the Federal Circuit. The circuit courts sometimes differ on certain points of tax law; as a result, tax and benefit planning may depend on what judicial circuit the taxpayer is located in. Where these differences exist, one or more taxpayers will eventually appeal a decision by the Court of Appeals to the United States Supreme Court to resolve differences of interpretation among various judicial circuits. However, this process takes many years and the Supreme Court may ultimately choose not to hear the case. Congress also sometimes amends the Code or other statute to resolve these interpretive differences.

Regulations

Regulations are interpretations of statutory law that are published by a government agency. In the benefits area, the most significant regulations are those published by the Treasury Department (the parent of the IRS), the Labor Department, and the PBGC.

Regulations are structured as abstract rules, like the statutory law itself. They are not related to a particular factual situation, although they often contain useful examples that illustrate the application of the rules. Treasury regulations currently are often issued in question-and-answer form.

The numbering system for regulations is supposed to make them more accessible by including an internal reference to the underlying statutory provision. For example, Treasury Regulation Section 1.401(k)-2 is a regulation relating to Section 401(k) of the Internal Revenue Code. Labor Regulation Section 2550.408b-3 relates to Section 408(b) of ERISA.

Issuance of regulations follows a prescribed procedure involving an initial issuance of *proposed regulations*, followed by hearings and public comment, then *final regulations*. The process often takes years. Where taxpayers have an urgent need to know answers, the agency will issue *regulations* that are both *temporary* and proposed. Technically, temporary regulations are binding while regulations issued only in proposed form are not. However, if a taxpayer takes a position contrary to such a proposed regulation, the taxpayer is taking the risk that the regulation will ultimately be finalized and be enforced against him.

Rulings and Other Information

IRS Rulings. IRS rulings are responses by the IRS to requests by taxpayers to interpret the law in light of their particular fact situations. A *Technical Advice Memorandum (TAM)* is similar to a ruling except that the request for clarification and guidance is initiated from an IRS agent in the field during a taxpayer audit, rather than directly from the taxpayer.

There are two types of IRS rulings—*Revenue Rulings*, which are published by the IRS as general guidance to all taxpayers, and *Private Letter Rulings (Let. Ruls.)*, which are addressed to only the specific taxpayers who requested the rulings. The IRS publishes its Revenue Rulings in IRS Bulletins (collected in Cumulative Bulletins—CB—each year). Revenue rulings are binding on IRS personnel on the issues covered in them, but often IRS agents will try to make a distinction between a taxpayer's factual situation and a similar one covered in a ruling if the ruling appears to favor the taxpayer.

Private letter rulings are not published by the IRS, but are available to the public with taxpayer identification deleted. These "anonymous" letter rulings are published for tax professionals by various private publishers. They are not binding interpretations of tax law except for the taxpayer who requested the ruling, and even then they apply only to the exact situation described in the ruling request and do not apply to even a slightly different fact pattern involving the same taxpayer. Nevertheless, letter rulings are very important in research since they are often the only source of information about the IRS position on various issues.

A *General Counsel Memorandum (GCM)* is an internal IRS document prepared by the General Counsel of the Service for its own staff's guidance in administering the Code. GCMs also give an indication of the probable approach the Service will take in a particular area.

A *Field Service Advice (FSA)* is an IRS document prepared for internal use within the IRS. Until 1998, these documents were not released to the public and, therefore, depending on when a particular FSA was written, may contain candid analysis of the issues involved. As a result of Freedom of Information Act litigation and subsequent legislation, FSAs issued after 1985 are required to be released to the public.[4] While FSAs are not binding even to the person to whom they are written, they do provide insight into the thinking of the IRS at the time they are written.

Because of frequent changes in the tax law, the IRS has been unable to promulgate regulations and rulings on a timely basis, and has increasingly used less formal approaches to inform taxpayers of its position. These include various types of published *Notices* and even speeches by IRS personnel. Finally, many important IRS positions are found only in *IRS Publications* (pamphlets available free to taxpayers) and *instructions* for filling out IRS forms. The IRS also maintains telephone question-answering services, but the value of these for information on complicated issues is minimal.

Other rulings. The Department of Labor and the PBGC issue some rulings in areas of employee benefit regulation under their jurisdiction. DOL rulings include the *Prohibited Transaction Exemptions (PTEs)*, which rule on types of transactions that can avoid the prohibited transaction penalties—for example, sale of life insurance contracts to qualified plans.

HOW TO FIND THE ANSWERS

Tax experts find it difficult to get answers to employee benefit tax questions, so non-experts should not be surprised if they also have trouble. The following approach is used by many successful financial planning professionals:

1. Investigate secondary sources, choose several that you find helpful, and keep them handy. Secondary sources are overviews of the law that give you a general understanding and direct you toward more detailed information. The *Tax Facts* and *Tools and Techniques* series of books are examples of secondary sources of information that provide rapid access to an overview and general explanation of the law.

2. When a tax or other benefit issue arises, review the secondary sources to get a general idea of the law in that area and where additional information can be found.

3. Review the statutory provisions and regulations (if any) relating to the issue—particularly the Internal Revenue Code and ERISA and the related regulations.

4. Review court cases and rulings dealing with the issue and compare their factual situations with the one you are dealing with.

5. The Internet as a source of information is becoming increasingly useful. Almost all IRS rulings, forms, and publications are available at www.irs.gov. In addition, many banks, investment firms, etc., post financial planning information on their websites. The most important caveat to using the Internet is to make sure the information is up-to-date; website owners can be careless about deleting obsolete information from their sites.

At this point, non-lawyer professionals must confront the problem of *unauthorized practice of law*. While the concept of "practice of law" is too complex to define here, in general a non-lawyer may not express an opinion to a client as to the specific law applicable to, and the legal implications of, the client's factual situation. A professional can, however, discuss the legal background of the client's situation in general and can advise the client to obtain an opinion of counsel as to the law's specific impact on the client. That should be the non-lawyer professional's role in a benefit planning situation involving complex or unsettled legal issues.

WHAT HAPPENS IF THE LAW IS NOT FOLLOWED?

There are both *criminal* and civil penalties that can apply if a taxpayer fails to abide by the tax law by taking too large a deduction or under-reporting items of income. Criminal penalties are those that can result in imprisonment.[5] Nothing will be said further here about criminal penalties except this: if a client discovers that the IRS is considering criminal tax sanctions against him, that client is in very serious trouble and needs immediate legal help from an expert in criminal tax law.

Most IRS audits that end unfavorably to the taxpayer do not result in penalties; the taxpayer merely has to pay back taxes plus interest—which can be substantial. However, certain penalties can also be assessed. These include penalties for:

- failure to file return or pay the tax indicated on the return. Penalty—5 percent of the underpayment per month, up to 25 percent.[6]

- substantial understatement of income tax (understatement of the greater of $5,000 or 10 percent of tax). Penalty—20 percent of the understatement.[7]

- negligence, imposed if a taxpayer fails to make a reasonable attempt to comply with the tax law. Penalty—20 percent of the underpayment.[8]

- fraud. Penalty—75 percent of the underpayment.[9]

- substantial valuation overstatement (for example, an overstatement of pension liabilities to inflate pension plan deductions). Penalty—20 to 40 percent of the underpayment.[10]

Legal opinion letters. Can a taxpayer rely on a legal opinion as to the tax consequences of a transaction—that is, will the taxpayer at least avoid the negligence or fraud penalties by doing so? Yes, generally speaking; however, there are some things the client should watch for:

- Many legal opinion letters avoid expressing an opinion on certain aspects of a transaction, so the client must read the opinion letter carefully.

- The client should be sure the legal opinion applies to the taxpayer and transaction in question and is not aimed at some other, similar transaction or is simply a generic opinion relating to a group of potential taxpayers. A "borrowed" opinion letter may provide useful information but taxpayer reliance on it is risky since the author of the opinion did not focus on the facts of the actual situation.

- If the transaction involves a tax shelter, the substantial underpayment penalty may be reduced under certain circumstances.[11] Tax shelter means: (1) a partnership or other entity; (2) any investment plan or arrangement; or (3) any other plan or arrangement if a significant purpose of such partnership, entity, plan, or arrangement is the avoidance or evasion of federal income tax.

CHAPTER ENDNOTES

1. Revenue Acts of 1921 and 1926.
2. Revenue Act of 1928.
3. Prior to October 30, 1992, the U.S. Court of Federal Claims was known as the U.S. Claims Court.
4. *Tax Analysts v. Internal Revenue Service*, 117 F.3d 607 (D.C. Cir. 1997); IRS Restructuring and Reform Act Section 3509.
5. A complete discussion of both criminal and civil penalties is contained in Saltzman, *IRS Practice and Procedure*: Warren, Gorham and Lamont, 2nd ed., 1990.
6. I.R.C. §6651.
7. I.R.C. §§6662(b)(2), 6662(d).
8. I.R.C. §§6662(b)(1), 6662(c).
9. I.R.C. §6663.
10. I.R.C. §§6662(b)(4), 6662(f), 6662(h).
11. I.R.C. §6662(d)(2)(C), as amended by AJCA 2004. In late 2004, the Service released final regulations affecting "covered opinions" and other written advice. See TD 9165, 69 Fed. Reg. 75839 (12-20-2004).

COMMON CONTROL RULES

CHAPTER 57

In designing qualified plans and other employee benefit plans, the plan designer often deals with employer organizations (incorporated or unincorporated) that are owned or controlled in common with other such organizations. Plan coverage must then sometimes be coordinated among members of the commonly controlled group of employers.

Common control must be taken into account in identifying the "employer" in an employee benefit plan under a variety of complex rules in the Internal Revenue Code. The objective of these rules is to prevent a business owner from getting around the coverage and nondiscrimination requirements for qualified plans by artificially segregating employees to be benefited from a plan into one organization, with the remainder being employed by subsidiaries or organizations with lesser plan benefits or no plan at all. While this is still technically possible, the controlled group rules restrict this practice considerably.

CONTROLLED GROUP RULES

The common control rules are inherently complicated, because the forms in which businesses can be owned are complicated. Complexity in the ownership structure of a business reflects many non-tax considerations such as capital structure and administrative needs; consequently these rules probably will always be complicated. There are three sets of these common control rules:

1. Under Code section 414(b), all employees of all corporations in a *controlled group* of corporations are treated as employed by a single employer for purposes of Code sections 401, 408(k), 408(p), 410, 411, 415, and 416.

   The major impact of this comes from the participation rules of Section 410, which, in effect, require the participation and coverage tests to be applied to the entire controlled group, rather than to any single corporation in the group. Code section 414(c) provides similar rules for commonly controlled partnerships and proprietorships.

2. Code section 414(m) provides that employees of an *affiliated service group* are treated as employed by a single employer. This requirement similarly has its major impact in determining participation in a qualified plan, but it applies to other employee benefit requirements as well.

3. A *leased employee* is treated as an employee of the lessor corporation under certain circumstances under Code section 414(n).

Some examples will give a general idea of the impact of these provisions on plan design; these are discussed in detail later. *Note*: The common thread of these examples is that the related organization's employees must be *taken into account* in applying the participation rules. This does not mean that these employees must necessarily be covered.

Example 1. Alpha Corporation owns 80 percent of the stock of Beta Corporation. Alpha and Beta are members of a parent subsidiary-controlled group of corporations. In applying the participation and coverage rules of Code section 410, Alpha and Beta must be considered as a single employer.

Example 2. Bert and Harry own stock as follows:

Owner	Corporation A	Corporation B
Bert	60%	60%
Harry	30	30
	90%	90%

Corporations A and B are a brother-sister controlled group. Thus, A and B must be considered as a single employer for purposes of Code section 410 and most other qualified plan rules.

Example 3. Medical Services, Inc., provides administrative and laboratory services for Dr. Sam and Dr. Joe, each of whom is an incorporated sole practitioner. Dr. Sam and Dr. Joe each own 50 percent of Medical Services, Inc. If either Dr. Sam or Dr. Joe adopts a qualified plan, employees of Medical Services, Inc., will have to be taken into account in determining whether plan coverage is nondiscriminatory.

Example 4. Calculators Incorporated, an actuarial firm, contracts with Temporary Services, Inc., an employee-leasing firm, to lease employees. If the leased employees perform services on a substantially full-time basis for at least one year, the leased employees will have to be taken into account in determining nondiscrimination in any qualified plan of Calculators, unless Temporary maintains a minimum (10 percent nonintegrated) money-purchase pension plan for the leased employees. See below for more information on leased employees.

Consequences of Controlled Group Status

Once again, all employees of all corporations that are members of a controlled group of corporations are treated as employed by a single employer for various purposes, specified in Code section 414(b). Probably the most significant of these consequences is the application of the coverage tests of Code section 410. All three tests will be applied to the group as a whole, except to the extent that the tests can be applied to a subgroup constituting a separate line of business under Code section 414(r). This does not necessarily mean that a plan cannot qualify if it involves employees of only one member of a controlled group. The plan for a single company in the controlled group could qualify if it meets one of the three tests, such as the average-benefit test in particular.

It is also possible that the controlled group aggregation rules can be applied to the advantage of the employer. For example, a plan for a controlled group might meet the average-benefit test, even though in a given corporation included in the group there might be only one or two participants, both among the highest paid employees of that corporation. Considered separately, the plan for that corporation would fail to qualify.

TYPES OF CONTROLLED GROUPS

Under Code sections 414(b) and 414(c), all employees of members of a controlled group of corporations or controlled group of trades or businesses (whether or not incorporated) that are under common control are treated as employed by a single employer for purposes of Sections 401, 408(k), 408(p), 410, 411, 415, and 416. This covers most provisions of the qualified plan law. The most important impact relates to the coverage requirements of Code section 410. Thus, all employees of employers in a controlled group must be taken into account when determining whether a qualified plan maintained by any employer in the controlled group satisfies the percentage participation tests or the discriminatory tests.

The existence of a controlled group is determined by applying the rules of Code section 1563(a), a section originally designed to inhibit corporations from breaking up into smaller units to take advantage of the graduated corporate tax rates. Under this provision, there are three types of controlled groups: parent-subsidiary controlled groups, brother-sister controlled groups, and combined groups.

Parent-Subsidiary Controlled Group

A parent-subsidiary controlled group is one or more chains of corporations connected through stock ownership with a common parent corporation if, with respect to the stock of each corporation (except the parent corporation):

At least 80 percent of the total combined voting power of all classes of stock entitled to vote or at least 80 percent of the total value of shares of all classes of stock is owned by one or more corporations in the group and the common parent corporation satisfies the same 80 percent test with at least one other corporation in the group. Stock owned directly by any other corporation in the group is excluded in determining the parent corporation's ownership.

In applying this test to unincorporated trades or businesses, the 80 percent test is applied to an interest in profits or to a capital interest.

Example. Suppose Alpha Corporation owns 80 percent of the total combined voting power of all classes of stock entitled to vote of Beta Corporation. Beta Corporation owns stock that possesses at least 80 percent of the total value of shares of all classes of stock of Gamma Corporation. Alpha is the common parent, and the parent-subsidiary controlled group consists of Alpha, Beta, and Gamma.

Brother-Sister Controlled Group

A brother-sister controlled group consists of two or more corporations in which five or fewer individuals, estates, or trusts own (with attribution, as described below) stock possessing:

At least 80 percent of the total combined voting power or value of all classes of stock (excluding nonvoting stock which is limited and preferred as to dividends) of each corporation, and more than 50 percent of the total combined voting power or value of all classes of stock (excluding nonvoting stock that is limited and preferred as to dividends) of each corporation, taking into account the stock ownership of each owner only to the extent that the owner's interest is identical in each corporation.

Example 1. Corporations M, N, and O have only one class of stock, which is owned by five unrelated individuals as follows:

	Percentage of Ownership in			Identical Ownership in
Investor	**M**	**N**	**O**	**MNO**
Alex	20%	10%	20%	10%
Bartley	20	30	10	10
Clay	20	20	30	20
Davis	20	20	20	20
Ensley	20	20	20	20
Total	100%	100%	100%	80%

Corporations M, N, and O constitute a brother-sister controlled group.

Example 2. Three corporations, Q, S, and T are owned by four unrelated individuals as follows:

	Percentage of Ownership in			Identical Ownership in		
Investor	**Q**	**S**	**T**	**Q-S**	**Q-T**	**S-T**
Walt	50%	25%	25.5%	25%	25.5%	25.0%
Xavier	50	25	25.5	25	25.5	25.0
Yolanda	0	25	24.5	0	0.0	24.5
Zorba	0	25	24.5	0	0.0	24.5
Totals	100%	100%	100%	50%	51%	99 %

Corporation Q and S do not constitute a brother-sister controlled group, because, although four individuals together own 100 percent of each, taking only identical ownership into account, there is only 50 percent common control. Although identical ownership in Q and T adds up to 51 percent, they are not a brother-sister group—see the next example. Finally, S and T constitute a brother-sister controlled group, with identical ownership adding up to a total of 99 percent.

At one time, the IRS included an example in the regulations which, somewhat simplified, went as follows:

	Percentage of Ownership in			Identical Ownership in		
Investor	**A**	**B**	**C**	**AB**	**AC**	**BC**
1	100%	60%	60%	60%	60%	60%
2	0	40	0	0	0	0
3	0	0	40	0	0	0
Total	100%	*	*	60%	60%	60%

*100 percent under prior regulations; 60 percent under current regulations. See below.

Prior regulations asserted that AB, AC, and BC constituted brother-sister controlled groups, even though some of the owners held no interest at all in A, B, or C. This interpretation was declared invalid by the U.S. Supreme Court in *U.S. v. Vogel Fertilizer Company*.[1] Current regulations now reflect this by providing that each person whose stock ownership is taken into account for purposes of the 80 percent requirement also must be a person whose stock ownership is counted toward the 50 percent requirement.[2] Under this interpretation, there are no brother-sister groups in this situation.

Combined Group

A combined group is three or more corporations each of which is a member of a parent-subsidiary group or a brother-sister group and one of which is a common parent of a parent-subsidiary group and also is included in a brother-sister group.

Example. Ken, an individual, owns 80 percent of the total combined voting power of all classes of stock of Steel Corporation and Lint Corporation. Lint Corporation owns 80 percent of the total combined voting power of all classes of the stock of Octopus Corporation. Steel and Lint are members of a brother-sister controlled group. Lint and Octopus are members of a parent-subsidiary group. Lint is the common parent of the parent-subsidiary group and also a member of the brother-sister group. Therefore, Steel, Lint, and Octopus constitute a combined group.

TYPES OF STOCK EXCLUDED FROM CONTROLLED GROUP DETERMINATION

Certain stock is excluded from consideration in computing the percentages in the controlled group tests.[3] In general, note that excluding stock from consideration makes it more likely that the tests will be met, because the target shareholder's stock will be a larger percentage of the amount outstanding. This is the purpose of these exclusionary rules; in general, they are designed to thwart attempts to get around controlled group tests by transferring stock to various trusts or other entities, as the rules indicate.

First of all, nonvoting preferred stock and treasury stock are not taken into account.

In addition, if the parent owns 50 percent or more of the total combined voting power or value of all classes of stock in the potential subsidiary corporation, the following are not taken into account in determining the existence of a parent-subsidiary controlled group:

- Stock in a subsidiary held by a trust that is part of a plan of deferred compensation for the benefit of the employees of the parent or the subsidiary.
- Stock in the subsidiary owned by an individual who is a principal shareholder (5 percent or more of voting power or total value) or an officer of the potential parent.
- Stock in the subsidiary owned by an employee of the subsidiary, if the stock is subject to conditions that run in favor of the parent or subsidiary and that substantially restrict the right to dispose of such stock. Stock subject to the typical buy-sell agreement generally would fall within this provision.
- Stock in the subsidiary owned by a tax-exempt organization that is controlled directly or indirectly by the parent or subsidiary or by an individual, estate, or trust that is a principal shareholder of the parent, by an officer of the potential parent, or by any combination of the above.[4]

For purposes of the brother-sister controlled group tests, the following stock is excluded whenever five or fewer potential common owners own at least 50 percent of the total combined voting power or value of all classes of stock:

- Stock held for the benefit of the employees of the corporation by a qualified retirement plan trust.
- Stock owned by an employee of the corporation, if the stock is subject to restrictions that run in favor of any of the common owners of the corporation and that substantially restrict the right to dispose of the stock (with an exception for a bona fide reciprocal stock-purchase agreement).
- Stock owned by a tax-exempt organization that is controlled directly or indirectly by

the corporation, by an individual, estate, or trust that is a principal shareholder of the corporation, by an officer of the corporation, or by any combination of these.[5]

Constructive Ownership (Attribution) Rules

In determining the existence of a controlled group, an individual may be deemed to own not only stock owned directly but also stock owned by certain related parties.[6]

The following rules apply for both parent-subsidiary and brother-sister determinations:[7]

- An option to acquire stock causes the option holder to be treated as owning the stock.
- Stock owned directly or indirectly by or for a partnership is considered owned by any partner having an interest of 5 percent or more in capital or profits, in proportion to the partner's interest in capital or profits (whichever is greater).
- Stock owned directly or indirectly by an estate or trust (excluding a qualified trust) is considered owned by a beneficiary who has an actuarial interest of 5 percent or more in such stock, to the extent of the actuarial interest.
- Stock owned directly or indirectly by or for any portion of a grantor trust is considered owned by the grantor.

Further attribution rules apply in the brother-sister situation.[8] These are:

- Stock owned directly by or for a corporation is considered owned by any person who owns 5 percent or more in value of its stock in proportion to the percentage of corporate value owned by the person.
- An individual is considered to own stock in a corporation owned directly or indirectly by or for his spouse (if not legally separated under a decree of divorce or separate maintenance), unless the person's ownership satisfies certain standards of remoteness set out in Section 1563(e)(5).
- A parent is deemed to own stock owned directly or indirectly by or for his children, including legally adopted children, who are less than twenty-one years of age, and an individual less than twenty-one years old is deemed to own stock owned directly or indirectly by or for his parents, including legally adoptive parents.
- If an individual owns more than 50 percent of the total combined voting power or value of all classes of stock in a corporation, the individual is considered as owning stock in the corporation owned directly or indirectly by or for his parents, grandparents, grandchildren, and children who have attained age twenty-one.

The above attribution rules all can be used to provide reattribution to another owner, except that stock attributed under the family attribution rules is not reattributed.[9] This can result in very complex attribution patterns, in some cases.

AFFILIATED SERVICE GROUP

The purpose and effect of the affiliated service group rules of Coe section 414(m) are best understood by looking at the loophole that this provision was designed to close. This loophole typically involved professional corporations or partnerships that desired to exclude rank-and-file employees from qualified plans maintained for the professional owners.

Example. Consider a situation in which two physicians enter into an equal partnership for the practice of medicine. A similar alternative practice was for each doctor to form a one-person professional corporation and then have the professional corporation enter into a partnership. The partnership could then form a separate support business to provide all support services for the medical practice, and the support business would become the employer of all the support employees. Each of the doctors would own just 50 percent of the support organization. Under all the other aggregation rules discussed here, except for the affiliated service group rules, the doctors could each adopt a qualified plan covering only themselves and none of the regular employees. The affiliated service group rules basically eliminate this type of planning or restrict it severely.

The affiliated service group provisions provide complex rules under which the employees of an *affiliated service group* must be included in any qualified plans that benefit the owners. An affiliated service group includes the *service organization* and the professional organization itself. For purposes of most of the pension provisions, including the coverage and nondiscrimination rules, all employees of an affiliated service group are treated as being employed by a single employer.

An affiliated service group means a service organization and one or more organizations that meet one of the following two tests:[10]

1. A service organization that is a shareholder or partner in the first organization and regularly performs services for the first organization or is regularly associated with the first organization in performing services for third persons.

2. An organization in which a significant portion of its business is the performance of services of a type historically performed for the first organization or for a service organization that is the shareholder or partner in the first organization. However, this applies only if 10 percent or more of the organization is owned by highly compensated employees (as defined in Chapter 13) of the first organization or any service organization that is a shareholder or partner in the first organization.

In addition, an affiliated service group also consists of a service recipient and an organization that performs management functions for the recipient.[11]

Under the proposed regulations, the rules apply primarily to service organizations of the type that provide professional services in the field of health, law, engineering, architecture, accounting, actuarial science, performing arts, consulting, or insurance. However, this list can be further expanded through regulations.[12]

Example. As an example of the operation of the affiliated service group rules, suppose Dr. VanDerslice incorporates and the corporation becomes a partner in the Butler Surgical Group. Doctor VanDerslice's corporation regularly associates with the Butler Surgical Group in performing services for third parties—individual patients, a hospital, and the like. Dr. VanDerslice's corporation and the Butler Surgical Group constitute an affiliated service group, as the corporation is a partner in the medical group and is regularly associated with the Butler Surgical Group in performing services for third parties.

As is readily apparent, the affiliated service group rules go considerably beyond the loophole they were initially intended to close. And the complexity of these rules is such that it is often difficult to determine whether they apply. Furthermore, many of the affiliated service group provisions involve a degree of subjective judgment—that is, ultimately they are up to the discretion of the IRS—unlike the controlled group rules which, though complex, are relatively mechanical. Thus, in doubtful cases, it is advisable to obtain a ruling from the IRS about whether an organization is a member of an affiliated service group.

EMPLOYEE LEASING

The leased employee provisions of Code section 414(n) were designed to reduce the discrimination potential from an employer's choosing to lease employees from an independent employee leasing organization, rather than employ them directly. The purpose of this practice is to keep the employees technically off the payroll of the lessee business and, thus, outside the coverage of its qualified plans.

This practice is limited under current law. A leased employee is considered an employee of the lessee organization for which the services are performed if:

- the employee has performed services on a substantially full-time basis for at least one year; and

- the services are "performed under the primary direction or control by the recipient."[13]

This rule does not apply if the leasing organization itself maintains a "safe-harbor" plan for the leased employees meeting certain minimum requirements:

- The plan must be a nonintegrated money-purchase plan with an employer contribution rate of at least 10 percent of compensation;

- the plan must provide immediate participation and full and immediate vesting; and

- All employees of the leasing organization with compensation of $1,000 or more over the past four years must be covered.

The safe-harbor exemption may not be used if leased employees constitute more than 20 percent of the recipient's (lessor's) nonhighly compensated work force.

Since 10 percent is a relatively modest plan contribution level, many leasing organizations adopt this approach. Thus, employee leasing remains a viable method for minimizing plan benefits and contributions for low-level employees, even with the restrictions of section 414(n).

Because of the one-year requirement, the leasing provision has no impact on most short-term temporary help. Attempts to technically avoid this requirement by rotating leased employees may not be effective, because the one-year requirement is determined on the basis of cumulative service for the recipient. The requirement of treating the leased employee as an employee of the recipient does not begin until the leased employee has met the one-year service requirement.

Because of the relatively low safe-harbor provision, some employers might be tempted to convert all their employees to leased employees through some arrangement with a leasing organization. However, the IRS has taken the position that the Code provision applies only to bona fide employee leases. If the lease is not deemed bona fide, the employees will be treated for qualified plan purposes as if they were employed directly.

CHAPTER ENDNOTES

1. 102 S. Ct. 821 (1982).
2. Treas. Reg. §1.1563-1(a)(3).
3. I.R.C. §1563(c).
4. I.R.C. §1563(c)(2)(A).
5. I.R.C. §1563(c)(2)(B).
6. I.R.C. §1563(e).
7. I.R.C. §1563(d).
8. I.R.C. §1563(d)(2).
9. I.R.C. §1563(f)(2).
10. I.R.C. §414(m)(2).
11. I.R.C. §414(m)(5).
12. Prop. Treas. Reg. §1.414(m)-2(f).
13. See I.R.C. §414(n).

FIDUCIARY BREACH LITIGATION

CHAPTER 58

INTRODUCTION

The Employee Retirement Income Security Act of 1974 ("ERISA") governs employee benefit plans sponsored by private companies. The statute defines who may be subject to liability under ERISA – most notably "fiduciaries" - and establishes the standards that govern fiduciaries' conduct. It also describes the types of claims that may be brought when disputes arise.

This chapter briefly discusses the duties that ERISA imposes upon fiduciaries.

WHO IS A FIDUCIARY?

In order to be liable under ERISA for a breach of fiduciary duty, one must be a fiduciary. While one's title may cause a person to be a fiduciary – for example, trustees are by definition fiduciaries – fiduciary status is also determined by the functions that a person performs relative to an employee benefit plan. Certain functions are considered non-fiduciary (or "settlor") functions. The term "settlor" is commonly used in trust law, and relates to the person establishing a trust. So-called settlor functions include establishing a plan and deciding the benefits that it will provide, amending a plan, and terminating a plan. When plan sponsors act in their settlor capacity, they are not subject to the rules governing fiduciaries. Additionally, some types of services that third parties provide to plans are considered non-fiduciary or "ministerial" functions. Those types of services include accounting and audit services, actuarial services, and generalized investment education services in which the service provider does not provide advice investment that is particularized to the needs of the plan or its participants.

However, ERISA provides that, when a person exercises discretionary control or authority over the management of a plan, or any authority or control over its assets, that person is a fiduciary. Many of the functions that plan sponsors perform for their plans are fiduciary functions. Buying and selling investments, appointing other fiduciaries and selecting service providers for the plan are all fiduciary functions. When fiduciaries perform those duties, they must adhere to ERISA's fiduciary requirements. Those duties are described in many of the cases as the "highest known to law." Breaching any of those duties may result in liability.

THE DUTY OF LOYALTY

A fiduciary's first obligation is to act "solely in the interest" of the plan's participants and beneficiaries.[1] This is often referred to as the "duty of loyalty."

Fiduciaries may breach their duty of loyalty when they engage in acts of self-dealing, rather than acting in the interest of the participants and beneficiaries. For example, when fiduciaries hire a plan service provider because the service provider offers the plan sponsor a special deal for services provided to the corporation, the fiduciaries may be liable for not acting with the required loyalty to the participants and beneficiaries. Fiduciaries may also breach the duty of loyalty not only by favoring their own interests, but when they act in the interests of third parties.

Fiduciaries have been sued for breaching their duty of loyalty in the following circumstances:

- An investment advisory firm invested significant plan assets in companies in which members of the firm had equity interests.[2]

- Fiduciaries were alleged to have used plan assets to purchase shares in companies in order to advance their own interests in those companies.[3]

- Corporate officers who were also plan trustees breached their duties to the plan when, in response to a tender offer to purchase the company's stock, the trustees not only failed to consider the offer, but used plan assets to purchase additional company stock, and failed to resign their posts as trustees when the conflict of interest became apparent.[4]

Alleged breaches of the duty of loyalty are often accompanied by claims that fiduciaries have engaged in certain transactions that are specifically prohibited by ERISA. Specifically, fiduciaries are prohibited from:

1. dealing with the assets of the plan in his own interest or for his own account;

2. acting in his individual capacity or in any other capacity in a transaction involving the plan on behalf of a party whose interests are adverse to the plan; or

3. receiving any consideration for his own personal account from any party dealing with the plan in connection with a transaction involving the assets of the plan.[5]

THE "PRUDENT MAN" RULE

ERISA requires fiduciaries to act with the prudence and skill as a person familiar with such matters acting under like circumstances. This is referred to as the "prudent man" rule, and it underlies all of the duties that a fiduciary owes to a plan. To comply with this rule, ERISA requires fiduciaries to appropriately investigate the merits of potential investments and to engage in a reasoned decision making process. The prudence requirement continues after the initial investment decision – fiduciaries must periodically monitor their investments to determine whether they continue to advance the needs of the plan's participants and beneficiaries. Whether an investment is appropriate for the plan at the time the investment is first made, and later, depends on the circumstances prevailing at the time. (The duty of prudence also extends to decisions to hire and retain service plan service providers, such as investment advisors and plan administrators).

Courts focus on a fiduciary's conduct in arriving at an investment decision or a decision to engage a service provider, not on the decision's results. The inquiry turns on whether a fiduciary used the appropriate methods to investigate and determine the merits of a decision.[6] As a result, some courts say that the rule requires prudence, not prescience.[7]

There is no one uniform checklist that fiduciaries must follow to satisfy their duty to act with prudence. Some factors that courts have considered to support a finding of procedural prudence include seeking outside legal and financial expertise, holding meetings to ensure fiduciary oversight of the investment decision, and continuing to monitor and receive regular updates on the investment's performance.[8] While ERISA does not have a specific requirement that fiduciaries operate according to a formal investment policy statement, at least one court has stated that the failure maintain such a policy, and act in accordance with it, may constitute a breach of fiduciary duty.[9] When plans do maintain investment policy statements, fiduciaries should be prepared to demonstrate that they referred to it and complied with its provisions, in connection with their investment decisions.

Fiduciaries who fail to engage in those types of processes subject themselves to liability under ERISA. For example, courts have criticized fiduciaries in the following circumstances:

1. Fiduciaries divested the plan of a favorable investment "arbitrarily," "without research" and without considering the plan's purpose of providing long term retirement income.[10]

2. Fiduciaries failed to understand:

   a. their duties to a plan;

   b. the assets owned by a plan;

   c. what the assets were worth; and

   d. whether it was prudent for the plan to own those assets.[11]

THE "EXCLUSIVE PURPOSE" RULE

Fiduciaries are also obligated to act "for the exclusive purpose" of providing benefits to participants and beneficiaries, and paying only reasonable expenses of administering the plan.[12] In recent years, much of the litigation involving alleged violations of the exclusive purpose rule focuses on the expenses incurred by the plan. More specifically, the focus is often on the expenses associated with plan investments.

To minimize the likelihood of liability, fiduciaries need to recognize who is receiving compensation in connection with their employee benefit plans, the manner in which they are receiving that compensation (i.e., direct compensation or "indirect" compensation such as revenue sharing payments made from one service provider – such as a mutual fund company – to another service provider such as a recordkeeper) and the amount of compensation that they receive. They must then engage in a prudent process of evaluating that compensation and determining whether the compensation is unreasonably high.

Allegations in recent cases have focused on such issues as whether plan fiduciaries have properly taken advantage of their plans' bargaining power by offering institutional share class mutual funds with lower expense ratios as opposed to "retail" share classes with correspondingly higher expenses.[13]

DUTY TO DIVERSIFY

Fiduciaries have a duty to diversify the plan's investments to minimize the risk of large losses, unless it is "clearly prudent" under the circumstances not to do so.[14] The duty to diversify is separate from the prudent man rule. It requires that fiduciaries not normally invest all or an unduly large portion of plan assets in a single security, or even in various types of securities.

There is no rigid rule regarding the percentage limit in any one investment. Rather, whether a fiduciary has satisfied the duty to diversify depends on the facts and circumstances surrounding each plan and investment.

In one case a court imposed liability on a fiduciary who directed a retirement plan to invest some 40 percent of its assets in deeds of trust on real property.[15]

DUTY TO ACT IN ACCORDANCE WITH THE PLAN'S TERMS

As long as a plan's terms are consistent with ERISA, the fiduciaries are obligated to act in accordance with those terms.[16] Failure to do so is both evidence of a breach of the prudent man rule and of the duty to follow the plan's provisions.[17] Conversely, fiduciaries may escape liability under this theory of they can establish that following the plan's terms would have violated ERISA.

ERISA 404(c)

ERISA contains a provision that provides a partial defense for fiduciaries of participant-directed plans, such as 401(k) plans. That provision, ERISA 404(c), provides that if a participant or beneficiary exercises control over the money in his account, the fiduciary will not be liable for any loss that results from the participant or beneficiary's exercise of that control. The statute does not explain what is needed in order to determine that the participant or beneficiary has exercised control. The Department of Labor has issued regulations that set the conditions that must be met for 404(c) protection to apply. However, even if those conditions are met, the fiduciaries must still prudently select and monitor the investments offered to the participants.

FREQUENTLY ASKED QUESTIONS

Question – Are changes anticipated in the area of fiduciary requirements?

Answer – Possibly. In April of 2015 the Department of Labor re-proposed a rule on conflicts of interest in the financial services field that would essentially require all financial advisors who work with clients' retirement funds to be subject to a fiduciary standard.[18] If adopted, this rule would create significant changes in the financial services industry and apply fiduciary standard to a much broader group of advisors than is currently the case. Due in large part to its scope, the rule as proposed is controversial and still faces a period of public comment and the potential to be altered before it is adopted, perhaps significantly. Financial advisors should be alert to any potential changes resulting from the adoption of such a rule.

CHAPTER ENDNOTES

1. ERISA §404(a)(1).
2. *Lowen v. Tower Asset Management*, 829 F.2d 1209 (2d Cir. 1987).

3. *Leigh v. Engle*, 727 F.2d 113 (7th Cir. 1984).
4. *Donovan v. Bierwirth*, 680 F.2d 263 (2nd Cir. 1982).
5. ERISA §406(b).
6. *In re Unisys Sav. Plan Litig.*, 74 F.3d 420, 434 (3rd Cir. 1996).
7. *DeBruyne v. Equitable Life Assurance Soc'y.*, 920 F.2d 457, 465 (7th Cir. 1990)
8. *Tatum v. RJR Pension Inv. Committee*, 761 F.3d 346 (4th Cir. 2014).
9. *Liss v. Smith*, 991 F.Supp. 278, 296 (S.D.N.Y. 1998).
10. *Tatum v. RJR Pension Inv. Committee, supra*, 761 F.3d at 358-359.
11. *Springate v. Weighmasters Murphy, Inc. Money Purchase Pension Plan*, 217 F.Supp.2d 1007 (C.D. Cal. 2002).
12. ERISA §404(a)(1)(A)(i), (ii).
13. *See, e.g., Tibble v. Edison Intern.*, 729 F.3d 1110 (9th Cir. 2013), *cert. granted*, 135 S.Ct. 43, 189 L.Ed.2d 895.
14. ERISA §404(a)(1)(C).
15. *Thomas, Head & Greisen v. Buster*, 24 F.2d 1114 (9th Cir. 1994). See also *Tibble v. Edison Int'l*,_U.S._ (May 18, 2015).
16. ERISA §404(a)(1)(D).
17. *Dardaganis v. Grace Capital, Inc.*, 889 F.2d 1237, 1241 (2d Cir.1989).
18. Definition of the Term ``Fiduciary''; Conflict of Interest Rule--Retirement Investment Advice, 80 Fed. Reg. 21,927 (proposed April 20, 2015) (to be codified at 29 C.F.R. pt. 2509-10).

AGE AND SEX DISCRIMINATION

CHAPTER 59

AGE DISCRIMINATION

The federal Age Discrimination in Employment Act (ADEA), as amended, provides that it is unlawful for an employer:

(1) to fail or refuse to hire or to discharge any individual or otherwise discriminate against any individual with respect to his compensation, terms, conditions, or privileges of employment, because of such individual's age;

(2) to limit, segregate, or classify its employees in any way which would deprive or tend to deprive any individual of employment opportunities or otherwise adversely affect his status as an employee, because of such individual's age; or

(3) to reduce the wage rate of any employee in order to comply with [ADEA].[1]

ADEA applies to workers and managers of any business that engages in interstate commerce (which the courts have defined very broadly) and employs at least twenty persons for each working day in each of twenty or more calendar weeks in the current or preceding calendar year.[2]

State laws are not preempted by ADEA. Therefore, it is possible that certain actions allowed under ADEA might be prohibited under applicable state law.

Pension Plans

The primary impact of ADEA on pension plans is that the language quoted above prohibits mandatory retirement at any age. However, mandatory retirement at age sixty-five is specifically permitted for an individual who has been in a "bona fide executive or high policy making position" for at least two years before retirement and who is entitled to a minimum fully vested pension of $44,000 annually calculated as a straight life annuity.[3]

Beyond the issue of compulsory retirement, the language of ADEA is general and does not provide specific guidance regarding its application to pension plans, qualified or nonqualified. The Equal Employment Opportunities Commission (EEOC) has issued some regulations in this area, but in light of the *Betts* case discussed below, the current validity of prior ADEA interpretations may be questionable.

For qualified plans, there are specific age discrimination provisions in the Internal Revenue Code, as discussed below, that are not affected by any controversy regarding ADEA.

Age Discrimination Provisions for Qualified Plans

Under Code section 411(b)(2), a *defined contribution* plan cannot reduce allocations (or the rate of allocations) of employer contributions, forfeitures, or income, gains or losses, in a participant's account because of the participant's age. However, the plan can have a "cap" on the number of years during which employer contributions and forfeitures will be allocated, or the total amount of contributions or forfeitures, provided that it is not based on age as such. For example, a plan can provide that employer contributions and forfeitures will be allocated only over the participant's first twenty-five years of service. Few plans use this approach.

Correspondingly, under Code section 411(b)(1)(H), in a *defined benefit* plan, the benefit formula cannot cut off accruals at a specified age, but it can provide that benefits are accrued fully after a specified number of years of service, such as twenty-five. Plans can continue to use age sixty-five as the "normal retirement age" for funding and benefit accrual purposes. If employees work past age sixty-five, the regulations provide alternative methods for benefit payment and/or accrual.[4]

Welfare Benefit Plans

Prior to the *Betts* case discussed below, in applying ADEA to benefit plans, an "equal cost" approach was developed for welfare benefit plans in court cases and in EEOC regulations. That is, an employer was not required to provide exactly the same benefits to older as to younger employees, but rather to provide benefits having the same cost level. Thus, for example, amounts of life insurance coverage (amounts of death benefit) could be reduced for older employees to reflect the increasing premium cost. EEOC regulations allowed the use of up to five-year age brackets for computing benefit costs. Costs were to be determined on a benefit by benefit basis under the EEOC regulations.[5]

ADEA contains a provision allowing an employer to "observe the terms of a bona fide employee benefit plan...that is a voluntary early retirement incentive plan consistent with the relevant purpose or purposes of [the ADEA]."[6] For many years the courts and the regulatory agencies have interpreted this as an authorization for adopting rules such as the EEOC regulations.

However, in 1989 the U. S. Supreme Court decided *Public Employees Retirement System of Ohio v. Betts*.[7] Specifically, the *Betts* case involved a disability retirement benefit that was not available to employees who retired after age fifty-nine. While the Court found that this benefit did not violate ADEA, it also ruled broadly that ADEA exempts all provisions of bona fide employee benefit plans, unless the plan is a subterfuge for discrimination in non-fringe benefit aspects of the employment relationship. In so holding, the Supreme Court invalidated the EEOC's "equal cost" regulation referred to above.

After the decision in the *Betts* case, Congress took up the age discrimination issue fairly quickly, and in 1990 passed corrective legislation that essentially restores and codifies the DOL's "equal benefit or equal cost" rule. Highlights of this legislation include:

1. The equal benefit or equal cost principle under prior EEOC regulations discussed above has now been adopted legislatively.

2. The law establishes minimum standards for employee waivers of rights under limited early retirement "window" provisions in which employees must decide whether or not to accept the program during a limited time period. If an employer adopts an early retirement incentive plan to encourage older employees to retire, employees must be given at least three weeks to decide if they want to accept the plan and must be advised in writing to consult a lawyer before accepting.

3. The law does not apply retroactively.

4. Like the original Age Discrimination in Employment Act, the amended Act applies to businesses that employ at least twenty persons during the year.

SEX DISCRIMINATION

Sex discrimination in employee benefit plans is governed primarily by the federal Civil Rights Act of 1964, which provides as follows:

> (a) It shall be an unlawful employment practice for an employer:
>
> (1) to fail or refuse to hire or to discharge any individual, or otherwise to discriminate against any individual with respect to his compensation, terms, conditions, or privileges of employment, because of such individual's race, color, religion, sex, or national origin; or
>
> (2) to limit, segregate, or classify its employees or applicants for employment in any way which would deprive or tend to deprive any individual of employment opportunities or otherwise adversely affect his status as an employee, because of such individual's race, color, religion, sex, or national origin.[8]

The Civil Rights Act covers all employers in interstate commerce who have at least fifteen employees for each working day in at least twenty calendar weeks in the current or preceding calendar year.[9]

There are no provisions in the Internal Revenue Code or ERISA directly dealing with sex discrimination, so court decisions and regulations under the Civil Rights Act are the primary source of authority in the benefits area.[10]

In the area of wage and benefit discrimination, the Civil Rights Act provisions overlap with another federal statute, the Equal Pay Act of 1963.[11] For most benefit purposes, it is adequate to discuss only the Civil Rights Act, since there are few, if any, benefit practices permitted by the Civil Rights Act that are prohibited by the Equal Pay Act. However, there is an important difference that affects smaller employers: the Equal Pay Act has *no small employer exception*.[12]

Sex discrimination raises obvious issues in employee benefits because so many common benefits involve actuarial differences in cost between men and women–life insurance, annuities (pensions), and health insurance, particularly with regard to coverage for pregnancy. The issues involved have been fought over in the courts and the regulatory agencies; the history will not be rehashed here, but instead the result–the state of current law–will be summarized as well as possible.

Pension Plans

Pension plans raise the issue of whether the law requires employers to make equal *contributions* or provide equal *benefits* for male and female employees. The court cases on this issue are not entirely clear, but the weight of Supreme Court decisions has convinced most commentators that an equal-benefit approach is required.[13] Specifically,

- A defined benefit plan should offer the same benefit for men and women retirees similarly situated (most always have done so).
- Employers with defined benefit plans can use sex-based actuarial assumptions for funding purposes, since this does not affect employees' benefits.
- If a retirement plan includes an incidental life insurance benefit, the same amount of life insurance must be provided to men and women employees with the same retirement benefits. If the plan is contributory, contributions must be based on unisex tables.
- If a defined contribution plan offers an annuity form of payout, either exclusively or as an option, unisex annuity rates must be used within the plan itself. (This will not prevent male retirees from taking a lump sum distribution and using the money to purchase a sex-based annuity providing higher monthly payments from an insurance company.)

Life Insurance

The same Supreme Court cases cited for pension plans have convinced most commentators that the courts will uphold prohibitions against sex-based life insurance benefits in an employer plan.[14] Therefore, any life insurance plan should provide the same amount of insurance to any participant, male or female, who is otherwise similarly situated (same compensation, same job classification, etc.). If plan participants must contribute to the plan (as in supplemental group coverage, for example) unisex premium rates must be used.

Health Insurance

In the area of health insurance, certain controversies have been settled only by federal legislation. Congress in 1978 added Section 701(k) to the Civil Rights Act to indicate that distinctions among employee benefits based on pregnancy or childbirth are considered sex-related. EEOC interpretive guidelines based on this Act[15] require pregnancy and childbirth-related medical expenses of employees to be treated the same as other medical expenses. Also, the EEOC guidelines require pregnancy benefits to be provided to spouses of male employees if spouses of female employees also receive health benefits.

Other EEOC regulations prohibit restricting spousal and family benefits to employees who are deemed "head of household" and also prohibit plans that provide benefits to spouses of male employees that are not available to female employees.[16]

CHAPTER ENDNOTES

1. ADEA, §4(a); 29 USC §623(a).
2. 29 USC §630(b).
3. ADEA §12(c)(1), 29 USC §631(a); 29 CFR (EEOC Reg.) §1627.17.
4. Prop. Treas. Reg. §1.411(b)-2(b)(4).
5. 29 CFR (EEOC Reg.) §1625.10.

6. ADEA §4(f)(2)(B), 29 USC §623(f)(2)(B). This exception does not permit involuntary retirement because of age or failure to hire because of age.
7. *Public Employees Retirement System of Ohio v. Betts*, 492 U.S. 158 (1989).
8. Civil Rights Act of 1964, §703(a), 42 USC §2000e-2(a).
9. 42 USC §2000e(b).
10. Some commentators have theorized that the fiduciary provisions of ERISA require impartial dealing with plan participants.
11. 29 USC §206.
12. Certain types of business are excepted, however, such as retail sales, fishing, agriculture, and newspaper publishing. 29 USC §§203(s), 213(a).
13. *Los Angeles Department of Water and Power v. Manhart*, 435 U.S. 702 (1978), involved a contributory pension plan of a municipality. The Court held that the plan could not require women to pay higher contributions than men to receive equal periodic benefits upon retirement. *Arizona Governing Committee v. Norris*, 463 U.S. 1073 (1983), involved a Section 457 deferred compensation plan (see Chapter 34) of a municipality. The plan provided a sex-based annuity table for retirees, so that for a given account balance, a female participant received a smaller monthly retirement payment. In both these cases, the Supreme Court found a violation of the Civil Rights Act.
14. Existing EEOC regulations prohibit sex discrimination in all fringe benefits. 29 CFR §§1604.9(b), 1620.4, 1604.9(e).
15. 44 Federal Register 23804 (April 20, 1979). The provision of these guidelines requiring pregnancy benefits to spouses of male employees was upheld by the Supreme Court in *Newport News Shipbuilding and Dry Dock Co. v. EEOC*, 462 U.S. 669 (1983).
16. 29 CFR §§1604.9(c), 1604.9(d).

ACCOUNTING FOR BENEFIT PLANS

CHAPTER 60

Accounting rules, including those affecting employee benefit plans, are promulgated by the Financial Accounting Standards Board (FASB). The FASB is a private organization designated by the accounting profession to promulgate general principles, practices and standards for accounting and financial disclosure. These FASB rules do not have the force of law as such, but they represent, de facto, the standards expected by shareholders, investors, and the government in financial reports of businesses, and they are generally followed by independent accountants for purposes of certifying financial statements. They are, therefore, quasi-regulatory in effect and should be considered along with state and federal government regulations in the design of executive benefit plans.

PENSION PLANS

The accounting rules for deferred compensation make no distinction between qualified and nonqualified plans. Instead, the applicable accounting rule depends on whether the plan constitutes one or more "individual deferred compensation contracts" on the one hand, or a "pension plan" on the other. While the balance sheet result is about the same either way, individual deferred compensation contracts are governed by the older Accounting Principles Board (APB) Opinion No. 12, as amended by FAS 106. Pension plans, however, are governed by FAS 87. APB No.12, FAS 106, and FAS 87 were amended by FAS 158 (discussed below).

Whether a plan is one or the other is to some extent a matter of the accountant's discretion. In general, if one or only a few executives are covered, APB No. 12 would be applied, while if the plan is a defined benefit plan or a pension plan as defined in ERISA, FAS 87 would apply.[1]

Under APB No. 12, the benefits accrued under a deferred compensation contract are charged to expense and spread ratably over the period of the executive's service. As amended by FAS 106, the period of service to be used is the period between the time the contract is entered into and the first year in which the executive is eligible for benefit payments (even if the executive might choose to further defer actual payment). Accrued benefits are charged to expense at their present value; the discount rate is not specified in APB No. 12 but accountants are likely to use current rates of return on high quality fixed-income investments. No funding method is specified in APB No. 12, but apparently either a level funding or accrued benefit approach can be used.

The following are highlights of FAS 87, "Employers' Accounting for Pensions":

1. Annual pension cost—the periodic cost charged against earnings, referred to as the "net periodic pension cost"—is determined under a uniform method prescribed by FAS 87. The employer may not simply charge the amount actually contributed to the plan to expense for the accounting year.

2. Generally, the unit credit (accrued benefit) method is used in determining the net periodic pension cost, regardless of the actuarial method used by the plan.

3. If the net periodic pension cost differs from the employer's actual plan contribution for the year, the difference will be shown as an asset or liability on the balance sheet.

4. If the plan's past service costs (accumulated benefit obligation) exceed the fair market value of

plan assets, a liability referred to as the *unfunded accumulated-benefit obligation* must be reflected on the balance sheet. This liability is balanced by an intangible asset on the balance sheet.

5. A specific format is prescribed for various financial statement footnotes relating to the pension plan, such as the fair market value of plan assets and any unamortized prior service costs.

For a plan that is terminating during the year, FAS 88, "Employers' Accounting for Settlements and Curtailments of Defined Benefit Pension Plans and Termination Benefits," provides rules for dealing with special accounting problems in plan termination.

FAS 158, "Employers' Accounting for Defined Benefit pension and Other Postretirement Plans—An Amendment of FASB Statements No. 87, 88, 106, and 132(R)," was issued in 2006 and significantly changes the balance sheet reporting for defined benefit pension plans. It requires companies to report their plans' funded status as either an asset or a liability on their balance sheets. Previously, this information was reported only in detailed pension footnotes.

Nonqualified and qualified plans must be reported separately by employers, since assets of qualified and nonqualified plans cannot be mingled. If a nonqualified plan is informally funded or financed—as such plans usually are (see Chapter 33)—the plan is considered to have no assets for accounting purposes, a fact which will increase the magnitude of the reported liabilities. The assets used for informal financing are corporate assets, not plan assets.

These accounting rules increase the balance sheet "visibility" of nonqualified plans, as compared with qualified plans, because of the fact that the liability will generally rise steadily in a plan that is not formally funded. Planners can generally mitigate this disadvantage by using an informal funding mechanism that produces a steadily increasing corporate asset, such as the cash value of an insurance policy; this asset can be pointed to as evidence of the company's financial responsibility with regard to the nonqualified plan liability.

CORPORATE-OWNED LIFE INSURANCE

Corporate-owned life insurance, whether held as an informal financing asset for a nonqualified pension plan (see above) or for other corporate or employee benefit purposes, is accounted for in accordance with FASB Technical Bulletin 85-4. The charge to corporate earnings is the premium less the cash value increase. Generally, this produces a charge to earnings only in the first few years of the policy, after which there is a profit. The policy's cash value appears as an asset on the balance sheet.

FASB Statement No. 109 (1992), superseding FAS 96 (1987), requires corporations to create a balance sheet liability to reflect taxes anticipated to be payable in the future (deferred taxes). If the corporation holds property with unrealized gain, it must generally show a liability for taxes on that gain, even if the gain is not realized during the accounting year. This rule potentially has an impact on corporate-owned life insurance, such as that held in a split-dollar plan, informally funded deferred compensation plan, or other plan. If the corporation's share of the cash value exceeds the corporation's basis, there is a potentially taxable gain. However, in the great majority of plans using corporate-owned life insurance, the corporation intends to hold the policy until the insured dies, at which point the corporation's realized gain will be nontaxable, except for possible alternative minimum tax liability.

FASB's previous statement on accounting for income taxes, FAS 96, stated the requirement of creating a tax liability in an inflexible way that appeared to apply to all insurance policies, regardless of whether the policy was likely to actually generate taxable income. However, FAS 109, which supersedes FAS 96, states that the difference between basis and cash value of a corporate-owned policy does not create a reportable liability if "the asset is expected to be recovered without tax consequence upon the death of the insured (there will be no taxable amount if the insurance policy is held until the death of the insured)."

FAS 109 does not directly discuss whether possible AMT on the death proceeds must be reflected as a balance sheet liability. However, it can be argued that the principles of the FAS would require the potential AMT to be so reported. As discussed in Chapter 48, the receipt of a death benefit, even though regular income-tax free, can result in an AMT liability.

HEALTH AND OTHER WELFARE BENEFIT PLANS

Health and life insurance benefit plans generally involve no significant accounting issues so long as the plans provide simply the usual year-to-year benefit and premium payment obligations. However, where employers provide benefits after employees retire, the FASB has recognized that there is a question as to how this obligation should be recognized for accounting purposes. The issue has become more important in light of recent court cases that restrict an employer's right to unilaterally modify or rescind benefits provided to retirees.

The FASB in 1989 issued an "exposure draft" of rules in this area, which was formalized as FAS 106, effective generally for fiscal years beginning after December 15, 1992, with a later date for certain small (under 500) nonpublic plans.

FAS 106 is based on the premise that post-retirement benefits of all types are, like pension benefits, a form of deferred compensation that is earned year by year by employees while they are actively working for the employer. Accordingly, FAS 106 requires an accrual of such benefits as they are earned, rather than as they are paid. This accrual will create a charge to earnings, and unfunded accrued benefits will create a growing balance sheet liability.

FAS 106 covers medical and life insurance, tuition assistance, day care, legal services, and housing subsidies, as well as other benefits provided during retirement in return for prior employment services. Retiree medical benefits have by far the greatest potential financial impact. FAS 106 includes specific guidelines for valuing post-retirement medical benefits.

This potential balance sheet liability will cause employers to seek to provide either funded plans or asset reserves or other financing assets such as life insurance contracts to cover the liabilities created by post-retirement benefits.

Under FAS 106, if assets are not segregated into a trust specifically for the purpose of funding the post-retirement benefits, they are not "plan assets" that directly reduce the balance sheet liability for post-retirement benefits. Thus, typical corporate-owned life insurance policies or asset reserves would not qualify as plan assets, nor would a Section 501(c)(9) trust (VEBA) if the VEBA included assets to fund benefits for active employees. However, Section 401(h) medical accounts (see Chapter 40) probably would qualify.

Although informal financing of retiree benefits will not reduce the balance sheet liability, the existence of assets can help to demonstrate the corporation's financial responsibility in planning to meet the projected liability. Corporate-owned life insurance can be used favorably for this purpose. Methods of financing retiree medical benefits are discussed further in Chapter 39.

STOCK OPTIONS AND OTHER SHARE-BASED PAYMENTS

After a long controversy, in 2004 the FASB issued FAS 123 (revised), which establishes accounting standards for "share-based" compensation; that is, compensation based on the value of the employer's stock. This includes stock options (an offer to sell stock to the employee at a specific price over a specified time period), a very common form of executive compensation.

Under FAS 123, a company must recognize the cost of options, or other share-based award of compensation to an employee, at the "grant-date fair value of the award." This cost is recognized over the period during which the employee is required to provide service in exchange for the award of compensation.

Under prior guidance (Opinion 25), the grant of an option generally resulted in recognition of no compensation cost because of the difficulty of pricing options other than those traded on an established market. The new statement requires the company to value the options, whether they are traded or not.

Options are valued based on the "observable market price of a [similar] option, or using a valuation technique such as an 'option pricing model.'"[2]

CHAPTER ENDNOTES

1. See *Tax Management Portfolio 393-2nd*, "Accounting for Pensions and Deferred Compensation," Bureau of National Affairs, Inc., Washington, D.C. (2001), page 11, for authors' views on how this distinction is made. According to their rationale, it would appear that most accountants would not apply FAS 87 to an unfunded plan, but this is not clear from FAS 87 itself.
2. FAS 123 (revised), paragraph 22. "Equity Share Options."

BENEFIT PLANS FOR PROPRIETORS, PARTNERS, AND S CORP SHAREHOLDERS

APPENDIX A

For benefit plan purposes, proprietorships and partnerships have one significant difference from corporations—the owners of these businesses are not technically *employees* of the business. By contrast, in a corporation an owner, even a 100 percent shareholder who works in the business is technically an employee of the corporation. For S corporations, the Internal Revenue Code requires that shareholder employees (those holding more than two percent of the S corporation's stock) be treated as partners for employee benefit purposes.[1]

Proprietorships, partnerships, and S corporations can have benefit plans for their employees that are exactly the same as those of regular or C corporations. Deductibility of benefit costs is the same, and tax treatment to these regular employees is also the same.

But—when the plan attempts to cover the business owners, some differences arise. Many sections of the Code providing favorable tax treatment of employee benefits apply only to employees. Thus, the benefit package for these organizations involves less favorable benefits for owners than if the organization was incorporated. If the situation is seriously adverse to the owners, the planner might even consider incorporating the organization (or, in the case of an S corporation, terminating the S corporation election).

Qualified retirement plans are a very significant exception to the unfavorable treatment of business owners in these organizations. Qualified plans can cover owners of unincorporated businesses or S corporations on much the same basis as regular employees. The differences are discussed in Chapter 29—HR 10 (Keogh) Plans. These differences are so small that it seldom pays to incorporate a business or terminate an S corporation election for qualified plan benefits alone.

PARTNERS AND PROPRIETORS

For federal income tax purposes, a proprietorship—an unincorporated business with one owner—is considered simply an extension of the owner. The proprietorship's profit or loss is computed on Schedule C of the owner's federal income tax return. The net income or loss from the business is added to the owner's adjusted gross income from other sources. As a result, business profits are added to other income, while losses are subtracted directly from other income.

This treatment allows all business expenses to be deducted off the top so they are available regardless of whether the taxpayer itemizes deductions. Proprietorship expense deductions are also available without any floor requirement that may be applicable to itemized deductions. For example, a proprietor can deduct all expenses for business use of an automobile, while an employee must itemize deductions and is subject to a two percent of adjusted gross income floor for employee business expenses.

The tax rates applicable to the business profits of a proprietorship are the same as those applicable to any other kind of individual income, and the income is taxed only once. By comparison, business income of a corporation is taxed at corporate rates, which are different from individual rates. Corporate income is taxed at the corporate level and then again at the shareholder level when it is paid out as dividends, although certain dividends may be taxed at capital gains rates.

With the exception of contributions to qualified plans, benefits and compensation paid to a proprietor are *not* deductible business expenses. Put another way, expenditures for employee benefits of a proprietor are treated the same as cash taken out by the proprietor.

For example, health insurance premiums, life insurance premiums, direct medical reimbursements, or any other form of benefit provided to the proprietor is nondeductible to the business and thus appears directly as income on the proprietor's Schedule C. The owner's benefits are nondeductible even if the business maintains the benefit plan for other, non-owner employees of the business as well as for the owner.

Partnerships, in principle, are treated for tax purposes the same as proprietorships. That is, the partners, not the partnership, are the taxable entities. However, because more than one taxpayer is involved, the tax rules for partnerships are complicated. In fact, they are among the most complex provisions of the tax law, but fortunately for benefit purposes most of the complexities can be overlooked.

A partnership typically pays no federal income taxes. All the taxes on the partnership's income are paid by the partners. However, a partnership must file a federal income tax return; the return is an information return that reports the partners' shares of income, losses, and other tax items.

Each partner must report and pay taxes on his distributive share of the partnership's income for the taxable year. A partner's distributive share is the amount of income that he is entitled to receive under the partnership agreement, even if it is not actually distributed to him during the taxable year. If the partnership has losses, each partner may deduct his share of the losses on his own tax return, subject to various limitations on passive loss deductions designed to deter tax shelter partnerships.

Employee benefits for partners are treated as follows:

- For qualified retirement plans (1) contributions for partners are deductible by the partnership along with those for regular employees, and (2) partners are taxed on qualified plan contributions and benefits much the same as regular employees. (See Chapter 13.)

- Costs for fringe benefits of any other type are deductible by the partnership in computing its taxable income—they are deductible under Section 162 as guaranteed payments to partners as defined in Code section 707(c). (This is the same way that guaranteed salary payments to partners are treated.) Alternatively, the partnership can treat the premium payment or other fringe benefit cost as a reduction in cash distributions to the partner.[2]

- Partners must then report as taxable income the value of all fringe benefits (other than qualified plans) provided for them by the partnership.[3]

S CORPORATION SHAREHOLDERS

The S corporation is a corporation that has elected (under Subchapter S of the Internal Revenue Code) to be taxed like a partnership for federal income tax purposes. (Most state income tax laws also recognize S corporations). "Like a partnership" is an oversimplification, of course—this will not come as any surprise to students of federal tax law. However, for fringe benefit purposes it is generally a close enough description.

In order to elect S corporation status, the corporation must comply with certain "don'ts"—it must *not*:[4]

- have more than one hundred shareholders (members of one family may elect to be treated as one shareholder)

- have a shareholder that is not an individual, an estate, or a certain type of trust

- be organized in a foreign country or have a nonresident alien shareholder

- have more than one "class of stock" (some differences in voting rights are allowed)

- be one of several specified ineligible types of corporation.

Qualified plans under Code section 401(a) and certain charitable organizations (Code section 501(c)(3)) may be S corporation shareholders.[5] An Individual Retirement Account (IRA) is not a qualified shareholder for this purpose. An Employee Stock Ownership Plan (ESOP) may hold S corporation stock.[6]

Some of these restrictions can have relevance in benefit planning that involves the use of employer stock. Such plans cannot violate the one-hundred-shareholder rule, or use a non-individual as a shareholder. Qualified plans and charitable organizations are treated as one shareholder for purposes of the one-hundred-shareholder rule. Also, benefit plans using stock must be designed so as not to violate the "one class of stock" requirement.[7]

Employee-shareholders Who Own More than 2 Percent

The Code provides that if an employee of an S corporation owns more than two percent of the stock (an MTTPSE—*m*ore-*t*han-*t*wo-*p*ercent *s*hareholder-*e*mployee—for purposes of this chapter), the MTTPSE is treated as a partner for fringe benefit purposes. Members of LLCs taxed as partners are treated similarly.[8] The Congressional committee reports on this provision[9] include the following specific fringe benefits (1) the tax exclusion for *benefits* under a health and accident plan, Section 105; (2) the tax exclusion for *coverage* under a health and accident plan, Section 106; (3) the tax benefits for group-term life insurance, Section 79; and (4) the exclusion for meals and lodging furnished for the convenience of the employer, Section 119. Qualified retirement plans are *not* covered by this provision; MTTPSEs are treated much like regular employees for qualified plan purposes.

Fringe benefits provided to MTTPSEs are treated as follows for tax purposes:

- The S corporation can deduct the cost of fringe benefits for MTTPSEs in determining its taxable income.[10]

- MTTPSEs must report—as compensation income—the value of any fringe benefits provided to them. These items must be included on the Form W-2 provided by the employer to the MTTPSE. Note that in the case of health and accident premiums, the amount of the premium is includable in full, but the MTTPSE is eligible for a deduction as set out in Code section 162(l). See Chapter 45.

- For FICA (social security) purposes, these fringe benefit amounts may or may not be includable, depending on the FICA rules for the type of plan involved. For example, health and accident premiums are not includable in the FICA tax base if there is a "plan or system" of health benefits for employees and dependents generally, or a class of employees. However, if the premiums are paid for a single employee or a few executives, the amounts may be includable in the FICA base.[11]

- Qualified retirement plans for MTTPSEs present some additional technical problems that are discussed in Chapter 13. The principal issue is, "What constitutes the MTTPSE's compensation for plan purposes?"

- Working condition fringe benefits (See Chapter 48) provided for partners or MTTPSEs are tax free if the partner could have deducted the item as a business expense.[12]

SPECIFIC FRINGE BENEFITS

The chart in Figure A.1 summarizes the treatment of specific fringe benefits for proprietors, partners, and MTTPSEs.

A "yes" in the chart indicates that the plan can be provided for these people with full tax benefits. A "no" indicates that the plan will provide no tax benefits for these key people. Note that some fringe benefit provisions of the Code such as dependent care (section 129) provide tax benefits for proprietors, partners, and MTTPSEs, despite the provisions discussed in this chapter.

Finally, in reviewing this chart, note that it reflects the treatment only of partners, proprietors, and MTTPSEs. All business organizations can adopt benefit plans providing full tax benefits for rank and file employees.

CHAPTER ENDNOTES

1. I.R.C. §1372.
2. Rev. Rul. 91-26, 1991-1 CB 184.
3. Under I.R.C. §61(a), all fringe benefits are currently taxable unless there is a specific provision of the Code that exempts or defers taxation of the benefit. Since most benefit exemptions or deferrals in the Code apply only to employees, partners are currently taxable on virtually all fringe benefits.
4. I.R.C. §1361.
5. I.R.C. §1361(c)(6).
6. *General Explanation of Tax Legislation Enacted in the 104th Congress* (JCT-12-96) pp. 130-131 (the Blue Book).
7. I.R.C. §1361(b)(1)(D).
8. I.R.C. §1372. See also Treas. Reg. §302.7701-1(b)(1)(i).
9. Committee Reports, Subchapter S Revision Act of 1982, P.L. 97-354, enacted October 19, 1982.
10. Rev. Rul. 91-26, 1991-1 CB 184.
11. Announcement 92-16, 1992-5 IRB 53.
12. Treas. Reg. §1.132-1(b)(2)(ii).
13. Source: Adapted from Jenkins, Gary E., "The Impact of Choice of Entity Selection upon Compensation and Fringe Benefit Planning after Tax Reform," *Journal of American Society of CLU and ChFC*, March 1988. See also Eule and Mustone, "Some Fringes and Still Free to S Corporation Owner-Employess," *Taxation for Lawyers*, April, 1992, and Trinz, "Which Tax-Free and Tax-Favored Fringe Benefits are Passthrough Owners Entitled To?" *RIA Pension and Benefits Week*, August 5, 2002. With regard to self-funded benefit plans, the correct treatment is unclear. See Eggertsen et al., "Guidence on Partner Health Leaves Self-Funding Questions Unanswered," *Journal of Taxation*, January, 1992.

Figure A.1

COMPARISON OF FRINGE BENEFITS BY ENTITY TYPE[13]				
Benefit	**Sole Prop.**	**Partnership**	**S Corp**	**C Corp**
Qualified plan	Yes	Yes	Yes	Yes
Deferred compensation	No	No	No	Yes
Salary continuation	No	Yes	Yes	Yes
Group life	No	No	No	Yes
Group healthYes	Yes	Yes	Yes	Yes
Group disability	No	No	No	Yes
Medical reimb. plans	No	No	No	Yes
Accidental death	No	No	No	Yes
Disability income plan	No	No	No	Yes
Employee death benefit				
–Employer provided	No	No	No	Yes
–Qualified plan	Yes	Yes	Yes	Yes
Educ. assistance plan	Yes	Yes	Yes	Yes
Dependent care	Yes	Yes	Yes	Yes
Meals & lodging	No	Yes	Yes	Yes
Cafeteria plan	No	No	No	Yes

QUALIFIED PLAN FACT FINDER

APPENDIX B

APP FORM 101

RETIREMENT PLAN DATA AND ABSTRACT FORM

Prepared for ______________________________

By ______________________________

Date ______________________________

SECTION I — RETIREMENT PLAN DATA

PART A — CLIENT PROFILE

A-1. Legal Name ____________________

Address ____________________

____________________ Zip __________

Telephone Number ____________________

Contact ____________________

A-2. Employer (Taxpayer) Identification Number ____________________

A-3. Nature of Enterprise (Check Appropriate Line)

3.1 _______ Sole proprietorship

3.2 _______ Partnership

3.3 _______ Business corporation

3.4 _______ S corporation

3.5 _______ Exempt org. (Sec. _________)

3.6 _______ Municipal corp. or government agency

3.7 _______ Professional corporation

3.8 _______ Business or real estate trust

3.9 _______ Other: specify

____

A-4. Nature of Business (Principal Business Activity)

____

____

IRS business code number __________

A-5. Accounting Method (Check One)

_________ Cash _________ Accrual

A-6. Fiscal Year Ends ____________________

(Month) (Day)

A-7. Date of Incorporation or Establishment

____________________ (Month and Year)

A-8. State of Incorporation or Domicile ____________________

A-9. Related Corporation or Unincorporated Entities, including Affiliated Service Groups (Names, Nature of Enterprises, Ownership Percentages of Related Enterprises)

____

____

____

____

A-10. Predecessor Entities

10.1 Name ________________________________

10.2 Nature of Entity ________________________________

10.3 Date of Establishment ________________________________

10.4 Date of Transfer ________________________________

A-11. What is the Approximate Rate of Employee Turnover as a Percent of the Active Group for the Past Five Years?

20____ ________%

20____ ________%

20____ ________%

20____ ________%

20____ ________%

A-12. Client Motives (For a New Benefit Program)

____

____

____

A-13. Employee Groups under Consideration (For a New Benefit Program)

13.1 ________ Salaried Employees

13.2 ________ Hourly Employees

13.3 ________ Collective-Bargaining Unit Employees

13.4 ________ Leased Employees

13.5 ________ Other

A-14. Competitors in Industry (Details as to Their Compensation Programs)

____

____

____

A-15. Local Nonindustry Employers (Details as to Their Compensation Programs)

____

____

____

____

PART B — FINANCIAL DATA

B-1. Attach Balance Sheets (Last Two or Three Years) and Summarize

____

____

B-2. Attach Profit and Loss Statements and Summarize

____

____

____

____

____

____

B-3. Summarize Earnings Projections

____

____

B-4. What Type of Cost Commitment Can Be considered for a Pension or a Profit-Sharing Plan or Both?

4.1 _________% of payroll

4.2 _________% of profit

4.3 _________% of profit in excess of $_________

4.4 $_________ Flat dollar amount

4.5 Other ____

____

PART C — CLIENT'S OTHER BENEFIT PROGRAMS

C-1. Nonqualified Retirement Plans

1.1 Plans of general application ______________________________

____

____

____

1.2 Personal plans (for individuals)

____

____

____

C-2. Group Life Insurance

2.1 How much ______________________________

2.2 Who is covered ______________________________

2.3 Beneficiary ______________________________

2.4 Premiums paid by

(a) ________ Employer

(b) ________ Employee

________ Payroll deduction

________ Other (specify) ______________________________

2.5 Carrier ______________________________

C-3. Accidental Death and Dismemberment

3.1 How much ______________________________

3.2 Who is covered ______________________________

3.3 Beneficiary ______________________________

3.4 Premiums paid by

(a) ________ Employer

(b) ________ Employee

________ Payroll deduction

________ Other (specify) ______________________________

3.5 Carrier ______________________________

3.6 Workmen's compensation offset

________ Yes ________ No Explain ______________________________

3.7 All accidents covered

_________ Yes _________ No Explain ______________________________

C-4. Long-Term Disability Coverage

4.1 How much ________________________ How long ________________________

4.2 Who is covered ____________________ Waiting period ____________________

4.3 Premiums paid by

_______ Employer

_______ Employee

_______ Payroll deduction

_______ Other (specify)____

4.4 Carrier ____

4.5 All causes

_________ Yes _________ No Explain ______________________________

4.6 Offsets

_________ Yes _________ No Explain ______________________________

4.7 Definition of disability ____

____

____

C-5. Existing Qualified Retirement Plans (list the following for each plan—use additional sheets if necessary)

5.1 Name of plan ____

5.2 Circle type of plan: Defined-Benefit Money-Purchase Target Profit-Sharing

5.3. a. Collectively bargained plan?_________No _________Yes (attach relevant portions of collective bargaining agreement)

b. Multiemployer plan? _________No _________Yes

5.4 Eligibility: a. age _________ b. Waiting period _________ c. employee classification _________

5.5 Contribution rate: By employer _____________ By employee

5.6 Benefit structure ____

5.7 Normal retirement benefit ______________________________At Age______________

5.8 Early retirement benefit ______________________________At Age______________

5.9 Death benefit ____

5.10 Disability benefit ____

Definition of disability ____

5.11 Vesting rate ____

5.12 Number of employees covered ____

5.13 Are there any employees who are covered by this plan to be covered by new plan?_____________

If so, are there to be offset provisions? ____

PART D — EMPLOYEE CENSUS DATA

Name	Sex	Date of Birth (or Age)	Date Hired (or Years of Service)	Position	Highly Compensated (HC) or Key (K) Employee?	Percent of Voting Stock	Annual Nondeferred Compensation				Social Security Number
							Basic	Bonus	Overtime	Total	

SECTION II — RETIREMENT PLAN ABSTRACT

PART E — PLAN CHARACTERISTICS AND PROVISIONS

E-1. Name of Plan ____

E-2. Type of Plan

2.1 _______ Defined-benefit: _______ Unit-benefit _______ Flat-benefit _______ Fixed-benefit

2.2 _______ Defined-contribution money purchase

2.3 _______ Target (assumed-benefit)

2.4 _______ Profit-sharing

2.5 _______ Thrift (savings)

2.6 _______ Section 401(k)

2.7 _______ Stock bonus

2.8 _______ ESOP

2.9 _______ Tax-deferred annuity (Section 403(b))

2.10 _______ Other or combination of types (specify ________________________________

E-3. Effective Date ____

E-4. Anniversary Date ____

E-5. Formal Name of Plan ____

E-6. Eligibility Requirements

6.1 Minimum age ____

6.2 Waiting period ____

6.3 Entry dates (explain) ____

6.4 Employee classification ____

____

6.5 Other (specify) ____

____

____

E-7. Past Service: Is Past Service with Prior Employer(s) to Count as Service with Company for Eligibility Purposes?

____

____

For benefit computation purposes?____

If yes, name prior employer(s)____

____

____

____

E-8. Integration

8.1 _______Nonintegrated

8.2 _______Social security (OASDI)

8.3 _______Railroad retirement act

E-9. Type of Integration

9.1 _______Excess (stepped up)

9.2 _______Offset

E-10. Integration Level

10.1_______Uniform integration break point $___________

10.2_______Covered compensation table I

10.3_______Covered compensation table II

10.4_______ Other ____

____

E-11. Integration Benefit Formula ______________________________

____

____

____

E-12. Other Offsets: Indicate the Contributions to or Benefits from Other Plans Which Are to be Used as Offsets to This Plan and Whether or Not Such Other Plans Are Qualified Plans under the Internal Revenue Code.

____

____

____

____

E-13. Normal Retirement Benefit

13.1 Formula

13.2 Age ______________________________

13.3 Minimum years of service ______________________________

13.4 Minimum years of plan participation ______________________________

13.5 Other ______________________________

E-14. Early Retirement Benefit

14.1 Formula

14.2 Age ______________________________

14.3 Minimum years of service ______________________________

14.4 Minimum years of plan participation ______________________________

14.5 Other ______________________________

E-15. Deferred Retirement Benefit

15.1 Formula

15.2 Maximum age ______________________________

15.3 Minimum years of service ______________________________

15.4 Minimum years of plan participation ______________________________

15.5 Other ______________________________

E-16. Disability Retirement

16.1 Formula

16.2 Minimum age ______________________

16.3 Minimum years of service ______________________

16.4 Minimum years of plan participation ______________________

16.5 Benefit commencement date ______________________

16.6 Definition of disability ______________________

(a) _______ Disability for social security purposes

(b) _______ Other (specify) ______________________

____

____

____

E-17. Death Benefits

17.1 Preretirement ______________________

____

____

17.2 Postretirement ______________________

____

____

E-18. Emergency Distributions ______________________

____

____

____

E-19. Describe Deferral or Salary Reduction Option (Section 401(k) Plan) ______________________

____

E-20. Withdrawal of Participant Contributions

20.1 When ______________________

20.2 How much ______________________

20.3 Earnings on contributions ______________________

20.4 Penalty ______

20.5 Notice requirement ______

E-21. Loans to participants

21.1 Maximum (if other than §72(p) limit ($50,000, ½ vested benefit, $10,000)) ______

21.2 Minimum ______

21.3 Interest rate ______

21.4 Duration ______

E-22. Other Benefits (specify) ______

______

______

E-23. Contributions

23.1 Rate of employer contributions

(a) ______ Discretionary

(b) ______ As actuarially determined

(c) ______ Formula (state formula)

23.2 Rate of Participant Contributions

(a) ______ Voluntary

Minimum ______

Maximum ______

(b) ______ Required

Amount of rate ______

Method of collection

______ Payroll withholding

______ Other (specify) ______

______

23.3 Employer Contributions To Be In

(a) ______ Cash

(b) ______ Stock

(c) ______ Other

E-24. Use of Forfeitures (If Any)

24.1_______To reduce subsequent employer contributions

24.2_______Reallocated among plan participants (defined-contribution only) state reallocation basis:

____

E-25. Employer Contribution Allocation Formula

25.1_______None. Unallocated funding

25.2_______Prorate according to compensation

25.3_______Prorate according to service

25.4_______Prorate according to compensation and service

25.5_______According to amounts contributed by employees

25.6_______Other (specify) ____

____

E-26. Vesting Schedule

26.1 Regular defined benefit plan _______________

26.2 Cash balance plan _______________

26.3 Defined contribution plan _______________

26.4 Set forth the vesting schedule in space below

____

____

____

____

____

____

E-27. Full and Immediate Vesting Is Required for Amounts, Earnings, and Benefits Derived from Employee Contributions.

E-28. Special Provisions Relating to Vesting in Individual Insurance Contracts ____________________

____

____

____

____

E-29. Definition of "Compensation" and "Hour of Service" for Plan Purposes (Indicate Status of Commissions, Bonuses, Overtime, etc., and for Defined-Benefit Plan Indicate Career Average, Final Average, or Other Basis for Determining Benefits)

____

____

____

____

E-30. Definition of "Net Income" or "Net Profits" for Plan Purposes (If Applicable)

30.1_______Profits for federal income tax purposes, but prior to reduction for contributions under (a) ________ this plan or (b) _______ qualified plans including this plan, but excluding

____

(state plans to be excluded) sponsored by employer

30.2_______Other (specify)

____

E-31. Beneficiary Designations

31.1_______None

31.2_______Automatic to spouse, if surviving, otherwise to estate of (a) _______ deceased participant or

(b) _______ deceased spouse

31.3_______Automatic to estate of deceased participant

31.4_______As per designation by employee

E-32. Earmarking of Contributions (Directed Investments)

32.1_______Yes

32.2_______No

If yes, indicate investment options and limitations ____________________

____

____

____

E-33. Mode of Distribution of Benefits (Normal Retirement)

33.1_______Joint life, participant and spouse (at least 50% to spouse)

33.2_______Full range of options (see below)

33.3_______Limited range of options (indicate which options are available below)

33.4_______Range of options

(a) _______ Life of participant only

(b) _______ Life of participant, 5 years certain

(c) _______ Life of participant, 10 years certain

(d) _______ Joint life, participant and spouse (at least 50% to spouse)

(e) _______ Joint life, participant and dependent

(f) _______ Joint life, participant and designated joint annuitant

(g) _______ Installments for 3 years

(h) _______ Installments for 5 years

(i) _______ Installments for 10 years

(j) _______ Installments for 15 years

(k) _______ Lump sum

(l) _______ Other (specify) ____

____

33.5 Method of determining actuarial equivalence ____

____

____

33.6 How options are elected ____

____

E-34. Timing of Distribution of Benefits

34.1 Normal retirement benefits

(a) _______ First day of month following normal retirement date

(b) _______ Other (specify) ____

____

34.2 Early Retirement Benefits

(a) _______ First day of month following early retirement date

(b) _______ First day of month following normal retirement date

(c) _______ First day of any month after early retirement date but not later than first day of month following normal retirement date

(d) _______ Combination of (b) & (c) above at employee's option

34.3 Disability benefits

(a) _______ First day of month following disability

(b) _______ First day of month following normal retirement date

(c) _______ First day of month following early retirement date after disability and before normal retirement date

(d) _______ Other (specify) ______________________________

____

(e) _______ Combination of (b) & (c) above at

_______ Employee's option

34.4 Preretirement death benefits

(a) _______ As promptly as practicable following death

(b) _______ Other (specify) ______________________________

____

34.5 Postretirement death benefits

(a) _______ As promptly as practicable following death

(b) _______ Pursuant to mode of retirement benefit election

(c) _______ Other (specify) ______________________________

____

34.6 Severance benefits

(a) _______ As promptly as practicable following termination of employment (not later than 60th day after close of plan year)

(b) _______ At normal retirement date

(c) _______ 10 years after plan participation

(d) _______ (a) or (c) at option of plan participant

E-35. Plan Administration

35.1 Plan administrator _______ Employer _______ Other (specify) ______________________________

____

35.2 Plan administrator to have investment power? __________Yes __________No

E-36. Insurance Provision and Restrictions ______________________________

____

____

____

E-37. Should There be Provisions in Plan and Trust Specifying That Insurance Company is Not a Party?

__________ Yes __________ No

E-38. Other Special Features and Notes as to Plan Provisions (Attach Additional Sheets if Necessary)

____

____

____

____

____

PART F — PLAN CENSUS DATA

Data for test under Section 410(b)(1) of the Internal Revenue Code

F-0. Is this data being provided for a separate line of business under Code Sec. 414(r)?

- ☐ Yes, eligible (describe) ____________
- ☐ No, not eligible
- ☐ No separate line of business

F-1. Total number of employees ____________

F-2. Number of employees in collective-bargaining unit (retirement benefits were subject to good faith bargaining) (Code Sec. 410(b)(3)(A)) ____________

F-3. Number of employees who have not yet satisfied proposed plan eligibility waiting period* and minimum age requirements (Code Sec. 410(b)(4)) ____________

F-4. Number of employees excluded under Code Secs. 410(b)(3)(B)-(C) ____________

F-5. Total Lines F-2 through F-4 ____________

F-6. Difference = Line F-1 minus Line F-5 ____________

F-6.1. Number of employees included in F-6 who are highly compensated (Code Sec. 414(q)) ____________

*NOTE: *If plan excludes part-time or seasonal employees, defined as other than employment for fewer than 1,000 hours per year, indicate here the definition used in the plan*

____

____

F-7. Employees excluded from coverage*

7.1 Ineligible due to being salaried ____________

7.2 Ineligible due to being hourly paid ____________

7.3 Ineligible due to job classification ____________

7.4 Ineligible due to being covered in another qualified plan ____________

7.5 Ineligible due to geographic location ____________

7.6 Ineligible for other reasons (specify) ____________

____________ ____________

____________ ____________

____________ ____________

7.8 Total excluded under F-7 ____________

**NOTE: No excluded employee should be counted in more than one category above.*

F-8. Number of employees presently eligible to participate in plan (F-6 minus F-7.8) ____________

F-9. Number of employees actually participating in plan ____________

F-10. Number of plan participants who are highly compensated ____________

Percentage test

F-11. Percentage of non-highly compensated employees participating—100 times

$$\left(\frac{\text{line F-9 minus line F-10}}{\text{line F-6 minus line F-6.1}}\right)$$ ______________________%*

Ratio test

F-12. Percentage of highly compensated employees participating—100 times (line F-10 divided by F-6.1) ______________________%

F-13. 0.7 times line F-11 ______________________%

F-14. Percentage of non-highly compensated employees participating—100 times

$$\left(\frac{\text{line F-9 minus line F-10}}{\text{line F-6 minus line F-6.1}}\right)$$ ______________________%**

Average Benefits Test

F-15. Describe nondiscriminatory classification of employees______________________

F-16. Average benefit percentage ______________________

____

* If F-11 is 70 or greater, the plan's coverage meets the percentage test and no further computation is required.

** If F-14 is equal to or greater than F-13, the plan meets the ratio test and no further compensation is required.

PART G — FUNDING

G-1. Type of Instrument

1.1 _______Self-administered trust

1.2 _______Group DA

1.3 _______Group IPG

1.4 _______Group annuity

1.5 _______Individual policy (fully insured)

1.6 _______Individual policy and investment fund

1.7 _______Other (specify) ____

____

G-2. Actuarial Assumptions and Cost Method

2.1 Actuarial assumptions

(a) _______Interest ____

(b) _______Turnover____

(c) _______Annuity form to be funded____

(d) _______Annuity purchase rate (dollar amount needed to purchase benefit of $10.00 per month at normal retirement)

Male ______________ Female ______________

or

(Dollar amount of monthly retirement income that can be purchased at normal retirement by $1,000)

Male ______________ Female ______________

(e) _______Preretirement mortality ____

(f) _______Salary scale ____

(g) _______Other (specify)____

____

2.2 Actuarial cost method ____

____

G-3. Type of Fiduciary Arrangement

3.1 _______Bank trustee

3.2 _______Individual trustee(s)

3.3 _______Insurance or annuity contracts

3.4 _______Custodial account

3.5 _______U.S. retirement bonds

3.6 _______Other (specify) ____

____

G-4. Annual Asset Valuation Date ______________________________

G-5. Trust (or Other) Fiscal Year ______________________________

G-6. Fund (Trust, Custodial Account, Annuity Plan) Identification Number ______________________________

G-7. SS-4 Needed? __________ Yes __________ No

G-8. Full Name and Address of Trustee or Other Fiduciary (Named Fiduciary) ______________________________

____

____

____

G-9. Is Trustee or Other Fiduciary Subject to Instruction by or Consent of Plan Committee, Advisor, or Other Party as to Acquisition, Retention, or Disposition of Investment Assets? ______________________________

If so, specify name and address of party whose consent is needed and acts for which consent is needed.

____

____

____

G-10. Situs of Trust ______________________________

G-11. Who Will Prepare and File Plan/Trust Returns and Reports with Internal Revenue Service and Department of Labor?

11.1 Form 5500 (or 5500-C or 5500-R—indicate which) ______________________________

11.2 Schedule A Form 5500 ______________________________

11.3 Schedule B Form 5500 ______________________________

11.4 Other reports ______________________________

____

____

____

G-12. Unusual Trust Agreement Provisions (Or Unusual Provisions to Be Included in Agreements Used in Lieu of or in Addition to Trust Agreement) ______________________________

____

____

____

G-13. Fiduciary Employer (Taxpayer) Identification Number ______________________________

G-14. Plan Administrator (If Other Than Employer) Identification Number ______________________________

PART H — AGENCY FILING RECORDS

H-1. Internal Revenue Service

1.1 Who will file for "Letter of Determination" ____________________

____

____

____

1.2 Indicate forms needed and date filed*

	Needed	Form No.	Date Filed	Response Received
(a)	______	SS-4 (Employer)	______	______
(b)	______	SS-4 (Plan Administrator)	______	______
(c)	______	2848 or 2848-D	______	______
(d)	______	5300	______	______
(e)	______	5302	______	______
(f)	______	5303	______	______
(g)	______	5307	______	______
(h)	______	5309	______	______
(i)	______	5310	______	______

*Form Index:

(a)/(b) SS-4—Application for employer (taxpayer) or plan administrator identification number

(c) 2848 or 2848-D—Power of attorney or authorization and declaration

(d) 5300—Application for determination

(e) 5302—Employee census

(f) 5303—Application for determination for collectively bargained plan

(g) 5307—Short form application for determination for employee benefit plan

(h) 5309—Application for determination of employee stock ownership plan

(i) 5310—Application for determination upon termination—notice of merger, consolidation or transfer of plan assets or liabilities

Where Letters of Determination are issued, indicate date of issuance and symbols in "response received" column.

H-2. State Government Filings (Preempted by Federal Law in Most Cases)

Filings Required	Forms to Be Submitted	Parties to Do Filing	Dates of Filing	Responses Received

H-3. Securities and Exchange Commission ____________________

H-4. Other ____________________

PART I — OTHER PROFESSIONALS

(Insert names, addresses, telephone numbers, and tax numbers)

I-1. Company's Accountant ____________________

____

____

I-2. Company's Counsel____________________

____

____

I-3. Actuary ____________________

____

____

I-4. Consultant ____________________

____

____

I-5. Fiduciary ____________________

____

____

I-6. Insurance Consultants (Indicate Lines of Coverage) ____________________

____

____

I-7. Union Representatives ____________________

____

____

I-8. Others (Specify) ____________________

____

____

____

LONG-TERM INCENTIVES: A COMPARATIVE ANALYSIS

APPENDIX C

Non-Qualified Stock Options (NQSOs) Public Companies

Description & Common Features

A right to purchase shares of company stock at a stated price ("option price") for a given period of time, frequently ten years.

Option exercise price normally equals 100% of the stock's fair market value on date of grant, but may be set below or above this level (i.e., "discount" or "premium"). However, recipients normally must wait a period of time (a "vesting period" of often one to four years) before they can exercise options, although vesting may be accelerated in certain circumstances (e.g., upon change in control). The option term may be shortened if the recipient's employment terminates before exercise.

NQSOs may be exercised by cash payment or by tendering previously owned shares of stock, depending on plan terms. NQSOs may be granted in tandem with stock appreciation rights or other devices.

Incentive Stock Options (ISOs) Public Companies

Description & Common Features

Option to purchase shares of company stock at 100% (or more) of stock's fair market value on date of grant ("option price") for a period of up to ten years, and designed to meet various other statutory requirements to qualify for ISO tax treatment, for example:

- $100,000 annual vesting limitation required.

- Stock must be held for at least two years after option grant and one year after exercise. Any sales before this time frame cause exercise to be taxed as nonqualified stock option.

- Post-termination exercise is limited (e.g., one year after disability terminations, three months after other terminations except for death). Any exercises after this time frame are taxed as nonqualified stock options.

- Shareholder approval required.

- ISO can only be granted to a company's employees, not to outside directors, contractors or consultants.

Incentive Stock Options (ISOs) Public Companies (cont'd)

Description & Common Features

- ISO must be repriced when ISO is materially amended after the grant (with the exercise price adjusted to at least the stock's fair market value on the amendment date).

Recipients normally must wait a period of time (a "vesting period" of often one to four years) before they can exercise options, although vesting may be accelerated in certain circumstances (e.g., upon change of control). The option term may be shortened if the recipient's employment terminates before exercise.

ISOs may be exercised by cash payment or by tendering previously owned shares of stock, depending on plan terms. ISOs may be granted in tandem with stock appreciation rights that have identical terms.

Phantom Stock/ Deferred Stock Units Public Companies

Description & Common Features

Units analogous to company shares, with a value generally equal to the full value of the underlying stock.

Units can be settled in cash and/or stock with the settlement date or event (e.g., termination of employment) fixed in advance and not controlled by the individual.

Note: The term "phantom stock" is used in other contexts (e.g., formula or appraised value stock for non-public companies or divisions). It also may be used to describe an arrangement like an SAR with a fixed exercise date. The treatments described here reflect only the definition given above.

Restricted Stock — Public Companies

Description & Common Features

An award of company stock with no or nominal cost that is non-transferable and subject to a substantial risk of forfeiture. As owners of the shares, holders normally have voting and dividend rights even while shares are subject to restrictions. These restrictions typically lapse over a period of three to five years.

Some companies grant restricted stock "units" under which shares of company stock will be granted when restrictions lapse. Such units have the same tax and expensing treatment as restricted stock; however, individuals do not have voting rights or beneficial ownership until actual shares are issued and balance sheet consequences will be different.

Performance Units/ Performance Cash Public Companies

Description & Common Features

A grant of a contingent number of units or a contingent cash award. Units may have a fixed dollar value, with the *number* earned varying with performance. Alternatively, a fixed number of units may be granted, with the *value* varying on the basis of performance.

Duration of performance cycle varies, but three to five years is typical. Financial objectives may relate to such measures as cumulative growth in earnings or improvements in rates of return.

At end of cycle, awards are paid in cash and/or stock according to the plan's earnout provisions and actual company performance.

Performance Shares — Public Companies

Description & Common Features

A contingent grant of a fixed number of common shares at the beginning of a performance cycle, with the *number* of shares payable at the end of the cycle dependent on how well performance objectives are achieved. The ultimate *value* of the performance shares depends on both the number of shares earned and their market value at the end of the cycle.

Duration of performance cycles varies, but three to five years is typical. Financial objectives may relate to such measures as cumulative growth in earnings or improvement in rates of return.

At end of cycle, awards are paid in cash and/or stock according to the plan's earnout provisions and actual company performance.

Stock Appreciation Rights (SARs) — Public Companies

Description & Common Features

Rights, normally granted in tandem with stock options, that permit the individual to receive a payment equal to the excess of the stock's value at exercise over the option price, in lieu of exercising the underlying stock option.

SARs may be attached to incentive stock options or nonqualified stock options or may be granted on a "freestanding" or "independent" basis without a tandem option.

SARS may be settled in cash, and/or stock.

Companies rarely grant SARs because individuals can enjoy the same economic benefits with cashless option exercises using broker loans without adverse variable accounting to the company.

GOVERNMENT BENEFITS

APPENDIX D

Though government benefits are not part of an employer's benefit plan per se, there availability does have some impact on the benefits planning process. This appendix outlines the eligibility and benefits of the three government programs that most commonly affect employees: Social Security, Medicare, and veteran's benefits. When designing an employee benefits plan, it is often important to keep these benefits in mind for coordination purposes. For instance, employees who have government health benefits from prior military service or through a spouse's prior service may need to report those benefits to the employer's group health provider.

SOCIAL SECURITY

Generally speaking, most employees in private industry, most self-employed persons, and members of the U.S. Armed Forces are covered by Social Security.

Some groups of employees are excluded from Social Security coverage and other groups are subject to special coverage provisions. The main groups excluded are federal employees hired before 1984, certain state and local employees, and railroad employees who come under the Railroad Retirement System.

A person becomes qualified for Social Security benefits by becoming "insured." Most types of benefits are payable if the person is either *fully* or *currently* insured. A special insured status is required for disability benefits.

A person becomes insured by acquiring a certain number of *quarters of coverage*.

A "quarter" is a *calendar* quarter; a period of three calendar months ending March 31, June 30, September 30, or December 31. Quarters of coverage can be acquired even before age twenty-one or after retirement age. Quarters of coverage determine insured status, not the size of a person's Social Security benefit. The law provides an exact method for computing benefits based on the person's Average Indexed Monthly Earnings.

A calendar quarter cannot be a quarter of coverage if: (1) it begins after the calendar quarter in which the person died, (2) it has not started yet, or (3) it is within a period of disability that is excluded from figuring benefit rights. (However, the beginning and ending quarters of a prior disability period may be counted as quarters of coverage if the earnings requirement is met in these quarters.)

Example: Assume Mr. Smith dies on June 24, 2015, after having earned $118,500 (the maximum earnings base for 2015). Normally, he would be credited with four quarters of coverage for that year. However, he is credited with only two because quarters after his death cannot be counted.

For 2015, an employee or self-employed person receives one quarter of coverage for each $1,220 of earnings up to a maximum of four.

Insured Status

Fully Insured

In addition to other requirements, a person must be fully insured to receive retirement benefits. A person is fully insured if he: (1) has at least six quarters of coverage, and (2) has acquired at least as many quarters of coverage as there are years elapsing *after* 1950 (or, if later, after the year in which he reaches age twenty-one) and *before* the year in which he dies, becomes disabled, or reaches, (or will reach) age sixty-two, whichever occurs first. (However, if a year, or any part of a year, fell within an established period of disability, that year need not be counted.) In any case, a person is fully insured for life if he has forty quarters of coverage.[1]

To determine the number of quarters of coverage needed to be fully insured at death, count the number of years *after* 1950 or, if later, after the year in which the person reached age twenty-one, and *before* the year in which the person dies. (But do not count a year any part of which was in an established period of disability.) A person needs at least this many quarters of coverage to be fully insured at death. However, as is the case for retirement benefits, no person can be fully insured with less than six quarters of coverage; and a person is fully insured in any event with forty quarters of coverage.

A person is insured for disability benefits if fully insured *and*:

(1) has at least twenty of the quarters during a forty-quarter period ending with the quarter in which the person is determined to be disabled, that is, the quarter the waiting period begins; and

(2) is fully insured in that quarter by having at least one credit for each calendar year after 1950, or if later, after the year in which the person attained age twenty-one, and prior to the year in which the person attains age sixty-two or dies or becomes disabled, whichever occurs earlier.[2]

In order to meet the twenty-out-of-forty quarters requirement, the twenty quarters of coverage need not be consecutive, but they must all be acquired during the forty-quarter period. (A quarter any part of which was included in a prior period of disability is not counted as one of the forty quarters unless it was a quarter of coverage and was either the first or last quarter of the period.) Generally speaking, this requirement is met if the person has worked five years in covered employment or covered self-employment out of the last ten years before disability.

Special insured status is needed by individuals who are disabled before age thirty-one to qualify for disability benefits or to establish a period of disability. The special insured status requirements are met if in the quarter that disability is determined to have begun or in a later quarter, a person:

(1) is disabled before the quarter in which age thirty-one is attained, and

(2) has credits in one-half of the quarters during the period beginning with the quarter after the quarter in which the person attained age twenty-one and ending with the quarter in which the person became disabled.

The credits must be earned in this period. If the number of elapsing quarters is an odd number, the next lower even number is used, and a minimum of six credits is required. If a person became disabled before the quarter in which age twenty-four is attained, the person must have six quarters of coverage in the twelve-quarter period ending with the quarter in which the disability began.

Currently Insured

A person is currently insured if he has acquired at least six quarters of coverage during the full thirteen-quarter period ending with the calendar quarter in which he: (1) died, (2) most recently became entitled to disability benefits, or (3) became entitled to retirement benefits.[3] The six quarters of coverage need not be consecutive, but they must be acquired *during* the thirteen-quarter period. Since insured status is based on quarters of coverage, one can work for as little as two months in two different years and be currently insured. (Calendar quarters any part of which are in an established prior period of disability are not counted in figuring the thirteen-quarter period, except that the first and last quarters of the disability period are counted if they are quarters of coverage.)

Child's benefits, mother's or father's benefits, and the lump sum death benefit are payable if a person is currently insured at death. Benefits for a surviving spouse age sixty or over, and benefits for a dependent parent, are payable only if the worker was *fully insured* at death.

Social Security Benefits

Retirement

An individual is entitled to a retirement benefit if he or she: (1) is fully insured; (2) is at least age sixty-two throughout the first month of entitlement, and (3) has filed application for retirement benefits.[4]

The retirement age is age sixty-six for workers reaching age sixty-two in 2006-2016; it then increases by two months a year for workers reaching age sixty-two in 2017-2022; and will be age sixty-seven for workers reaching age sixty-two after 2022 (i.e., reaching age sixty-seven in 2027).[5]

The normal retirement age for spouse's benefits (presently age sixty-six) moves upward in exactly the same way as that for workers; the normal retirement age for a surviving spouse's benefits also rises but in a slightly different manner (beginning for surviving spouses who attained age sixty in 2000 and reaching a normal retirement age of sixty-seven in 2029).

Reduced benefits will continue to be available at age sixty-two, but the reduction factors will be revised so that there is a further reduction (up to a maximum of 30 percent for workers entitled at age sixty-two after the retirement age is increased to age sixty-seven, rather than only up to 20 percent for entitlement at age sixty-two under previous law.

A retirement benefit that starts at or after normal retirement age equals the worker's PIA (primary insurance amount). But a worker who elects to have benefits start before normal retirement age will receive a monthly benefit equal to only a percentage of the PIA (the PIA will be reduced by 5/9 of 1 percent for each of the first thirty-six months the worker is under normal retirement age when payments commence and by 5/12 of 1 percent for each such month in excess of thirty-six).[6]

As a general rule, a person taking reduced retirement benefits before normal retirement age will continue to receive a reduced rate after normal retirement age.

Disability

A worker is entitled to disability benefits if he or she: (1) is insured for disability benefits, (2) is under age sixty-five, (3) has been disabled for twelve months or is expected to be disabled for at least twelve months, or has a disability which is expected to result in death, (4) has filed application for disability benefits, and (5) has completed a five-month waiting period or is exempted from this requirement.[7]

The amount of a disabled worker's benefit generally equals his PIA (primary insurance amount), determined as if the worker were at normal retirement age and eligible for retirement benefits in the first month of his waiting period.

However, the formula for determining a disabled worker's AIME (Average Indexed Monthly Earnings) and PIA differs from the formula used for a retiring worker. There are also different limits on the amount of family benefits that can be paid to a disabled worker and his family.

Spouse's Benefit

An individual is entitled to spouse's benefits on a worker's Social Security record if: (1) the worker is entitled to retirement or disability benefits, (2) the spouse has filed an application for spouse's benefits, (3) the spouse is not entitled to a retirement or disability benefit based on a primary insurance amount equal to or larger than one-half of the worker's primary insurance amount, and (4) the spouse is either age sixty-two or over, or has in care a child under age 16, or disabled, who is entitled to benefits on the worker's Social Security record.[8]

The spouse of a worker must also meet *one* of the following conditions: (1) the spouse must have been married to the worker for at least one year just before filing an application for benefits, or (2) the spouse must be the natural mother or father of the worker's child, or (3) the spouse was entitled or potentially entitled to spouse's, surviving spouse's, parent's, or childhood disability benefits in the month before the month of marriage to the worker, or (4) the spouse was entitled or potentially entitled to a surviving spouse's, parent's, or child's (over 18) annuity under the Railroad Retirement Act in the month before the month of marriage to the worker. A spouse is "potentially entitled" if he or she meets all the requirements for entitlement other than the filing of an application and attaining the required age.

The spouse is entitled to a divorced spouse's benefit on the worker's social security record if: (1) the worker is entitled to retirement or disability benefits, (2) the spouse has filed an application for divorced spouse's benefits, (3) the spouse is not entitled to a retirement, survivor's, or disability benefit based on a primary insurance amount which equals or exceeds one half the worker's primary insurance amount, (4) the spouse is age sixty-two or over, (5) the spouse is not married, and (6) the spouse had been married to the worker for 10 years before the date the divorce became final.

If the spouse of a retired or disabled worker is caring for the worker's under-age-sixteen or disabled child, the monthly benefit equals 50 percent of the worker's PIA regardless of his or her age. If the spouse is not caring for a child, monthly benefits starting at normal retirement age likewise equal 50 percent of the worker's PIA; but if the spouse chooses to start receiving benefits at or after age sixty-two, but before normal retirement age, the benefit is reduced.

If the spouse chooses to receive, and is paid, a reduced spouse's benefit for months before normal retirement age, he or she is not entitled to the full spouse's benefit rate upon reaching normal retirement age. A reduced benefit rate is payable for as long as he or she remains entitled to spouse's benefits.

Survivor Benefits: Mother's or Father's Benefits

The surviving spouse of a fully or currently insured worker is entitled to a mother's or father's benefit at any age if: (1) caring for a child under age sixteen, or disabled before age twenty-two, who is entitled to a child's benefit on the deceased worker's account; (2) the child is the survivor's own child or is legally adopted; (3) the surviving spouse is unmarried; (4) no widow's or widower's benefit is available; (5) no retirement benefit is available based on the surviving spouse's own work record which is equal to or larger than the mother's or father's benefit; and (6) application has been filed for benefits.[9]

The amount of a mother's or father's benefit is equal to 75 percent of the deceased spouse's PIA (primary insurance amount). However, because of the family maximum limit, the monthly benefit actually received by the surviving spouse may be less. (See Maximum Family Benefits below.) A surviving divorced mother's or father's benefit is the same amount. However, benefits paid to a divorced mother or father will not be reduced because of the limit on total family benefits; and such benefits are not counted in figuring the total benefits payable to others on the basis of the deceased worker's account.

A mother's or father's benefit ceases when the youngest child reaches age sixteen (unless a child is disabled). The surviving spouse can receive no further benefits until becoming entitled to a surviving spouse's benefit at age sixty (or a disabled widow's or widower's benefit at age fifty). The period during which the surviving spouse is entitled to no benefits is known as the Black-Out Period. The fact that a child's benefits will continue after age sixteen does not entitle his mother or father to a continuation of benefits.

Survivor Benefits: Child of Deceased Worker

If a worker dies either fully *or* currently insured, each child who meets the relationship requirements is entitled to a child's benefit if: (1) under age eighteen, or over age eighteen and disabled by a disability that began before age twenty-two, or under age nineteen and a full-time elementary or secondary school student, (2) not married, (3) dependent upon the deceased parent, and (4) an application has been filed for benefits.[10]

The surviving child's benefit is equal to 75 percent of the deceased worker's PIA (primary insurance amount). However, because of the family maximum limit, the monthly benefit actually received by the child may be less. (See Maximum Family Benefits below.)

A child's benefits end: (1) at death, or (2) at age eighteen (nineteen if a full-time elementary or secondary student), or (3) when disability ceases if benefits are being received only because the child was disabled before age twenty-two (but further benefits may be available if disability occurs again within seven years after childhood disability benefits terminate), or (4) when married. However, marriage of a disabled child over age eighteen to another Social Security beneficiary over age eighteen will ordinarily not terminate the child's benefits.

Widow or Widower's Benefits

A surviving spouse is entitled to benefits based on the deceased spouse's earnings if: (1) the surviving spouse is age sixty or over, or is at least age fifty but not age sixty and is disabled, (2) the worker died fully insured, (3) the surviving spouse is not entitled to a retirement benefit that is equal to or larger than the worker's primary insurance amount (PIA), (4) the surviving spouse has filed an application for benefits, and (5) in most circumstances the surviving spouse has not remarried unless the remarriage happened after the surviving spouse turned sixty.[11]

In addition, one of the following conditions must be met: (1) the surviving spouse was married to the deceased worker for at least nine months just before he or she died (see exceptions below); (2) the surviving spouse is the biological mother or father of the worker's child (this requirement is met if a live child was born to the worker and the surviving spouse, although the child need not still survive); (3) the surviving spouse legally adopted the worker's child during their marriage and before the child reached age eighteen; (4) the surviving spouse was married to the worker when they both legally adopted a child under age eighteen; (5) the worker legally adopted the surviving spouse's child during their marriage and before the child reached age eighteen; or (6) the surviving spouse was entitled or potentially entitled to wife's, husband's, father's, mother's, parent's, or childhood disability benefits, or to a survivor spouse's, child's (age eighteen or over) or parent's annuity under the Railroad Retirement Act, in the month before the month the surviving spouse married the deceased worker.

The nine-month duration of marriage requirement is waived if the worker's death was accidental or it occurred in the line of duty while a member of a uniformed service serving on active duty, or if the surviving spouse who was married to the worker at the time of death, was previously married to and divorced from the worker and the previous marriage had lasted nine months.

If the surviving spouse is normal retirement age or older when benefits commence, the monthly benefit is equal to 100 percent of the deceased worker's PIA (the amount the worker would have been entitled to receive upon normal retirement age) plus any additional amount the deceased worker was entitled to because of delayed retirement credits (the delayed retirement credit is discussed below). If the worker was receiving benefits before normal retirement age, the surviving spouse is entitled to an amount equal to the reduced benefit the worker would have been receiving had he lived (but not less than 82.5 percent of the PIA).

Computing Social Security Benefits

The Primary Insurance Amount (PIA) is the basic unit used to determine the amount of each monthly benefit payable under social security, and applies to both the old and new method of computing benefits. A disabled worker – or a retired worker whose old-age benefits start at normal retirement age – receives monthly benefits equal to the PIA. Retired workers whose old-age benefits start *after* normal retirement age also receive an additional delayed retirement credit.

Monthly benefits for members of an insured's family (dependent's and survivor's benefits) are all figured as percentages of the worker's PIA. The total amount of monthly benefits payable on a worker's social security account is limited by a "maximum family benefit" which is also related to the worker's PIA.

The Wage Indexing Method is what is used to calculate a person's PIA. This method is based on "indexed" earnings over a fixed number of years after 1950. (Indexing is a mechanism for expressing prior year's earnings in terms of their current dollar value.)

The "wage indexing" method uses a formula to determine the PIA.[12]

Step I. Index the earnings record.

Step II. Determine the individual's Average Indexed Monthly Earnings (AIME).

Step III. Apply the PIA formula to the AIME.

The AIME is based on Social Security earnings for years after 1950. This includes wages earned as an employee and/or self-employment income.

Only earnings credited to the person's Social Security account can be used up to the Social Security wage base for that year ($118,500 in 2015).

The AIME is based on the earnings record after wages have been indexed. Indexing creates an earnings history which more accurately reflects the value of the individual's earnings in comparison with the national average wage level at the time of eligibility. Earnings for each year are indexed up to and including the "indexing year," the second year before the worker reaches age sixty-two, or dies or becomes disabled before age sixty-two.

Wages are indexed by applying a ratio to the worker's earnings for each year beginning with 1951. The ratio is the "indexing average wage" for the second year before the year of the worker's eligibility for benefits or death, divided by the "indexing average wage" for the year being indexed. Thus, indexed earnings for each year are computed as follows:

$$\text{Worker's Actual Earnings (Up to the Social Security Maximum) for Year to be Indexed} \times \frac{\text{Average Earnings of all workers in Indexing Year (Second Year before Eligibility or Death)}}{\text{Average Earnings of all workers for Year being Indexed}}$$

Example. Mr. Martin earned $15,000 in 1989 and reached age sixty-two in 2015. The indexing average wage for 2013 (his "indexing year") was $44,888.16 and the indexing average wage for 1989 was $20,099.55. Indexed earnings for 1989 are computed as follows:

$$\$15{,}000 \times \frac{\$44{,}888.16}{\$20{,}099.55} = \$33{,}499.38$$

Indexed earnings of $34,987.32 are used in place of actual earnings for 1987 in Mr. Martin's AIME computation.

In computing a person's AIME, the following steps are taken:

Step I. Count the *number* of years *after* 1950 (or after year person reached age twenty-one, if later) and *up to* (not including) the year of attaining age sixty-two (or the year of disability or death, if before age sixty-two). The number of years counted is the number of *computation elapsed years*.

Step II. Subtract five from the number of computation elapsed years when computing the AIME for *retirement* or *death benefits*. The number remaining (if less than two, use two) is the *number of computation base years* to be used in computing the AIME.

The number of years to be subtracted for *disability benefits* is scaled according to the worker's age, under the following schedule:

Worker's age at disability	Number of dropout years to be subtracted
Under 27	0
27 through 31	1
32 through 36	2
37 through 41	3
42 through 46	4
47 and over	5

Example: An insured woman attained age forty in January 2015 and is found to be entitled to disability benefits. It is determined that her waiting period began on March 1, 2015. The elapsed years run from 1997 (age twenty-two) through 2014 and total 18 years. Because the woman is forty years old, there are 15 computation years (18 minus 3).

Step III. List Social Security earnings in the *computation base years*. (Social Security earnings limits are listed under the heading "AIME.") Computation base years are years *after* 1950, up to and *including* the year of death, or the year *before* entitlement to retirement or disability benefits. (A person is not entitled to benefits until an application for benefits is filed.)

Notice that the year of death is included as a computation base year – but the year in which an application is made for retirement or disability benefits is not included. However, for benefits payable for the next year after application is made for retirement or disability benefits, the AIME for retirement or disability benefits will be recomputed, and earnings for this final year substituted for the lowest year if the result is a higher AIME.

Where benefits are being estimated for entitlement at some future time, use anticipated earnings (but not over the Social Security maximum) for future computation base years.

Step IV. Index earnings in each computation base year up to but not including the "indexing year."

Step V. From the list of indexed earnings (and non-indexed earnings for and after the "indexing year"), select years of highest earnings (same number as found in **Step II**). Selected years need not be in consecutive order.

Step VI. Total indexed and nonindexed earnings for selected years are divided by the number of months in the number of years found in **Step II**, dropping cents. This is the person's Average Indexed Monthly Earnings (AIME).

If a person does not have earnings covered by Social Security in as many years as are required to be used as benefit computation years, total earnings must nevertheless be divided by the number of months in the required number of years. In other words, one or more years of zero earnings must be used.

The Primary Insurance Amount is determined by applying a formula to the Average Indexed Monthly Earnings (AIME). Where first eligibility is in calendar year 2015, the Primary Insurance Amount is the sum of three separate percentages of portions of the AIME. It is found by adding 90 percent of the first $826 or less of the AIME, plus 32 percent of the AIME from $827 through $4,980, plus 15 percent of the AIME in excess of $4,980.

If the resulting PIA is not an even multiple of 10¢, it is rounded to the next lower multiple of 10¢.

The PIA is then subject to cost-of-living increases beginning with the year of first eligibility.

Maximum Family Benefits

The following formula determines the Maximum Family Benefit for those who reach age sixty-two or dying before age sixty-two in 2015:[13]

(1) 150 percent of the first $1,056 of PIA, plus

(2) 272 percent of PIA over $1,056 through $1,524, plus

(3) 134 percent of PIA over $1,524 through $1,987, plus

(4) 175 percent over $1,987.

The result is the family maximum. (The final figure should be rounded to the next lower multiple of $0.10 if not an even multiple of $0.10.) The Maximum Family Benefit is subject to cost-of-living increases beginning with the year of first eligibility. The numbers in the calculation change each year based on the change in the nation's average wages, but the percentages stay the same.

For a disabled worker and family, benefits may not exceed the lesser of 85 percent of the Average Indexed Monthly Earnings (AIME) on which the worker's disability benefit is based, or 150 percent of the disability benefit payable to the worker alone. However, in no case will a family's benefit be reduced below 100 percent of the benefit which would be payable to the worker alone.

Cost-of-Living Increases

The Social Security Act provides for automatic increases in benefits and in the maximum earnings base (earnings subject to social security taxes) due to changing economic conditions.[14]

The automatic increases in benefits are determined by increases in the Consumer Price Index for All Urban Wage Earners and Clerical Workers prepared by the Department of Labor. The increases in the maximum earnings base are determined from increases in average nationwide wages, if there has been a cost-of-living increase in benefits for the preceding December.

Individuals using the "wage indexing" benefit computation method are entitled to cost-of-living increases beginning with the year of first eligibility (the year of attaining age sixty-two, or disability or death before age sixty-two). The PIA is calculated for the year of first eligibility and the cost-of-living increases in that year and subsequent years will be added. As long as eligibility exists in any month of the year, the PIA will be increased by the automatic benefit increase percentage applicable to the check sent in January of the following year.

Example: Mr. Jones attains age sixty-two in November 2013 and waits until January 2015 to apply for benefits. The PIA is calculated and will be increased by the automatic cost-of-living benefit increases applicable to December 2013 and December 2014. The resultant PIA will be payable in the benefit paid for January 2015.

Delayed Retirement Credit

Workers who continue on the job receive an increase in retirement benefits for each year they work between normal retirement age and seventy.[15] Note that this is *not* an increase in the worker's PIA. Other benefits based on the PIA, such as those payable to a spouse, are not affected.

For those individuals who turn age sixty-two in 2005 or later, delaying the receipt of Social Security benefits past normal retirement age will increase the person's benefits by 2/3 of 1 percent for each month (or 8 percent per year) after reaching normal retirement age. A person's maximum delayed retirement credit will be reached at age seventy.

Delayed Retirement Credit Rates

Attain Age 62	Monthly Percentage	Yearly Percentage
1979 – 86	1/4 of 1%	3%
1987 – 88	7/24 of 1%	3.5%
1989 – 90	1/3 of 1%	4.0%
1991 – 92	3/8 of 1%	4.5%
1993 – 94	5/12 of 1%	5%
1995 – 96	11/24 of 1%	5.5%
1997 – 98	1/2 of 1%	6%
1999 – 2000	13/24 of 1%	6.5%
2001 – 2002	7/12 of 1%	7%
2003 – 2004	5/8 of 1%	7.5%
2005 or after	2/3 of 1%	8%

Working After Retirement

A Social Security beneficiary will lose part or all of his benefits if he is under the normal retirement age for all of 2015 and earns over $15,720. However, an alternative test applies in the initial year of retirement if it produces a more favorable result. A beneficiary will lose benefits if he reaches normal retirement age in 2015 and earns more than $41,880. Earnings in and after the month in which a person reaches normal retirement age are not included in determining total earnings for the year.[16]

The annual exempt amounts ($15,720 and $41,880 in 2015) will be increased each year as wage levels rise.

A beneficiary who has reached normal retirement age before the current year can earn any amount without loss of benefits. Regardless of how much earnings are earned in the year of attaining normal retirement age, no benefits are withheld for the month in which normal retirement age is reached, or for any subsequent month.

If the beneficiary is at normal retirement age or older, no benefits will be lost because of his earnings. If he is under the normal retirement age, the following rules apply:

- If no more than $41,880 is earned in 2015 by a beneficiary who reaches the normal retirement age in 2015, no benefits will be lost for that year.

- If more than $41,880 is earned in 2015 before the month the beneficiary reaches normal retirement age, $1 of benefits will be lost for each $3 of earnings over $41,880.

- If not more than $15,720 is earned in 2015 by a beneficiary under normal retirement age for the entire year, no benefits will be lost for that year.

- If more than $15,720 is earned in 2015 by a beneficiary under normal retirement age for the entire year, $1 of benefits will ordinarily be lost for each $2 of earnings over $15,720.

- But, no matter how much is earned during 2015, no *retirement* benefits in the *initial year of retirement* will be lost for any month in which the beneficiary neither: (1) earns over $1,310 if retiring in a year before the year he reaches normal retirement age, nor (2) renders any substantial services in self-employment.

The initial year of retirement is the first year in which he is both entitled to benefits and has a month in which he does not earn over the monthly exempt wage amount (as listed above) and does not render substantial services in self-employment.

In determining the amount of benefits for a given year that will be lost, two factors must be taken into consideration: (1) the amount of the person's excess earnings for the year, and (2) the months in the year that can actually be charged with all or a portion of the excess earnings potentially chargeable in the initial year of retirement.

Both wages earned as an employee and net earnings from self-employment are combined for purposes of determining the individual's total earnings for the year. Only "excess earnings" are potentially chargeable against benefits.

Excess earnings are charged first against all benefits payable on the worker's account for the first month of the year. If any excess earnings remain, they are charged against all benefits payable for the second month of the year, and so on until all the excess earnings have been charged, or no benefits remain for the year. However, a month cannot be charged with any excess earnings and must be skipped if: (1) the individual was not entitled to benefits for that month, (2) was over normal retirement age in that month; (3) in the initial year of retirement he did not earn over $1,310 (using 2015 figures) in a year before the year he reaches normal retirement age; or (4) did not render substantial services as a self-employed person in that month.

If the excess earnings chargeable to a month are less than the benefits payable to the worker and to other persons on his account, then the excess is chargeable to each beneficiary in the proportion that the original entitlement rate of each bears to the sum of all their original entitlement rates.

Example 1. Dr. Brown partially retires in January 2015 at the age of sixty-two. Based on his earnings history and the age he starts receiving benefits, his Social Security benefit is $1,200 per month. He practices for three months in 2015 and earns $30,000. The remainder of his initial year of retirement is spent in Florida playing golf. Despite the fact that Dr. Brown has excess earnings in 2015 that would, under the annual test, cause a benefit loss of $7,440, he will lose only the $3,600 in benefits for the three months during which he performed substantial services in self-employment because 2015 is his initial year of retirement.

Example 2. Dr. Smith, who partially retired in 2014 at age sixty-two, practices for four months in 2015 and earns $32,000. As 2015 is his second year of retirement, the monthly earnings test does not apply. His benefits will be reduced by $1 for each $2 of earnings over $15,720. This means that Dr. Smith's benefits in 2015 will be reduced by $8,140 (half of the amount in excess of $15,720).

Example 3. Mr. Martin is sixty-eight years old and has not retired. He earns $45,000 a year. Mr. Martin receives retirement benefits of $700 a month. Because he is over the normal retirement age, he loses none of his benefits by working.

Income Taxation of Social Security Benefits

Social Security retirement, survivor, and disability benefits may be subject to income taxation in some cases.[17] The person who has the legal right to receive the benefits must determine if the benefits are taxable. For example, if a parent and child both receive benefits, but the check for the child is made out in the parent's name, the parent must use only the parent's portion of the benefits in figuring if benefits are taxable. The portion of the benefits that belongs to the child must be added to the child's other income to see if any of those benefits are taxable.

If the only income a person receives is Social Security benefits, the benefits generally are not taxable and he probably does not need to file a return. However, if a person has other income in addition to benefits, he may have to file a return even if none of the benefits are taxable.

If the total of a person's income plus half of his benefits is more than the *base amount*, some of the benefits are taxable. Included in the person's total income is any tax-exempt interest income, excludable interest from United States savings bonds, and excludable income earned in a foreign country, United States possession, or Puerto Rico.

The base amount is as follows depending upon a person's filing status:

- $32,000 for married couples filing jointly.
- $-0- for married couples filing separately and who lived together at any time during the year.
- $25,000 for other taxpayers.

If a person is married and files a joint return, the person and his spouse must combine their incomes and their Social Security benefits when figuring if any of their combined benefits are taxable. Even if the spouse did not receive any benefits, the person must add the spouse's income to his when figuring if any of his benefits are taxable.

Example: Jim and Julie Smith are filing a joint return for 2015 and both received Social Security benefits during the year. Jim received net benefits of $6,600, while Julie received net benefits of $2,400. Jim also received a taxable pension of $10,000 and interest income of $500. Jim did not have any tax-exempt interest income. Jim and Julie's Social Security benefits are not taxable for 2015 because the sum of their income ($10,000 + 500 = $10,500) and one-half their benefits ($9,000 ÷ 2 = $4,500) $15,000 ($10,500 + 4,500), is not more than their base amount ($32,000).

The amount of benefits to be included in taxable income depends on the person's total income plus half his Social Security benefits. The higher the total, the more benefits a person must include in taxable income. Depending upon a person's income he may be required to include either up to 50 percent or up to 85 percent of benefits in income.

50 Percent Taxable

If a person's income plus half of his Social Security benefits is more than the following *base amount* for his filing status, up to 50 percent of his benefits will be included in his gross income.

- $32,000 for married couples filing jointly.
- $-0- for married couples filing separately and who lived together at any time during the year.
- $25,000 for all other taxpayers.

85 Percent Taxable

If a person's income plus half of his Social Security benefits is more than the following *adjusted base amount* for his filing status, up to 85 percent of his benefits will be included in his gross income.

- $44,000 for married couples filing jointly.
- $-0- for married couples filing separately and who lived together at any time during the year.
- $34,000 for other taxpayers.

If a person is married filing separately and *lived with* his spouse at any time during the year, up to 85 percent of his benefits will be included in his gross income.

MEDICARE

Medicare is the federal health insurance program that covers most people who are age sixty-five or older. Medicare also covers people of any age who suffer from permanent kidney failure, and certain disabled people.

Medicare generally consists of four parts:

1. Hospital Insurance (Part A),
2. Medical Insurance (Part B),
3. Medicare Advantage (Part C), and
4. Prescription Drug Insurance (Part D).

Hospital Insurance (Part A)

Hospital Insurance (Part A) provides institutional care, including inpatient hospital care, skilled nursing care, post-hospital home health care, and, under certain conditions, hospice care. Part A is financed mostly by Social Security payroll tax deductions which are deposited in the Federal Hospital Insurance Trust Fund. Medicare beneficiaries also participate in the financing of Part A by paying deductibles, coinsurance, and premiums.

Medical Insurance (Part B)

Medical Insurance (Part B) is a voluntary program of health insurance. It covers physician's services, outpatient hospital care, physical therapy, ambulance trips, medical equipment, prosthesis, and a number of other services not covered under Part A. It is financed through monthly premiums paid by those who enroll and contributions from the federal government, both of which are deposited into the Federal Supplementary Medical Insurance Trust Fund. The government's share of the cost of Medicare Part B is approximately 75 percent.

Medicare Advantage (Part C)

Medicare Advantage (Part C) permit contracts between CMS and a variety of different private managed care and fee-for-service organizations. Most Medicare beneficiaries can choose to receive benefits through the original Medicare fee-for-service program (Part A and Part B) or through one of the following Medicare Advantage plans:

1. Coordinated care plans, including Health Maintenance Organizations (HMOs), Preferred Provider Organizations (PPOs), and Provider Sponsored Organizations (PSOs).

2. Religious fraternal benefit society plans that may restrict enrollment to members of the church, convention, or group with which the society is affiliated.

3. Private fee-for-service plans that reimburse providers on a fee-for-service basis.

Prescription Drug Insurance (Part D)

Medicare Part D is the Prescription Drug Insurance program added to Medicare by the Medicare Prescription Drug, Improvement, and Modernization Act of 2003. In exchange for a monthly premium, Medicare Part D participants receive limited coverage for prescription drug benefits up to a catastrophic coverage threshold, above which Part D will cover roughly 95 percent of prescription drug costs.

Medicare Supplement Insurance (Medigap Insurance)

Medigap insurance is designed to help pay the deductibles and coinsurance incurred by beneficiaries who are in the original Medicare plan (Part A and Part B). A Medigap policy may also pay for certain items or services not covered by Medicare at all. Medigap only works with the original Medicare plan. It will not cover out-of-pocket expenses, such as co-payments, in a managed care plan.

Eligibility and Enrollment

Hospital Insurance (Part A)

Hospital Insurance is available to all persons age sixty-five and over who are entitled to monthly Social Security cash benefits or monthly cash benefits under Railroad Retirement programs (whether retired or not). A Social Security disability beneficiary is covered under Medicare generally after he or she has been entitled to disability benefits for twenty-four months or more.

A dependent or survivor of a person entitled to Hospital Insurance benefits, or a dependent of a person under age sixty-five who is entitled to retirement or disability benefits is also eligible for Hospital Insurance (Part A) benefits if the dependent or survivor is at least sixty-five years old.

Workers who are considered insured under Social Security (and certain of their dependents) with end-stage renal disease who require dialysis or a kidney transplant are deemed disabled for Medicare coverage purposes even if they are working.

Medical Insurance (Part B)

All persons entitled to premium-free Hospital Insurance (Part A), or premium Hospital Insurance (Part A) for the working disabled under Medicare, may voluntarily enroll in Medical Insurance (Part B). Social Security and Railroad Retirement beneficiaries, age sixty-five or over, are, therefore, automatically eligible. However, any other person age sixty-five or over may enroll provided that he or she is a resident of the United States and is either: (1) a citizen of the United States, or (2) an alien lawfully admitted for permanent residence who has resided in the United States continuously during the five years immediately prior to the month in which he or she applies for enrollment.

The initial enrollment period is a period of seven full calendar months, the beginning and end of which are determined for each person by the day on which he or she is first eligible to enroll. The initial enrollment period begins on the first day of the third month before the month a person first becomes eligible to enroll and ends with the close of the last day of the third month following the month a person first becomes eligible to enroll. For example: If the person's sixty-fifth birthday is April 10, 2015, the initial enrollment period begins January 1, 2015 and ends July 31, 2015. Anyone who fails to enroll during the initial enrollment period may enroll during a general enrollment period. There are general enrollment periods each year from January 1st through March 31st. Coverage begins the following July 1st.

The premium will be higher for a person who fails to enroll within twelve months, or who drops out of the plan and later re-enrolls. The monthly premium will be increased by 10 percent for each full twelve months during which he or she could have been, but was not, enrolled.

If a person declines to enroll (or terminates enrollment) at a time when Medicare is secondary payer to his or her employer group health plan, the months he or she was covered under the employer group health plan (based on current employment) and Hospital Insurance will not be counted as months during which he or she could have been enrolled in Medical Insurance for the purpose of determining if the premium amount should be increased above the basic rate. These people may then enroll during the "special enrollment period," lasting for seven months and starting the first month the person is not covered by a group health plan.

Medicare Advantage (Part C)

Beneficiaries entitled to Hospital Insurance (Part A) and enrolled in Medical Insurance (Part B) are eligible to enroll in a Medicare Advantage plan. Beneficiaries with end-stage renal disease may not enroll in a Medicare Advantage plan, but may remain in a plan if already enrolled. Beneficiaries receiving inpatient hospice care may not enroll in or remain in a Medicare Advantage plan. Part B only enrollees are ineligible.

Beneficiaries may choose a Medicare Advantage plan at initial eligibility or during one of the enrollment periods described below. Through 2004, they could enroll or disenroll on a monthly basis. For the first six months of 2005 (or the first six months of eligibility in year 2005, in the case of a person first eligible for Medicare Advantage in 2005), beneficiaries could enroll and disenroll from plans once during that period. In years after 2005, changes must be made in the first three months of the year (or the first three months of eligibility), or during the annual coordinated enrollment period.

The annual coordinated enrollment period runs from October 15 through December 7 of each year. Enrollments at this time are effective the following January 1.

Plans must accept all beneficiaries on a first-come, first-served basis, subject to capacity limits.

Prescription Drug Insurance (Part D)

Anyone who is entitled to Medicare Part A or enrolled in Part B is eligible to participate in Prescription Drug Insurance (Part D). All Medicare participants are similarly eligible for the prescription drug discount card, except those enrolled in Medicaid and entitled to Medicaid drug coverage. The enrollment periods for drug-only plans and Medicare Advantage plans run concurrently.

Medicare Supplement Insurance (Medigap)

There is an open enrollment period for selecting Medigap policies that guarantees that a person age sixty-five or older cannot be denied Medigap insurance or charged higher premiums because of health problems. The open enrollment period starts on the first day of the month in which a person is both over sixty-five and enrolled in Medicare Part B, and lasts for six months.

Even when a person buys a Medigap policy in this open enrollment period, the policy may still exclude coverage for "pre-existing conditions" during the first six months the policy is in effect. Pre-existing conditions are conditions that were either diagnosed or treated during the six-month period before the Medigap policy became effective.

To individuals enrolled in Medicare prior to age sixty-five, Medigap insurers are required to offer coverage, regardless of medical history, for a six-month period when the individual reaches age sixty-five. Insurers are prohibited from discriminating in the price of policies for such an individual, based upon the health status of the policyholder.

Hospital Insurance (Part A) Benefits

Over and above the "deductible" and "coinsurance" amounts that must be paid by the patient, the following services are covered under Medicare Part A:

1. Inpatient hospital care for up to ninety days in each "benefit period." The patient pays a deductible of $1,260 (in 2015) for the first sixty days and coinsurance of $315 per day (in 2015) for each additional day up to a maximum of thirty days. In addition, each person has a nonrenewable lifetime "reserve" of sixty additional hospital days with coinsurance of $630 per day (in 2015).

2. Post-hospital extended care in a skilled nursing facility for up to one hundred days in each "benefit period." The patient pays nothing for the first twenty days. After twenty days the patient pays coinsurance of $157.20 per day (in 2015) for each additional day up to a maximum of eighty days.

3. The first one hundred post-hospital home health service visits following a hospital or skilled nursing facility stay. The services must be made under a plan of treatment established by a physician, except that there is 20 percent cost-sharing payable by the patient for durable

medical equipment (other than the purchase of certain used items).

4. Hospice care for terminally ill patients.

Inpatient Hospital Care

Except for the "deductible" and "coinsurance" amounts that must be paid by the patient, Medicare helps pay for inpatient hospital service for up to ninety days in each "benefit period." Medicare will also pay (except for a coinsurance amount) for sixty additional hospital days over each person's lifetime (applies to disabled beneficiaries at any age; others after age sixty-five).

The ninety-day benefit period starts again with each spell of illness. A benefit period is a way of measuring the patient's use of services under Hospital Insurance. The patient's first benefit period starts the first time the patient receives inpatient hospital care after Hospital Insurance coverage begins. A benefit period ends when the patient has been out of a hospital or other facility primarily providing skilled nursing or rehabilitative services for sixty days in a row (including the day of discharge). After one benefit period has ended, another one will start whenever the patient again receives inpatient hospital care.

Example 1. Mr. Smith enters the hospital on February 5. He is discharged on February 15. He has used 10 days of his first benefit period. Mr. Smith is not hospitalized again until August 20. More than sixty days elapsed between his hospital stays, so he begins a new benefit period, his Hospital Insurance coverage is completely renewed, and he will again pay the hospital deductible.

Example 2. Mr. Jones enters the hospital on September 14. He is discharged on September 24. He also has used ten days of his first benefit period. However, he is then readmitted to the hospital on October 20. Fewer than sixty days have elapsed between hospital stays, so Mr. Jones is still in his first benefit period and will not be required to pay another hospital deductible. This means that the first day of his second admission is counted as the eleventh day of hospital care in that benefit period. Mr. Jones will not begin a new benefit period until he has been out of the hospital (and has not received any skilled care in a skilled nursing facility) for sixty consecutive days.

Lifetime reserve days are extra hospital days to use if a patient has a long illness and needs to stay in the hospital for more than ninety days in a benefit period. Each person has only sixty lifetime reserve days. Thus, if a patient uses eight lifetime reserve days in his or her first hospital stay this year, the next time he or she visits a hospital he or she will have only fifty-two lifetime reserve days left to use, whether or not he or she has a new benefit period. A patient can decide when he or she wants to use his or her lifetime reserve days.

Skilled Nursing Facility Care

In order to qualify for skilled nursing facility benefits under Hospital Insurance, the patient must meet all of the following five conditions:

1. The patient's condition requires daily skilled nursing or skilled rehabilitative services which can only be provided in a skilled nursing facility.

2. The patient has been in a hospital at least three days in a row before being admitted to a participating skilled nursing facility.

3. The patient is admitted to the skilled nursing facility within a short time (generally within thirty days) after leaving the hospital.

4. The patient's care in the skilled nursing facility is for a condition that was treated in the hospital, or for a condition that arose while receiving care in the skilled nursing facility for a condition which was treated in the hospital.

5. A medical professional certifies that the patient needs, and receives, skilled nursing or skilled rehabilitation services on a daily basis.

There is no lifetime limit on the amount of skilled nursing facility care provided under Hospital Insurance. Except for the coinsurance (which must be paid after the first twenty days in each benefit period), the plan will pay the cost of one hundred days' post-hospital care in each benefit period, regardless of how many benefit periods the person may have. After one hundred days of coverage in a benefit period, the patient must pay the full cost of skilled nursing facility care.

Home Health Care

Hospital Insurance pays for the first one hundred home health visits in a "home health spell of illness" if all six of the following conditions are met:

1. The care is post-institutional home health services.
2. The care includes intermittent skilled nursing care, physical therapy, or speech therapy.
3. The person is confined at home.
4. The person is under the care of a physician who determines the need for home health care and sets up a home health plan for the person.
5. The home health agency providing services participates in Medicare.
6. The services are provided on a visiting basis in the person's home, or if it is necessary to use equipment that cannot be readily made available in the home, on an outpatient basis in a hospital, skilled nursing facility, or licensed rehabilitation center.

The term "home health spell of illness" means a period of consecutive days: (1) beginning with the first day a person is furnished post-institutional home health services (in a month in which the person is entitled to benefits under Part A), and (2) ending with the close of the first period of sixty consecutive days thereafter for which the person is neither an inpatient in a hospital or skilled nursing facility nor provided home health services.

Hospice Care

Hospice care is an approach to treatment that recognizes that the impending death of an individual warrants a change in focus from care that is designed to cure, to care that is designed to provide relief from pain and other uncomfortable symptoms. The goal of hospice care is to help terminally ill individuals continue life with minimal disruption to normal activities while remaining primarily in the home environment.

Under the Medicare hospice benefit, Medicare pays for services every day and also permits a hospice to provide appropriate custodial care, including homemaker services and counseling. Hospice care under Medicare includes both home care and inpatient care, when needed, and a variety of services not otherwise covered under Medicare.

Hospice care is covered under Hospital Insurance (Part A) when the beneficiary: (1) is eligible for Hospital Insurance benefits, (2) is certified by a doctor as terminally ill (i.e., life expectancy of six months or less), and (3) files a statement electing to waive all other Medicare coverage for hospice care from hospice programs other than the one chosen, and elects not to receive other services related to treatment of the terminal condition. (The beneficiary can later revoke the election.)

There are no deductibles under the hospice benefit. The beneficiary does not pay for Medicare-covered services for the terminal illness, except for small coinsurance amounts for outpatient drugs and inpatient respite care. For outpatient prescription drugs, the patient is responsible for 5 percent of the cost of drugs or $5, whichever is less. For inpatient respite care, the patient pays 5 percent of the amount paid by Medicare for a respite care day.

Medical Insurance (Part B) Benefits

Under Medical Insurance, Medicare usually pays 80 percent of the approved charges for doctors' services and the cost of other services that are covered under Medical Insurance after the patient pays an annual deductible. Medical Insurance helps pay for covered services received from a doctor in the doctor's office, in a hospital, in a skilled nursing facility, in the patient's home, or any other location. Doctors' services are covered wherever furnished in the United States. This includes the cost of house calls, office visits, and doctors' services in a hospital or other institution. It also includes the fees of physicians, surgeons, pathologists, radiologists, anesthesiologists, physiatrists, and osteopaths.

In addition, Medical Insurance covers: (1) medical and surgical services, including anesthesia, (2) diagnostic tests and procedures that are part of the patient's treatment, (3) radiology and pathology services by doctors while the patient is a hospital inpatient or outpatient, (4) treatment of mental illness (Medicare payments are limited), (5) X-rays, (6) services of the doctor's office nurse, (7) drugs and biologicals that cannot be self-administered, (8) transfusions of blood and blood components, (9) medical supplies, and (10) physical/occupational therapy and speech-language pathology services.

Medical Insurance does not cover the following: (1) most routine physical examinations, and tests directly related to those examinations (except some Pap smears and mammograms), (2) most routine foot care and dental care, (3) examinations for prescribing or fitting eyeglasses or hearing aids and most eyeglasses and hearing aids, (4) immunizations (except annual flu shots, pneumococcal vaccinations or immunizations required because of an injury or immediate risk of infection, and hepatitis B for certain persons at risk), (5) cosmetic surgery, unless it is needed because of accidental injury or to improve the function of a malformed part of the body, (6) most prescription drugs, (7) custodial care at home or in a nursing home, and (8) orthopedic shoes.

Major outpatient hospital services covered by Medical Insurance include: (1) services in an emergency room or outpatient clinic, including same-day surgery, (2) laboratory tests billed by the hospital, (3) mental health care in a partial hospitalization psychiatric program, if a physician certifies that inpatient treatment would be required without it, (4) X-rays and other radiology services billed by the hospital, (5) medical supplies such as splints and casts, (6) drugs and biologicals that cannot be self-administered, and (7) blood transfusions furnished to the patient as an outpatient (after the first three pints).

Payments by the government under Medical Insurance program can be made in one of two ways, (1) directly to the doctor or supplier, which is called "assignment," or (2) directly to the patient. Under the assignment method, the doctor or supplier agrees to accept the amount approved by the Medicare carrier as total payment for covered services.

If a doctor does not accept assignment, for most covered services, there are limits on the amount that a patient can be charged. The most a doctor can charge is 115 percent of what Medicare approves. The 115 percent limit also applies to fees for physical and occupational therapy services, suppliers, injections, and other services billable under the physician fee schedule.

Medicare Advantage (Part C) Benefits

All Medicare Advantage plans are required to provide the current Medicare benefit package (excluding hospice services), and any additional health services required under the adjusted community rate (ACR) process. Part C plans may offer mandatory supplemental benefits, subject to approval by the Centers for Medicare & Medicaid Services, and may also offer optional supplemental benefits. Private fee-for-service plans may offer supplemental benefits that include payment for some or all of the permitted balance billings amounts and additional services that the plan determines are medically necessary.

Medicare Advantage plans are permitted to select the providers who may furnish benefits to enrollees, as long as benefits are available and accessible to all enrollees with reasonable promptness and assured continuity, twenty-four hours a day, seven days a week. Medicare Advantage plans are required to pay for emergency services without regard to prior authorization or whether the provider has a contractual relationship with the plan. An emergency medical condition is defined using a "prudent layperson" standard (including conditions that may be manifested by "severe pain").

Prescription Drug Insurance (Part D) Benefits

Prescription Drug Insurance will offer a standard benefit to most participants. Part D offers the following standard benefit in 2015:

Drug Expense	Patient Pays	Medicare Part D Pays
First $320	100%	Nothing
$320-$2,960	25%	75%
$2,960-$6,680	100%	Nothing
Above $6,680	Up to 5%	95% or more (based on income)

Participants with incomes below 150 percent of the federal poverty guidelines have lower cost sharing requirements than under the standard benefit. Beneficiaries with incomes below 135 percent of the federal poverty guidelines have no cost-sharing obligation for prescription drug expenses above $6,680. Beneficiaries with incomes between 135 and 150 percent of the federal poverty guidelines have $2.65 co-pays for generic prescriptions and $6.60 co-pays for name-brand prescriptions. Those with incomes above 150 percent of the federal poverty level have 5 percent co-pays.

For 2015, 135 percent of the federal poverty guidelines is $15,754.50 for a single person, and $21,235.50 for a married couple; 150 percent of the poverty level is $17,655.00 for a single person, and $23,895.00 for a married couple.[18] Sponsoring organizations may offer alternative prescription drug coverage through plans that (1) provide coverage, the actuarial value of which is at least equal to the actuarial value of the standard prescription drug coverage, (2) offer access to negotiated prices, and (3) are approved by CMS.

Part D plans may also provide supplemental prescription drug coverage that offers cost-sharing reductions and enhanced benefits. A plan may charge a supplemental premium for the supplemental coverage. However, a sponsoring organization offering supplemental coverage in an area must also offer a prescription drug plan in the area that provides only basic coverage. Basic coverage is either the statutorily-defined standard benefit or the alternative prescription drug coverage without any supplemental benefits.

Medicare Supplement Insurance (Medigap) Benefits

Congress established federal standards for Medigap policies in 1990 and again in 2010. Most states have adopted regulations limiting the sale of Medigap insurance to no more than ten standard policies identified by the letters A, B, C, D, F, G, K, L, M, and N. Plan A is a basic policy offering a "core package" of benefits. Plans B, C, D, F, G, M, and Neach have a different combination of benefits, but they all include the core package. Plans K and L do not included the core benefit package; they instead offer catastrophic coverage. The basic policy, offering the core package of benefits, is available in all states. The availability of other plans varies from state to state.

The core package of benefits that policies A through G, M, and N contain includes the following benefits:

- Hospital Insurance (Part A) coinsurance for the 61st through 90th day of hospitalization in any Medicare benefit period
- Hospital Insurance coinsurance for the 91st through 150th day
- Hospital Insurance expenses for an extra 365 days in the hospital
- Hospital Insurance (Part A) and Medical Insurance (Part B) deductible for the cost of the first three pints of blood
- Medical Insurance (Part B) coinsurance (20 percent of allowable charges), and
- Hospice (Part A) coinsurance.

Plan A is the core benefit package. Medigap policies B through G, M, and N offer the core benefit package and cover one or more of the following additional expenses:

1. the Hospital Insurance (Part A) deductible
2. the Medical Insurance (Part B) deductible
3. Blood (3 pints)
4. Part A Hospice Care
5. the coinsurance for care in a skilled nursing home
6. Medicare Part A deductible
7. Medicare Part B deductible
8. Medicare Part B excess charges (80 percent of balance billing, 100 percent of lawful billing)
9. foreign travel emergencies
10. coverage of 50 percent of the cost of outpatient prescription drugs after payment of a $250 deductible, up to a maximum benefit of $1,250 or $3,000 (*This may no longer be offered to new customers.*)

Details on the additional expenses covered by each plan can be found in Figure D.1.

Beginning in 2006, two new standard plans became available. These two plans do not include the entire core benefit package.

- *Plan K* includes: (1) coverage of 50 percent of the cost-sharing otherwise applicable under Parts A and B, except for the Part B deductible, (2) coverage of 100 percent of hospital inpatient coinsurance and 365 extra lifetime days of coverage of inpatient hospital services, (3) coverage of 100 percent of any cost-sharing otherwise applicable for preventive benefits, and (4) a limit on annual out-of-pocket spending under Part A and Part B of $4,940 (in 2015).

Figure D.1

MEDIGAP PLAN BENEFITS CHART	
Medigap Plan	**Additional Expenses Covered**
B	1, 2, 3, 4, 6
C	1, 2, 3, 4, 5, 6, 7, 9
D	1, 2, 3, 4, 5, 6, 9
F	1, 2, 3, 4, 5, 6, 7, 8, 9
G	1, 2, 3, 4, 5, 6, 8, 9
K	1, 2-6 (50%)
L	1, 2-6 (75%),
M	1, 2, 3, 4, 5, 6 (50%), 9
N	1, 2, 3, 4, 5, 6, 9

- *Plan L* includes: (1) coverage of 75 percent of the cost-sharing otherwise applicable under Parts A and B, except for the Part B deductible, (2) coverage of 100 percent of hospital inpatient coinsurance and 365 extra lifetime days of coverage of inpatient hospital services, (3) coverage of 100 percent of any cost-sharing otherwise applicable for preventive benefits, and (4) a limit on annual out-of-pocket spending under Part A and Part B of $2,470 (in 2015).

Effective June 1, 2010, changes to Medigap policies include: (1) the addition of hospice benefits to the core package (see Policy A, above); (2) the elimination of preventive benefits and at-home recovery benefits as of June 1, 2010; (3) the elimination of Plans E, H, I, and J; and (4) the addition of Plans M and N.

Medicare SELECT is similar to Medigap coverage except that a Medicare SELECT policy may (except in emergencies) limit Medigap benefits to items and services provided by certain selected health care professionals or may pay only partial benefits when the patient gets health care from other health care professionals.

Medicare Taxation and Financing

Hospital Insurance (Part A)

Hospital Insurance is financed by a payroll tax imposed upon most employers and employees, as well as by taxes on self-employment income. The tax must be paid by individuals, regardless of age, who are subject to the regular Social Security tax or to the Railroad Retirement tax. It is also paid by all federal employees and by all state and local government employees: (1) hired after March 1986, or (2) not covered by a state retirement system in conjunction with their employment (beginning July 2, 1991). The tax is imposed upon all earnings. The rate of the Hospital Insurance tax is 1.45 percent each for employees and employers, and 2.90 percent for the self-employed. There is an additional Hospital Insurance tax of 0.9 percent on earned income exceeding $200,000 for individuals and $250,000 for married couples filing jointly. Also, a Medicare tax is applied to investment income. A new 3.8 percent tax will be imposed on net investment income of single taxpayers with adjusted gross income above $200,000 and join filers with AGI over $250,000.

There is a special federal income tax deduction of 50 percent of the Hospital Insurance self-employment tax. Most states also allow this same deduction for state income tax purposes. This deduction, which is available regardless of whether or not a taxpayer itemizes deductions, is designed to treat the self-employed in the same manner as employees and employers are treated for Social Security and income tax purposes.

Medical Insurance (Part B)

Medical Insurance is financed through premiums paid by people who enroll and through funds from the federal government. Most persons enrolled pay a basic monthly premium of $104.90 per month (in 2015). The basic Medical Insurance premium is designed to cover 25 percent of program costs each year.

The federal government pays the remaining 75 percent of the program's costs from general revenues. In September or October of each year, the Centers for Medicare & Medicaid Services announces the premium rate for the twelve-month period starting the following January. These monthly premiums are in addition to the deductible and coinsurance amounts that must be paid by the patient.

Single persons with annual incomes over $85,000 and married couples with incomes over $170,000 (both indexed for 2015) will pay a higher percentage of the cost of Medicare Insurance. These higher-income beneficiaries will pay a monthly premium equal to 35, 50, 65, or 80 percent of the total cost, depending on their income level.

The premium rate for a person who enrolls after the first period when enrollment is open, or who re-enrolls after terminating coverage, will be increased by 10 percent for each full twelve months the person stayed out of the program.

Income-Adjusted Monthly Premium Medical Insurance (2015)

Single Taxpayer	Married Taxpayers Filing Jointly	Total Premium
Not greater than $85,000	Not greater than $170,000	$104.90
$85,000 – $107,000	$170,000 – $214,000	146.90
$107,000 – $160,000	$214,000 – $320,000	209.90
$160,000 – $214,000	$320,000 – $428,000	272.70
More than $214,000	More than $428,000	335.70

Married Taxpayers Filing Separately	Total Premium
Not greater than $85,000	$104.90
$85,000 - $129,000	272.70
More than $129,000	335.70

Medicare Advantage (Part C)

Medicare Advantage is financed through the same taxes and premiums as the traditional Hospital Insurance and Medical Insurance programs. In addition, a Medicare Advantage plan may charge additional premiums for additional benefits offered through the plan.

Prescription Drug Insurance (Part D)

Prescription Drug Insurance will be partially financed through premiums paid by participants, whether for drug-only plans or as part of Medicare Advantage premiums. For 2015, the monthly premium averages $33.13.[19]

Beneficiaries who choose not to enroll in Prescription Drug Insurance during their initial enrollment period may face a late enrollment penalty if they later choose to enter the program. The late enrollment penalty is the greater of "an amount that [CMS] determines is actuarially sound for each uncovered month" or "1 percent of the base beneficiary premium" per month. This penalty is similar to the penalty currently in place for late enrollment in Medicare Part B, 10 percent per twelve-month period. For those enrolling in 2015, the penalty will be $0.33 per full month in which they were eligible to enroll in Prescription Drug Insurance but did not.

Beneficiaries who have other sources of drug coverage may be able to maintain that coverage and not enroll in Prescription Drug Insurance without penalty. If a beneficiary's existing coverage is at least as good as Prescription Drug Insurance (i.e., considered "creditable coverage") then the beneficiary can avoid any late enrollment penalties if he later enrolls in Prescription Drug Insurance. Creditable coverage is coverage that is actuarially equivalent to Part D Prescription Drug Insurance. Failure to maintain creditable prescription drug coverage for a period of sixty-three days or longer may subject an individual to a later enrollment penalty.

Entities (such as a former employer) offering prescription drug coverage to Part D eligible individuals must disclose to those individuals whether the coverage they provide is creditable coverage as defined by CMS. These entities must also inform CMS of the status of this coverage.

Medicare Supplement Insurance

Medicare supplement (Medigap) insurance is private insurance funded through premiums paid by plan participants.

VETERANS BENEFITS

A Veteran is defined as an individual who has served in the armed forces (either for their entire career or only one tour of duty) and was discharged or released therefrom with other than a dishonorable discharge. As a result of this service to our country they are eligible for specific federal and state benefits and programs. Eligibility for these benefits and programs is based upon each veteran's service record and other factors.

Types of Benefits

Thrift Savings Plan

A Thrift Savings Plan (TSP) is a defined contribution plan for Federal employees and members of the uniformed services. Established by Congress under the Federal Employees' Retirement System Act of 1986, it offers the same types of retirement savings and investment plan savings and tax benefits as many traditional private sector 401(k) plans. Members of the uniformed services may contribute to their TSP from their basic pay, incentive pay, special pay, or bonus pay. However, catch-up contributions are limited to basic pay only and can't be made from tax-exempt pay in a combat zone.

Employees who fall under the Federal Employees' Retirement System (FERS) or Civil Service Retirement Services (CSRS) after July 31, 2010, will be automatically enrolled, unless a contribution election is made to stop or change the contribution amount, into the TSP. Three percent (3 percent) of their basic pay will be automatically deducted each pay period and deposited in their TSP account. A FERS employee will also receive contributions from their respective government agency. A FERS employee, hired before August 1, 2010, who is not making TSP contributions will still receive an automatic one percent (1 percent) agency contribution.

Employees age fifty or older may be eligible to make catch-up contributions to their TSP. Eligibility to make catch-up contributions requires the employee to already be contributing the annual Internal Revenue Code elective deferral limit. A new catch-up contribution election must be made for each calendar year.

Military Pension System

Military pensions are classified under three distinct programs, each dependent upon when the service member entered the armed forces. Service members who entered the armed forces (i) before September 1980 are eligible for the Final Pay Retirement System (pension based on their last month of compensation); (ii) between September 1980 and August 1986 are eligible for the High-3 system (pension is an average of the thirty-six highest months of base pay);[20] and (iii) after August 1986 are eligible for the REDUX system (choose between the High-3 system and the REDUX retirement system). The REDUX retirement system is similar to the High-3 in that a service member's pension will be based on the average of the highest thirty-six months base pay. However, it differentiates itself in that a service member will receive a 3.5 percent increase for each additional year of service past twenty years, instead of 2.5 percent under the High-3 system.

A service member who retires with at least twenty years of active duty service will be eligible to immediately begin receiving their pension. In contrast, a member of the ready reserve forces will not begin collecting their pension until age sixty. However, the 2008 Defense Authorization Act allows members of the ready reserve to begin drawing retirement pay three months earlier than age sixty for every three months of active duty under certain mobilization authorities in support of contingency operations, down to a limit of age fifty. Only qualifying active duty service performed after Jan. 28, 2008 will count toward the lower retirement age.

The Survivor Benefit Plan

Prior to receiving a military pension, a service member must consider what would happen upon their death and the end of their pension benefits. Without proper advanced planning, a surviving spouse could be left without a substantial income source. To offset this potential problem, a service member may utilize the Survivor Benefit Plan (SBP), which is an insurance plan that will pay a monthly annuity to a surviving spouse. A retiring service member will be automatically enrolled in SBP, with maximum coverage, if they have a spouse or dependent children, unless an election is made for lesser or no coverage. Surviving family members can be eligible for up to fifty-five (55 percent) percent of retired pay through SBP coverage. Alternatively, SBP coverage may be elected for a former spouse or parent.

Participation in the SBP will require the service member to pay a monthly premium (based on the "base amount" or benefit level elected). Effective October 1, 2008, SBP participants who reach seventy years of age and have made 360 payments (thirty years) will no longer be required to pay premiums for continued SBP coverage. Monthly SBP costs will not be included in the retired service members taxable Federal and state income.

The Veterans Pension Program

A wartime veteran, with a limited income and inability to work, may qualify for a Veterans Disability Pension or the Veterans Pension for Veterans sixty-five or older. Eligibility for the pension requires:

1. enlistment prior to September 7, 1980;
2. the service member to have been discharged under other than dishonorable conditions;
3. ninety days or more of active duty with at least one day during a period of war time;
4. permanent and total disability (does not need to be service-connected), or are age sixty-five or older; and
5. countable family income below an annual limit set by law.

However, a veteran who enlisted after September 7, 1980, must (i) have served at least twenty-four months; or (ii) the full period for which they were called or ordered to active duty.[21]

The VA Payment Rates

The VA will pay the veteran the difference between their countable family income and the yearly income limit which describes their situation. This difference will be paid in twelve equal monthly payments rounded down to the nearest dollar. The amount of annual benefits received will be based upon the retired service member's marital status, their number of dependents, whether they are housebound or require aid and attendance.

Example: Sally (a single veteran) has an annual income of $7,000. Her annual income limit is $12,256. To determine Sally's pension subtract her annual income of $7,000 from the $12,256 income limit which gives her an annual pension rate of $5,256. This translates into a monthly pension check of approximately $438.

Aid and Attendance Pension

The Aid and Attendance Pension is a federal assistance program for veterans that was established in 1952. The program provides a monthly VA pension to assist with the cost of caring for qualifying veterans (disabled or frail and have trouble living on their own). These benefits may be utilized for assisted living expenses or home health care. Every veteran receiving the pension will automatically qualify for VA health care benefits (prescription coverage, hospital, and physician care).

A veteran's eligibility for the Aid and Attendance Pension is predicated upon (i) ninety days of active duty service; (ii) at least one day during a period of war; and (iii) an honorable discharge. A veteran who entered active duty service after September 7, 1980, must have served at least twenty-four months or the full period of his or her obligation to qualify for the Aid and Attendance Pension.

A surviving spouse (marriage must have ended due to the veteran's death) of a qualifying veteran may also be eligible for the Aid and Attendance Pension.

To qualify medically, a veteran or surviving spouse must: (i) require the assistance of another person to perform daily tasks (eating, dressing, adjusting prosthetic devices, etc.); or (ii) be blind; or (iii) be in a nursing home or assisted living facility for mental or physical incapacity (lacks the capacity to contract or to manage his or her own affairs).

To qualify financially, a veteran must have (i) less than $80,000 in assets, excluding his/her personal residence and automobile; and (ii) insufficient "countable income" (earnings, disability and retirement payments, interest, and dividends). For countable income purposes, welfare benefits and Supplemental Security Income (SSI) will not be included. SSI is described in more detail under Social Security Disability Benefits.

A qualifying veteran will receive (i) full VA health care and prescription benefits; and (ii) a monthly pension (based on the number of dependents and entitlement to housebound or aid and attendance benefits). The pension amount will be based on the veteran's annual income less the cost of care (assisted living or nursing facility, doctor appointments and prescription drugs, medical supplies, eye glasses, hearing aids, etc.) provided to them.

Social Security Disability Benefits

Many disabled service members are surprised to learn that they are not only entitled to disability benefits from the Department of Veteran Affairs, but also from the Social Security Administration. Although a separate application is required, service members who become disabled during service to our country on or after October 1, 2001, will receive expedited processing of disability claims.

Entitlement to Social Security disability benefits is predicated upon the disabled service member's (i) inability to perform substantial work due to his or her medical condition; and (ii) the medical condition(s) must last, or be expected to last, at least one year or be expected to result in death. Eligible service members will receive disability benefits through two distinct programs: Social Security Disability Insurance (SSDI) and Supplemental Security Income (SSI).

The SSDI program provides benefits to "insured" disabled veterans (worked long enough to qualify and paid Social Security taxes) and certain members of his or her family. The SSI program provides benefits based upon financial need. Military status and receipt of military pay will not, by themselves, prevent the receipt of Social Security disability benefits. The service member's actual work activity will be the determining factor. Even if the wounded service member is still receiving pay while disabled, he or she can receive Social Security disability benefits. For example, if a wounded or injured service member is recovering in a hospital, and is expected to be unable to work for at least a year, he or she may be eligible to receive disability benefits while continuing to receive military pay.

Others Eligible for Benefits

Certain members of a service member's family may also qualify for Social Security disability benefits. These include: (i) a spouse (if older than age sixty-two or any age if caring for a child of the disabled service member who is under age sixteen or disabled); (ii) an unmarried child (adopted, stepchild, or grandchild) under age eighteen (under age nineteen if in elementary or secondary school full time); and (iii) an unmarried disabled child older than age eighteen (disability must have started prior to age twenty-two). In limited circumstances a divorced spouse may qualify for disability benefits based on the disabled service member's earnings. Spousal eligibility requires: (i) at least ten years of marriage; (ii) not currently married; and (iii) at least age sixty-two. Any amount received by the disabled service member's former spouse will not reduce the disabled service member's benefits.

Benefits Timeframe

By law, Social Security disability payments cannot begin until the service member has been disabled for at least five full months. Payments will then continue as long as the disability has not improved and the service member cannot work. Each service member's case will be reviewed on a regular basis.

Special Veteran Benefits

Older service members may additionally qualify for Special Veteran Benefits. Eligibility requires the service member to be: (i) age sixty-five or older as of December 14, 1999; (ii) a World War II veteran; (iii) eligible for Supplemental Security Income (SSI) for December 1999 or for the month they apply for special veterans benefits; and (iv) have other benefit income that is less than seventy-five (75 percent) percent of the current SSI federal benefit rate. However, a veteran's dependents or survivors are not eligible for the special benefit.

Tax Planning Considerations

State Retirement Income Tax

While disability compensation is exempt from both Federal and state income taxation, only some states (Alaska, Florida, Nevada, South Dakota, Texas, Washington, Wyoming Alabama, Hawaii, Illinois, Kansas, Kentucky, Louisiana, Massachusetts, Michigan, Mississippi, Missouri, New Jersey, New York, North Carolina, Ohio, Pennsylvania, and Wisconsin) exempt all or a portion of a service member's retirement pension from income taxation. State income tax will not be withheld from a service member's pension unless their state of residence has entered into an agreement with the Department of Defense (DoD) to permit finance centers to withhold state income tax. Service members who live in a state without a DoD agreement may request withholding directly from Defense Finance Accounting Services (DFAS).

Combat Zone Retirement Planning

The biggest benefit of combat-zone service is that all compensation received by enlisted service members and warrant officers is tax-free (excluded from their taxable gross income). Officers only receive tax-free compensation up to the highest senior enlisted service member rate of basic pay. The tax-free compensation, coupled with all other tax-free benefits (hazard duty pay, family separation pay, etc.) each service member receives, provides several financial and tax planning opportunities.

Differential Pay

Employees who receive differential pay (the difference between their civilian compensation and military compensation) from their employer should consider utilizing these funds to maximize their employer sponsored 401(k) account first. In many cases, the contributed funds or a portion thereof will be matched by the employer. In addition, if the differential pay is contributed to an employer sponsored 401(k) account it will not constitute taxable income to the service member and will allow them to maintain themselves in the lowest possible Federal income tax bracket while saving for the future.

The differential pay can be subsidized by state grants to employers. In Florida, the "Citizen Soldier Program" provides matching grants to employers who pay wages to employees while they are serving in the Reserves or the Florida National Guard on federal active duty.

Additional Combat Zone Contributions

While there is not a direct income tax benefit derived from contributing tax-free combat zone compensation to a Thrift Savings Plan (TSP) or other form of retirement account, the earnings on the contributions will grow tax-deferred until withdrawn. Notwithstanding the elective deferral limits, service members in a tax-free combat zone are eligible to contribute a larger portion of their tax-free compensation to his or her TSP and other retirement accounts. The contributions may include both tax-exempt combat zone contributions and regular deferred contributions. Each type of contribution will be listed separately on the service member's monthly TSP account statement.

Once the service member reaches the age of retirement the TSP account withdrawals will be taken proportionally from both the taxable and tax-exempt funds. The amount attributable to tax-exempt contributions will not be subject to income tax upon withdrawal.

If the service member leaves military service prior to retirement, the taxable and tax-exempt TSP funds can be transferred or rolled over into a traditional IRA or a Roth IRA, the funds may be or transferred to certain eligible employer plans (only if the IRA or plan certifies that it accepts tax-exempt balances).

Alternatively, upon termination of military service or retirement, the tax-exempt funds can be rolled over directly into a Roth IRA. The funds and earnings will then grow tax-free and be tax-free to the recipient upon withdrawal from the Roth IRA.

Roth-IRA

Service in a combat zone may provide a service member, who does not have a working spouse or is single, with negative taxable income after subtracting the personal exemption, standard deduction, or itemized deductions. This may create the perfect opportunity to convert an existing IRA into a Roth IRA.

Contributions to a Roth IRA come from after-tax compensation (unless you are in a combat zone and the compensation is not taxable). The benefits of a Roth IRA are that contributed funds grow tax free and will not be subject to income tax upon their withdrawal. In addition, there is no mandatory requirement that any funds be withdrawn from the account after reaching age 70½.

The lack of taxable income further provides a service member with an excellent opportunity to convert an existing IRA into a Roth-IRA. While the conversion will be a taxable event, the tax will be minimized by the service member being in one of the lower Federal income tax brackets. The payment of a little tax today can turn a tax-deferred account into a tax-free future account.

Retirement Savings Contributions Credit

Tax-free combat zone compensation and benefits will increase the number of service members (enlisted and officers) eligible to take advantage of "The Retirement Savings Contribution Credit" (the "Credit"). Eligible service members will receive a tax credit of up to $1,000 ($2,000 if filing jointly) on their Federal income tax return for each year they contribute to a TSP.

Capital Gains Tax

Today's capital gain tax rates of 0 percent (for taxpayers failing into the 10 or 15 percent Federal income tax brackets) and 15 percent (for taxpayers falling into the 28, 31, 36, or 39.6 percent Federal income tax brackets) provide many tax planning options for those serving in a combat zone. Service members in a combat zone, as a result of their tax free income and low income tax bracket, can take advantage of the 0 percent capital gains tax rate by (i) selling an appreciated long-term capital asset (stock, bonds, mutual funds, etc.) for needed cash funds, (ii) selling an appreciated long-term capital asset to reset its basis to a higher amount (selling the asset, realizing the tax-free gain, and repurchasing the same asset at a higher price), or (iii) rebalancing (revision of asset-allocation percentages) a portfolio. The tax savings from the 0 percent rate will depend upon what the service member's applicable tax rate would otherwise have been.

Other Planning Considerations for Veterans

VA Disability Compensation

The VA Disability Compensation program is a tax-free benefit paid to honorably discharged veterans who served for at least ninety days, of which at least one day was during war.

Eligibility for the benefits requires the service member to have a disability caused during service or made worse in service.

The amount of benefits the veteran receives will be predicated upon their degree of disability (a scale from 0 to 100 percent). Even though they may arise after discharge from military service, compensation may also be paid for disabilities considered related or secondary to disabilities occurring during military service and for disabilities presumed to be related to circumstances of military service.

Surviving family members may be eligible for several benefits and compensation. These include Dependent Indemnity Compensation, a Death Gratuity payment, and TRICARE benefits.

Dependency and Indemnity Compensation (DIC)

This is a monthly benefit paid to eligible survivors of a (i) service member who died while on active duty or (ii) veteran whose death resulted from a service-related injury or disease, or (iii)veteran whose death resulted from a non-service related injury or disease, and who was receiving, or was entitled to receive VA Compensation for service-connected disability that was rated as totally disabling for at least ten years immediately before death, or since the veteran's release from active duty and for at least five years immediately preceding death.

Death Gratuity

A $100,000 death gratuity (100 percent tax free) will be paid to the next of kin for the following service members: (i) service member who dies while on active duty or while performing authorized travel to or from active duty; and (ii) a reservist who dies while on inactive duty training (including while traveling directly to or from that active duty for training or inactive duty training) or while performing annual training duty (including while performing authorized travel to or from that annual training duty).

Death Pension

A death pension is a benefit paid to eligible dependents of deceased wartime veterans. A service member's family may be eligible if: (i) the deceased veteran was discharged from military service under other than dishonorable conditions; and (ii) served ninety days or more of active duty with at least one day during a period of war time;[22] and (iii) they are a surviving spouse or unmarried child of the deceased veteran; and (iv) the recipient's countable income is below a yearly limit set by law.

Impact of Divorce on a Service Member's Pension

Divorce rates for service members are higher than those for the general population. The Uniformed Services Former Spouses Protection Act (USFSPA) governs the terms and conditions for the division of a retired service member's pension during a divorce. There are four methods to divide a retired service member's pension: (i) stated dollar amount (most advantageous option as it precludes a former spouse from a Cost of Living Adjustment (COLA)); (ii) percentage amount (less advantageous method as it allows a former spouse to benefit from any additional years of military service); (iii) coverture fraction formula (division of the number of years of military service during marriage (numerator) into the total number of years of military service at retirement (denominator)); and (iv) delayed order option (best utilized when there is an impasse). When contemplating which option to utilize it is important to limit the former spouse's potential benefit from additional years of service or earnings gain from promotion(s).

When a marriage overlaps a service member's period of service by at least ten years, the government will automatically send the former spouse's benefit directly to them. However, if the overlapping period was less than ten years, it will not automatically enforce the court order.

FREQUENTLY ASKED QUESTIONS

Question – If a client receives a military retirement pension will it impact their Social Security benefits?

Answer – A retired service member may receive both full Social Security benefits and their military retirement without any offset. Social Security benefits will be based on the retired service member's earnings and may only be reduced if they also receive a government pension based on a job in which they did not pay Social Security taxes.

Question – Is a military pension subject to state income tax?

Answer – Only residents of the states of Alaska, Florida, Nevada, South Dakota, Texas, Washington, Wyoming Alabama, Hawaii, Illinois, Kansas, Kentucky, Louisiana, Massachusetts, Michigan, Mississippi, Missouri, New Jersey, New York, North Carolina, Ohio, Pennsylvania and Wisconsin will be able to exempt all or a portion of their retirement pension from income taxation.

Question – When can a client collect retirement pension if the client served on active duty for ten years and then completed ten years of service in the reserve forces?

Answer – Unless the service member retires with at least twenty years of active duty service they will not be eligible to collect their military pension until age sixty.

WHERE CAN I FIND OUT MORE?

Social Security and Medicare Facts, Cincinnati, OH: The National Underwriter Co., (revised annually).

CHAPTER ENDNOTES

1. 42 USC §414(a).
2. 42 USC §423(c)(1).
3. 42 USC §414(b).
4. 42 USC §402(a).
5. 42 USC §416(l).
6. 42 USC §402(q).
7. 42 USC §423(a).
8. 42 USC §402(b).
9. 42 USC §402(g).
10. 42 USC §402(d).
11. 42 USC §§402(e), (f).
12. 20 CFR Part 404.
13. 42 USC §403.
14. 42 USC §415(i).
15. 42 USC §402(w).
16. 42 USC §403(b).
17. I.R.C. §86.
18. For the forty-eight contiguous states and the District of Columbia. The amounts are higher in Alaska and Hawaii.
19. Center for Medicare, "Annual Release of Part D National Average Bid Amount and other Part C & D Bid Information" (July 31, 2014).
20. The system provides a service member with 2.5 percent of their base pay per year of service or up to a maximum of 100 percent for forty years of service.
21. 38 CFR 3.12a.
22. A service member is anyone who enlists after 9/7/80 generally has to serve at least twenty-four months or the full period for which a person was called or ordered to active duty in order to receive any benefits based on that period of service. With the advent of the Gulf War on 8/2/90 (and still not ended by Congress to this day), veterans can now serve after 9/7/80 during a period of wartime. When they do, they generally now must servetwenty-four4 months to be eligible for pension or any other benefits. But note the exclusions in 38 CFR 3.12(d).

INDEX

A

B

C

L

M

N

O

P

T

U

V

W